A Companion to the Intellectual Life of the Palaeologan Period

Brill's Companions to the Byzantine World

Managing Editor

Wolfram Brandes

VOLUME 12

The titles published in this series are listed at *brill.com/bcbw*

A Companion to the Intellectual Life of the Palaeologan Period

Edited by

Sofia Kotzabassi

BRILL

LEIDEN | BOSTON

Cover illustration: Kariye Camii (Chora Monastery). Exonarthex, west wall, lower part of a fresco painting with the Palaiologoi-family monogram (photo by Sofia Kotzabassi).

The Library of Congress Cataloging-in-Publication Data is available online at https://catalog.loc.gov
LC record available at https://lccn.loc.gov/2022946117

Typeface for the Latin, Greek, and Cyrillic scripts: "Brill". See and download: brill.com/brill-typeface.

ISSN 2212-7429
ISBN 978-90-04-52706-5 (hardback)
ISBN 978-90-04-52708-9 (e-book)

Copyright 2023 by Koninklijke Brill NV, Leiden, The Netherlands.
Koninklijke Brill NV incorporates the imprints Brill, Brill Nijhoff, Brill Hotei, Brill Schöningh, Brill Fink, Brill mentis, Vandenhoeck & Ruprecht, Böhlau, V&R unipress and Wageningen Academic.
All rights reserved. No part of this publication may be reproduced, translated, stored in a retrieval system, or transmitted in any form or by any means, electronic, mechanical, photocopying, recording or otherwise, without prior written permission from the publisher. Requests for re-use and/or translations must be addressed to Koninklijke Brill NV via brill.com or copyright.com.

This book is printed on acid-free paper and produced in a sustainable manner.

Contents

Acknowledgments VII
List of Maps VIII
Notes on Contributors IX

Introduction: Intellectual Life in the Palaeologan Period:
Persons, Genres and Trends 1
   Sofia Kotzabassi

1 The "Legacy" of Aphthonios, Hermogenes and Pseudo-Menander:
Aspects of Byzantine Rhetoric under the Palaiologoi 15
   Eleni Kaltsogianni

2 Intellectual Pursuits for Their Own Sake 76
   Sophia Mergiali-Sahas

3 Continuity and Evolution in Autobiographical Literature 112
   Sofia Kotzabassi

4 Writing the History of Decline 133
   Apostolos Karpozilos

5 Spirituality and Emotion: Poetic Trends in the Palaeologan Period 172
   Ioannis Vassis

6 Epistolography, Social Exchange and Intellectual Discourse
(1261–1453) 211
   Alexander Riehle

7 The Reappropriation of Philosophy in the Palaeologan Period 252
   Pantelis Golitsis

8 Κόσμου θεωρία: Cosmic Vision and Its Significance in the Works of
Theodore Metochites and Other Contemporary Intellectuals 281
   Ioannis Polemis

9 Monasticism and Intellectual Trends in Late Byzantium 322
   Demetra Samara and Ilias Taxidis

VI

CONTENTS

10   The Hesychast Controversy: Events, Personalities,
Texts and Trends   345
Ioannis Polemis

11   Working in the Imperial and Patriarchal Chanceries   399
Giuseppe De Gregorio

12   Public and Private Libraries in Byzantium   458
Ilias Taxidis

General Bibliography   491
Index of Manuscripts and Documents   503
Index of Places   507
General Index   510

Acknowledgments

My thanks go to the managing editor of *Brill's Companions to the Byzantine World*, Wolfram Brandes, who welcomed this volume into his series, and to the authors of the individual chapters for their excellent cooperation and patience. Unfortunately not all invited scholars were able to contribute to this volume. I would also like to thank the two anonymous reviewers for their valuable suggestions; Demetra Samara who revised references and bibliographies; George Alexakis who copyedited the text of the manuscript; and the publisher's former and current editorial staff, in particular Julian Deahl, Alessandra Giliberto and Peter Buschman, for their tireless support.

Maps

9.1   Monasteries in Constantinople   338
9.2   Monastic centers outside of Constantinople   339
12.1   Libraries in Constantinople   481
12.2   Monastic libraries in Asia Minor   482

Notes on Contributors

Giuseppe De Gregorio

is Professor for Greek Palaeography at the University of Bologna. His main fields of investigation are Greek manuscripts and documents, especially of the Palaeologan era as well as of the early modern period (in Western Europe and in the Ottoman East), history and reception of ancient Greek texts in Byzantium, Byzantine chanceries, and Byzantine epigrams.

Pantelis Golitsis

is a researcher at the Aristoteles-Archiv of the Freie Universität Berlin and an Assistant Professor at the Aristotle Unversity of Thessaloniki. He is the author of *Les Commentaires de Simplicius et de Jean Philopon à la* Physique *d'Aristote. Tradition et innovation* (Berlin & New York, 2008) and has published several articles on topics of Late antique and Byzantine philosophy.

Eleni Kaltsogianni

is Assistant Professor of Byzantine literature at the University of Ioannina. Her research interests focus on learned literature, especially rhetoric and hagiography, of the Middle and Late Byzantine period (from the 12th to the 15th centuries). In collaboration with Ioannis Polemis, she has published an edition of Theodore Metochites' rhetorical works in the *Bibliotheca Teubneriana*.

Apostolos Karpozilos

is Professor emeritus of the University of Ioannina. He taught Medieval Greek Literature. He provided critical editions of *The Letters of Ioannes Mauropous* and of Theodore Hyrtakenos (with George Fatouros). He is the author of several works on Byzantine epistolography and historiography (*Byzantine Historian and Chroniclers*, 4 vols.), and has also written articles on the material culture of Byzantium.

Sofia Kotzabassi

is Professor of Byzantine Philology at the Aristotle University of Thessaloniki. Her research interests include Byzantine rhetoric and epistolography, historiography and prosopography, and Greek paleography. Her recent publications include *Das hagiographische Dossier der heiligen Theodosia von Konstantinopel* (Berlin, 2009) and *Greek Manuscripts at Princeton. A Descriptive Catalogue* (with Nancy Ševčenko, Princeton, 2010).

Sophia Mergiali-Sahas

is Associate Professor of Byzantine History at the University of Athens. Her publications include, *L'Enseignement et les Lettrés pendant l'Époque des Paléologues* (Athens, 1996), *Writing history with the saints: From the society of the saints to the society of the Palaeologan era (1261–1453)* (in Greek; forthcoming), and some twenty articles on intellectual history, social issues, holy relics and political power, diplomacy, piracy, slave trade, and other aspects of Byzantine history.

Ioannis Polemis

is Professor of Byzantine Literature at the Athens University. He specializes in Late Byzantine literature, and has produced editions and translations of *Ethikos* and the orations of Theodore Metochites, the Funeral Orations of Michael Psellos. He is the author of a number of articles on the hesychastic quarrels of the 14th century, and has published various texts of the late 14th century referring to the Palamite controversy.

Alexander Riehle

is Assistant Professor of the Classics at Harvard University. He specializes in the rhetorical and epistolary literature of late Byzantium. He is the editor of *A Companion to Byzantine Epistolography* (Leiden, 2020) and is currently preparing an edition and translation of the letter-collections of Nikephoros Choumnos.

Demetra Samara

taught Byzantine Philology at the Aristotle University of Thessaloniki. Her research deals with the literature of the Palaeologan period. She is the author of *Theodore Mouzalon. The Life and writings of a 13th Century Scholar* (in Greek, 2018) and is preparing a critical edition and translation of Manuel Philes.

Ilias Taxidis

is Associate Professor of Byzantine Philology at the Aristotle University of Thessaloniki. His main interests are Byzantine epistolography, rhetoric and poetry. His most recent publications include *Les epigrammes de Maxime Planude* (Berlin 2017) and *The Ekphraseis in the Byzantine Literature of the 12th century* (Alessandria, 2021).

NOTES ON CONTRIBUTORS

Ioannis Vassis

is Professor of Medieval Greek Literature at the Aristotle University of Thessaloniki. He specializes in Byzantine Poetry and his recent publications include *Leon Magistros Choirosphaktes, Chiliostichos Theologia* (Berlin, 2002), *Initia Carminum Byzantinorum* (Berlin, 2005), and, with Ioannis Polemis, *A Greek Exile in 12th-century Malta. The Poem of the Ms. Matritensis BN 4577. A New Critical Edition with Translation and Notes* (in Greek, Athens, 2016).

INTRODUCTION

Intellectual Life in the Palaeologan Period: Persons, Genres and Trends

Sofia Kotzabassi

1 Renaissance or Not Renaissance?

The publication in book form of four lectures given by Sir Steven Runciman at Queen's University, Belfast as the very well-known *The Last Byzantine Renaissance* (1970)[1] was decisive in directing the interest of a broad and educated public to Byzantium's last two centuries. It followed Ihor Ševčenko's systematic study of such eminent scholars of the period as the *mesazon* Nikephoros Choumnos (*c.*1250/55–1327), *megas logothetes* Theodore Metochites (1270–1332) and Nicholas Kabasilas (*c.*1319–after 1391),[2] and also the admiration aroused by the unveiling of the famous mosaics and frescoes in the Chora Monastery (Kariye Camii) in 1966, by Paul Underwood,[3] after years devoted to their conservation and restoration, and their publication in a monumental four-volume edition. The direct connection between this splendid set of works and Theodore Metochites, one of the most important figures and eminent scholars of the period, whose portrait – on his knees offering the church to Christ – appears in an impressive scene above the entrance to the nave, served indirectly to encourage exploration of his personality and rich body of writings.

It may be true, as Runciman observes in the preface to his book, that "The product of Byzantine scholars is less attractive to us today than the product of Byzantine artists. But scholarship should be judged by the standards of its age, not by the tastes of subsequent generations", but in the intervening years study of the Palaeologan *literati* has brought to light many exceptionally interesting "products" and persons.

---

1 Runciman, *The Last Byzantine Renaissance*.
2 Cf. among others Ševčenko, "Nicolas Cabasilas' Anti-Zealot Discourse"; id., "The Author's Draft of Nicholas Cabasilas Anti-Zealot Discourse"; id., *La vie intellectuelle et politique à Byzance sous les premiers Paléologues*.
3 Underwood, *The Kariye Djami, vol. 1: Historical Introduction and Description of the Mosaics and Frescoes, vol. 2: The Mosaics, vol. 3: The Frescoes*.

© KONINKLIJKE BRILL NV, LEIDEN, 2023 | DOI:10.1163/9789004527089_002

Although the characteristics of the literary and artistic productions of the Palaeologan age were quite different from those of the Italian Renaissance, it is also generally accepted that, despite being preceded by the dissolution and fragmentation of the Byzantine Empire as a consequence of the Crusaders' capture of Constantinople in 1204, the situation in Byzantium just prior to the Palaeologan period did not resemble that preceding the Renaissance in Western Europe.

The Palaeologan age is the longest and most turbulent period in Byzantine history. It begins with the restoration of Byzantine imperial authority in Constantinople in 1261, after 57 years of Latin rule, and ends with the fall of the city to the Turks in 1453.

Although Byzantine territory was then far smaller than it had been, and was perpetually shrinking as its neighbours, and especially the Turks, gradually expanded, a situation that had serious economic consequences for the empire, the Palaeologan period can nonetheless show important achievements in the interlinked domains of art, letters and the sciences, which operated interactively and express the intellectual life of Byzantium in its final centuries.

Political power went hand in hand with erudition far more than at any other time, as witness the lively interest of Andronikos II Palaiologos in literature and the arts and his support for scholars and *literati* throughout his forty five-year reign (1282–1328); as witness also the prolific literary activity of the Emperors John VI Kantakouzenos (1341–1347) and Manuel II Palaiologos (1391–1425), who some four centuries after Constantine VII Porphyrogennetos (913–959) once again combined the conditions of emperor and scholar. Moreover, in no other period do we find in Byzantium so many men of letters in such high-ranking state offices as those of *logothetes tou genikou*, grand logothete (*megas logothetes*), or *mesazon*, which were held by (among others) George Akropolites (1217–1282), his son Constantine Akropolites (*c.*1250–1323/24), Theodore Mouzalon (1256/58–1294), Nikephoros Choumnos, Theodore Metochites, and Demetrios Kydones (*c.*1324–1397).

2 The Role of the Women

At the same time, we also find the women of the Byzantine aristocracy playing a more active role in public life in the Palaeologan era than in any previous period. Well educated and with commanding personalities, these women engaged actively in the political and cultural life of the empire and enjoyed the esteem of eminent scholars.

INTRODUCTION

One of those distinguished for her strength of character was Irene-Eulogia Palaiologina (before 1220–1284), sister of Michael VIII Palaiologos (1259–1282), who opposed her brother's policy on Church Union and was in consequence exiled to Asia Minor with her daughter, *protobestiarissa* Theodora Raoulaina (*c*.1240–1300). With her encouragement, Theodora Raoulaina would write a *Life* of St. Theodore and St. Theophanes the *Graptoi* (the Branded), a work distinguished for its elegance and rhetorical perfection. Irene-Eulogia Palaiologina was also responsible, at least in part, for the exceptionally fine education which won her daughter a prominent place among the *literati* of the early Palaeologan period.[4] Indeed, she is described in the most flattering terms by the *orator of orators* Manuel Holobolos (*c*.1245–1310/14) in a letter of condolence to her daughter, Theodora Raoulaina, upon the death of the latter's husband, the *protovestiarios* John Raoul, and by the scholarly Patriarch Gregory of Cyprus (1241–1289) upon the occasion of her own death.[5] Theodora Raoulaina was considered by many scholars of the late 13th century as a worthy interlocutor, because of her general culture, her philological knowledge, her activity as a copyist, and her extensive library.[6]

Apart from her friendship and regular correspondence with Gregory of Cyprus, which was largely concerned with exchanges of manuscripts, mainly of ancient orators, but also occasionally with comments on the style of the Patriarch's letters, Theodora Raoulaina also demonstrated an interest in the physical sciences and in music. In his Letter 68 to Theodora Raoulaina, Manuel-Maximos Planoudes (1255–1305) complains of the loss of a manuscript containing Bryennios' *Harmonics* which he had been intending to use as a basis for corrections to a manuscript of hers on the same subject, while Constantine Akropolites corresponded with her on the subject of a treatise on astrology.[7] She herself was the copyist of one of the most important manuscripts of Simplikios' commentary on Aristotle's *Physics*, and her name is associated with other manuscripts as well, including a manuscript of Thucydides (Munich, Bayerische Staatsbibliothek, MS Monac. gr. 430) and a 12th-century parchment manuscript of the commentaries of Theophylact of Bulgaria on the Gospels (Paris, Bibliothèque National de France, Paris. Coisl. gr. 128) which she presented to the Athonite monastery of Megiste Lavra in 1300; she may also have

---

4 See in this regard chapter 9, pp. 335–36.
5 Cf. Kotzabassi, "Manuel Holobolos' Letter of Consolation to Theodora Raoulaina" and ead., "Scholarly Friendship in the Thirteenth Century", pp. 145–47.
6 See Zorzi, "Una copista, due copisti, nessuna copista?" and chapter 9, pp. 334–35.
7 See Kotzabassi, "Scholarly Friendship in the Thirteenth Century: Patriarch Gregorios II Kyprios and Theodora Raoulaina", esp. pp. 115–19.

been the sponsor of fifteen precious liturgical manuscripts ascribed by Buchtal and Belting to the "atelier of Palaiologina".[8]

Theodora Raoulaina may have been the most erudite and active of the female scholars of the Palaeologan period, but she was not alone. Many ladies of the highest rank were extremely well educated, among them Irene-Eulogia Choumnaina, daughter of Nikephoros Choumnos and wife of John Palaiologos († 1307), the son of Andronikos II, who studied with her father and was praised by Nikephoros Gregoras (1290/94–1358/61) for her quick wit and theological learning.[9] She herself, as founder of the convent *tou Philanthropou Soteros*, corresponded with both her father and her spiritual father, Theoleptos of Philadelphia, and later with Gregory Akindynos (ca. 1300–1348).[10] The Empress Helen (1333/4–1397), daughter of John VI Kantakouzenos and wife of John V Palaiologos, who corresponded with Nikephoros Gregoras and Demetrios Kydones, was also formidably well educated.[11]

The manuscripts dedicated to the libraries of their foundations by many of the female founders of monasteries in that period, such as Theodora Synadene (before 1270–after 1342), founder of the Bebaias Elpidos Nunnery (Virgin of Sure Hope)[12] and the *protostratorissa* Anna Komnene Raoulaina Strategopoulina (*PLP* 26893), daughter of Theodora Raoulaina and founder of the Monastery of Christ Krataios,[13] show that the convents, too, had nuns who could read lives and encomia of saints and other religious works. Indeed, in the *Typikon* of her monastery Theodora Synadene urged the nuns to do so.[14]

Thomaïs, later an abbess in Constantinople, lived in the late 14th and early 15th century. She was an orphan who was raised in the household of the mother of Nicholas Kabasilas (*c*.1319–after 1391), where she acquired a basic education. She later studied with the hymnographer Palaiologina at the Monastery of St. Theodora in Thessaloniki and returned to Constantinople with a knowledge of the Scriptures that drew the attention of the Empress and the Patriarch.[15]

Some of the female relatives of the Byzantine emperors embroiled themselves in the religious disputes of their day. Among these were Maria-Martha Tarchaneiotissa (*c*.1214/16–after 1267, *PLP* 21389), sister of Michael VIII

---

8 Buchtal/Belting, *Patronage in Thirteenth Century Constantinople*. See also Talbot, "Bluestocking Nuns", pp. 611–12 and chapter 9, p. 334.

9 Cf. Talbot, "Bluestocking Nuns", pp. 606–607.

10 Talbot, "Bluestocking Nuns", pp. 612–13.

11 Cf. *PLP* 21365.

12 See Talbot, "Bluestocking Nuns", p. 612 and below chapter 3.

13 Demirtiken, "Changing Profiles of Monastic Founders in Constantinople", p. 282.

14 Talbot, "Bluestocking Nuns", pp. 608 and 612.

15 Talbot, "Bluestocking Nuns", p. 607.

INTRODUCTION

Palaiologos and founder of the monastery that bears her name, who supported the Arsenites, Theodora Raoulaina and her mother Irene-Eulogia Palaiologina, who opposed Church Union, and Irene-Eulogia Choumnaina, who supported Gregory Akindynos and the anti-Hesychasts.[16]

3 Manuscripts and the Role of Thessaloniki

A significant factor in the blossoming of intellectual life in the Palaeologan age was the change in writing material with the progressively increasing use of paper. Parchment continued to be used, but paper was both far less expensive and much easier for non-professional scribes to use. Paper made it possible for scholars to set down their own works without having to employ a professional scribe, and it also helped their writings circulate: there are many references to scholars hearing of a new work and asking for a copy from the author or a friend. In the same way, paper facilitated the copying of Ancient Greek and Byzantine literature, since anyone interested in a particular work could borrow a manuscript from a friend and make his own copy.[17]

Many of the scholars of that age studied the Ancient Greek literature intensively, copied new manuscripts, and attempted to correct existing manuscripts.[18] Three of the most important Byzantine philologists, Thomas Magistros (c.1275–after 1347), Manuel Moschopoulos (end 13th–after 1305/6) and Demetrios Triklinios (c.1280–1340), dealt mainly with the tragic poets,[19] Planoudes with Plutarch and Ptolemy's *Geography*,[20] and John Pediasimos (c.1240–1301/14) with Cleomedes' *The Heavens*.[21]

It would be remiss, in speaking of these scholars, to fail to mention the significance of presence of Thessaloniki in the intellectual and literary production of the Palaeologan period.

---

16 Talbot, "Bluestocking Nuns", pp. 614–17.
17 Mentions of searches for manuscripts by different writers and information about the copying of them abound in the letters of almost all the scholars of the period. There also exist a fair number of manuscripts of works of Ancient Greek literature copied by the hand of renowned scholars and of manuscripts in which Byzantine scholars collected fragments of older writers.
18 Here, too, the letters and manuscripts provide considerable information about the process.
19 Cf. Gaul, Thomas *Magistros und die spätbyzantische Sophistik*.
20 See Taxidis, *Μανουήλ-Μάξιμος Πλανούδης. Συμβολή στη μελέτη του βίου και του έργου του*.
21 Cf. Acerbi, "Logistic, Arithmetic, Harmonic Theory, Geometry, Metrology, Optics and Mechanics".

Many eminent scholars of that age were natives of the city or lived there for a time. Apart from the three philologists already mentioned, Thessaloniki was the birthplace of Nicholas Kabasilas, Patriarch Philotheos Kokkinos, an active participant in the Hesychast controversy, and Demetrios Kydones, while among those who spent some years living and working there were Nikephoros Choumnos, Theodore Metochites, the philosopher Joseph Rhakendytes, and Metropolitans Gregory Palamas and Symeon of Thessaloniki. One of the subjects upon which Symeon (who was metropolitan of the city shortly before it fell to the Turks) wrote, was an interpretation of the Liturgy, a topic with which Nicholas Kabasilas had also engaged some years earlier but until then had seemingly been of no interest to Byzantine scholars.

Others connected with Thessaloniki include three of the most distinguished jurists of the age. The Palaeologan period may have little to show in the way of original jurisprudence, but a number of efforts were made to systematise the laws in use. One of these was the *Synopsis minor*, a compilation attributed to the *dikaiophylax* of Thessaloniki George Phobenos.[22] The work was cited a few decades later by the author of the *Hexabiblos* (ca. 1345), Constantine Harmenopoulos.[23] Although his origins are unknown, Harmenopoulos served as *nomophylax* and *katholikos krites* of Thessaloniki, while his *Hexabiblos* was the most important legal work of the period. Some years earlier, also in Thessaloniki, Matthew Blastares (*c.*1280–*c.*1350) had written a lengthy legal work, the *Alphabetical Treatise* (Σύνταγμα κατά στοιχεῖον),[24] a compendium of canon and civil law organised in twenty-four sections according to the letters of the Greek alphabet.

Thessaloniki is also associated with a rich body of hagiographical literature and hymnography, relating primarily but far from exclusively to the city's patron and protector, St. Demetrios. Many scholars, both lay-persons and churchmen, composed encomia on saints from various times in this period, among them Constantine Acropolites, Theodore Metochites, Nikephoros Gregoras, Philotheos Kokkinos and Nicholas Kabasilas, while several, including Philotheos Kokkinos, Symeon of Thessaloniki and Mark Eugenikos, Metropolitan of Ephesos (15th c.), were also hymnographers.

---

22   See Troianos, *Die Quellen des byzantinischen Rechts*, pp. 314–15, 323. Phobenos lived in the late 13th century.

23   See Troianos, *Die Quellen des byzantinischen Rechts*, pp. 316–21.

24   See Troianos, *Die Quellen des byzantinischen Rechts*, pp. 317, 329–31.

INTRODUCTION

4   Sciences and Curriculum

That age was one of markedly increased interest in mathematics, astronomy and medicine.[25] In the early years after the recovery of Constantinople by Michael VIII Palaiologos in 1261 the *megas logothetes* George Akropolites taught Nicomachian arithmetic and Euclidian geometry.[26] Theodore Metochites sought someone to teach him astronomy, which he later taught to his pupil Nikephoros Gregoras, who in turn wrote an *Elements of Astronomical Science* following Ptolemy's *Almagest*.[27] In their study of astronomy some scholars adopted elements from the Persian and Arabic traditions as well; among these are George Chionades (1240–1320), Nicholas Rhabdas, George Chrysokokkes, Isaac Argyros, Nicholas Kabasilas and Theodore Meliteniotes.[28] Medicine was also a subject of interest to Palaeologan scholars, as evidenced by the works of Nicholas Myrepsos and John Aktouarios.[29]

Although Ancient Greek philosophy had always been part of the *Trivium* and a perennial interest of Byzantine *literati*, interest in the subject in the Palaiologan period was noticeably heightened. This is expressed both in the copying of manuscripts of Plato and Aristotle by Byzantine scholars like Gregory of Cyprus[30] and George Pachymeres (*c*.1242–1310) and in the writing of commentaries or paraphrases, particularly of the works of Aristotle. In this regard one might mention the commentaries of Theodore Metochites on many of Aristotle's works, the surviving commentaries of Nikephoros Gregoras, Neophytos Prodromenos and George Scholarios, and the paraphrases of George Pachymeres and Joseph Rakendytes.[31]

Another activity that influenced the intellectual life of the age was the translation of secular and theological Latin literature. The first Byzantine scholars to engage in translation were Maximos Planoudes, who among other things translated works by Cato, Ovid and Augustine, and Manuel Holobolos, who translated Boethius. They were followed by Demetrios Kydones, who translated

---

25   See Tihon, "Science in the Byzantine Empire".

26   See below chapter 3, p. 116.

27   See chapter 3, pp. 120–21.

28   For Byzantine work in the mathematical sciences see Tihon, "Science in the Byzantine Empire", pp. 192–197 and Acerbi, "Logistic, Arithmetic, Harmonic Theory, Geometry, Metrology, Optics and Mechanics".

29   See Touwaide, "Medicine and Pharmacy".

30   See below chapter 3, p. 117 and chapter 8, p. 258.

31   See below chapter 7.

Thomas Aquinas and some works of Augustine, and George-Gennadios Scholarios, who would later become Patriarch.[32]

Despite the friction created between Byzantium and the West by the two attempts at church union with the Council of Lyon (1274) and the Council of Ferrara/Florence (1438–39), communication between the two sides was cultivated, particularly in the 15th century. With the Renaissance in Italy came a turn towards Antiquity and interest in Ancient Greek writers, spurring numerous Italians to go to Byzantium in search of manuscripts and to learn Greek, while Byzantine scholars moved to Italy, seeking to escape the looming Turkish conquest and in hopes of better fortunes.

In the Palaeologan age intellectual and artistic activity were connected. Members of the Byzantine aristocracy restored monasteries[33] and dedicated icons, and poets composed epigrams about them: Maximos Planoudes, for example, wrote three epigrams on the monastery renovated by Theodora Raoulaina,[34] and Manuel Philes composed the lines carved in relief on the cornice in the Pammakaristos Monastery.[35]

Through their active engagement with and systematic promotion of every branch of knowledge, through works of their own dealing with the teaching of the *Trivium* and the *Quadrivium*,[36] and through their personal literary and philological production, the Byzantine *literati* demonstrated their "ability to think and understand things, especially complicated ideas",[37] creating an intellectual environment that went beyond the limited number of "chancery" scholars to pervade society and shape the life of the Byzantine citizens of that age.

The way in which the intellectual life of the Palaeologan period is reflected and described in the works and activities of its writers and scholars is presented in the chapters that follow.

For the Byzantines, rhetoric (Chapter 1) had always been a fundamental element of any intellectual activity. At all times forming part of the Byzantine curriculum and serving as a means of stabilizing the political system through the

---

32 Cf. Athanasopoulos (ed.), *Translation Activity in Late Byzantine World.*

33 Cf. Talbot, "Building Activity in Constantinople under Andronikos II" and Kidonopoulos, Bauten in Konstantinopel 1204–1328.

34 Cf. Taxidis, *Les épigrammes de Maxime Planude*, pp. 118–33 (nos 15–17); see also below chapter 9, p. 335.

35 Cf. Belting/Mouriki/Mango, *Mosaics and Frescoes of St. Mary Pammakaristos (Fethiye Camii)*, and Demirtiken, "Changing Profiles of Monastic Founders in Constantinople", pp. 274–75.

36 Cf. Acerbi, "Logistic, Arithmetic, Harmonic Theory, Geometry, Metrology, Optics and Mechanics", pp. 113–16.

37 *Cambridge English Dictionary*, s.v.

INTRODUCTION

propagation of official ideology, rhetoric continued to play a significant role in the intellectual life of the Palaeologan era. Court oratory flourished under the patronage of learned rulers, while the death of emperors or other prominent persons was often commemorated in funerary orations of lofty style. Significant historical events, such as the siege or fall of Byzantine cities, also offered an occasion for the composition of rhetorical speeches of epideictic or advisory character, while the uncertain historical conjuncture led to a revival of counselling oratory, a genre that had previously been neglected. The aim of Chapter 1 is to give a taste of the various forms of rhetorical discourse that were produced in the late Byzantine period and point out the basic trends to be observed in each individual genre (*e.g.*, imperial panegyrics, funeral orations, praises of cities, counselling texts, speeches on historical occasions), with reference, of course, to their main representatives.

Although for the vast majority of Byzantines the norm was that learning was sought for its practical benefits or as a means towards divine knowledge but never for its own sake, in the intellectual history of the Palaiologan era we are presented with what appears to be a converse trend. In the case of some specific (albeit few) intellectuals of high cultural awareness, we encounter a novel mentality in terms of a pursuit of scientific and literary knowledge that becomes an end in itself. Five representative figures are examined in Chapter 2: the *megas logothetes* Theodore Metochites, lover of astronomy, the court physician John Zacharias, astrologer; the physician Gregory Chioniades, devoted to Persian astronomy, the *mesazon* Demetrios Kydones, dedicated to Western theology, and the Emperor Manuel Palaiologos, one of the most prolific authors of his time. Devotion to learning for its own sake may be seen as a luxury, especially under circumstances of political decline. But for those few, such a devotion was believed to imbue the intellectual environment and make life worth living, especially at a time when the looming eclipse of the Byzantine Empire was imminent and irreversible.

Interest in seeking knowledge and acquiring scientific learning is also reflected in the autobiographical texts of the age (Chapter 3), whose *literati*, more than in any preceding period, reveal considerable autobiographical information in their works, some of them indeed writing entirely autobiographical texts either as self-contained works or as introductions to some other composition. The characteristic feature of these texts is that their authors chose to relate not an account of their lives but a description of their adventures in search of knowledge.

The framework within which the intellectual life of the last two centuries of Byzantium unfolded and the impact of the various political, military and religious conflicts are described by the historians of the age (Chapter 4). The political circumstances of the Palaeologan period made some historians more outspoken and often critical of the rulers and protagonists of the events. Others used their histories as a propaganda tool, for a variety of reasons – ideological, religious or for personal gain. Regardless of their motives, they depicted military disasters, civil wars and the prevailing political unrest in cities and the countryside – those factors that contributed to the collapse of the State. And yet for about one hundred years – from the middle of the fourteenth century to the Fall of Constantinople – no major historical work was written. The Turkish advance must be the main reason for this gap in historiography, and those who recorded their victorious deeds felt apologetic towards their Christian readers. In their outlook they remained traditional, attributing the disintegration of the State to the will of the divine. For current events they found parallels in the classics and the Scriptures. Their views on history and its dynamics were antiquarian and as such differed little from older works.

Poetry was indisputably a major element of intellectual life (Chapter 5). Poets and patrons were members of the same elite, which was also the audience for the poems. Poets were not only able to demonstrate their skill in handling language but could also present their works publicly, either at the imperial court or in what were described as "theatres", and might even see some of them preserved as inscriptions on works of art, icons, churches, etc., or as prefaces to prose works. In their poems they often expressed not only their own sentiments but also those in whose name they were writing and which related to ecclesiastical as well as to secular matters.

Another window into the intellectual life of the *literati* of the age is afforded by the numerous letters that have survived. Chapter 6 examines the role that letter-writing played within the circles of the educated elites of the late Byzantine period. It argues that epistolography was an essential medium of social exchange, which enabled *literati* to communicate with one another and to reaffirm themselves as a distinctive group based on the principles of friendship and shared intellectual ideals. While the general "conservatism" of Byzantine literary culture fostered the stabilisation of social and linguistic codes within this framework, this essay shows that the transformation that Byzantine society underwent due to the severe crisis it experienced in this period challenged traditional values and profoundly affected the constitution of networks and behaviour of educated elites.

Philosophy held a special place in the lives and work of the *literati* of the Palaiologan period. Chapter 7 provides an outline of the two main features of that era in this regard: 1) the production of new copies of ancient philosophical texts, as well as the composition of new commentaries on them, which made possible an extensive knowledge of Plato and Aristotle during this period;

INTRODUCTION   11

and 2) the intervention of ancient philosophy into theology and religious life, as may be seen primarily through the Palamist controversy and its various extensions.

It would not be possible to speak of philosophy without mentioning one of the most important scholars of this period, the *megas logothetes* Theodore Metochites. Chapter 8 essays an examination of various aspects of the contemplation of the world in his main writings. Metochites introduced the study of the four mathematical sciences into Late Byzantium, and the idea of the contemplation of the world is therefore rather frequently discussed in his treatises. As an heir of the Late Antique tradition of cosmic theology, he stresses that contemplation of the world or nature may lead man towards God. Drawing upon the works of Philo of Alexandria, in the *Ethikos*, one of his most important treatises, he depicts an impressive image of the sage who contemplates the world, free of all distractions. He even goes so far as to compare some of the objects described in his treatises with the world: Constantinople is a microcosm of the whole universe, while the Byzantine provinces in Asia Minor are aptly compared to the well-ordered *kosmos*. In some cases, however, Metochites does not hesitate to give the term "nature" a negative connotation, stressing its instability. Despite all appearances, the world in Metochites' works is presented as something ambiguous, or even terrifying. That ambiguity allows Metochites to pose the question whether human life is worth living. Although he admits that life is a gift from God, the fact that he dares to ask such a question indicates the author's inner estrangement from the basic tenets of official Byzantine ideology.

Intellectual life was also closely connected with the monasteries (Chapter 9), both in Constantinople and near other cities. Several of these had been founded by members of the elite and were centres promoting and disseminating knowledge and ideas, support for which often created conflict. Despite the fact that Byzantine monasticism flourished in the early second millennium, the gradual expansion of the Seljuks into Asia Minor led little by little to the destruction of the monastic centres in that area, such as Mount Latros in Miletos, Mount Galesion in the region of Ephesos and Mount Auxentios in Bithynia, which, however, survived until the beginning of the 14th century, contributing decisively to the intellectual blossoming of the Palaeologan era. At the same time, the progressive development of large monastic centres in the European part of the Byzantine Empire, such as Mount Athos, Meteora or Mount Ganos in Thrace, somewhat restored the lost balance, while in the meantime strong and important monastic complexes founded during the previous centuries in the empire's two great urban centres, Constantinople and Thessaloniki, continued to flourish during the Palaelogan period. In any case, it seems that the monasticism of the Palaeologan era contributed significantly to the intellectual movement of the time, either in the form of direct or indirect participation in the so-called "Palaeologan renaissance" or by supporting and disseminating Hesychastic theology (Chapter 10), proving that at a time when the empire was in decline, monasticism experienced a rich period on the intellectual, ideological and artistic levels, reflecting the beauty of every form of Byzantine spirituality. Gregory Palamas, one of the few original thinkers of late Byzantium, had the audacity to raise the question of God's relations with his creatures in 14th-century Byzantium and to apply that distinction to the problem of man's union with God in a consistent manner, using a precise philosophical vocabulary.

An important role in the intellectual life of the Palaeologan period was played by the imperial and patriarchal chancery and Byzantium's public and private libraries. Chapter 11 provides a detailed reconstruction of the inner workings and mechanisms of production in these offices, which were in charge of copying the acts of both the Byzantine sovereign and the Great Church, and highlights evidence that demonstrates the chanceries' value in assembling a rhetorical toolbox that could be used in the service of political ideology and religious Orthodoxy (for example in documentary prefaces – among the highest expressions of intellectual production, used as exercises even by the most important *literati*). Moreover, it examines certain cases that exemplify the activity of well-known officials/intellectuals within the imperial court and the patriarchal entourage, as well as within Byzantine society in general. Finally, it identifies several key intersections between the writing practices of these two offices, which often constituted a sort of graphic training ground for the scribes who worked in them.

Some of the scribes of the imperial and patriarchal chancery, such as Michael Klostomalles and George Galesiotes, made an important contribution to the production of manuscripts at this time and to the reconstruction of public and private libraries. The contents of the books belonging to those public, monastic and private libraries that were active, as described by the sources, during 1261–1453 are examined in the last chapter of this volume, which provides a full and broader view of libraries and manuscripts in Byzantium during the Palaeologan era.

Regardless of political dissensions, civil strife and military conflicts, the Palaeologan age was a brilliant period for the arts and letters. In perhaps no other era had there been such intense dedication to classical studies and the sciences, such extensive philological and publishing activity, or such great literary production. Intellectual disputes such as those between Nikephoros Choumnos and Theodore Metochites or Nikephoros Gregoras and Barlaam of

INTRODUCTION 13

Calabria, and those created by the theological conflicts surrounding the union of the churches and Hesychasm, provided ample material for public debate and the writing of new works, but also for revealing aspects of the personality of the scholars and the society they lived in, and give us an eloquent image of intellectual life in the Palaeologan age.

This image cannot, of course, be captured in its entirety within the scope of this book. It is, however, our hope and intention that it presents the protagonists and the main sectors of intellectual life in the last two centuries of Byzantium and gives the reader both an overall picture of that life and the urge to study it more closely.

Bibliography

Secondary Literature

Acerbi, F., "Logistic, Arithmetic, Harmonic Theory, Geometry, Metrology, Optics and Mechanics", in Lazaris (ed.), *A Companion to Byzantine Science*, pp. 105–59.

Athanasopoulos, P. (ed.), *Translation Activity in Late Byzantine World. Context, Authors and Texts* (Byzantinisches Archiv – Series Philosophica, 4), Berlin/Boston 2022.

Belting, H./D. Mouriki/C. Mango, *Mosaics and Frescoes of St. Mary Pammakaristos (Fethiye Camii) at Istanbul*, Washington, DC 1978.

Buchtal H./H. Belting, *Patronage in Thirteenth Century Constantinople. An Atelier of Late Byzantine Book Illumination and Calligraphy* (Dumbarton Oaks Studies, 16), Washington, DC 1978.

Demirtiken, E., "Changing Profiles of Monastic Founders in Constantinople, From the Komnenoi to the Palaiologoi: The Case of the Theotokos Pammakaristos Monastery in Context", in M. Kinloch/A. MacFarlane (eds.), *Trends and Turning Points. Constructing the Late Antique and Byzantine World* (The Medieval Mediterranean, 117), Leiden/Boston 2019, pp. 266–86.

Gaul, N., *Thomas Magistros und die spätbyzantische Sophistik: Studien zum Humanismus urbaner Eliten der frühen Palaiologenzeit* (Mainzer Veröffentlichungen zur Byzantinistik, 10), Wiesbaden 2011.

Kidonopoulos, V., *Bauten in Konstantinopel 1204–1328. Verfall und Zerstörung, Restaurierung, Umbau und Neubai von Profan- und Sakralbauten* (Mainzer Veröffentlichungen zur Byzantinistik, 1), Wiesbaden 1994.

Kotzabassi, S., "Manuel Holobolos' Letter of Consolation to Theodora Raoulaina", *Parekbolai* 10 (2020), 151–60.

Kotzabassi, S., "Scholarly Friendship in the Thirteenth Century: Patriarch Gregorios II Kyprios and Theodora Raoulaina", *Parekbolai* 1 (2011), 115–70.

Lazaris, S. (ed.), *A Companion to Byzantine Science* (Brill's Companions to the Byzantine World, 6), Leiden 2020.

Runciman, S., *The Last Byzantine Renaissance*, Cambridge 1970 (repr. 2008).

Ševčenko, I., *La vie intellectuelle et politique à Byzance sous les premiers Paléologues. Études sur la polémique entre Théodore Métochite et Nicéphore Choumnos* (Corpus Bruxellense Historiae Byzantinae. Subsidia, 3), Brussels 1962.

Ševčenko, I., "Nicolas Cabasilas' Anti-Zealot Discourse: A Reinterpretation", *Dumbarton Oaks Papers* 11 (1957), pp. 79–171.

Ševčenko, I., "The Author's Draft of Nicholas Cabasilas Anti-Zealot Discourse: Parisinus Graecus 1276", *Dumbarton Oaks Papers* 14 (1960), pp. 181–201.

Talbot, A.-M., "Bluestocking Nuns: Intellectual Life in the Convents of Late Byzantium", in *Okeanos: Essays presented to Ihor Ševčenko on his Sixtieth Birthday by his Colleagues and Students, Harvard Ukrainian Studies* 7 (1983), 604–18 (repr. in ead., *Women and Religious Life in Byzantium*, Aldershot 2001, no. XVIII).

Talbot, A.-M., "Building Activity in Constantinople under Andronikos II: The Role of Women Patrons in the Construction and Restoration of Monasteries", in N. Necipoğlu (ed.), *Byzantine Constantinople: Monuments, Topography and Everyday Life*, Leiden 2001, pp. 329–43.

Taxidis, I., *Les épigrammes de Maxime Planude: introduction, édition critique, traduction française et annotation* (Byzantinisches Archiv, 32), Berlin/Boston 2017.

Taxidis, I., *Μάξιμος Πλανούδης: Συμβολή στη μελέτη του corpus των επιστολών του* (Βυζαντινά Κείμενα και Μελέτες, 58), Thessaloniki 2012.

Tihon, A., "Science in the Byzantine Empire", in D.C. Lindberg/M.H. Shank (eds.), *The Cambridge History of Science. Vol. 2: Medieval Science*, Cambridge 2013, pp. 190–206.

Touwaide, A., "Medicine and Pharmacy", in Lazaris (ed.), *A Companion to Byzantine Science*, pp. 354–403.

Troianos, S., *Die Quellen des byzantinischen Rechts*, Berlin/Boston 2017.

Underwood, P.A. (ed.), *The Kariye Djami, vol. 1: Historical Introduction and Description of the Mosaics and Frescoes, vol. 2: The Mosaics, vol. 3: The Frescoes* (Bollingen Series, 70), New York 1966.

Zorzi N., "Una copista, due copisti, nessuna copista? Teodora Raulena e i due codici attribute alla sua mano", *Medioevo greco* 19 (2019), 259–82.

CHAPTER 1

The "Legacy" of Aphthonios, Hermogenes and Pseudo-Menander: Aspects of Byzantine Rhetoric under the Palaiologoi

Eleni Kaltsogianni

1 Introduction

> At first you should pursue those arts that are common and necessary to all, and be trained in them. These are rhetoric and the art of law. No one who lacks these (skills) can ever act the right way in his life. For, how can one talk to his fellow-men, when he doesn't know how to speak? How can one have dealings with others, when he ignores the law?[1]

With these words the Cypriot scholar George Lapithes summarizes, around the middle of the 14th century, the skills one should possess in order to succeed in life; for Lapithes rhetoric is, along with the art of law, a prerequisite for a "successful" life, which in its turn points to the importance ascribed to rhetoric in his times, that is in the Palaeologan age; it is rhetoric that helps one obtain and maintain contact with other people, and as such it can be considered the foundation of social life.

The fundamental role of rhetoric in Byzantine intellectual life and society in general was not, of course, stressed for the first time in the Palaelogan age. However, as documented by transmitted works, this era, like the Comnenian era before it, witnessed a wealth of rhetorical production. What Lapithes says here is what H.-G. Beck has summarized for the whole of Byzantine culture as follows:

> Rhetoric was for the Byzantines equal to *paideia* ... The *logos peistikos* taught by rhetoric was the foundation of social life and of every

---

1 George Lapithes, *Improvised verses*, ed. Chatzisavvas, p. 84, lines 147–53: Μάλιστα χρὴ δὲ τὰς κοινὰς καὶ πᾶσιν ἀναγκαίας / τέχνας διώκειν ἅπαντας, καὶ ταύταις ἐνασκεῖσθαι. / Αὗται δ᾽ εἰσὶ ῥητο- ρικὴ καὶ ἡ τῶν νόμων τέχνη. / Οὐδεὶς γὰρ ὅλως δύναται, τούτων ἐστερημένος, / πράττειν ὀρθῶς οὐδέποτε τὰς ἐν τῷ βίῳ πράξεις. / Πῶς γὰρ ὁ λέγειν μὴ εἰδὼς τοῖς πέλας ὁμιλήσει; / Πῶς ὁ τὸ δίκαιον μὴ γνοὺς πρός τινας συναλλάξει;. On George Lapithes, see *PLP* no. 14479.

© KONINKLIJKE BRILL NV, LEIDEN, 2023 | DOI:10.1163/9789004527089_003

communal and political organization. Rhetorical speech, *logos* was the logically structured expression of man's inner thoughts and images, and as such it served the communication between members of society. Thus, the rhetor was, in the sense of Isocrates, the ideal teacher, the ideal politician, and the ideal statesman.[2]

"Education" and "politics" are two keywords one should bear in mind when dealing with Byzantine rhetoric, and rhetoric in general. The connection goes back to the ancient sophists, who trained young aristocrats in the art of rhetoric as a means of acquiring prestige and political influence: in order to be socially and politically effective, one should speak (and write) in a way that was stylistically elegant and syntactically correct; rhetoric was in this framework the art of elegant and, thus effective, discourse. Later on, rhetorical discourse became synonymous with the pure "Attic" discourse, and ancient Greek orators were considered as models worthy of *mimesis*.[3]

Rhetorical education, which was in this vein equal to classical education, was adopted in the 4th century by the Byzantine state and Church, and became thereafter one of the most distinctive and all-pervasive elements of Byzantine intellectual life and culture.[4] Both the state and the Church recruited their officials from among the better-trained students in rhetoric, because the drawing up of official documents (in particular the preambles/arengas to these documents) presupposed a high level of diction that was clear, precise, and elegant at the same time.[5] These documents propagated the official political and ecclesiastical ideology of Byzantium, and it is especially this role of rhetoric as a means of stabilizing the system that made it "ubiquitous" throughout the Byzantine millennium.[6]

---

2 Beck, "Antike Beredsamkeit", p. 98 (translated and slightly paraphrased).
3 On the origins and evolution of rhetoric, see Hunger, *Literatur*, vol. 1, pp. 65–68.
4 Jeffreys, "Rhetoric in Byzantium", p. 166.
5 Constantinides, "Rhetoric", pp. 41–42. See also the capter on the imperial and patriarchal chanceries in this volume, esp. section 2.1 ("Prefaces to Documents as Expressions of Intellectual Production") focusing on preambles for official documents that were composed by prominent intellectuals of the Palaeologan era and have been transmitted along with other rhetorical/literary works of theirs.
6 On the social and political function of rhetoric in Byzantium, see Hunger, *Literatur*, vol. 1, pp. 69–74.

2 The Flourishing of Rhetoric: Prerequisites and General Characteristics

The recapture of Constantinople in 1261, which marks the official beginning of the Palaeologan age, was somehow equal to a "re-establishment" of the Byzantine state, although the sense of (political and cultural) continuity of the Empire had not been lost during the period of the Nicaean exile. Given the primarily political role of rhetoric, it comes as no surprise that the education of lay and ecclesiastical officials was among the priorities of the first Palaeologan emperor Michael VIII, and that rhetoric held the central position within the framework of the restored educational system.

The revival of learning (and rhetoric) after 1261 is linked to the person of the *megas logothetes* George Akropolites,[7] who was already a distinguished scholar in the Nicaean Empire. In the words of his student, Gregory of Cyprus, "Akropolites was the most erudite man of his time and he was deeply concerned with the drought of learning in the newly recaptured Byzantine capital; thus, the emperor relieved him of his duties in the civil service, so that he could devote himself to his teaching activities."[8] Among the materials taught by Akropolites we find, of course, rhetoric, that was considered one of the highest disciplines. It was placed at an intermediate level in the curriculum, between syllogistics viz. analytics and the higher stages of Aristotelian philosophy.[9]

The Church also showed its concern for the education of its future officials, and the first step taken towards this direction was the appointment of Manuel Holobolos as *rhetor c.*1265.[10] Holobolos was officially appointed as a teacher in logic, but his duties as *rhetor* of the Church were rather linked to the imperial ceremonial, since he delivered orations and poems for the emperor on special occasions, and it was through his writings (along, of course, with the official documents) that the imperial image of Michael VIII was articulated and disseminated, something which again points to the close connection between

---

7   On George Akropolites, see *PLP* no. 518.

8   Gregory of Cyprus, *Autobiography*, ed. Lameere, p. 185, lines 7–11 (text slightly paraphrased). On Gregory of Cyprus, see *PLP* no. 4590.

9   Gregory of Cyprus, *Autobiography*, ed. Lameere, p. 185, lines 20–23. Cf. Constantinides, *Higher Education*, pp. 32–35, id., "Rhetoric", p. 50, and Mergiali, *L'enseignement*, pp. 15–16.

10   Constantinides, *Higher Education*, pp. 52–56, id., "Rhetoric", p. 45, Mergiali, *L'enseignement*, p. 30, and recently Kountoura-Galake, "Ο Μανουήλ Ολόβωλος και η Λατίνων φωνή", pp. 385–91. On Manuel Holobolos, see *PLP* no. 21047 and the section on imperial orations below, as well as the chapter on the imperial and patriarchal chanceries in this volume. The initiative for the re-establishment of the post of the professional *rhetor* of the patriarchate is attributed to the patriarch Germanos III (1265–66), on whom see *PLP* no. 17091.

rhetoric and politics.[11] The flourishing of rhetoric under Michael VIII is especially praised by Holobolos in one of his orations in honour of the emperor, where he observes that "the torches of rhetoric that had (long) blown out, light now again."[12]

We do not possess any evidence about other Palaeologan emperors encouraging and supporting the study of rhetoric until the reigns of Manuel II and John VIII, who intervened in favor of a school run by John Argyropoulos;[13] nevertheless the information we have – especially from the rich correspondence between scholars – proves that rhetoric remained an essential part of the so-called *enkyklios paideia* throughout the Palaeologan era, until the fall of the Byzantine Empire.[14] Another factor that also fostered the flourishing of rhetoric in the period under examination was the intensification of the study of the classical past, usually described with the term "Palaeologan Renaissance". The classical heritage was, of course, present in Byzantine culture in all its phases, but during the Palaeologan period the links to the classical past were strengthened and Hellenism, that is the consciousness of being the heirs of ancient Greek language and culture, often worked for the Byzantines as a counterbalance to the gradual political decline of their state.[15] In this vein grammar, poetry, and rhetoric were the disciplines that offered the keys to the knowledge of the classical/Hellenic past.

Throughout the Palaeologan period we come across the so-called *theatra*, that is circles of intellectuals, who gathered to present their rhetorical works and to listen to the works of their colleagues being performed.[16] At the top of these *theatra* stood that of the emperor, to which every rhetor aspired with the prospect of improving his social prestige and status. A rhetorical performance before the emperor has often marked the beginning of a career in the civil/imperial service, as in the case of Theodore Metochites, the most distinguished

---

11 Angelov, "The Confession of Michael VIII Palaiologos and King David", p. 204.

12 Manuel Holobolos, *Orations*, ed. Treu, p. 96, lines 4–5: τί δαί; σήμερον οὐ καὶ τὰ τῆς ῥητορικῆς σβεσθέντα πάλιν ἀνάπτει πυρσά; On Holobolos' orations in honour of Michael VIII, see below.

13 See below, p. 22.

14 Mergiali, *L'enseignement*, pp. 27, 93, 163, 230, and passim.

15 See Ševčenko, "The Decline of Byzantium", pp. 172–75, Hunger, "Klassizistische Tendenzen", p. 147, and Vryonis, "Byzantine Cultural Self-Consciousness". From the most recent titles on Hellenism in late Byzantium, see, e.g., Monfasani, "The Greeks and Renaissance Humanism", and Lamers, *Greece Reinvented*.

16 For the *theatra* in the Palaeologan period, see Gaul, *Thomas Magistros und die spätbyzantinische Sophistik*, pp. 18–53, id., "Performative Reading", and Leonte, *Imperial Visions of Late Byzantium*, pp. 59–64.

THE "LEGACY" OF APHTHONIOS, HERMOGENES AND PSEUDO-MENANDER   19

scholar and powerful statesman in the court of Andronikos II Palaiologos.[17] But except for the court or other private *theatra*, the rhetors of the Palaeologan era occasionally claimed the right to address a wider audience, that is certain urban circles, and to take a stand on contemporary social/political matters, thus reviving the so-called *genos symbouleutikon* that had fallen into disuse since the Roman imperial period.[18]

About 70 (or slightly more) out of the *c*.180 known scholars of the Palaeologan period have composed at least one piece of secular oratory (theoretical texts and rhetorical exercises included), that is *c*.38–40 per cent;[19] 10 of them are known to us only from their rhetorical works, mostly encomia/epitaphs on emperors/members of the imperial family or other prominent individuals. Of course, training in rhetoric should be presumed for almost all intellectuals of the period. As for the social status of the rhetoricians, they came from the three basic social groups to which the intellectuals of the time belonged:[20] they were either state/court officials/dignitaries (among them high-ranking ones, such as George and Constantine Akropolites, Theodore Metochites, Nikephoros Choumnos, and Demetrios Kydones) or ecclesiastics, that is learned monks, Church officials, metropolitans, bishops or even patriarchs, while a relatively small number earned their living as free-lance teachers of grammar and rhetoric. Thus, the connection with the court and/or the Church, an inherent characteristic of Byzantine rhetoric as described above, is also reflected in the social status of its representatives.

The absolute number of rhetorical texts produced in the Palaeologan period is not easy to define; those surviving amount to over 300, but we also have evidence of rhetorical pieces that have not come down to us. The lion's share belongs, of course, to epideictic oratory, the rhetorical genre that was mostly cultivated in Byzantium.[21] Encomia and addresses to the emperors, along with epitaphs, are the two predominant genres, in which the rhetorical production of the Palaeologan era almost surpasses that of all other periods of Byzantine literature. Encomia/*ekphraseis* of cities – either free-standing or integrated

---

17   On Theodore Metochites and his rhetorical work, see below.

18   Gaul, *Thomas Magistros und die spätbyzantinische Sophistik*, pp. 172–74.

19   For a list of the intellectuals in the Palaeologan period, see Matschke/Tinnefeld, *Die Gesellschaft im späten Byzanz*, pp. 373–85.

20   Ševčenko, "Society and Intellectual Life in the 14th Century", and Matschke/Tinnefeld, *Die Gesellschaft im späten Byzanz*, pp. 232–59.

21   Hunger, *Literatur*, vol. 1, pp. 67–68, and id., *Aspekte*, p. 4. For a different approach, see recently Riehle, "Rhetorical Practice", pp. 294–97; Riehle suggests that both judicial and deliberative oratory "persisted (in Byzantium), even if in a different guise than in classical antiquity".

into other texts – also flourished especially in this period. On the other hand, the historical circumstances of the time often gave the occasion for the composition of speeches related to contemporary events, such as the siege or the fall of Byzantine cities to their enemies, but also for the composition of advisory speeches addressed to wider audiences, as already mentioned above. Even in the field of school rhetoric the Palaeologan era has some 'innovations' to display, such as the revival of the so-called *meletai* or *gymnasiai*, a type of advanced rhetorical exercise that had been neglected since the 6th century.[22]

3   Theory of Rhetoric, Rhetorical Manuscripts and Exercises

The rich rhetorical production of the Palaeologan era naturally presupposed a good rhetorical training, which in its turn was based on handbooks containing the theory of rhetoric, i.e. the rules for the composition of various kinds of rhetorical texts. Throughout the Byzantine millennium the teaching of rhetoric was based on certain key texts of the 3rd and 4th centuries AD, more specifically on the various treatises of Hermogenes of Tarsos, the so-called *Corpus Hermogenianum*, and the *Progymnasmata* of Aphthonios. These canon-texts were copied in the next centuries and served as teaching material, while they generated a significant number of commentaries, which testify to their importance in the instruction process.[23] Apart from the works of Aphthonios and Hermogenes, the treatises attributed to Menander of Laodikeia on the various forms of epideictic oratory also provided an important tool for rhetorical composition, especially if we take into consideration the dominant role of epideictic oratory in Byzantium.[24] However, they never gained a place in the rhetorical curriculum, and only rarely were they included in handbooks of rhetoric, such as the *Synopsis* by Joseph the Philosopher, which we will discuss below.

The first to deal with the theory of rhetoric in the Palaeologan period was Maximos Planoudes (1255–1305), a learned monk and one of the most erudite scholars of the time, who was also active as a teacher.[25] Planoudes re-edited the whole Hermogenian corpus, along with a commentary based on the *P-Corpus*, as well as on John Doxapatres' commentary on Aphthonios,

---

22   For the genre of *meletai* in the Palaeologan period, see below, pp. 28–30.

23   Hunger, *Literatur*, vol. 1, pp. 75–88.

24   Hunger, *Literatur*, vol. 1, pp. 68, and 88–89. For a different approach, see Papaioannou, "Rhetoric and Rhetorical Theory", pp. 109–10.

25   On Maximos Planoudes, see *PLP* no. 23308, Fryde, *Renaissance*, pp. 226–67, and Pontani, "Scholarship in the Byzantine Empire", pp. 483–90.

THE "LEGACY" OF APHTHONIOS, HERMOGENES AND PSEUDO-MENANDER   21

and added his own *Prolegomena*.[26] Although not original, Planoudes' work is indicative of what was regarded as useful in the study of rhetoric by the end of the 13th century,[27] and also points to the traditional character of rhetorical education in Byzantium.

At the beginning of the 14th century another erudite scholar, Demetrios Triklinios,[28] who was based in Thessaloniki, copied in his own hand a manuscript containing the works of Aphthonios and Hermogenes. This manuscript is the codex Oxon. New College 258, dating from August 1308.[29]

The importance given to rhetorical education in the Palaeologan period as a part of one's universal learning can be verified in the case of Joseph the Philosopher (c.1280–1330).[30] Joseph's only surviving work is his *Encyclopedia*, an introduction to the liberal arts, such as physics, anthropology, mathematics, ethics, and theology; in this context rhetoric is the first discipline to be treated, and it is this part of the whole *Encyclopedia* that has been mostly transmitted in the manuscripts.[31] Interestingly, Joseph devoted a chapter of his *Synopsis of Rhetoric* to epideictic oratory, deriving from Pseudo-Menander,[32] as already pointed out above.

A *Synopsis of Rhetoric* has also been preserved under the name of Matthew Blastares, a priestmonk from Thessaloniki, who was active c.1335–50.[33] The text, except for the *Prolegomena*, remains unedited, and survives in the codex Paris. gr. 2830 (fols. 201r–216v); it is largely a summary based on Blastares' reading of the rhetorical manuals.[34] Later in the century an anonymous (teacher of rhetoric?) compiled a new collection of theoretical texts on rhetoric, along with scholia, which presupposes the rhetorical corpus of Maximos Planoudes;

---

26   The work has been edited by Walz, *Rhetores Graeci*, vol. 5, pp. 212–610 (cf. Rabe, *Prolegomenon Sylloge*, pp. 64–73 [*Prolegomena*]). See also Rabe, *Rhetoren-Corpora*, pp. 332–37, Wendel, "Planudes Maximos", cols. 2230–32, and Kennedy, *Greek Rhetoric*, pp. 323–24.

27   Kennedy, *Greek Rhetoric*, p. 324.

28   On Demetrios Triklinios, see PLP no. 29317, Fryde, *Renaissance*, pp. 268–94, Bianconi, *Tessalonica nell'età dei Paleologi*, pp. 91–118, and Pontani, "Scholarship in the Byzantine Empire", pp. 498–502.

29   For the manuscript, see Turyn, *Dated Greek Manuscripts*, pp. 71–72.

30   On Joseph the Philosopher, see PLP no. 9078, and Gielen, "Joseph the Philosopher".

31   On the *Encyclopedia*, see Gielen, "Ad Maiorem Dei Gloriam" (with references to older literature). The *Synopsis* has been edited by Walz, *Rhetores Graeci*, vol. 3, pp. 465–569; on this, see De Falco, "Sulla Rhetorica del filosofo Giuseppe".

32   Joseph the Philosopher, *Synopsis of Rhetoric*, ed. Walz, pp. 547–58. See also Toth, "Rhetorical *Theatron*", pp. 433–34, and Angelov, *Imperial Ideology*, pp. 53–54.

33   On Matthew Blastares, see PLP no. 2808.

34   Paschos, Ματθαῖος Βλάσταρης, pp. 115–17.

it is the so-called *Rhetor Monacensis* (from the codex Monac. gr. 505, where the compilation survives).[35]

With John Chortasmenos we move to the beginning of the 15th century.[36] The famous bibliophile and copyist wrote his own *Prolegomena* to rhetoric, which he included in his "Hausbuch", the codex Vind. suppl. gr. 75; among others he excerpted from the works of John Doxapatres and Maximos Planoudes.[37] In two other manuscripts, the codices Londin. Harley 5697 and Riccard. gr. 58, Chortasmenos appears as the author of commentaries to the *Progymnasmata* of Aphthonios and Hermogenes' *Art of Rhetoric*.[38]

A younger contemporary of Chortasmenos was John Argyropoulos, chiefly known as a teacher of Greek philosophy in Italy.[39] Early on in his career he was named head of a school in Constantinople, where he must have taught grammar and rhetoric.[40] For the purposes of his teaching he composed his *Prolegomena* to the *Progymnasmata* of Aphthonios, based on John Doxapatres and the Suda-Lexikon.[41]

The scholars of the Palaeologan period were not only interested in the traditional theoretical texts on rhetoric, but also endeavored to acquire and produce manuscripts with the works of the ancient rhetors, such as Demosthenes, Aelius Aristeides, and Libanios, who also served as their models in the rhetorical praxis. This concern derived primarily from the lack of books after the sack of 1204, and it was enhanced by the rising classicism of the time.[42]

The case of Gregory of Cyprus, who studied rhetoric under George Akropolites,[43] is illuminating in this respect: in his correspondence Gregory speaks about his efforts to acquire or prepare his own copies with works of the ancient rhetors, primarily Aelius Aristeides, who became fashionable among

---

35 For the *Rhetor Monacensis*, see Rabe, "Rhetoren-Corpora", pp. 345–57.

36 On John Chortasmenos, see PLP no. 30897, Mergiali, *L'enseignement*, pp. 178–82, and Petrou, *Η παιδεία στην Κωνσταντινούπολη τον 15ο αι.*, passim.

37 John Chortasmenos, *Opera*, ed. Hunger, pp. 29–30, and Petrou, *Η παιδεία στην Κωνσταντινούπολη τον 15ο αι.*, pp. 194–98.

38 John Chortasmenos, *Opera*, ed. Hunger, pp. 30–31, and Petrou, *Η παιδεία στην Κωνσταντινούπολη τον 15ο αι.*, pp. 198–99.

39 On John Argyropoulos, see PLP no. 1267, Mergiali, *L'enseignement*, pp. 227–34, and Petrou, *Η παιδεία στην Κωνσταντινούπολη τον 15ο αι.*, passim.

40 Mergiali, *L'enseignement*, pp. 190, 230, and 232–33.

41 John Argyropoulos, *Prolegomena to the Progymnasmata of Aphthonios*, ed. Rabe; an older edition can be found in Lampros, *Ἀργυροπούλεια*, pp. 175–80. See also Hunger, *Literatur*, vol. 1, p. 79, and Petrou, *Η παιδεία στην Κωνσταντινούπολη τον 15ο αι.*, pp. 199–201.

42 Cf. Constantinides, "Rhetoric", p. 46.

43 See above, p. 17.

THE "LEGACY" OF APHTHONIOS, HERMOGENES AND PSEUDO-MENANDER 23

the scholars of the time.[44] The codex Paris. gr. 2998, for example, an autograph of Gregory, is a rhetorical collection comprising works of Aelius Aristeides, along with works of Demosthenes, Aeschines, Libanios, Themistios, and Synesios of Cyrene.[45]

Gregory's opponent, the unionist Patriarch John Bekkos,[46] also possessed his own copies of the ancient rhetorical works. Among the books he bequeathed with his testament to his spiritual son, Constantine Sinaites, we find Aristotle's *Rhetoric*, commentaries on Hermogenes' *On Staseis* and *On Ideas*, as well as on Aphthonios' *Progymnasmata*, and the *Declamations* of Libanios.[47] None of these books has been identified in the surviving manuscripts as of yet.

Demosthenes, Aelius Aristeides, Libanios and Synesios of Cyrene were especially popular among the scholars of the time. About 18 manuscripts containing works of these rhetors were copied in the first half of the 14th century in Thessaloniki, the second city and major cultural center of the empire,[48] and are more or less linked to the circle of Demetrios Triklinios, who has already been mentioned for his copy of Aphthonios and Hermogenes.[49] Triklinios prepared two manuscripts with works of Synesios (Paris. Mazarine 4453 and Laur. Plut. 80.19),[50] while he participated in the copying of three manuscripts with works of Libanios (Mosqu. Synod. gr. 489, Neap. II.E.17, and Vatic. gr. 83).[51] Another member of the Triklinios family, Nikolaos Triklines, also prepared a collection with works of Demosthenes, Libanios, and Aelius Aristeides (codex Escor. R.I.20).[52] John Katrares, who was active in Thessaloniki in the first half of the 14th century, copied the codex Vatic. gr. 1299 with works of Aelius Aristeides, and he was also one of the copyists of the codex Vatic. gr. 224, a collection of Lucian, Libanios, and Aelius Aristeides.[53]

---

44 See Kotzabassi, *Die handschriftliche Überlieferung*, pp. 6–9, Constantinides, "Rhetoric", pp. 46–47, and Chrysostomidis, *Τὸ corpus τῶν ἐπιστολῶν τοῦ Γεωργίου-Γρηγορίου Κυπρίου*, passim.

45 See Pérez Martín, *El patriarca Gregopio de Chipre*, pp. 25–28, Kotzabassi, *Die handschriftliche Überlieferung*, pp. 5–7, and Constantinides, "Rhetoric", p. 47.

46 On John Bekkos, see PLP no. 2548.

47 Kotzabassi, "The Testament of John Bekkos", pp. 28–29 and 34, lines 51–58 (text).

48 On Thessaloniki as a cultural center in the Palaeologan period, see e.g., Tinnefeld, "Intellectuals in Late Byzantine Thessaloniki".

49 See above, p. 21.

50 Bianconi, *Tessalonica nell'età dei Paleologi*, pp. 106, 180, and 249.

51 Bianconi, *Tessalonica nell'età dei Paleologi*, pp. 116–17, 181, and 249.

52 Bianconi, *Tessalonica nell'età dei Paleologi*, pp. 128, 134, 180, and 251. On Nikolaos Triklines, see PLP no. 29315.

53 Bianconi, *Tessalonica nell'età dei Paleologi*, pp. 146, 148–49, 180, and 250. On John Katrares, see PLP no. 11544.

A certain predilection for Libanios can be observed in the case of John Chortasmenos. The codex Ambros. L 64 sup., containing works of the rhetor, was in Chortasmenos' possession, while the codex Vatic. Chis. R.VI.43 is partly an autograph of his and Vatic. gr. 939 features marginalia and corrections by his hand.[54]

In addition to the models of the distant past, the scholars of the Palaeologan period kept in contact with earlier Byzantine oratory, especially from the Comnenian era.[55] Notes in the margins of the famous Escor. Y.II.10 with 12th-century rhetorical works are an indication that the manuscript circulated in late Byzantium and was available to the rhetoricians of the time.[56] The codex Bodl. Barocci 131 is a manuscript of the second half of the 13th century that also transmitted rhetorical works of the 11th and 12th centuries, as well as parts of Menander's treatise *De epideicticis*;[57] a closely similar case is that of codex Vind. Phil. gr. 321, which was copied in Constantinople around the same period and contains works by court authors from the middle of the 13th century, along with 12th-century rhetorical works.[58] The exact impact of earlier Byzantine oratory on the rhetorical production of the Palaeologan period has yet to be investigated.

The first stage of rhetorical training comprised the composition of rhetorical exercises based on the models provided by Hermogenes, and especially Aphthonios in their *Progymnasmata*, a set of 14 exercises arranged according to their difficulty, from the simplest to the most complicated.[59] Teachers of rhetoric composed their own sets of *progymnasmata* for their teaching purposes, but complete sets are rather rare, and in most cases we possess more or less free-standing examples on certain chapters of Aphthonios, which are not always linked directly to the school praxis.

Gregory of Cyprus wrote, probably during his student years, 17 fables (*mythoi*), a tale (*diegema*) on the sacrifice of Iphigeneia, and a characterization (*ethopoiia*).[60] These exercises have a relatively sparse manuscript transmission compared to Gregory's later rhetorical works, among which we also

---

54   John Chortasmenos, *Opera*, ed. Hunger, p. 52, and Petrou, *Η παιδεία στην Κωνσταντινούπολη του 15ο αι.*, pp. 295 and 300.

55   Angelov, *Imperial Ideology*, p. 56, and Spingou, *Words and Artworks*, pp. 51–60 (both with references to older literature).

56   De Andrés, *Catálogo*, pp. 120–31.

57   Wilson, "A Byzantine Miscellany".

58   Agapitos/Angelov, "Six Essays", pp. 48–60.

59   For the *progymnasmata* in general, see Hunger, *Literatur*, vol. 1, pp. 92–120, Webb, "The *Progymnasmata* as Practice", and Kennedy, *Progymnasmata*.

60   Gregory of Cyprus, *Progymnasmata*, ed. Kotzabassi.

THE "LEGACY" OF APHTHONIOS, HERMOGENES AND PSEUDO-MENANDER   25

find two small rhetorical exercises: a *chreia*[61] on Socrates' saying that reason is the sculptor of virtuous souls,[62] and an encomium of the sea, which praises the goods of water for the human life and is probably due to Gregory's origin from an island.[63]

A complete set of *progymnasmata* survives under the name of George Pachymeres, the famous historian of the early Palaeologan period.[64] It is not clear whether Pachymeres composed these exercises during his student years, like Gregory of Cyprus, or later, as *rhetor* of the Church.[65] Some of the topics he deals with had already been treated by earlier authors of *progymnasmata*: this is the case, for example, with his *diegema* on Odysseus and Palamedes, a subject also treated by Nikephoros Basilakes in the 12th century,[66] as well as his *gnome* on Demosthenes' saying that money is the driving force in all things,[67] and his comparison (*synkrisis*) between the olive-tree and the vine.[68]

The church historian Nikephoros Kallistou Xanthopoulos wrote *progymnasmata* for the purposes of his rhetorical teaching, as is evident from the title that accompanied these pieces in the unique manuscript that preserves them.[69] Only the examples on the first four chapters of Aphthonios (fable, tale, *chreia* and *gnome*) have come down to us, but there is a strong possibility that Nikephoros had written examples on all of Aphthonios' chapters.[70] It is interesting to note that in the case of *gnome* Nikephoros analyzes a saying contrasting with the one treated by Pachymeres, and praises (based on a citation from

---

61   A *chreia* would be a short essay that made a point on a saying or action attributed to a specific person. See Hock/O'Neil, *The Chreia and Ancient Rhetoric*.

62   Gregory of Cyprus, *Chreia*, ed. Boissonade. See also Hock/O'Neil, *The Chreia and Ancient Rhetoric*, pp. 308–33.

63   Gregory of Cyprus, *Encomium of the sea*, ed. Boissonade. For Gregory's motives, cf. Kotzabassi, *Die handschriftliche Überlieferung*, p. 11.

64   George Pachymeres, *Progymnasmata*, ed. Walz. On George Pachymeres, see PLP no. 22186, and Lampakis, Γεώργιος Παχυμέρης. For an analysis of the texts, see ibid., pp. 136–50.

65   Lampakis, Παχυμέρης, p. 136. According to Golitsis, "George Pachymère comme didascale", p. 62 (with n. 46), Pachymeres may have succeeded Manuel Holobolos as *rhetor* after 1273, when the latter was forced to abandon his post, because of his opposition to the Union of the Churches.

66   Taxidis, "Die Episode des Palamedes in den byzantinischen Progymnasmata".

67   Lampakis, Παχυμέρης, pp. 140–41.

68   Lampakis, Παχυμέρης, p. 146.

69   Nikephoros Xanthopoulos, *Progymnasmata*, ed. Glettner. On Nikephoros Kallistou Xanthopoulos, see PLP no. 20826.

70   Nikephoros Xanthopoulos, *Progymnasmata*, ed. Glettner, pp. 6–7.

Gregory of Nazianzos) the virtues of poverty and humbleness.[71] All four pieces testify to Xanthopoulos' strong dependence on Aphthonios.[72]

The *progymnasmata* of Constantine Akropolites form a rather exceptional case. Constantine was the elder son of George Akropolites, and is chiefly known for his rhetorical reworkings of older hagiographical texts.[73] Like many of his hagiographical works, his *progymnasmata* also seem to have been written on the instigation of his friends and may not have served teaching purposes, as has been suggested.[74] The collection consists of 14 pieces, which correspond to seven of Aphthonios' chapters.[75] Also worth mentioning is Akropolites' predilection for religious topics, especially in his five characterizations, a tendency also exhibited by the 12th-century rhetor Nikephoros Basilakes,[76] although the two authors do not appear to share any common topics. For example, Akropolites reconstructs Lazarus' words after his resurrection, or the reaction of Constantine the Great after his healing from leprosy; the idea of salvation of the faithful through God is common in all these pieces.[77]

A series of free-standing rhetorical exercises based on the relevant *progymnasmata* also survives from the Palaeologan period. These pieces often surpassed mere school purposes and formed literary works of their own merit. The school environment still lies behind Maximos Planoudes' lengthy *Comparison between Winter and Spring*,[78] since the four seasons offered a suitable topic for many chapters of the *progymnasmata*, as is evident from the surviving examples.[79] Planoudes highlights the merits of Winter against the shortcomings of Spring, but his arguments go far beyond those found in the rhetorical handbooks. Moreover, Planoudes' text should rather be read as part

---

71 Nikephoros Xanthopoulos, *Progymnasmata*, ed. Glettner, pp. 10–12, 264–68.

72 Nikephoros Xanthopoulos, *Progymnasmata*, ed. Glettner, pp. 268–69.

73 On Constantine Akropolites, see *PLP* no. 520.

74 Constantine Akropolites, *Ethopoiiai*, ed. Romano, p. 313 (with n. 19). Constantinides (*Higher education*, p. 101) suggested that Akropolites' *progymnasmata* could have been composed for ecclesiastical students.

75 For a complete list, see Romano, *Constantino Acropolita*, pp. 25–26, and Constantinides, "Rhetoric", p. 49.

76 Hunger, *Literatur*, vol. 1, pp. 112–13, and Constantinides, "Rhetoric", p. 49.

77 Constantine Akropolites, *Ethopoiiai*, ed. Romano, p. 319.

78 Maximos Planoudes, *Comparison between Winter and Spring*, ed. Treu; the text was first edited by Boissonade, *Anecdota Graeca*, vol. 2, pp. 310–39.

79 A comparison between Winter and Summer can be found, e.g., in the model exercises of Nikolaos the Sophist, and it proves the superiority of the former over the latter. See Walz, *Rhetores Graeci*, vol. 1, pp. 366–67.

THE "LEGACY" OF APHTHONIOS, HERMOGENES AND PSEUDO-MENANDER   27

of a literary controversy, as it is supposed to be a response to a contemporary rhetorical work that supported the opposite view.[80]

The comparison between Demosthenes and Aelius Aristeides by Theodore Metochites was not, of course, conceived as a school exercise.[81] Metochites composed this text in 1330–31, at the age of 60.[82] This kind of *synkrisis* goes back to Dionysios of Halikarnassos and his comparison between Isaios and Lysias, while the analysis of the literary merits of the ancient rhetors was a subject treated by many late antique authors, such as Lucian, Plutarch, and Hermogenes, as well as by Byzantine ones, among them Photios and Michael Psellos.[83] Demosthenes was regarded as the top representative of political/counseling oratory; Aristeides, on the other hand, devoted himself to epideictic oratory, since he lived in an absolute monarchy. For Metochites, the latter was better suited as a model for the students of his time, because they lived under the same kind of regime.[84]

Another type of *progymnasma* that gave some free-standing pieces in the Palaeologan period was the characterization (*ethopoiia*). The two texts in

---

80 Maximos Planoudes, *Comparison between Winter and Spring*, ed. Treu, p. 3, lines 9–20: καὶ οὐχ ἥκιστα νῦν, ὅτε τις τῶν τοῦ ἡμετέρου συστήματος, τοῦ λογικοῦ καταλόγου, ἀνὴρ τὰ μὲν ἄλλα φίλτατος πάντων ἐμοί, καὶ φιλοσοφίας ἄκρως ἐχόμενος, δεινότατος δὲ εἰπεῖν, καὶ λόγους πράγμασιν ἱκανὸς ἐξισῶσαι, ἔστι δὲ οὗ καὶ ὑπερβαλέσθαι, ἔαρος μὲν καὶ τῶν κατ᾽ αὐτὸ μακρὸν διεξῆλθε τὸν ἔπαινον ἐν μέρει λογικῆς παιδιᾶς τε καὶ διαχύσεως, χειμῶνα δὲ πολλά τε καὶ ἀηδῆ ἐξωνείδισε, τόσον δέ τι πειθοῖ ξυμμιγῆ τὸν λόγον καὶ χάριτι κερασάμενος, ὥστ᾽, εἰ μὴ γυμνασία τις ἦν, μηδ᾽ ἐπίδειξις τῆς περὶ λόγους ἀσκήσεως, ἄντικρυς ἀλήθειαν ὑπειλῆφθαι τὰ εἰρημένα, τὸν χειμῶνά τε κινδυνεύειν ἐντεῦθεν οὐχ ὅπως τοῦ ἀρίστου ἀποπίπτειν, ἀλλὰ μηδὲ ταῖς ὥραις συνεξετάζεσθαι (and even more now that someone from our community, the group of intellectuals, a man who for the rest is the dearest of all to me, who is clung to philosophy at the highest degree, who is very skilful at speaking and competent in making words equal to things, or even exceed them (i.e. the things) sometimes, (this man) went in detail through the praise of Spring and its merits as a kind of intellectual game and (expression of) amusement, while on the other hand he threw so many and odious reproaches on Winter mixing up in his speech persuasiveness together with the beauty (of words), so that if it were not an exercise and display of his training in the *logoi*, his sayings would be perceived as the truth, and thus Winter would run the risk not only of failing to be considered the best, but also of not even being reckoned among the seasons).

81 Theodore Metochites, *Orations*, eds. Polemis/Kaltsogianni, pp. 673–96, and Theodore Metochites, *Comparison between Demosthenes and Aelius Aristeides*, ed. Gigante. On Theodore Metochites, see PLP no. 17982, Fryde, *Renaissance*, pp. 322–36, as well as the relevant chapter in this volume.

82 Ševčenko, *Études*, p. 143.

83 Theodore Metochites, *Comparison between Demosthenes and Aelius Aristeides*, ed. Gigante, pp. 15–19.

84 Theodore Metochites, *Orations*, eds. Polemis/Kaltsogianni, p. 695, lines 73–84. Cf. Theodore Metochites, *Comparison between Demosthenes and Aelius Aristeides*, ed. Gigante, pp. 36–38.

question date from the late 14th/early 15th century, and are both linked directly to historical circumstances. In the 1390s John Chortasmenos wrote a fictitious address of Tamerlane to the heads of his troops, when the "Persians" were fighting against the "Scyths" of Tohtamyš; Chortasmenos not only invents the words of Tamerlane, but he also calls upon a supposed ear-witness.[85] Some years later Manuel II Palaiologos composed another rhetorical piece starring Tamerlane: in this short *ethopoiia* Tamerlane addresses the Turkish sultan Bayezid after the battle of Ankara (1402), and castigates him for not bearing his defeat like a man.[86]

The unlimited potential of rhetoric can be demonstrated by two more rhetorical pieces from the last century of Byzantium. Both belong to the genre of *encomium*, deal with animals, and are addressed to eminent persons of the time. The first was by the hand of Demetrios Chrysoloras, who wrote a eulogy of the flea – a subject treated in the past by Michael Psellos – and sent it to the Emperor Manuel II Palaiologos.[87] The second is the encomium of a dog, written by Theodore Gazes and addressed to an "illustrious" man and "lover of the Muses" who remains anonymous.[88] The text was meant to accompany the gift Gazes sent to this person, a female dog;[89] as the author explicitly states, the composition of the encomium was for him a kind of literary game.[90]

Except for the *progymnasmata*, another type of rhetorical exercise that was cultivated during the Palaeologan period was the *melete* or *gymnasia*, that is a fictitious speech, which the student composed on a given historical/ mythological situation, and which he was supposed to deliver in the name of a historical/mythological person; in this sense, *melete* was close to *ethopoiia*,

---

85   John Chortasmenos, *Ethopoiia of Tamerlane*, ed. Treu. See also Hunger, "Zeitgeschichte", pp. 155–56.

86   Manuel II Palaiologos, *Ethopoiia of Tamerlane*, ed. Legrand. See also Hunger, "Zeitgeschichte", pp. 156–57, and Çelik, *Manuel II Palaiologos*, pp. 248–49, 394 (English translation of the text). On Manuel Palaiologos, see PLP no. 21513; especially on his literary activity, see the monographs of Lamprou, *Ὁ αὐτοκράτωρ Μανουὴλ Β΄ Παλαιολόγος ὡς θεολόγος*, Leonte, *Imperial Visions of Late Byzantium*, and Çelik, *Manuel II Palaiologos*.

87   Demetrios Chrysoloras, *Encomium of the Flea*, ed. De Andrés. See also Taxidis/Nikou/ Chrysostomidis, *The Ekphraseis in the Literature of the Palaeologan Era*, pp. 283–84. On Demetrios Chrysoloras, see PLP no. 31156.

88   Theodore Gazes, *Encomium of a Dog*. See also Gibson, "In Praise of Dogs", pp. 31–35, and Rhoby, "Hunde in Byzanz", p. 809. The anonymous addressee has usually been identified in the modern secondary literature with Muhammad the Conqueror; cf. Hunger, "Literatur", vol. 1, p. 106. On Theodore Gazes, see PLP no. 3450, Wilson, *From Byzantium to Italy*, passim, and Pontani, "Scholarship in the Byzantine Empire", p. 521.

89   Gibson, "In Praise of Dogs", p. 31.

90   Theodore Gazes, *Encomium of a Dog*, in *Patrologia Graeca*, vol. 161, col. 997: ἐβουλήθην δ᾽ αὐτοσχεδιάσαι τὸν λόγον, κυνὶ μὲν ἐγκώμιον, ἐμοὶ δὲ παίγνιον, σοὶ δ᾽ ἀθυρμάτιον. See also Gibson, "In Praise of Dogs", p. 35, and Rhoby, "Hunde in Byzanz", p. 809.

THE "LEGACY" OF APHTHONIOS, HERMOGENES AND PSEUDO-MENANDER   29

but in the case of *melete* emphasis was placed on the complete treatment of the subject, and not so much on the depiction of the character of the speaking person.[91] *Meletai* had been especially fashionable during Late Antiquity, and were composed for public recitation/performance in the *theatra*. Their subjects derived mainly from the speeches of Demosthenes, the Persian and the Peloponnesian wars, the history of Alexander the Great, as well as Greek mythology. In Byzantium the genre had been neglected after the 6th century, and only found its place again in the rhetorical production of the scholars in the early Palaeologan period.[92]

The revival of the genre of *meletai* in the early Palaeologan period may be linked to the figure of George Akropolites, although no relevant text of his has been preserved. However, both Gregory of Cyprus and George Pachymeres, who cultivated this genre, were Akropolites' students, therefore the original inspiration likely goes back to him.[93] Gregory of Cyprus wrote four *meletai*: two of them are responses to the relevant *meletai* of Libanios,[94] while another one is a response to Synesios' *Encomium of Baldness*.[95] The *meletai* of George Pachymeres, on the other hand, amount to 13, and the number probably points to the author's effort to systematically revive the genre.[96] Pachymeres derives his subjects from Hermogenes' *On Staseis*, and each one of his *meletai* corresponds to a different argumentative strategy (*stasis*).[97] Two of the texts refer to historical personalities (Demosthenes, Pericles),[98] while we also have examples on the supposed errors of generals and the accusations brought against them,[99] on cases of distinction for bravery,[100] and on several issues of social interest.[101]

---

91   On the genre of *meletai* in general, see Russell, *Greek Declamation*.

92   Hunger, *Literatur*, vol. 1, pp. 93–94, and Gaul, *Thomas Magistros und die spätbyzantinische Sophistik*, pp. 129–68.

93   Gaul, *Thomas Magistros und die spätbyzantinische Sophistik*, p. 172.

94   These have been edited along with the works of Libanios; see Foerster, *Libanii opera*, vol. 6, pp. 52–82, and ibid., vol. 7, pp. 142–79.

95   Gregory of Cyprus, *Melete*, ed. Pérez Martín.

96   George Pachymeres, *Meletai*, ed. Boissonade. For an analysis of the texts, see Lampakis, *Παχυμέρης*, pp. 150–80, and id., "Οι μελέτες του Γεωργίου Παχυμέρη".

97   Cf. Lampakis, *Παχυμέρης*, pp. 152–53.

98   George Pachymeres, *Meletai*, ed. Boissonade, pp. 1–19, 82–89 (*meletai* 1 and 5). Cf. Lampakis, *Παχυμέρης*, pp. 153–57.

99   George Pachymeres, *Meletai*, ed. Boissonade, pp. 59–81, 229–48, and 249–51 (*meletai* 4, 12, and 13). Cf. Lampakis, *Παχυμέρης*, pp. 163–70.

100   George Pachymeres, *Meletai*, ed. Boissonade, pp. 90–112, 112–34, and 207–29 (*meletai* 6, 7, and 11). Cf. Lampakis, *Παχυμέρης*, pp. 170–74.

101   George Pachymeres, *Meletai*, ed. Boissonade, pp. 134–59, 159–86, and 186–207 (*meletai* 8, 9, and 10). Cf. Lampakis, *Παχυμέρης*, pp. 174–80.

An exceptional case is the *melete* of Sophonias the monk, who may likely be the homonymous paraphrast of Aristotle who lived in the late 13th/early 14th century.[102] Unlike its contemporary *meletai*, which draw upon the classical tradition, Sophonias' text elaborates on a subject from the New Testament, the famous discourse of the Apostle Paul in the Areopagus, thus creating a parallel to the *ethopoiiai* of Constantine Akropolites.[103]

Apart from its pedagogical role, the re-enactment of the classical past in the *meletai* could occasionally function on a different level, and serve as a means of alluding to contemporary events. This has been argued for the *meletai* of Thomas Magistros, and especially for the two texts that are based on Demosthenes' speech *Against Leptines*. Magistros was one of the leading classical scholars of the Palaeologan era, but he is also known, as we shall see, for his political speeches.[104] His six *meletai* draw on ancient Greek history and form three pairs, each subject being treated in both its positive and its negative aspect.[105] The example of the two Leptinean *meletai* shows that Magistros sometimes deliberately altered the details of the original situation, in order to create parallels with contemporary political affairs.[106]

A final point worth mentioning is a single *melete* by the learned Emperor Manuel II Palaiologos. Rather than being a school exercise, the text seems to have been inspired by the same playful mood that lies behind Manuel's characterization of Tamerlane discussed above.[107] The situation treated in this case has nothing to do with ancient Greek history or mythology: the author presents a drunkard appealing to the court against his son – who as a ruler of the city has ordered the devastation of vineyards, in order to bring his father to reason – and seeking to prove that this is not a legitimate child of his.[108]

---

102 Sophonias the Monk, *Melete*, eds. Searby/Sjörs. On Sophonias the Monk, see PLP no. 26424.

103 Cf. above, p. 26.

104 On Thomas Magistros, see PLP no. 16045, Gaul, *Thomas Magistros und die spätbyzantinische Sophistik*, and Pontani, "Scholarship in the Byzantine Empire", pp. 496–98.

105 For the texts and their editions, see Gaul, *Thomas Magistros und die spätbyzantinische Sophistik*, pp. 402–403.

106 The author must have seen a connection between the *ateleiai* that Leptines tried to reduce with his law, and the *pronoiai* that Andronikos II Palaiologos was trying to reduce during his reign, in order to rectify the critical economic and military situation of the empire; cf. Martin, "Rhetorical Exercise or Political Pamphlet?".

107 Cf. above, p. 28.

108 Manuel II Palaiologos, *Melete on a Drunkard*, ed. Boissonade. See also Lamprou, Ὁ αὐτοκράτωρ Μανουὴλ Βʹ Παλαιολόγος, pp. 214–16, and Çelik, *Manuel II Palaiologos*, passim.

THE "LEGACY" OF APHTHONIOS, HERMOGENES AND PSEUDO-MENANDER   31

4   Practical Uses of Rhetoric: Imperial Orations

The demanding school training was, of course, a prerequisite for the practical uses of rhetoric, which, as already stressed, centered on the field of epideictic oratory.[109] The main genre cultivated by the Byzantines in this field was the *basilikos logos* (imperial oration), an encomium addressed to the emperor, according to its definition by Pseudo-Menander, who set out the rules for the composition of such texts.[110] An imperial oration dealt with the emperor's origins, his physical appearance, his virtues and his achievements in war and peace.[111] Given the chiefly political function of rhetoric, it is clear that imperial panegyric was the principal medium for the propagation of the official ideology, since it projected the image of the ideal emperor; thus, it comes as no surprise that this specific rhetorical genre flourished almost throughout the Byzantine era,[112] and gave some of its masterpieces in the Palaeologan period. The flowering of imperial orations in the late Byzantine period was further fostered by certain historical facts, which contributed to the "revival" of the genre, especially during the reigns of the first two Palaeologan emperors, Michael VIII and Andronikos II. The Palaiologoi were the new dynasty on the imperial throne, after the usurpation of the imperial office by Michael VIII, and therefore sought to legitimize their rule. Moreover, the seizure of power by the new dynasty coincided with the recapture of Constantinople in 1261, a fact that also had an impact on the official ideology of the Byzantine state and left its mark on contemporary rhetorical praxis.[113]

The first surviving rhetorical texts reflecting this "renewed" imperial ideology are three imperial orations for Michael VIII Palaiologos penned by Manuel Holobolos.[114] Holobolos has been mentioned above as the first holder of the

---

109   See above, p. 19.

110   Menander of Laodikeia, *De epideicticis* 368.3, eds. Russell/Wilson, p. 76: ὁ βασιλικὸς λόγος ἐγκώμιόν ἐστι βασιλέως. On the theory of imperial oration according to Byzantine rhetorical manuals, see Toth, *Imperial Orations*, pp. 13–21.

111   On the character of Byzantine imperial orations in general, see Previale, "Teoria e prassi del panegirico bizantino", Dennis, "Imperial Panegyric", and Toth, *Imperial Orations*, pp. 31–45. In the following I use the term *imperial oration* in the wider sense of an encomiastic/panegyrical speech addressed to the emperor; on the issue of terminology, see Toth, *Imperial Orations*, pp. 169–83, and ead., "Rhetorical *Theatron*", pp. 433–36.

112   For a gap in the production of imperial panegyrics in the middle Byzantine period, see Kaldellis, "The Discontinuous History of Imperial Panegyric in Byzantium".

113   Angelov, *Imperial Ideology*, p. 42.

114   Manuel Holobolos, *Orations*, ed. Treu, pp. 30–98; the first oration has been edited anew by Sideridis, "Μανουὴλ Ὁλοβώλου ἐγκώμιον". See also Macrides, "New Constantine", and Toth, *Imperial Orations*, pp. 80–85. On Holobolos' involvement in promoting the official

reinstated position of the *rhetor* of the Church.[115] Under the Komnenoi the *rhetor*'s duty was to deliver panegyrics in honour of the emperor at Epiphany; the custom was slightly modified under the Palaiologoi, and the recitation of imperial panegyrics was held at Christmas.[116] Holobolos must have been the first *rhetor* of the Church to deliver such orations in honour of the emperor in the Palaeologan period.

Holobolos' orations were delivered in the course of three subsequent years, in all likelihood 1265–1266–1267.[117] The three texts were conceived as part of a series, as is evident from the fact that at the beginning of each oration the author summarizes the contents of the previous one.[118] Moreover, Holobolos places his orations within the realm of the former rhetorical tradition, and describes them as an "annual verbal tribute" to the emperor according to an ancient custom, thus providing the link with older rhetorical practices.[119] Although he is aware of the rhetorical rules for the composition of an encomium,[120] nevertheless he does not follow them strictly. The first oration begins with Michael's birth and upbringing, documents his accession to the throne, which is described as a reward for his pains for the sake of the Romans, and deals with certain major events of his early reign in Asia Minor. The second oration is dedicated to the reconquest of Constantinople and the emperor's triumphal entry into the Byzantine capital; in this context Michael is described as the "New Constantine", that is, as a new founder of Constantinople.[121] Finally, the third oration deals with the emperor's efforts to restore the capital and re-establish the educational system. All three texts are composed in the high Attic style, with numerous rare words and references to ancient literature (e.g., Homer, Pindar, Plato, Aristotle, Plutarch, even Virgil). However, there are far more references to the Scriptures, while the *synkriseis* of the emperor with

---

      ideology and politics of Michael VIII, see Angelov, "The Confession of Michael VIII Palaiologos and King David", and Pieralli, *La corrispondenza diplomatica dell'imperatore bizantino*, passim.

115   See above, p. 17.

116   Macrides, "New Constantine", pp. 25–31, 40–41, ead., "From the Komnenoi to the Palaiologoi", pp. 270–73, and Angelov, *Imperial Ideology*, pp. 44–45.

117   Macrides, "New Constantine", pp. 19, 37 (with no. 137).

118   Macrides, "New Constantine", pp. 16, 18.

119   Macrides, "New Constantine", pp. 27, 30.

120   Manuel Holobolos, *Orations*, ed. Treu, p. 32, lines 16–35. See also the discussion in Toth, *Imperial Orations*, pp. 173–75, and ead., "Rhetorical *Theatron*", p. 434.

121   Manuel Holobolos, *Orations*, ed. Treu, p. 57, lines 1–4. Cf. Macrides, "New Constantine", pp. 23–24 (with n. 55), and Lauritzen, "Il modello constantiniano", pp. 313–14.

THE "LEGACY" OF APHTHONIOS, HERMOGENES AND PSEUDO-MENANDER   33

older rulers, prescribed by the rhetorical theory,[122] derive almost equally from the Old Testament and ancient history.[123]

Holobolos' encomia for Michael VIII are the only imperial orations of the Palaeologan period that are known to have been delivered within the fixed annual cycle of court ceremonial. Although the genre flourished much more under Michael's son, Andronikos II, who is, along with Manuel I Komnenos, one of the most eulogized Byzantine emperors of all times, most of the panegyrics in his honour were recited within the framework of rhetorical performances at the court, in the presence of the emperor's entourage. We have in some cases evidence of rhetorical shows, in which the orators participated and which lasted for several days. The intended audience of the orations must not have been very wide, including mostly the emperor himself and members of the court, that is high officials and prominent ecclesiastics.[124]

Gregory of Cyprus provides the link between the reigns of Michael VIII and Andronikos II, as he eulogized both emperors. His panegyric for Michael VIII dates from the early 1270s, when Gregory had just completed his higher education and had joined the imperial clergy as *protoapostolarios*, probably through the intervention of Akropolites.[125] In the text he praises the revival of learning in Byzantium after 1261, thus paying tribute to his teacher, who had been the mastermind behind this.[126] The oration more or less follows the instructions of Pseudo-Menander and begins with a lengthy praise of Constantinople, the imperial city and the emperor's fatherland;[127] the praise of the Byzantine capital appears as a structural element especially in the imperial orations of the early Palaeologan period, and must be correlated with the impact of the reconquest of Constantinople.[128] Gregory presents the course of Michael's life from his birth to his accession to the throne and the recapture of the old seat of the empire, which crowns the emperor's deeds; the influence of Holobolos' orations is perceptible not only in the subjects the author deals with, but even in the wording of certain passages. The panegyric for Andronikos II, which

---

122 Menander of Laodikeia, *De epideicticis* 376.31–377.9, eds. Russell/Wilson, p. 92.

123 See the table in Angelov, *Imperial Ideology*, p. 87.

124 Toth, *Imperial Orations*, pp. 205–14, ead., "Rhetorical *Theatron*", pp. 436–46, and Angelov, *Imperial Ideology*, pp. 46–50.

125 Gregory of Cyprus, *Encomium for Michael VIII*, ed. Boissonade. See also Toth, *Imperial Orations*, pp. 89–90. For the dating, see Angelov, *Imperial Ideology*, p. 71 (with n. 160).

126 Gregory of Cyprus, *Encomium for Michael VIII*, ed. Boissonade, pp. 352, line 2–354, line 5. See also above, p. 17.

127 Gregory of Cyprus, *Encomium for Michael VIII*, ed. Boissonade, pp. 316, line 21–319, line 25.

128 Fenster, *Laudes*, pp. 185–96, and recently Parlier, "Constantinople dans les éloges impériaux de Michel VIII et d'Andronic II".

dates from the early months of his reign (before March 1283),[129] is modelled on the same patterns, and focuses on the termination of the Union of Lyons, one of the first political acts of Andronikos II, which dominates the image of the emperor in contemporary literature.[130]

Gregory's encomium for Andronikos II itself served as a model for later imperial orations, such as those composed by Nikephoros Choumnos and Theodore Metochites. Choumnos was the older of the two orators and delivered his encomium between 1283–85.[131] His panegyric closely follows that of Gregory of Cyprus – of course, with variations of accent – and adds certain new features to the literary image of Andronikos II that would be repeated in later texts, such as the emperor's mildness and his aversion towards corporeal punishment,[132] as well as his fondness of philosophical discussions and participation in intellectual gatherings at court.[133]

It was the rhetorical skills of the twenty-year old Theodore Metochites that attracted Andronikos II and marked the beginning of Metochites' brilliant political career, which made him the most powerful man in the Empire.[134] Metochites' two orations in honour of Andronikos II date from the 1290s.[135] The first one is more traditional in its contents and structure, and bears outspoken resemblances to the older encomia of Gregory of Cyprus and Nikephoros Choumnos.[136] However, Metochites knows to innovate when resorting to late antique authors such as Synesios of Cyrene and Philo Judaeus, in order to present traditional material in a new light.[137] The second oration is not a typical encomium according to the instructions of Pseudo-Menander, but fits rather

---

129 Gregogy of Cyprus, *Encomium for Andronikos II*, ed. Boissonade. See also Toth, *Imperial Orations*, pp. 91–92.

130 Gregory of Cyprus, *Encomium for Andronikos II*, ed. Boissonade, pp. 380, line 15–384, line 24.

131 Nikephoros Choumnos, *Encomium for Andronikos II*, ed. Boissonade. See also Toth, *Imperial Orations*, pp. 95–97. For the dating, see Verpeaux, *Nicéphore Choumnos*, pp. 36 (with n. 3) and 89–90 (he dates the text to 1284–85), and Riehle, "Funktionen der byzantinischen Epistolographie", pp. 11–12 (he dates the text a year earlier, to 1283–84). On Nikephoros Choumnos, see PLP no. 30961.

132 Nikephoros Choumnos, *Encomium for Andronikos II*, ed. Boissonade, pp. 46, line 20–47, line 12.

133 Nikephoros Choumnos, *Encomium for Andronikos II*, ed. Boissonade, p. 36, lines 14–26.

134 Theodore Metochites, *Orations*, eds. Polemis/Kaltsogianni, pp. 149–75, 267–90, and Theodore Metochites, *Imperial Orations*, ed. Polemis. For the dating, see, Theodore Metochites, *Imperial Orations*, ed. Polemis, pp. 33–42.

135 Theodore Metochites, *Imperial Orations*, ed. Polemis, pp. 33–42.

136 Theodore Metochites, *Imperial Orations*, ed. Polemis, pp. 65–72.

137 Theodore Metochites, *Imperial Orations*, ed. Polemis, pp. 73–98.

THE "LEGACY" OF APHTHONIOS, HERMOGENES AND PSEUDO-MENANDER   35

in the generic category of *prosphonetikos logos* (laudatory address);[138] it deals with the emperor's expedition to Asia Minor in the years 1290–93, yet was delivered in Constantinople some years later.[139]

The coronation of Andronikos' son Michael IX as co-emperor on 21 May 1294 was celebrated for several days, with feasts and the delivery of panegyrics. Invited by the emperor, Maximos Planoudes delivered on this occasion his *Basilikos*, a panegyric on Michael IX, mixing the praise with some pieces of counsel.[140] This oration has been classified by modern scholars as a sample of the so-called "political panegyric", a genre described by Hermogenes and also discussed by Planoudes in his commentary on the Hermogenian corpus. In the counseling part of his speech the rhetor sought to influence the military policy of the future emperor and indirectly criticized Andronikos' decision to dismantle the Byzantine fleet in 1285.[141]

Naturally, the first encounter of a rhetorician with the emperor offered a suitable occasion for the delivery of an encomium in the latter's honour. This was the case with Nikephoros Gregoras' first panegyric for Andronikos II, which the author addressed to the emperor on the occasion of their first meeting in 1321–22.[142] Gregoras was a student of Metochites, and entered the intellectual circles of Andronikos II probably through the intervention of his master. He wrote three panegyrical addresses to the old emperor in total, praising primarily his intellectual and rhetorical skills. The second panegyric seeks to prove that Andronikos II is an admirer of Plato, thus presenting some of the emperor's traditional virtues in the light of Platonic philosophy.[143] The originality

---

138   Menander of Laodikeia, *De epideicticis* 414.31–418.4, eds. Russell/Wilson, pp. 164–72. See also the discussion in Theodore Metochites, *Imperial Orations*, ed. Polemis, pp. 34–35.
139   On the historical circumstances, see Theodore Metochites, *Imperial Orations*, ed. Polemis, pp. 42–59.
140   Maximos Planoudes, *Basilikos*, ed. Westerink, and Kourousis, "Νέος κῶδιξ τοῦ *Βασιλικοῦ* Μαξίμου τοῦ Πλανούδη" (addenda to the edition of Westerink from the codex Ambrosianus G 14 sup.). See also Toth, *Imperial Orations*, pp. 106–108, and Giannouli, "Coronation Speeches", pp. 206–13.
141   Angelov, "Byzantine Imperial Panegyric as Advice Literature", pp. 58–65, and id., *Imperial Ideology*, pp. 172–79.
142   On Nikephoros Gregoras, see *PLP* no. 4443, and Fryde, *Renaissance*, pp. 357–73. For the text, which the author later incorporated in his historical work, see Nikephoros Gregoras, *Roman History* VIII.8, ed. Schopen, vol. 1, pp. 328, line 9–339, line 20. See also Toth, *Imperial Orations*, pp. 125–26. For the dating, see Nikephoros Gregoras, *Roman History*, trans. van Dieten, vol. 1/2, p. 153.
143   Nikephoros Gregoras, *Encomia for Andronikos II*, ed. Leone, pp. 503–10. See also Guilland, *Essai*, pp. 148–49, and Toth, *Imperial Orations*, pp. 126–27.

of the third oration lies rather in its linguistic form than in its contents, as Gregoras composed it in the Ionic dialect.[144]

The unparalleled flowering of court culture during the reign of Andronikos II Palaiologos did not continue under his successors. The civil war of the 1340s for the succession of Andronikos III, and later the conflict between Matthew Kantakouzenos and John V Palaiologos, along with the rapid diminishing of Byzantine territories, did not offer favourable conditions for the flourishing of court oratory and intellectual life in general.[145] Very few imperial orations survive from this period, and they rather have the form of short laudatory addresses, such as the oration of Demetrios Kydones to John VI Kantakouzenos shortly after the latter's entry to Constantinople in 1347[146] or the orations of Nicholas Kabasilas for Anna of Savoy and Matthew Kantakouzenos, dating from 1347–51 and 1354 respectively.[147]

It was under the learned Emperor Manuel II and his son John VIII Palaiologos that court oratory, and thus the genre of imperial oration, flourished again, although not to the same extent as under the first two rulers of the dynasty; but the historical circumstances had also changed.[148] Manuel himself was the addressee of four panegyrics, the earliest dating from shortly after his return to Constantinople from his long journey to the West in 1403. The text has traditionally been attributed to Isidore of Kiev, yet his authorship cannot be certain;[149] apart from the emperor's pains for the sake of his subjects, the author also praises Manuel for his rhetorical skills that make him a philosopher on the imperial throne, just like Plato's ideal king, a standard

---

144 Nikephoros Gregoras, *Encomia for Andronikos II*, ed. Leone, pp. 510–15. See also Guilland, *Essai*, pp. 149–50, and Toth, *Imperial Orations*, pp. 127–28.

145 Cf. Toth, *Imperial Orations*, p. 60.

146 Demetrios Kydones, *Encomium for John VI Kantakouzenos*, ed. Cammelli. See also Toth, *Imperial Orations*, pp. 136–37. On Demetrios Kydones, see PLP no. 13876, and Ryder, *The Career and Writings of Demetrius Kydones*.

147 Nicholas Kabasilas, *Encomia for Matthew Kantakouzenos and Anna of Savoy*, ed. Jugie, and Laurent, "Un nouveau témoin", pp. 201–204 (different readings from the codex Barlaam 202, as well as the end of the encomium for Anna of Savoy missing from the edition of Jugie). Especially on the encomium for Matthew Kantakouzenos, see Toth, *Imperial Orations*, 140–41, and Congourdeau, "Nicolas Cabasilas and Matthieu Cantacuzène". On Nicholas Kabasilas, see PLP no. 30539.

148 This late "revival" of court oratory should be regarded as an effect of the Turkish defeat in the battle of Ankara, which led to a temporary halt in their expansion and gave the Byzantines the opportunity to reconquer some territories, thus enhancing their self-confidence; cf. Schmitt, "Kaiserrede und Zeitgeschichte", p. 210.

149 Isidore of Kiev, *Encomium for Manuel II*, ed. Polemis. On Isidore of Kiev, see PLP no. 8300, and Philippides/Hanak, *Cardinal Isidore*.

motif in the praises of Manuel.[150] One more panegyric has recently been attributed to Manuel's friend Makarios Makres, and must have been delivered in Thessaloniki sometime around 1408–10,[151] while the other two encomia date from *c.*1417–18 and were penned by Demetrios Chrysoloras[152] and John Chortasmenos.[153] Chrysoloras' text, in the form of a *synkrisis* between Manuel and the ancient rulers, is an important source for the emperor's activity in the Peloponnese in the years 1414–16 and the re-building of the Hexamilion, a barrier-wall across the Isthmus of Corinth covering a distance of about six miles;[154] moreover, the author extols Manuel's literary achievements, with reference to his works,[155] thus exploiting a common motif of contemporary encomiastic literature, as pointed out above. Of interest on the other hand, in the case of Chortasmenos, is the fact that the author provided his text with a preface (*protheoria*), in which he analyzes the rhetorical character of his speech drawing on Hermogenes' treatise *On Ideas*;[156] literary analyses of this kind, not attested for earlier rhetorical texts, must have become fashionable in the circle of Manuel II Palaiologos, as will become clear in the case of the emperor's epitaph on his brother Theodore.[157]

Manuel's figure is also present in some of the encomia that were written for his son, John VIII Palaiologos, who succeeded him to the throne in 1425. Of special interest is the lengthy panegyric composed by Isidore of Kiev and delivered by the author himself in Constantinople sometime between spring

---

150 Polemis, "Two Praises", p. 713 (with n. 63), and Leonte, *Imperial Visions of Late Byzantium*, pp. 95–96.

151 Makarios Makres, *Encomium for Manuel II*, ed. Dendrinos. Dendrinos has considered the text to be an epitaph, yet it has been argued convincingly that we rather have to do with an encomium, composed while the emperor was still alive; see Polemis, "Two Praises", pp. 699–704, where the text is attributed to Makarios Makres. On Makarios Makres, see *PLP* no. 16379.

152 Demetrios Chrysoloras, *Comparison between Rulers of the Old and the New Emperor Manuel Palaiologos*, ed. Lampros.

153 John Chortasmenos, *Opera*, ed. Hunger, pp. 217–24. For the dating of the text, see ibid., pp. 55–57. See also Toth, *Imperial Orations*, pp. 149–50.

154 Demetrios Chrysoloras, *Comparison between Rulers of the Old and the New Emperor Manuel Palaiologos*, ed. Lampros, pp. 239, line 23–245, line 3. See also Leonte, *Imperial Visions of Late Byzantium*, p. 92.

155 Demetrios Chrysoloras, *Comparison between Rulers of the Old and the New Emperor Manuel Palaiologos*, ed. Lampros, p. 232, lines 1–26. See also Leonte, *Imperial Visions of Late Byzantium*, pp. 97–98.

156 John Chortasmenos, *Opera*, ed. Hunger, pp. 225–26.

157 See below, p. 40–41.

and early autumn of the year 1429.[158] The text is in keeping with the panegyrics composed in the times of Michael VIII and Andronikos II Palaiologos; a common feature it shares with the older texts is, e.g., the extensive *laus Constantinopolitana*.[159] Moreover, Isidore's panegyric constitutes an important historical source, containing a detailed account of contemporary events, which is unusual for rhetorical texts, an indication that rhetoric in this period assumed some of the traditional functions of historiography.[160] In reconstructing the glorious past of the City and the family of the Palaiologoi, and praising *in extenso* the emperor's deeds, the author might have been attempting to breathe courage and self-confidence into his contemporary Byzantines on the eve of their definite fall.[161] Furthermore, in the case of Isidore's panegyric, the manuscript tradition provides evidence for a redrafting of the text before its final version, a practice that is also attested for other major rhetorical texts of the time, and points to the importance given to these pieces, which were not always conceived as ephemeral compositions.[162]

Even the last Byzantine emperor, Constantine XI Palaiologos, was the addressee of some panegyrics on various occasions, before and after his accession to the throne. Three of them were penned by John Dokeianos, who is also known as a copyist and owner of manuscripts.[163] The earliest dates from c.1441 in its first redaction,[164] and was probably delivered in Constantinople;[165] it is

---

158   Isidore of Kiev, *Encomium for John VIII*, ed. Lampros. For the dating, see Schmitt, "Kaiserrede und Zeitgeschichte", pp. 241–42. See also Toth, *Imperial Orations*, pp. 158–61.

159   Isidore of Kiev, *Encomium for John VIII*, ed. Lampros, pp. 136, line 13–138, line 32. See also Fenster, *Laudes*, pp. 255–57, and recently Leonte, "Visions of Empire" (Leonte examines the spatial representations in the encomium and argues that Isidore emphasizes the preeminent position of Constantinople in the empire as an answer to the attempts of his contemporaries to promote the importance of other urban centers in late Byzantium).

160   See Schmitt, "Kaiserrede und Zeitgeschichte", pp. 217–19, and Leonte, *Imperial Visions of Late Byzantium*, pp. 77–78.

161   See Schmitt, "Kaiserrede und Zeitgeschichte", pp. 219–24 and 237–41.

162   For the different versions of Isidore's text, see Mercati, *Scritti di Isidoro, il cardinale Ruteno*, pp. 6–7. See also Schmitt, "Kaiserrede und Zeitgeschichte", p 214 (with n. 25), and Toth, "Rhetorical *Theatron*", pp. 446–47.

163   On John Dokeianos, see PLP no. 5577, and Calia, *Giovanni Dokeianos*.

164   John Dokeianos, *Encomium for Constantine XI (red. A)*, ed. Calia. An older edition by Lampros can be found in *Παλαιολόγεια καὶ Πελοποννησιακά*, vol. 1, pp. 221–31. For the dating, see Topping, "Dokeianos", p. 5, and Calia, *Giovanni Dokeianos*, pp. 223–24.

165   Lampros (*Παλαιολόγεια καὶ Πελοποννησιακά*, vol. 1, p. μθ´) suggested that the encomium was composed in Constantinople, based on the use of the demonstrative pronoun ἥδε with reference to the Byzantine capital; his view is rejected by Calia (*Giovanni Dokeianos*, p. 223), who suggests that the text was written in Mistras. However, there is a passage in the text which leaves no doubt that it was meant for a Constantinopolitan audience; see Calia, *Dokeianos*, p. 209, lines 157–164: Ῥωμαῖοι δὲ συμπολῖται, τὸν αὑτῶν στρατηγὸν καὶ

THE "LEGACY" OF APHTHONIOS, HERMOGENES AND PSEUDO-MENANDER   39

defined as an encomium, and echoes some of the traditional *topoi* of the genre,[166] yet is not devoid of historical value, especially with regards to Constantine's earlier life (capture of Patras, first despotate in the Peloponnese). Dokeianos later prepared a revised version of the text, which is about 1/3 longer and adds an *excursus* on the siege of Constantinople by the Turks in 1442.[167] On occasion of Constantine's return to Mistras (end of 1443)[168] Dokeianos composed a short address (*prosphonemation*), which also survives in two versions,[169] while a much shorter oration was written by the rhetorician in order to welcome the emperor in the capital in the spring of 1449;[170] this last text may have been presented by a member of the imperial family, for Dokeianos seems to have a Constantinopolitan audience in mind.[171]

πρύτανιν εὐφημοῦντες, καὶ πρὸς γῆν ἑτέραν τὴν καλοῦσαν αὐτὸν ὁρμώμενον, σὺν δορυφορίᾳ καὶ κρότοις προπέμπουσιν, ἀβουλητὶ μὲν δήπουθεν καὶ δυσχερῶς, διακρίσει δ᾽ εὐλόγῳ, τὸν κοινὸν εὐεργέτην πιεζόμενοι καὶ ἄλλοις μεταδιδόντες ἀπόνασθαι τῶν καλῶν, ταῖς σφῶν εὐχαῖς εὐλόγως τεθαρρηκότες, ἐπανήξειν αὖθις αὐτὸν προσδοκῶντες εἰς Κωνσταντίνου καὶ τῶν ἐλπίδων οὐ ψευσάμενοι, μετὰ κρείττονος προσηγορίας τῶν σῶν νῦν εὐφημιῶν ἀπολαύουσιν. The whole passage is omitted in the second redaction of the encomium, on which see below.

166 E.g., the reference to Achilles' apprenticeship with Cheiron, when it comes to speak about the emperor's education. See John Dokeianos, *Encomium for Constantine XI* (*red. A*), ed. Calia, p. 207, lines 123–131; cf. Menander of Laodikeia, *De epideicticis* 371.23–24, eds. Russell/Wilson, p. 82.

167 John Dokeianos, *Encomium for Constantine XI* (*red. B*), ed. Calia. This second redaction dates from *c*.1443, and was probably meant to be delivered in Mistras, as we can infer from the following passage missing from the red. A: οὐ γὰρ ὡς οὕτω φανῆναι τὸ παρὸν ἤρχθη δουλοπρεπὲς (δουλωπρεπὲς cod., Calia) τόλμημα· ἀλλ᾽ ὡς κατὰ τὴν νῆσον (sic cod., Calia: Πελοπόννησον legendum) προϋπαντῆσον σοι, καὶ τὰ λαμπρά σου μηνῦσον (μήνυσον Calia) εὐφήμως ἐγκώμια. See Calia, *Giovanni Dokeianos*, p. 218, lines 352–54.

168 See Topping, "Dokeianos", p. 5, and Calia, *Giovanni Dokeianos*, p. 259. In the older literature the text has commonly been associated with Constantine's assumption of imperial power and thus, dated to 1449; see, e.g., Lampros, *Παλαιολόγεια καὶ Πελοποννησιακά*, vol. 1, p. ν′, and Toth, *Imperial Orations*, p. 163.

169 John Dokeianos, *Prosphonemation for Constantine XI* (*red. A*), ed. Calia, and id., *Prosphonemation for Constantine XI* (*red. B*), ed. Calia. The red. A of the text was edited in the past by Sp. Lampros in *Παλαιολόγεια καὶ Πελοποννησιακά*, vol. 1, pp. 232–35. Dokeianos defines his text more specifically as an *epibaterios logos* (speech of arrival); see John Dokeianos, *Prosphonemation for Constantine XI* (*red. A*), ed. Calia, p. 255, lines 58–59, and id., *Prosphonemation for Constantine XI* (*red. B*), ed. Calia, p. 254, lines 46–47. On the *epibaterios logos*, see Menander of Laodikeia, *De epideicticis* 377.31–388.15, eds. Russell/Wilson, pp. 94–114.

170 John Dokeianos, *Oration for Constantine XI*, ed. Calia. A short fragment of the text was also edited by Lampros, *Παλαιολόγεια καὶ Πελοποννησιακά*, vol. 1, p. 250.

171 A possible candidate would be Eleni Palaiologina (*PLP* no. 21363), the daughter of Demetrios Palaiologos (*PLP* no. 21454). See Topping, "Dokeianos", pp. 7–8, and Calia, *Giovanni Dokeianos*, p. 287.

5   Practical Uses of Rhetoric: Funeral Orations

The second major type of epideictic oratory that was cultivated in the Palaeologan period was the *epitaphios logos* (funeral oration) in its various forms. The instructions for the composition of this kind of speech were also provided by Pseudo-Menander, who made the distinction between the "monody", that is a *threnos* (lamentation) for the loss of a person,[172] and the "epitaph" proper, which focused on the praise of the deceased.[173] Most of the funeral orations produced during the Palaeologan period belong rather to the genre of monody,[174] although the elements of mourning and praise are very often combined. These texts would be presented in the course of a funeral or memorial service, but despite their conventional character, they provide us in some cases with useful prosopographical and historical information. The number of funeral orations that survive from the period under consideration amount to 74, that is more than 50 per cent of the total 142 texts that have come down to us from the whole Byzantine era.[175]

The earliest surviving funeral oration from the Palaelogan age was written by Theodore Metochites and is dedicated to the Empress Theodora Palaiologina, wife of Michael VIII, who passed away on 4 March 1303.[176] The oration was delivered during the empress' burial,[177] in the presence of her son, Andronikos II, to whose grief the author makes special reference.[178] Metochites develops his subject – according to the rhetorical theory – on two levels, present and past,[179] which alternate with each other: on the level of the present he extols the enormity of the bereavement for all the Romans,[180] while on the level of past he praises the virtues of the deceased empress, with reference to her philanthropy and her role in the restoration of churches and monasteries.[181] A further text of Metochites, which has often been classified as an epitaph, is concerned with Joseph the Philosopher and was written after

---

172   Menander of Laodikeia, *De epideicticis* 434.10–437.4, eds. Russell/Wilson, pp. 200–207.
173   Menander of Laodikeia, *De epideicticis* 418.5–422.4, eds. Russell/Wilson, pp. 170–79.
174   Cf. Sideras, *Grabreden*, p. 245.
175   Cf. Sideras, *Grabreden*, p. 245.
176   Theodore Metochites, *Orations*, eds. Polemis/Kaltsogianni, pp. 329–46. See also Sideras, *Grabreden*, pp. 262–64. On Theodora Palaiologina, see PLP no. 21380.
177   Sideras, *Grabreden*, p. 264.
178   Theodore Metochites, *Orations*, eds. Polemis/Kaltsogianni, pp. 339, line 10–341, line 31.
179   Menander of Laodikeia, *De epideicticis* 435.16–436.10, eds. Russell/Wilson, p. 204.
180   See, e.g., Theodore Metochites, *Orations*, eds. Polemis/Kaltsogianni, pp. 331, line 11–333, line 55, and 334, line 16–336, line 56.
181   See, e.g., Theodore Metochites, *Orations*, eds. Polemis/Kaltsogianni, pp. 336, line 1–337, line 30, and 338, line 1–339, line 3. See also Talbot, "Empress Theodora Palaiologina".

1328; its literary character could be better described as an "encomium in the form of an epistle".[182]

Apart from the emperors and empresses, a substantial number of funeral orations in the Palaeologan period were dedicated to other members of the imperial family. The two sons of Andronikos II, John and Michael IX Palaiologos,[183] who died in 1307 and 1320 respectively, were honoured with more than one epitaph each. Alexios Lampenos, a person known only from his funeral orations for members of the Palaeologan family,[184] composed a total of four monodies in honour of John Palaiologos, each one linked to a different occasion (announcement of death, memorial services, translation of mortal remains).[185] All four texts share common motifs and stylistic devices, with the *topos* of *mors immatura* – John died at the age of 21 – being the dominant one; the balance between lamentation and praise varies in each case, but the encomiastic element prevails over the wailing as time passes.[186] The situation is similar with the orations on the death of Michael IX Palaiologos: John Staphidakis composed a monody to be delivered probably during Michael's funeral in Thessaloniki;[187] the text is full of apostrophes to persons, cities, and elements of nature, in order to widen participation in the lamentation for the death of the co-emperor.[188] A second monody, written by Theodore Hyrtakenos, was delivered in Constantinople on the occasion of a memorial service for Michael IX;[189] in this case the author turns the *threnos* into an indirect encomium of the deceased, employing numerous citations from and allusions to ancient Greek literature, which serve occasionally as a mere display of Hyrtakenos' erudition.[190]

A special reference should be made to the funeral orations on two prominent intellectuals and statesmen of the early Palaeologan period, Nikephoros

---

182 Theodore Metochites, *Orations*, eds. Polemis/Kaltsogianni, pp. 633–72. For the literary character of the text, see the discussion in Sideras, *Grabreden*, pp. 55–56.

183 See *PLP* nos. 21475 and 21529 respectively.

184 On Alexios Lampenos, see *PLP* no. 14423.

185 Alexios Lampenos, *Monodies on John Palaiologos*, ed. Lampros. See also Sideras, *Grabreden*, pp. 275–79, and Taxidis, "Les monodies et les oraisons funèbres".

186 Taxidis, "Les monodies et les oraisons funèbres", pp. 271–72.

187 John Staphidakis, *Monody on Michael IX*, ed. Pignani; see also Sideras, *Grabreden*, pp. 280–82. On John Staphidakis, see *PLP* no. 26734.

188 Taxidis, "Les monodies et les oraisons funèbres", pp. 282–83.

189 Theodore Hyrtakenos, *Funeral Oration on Michael IX*, ed. Chrysostomidis; an older edition can be found in Boissonade, *Anecdota Graeca*, vol. 1, pp. 254–68. See also Sideras, *Grabreden*, pp. 259–60. On Theodore Hyrtakenos, see *PLP* no. 29507, and Mergiali, *L'enseignement*, pp. 90–95.

190 Taxidis, "Les monodies et les oraisons funèbres", pp. 281–82.

Choumnos and Theodore Metochites. Choumnos died in 1327 and was honoured with an epitaph by Theodore Hyrtakenos, with whom he was also in correspondence. The intellectual merits of the deceased are in this case in the foreground, yet the encomium culminates in Choumnos' relationship with the Emperor Andronikos II, which is presented as the crown of his bliss.[191] In the epitaph on Theodore Metochites by Nikephoros Gregoras, which the author himself probably delivered during Metochites' burial, the close relationship between Metochites and Andronikos II is the main subject; the temporal proximity of the death of the two men – Metochites died exactly one month after the emperor – must have also played a role in Gregoras' choice to emphasise this point.[192]

Nikephoros Gregoras integrated in his historical work two more epitaphs dedicated to Andronikos II and Andronikos III Palaiologos respectively. The epitaph on Andronikos II was delivered on the second day after the emperor's death (14/15 February 1332) on the instigation of the latter's daughter Simonis. Gregoras defines his text as a *threnos* and adheres strictly to Menander's instruction for the composition of monodies, according to which the author of a monody should present the encomium of the deceased as the occasion for the lament.[193] The encomium of Andronikos II runs on the basic *topoi* of Byzantine imperial ideology (wakefulness, providence, benefaction, philanthropy), and repeats some of the motifs of the panegyrics in honour of the emperor (piety, patronage of learning), while the participation of the elements of nature in the lamentation underlines the enormity of the disaster.[194] Gregoras' epitaph on Andronikos III, on the other hand, was delivered in the imperial palace on the third day after the emperor's death (17/18 June 1341); it displays certain common motifs with the epitaph on Andronikos II, yet it is the military virtues of Andronikos III that stay in the foreground, as well as his personal intervention in the controversy between Barlaam and Palamas in the Council of 1341.[195]

---

191 Theodore Hyrtakenos, *Funeral Oration on Nikephoros Choumnos*, ed. Chrysostomidis; an older edition can be found in Boissonade, *Anecdota Graeca*, vol. 1, pp. 282–92. See also Sideras, *Grabreden*, pp. 260–61.

192 The epitaph has been incorporated by Gregoras in his historical work; see Nikephoros Gregoras, *Roman History* X.2, ed. Schopen, vol. 1, pp. 475, lines 1–481, line 13. See also Sideras, *Grabreden*, pp. 293–95.

193 Menander of Laodikeia, *De epideicticis* 434.18–23, eds. Russell/Wilson, p. 202.

194 See Nikephoros Gregoras, *Roman History* X.1, ed. Schopen, vol. 1, pp. 465, line 1–472, line 6. See also Sideras, *Grabreden*, pp. 292–93. On Simonis Palaiologina, see PLP no. 21398.

195 Nikephoros Gregoras, *Roman History* XI.11, ed. Schopen, vol. 1, pp. 560, line 8–565, line 13. See also Sideras, *Grabreden*, pp. 295–97.

THE "LEGACY" OF APHTHONIOS, HERMOGENES AND PSEUDO-MENANDER   43

Most prominent among the epitaphs of the Palaeologan period is the one composed by the Emperor Manuel II for his brother Theodore, the Despot of Mistras. Theodore I Palaiologos was the third son of John V Palaiologos, and was appointed c.1382 as a ruler in Peloponnese, where he stayed until his death in 1407.[196] Shortly thereafter Manuel composed a lengthy epitaph for his brother, which was delivered on the occasion of a memorial service in Mistras, partly by Isidore of Kiev and partly by a certain Gazes.[197] Covering about 100 printed pages in its modern edition, it is the lengthiest epitaph of the whole Byzantine era. For the most part it is concerned with the Byzantine affairs in the Peloponnese under the rule of Theodore, thus serving as an official apology for the policies of the Palaiologoi.[198] In terms of literary structure, the text is organized basically as an encomium (praise of the fatherland and parents, natural gifts of the deceased, praise of the latter's deeds),[199] and also contains some dialogical parts, a feature found mostly in metrical epitaphs.[200] Furthermore, the study of the manuscript tradition reveals at least seven different stages of reworking of the text by its author, which testify to the literary value attributed to it.[201] This is further evidenced by the fact that Manuel sent the epitaph to his contemporaries, among them Guarino of Verona and Manuel Chrysoloras, asking for their criticism. In fact, Chrysoloras replied with a long epistolary treatise, which analyses the literary merits of Manuel's work in terms of content and style.[202] Two shorter *protheoriai* on the content and

---

196 On Theodore I Palaiologos, see *PLP* no. 21460.

197 Manuel II Palaiologos, *Funeral Oration on his Brother Theodore*, ed. Chrysostomides. See also Sideras, *Grabreden*, pp. 315–20.

198 Cf. Leonte, "A Brief *History of Morea*". Radošević, "Waiting for the End", pp. 61–63 and 67–68 also discusses briefly Manuel's epitaph as a means of advertising the emperor's political concerns.

199 For the structure of the text, see Manuel II Palaiologos, *Funeral Oration on his Brother Theodore*, ed. Chrysostomides, pp. 61–62, and Leonte, *Imperial Visions of Late Byzantium*, pp. 199–236.

200 Cf. Sideras, *Grabreden*, p. 316 (with n. 13).

201 Manuel II Palaiologos, *Funeral Oration on his Brother Theodore*, ed. Chrysostomides, pp. 43–53.

202 Manuel Chrysoloras, *Epistolary Treatise on Manuel II Palaiologos' Epitaph for his Brother*, eds. Patrinelis/Sophianos. See also Nuti, "Manuel Chrysoloras' Περὶ τοῦ βασιλέως λόγου". On Manuel Chrysoloras, see *PLP* no. 31165, Thorn-Wickert, *Manuel Chrysoloras*, and Pontani, "Scholarship in the Byzantine Empire", pp. 514–16.

literary character of the oration were penned by George Gemistos Plethon[203] and Ioasaph of Ephesos.[204]

Manuel Palaiologos' epitaph marked the beginning of a new flourishing of the rhetorical genre during the first half of the 15th century. We have in total 40 surviving epitaphs from this period, which proves to be the richest in the production of funeral orations compared to the whole Byzantine era.[205] Two of the texts are dedicated to Manuel himself, who died in 1425; the one was penned by his friend Makarios Makres,[206] while the other is the work of Bessarion.[207] Both texts were delivered on the tomb of the emperor during a memorial service, which, however, cannot be further specified. A point of interest in both of them is the address of the rhetoricians to the letters, which should lament the loss of their wise patron.

Ten of the forty 15th-century Byzantine epitaphs were produced in Mistras for prominent figures of the Despotate.[208] A case worth mentioning is the epitaphs on Kleopa Palaiologina, the prematurely deceased wife of the Despot Theodore II Palaiologos.[209] Kleopa died on Good Friday of the year 1433, and was honoured with at least five funeral orations written by scholars of the time, among them Bessarion and George Gemistos Plethon.[210] Most of the orations praise the dead princess for her piety, her devotion to her husband, and her love for the neighbour; Plethon's text stands alone for the absence of lament and its final digression on the immortality of the soul.[211]

Both Plethon and Bessarion, who have been mentioned so far as authors of epitaphs, were honoured in their turn with funeral orations by their contemporaries. Plethon marked with his personality and innovative ideas the

---

203 Manuel II Palaiologos, *Funeral Oration on his Brother Theodore*, ed. Chrysostomides, pp. 67–69. An English translation can be found in Leonte, *Imperial Visions of Late Byzantium*, pp. 288–90. On Plethon, see below.

204 Manuel II Palaiologos, *Funeral Oration on his Brother Theodore*, ed. Chrysostomides, p. 70. On Ioasaph of Ephesos, see PLP no. 8916.

205 Sideras, *Grabreden*, pp. 63 and 245.

206 Makarios Makres, *Funeral Oration on Manuel II Palaiologos*, ed. Sideras. See also Sideras, *Grabreden*, pp. 344–45.

207 Bessarion, *Funeral Oration on Manuel II Palaiologos*, ed. Lampros. See also Sideras, *Grabreden*, pp. 361–62. On Bessarion, see below.

208 Sideras, *Grabreden*, pp. 463–64.

209 On Kleopa Palaiologina, see PLP no. 21385, and Dąbrowska, "'Vasilissa, ergo gaude ...'".

210 For the epitaphs on Kleopa Palaiologina, see Sideras, *Grabreden*, pp. 322–26, 333–34, 335–36, 356–57, and 365–66.

211 George Gemistos Plethon, *Funeral Oration on Kleopa Palaiologina*, ed. Lampros, pp. 161–75 (especially, pp. 171, line 1–174, line 4).

THE "LEGACY" OF APHTHONIOS, HERMOGENES AND PSEUDO-MENANDER   45

intellectual life in Mistras during the first half of the 15th century;[212] he died on 26 June 1452. During his burial his disciple Gregory the monk, who is otherwise unknown, delivered a funeral oration praising the universal learning of his master and comparing him to wise men of the past; in the consolatory part of his oration Gregory speaks about the immortality of the soul, drawing mainly on Plato.[213] Another disciple of Plethon, Charitonymos Hermonymos, dedicated an epitaph to his master at a later stage. Like Gregory, he also praised Plethon's wisdom, comparing him to Socrates and Plato, and maintained that the death of a wise man is a greater loss than the death of a king.[214]

The only surviving Greek epitaph on Bessarion, on the other hand, is chronologically the last piece of this rhetorical genre and goes, in fact, beyond the limits of the Byzantine era. Bessarion was born in Trebizond and is also counted among the disciples of Plethon. As bishop of Nicaea, he participated in the Council of Ferrara/Florence in 1438–39; being a fervent supporter of the Union of the Churches, he later espoused the Catholic creed and became a cardinal of the Roman Church. He died in November 1472 in Ravenna.[215] It was a Latin epitaph that was delivered during his funeral, yet his protégé Michael Apostoles also composed a Greek epitaph, when news of Bessarion's death reached Crete, where Apostoles was established at the time.[216] The encomiastic element prevails over the wailing in this case; as the author explicitly states, the lament limits itself to the preamble, while the rest of the text has a pure encomiastic character.[217] It is interesting to observe that Apostoles drew, among other sources, on Plethon's epitaph on Kleopa Palaiologina,[218] a literary choice indicative of the influence of Plethon and his text.

---

212   On Plethon, see *PLP* no. 3630, as well as the monographs of Tambrun-Krasker, *Pléthon: Le retour de Platon*, Siniossoglou, *Radical Platonism in Byzantium*, and Hladký, *The Philosophy of Gemistos Plethon*. Plethon's ideas on the reform of the Byzantine state will be discussed below, in the section on symbouleutic oratory.

213   Gregory the Monk, *Funeral Oration on Plethon*; see also Sideras, *Grabreden*, pp. 358–59. On Gregory the Monk, see *PLP* no. 4605.

214   Charitonymos Hermonymos, *Funeral Oration on Plethon*; see also Sideras, *Grabreden*, pp. 377–78. On Charitonymos Hermonymos, see *PLP* no. 6126.

215   On Bessarion, see *PLP* no. 2707. For more recent bibliography, see Giarenis/Maras/Baloglou/Kyriakidis, *Βησσαρίων ἐκ Τραπεζοῦντος τοῦ Πόντου*, Mariev, *Bessarion's Treasure*, and Rigo/Zorzi, *I libri di Bessarione*

216   Michael Apostoles, *Funeral Oration on Bessarion*, ed. Riehle; see also Sideras, *Grabreden*, pp. 387–88. On Michael Apostoles, see *PLP* no. 1201, and Georgakopoulos, *Μιχαὴλ Ἀποστόλης*.

217   Michael Apostoles, *Funeral Oration on Bessarion*, ed. Riehle, pp. 20*–25*.

218   Michael Apostoles, *Funeral Oration on Bessarion*, ed. Riehle, p. 29*.

Among the epitaphs of the Palaeologan period there is also one text dedicated not to a single person, but to a group of persons, just like in the case of the ancient *epitaphios logos*. The text was written by Demetrios Kydones, a prominent scholar of the second half of the 14th century who served as *mesazon* under John VI Kantakouzenos and was later in the service of John V Palaiologos.[219] Kydones' oration is concerned with the Zealot revolt in Thessaloniki in 1345 and the massacre of the about one hundred partisans of Kantakouzenos in the city, to whose party the author belonged.[220] It stands out for the vivid description of the hostilities on the one hand and the encomiastic *ekphrasis* of Thessaloniki on the other, which is skillfully placed at the beginning of the oration, in order to underline the contrast with the current situation in the city.[221]

Natural phenomena and disasters could also provide the occasion for the composition of monodies. Aelius Aristeides and Libanios had, for example, written speeches on the destruction of cities or monuments after an earthquake or a fire.[222] A few such texts survive from the Palaeologan period, such as the short monody of George Galesiotes on the partial collapse of the Hagia Sophia due to an earthquake in 1346.[223] The symbolic role of the Church for Byzantine culture as a whole justifies the great impact of the fact in contemporary literature and the eschatological dimensions attributed to it; when the monument was restored in 1353–54, Alexios Makrembolites composed another rhetorical text, in which he presented the fall of Hagia Sophia as a sign of the imminent end of the world.[224]

Finally, a reference should be made to a group of monodies, which were produced in the late years of the Byzantine Empire and are concerned with the fate of Byzantine cities, which fell, one after the other, into the hands of the Turks. Thessaloniki first came under Turkish occupation in 1430, a fact which gave the occasion for the composition of three monodies lamenting the lost grandeur of the city: one of them has been attributed to John Anagnostes, who

---

219 On Demetrios Kydones, see above, p. 36.
220 On the Zealot rising, see Congourdeau, *Les Zélotes*.
221 Demetrios Kydones, *Monody on Those who Fell in Thessaloniki*. See also Sideras, *Grabreden*, pp. 73 and 302–304, Kaltsogianni/Kotzabassi/Paraskevopoulou, *Η Θεσσαλονίκη στη βυζαντινή λογοτεχνία*, pp. 54–58, Kushch, "Dèmètrios Kydonès, source pour l'histoire du mouvement zélote", and Taxidis/Nikou/Chrysostomidis, *The Ekphraseis in the Literature of the Palaeologan Era*, pp. 230–31.
222 Sideras, *Grabreden*, pp. 48 (with n. 17) and 49 (with n. 18).
223 George Galesiotes, *Monody on the Fall of Hagia Sophia*, ed. Kourousis. On George Galesiotes, see PLP no. 3527.
224 Alexios Makrembolites, *On the Fall of Hagia Sophia*, ed. Kourousis. On Alexios Makrembolites, see PLP no. 16352.

THE "LEGACY" OF APHTHONIOS, HERMOGENES AND PSEUDO-MENANDER   47

also wrote a historical account of the events,[225] while the other two are the works of the brothers Mark[226] and John Eugenikos,[227] both known for their vigorous opposition to the Union of the Churches. As is typical for monodies, the lament intermingles with the encomium of the fallen city and the glorious past of Thessaloniki is contrasted to its gloomy present.[228] The same scheme was repeated 23 years later in the monodies on the fall of Constantinople. Most of them prove to be indirect encomia of the Byzantine capital dressed with a veil of mourning. Among their authors we find again John Eugenikos,[229] as well as Andronikos Kallistos, who was a teacher of the Greek language in Italy.[230] A common attribute of most of the texts is the description of the fall of Constantinople as an earthquake and a storm with universal dimensions, and the comparison with the fall of other cities, such as Troy, Jerusalem and Babylon. However, the emphasis varies in each case: Andronikos Kallistos, e.g., gives a comprehensive (though indirect) encomium of Constantinople, which comprises most of the *topoi* of the *laudes Constantinopolitanae*, in order to stress the enormity of the disaster for the whole world; John Eugenikos, on the other hand, limits his praise to a few adjectives and attributes and addresses his lament to the Theotokos, who has denied her protection to the City.[231]

6   Encomia/*Ekphraseis* of Cities

Among the rhetorical genres that flourished especially in the Palaeologan period were the encomia of cities. The genre had a long tradition going back to ancient Greece, yet it was Aelius Aristeides that systematically cultivated it

---

225   John Anagnostes, *Monody on the Fall of Thessaloniki*, ed. Tsaras. On John Anagnostes, see *PLP* no. 839.

226   Mark Eugenikos, *Monody on the Fall of Thessaloniki*, ed. Pilabakis. On Mark Eugenikos, see *PLP* no. 6193.

227   John Eugenikos, *Monody on the Fall of Thessaloniki*, ed. Pilabakis. On John Eugenikos, see *PLP* no. 6189.

228   Kaltsogianni/Kotzabassi/Paraskevopoulou, *Η Θεσσαλονίκη στη βυζαντινή λογοτεχνία*, pp. 76–85.

229   John Eugenikos, *Monody on the Fall of Constantinople*, ed. Lampros.

230   Andronikos Kallistos, *Monody on the Fall of Constantinople*, ed. Pertusi. On Andronikos Kallistos, see *PLP* no. 10484, Wilson, *From Byzantium to Italy*, passim, and Pontani, "History of Byzantine Scholarship", pp. 523–24.

231   Fenster, *Laudes*, pp. 281–89. For Kallistos' text, see also Taxidis/Nikou/Chrysostomidis, *The Ekphraseis in the Literature of the Palaeologan Era*, pp. 216–17.

in the 2nd century AD[232] Menander of Laodikeia in his *De epideicticis* also gave instructions on the composition of such kind of texts. According to Menander, the encomium of a city should include chapters on the countryside and on individuals; in praising the countryside, the rhetor should refer to the geographical setting, climate, and nature; the praise of the individuals, on the other hand, should draw on their origins, actions, and accomplishments.[233] The flourishing of the genre in the Palaeologan period should be attributed to a combination of factors: at first it was the impact of the reconquest of the Byzantine capital in 1261 that gave the motivation for the composition of praises of the imperial city, both free-standing and integrated into other texts (e.g., imperial orations).[234] Furthermore, the Byzantine state at the time was hardly more than a set of individual cities (Constantinople, Thessaloniki, and later Mistras) with their surrounding countryside, a historical development that somewhat enhanced their political role and importance.[235] To this, one should add the interest of the intellectuals of the period in Aelius Aristeides, as attested in their efforts to acquire manuscripts with the works of the rhetor, as well as in the citations from the latter that can be traced in contemporary rhetorical works.[236] In the following I shall discuss only the free-standing encomia/encomiastic *ekphraseis* of cities produced in the Palaeologan period.[237]

The first two examples may be found among the rhetorical works of Theodore Metochites. The earliest is a praise of the city of Nicaea, which served as capital of the exiled Byzantine Empire from 1204 to 1261.[238] Metochites composed

---

232   Fenster, *Laudes*, pp. 1–8, and Voudouri, *Αυτοτελή εγκώμια πόλεων της ύστερης βυζαντινής περιόδου*, pp. 75–254.

233   Menander of Laodikeia, *De epideicticis* 346.26–367.8, eds. Russell/Wilson, pp. 32–75. See also Fenster, *Laudes*, pp. 8–13, and Voudouri, *Αυτοτελή εγκώμια πόλεων της ύστερης βυζαντινής περιόδου*, pp. 149–53.

234   Fenster, *Laudes*, pp. 185–226 and 318. See also above, pp. 33 and 38.

235   Saradi, "Monuments", p. 179, Voudouri, *Αυτοτελή εγκώμια πόλεων της ύστερης βυζαντινής περιόδου*, p. 276, and Taxidis/Nikou/Chrysostomidis, *The Ekphraseis in the Literature of the Palaeologan Era*, p. 179.

236   Voudouri, *Αυτοτελή εγκώμια πόλεων της ύστερης βυζαντινής περιόδου*, pp. 256–57, and Taxidis/Nikou/Chrysostomidis, *The Ekphraseis in the Literature of the Palaeologan Era*, p. 179. See also above, pp. 22–23.

237   On free-standing city encomia in late Byzantium, see the detailed study of Voudouri, *Αυτοτελή εγκώμια πόλεων της ύστερης βυζαντινής περιόδου*; on the distinction between free-standing and integrated encomia/encomiastic *ekphraseis*, see ibid., pp. 257–68, and Taxidis/Nikou/Chrysostomidis, *The Ekphraseis in the Literature of the Palaeologan Era*, 178–82.

238   Theodore Metochites, *Orations*, eds. Polemis/Kaltsogianni, pp. 1–14, and Theodore Metochites, *Nicaeus*, ed. Mineva. An English translation with commentary can be found in Foss, *Nicaea*, pp. 164–203.

THE "LEGACY" OF APHTHONIOS, HERMOGENES AND PSEUDO-MENANDER   49

this text c.1290 and delivered it in Nicaea, in the presence of the Emperor Andronikos II Palaiologos, who is directly addressed at the end of the speech as the most precious ornament of the city.[239] The structure of *Nicaeus* closely follows Menander's guidelines:[240] it begins with a reference to the past of Nicaea and its renovation by the emperor Trajan, and then the author praises the setting and the surroundings of the city, its walls, and the public buildings (especially churches, monasteries, and philanthropic institutions);[241] the encomium culminates in the praise of Nicaea as host of the First and Seventh Ecumenical Councils,[242] as well as the city that preserved the seeds for the later "revival" of the empire.

Metochites' second encomium is entitled *Byzantios or About the Imperial Megalopolis* and constitutes a long praise of Constantinople, which the author composed as a gift for his native city and nurse in letters.[243] *Byzantios* was written between 1305 and 1320.[244] In terms of length, it is approximately nine times longer than the *Nicaeus*, and it is thus uncertain whether the speech was delivered in public at all.[245] Its overall structure is (on the surface) similar to that of the *Nicaeus* and the basic precepts of Menander can easily be detected throughout the text:[246] the praise of Constantinople's setting as

---

239   For the dating see Ševčenko, *Études*, pp. 136–39. See also Rhoby, "*Byzantios* and Other City *Encomia*", p. 83.

240   For a summary of the text, see Hunger, *Literatur*, vol. 1, pp. 173–74, Foss, *Nicaea*, p. 128, and Theodore Metochites, *Nicaeus*, ed. Mineva, pp. 326–27. See also Voudouri, Αυτοτελή εγκώμια πόλεων της ύστερης βυζαντινής περιόδου, pp. 339–49, and Taxidis/Nikou/Chrysostomidis, *The Ekphraseis in the Literature of the Palaeologan Era*, pp. 120–23.

241   For the description of churches and other public buildings in the *Nicaeus*, see Saradi, "The *Kallos* of the Byzantine City", pp. 45–46, and ead., "Monuments", pp. 186–89.

242   Cf. Rhoby, "*Byzantios* and Other City *Encomia*", pp. 87–88.

243   Theodore Metochites, *Orations*, eds. Polemis/Kaltsogianni, pp. 430–552, and Theodore Metochites, *Byzantios*, ed. Polemis. For Metochites' motives, cf. Rhoby, "*Byzantios* and Other City *Encomia*", p. 86, and Taxidis/Nikou/Chrysostomidis, *The Ekphraseis in the Literature of the Palaeologan Era*, pp. 123–24.

244   Theodore Metochites, *Byzantios*, ed. Polemis, pp. 20–21. See also Voudouri, "Representations of Power", pp. 110–11 and 118, where the author suggests as a possible *terminus post quem* the years 1306–1307, and ead., Αυτοτελή εγκώμια πόλεων της ύστερης βυζαντινής περιόδου, pp. 352–58 (she dates the text to 1308–1309); Voudouri's dating is repeated by Taxidis/Nikou/Chrysostomidis, *The Ekphraseis in the Literature of the Palaeologan Era*, p. 134.

245   Rhoby, "*Byzantios* and Other City *Encomia*", p. 85, and Theodore Metochites, *Byzantios*, ed. Polemis, p. 27. On the contrary, Voudouri, "Representations of Power", pp. 111–13, and ead., Αυτοτελή εγκώμια πόλεων της ύστερης βυζαντινής περιόδου, pp. 358–59, as well as Taxidis/Nikou/Chrysostomidis, *The Ekphraseis in the Literature of the Palaeologan Era*, p. 134 suggest that the speech was probably delivered orally in a rhetorical *theatron*.

246   For a summary of *Byzantios*' contents and structure, see Fenster, *Laudes*, pp. 196–204, Theodore Metochites, *Byzantios*, ed. Polemis, pp. 31–40, Voudouri, Αυτοτελή εγκώμια

a bridge between Europe and Asia is followed by chapters on the establishment of the City by Constantine the Great, the description of its fortifications and buildings (with special reference to the church of Hagia Sophia), and the comparison with renowned cities of the past, such as Babylon, Alexandreia, Antioch, and Rome: all of them are defeated by Constantinople, which blossoms eternally and constantly renews itself, thus resembling the nature of the world. The ecumenical role of the Byzantine capital is expressed in a variety of motifs and pictures, while *Byzantios* also reflects some of the discussions among the intellectuals of the time, as well as the author's philosophical preoccupations, an element that elevates the text above the narrow limits of rhetorical theory.[247]

Fully developed praises of cities, such as the aforementioned texts of Theodore Metochites and those integrated into imperial orations, are a special characteristic of early Palaeologan rhetoric.[248] Moreover, the "rhetorization" of hagiography in the same period had as a result that many learned hagiographers, following the prescriptions of rhetorical theory, included praises of a saint's native city in their works.[249] Thessaloniki in particular was heavily praised in this context, in the texts dedicated to Saint Demetrios and other local saints. Authors such as Constantine Akropolites, Theodore Metochites, Nikephoros Gregoras, Nicholas Kabasilas, and especially Philotheos Kokkinos payed their tribute to the second city of the empire and extolled the virtues of Thessaloniki, occasionally using the same *topoi* that appear in the contemporary encomia of Constantinople.[250]

There are also certain free-standing city encomia surviving from the 15th century, but they are concerned in their majority with cities of the periphery, as we shall see below. As far as Constantinople is concerned, a reference should be made to a text composed by Manuel Chrysoloras and often cited as *Comparison between the Old and the New Rome*.[251] In fact, this is a lengthy epistle of Chrysoloras to the Emperor Manuel II Palaiologos dating from 1411,

---

πόλεων της ύστερης βυζαντινής περιόδου, pp. 360–90, and Taxidis/Nikou/Chrysostomidis, *The Ekphraseis in the Literature of the Palaeologan Era*, pp. 123–35.

247 Cf. the contribution of I. Polemis in this volume.

248 Fenster, *Laudes*, p. 225, and Rhoby, "Die Rezeption der spätantiken Rhetorik", p. 119.

249 Fenster, *Laudes*, p. 219, Stamouli, Οι «εκφράσεις» στα αγιολογικά κείμενα της παλαιολόγειας εποχής, pp. 203–542, and Taxidis/Nikou/Chrysostomidis, *The Ekphraseis in the Literature of the Palaeologan Era*, pp. 180–81, 193–95, 225–26, 243–44, 288, 290, 293, 294.

250 Kaltsogianni/Kotzabassi/Paraskevopoulou, Η Θεσσαλονίκη στη βυζαντινή λογοτεχνία, pp. 143–213.

251 Manuel Chrysoloras, *Comparison between the Old and the New Rome*, ed. Billò. The title does not seem to go back to the author himself and does not fully correspond to the content.

THE "LEGACY" OF APHTHONIOS, HERMOGENES AND PSEUDO-MENANDER   51

in which the former narrates to the latter his first impressions of Rome, where he was established at the time.[252] Taking as a starting-point the encomiastic words of past authors, such as Libanios and John Chrysostom, for Rome, Chrysoloras seeks to prove that the greatness of the city's past is still reflected in the ruins of public buildings;[253] above all, Rome is a city rich in relics, as well as the one that hosts the tombs of the Apostles Peter and Paul, elements that underline its role as seat of Christianity. Constantinople, on the other hand, is for Chrysoloras the "New Rome", the "daughter of the "Old Rome" that has surpassed the beauty of her "mother" in all aspects. However, after the lengthy *ekphrasis* of Constantinople, which comprises most of the *topoi* prescribed by the rhetorical theory, the author concludes that both cities – and especially Rome – offer proofs for the transience of glory and power.[254]

As for the free-standing city encomia that survive from the first half of the 15th century, the most prominent among these is Bessarion's lengthy encomium for his native city, Trebizond.[255] Like Theodore Metochites in his *Byzantios*, Bessarion also states that he composed the speech as an expression of gratitude to the place that gave him the gift of life.[256] The encomium dates probably from 1436–37,[257] but the circumstances of its composition and/or

252   For the addressee of the epistle, see Rollo, "Sul destinatario della *Σύγκρισις τῆς παλαιᾶς καὶ νέας Ῥώμης*".

253   For the role of antiquities in late Byzantine encomia of cities, especially *Byzantios* and the *Comparison* of Chrysoloras, see Magdalino, "The Beauty of Antiquity in Late Byzantine Praises of Constantinople". For Chrysoloras' debt to the rhetorical tradition of the Second Sophistic as reflected especially in the *ekphrasis* of the ancient monuments of Rome, see Webb, "Describing Rome in Greek".

254   See the summary of the contents in Fenster, *Laudes*, pp. 234–37. See also the analysis in Maltese/Cortassa, *Roma parte del cielo*, pp. 15–44.

255   Bessarion, *Encomium of Trebizond*, ed. Lampsidis; an older edition of the text was published by Sp. Lampros in *Νέος Ἑλληνομνήμων* 13 (1916), 145–204. See also Giarenis, "Ὁ λόγιος καὶ ὁ γενέθλιος τόπος", Saradi, "Η ἔκφρασις της Τραπεζούντας από τον Βησσαρίωνα", ead., "Monuments", pp. 189–91, Akişik, "Praising a City", pp. 10–21, Lauritzen, "Bessarion's Political Thought", Lamers, *Greece Reinvented*, pp. 94–112, Voudouri, *Αυτοτελή εγκώμια πόλεων της ύστερης βυζαντινής περιόδου*, pp. 476–594, Giarenis, "Η Ἔκφρασις του Βησσαρίωνα για την Τραπεζούντα", and Taxidis/Nikou/Chrysostomidis, *The Ekphraseis in the Literature of the Palaeologan Era*, pp. 73–80.

256   Bessarion, *Encomium of Trebizond*, ed. Lampsidis, p. 21, lines 12–22. Cf. Giarenis, "Ὁ λόγιος καὶ ὁ γενέθλιος τόπος", pp. 268–69.

257   For the dating, see Lampsidis, "Περὶ τὰ Ἐγκώμια εἰς Τραπεζοῦντα τοῦ Βησσαρίωνος", pp. 159–60, and Voudouri, *Αυτοτελή εγκώμια πόλεων της ύστερης βυζαντινής περιόδου*, pp. 505–507. Akişik ("Praising a City", p. 16 with n. 90) proposes a later date, *c*.1439–40, with which Giarenis also concurs ("Η Ἔκφρασις του Βησσαρίωνα για την Τραπεζούντα", pp. 186–87). Spyridon Lampros, the first editor of the text, dated it to the reign of Alexios IV Grand Komnenos, and more specifically between 1426–29; see Lampros, *Παλαιολόγεια καὶ*

delivery are not clear.[258] Trebizond was the capital of the independent state that was established after 1204 by members of the Comnenian family along the south-eastern coastline of the Black Sea, and led an autonomous existence until its conquest by the Turks in 1461.[259] Bessarion gives details on the history of the city during antiquity – its establishment, though indirectly, goes back to Athens – drawing on Herodotus and Plutarch, he vividly describes the commercial activity in the market, which is due to the favourable location of Trebizond and the natural harbours of the area, and praises the military skills of the inhabitants, who are constantly trained, in order to be ready to defend their country against invaders.[260] Although it deals with some of the basic topics proposed by the rhetorical theory for the encomium of a city, Bessarion's speech is nevertheless quite unique in its contents and disposition, and proves to be more than a rhetorical exercise; Libanios' *Antiochikos* has been identified as the author's basic model.[261] It has also been suggested that in praising the great past and other virtues of Trebizond, Bessarion sought to encourage his contemporaries to defend their city against the Turkish threat.[262]

A much shorter encomiastic *ekphrasis* of Trebizond was penned about a decade later by John Eugenikos.[263] Eugenikos wrote a total of four topographical

---

     Πελοποννησιακά, vol. 4, p. 197. Lampros' dating is accepted by Lauritzen ("Bessarion's Political Thought", p. 154).

258   According, to Lampsidis ("Περὶ τὸ Ἐγκώμιον εἰς Τραπεζούντα τοῦ Βησσαρίωνος", p. 160), the text was written in Constantinople, and was either sent by the author to Trebizond, in order to be circulated among the citizens, or was read by Bessarion himself to the Trebizondians during a private visit to the city, but not on a public occasion. Giarenis ("Ὁ λόγιος καὶ ὁ γενέθλιος τόπος", p. 278, and "Περὶ τὸ Ἐγκώμιον εἰς Τραπεζούντα τοῦ Βησσαρίωνος", pp. 182, 200–201, 204) argues against an oral delivery; this view is also shared by Akişik ("Praising a city", pp. 10–11). Voudouri (*Αὐτοτελή ἐγκώμια πόλεων τῆς ὕστερης βυζαντινῆς περιόδου*, pp. 507 and 582), on the other hand, favours the idea that Bessarion wrote the encomium with the intention for it to be read first in Trebizond and possibly later in Constantinople; as to the audience, she identifies it either with the citizens of Trebizond or with the members of a rhetorical *theatron*.

259   See Karpov, S., *Istorija Trapezundskoj imperii*, St. Petersburg 2007.

260   For a summary of the text's contents, see Lampsidis, "Περὶ τὸ Ἐγκώμιον εἰς Τραπεζούντα τοῦ Βησσαρίωνος", pp. 161–68, Hunger, *Literatur*, vol. 1, pp. 175–76, Voudouri, *Αὐτοτελή ἐγκώμια πόλεων τῆς ὕστερης βυζαντινῆς περιόδου*, pp. 572–94, and Taxidis/Nikou/Chrysostomidis, *The Ekphraseis in the Literature of the Palaeologan Era*, pp. 74–79.

261   Fatouros, "Bessarion und Libanios".

262   Cf. Lampsidis, "Περὶ τὸ Ἐγκώμιον εἰς Τραπεζοῦντα τοῦ Βησσαρίωνος", pp. 160, 168, and 184.

263   John Eugenikos, *Ekphrasis of Trebizond*, ed. Lampsidis. See also Voudouri, *Αὐτοτελή ἐγκώμια πόλεων τῆς ὕστερης βυζαντινῆς περιόδου*, pp. 594–618, and Taxidis/Nikou/Chrysostomidis, *The Ekphraseis in the Literature of the Palaeologan Era*, pp. 88–92.

THE "LEGACY" OF APHTHONIOS, HERMOGENES AND PSEUDO-MENANDER   53

ekphraseis: In addition to Trebizond, he praised Imbros,[264] Corinth[265] and the village of Petrina in Lakonia.[266] All four texts share common motifs and expressions, an indication that the author probably drew on a standard repertoire: the four places with their surroundings are presented as *loci amoeni*, there are references to the flora and fauna, the author makes puns with the place-names and in conclusion defines his texts as gifts to the respective places, mostly for their hospitality.[267]

7   The "Revival" of the *Genos Symbouleutikon*

It has already been mentioned that advisory oratory in the form it had been practiced by the Attic rhetors of the 5th and 4th centuries BC had fallen into disuse since Late Antiquity, due to the historical and political developments that led from the Athenian democracy to the Hellenistic states and later to the Roman Imperium.[268] Very few rhetorical texts from the Byzantine era can be classified as counseling speeches, and most of them were produced at court by persons who were close to the emperor – one should think, e.g., of the so-called "mirrors of princes", which contained advice for the emperor, yet they were composed in their majority by men of his milieu, and only rarely deviated from the patterns of official imperial ideology.[269] However, traces of counseling and criticism can even be detected in "propaganda texts" such as imperial orations, as we have seen, e.g., in the case of the *Basilikos* of Maximos Planoudes.[270] Furthermore, there exist a few rhetorical works from the Palaeologan period which are concerned with social and political matters of the time and are not directly linked to the court, and thus can be evaluated as pieces of "independent" political thought; interestingly enough, these works were not produced

---

264   John Eugenikos, *Ekphrasis of Imbros*, ed. Boissonade. See also Taxidis/Nikou/Chrysostomidis, *The Ekphraseis in the Literature of the Palaeologan Era*, pp. 86–88.

265   John Eugenikos, *Ekphrasis of Corinth*, ed. Lampros. See also Voudouri, Αυτοτελή εγκώμια πόλεων της ύστερης βυζαντινής περιόδου, pp. 618–27, and Taxidis/Nikou/Chrysostomidis, *The Ekphraseis in the Literature of the Palaeologan Era*, pp. 92–94.

266   John Eugenikos, *Ekphrasis of Petrina*, ed. Lampros. See also Rhoby, "Bemerkungen zur κώμης ἔκφρασις des Johannes Eugenikos", and Taxidis/Nikou/Chrysostomidis, *The Ekphraseis in the Literature of the Palaeologan Era*, pp. 94–97.

267   Cf. Rhoby, "Die Rezeption der spätantiken Rhetorik", pp. 121–23, and recently Chrysostomidin/Nikou/Taxidis, "Some Remarks on the Structure of John Eugenikos' *Ekphraseis* of Cities and Places".

268   Cf. above, p. 19 (with n. 21).

269   On this rhetorical genre, see below, pp. 56–58.

270   Cf. above, p. 35.

in the capital, but in Thessaloniki, whose role as an urban centre was enhanced during the late Byzantine period.

The first two texts to be discussed in this section are actually concerned with the historical developments in Thessaloniki during the first half of the 14th century. The earliest was written by Nikephoros Choumnos, who served as judge in the city sometime between 1286–95.[271] Choumnos' text is defined in the title as a "counseling speech", and is addressed to the people of Thessaloniki (and especially to the city's Senate), in order to counsel them on the issue of justice.[272] Writing from Constantinople between 1295–1316 (probably c.1310),[273] the author initially expresses his "erotic" disposition towards Thessaloniki, which is developed in a lengthy encomium of the city according to the rules of Menander; this part of the speech serves somewhat as *captatio benevolentiae*, before Choumnos proceeds to the main, counseling part, in which he castigates the greed of the rich people who appropriate the estates of the poor, and urges the Senate of Thessaloniki to take the matter in hand.[274] The speech culminates in an encomium of the Emperor Andronikos II, who is especially concerned with the maintenance of law and order in Thessaloniki, an element that makes the author appear as the emperor's voice.[275]

In the case of Thomas Magistros' speech *To the Thessalonians on Unity*, on the other hand, we hear the voice of a citizen preoccupied with urban affairs. Magistros' concern for the affairs of his native city is demonstrated in a variety of texts, such as his speech in defense of the general Chandrenos, which he delivered as an official envoy of Thessaloniki before Andronikos II.[276] His speech *On Unity* dates from the period of the civil war between Andronikos II and Andronikos III (1321–28), when part of Thessaloniki's population sided with the latter, thus bringing the conflict into the city and causing social and

---

271   For the person, see above, p. 34.

272   Nikephoros Choumnos, *To the Thessalonians on Justice*, ed. Boissonade.

273   Verpeaux, *Nicéphore Choumnos*, pp. 49–51, and Gaul, *Thomas Magistros und die spätbyzantinische Sophistik*, p. 66 (with n. 24).

274   On the structure and contents of the speech, see Nerantzi-Barmazi, "Ὁ λόγος τοῦ Νικηφόρου Χούμνου *Θεσσαλονικεῦσι Συμβουλευτικός*", Konstantakopoulou, *Βυζαντινή Θεσσαλονίκη*, pp. 149–53, Kaltsogianni/Kotzabassi/Paraskevopoulou, *Η Θεσσαλονίκη στη βυζαντινή λογοτεχνία*, pp. 36–47, Gaul, *Thomas Magistros und die spätbyzantinische Sophistik*, pp. 66–82, and Taxidis/Nikou/Chrysostomidis, *The Ekphraseis in the Literature of the Palaeologan Era*, pp. 279–81.

275   Gaul, *Thomas Magistros und die spätbyzantinische Sophistik*, p. 82.

276   Gaul, *Thomas Magistros und die spätbyzantinische Sophistik*, pp. 87–113. For the edition of the speech, see Boissonade, *Anecdota Graeca*, vol. 2, pp. 188–211.

THE "LEGACY" OF APHTHONIOS, HERMOGENES AND PSEUDO-MENANDER   55

political upheaval.[277] Magistros juxtaposes the benefits of unity to the evils of conflict: unity is extolled as the foundation of civil life and as a prerequisite for the prosperity of a city/state; it was unity that lay behind the glorious deeds of the Athenians during the Persian wars, while they lost their power when they started having internal political conflicts. The people of Thessaloniki should cease hostilities, live in concord with each other, and make their city a model of civil life.[278] Among Magistros' sources modern scholars have identified Aelius Aristeides' oration *On Unity of the Cities*; it has been suggested that this creates a parallel between the social/political preoccupations of the rhetors of the Second Sophistic and the concerns of the intellectuals in the early Palaeologan period.[279]

A number of counseling speeches from the Palaeologan period were motivated by the critical historical circumstances of the time; high state officials, patriarchs, and emperors addressed the Byzantine citizens in the face of the growing Turkish threat, in order to boost their spirit or to encourage them to take specific actions. In 1354 the Turks conquered Kallipoli and established their first beachhead on European ground. In 1366 Amadeus of Savoy reconquered the peninsula and offered it back to the Byzantines, on the condition that they espoused the Catholic creed; it was on this occasion that the "prime minister" of the emperor John v Palaiologos, Demetrios Kydones, who had already professed himself Catholic, composed a counseling speech, in which he urged his contemporaries to accept the alliance offered to them by the Latin West and reminded the Byzantines of their common Roman past with the Latins.[280] Some years later (in 1371) Kydones addressed another counseling speech to his contemporaries, advising them not to give Kallipoli back to the Turks, who had requested it as a condition for a peace treaty.[281]

The next two pieces we shall discuss are concerned with the fate of the two major Byzantine cities, Constantinople and Thessaloniki, in the face of an imminent Turkish attack. Thessaloniki and its environs were besieged by the Turks from 1382 to 1387, when the city was first conquered. Manuel II Palaiologos,

---

277   Thomas Magistros, *To the Thessalonians on Unity*, ed. Laourdas. For the existing translations and commentaries in modern language and the basic secondary literature, see Gaul, *Thomas Magistros und die spätbyzantinische Sophistik*, p. 407.

278   See the analysis of the contents in Gaul, *Thomas Magistros und die spätbyzantinische Sophistik*, pp. 144–59. See also Kaltsogianni/Kotzabassi/ Paraskevopoulou, *Η Θεσσαλονίκη στη βυζαντινή λογοτεχνία*, pp. 49–51.

279   Gaul, *Thomas Magistros und die spätbyzantinische Sophistik*, pp. 156–59.

280   Demetrios Kydones, *Oratio pro subsidio Latinorum*. See also Ryder, *The Career and Writings of Demetrius Kydones*, pp. 43, 144–46, and 153–60.

281   Demetrios Kydones, *Oratio de non reddenda Callipoli*. See also Ryder, *The Career and Writings of Demetrius Kydones*, pp. 43–44, 144–46, and 153–60.

who had served as ruler of Thessaloniki between 1369–1373 and was residing in the city at the beginning of the siege, spoke in the autumn of 1383 before the assembly of the people of Thessaloniki and delivered a counseling speech, in which he advised against a potential capitulation to the Turks and urged the Thessalonians to resist to the death in order to defend their city and the surrounding territories.[282] At the end of the 14th century Constantinople was also blockaded for the first time by the Turks of Bayezid (from 1394 to 1402), but the City remained unassailable for the time being thanks to its strong walls; the walls were, indeed, the only means of defense for the Byzantine capital, although they had suffered serious damage over the course of time. The refurbishment of the City's walls is the subject of a short oration by the priestmonk Joseph Bryennios, which the author delivered in the imperial palace shortly after 1415, in the presence of the emperor, the patriarch, high state officials and the clergy.[283] Bryennios urges all citizens of Constantinople, both the rich and the poor, to contribute to the restoration of the walls, in order to safeguard the city, which is the seat of the Orthodox faith and, thus, the "mother" of all Christians. A short *laus Constantinopolitana* belongs, of course, to the basic structural elements of the speech.[284]

As a subgenre of deliberative oratory we should also consider the so-called "mirrors of princes". These were counseling texts addressed to the emperor/the heir of the throne and projecting the image of the ideal ruler, according to the traditional tenets of the official imperial ideology; they shared many features with the imperial orations proper, but had a clear prescriptive and instructive character. Traditional manuals of rhetoric did not contain rules for the composition of "mirrors of princes" – the term itself is of western origin – despite the fact that such texts had a long tradition going back to the pseudo-Isocratic speeches *To Nicocles* and *To Demonicus*, and the authors themselves seem to recognize them as a distinct literary genre.[285]

---

282 Manuel II Palaiologos, *Admonitory Address to the Thessalonians*, ed. Laourdas. See also Kaltsogianni/Kotzabassi/Paraskevopoulou, *Η Θεσσαλονίκη στη βυζαντινή λογοτεχνία*, pp. 60–62, Lamprou, *Ὁ αὐτοκράτωρ Μανουὴλ Β΄ Παλαιολόγος*, pp. 217–19, Leonte, *Imperial Visions of Late Byzantium*, pp. 109–10, and Çelik, *Manuel II Palaiologos*, 94–102.

283 Joseph Bryennios, *On the Rebuilding of the City*, ed. Tomadakis. See also Gounaridis, "Ἰωσὴφ Βρυέννιος, προφήτης τῆς καταστροφῆς", and Kiousopoulou, *Emperor or Manager*, pp. 150–52. On Joseph Bryennios, see *PLP* no. 3257.

284 Fenster, *Laudes*, pp. 250–53.

285 For the "mirrors of princes" in general, see Hunger, *Literatur*, vol. 1, pp. 158–65. For the differentiation between "mirrors of princes" and "imperial panegyrics", which is underlined in the texts themselves, see Giannouli, "Paränese zwischen Enkomion und Psogos", especially p. 123. Against the traditional concept of "mirrors of princes" as a distinct literary genre argues Odorico, "Les miroirs des princes à Byzance".

The earliest surviving "mirror of a prince" from the Palaeologan period was written by the politically engaged and frequently mentioned Thomas Magistros.[286] The date of composition, as well as the addressee of the speech cannot be determined with certainty: the earliest date proposed is c.1304, while other scholars have dated it to the second, third or even the fourth decade of the 14th century; as for the person of the ruler, he has been identified alternatively with Andronikos II, Michael IX, the Despot Constantine Palaiologos, and Andronikos III.[287] Magistros' text is entitled *On Kingship*, and the title itself creates a parallel to the homonymous oration that Synesios of Cyrene addressed to the Emperor Arcadius in 398; common expressions and ideas testify to the author's familiarity with the older text, which he utilized not only as a literary model, but also as a model of criticism on contemporary policies.[288] Magistros begins his oration with common tenets of the Byzantine imperial ideology, already established in the relevant tradition: the emperor should be an imitator of God in terms of mildness, philanthropy, and generosity/charity, he should provide for the well-being of his subjects, select able and honest officials, and make ready for war;[289] however, in the course of the speech the author gives more concrete counsel, especially on fiscal issues,[290] he attacks the policy of employment of foreign mercenaries (most likely with the so-called "Catalan company" in mind), and criticizes the dismantling of the Byzantine fleet,[291] an issue also discussed by Maximos Planoudes in his *Basilikos*.[292] What crowns the image of the ideal emperor in the view of an intellectual like Magistros is, of course, learning, which the emperor should patronize so that his state resembles a *theatron* of the Muses;[293] this concept

---

286 Thomas Magistros, *On Kingship*, ed. Volpe-Cacciatore. For the existing translations and commentaries in modern language and the basic secondary literature, see Gaul, *Thomas Magistros und die spätbyzantinische Sophistik*, pp. 406–407.

287 Angelov, *Imperial Ideology*, pp. 189–90, Giannouli, "Paränese zwischen Enkomion und Psogos", pp. 127–28, and Gaul, *Thomas Magistros und die spätbyzantinische Sophistik*, pp. 330–37 (all three with references to older literature).

288 Angelov, *Imperial Ideology*, pp. 189–91.

289 For the imperial ideology as expressed through the "mirrors of princes" in the early and middle Byzantine period, see Paidas, *Η θεματική των βυζαντινών 'κατόπτρων ηγεμόνος' της πρώιμης και μέσης περιόδου*.

290 Angelov, *Imperial Ideology*, pp. 298–303. For Magistros' critique on imperial taxation, see also Laiou, "Le débat sur le droit du fisc et les droits régaliens au début du 14ᵉ siècle".

291 Cf. Angelov, *Imperial Ideology*, p. 303.

292 See above, p. 35.

293 Thomas Magistros, *On Kingship*, ed. Volpe-Cacciatore, p. 79, lines 1253–1271.

stands in line with the image of Andronikos II in contemporary imperial panegyrics, and likely points to the real addressee of the speech.[294]

The second surviving "mirror of a prince" forms part of the literary production of Manuel II Palaiologos. Manuel composed this text for his son and heir to the throne John VIII, and must have presented it to the latter *c.*1406.[295] In contrast to Magistros' text, Manuel's mirror is not structured like an oration proper, but is divided into 100 chapters. As H. Hunger has already pointed out, moral and theological issues stay here in the foreground, such as, e.g., the vanity of worldly matters or the relationship between the emperor and the Church;[296] practical issues, on the other hand, are rarely touched upon, although they are not totally absent from Manuel's reasoning (e.g., the strategy to lead an army on the battlefield).[297] There are, of course, some common topics which link Manuel's work to the older tradition of advisory texts for rulers,[298] yet it appears that the learned emperor was more interested in projecting the image of the ideal moral human character and not only that of the ideal ruler, thus expanding the scope of his text and making approaches to other kinds of advice literature, such as the *gnomologia* and *kephalaia*.[299]

One more text to discuss in this context is the *Basilikos or On Kingship*, addressed by John Argyropoulos to Constantine XI.[300] In modern secondary literature the text has been classified as a *stephanotikos logos*, associated with Constantine's coronation in 1449.[301] However, as Antonia Giannouli has convincingly argued, in terms of content we have to do rather with a theoretical treatise on kingship and a "mirror" of the ideal emperor.[302] After analysing the merits of kingship as a political system along with the basic imperial virtues (piety, prudence, bravery, justice, providence, mildness, intelligence),

---

294 Cf. Hunger, *Literatur*, vol. 1, p. 164.

295 Manuel Palaiologos, *Precepts of Imperial Conduct*. For the dating, see Leonte, *Imperial Visions of Late Byzantium*, pp. 126–28 (with references to older literature).

296 Cf. Hunger, *Literatur*, vol. 1, pp. 164–65, and Paidas, *Τὰ βυζαντινά 'κάτοπτρα ἡγεμόνος' τῆς ὕστερης περιόδου*, pp. 54–58.

297 On the contents and structure of the "Precepts", see Leonte, *Imperial Visions of Late Byzantium*, pp. 128–35, and ibid., Appendix 2, as well as Çelik, *Manuel II Palaiologos*, 319–30.

298 It has been suggested that the author used Agapetos' mirror of Justinian as one of his basic models; cf. Ševčenko, "Agapetos East and West", pp. 8–9, Leonte, *Imperial Visions of Late Byzantium*, pp. 146–48, and Çelik, *Manuel II Palaiologos*, 325–26.

299 See the discussion in Leonte, *Imperial Visions of Late Byzantium*, pp. 135–43.

300 John Argyropoulos, *Basilikos or On Kingship*, ed. Lampros.

301 See, e.g., Lampros, *Ἀργυροπούλεια*, pp. κ΄–κα΄, and Hunger, *Literatur*, vol. 1, p. 151. See also Giannouli, "Coronation Speeches", pp. 217–18.

302 Giannouli, "Coronation Speeches", pp. 218–20, and 221. See also Angelov, *Imperial Ideology*, p. 63.

THE "LEGACY" OF APHTHONIOS, HERMOGENES AND PSEUDO-MENANDER   59

Argyropoulos concludes his oration with an exhortation to the emperor to intensify his efforts for the salvation of the Greeks (*sic*) by turning for help to the West;[303] the advisory elements in the speech, either theoretical or practical, prevail over the panegyrical, thus justifying its classification as a piece of deliberative oratory.

Finally, a reference should be made to the so-called *memoranda* of George Gemistos Plethon. These texts are discussed in this session, for, like the "mirrors of princes", they offer advice for an effective conduct of state affairs, although they do not belong to this specific literary genre. Plethon was exiled to Mistras by Manuel II Palaiologos in 1405 over suspicions of heresy and paganism, but was later rewarded with various public offices and became head of the circle of intellectuals at the Despotate. Between 1416–18 he addressed a counseling speech to the Despot Theodore II Palaiologos, in which he expressed his concern for the defense of the Peloponnese in the face of the Turkish threat and proposed reforms for the improvement of the economic and military conditions in Morea. Plethon suggested that the state should rely on a citizen army rather than mercenaries and insisted on the exemption of soldiers from taxation, so that they could devote themselves to the defense of their fatherland; taking this principle as a starting point, he proposed a new state organization for the Despotate of Morea, according to which the population should be divided into three separate classes with a specific function: manual workers, service workers, and ruling class, including military.[304] This model, roughly based on Plato's *Politeia* and the accounts of the socio-political organization of ancient Sparta,[305] was repeated by Plethon in a later counseling address to Manuel II Palaiologos in 1418.[306]

---

303   John Argyropoulos, *Basilikos or On Kingship*, ed. Lampros, p. 47, lines 2–18.

304   George Gemistos Plethon, *Address to Theodore II Palaiologos on the Peloponnesian Affairs*, ed. Lampros. For the existing translations and commentaries in modern languages, see Hladký, *The Philosophy of Gemistos Plethon*, p. 326 (with n. 11). See also Siniossoglou, *Radical Platonism in Byzantium*, pp. 328–47, Hladký, *The Philosophy of Gemistos Plethon*, pp. 11–19, and Lamers, *Greece Reinvented*, pp. 36–42.

305   See Baloglou, "The Institutions of Ancient Sparta in the Work of Pletho", and Schawcross, "A New Lykourgos for a New Sparta".

306   George Gemistos-Plethon, *Address to Manuel II Palaiologos on the Peloponnesian Affairs*, ed. Lampros. For the existing translations and commentaries in modern languages, see Hladký, *The Philosophy of Gemistos Plethon*, p. 326 (with n. 8).

8   Concluding Remarks

Not all aspects of Palaeologan rhetoric can be discussed within the limits of this chapter. The above presentation has concentrated only on free-standing rhetorical texts, and has not considered embedded uses of rhetoric, e.g., in historiography, hagiography or epistolography;[307] it has also (arbitrarily) not taken into account the field of ecclesiastic oratory, which followed to a great extent the same patterns and – especially by the end of the period – touched very often upon secular issues,[308] as well as versified rhetorical texts (primarily imperial encomia and epitaphs).[309]

The volume and versatility of rhetorical texts produced in the Palaeologan era makes it, of course, difficult to summarize some basic developments: the focus on epideictic oratory is common with the previous periods, and the same applies to the close connection of the rhetors with the imperial court. Traditional forms continued to serve as the basis for rhetorical composition, as is evident both from the manuscripts of and commentaries on the manuals of Hermogenes and Aphthonios that were produced in the late Byzantine period and from the texts themselves. Nevertheless, the rhetors of the Palaeologan period "re-discovered" authors of the Second Sophistic such as Aelius Aristeides, and payed their tribute to the "master" of epideictic oratory, Menander of Laodikeia, by incorporating a basic chapter of his treatise in their rhetorical manuals. Moreover, neglected forms were brought into light, sometimes in order to give (even if indirectly) expression to contemporary preoccupations, like in the case of *meletai*.

Despite the fact that rhetoric flourished throughout the Palaeologan period, the vast majority of rhetorical production belongs either to the reigns of the first two Palaiologoi, Michael VIII and Andronikos II, or to the first half of the 15th century; as can be expected, the desperate historical situation of the second half of the 14th century did not favor rhetoric and literary activity in general. Although it remained "traditional" in its basic forms and subjects,

---

307   For embedded uses of rhetoric in Byzantine literature, see Jeffreys, "Rhetoric in Byzantium", pp. 175–77. Especially on rhetoric in Byzantine epistolography, see recently Kotzabassi, "Epistolography and Rhetoric".

308   One should bear in mind, for instance, the homilies of Isidore Glabas, where the author often discussed social matters of his time (see Christophoridis, "Ὁ ἀρχιεπίσκοπος Θεσσαλονίκης Ἰσίδωρος Γλαβᾶς καὶ τὰ κοινωνικὰ προβλήματα τῆς ἐποχῆς του"), or the politico-historical orations of Symeon of Thessaloniki (see Balfour, *Politico-Historical Works of Symeon Archbishop of Thessalonica*).

309   See, e.g., Papadogiannakis, *Studien zu den Epitaphien des Manuel Philes*, and Kubina, *Die enkomiastische Dichtung des Manuel Philes*.

THE "LEGACY" OF APHTHONIOS, HERMOGENES AND PSEUDO-MENANDER   61

during the last centuries of the Byzantine Empire rhetoric assumed under circumstances a more "pragmatic" role, and occasionally served as a means of approaching contemporary events, yet in a refined way.

Bibliography

Primary Sources

Alexios Lampenos, *Monodies on John Palaiologos*, ed. Sp. Lampros, "Αἱ μονῳδίαι Ἀλεξίου τοῦ Λαμπηνοῦ καὶ ὁ οἶκος τοῦ Ἀνδρονίκου Α΄ Παλαιολόγου", *Νέος Ἑλληνομνήμων* 11 (1914), 386–400.

Alexios Makrembolites, *On the Fall of Hagia Sophia*, ed. Kourousis, "Αἱ ἀντιλήψεις περὶ τῶν ἐσχάτων τοῦ κόσμου", pp. 235–40.

Andronikos Kallistos, *Monody on the Fall of Constantinople*, ed. A. Pertusi, *La caduta di Costantinopoli. L'eco nel mondo*, vol. 2, Verona 1976, pp. 354–63, 483–84.

Bessarion, *Encomium of Trebizond*, ed. O. Lampsidis, "Ὁ εἰς Τραπεζοῦντα λόγος τοῦ Βησσαρίωνος", *Ἀρχεῖον Πόντου* 31 (1984), 3–82.

Bessarion, *Funeral Oration on Manuel II Palaiologos*, ed. Lampros, *Παλαιολόγεια καὶ Πελοποννησιακά*, vol. 3, pp. 284–90.

Charitonymos Hermonymos, *Funeral Oration on Plethon*, in *Patrologia Graeca*, vol. 160, cols. 805–12.

Constantine Akropolites, *Ethopoiiai*, ed. R. Romano, "Etopee inedite di Constantino Acropolita", in *Ταλαρίσκος: Studia Graeca Antonio Garzya sexagenario a discipulis oblata*, Naples 1987, pp. 311–38.

Demetrios Chrysoloras, *Encomium of the Flea*, ed. G. de Andrés, "Demetrio Crisoloras el Palaciego, Encomio de la pulga", *Helmantica* 35 (1984), 51–69.

Demetrios Chrysoloras, *Comparison between Rulers of the Old and the New Emperor Manuel Palaiologos*, ed. Lampros, *Παλαιολόγεια καὶ Πελοποννησιακά*, vol. 3, pp. 222–45.

Demetrios Kydones, *Encomium for John VI Kantakouzenos*, ed. G. Cammelli, "Demetrii Cydonii ad Ioannem Cantacuzenum imperatorem oratio altera", *Byzantinisch-Neugriechische Jahrbücher* 4 (1923), 77–83.

Demetrios Kydones, *Monody on Those who Fell in Thessaloniki*, in *Patrologia Graeca*, vol. 109, cols. 639–52.

Demetrios Kydones, *Oratio de non reddenda Callipoli*, in *Patrologia Graeca*, vol. 154, cols. 1009–36.

Demetrios Kydones, *Oratio pro subsidio Latinorum*, in *Patrologia Graeca*, vol. 154, cols. 961–1008.

George Galesiotes, *Monody on the Fall of Hagia Sophia*, ed. Kourousis, "Αἱ ἀντιλήψεις περὶ τῶν ἐσχάτων τοῦ κόσμου", pp. 241–50.

62 KALTSOGIANNI

George Gemistos Plethon, *Address to Manuel II Palaiologos on the Peloponnesian Affairs*, ed. Lampros, Παλαιολόγεια καὶ Πελοποννησιακά, vol. 3, pp. 246–65.

George Gemistos Plethon, *Address to Theodore II Palaiologos on the Peloponnesian Affairs*, ed. Lampros, Παλαιολόγεια καὶ Πελοποννησιακά, vol. 4, pp. 113–35.

George Gemistos Plethon, *Funeral Oration on Kleopa Palaiologina*, ed. Lampros, Παλαιολόγεια καὶ Πελοποννησιακά, vol. 4, pp. 161–75.

George Lapithes, *Improvised verses*, ed. A. Chatzisavvas, Στίχοι πολιτικοὶ αὐτοσχέδιοι εἰς κοινὴν ἀκοὴν τοῦ σοφωτάτου κυρίου Γεωργίου Λαπίθου τοῦ Κυπρίου (Lapithos, 15), Besançon 2001.

George Pachymeres, *Meletai*, ed. J.F. Boissonade, *Georgii Pachymeris Declamationes XIII*, Paris 1848.

George Pachymeres, *Progymnasmata*, ed. Walz, *Rhetores Graeci*, vol. 1, pp. 551–96.

Gregory of Cyprus, *Autobiography*, ed. W. Lameere, *La tradition manuscrite de la correspondance de Grégoire de Chypre Patriarche de Constantinople*, Brussels 1937, pp. 173–91.

Gregory of Cyprus, *Chreia*, ed. Boissonade, *Anecdota Graeca*, vol. 2, pp. 269–73.

Gregory of Cyprus, *Encomium for Andronikos II*, ed. Boissonade, *Anecdota Graeca*, vol. 1, pp. 359–93.

Gregory of Cyprus, *Encomium for Michael VIII*, ed. Boissonade, *Anecdota Graeca*, vol. 1, pp. 313–58.

Gregory of Cyprus, *Encomium of the Sea*, in *Patrologia Graeca*, vol. 142, cols. 433–44.

Gregory of Cyprus, *Meletai*, ed. R. Foerster, *Libanii opera*, 12 vols., Leipzig 1843–1922 (repr. Hildesheim 1963), vol. 6, pp. 52–82, and ibid., vol. 7, pp. 142–79.

Gregory of Cyprus, *Melete*, ed. Pérez Martín, *El patriarca Gregorio de Chipre*, pp. 361–96.

Gregory of Cyprus, *Progymnasmata*, ed. S. Kotzabassi, "Die Progymnasmata des Gregor von Zypern. Fabeln, Erzählung und Ethopoiie", Ἑλληνικά 43 (1993), 45–63.

Gregory the Monk, *Funeral Oration on Plethon*, in *Patrologia Graeca*, vol. 160, cols. 811–20.

Isidore of Kiev, *Encomium for John VIII*, ed. Lampros, Παλαιολόγεια καὶ Πελοποννησιακά, vol. 3, pp. 132–99.

Isidore of Kiev (?), *Encomium for Manuel II*, ed. Polemis, "Two Praises", pp. 705–14.

John Anagnostes, *Monody on the Fall of Thessaloniki*, ed. G. Tsaras, Ἡ τελευταία ἅλωση τῆς Θεσσαλονίκης (1430), Thessaloniki 1985, pp. 70–77.

John Argyropoulos, *Basilikos or On Kingship*, ed. Lampros, Ἀργυροπούλεια, pp. 29–47.

John Argyropoulos, *Prolegomena to the Progymnasmata of Aphthonios*, ed. Rabe, *Prolegomenon Sylloge*, pp. 156–58.

John Chortasmenos, *Ethopoiia of Tamerlane*, ed. M. Treu, "Eine Ansprache Tamerlans", *Byzantinische Zeitschrift* 19 (1910), 15–28.

THE "LEGACY" OF APHTHONIOS, HERMOGENES AND PSEUDO-MENANDER   63

John Chortasmenos, *Opera*, ed. H. Hunger, *Johannes Chortasmenos (ca.1370–ca.1436/37). Briefe, Gedichte und kleine Schriften. Einleitung, Regesten, Prosopographie, Text* (Wiener Byzantinistische Studien, 7), Vienna 1969.

John Dokeianos, *Encomium for Constantine XI (red. A)*, ed. Calia, *Giovanni Dokeianos*, pp. 199–213.

John Dokeianos, *Encomium for Constantine XI (red. B)*, ed. Calia, *Giovanni Dokeianos*, pp. 198–220.

John Dokeianos, *Prosphonemation for Constantine XI (red. A)*, ed. Calia, *Giovanni Dokeianos*, pp. 253–57.

John Dokeianos, *Prosphonemation for Constantine XI (red. B)*, ed. Calia, *Giovanni Dokeianos*, pp. 252–54.

John Dokeianos, *Oration for Constantine XI*, ed. Calia, *Giovanni Dokeianos*, p. 286.

John Eugenikos, *Ekphrasis of Corinth*, ed. Lampros, Παλαιολόγεια καὶ Πελοποννησιακά, vol. 1, pp. 47–48.

John Eugenikos, *Ekphrasis of Imbros*, ed. J.F. Boissonade, *Anecdota Nova*, Paris 1844, pp. 329–31.

John Eugenikos, *Ekphrasis of Petrina*, ed. Lampros, Παλαιολόγεια καὶ Πελοποννησιακά, vol. 1, pp. 49–55.

John Eugenikos, *Ekphrasis of Trebizond*, ed. O. Lampsidis, "Ἰωάννου Εὐγενικοῦ ἔκφρασις Τραπεζοῦντος. Χρονολόγησις καὶ ἔκδοσις", Ἀρχεῖον Πόντου 20 (1955), 3–39.

John Eugenikos, *Monody on the Fall of Constantinople*, ed. Sp. Lampros, "Μονῳδίαι καὶ θρῆνοι ἐπὶ τῇ ἁλώσει τῆς Κωνσταντινουπόλεως", Νέος Ἑλληνομνήμων 5 (1908), 219–26.

John Eugenikos, *Monody on the Fall of Thessaloniki*, ed. Pilabakis, Ἑάλω Θεσσαλονίκη, pp. 76–85.

John Staphidakis, *Monody on Michael IX*, ed. A. Meschini, *La monodia di Stafidakis*, Padova 1974.

Joseph Bryennios, *On the Rebuilding of the City*, ed. N. Tomadakis, "Ἰωσὴφ Βρυεννίου δημηγορία περὶ τοῦ τῆς πόλεως ἀνακτίσματος (1415 μ.Χ.)", Ἐπετηρὶς Ἑταιρείας Βυζαντινῶν Σπουδῶν 36 (1968), 1–15.

Joseph the Philosopher, *Synopsis of Rhetoric*, ed. Walz, *Rhetores Graeci*, vol. 3, pp. 465–569.

Makarios Makres, *Encomium for Manuel II*, ed. C. Dendrinos, "An Unpublished Funeral Oration on Manuel II Palaeologus", in C. Dendrinos/J. Harris/E. Charvalia-Crook/J. Herrin (eds.), *Porphyrogenita. Essays on the History and Literature of Byzantium and the Latin East in Honour of Julian Chrysostomides*, Aldershot 2003, pp. 423–56

Makarios Makres, *Funeral Oration on Manuel II*, ed. A. Sideras, 25 Ἀνέκδοτοι Βυζαντινοί Ἐπιτάφιοι. Unedierte byzantinische Grabreden, Thessaloniki 1991, pp. 299–307.

64 KALTSOGIANNI

Manuel Chrysoloras, *Epistolary treatise on Manuel II Palaiologos' Epitaph for his Brother Theodore*, ed. G. Patrinelis/D. Sophianos, Μανουὴλ Χρυσολωρᾶ Λόγος πρὸς τὸν αὐτοκράτορα Μανουὴλ Β΄ Παλαιολόγο, Athens 2001.

Manuel Chrysoloras, *Comparison between the Old and the New Rome*, ed. C. Billò, "Manuele Crisolora, *Confronto tra l'Antica e la Nuova Roma*", *Medioevo Greco* 0 (2000), 1–26.

Manuel Holobolos, *Encomium for Michael VIII*, ed. X.A. Sideridis, "Μανουὴλ Ὁλοβώλου ἐγκώμιον εἰς τὸν αὐτοκράτορα Μιχαὴλ Η΄ τὸν Παλαιολόγον", Ἐπετηρὶς Ἑταιρείας Βυζαντινῶν Σπουδῶν 3 (1926), 168–91.

Manuel Holobolos, *Orations*, ed. M. Treu, *Manuelis Holoboli Orationes*, Programm des Victoria Gymnasiums zu Potsdam 1906–1907.

Manuel II Palaiologos, *Admonitory Address to the Thessalonians*, ed. B. Laourdas, "Ὁ 'Συμβουλευτικὸς πρὸς τοὺς Θεσσαλονικεῖς' τοῦ Μανουὴλ Παλαιολόγου", Μακεδονικά 3 (1953–55), 290–307.

Manuel II Palaiologos, *Ethopoiia of Tamerlane*, ed. E. Legrand, *Correspondence. Lettres de l'empereur Manuel Paléologue*, 2nd ed., Paris 1962, pp. 103–104.

Manuel II Palaiologos, *Funeral Oration on his Brother Theodore*, ed. J. Chrysostomides, *Manuel II Palaeologus. Funeral Oration on his Brother Theodore* (Corpus Fontium Historiae Byzantinae, 26), Thessaloniki 1985.

Manuel II Palaiologos, *Melete on a Drunkard*, ed. Boissonade, *Anecdota Graeca*, vol. 2, pp. 274–307.

Manuel II Palaiologos, *Precepts of Imperial Conduct*, in *Patrologia Graeca*, vol. 156, cols. 320–84.

Mark Eugenikos, *Monody on the Fall of Thessaloniki*, ed. Pilabakis, Ἑάλω Θεσσαλονίκη, pp. 13–65.

Maximos Planoudes, *Basilikos*, ed. L. Westerink, "Le Basilikos de Maxime Planude", *Byzantinoslavica* 27 (1966), 98–103; 28 (1967), 54–67; 29 (1968), 34–50.

Maximos Planoudes, *Commentary on Hermogenes*, ed. Walz, *Rhetores Graeci*, vol. 5, pp. 212–610.

Maximos Planoudes, *Comparison between Winter and Spring*, ed. M. Treu, *Maximi monachi Planudis comparatio hiemis et veris*, Progr. Gymnas. Ohlau 1878.

Menander of Laodikeia, *De epideicticis*, eds. D.A. Russell/N.G. Wilson, *Menander Rhetor*, Oxford 1981, pp. 76–224.

Michael Apostoles, *Funeral Oration on Bessarion*, ed. A. Riehle, *Die Grabrede des Michaelos Apostoles auf Bessarion*, Munich 2006.

Nikephoros Choumnos, *Encomium for Andronikos II*, ed. Boissonade, *Anecdota Graeca*, vol. 2, pp. 1–56.

Nikephoros Choumnos, *To the Thessalonians on Justice*, ed. Boissonade, *Anecdota Graeca*, vol. 2, pp. 137–87.

THE "LEGACY" OF APHTHONIOS, HERMOGENES AND PSEUDO-MENANDER   65

Nikephoros Gregoras, *Encomium for Andronikos II*, in Nikephoros Gregoras, *Roman History* VIII.8, ed. Schopen, vol. 1, pp. 328, line 9–339, line 20.

Nikephoros Gregoras, *Encomia for Andronikos II*, ed. P.A.M. Leone, "Nicephori Gregorae ad imperatorem Andronicum II Palaeologum Orationes", *Byzantion* 41 (1971), 497–519.

Nikephoros Gregoras, *Funeral Oration on Andronikos II*, in Nikephoros Gregoras, *Roman History* X.1, ed. Schopen, vol. 1, pp. 465, line 1–472, line 6.

Nikephoros Gregoras, *Funeral Oration on Andronikos III*, in Nikephoros Gregoras, *Roman History* XI.11, ed. Schopen, vol. 1, pp. 560, line 8–565, line 13.

Nikephoros Gregoras, *Funeral Oration on Theodore Metochites*, in Nikephoros Gregoras, *Roman History* X.2, ed. Schopen, vol. 1, pp. 475, line 1–481, line 13.

Nikephoros Gregoras, *Roman History*, eds. L. Schopen/I. Bekker, *Nicephori Gregorae Byzantina Historia* (Corpus Scriptorum Historiae Byzantinae, 19), 3 vols., Bonn 1829–55.

Nikephoros Gregoras, *Roman History*, trans. J.L. van Dieten, *Rhomäische Geschichte. Historia Rhomaike* (Bibliothek der griechischen Literatur, 4), 6 vols., Stuttgart 1973–2003.

Nikephoros Kallistou Xanthopoulos, *Progymnasmata*, ed. J. Glettner, "Die Progymnasmata des Nikephoros Kallistos Xanthopulos", *Byzantinische Zeitschrift* 33 (1933), 1–22, 255–70.

Nicholas Kabasilas, *Encomia for Matthew Kantakouzenos and Anna of Savoy*, ed. M. Jugie, "Nicolas Cabasilas, Panégyriques inédits de Mathieu Cantacuzène et d'Anne Paléologine", *Izvěstija Russkago Archeologičeskago Instituta v Konstantinopolě* 15 (1911), 112–21.

Prolegomenon Sylloge, ed. H. Rabe (Rhetores Graeci, 14), Leipzig 1931 (repr. Leipzig 1995).

Rhetores Graeci, ed. C. Walz, 9 vols., Stuttgart 1832–36 (repr. Osnabrück 1968).

Sophonias the Monk, *Melete*, eds. D.M. Searby/A. Sjörs, "A Rhetorical Declamation of Sophonias the Monk and Paraphrast", *Byzantinische Zeitschrift* 104 (2011), 147–82.

Theodore Gazes, *Encomium of a Dog*, in *Patrologia Graeca*, vol. 161, cols. 985–97.

Theodore Hyrtakenos, *Funeral Oration on Michael IX*, ed. I. Chrysostomidis, "Η Μονῳδία ἐπὶ τῷ θανάτῳ τοῦ ἀοιδίμου βασιλέως κυροῦ Μιχαὴλ Παλαιολόγου τοῦ νέου του Θεοδώρου Ὑρτακηνοῦ", *Βυζαντινά* 38 (2022), 255–76.

Theodore Hyrtakenos, *Funeral Oration on Nikephoros Choumnos*, ed. Chrysostomidis, *Οι μονωδίες του Θεοδώρου Υρτακηνού*, pp. 101–108.

Theodore Metochites, *Byzantios*, ed. I. Polemis, Θεόδωρος Μετοχίτης. Βυζάντιος ἢ περὶ τῆς βασιλίδος μεγαλοπόλεως. Κοσμολογία καὶ ῥητορικὴ κατὰ τὸν ΙΔ ΄ αἰῶνα (Βυζαντινοί συγγραφείς, 18), Thessaloniki 2013.

Theodore Metochites, *Imperial Orations*, ed. I. Polemis, Θεόδωρος Μετοχίτης. Οἱ δύο βασιλικοὶ λόγοι (Κείμενα βυζαντινῆς λογοτεχνίας, 4), Athens 2007.

Theodore Metochites, *Nicaeus*, ed. E. Mineva, "Ὁ 'Νικαεὺς' τοῦ Θεοδώρου Μετοχίτου", *Δίπτυχα* 6 (1994–95), 307–27.

Theodore Metochites, *Orations*, eds. I. Polemis/E. Kaltsogianni, *Theodorus Metochites. Orationes* (Bibliotheca Teubneriana, 2031), Berlin/Boston 2019.

Theodore Metochites, *Synkrisis between Demosthenes and Aelius Aristeides*, ed. M. Gigante, *Teodoro Metochites. Saggio critico su Demostene e Aristide*, Milan 1969.

Thomas Magistros, *On Kingship*, ed. P. Volpe-Cacciatore, *Toma Magistro. La regalità*, Naples 1997.

Thomas Magistros, *To the Thessalonians on Unity*, ed. B. Laourdas, "Θωμᾶ Μαγίστρου Τοῖς Θεσσαλονικεῦσι περὶ ὁμονοίας", *Ἐπιστημονικὴ Ἐπετηρὶς Σχολῆς Νομικῶν καὶ Οἰκονομικῶν Ἐπιστημῶν Ἀριστοτελείου Πανεπιστημίου Θεσσαλονίκης* 12/5 (1969), 751–75.

Secondary Literature

Agapitos, P./D. Angelov, "Six Essays by Theodore II Laskaris in Vindobonensis Phil. Gr. 321: Edition, Translation, Analysis", *Jahrbuch der Österreichischen Byzantinistik* 68 (2018), 39–75.

Akişik, A., "Praising a City: Nicaea, Trebizond, and Thessalonike", in N. Necipoğlu/ C. Kafadar (eds.), *In memoriam Angeliki E. Laiou. Journal of Turkish Studies* 33 (2011), 1–25.

de Andrés, G., *Catálogo de los códices Griegos de la Real Biblioteca de el Escorial*, Madrid 1965.

Angelov, D., "Byzantine Imperial Panegyric as Advice Literature", in Jeffreys (ed.), *Rhetoric in Byzantium*, pp. 55–72.

Angelov, D., *Imperial Ideology and Political Thought in Byzantium, 1204–1330*, Cambridge, MA 2007.

Angelov, D., "The Confession of Michael VIII Palaiologos and King David. On a Little Known Work of Manuel Holobolos", *Jahrbuch der Österreichischen Byzantinistik* 56 (2006), 193–204.

Balfour, D., *Politico-Historical Works of Symeon Archbishop of Thessalonica [1416/17 to 1429]. Critical Greek Text with Introduction and Commentary* (Wiener Byzantinistische Studien, 13), Vienna 1979.

Baloglou, C.P., "The Institutions of Ancient Sparta in the Work of Pletho", in L.G. Benakis/C.P. Baloglou (eds.), *Proceedings of the International Congress on Plethon and His Time*, Athens/Mistras 2003, 311–26.

Beck, H.-G., "Antike Beredsamkeit und byzantinische Kallilogia", *Antike und Abendland* 15 (1969), 91–101.

Bianconi, D., *Tessalonica nell'età dei Paleologi. Le pratiche intellettuali nel riflesso della cultura scritta* (Dossiers byzantins, 5), Paris 2005.

Boissonade, J.F., Ἀνέκδοτα. *Anecdota Graeca e codicibus regiis*, 5 vols., Paris 1829–33 (repr. Hildesheim 1962).

Calia, A., *Meglio il turbante del sultano della tiara latina: Giovanni Dokeianos e la transizione bizantino-ottomana a Constantinopoli nel secondo Quattrocento*, PhD Thesis, University of San Marino and École Pratique des Hautes Études 2016.

Çelik, S., *Manuel II Palaiologos (1350–1425). A Byzantine Emperor in a Time of Tumult*, Cambridge 2021.

Christophoridis, B., "Ὁ ἀρχιεπίσκοπος Θεσσαλονίκης Ἰσίδωρος Γλαβᾶς καὶ τὰ κοινωνικὰ προβλήματα τῆς ἐποχῆς του", *Ἐπιστημονικὴ Ἐπετηρὶς Θεολογικῆς Σχολῆς Ἀριστοτελείου Πανεπιστημίου Θεσσαλονίκης* 29 (1986–89), 519–90.

Chrysostomidis, I., *Οι μονωδίες του Θεοδώρου Υρτακηνού*, MA Thesis, Aristotle University of Thessaloniki 2008.

Chrysostomidis, I., *Το corpus των επιστολών του Γεωργίου-Γρηγορίου Κυπρίου*, PhD Thesis, Aristotle University of Thessaloniki 2015.

Chrysostomidis, I./D. Nikou/I. Taxidis, "Some Remarks on the Structure of John Eugenikos' *Ekphraseis* of Cities and Places", *Parekbolai* 11 (2021), 81–90.

Congourdeau, M.-H. (ed.), *Les Zélotes. Une révolte urbaine à Thessalonique au 14ᵉ siècle. Le dossier des sources*, Paris 2013.

Congourdeau, M.-H., "Nicolas Cabasilas et Matthieu Cantacuzène", in S. Efthymiadis/ C. Messis/P. Odorico/I. Polemis (eds.), *«Pour une poétique de Byzance». Hommage à Vassilis Katsaros* (Dossiers byzantins, 16), Paris 2015, pp. 85–98.

Constantinides, C.N., *Higher Education in Byzantium in the Thirteenth and Early Fourteenth Centuries (1204–ca 1310)* (Texts and Studies of the History of Cyprus, 11), Nicosia 1982.

Constantinides, C.N., "Teachers and Students of Rhetoric in the Late Byzantine Period", in Jeffreys, *Rhetoric in Byzantium*, pp. 39–53.

Dąbrowska, M., "'Vasilissa, ergo gaude…'. Cleopa Malatesta's Byzantine CV", *Byzantinoslavica* 63 (2005), 217–24.

de Falco, V., "Sulla Rhetorica del filosofo Giuseppe", *Historia* 5 (1931), 627–43.

Dennis, G.T., "Imperial Panegyric: Rhetoric and Reality", in Maguire, H. (ed.), *Byzantine Court Culture from 829 to 1204*, Washington, DC 1997, pp. 131–40.

Fatouros, G., "Bessarion und Libanios. Ein typischer Fall byzantinischer Mimesis", *Jahrbuch der Österreichischen Byzantinistik* 49 (1999), 191–204.

Fenster, E., *Laudes Constantinopolitanae* (Miscellanea Byzantina Monacensia, 9), Munich 1969.

Foss, C., *Nicaea: A Byzantine Capital and its Praises*, Brookline, MA 1996.

Fryde, E., *The Early Palaeologan Renaissance (1261–c.1360)* (The Medieval Mediterranean, 27), Leiden/Boston 2000.

Gaul, N., "Performative Reading in the Late Byzantine *Theatron*", in T. Shawcross/I. Toth (eds.), *Reading in the Byzantine Empire and Beyond*, Cambridge 2018, pp. 215–33.

Gaul, N., *Thomas Magistros und die spätbyzantinische Sophistik. Studien zum Humanismus urbaner Eliten in der früher Palaiologenzeit* (Mainzer Veröffentlichungen zur Byzantinistik, 10), Wiesbaden 2011.

Georgakopoulos, D.S., *Μιχαὴλ Ἀποστόλης. Ὁ βυζαντινὸς λόγιος καὶ τὸ ἔργο του στὴ βενετοκρατούμενη Κρήτη (1420/22–1478)*, Athens 2022.

Gerstel, S. (ed.), *Viewing the Morea*, Washington, DC 2013.

Giannouli, A., "Paränese zwischen Enkomion und Psogos. Zur Gattungseinordnung byzantinischer Fürstenspiegel", in A. Rhoby/E. Schiffer (eds.), *Imitatio – Aemulatio – Variatio. Akten des internationalen wissenschaftlichen Symposions zur byzantinischen Sprache und Literatur* (Wien, 22.–25. Oktober 2008) (Veröffentlichungen zur Byzanzforschung, 21), Vienna 2010, pp. 119–28.

Giannouli, A., "Coronation Speeches in the Palaeologan Period?", in A. Beihammer/ S. Constantinou/M. Parani (eds.), *Court Ceremonies and Rituals of Power in Byzantium and the Medieval Mediterranean. Comparative Perspectives*, Leiden/Boston 2013, pp. 203–23.

Giarenis, I., "Ὁ λόγιος καὶ ὁ γενέθλιος τόπος. Ἡ Τραπεζούντα μὲ τὸν τρόπο τοῦ Βησσαρίωνος", *Ἐπετηρὶς Ἑταιρείας Βυζαντινῶν Σπουδῶν* 53 (2007–2009), 265–80.

Giarenis, I., "Ἡ Ἔκφρασις τοῦ Βησσαρίωνα για την Τραπεζούντα. Ἡ χρονολόγηση του ἔργου και το εγκώμιο των Μεγαλοκομνηνῶν αυτοκρατόρων", in Giarenis/Maras/Baloglou/ Kyriakidis, *Βησσαρίων ἐκ Τραπεζοῦντος τοῦ Πόντου*, pp. 175–208.

Giarenis, I./A.G. Maras/C.P. Baloglou/T.A. Kyriakidis (eds.), *Βησσαρίων ἐκ Τραπεζοῦντος τοῦ Πόντου. Λόγιος του Βυζαντινοῦ και του Δυτικοῦ Αναγεννησιακοῦ 15ου αιώνα = Βυζαντινὸς Δόμος* 25 (2016–2017), Thessaloniki 2017.

Gibson, C.A., "In Praise of Dogs: An Encomium Theme from Classical Greece to Renaissance Italy", in L.D. Gelfand (ed.), *Our Dogs, Our Selves. Dogs in Medieval and Early Modern Art, Literature, and Society* (Art and Material Culture in Medieval and Renaissance Europe, 6), Leiden/Boston 2016, pp. 19–40.

Gielen, E., "Joseph the Philosopher, an Outstanding Outsider: Philosophy and Rhetoric at the Court of Andronicus II", in G. Nathan/L. Garland (eds.), *Basileia: Essays on Imperium and Culture in Honour of E.M. and M.J. Jeffreys* (Byzantina Australiensia, 17), Brisbane 2011, pp. 205–15.

Gielen, E., "*Ad Maiorem Dei Gloriam*. Joseph Rhakendytes' Synopsis of Byzantine Learning", in J. König/G. Woolf (eds.), *Encyclopaedism from Antiquity to the Renaissance*, Cambridge 2013, pp. 259–76.

Golitsis, P., "George Pachymère comme didascale. Essai pour une reconstitution de sa carrière et de son enseignement philosophique", *Jahrbuch der Österreichischen Byzantinistik* 58 (2008), 53–68.

THE "LEGACY" OF APHTHONIOS, HERMOGENES AND PSEUDO-MENANDER   69

Gounaridis, P., "Ἰωσήφ Βρυέννιος, προφήτης τῆς καταστροφῆς", in T. Kiousopoulou (ed.), *1453: Η άλωση της Κωνσταντινούπολης και η μετάβαση από τους μεσαιωνικούς στους νεώτε-ρους χρόνους*, Heraklio 2005, pp. 133–45.

Guilland, R., *Essai sur Nicéphore Grégoras. L'homme et l'oeuvre*, Paris 1926.

Hladký, V., *The Philosophy of Gemistos Plethon: Platonism in Late Byzantium, between Hellenism and Orthodoxy*, Farnham 2014.

Hock, R.F./E.N. O'Neil, *The Chreia and Ancient Rhetoric. Classroom Exercises* (Society of Biblical Literature. Writings from the Greco-Roman World, 2), Atlanta 2002.

Hunger, H., *Die hochsprachliche profane Literatur der Byzantiner* (Byzantinisches Handbuch: Handbuch der Altertumswissenschaft, 12.5), 2 vols., Munich 1978.

Hunger, H., "Klassizistische Tendenzen in der byzantinischen Literatur des 14. Jh.", in *Actes du XIV Congrès International des études byzantines*, vol. 1, Bucarest 1974, pp. 139–51.

Hunger, H., "Zeitgeschichte in der Rhetorik des sterbenden Byzanz", *Wiener Archiv für Geschichte des Slawentums und Osteuropas* 3 (1959), 152–61.

Jeffreys, E. (ed.), *Rhetoric in Byzantium. Papers from the Thirty Fifth Spring Symposium of Byzantine Studies, Exeter College, University of Oxford, March 2001* (Society for the Promotion of Byzantine Studies. Publications, 11), Aldershot 2003.

Jeffreys, E., "Rhetoric in Byzantium", in I. Worthington (ed.), *A Companion to Greek Rhetoric*, Oxford 2007, pp. 166–83.

Kaldellis, A., "The Discontinuous History of Imperial Panegyric in Byzantium and its Reinvention by Michael Psellos", *Greek, Roman, and Byzantine Studies* 59 (2019), 693–713.

Kaltsogianni, E./S. Kotzabassi/I. Paraskevopoulou, *Η Θεσσαλονίκη στη βυζαντινή λογοτε-χνία. Ρητορικά και αγιολογικά κείμενα* (Βυζαντινά Κείμενα και Μελέτες, 32), Thessaloniki 2002.

Kennedy, G.A., *Greek Rhetoric under Christian Emperors*, Princeton 1983.

Kennedy, G.A., *Progymnasmata. Greek Textbooks of Prose Composition and Rhetoric*, Leiden/Boston 2003.

Kiousopoulou, T., *Βασιλεύς ή Οικονόμος. Πολιτική εξουσία και ιδεολογία πριν την Άλωση*, Athens 2007 (trans. P. Magdalino, *Emperor or Manager: Power and Political Ideology in Byzantium before 1453*, Genoa 2011).

Konstantakopoulou, A., *Βυζαντινή Θεσσαλονίκη. Χώρος και Ιδεολογία*, Ioannina 1996.

Kotzabassi, S., *Die handschriftliche Überlieferung der rhetorischen und hagiographi-schen Werke des Gregor von Zypern* (Serta Graeca, 6), Wiesbaden 1998.

Kotzabassi, S., "Epistolography and Rhetoric", in A. Riehle (ed.), A Companion to Byzantine Epistolography (Brill's Companions to the Byzantine World, 7), Leiden/Boston 2020, pp. 177–99.

Kotzabassi, S., "The Testament of John Bekkos", *Βυζαντινά* 32 (2012), 25–35.

Kountoura-Galake, E., "Ὁ Μανουὴλ Ὁλόβωλος καὶ η Λατίνων φωνή: διανόηση καὶ πολιτική", in V.N. Vlyssidou (ed.), *Byzantine Authors and their Times* (National Hellenic Research Foundation, Institute of Historical Research. Research Series, 8), Athens 2021, pp. 371–95.

Kourousis, S.I., "Αἱ ἀντιλήψεις περὶ τῶν ἐσχάτων τοῦ κόσμου καὶ ἡ κατὰ τὸ ἔτος 1346 πτῶσις τοῦ τρούλλου τῆς Ἁγίας Σοφίας", *Ἐπετηρὶς Ἑταιρείας Βυζαντινῶν Σπουδῶν* 37 (1969–70), 211–50.

Kourousis, S.I., "Νέος κῶδιξ τοῦ *Βασιλικοῦ* Μαξίμου τοῦ Πλανούδη", *Ἀθηνᾶ* 73–74 (1973), 426–34.

Kubina, K., *Die enkomiastische Dichtung des Manuel Philes. Form und Funktion des literarischen Lobes in der frühen Palaiologenzeit* (Byzantinisches Archiv, 38), Berlin/ Boston 2000.

Kusch, T., "Dèmètrios Kydonès, source pour l'histoire du mouvement zélote", in M.-H. Congourdeau (ed.), *Thessalonique au temps des Zélotes, Actes de la table ronde organisée dans le cadre du 22ᵉ Congrès international des études byzantines, à Sofia, le 25 août 2011*, Paris 2014, pp. 89–98.

Laiou, A.E., "Le débat sur le droit du fisc et les droits régaliens au début du 14ᵉ siècle", *Revue des Études Byzantines* 58 (2000), 97–122.

Lambakis, S., *Γεώργιος Παχυμέρης, πρωτέκδικος καὶ δικαιοφύλαξ: Εἰσαγωγικὸ δοκίμιο*, (Ἐθνικὸ Ἵδρυμα Ἐρευνῶν – Μονογραφίες, 5), Athens 2004.

Lamers, H., *Greece Reinvented: Transformations of Byzantine Hellenism in Renaissance Italy* (Brill's Studies in Intellectual History, 247), Leiden 2015.

Lampros, S., *Ἀργυροπούλεια*, Athens 1910.

Lampros, S., *Παλαιολόγεια καὶ Πελοποννησιακά*, 4 vols., Athens 1912–30.

Lamprou, S., *Ὁ αὐτοκράτωρ Μανουὴλ Β´ Παλαιολόγος ὡς θεολόγος. Συμβολὴ στὴν ἔρευνα τῆς Παλαιολόγειας Γραμματείας*, Thessaloniki 2012.

Lampsides, O., "Περὶ τὸ Ἐγκώμιον εἰς Τραπεζοῦντα τοῦ Βησσαρίωνος", *Ἀρχεῖον Πόντου* 37 (1980), 153–84.

Laurent, V., "Un nouveau témoin de la correspondance de Démétrius Cydonès et de l'activité littéraire de Nicolas Cabasilas Chamaétos: le codex Meteor. Barlaam 202", *Ἑλληνικὰ* 9 (1936), 185–205.

Lauritzen, F., "Bessarion's Political Thought: The Encomium to Trebizond", *Bulgaria Mediaevalis* 2 (2011), 153–59.

Lauritzen, F., "I panegyrici bizantini dal VII al XV secolo: Il modello constantiniano alla corte di Constantinopoli", in *Constantino I. Enciclopedia Constantiniana sulla figura e l'imagine dell'imperatore del cosiddetto editto di Milano, 313–2013*, vol. 2, Roma 2013, pp. 309–19.

Leonte, F., "A Brief *History of Morea* as Seen through the Eyes of an Emperor-Rhetorician: Manuel II Palaiologos's Oration for Theodore, Despot of Morea", in Gerstel, *Viewing the Morea*, pp. 397–417.

Leonte, F., *Imperial Visions of Late Byzantium. Manuel II Palaiologos and Rhetoric in Purple* (Edinburgh Byzantine Studies), Edinburgh 2020.

Leonte, F., "Visions of Empire. Gaze, Space, and Territory in Isidore's Encomium for John VIII Palaiologos", *Dumbarton Oaks Papers* 71 (2017), 249–72.

Macrides, R., "From the Komnenoi to the Palaiologoi: Imperial Models in Decline and Exile", in P. Magdalino (ed.), *New Constantines: The Rhythm of Imperial Renewal in Byzantium, 4th–13th Centuries*, Aldershot 1994, pp. 269–83.

Macrides, R., "The 'New Constantine' and the New Constantinople – 1261?", *Byzantine and Modern Greek Studies* 6 (1980), 13–41.

Magdalino, P., "The Beauty of Antiquity in Late Byzantine Praises of Constantinople", in Odorico/Messis (eds.), *Villes de toute beauté*, pp. 101–21.

Maltese, E.V./G. Cortassa, *Roma parte del cielo. Confronto tra l'Antica et la Nuova Roma di Manuele Crisolora*, Torino 2000.

Mariev, S. (ed.), *Bessarion's Treasure. Editing, Translating and Interpreting Bessarion's Literary Heritage* (Byzantinisches Archiv – Series Philosophica, 3), Berlin/Boston 2021.

Martin, G., "Rhetorical Exercise or Political Pamphlet? Thomas Magistros' Exploitation of Demosthenes' *Against Leptines*", *Greek, Roman and Byzantine Studies* 46 (2006), 207–26.

Matschke, K.-P./F. Tinnefeld, *Die Gesellschaft im späten Byzanz. Gruppen, Strukturen und Lebensformen*, Cologne/Weimar/Vienna 2001.

Mergiali, S., *L'enseignement et les lettrés pendant l'époque des Paléologues (1261–1453)* (Ἑταιρεία τῶν Φίλων τοῦ Λαοῦ: Κέντρον Ἐρεύνης Βυζαντίου, 5), Athens 1996.

Mercati, G., *Scritti di Isidoro, il cardinale Ruteno, e codici a lui appartenuti* (Studi e Testi, 46), Rome 1926.

Mercati, G., "The Greeks and Renaissance Humanism", in D. Rundle (ed.), *Humanism in Fifteenth-Century Europe*, Oxford 2012, pp. 31–78.

Nerantzi-Barmazi, B., "Ὁ λόγος του Νικηφόρου Χούμνου *Θεσσαλονικεῦσι Συμβουλευτικός*", *Βυζαντινά* 21 (2000), 271–77.

Nuti, E., "Manuel Chrysoloras' Περὶ τοῦ βασιλέως λόγου: Genre, Aims, Content, and Sources", *Greek, Roman, and Byzantine Studies* 56 (2016), 164–94.

Odorico, P., "Les miroirs des princes à Byzance. Une lecture horizontale", in P. Odorico (ed.), *L'éducation au gouvernement et à la vie. La tradition des "règles de vie" de l'Antiquité au Moyen Age* (Autour de Byzance, 1), Paris 2009, 223–46.

Odorico, P./C. Messis (eds.), *Villes de toute beauté. L'ekphasis des cités dans les littératures Byzantine et Byzantino-Slaves* (Dossiers byzantins, 12), Paris 2012.

Paidas, K., *Η θεματική των βυζαντινών 'κατόπτρων ηγεμόνος' της πρώιμης και μέσης περιόδου. Συμβολή στην πολιτική θεωρία των Βυζαντινών*, Athens 2005.

Paidas, K., *Τα βυζαντινά 'κάτοπτρα ηγεμόνος' της ύστερης περιόδου (1254–1403). Εκφράσεις του βυζαντινού βασιλικού ιδεώδους*, Athens 2006.

Papadogiannakis, N., *Studien zu den Epitaphien des Manuel Philes. Inaugural-Dissertation zur Erlangung des Grades eines Doktors der Philosophie des Fachbereichs Altertumswissenschaften der Freien Universität Berlin*, Heraklio 1984.

Papaioannou, S., "Rhetoric and Rhetorical Theory", in A. Kaldellis/N. Siniossoglou (eds.), *The Cambridge Intellectual History of Byzantium*, Cambridge 2017, pp. 101–12.

Parlier, M., "Constantinople dans les éloges impériaux de Michel VIII et d'Andronic II (1259–1328). Entre Rome et Jérusalem", *Histoire Urbaine* 45/1 (2016), 125–43.

Paschos, P.B., *Ὁ Ματθαῖος Βλάσταρης καὶ τὸ ὑμνογραφικὸν ἔργον του*, Thessaloniki 1978.

Pérez Martín, I., *El patriarca Gregorio de Chipre (ca. 1240–1290) y la transmisión de los textos clásicos en Bizancio* (Nueva Roma, 1), Madrid 1996.

Petrou, I.P., *Η παιδεία στην Κωνσταντινούπολη τον 15ο αι.*, PhD Thesis, University of Ioannina 2017.

Philippides, M./W.K. Hanak (eds.), *Cardinal Isidore, c.1390–1462. A Late Byzantine Scholar, Warlord, and Prelate*, New York 2018.

Pieralli, L., *La corrispondenza diplomatica dell'imperatore bizantino con le potenze estere nel tredicesimo secolo (1204–1282). Studio storico-diplomatistice ed edizione critica* (Collectanea Archivi Vaticani, 54), Vatican City 2006.

Pilabakis, M., *Ἑάλω Θεσσαλονίκη. Θρῆνος γιὰ τὴν ἅλωση του 1430*, Athens 1997.

Polemis, I., "Two Praises of the Emperor Manuel II Palaiologos: Problems of Authorship", *Byzantinische Zeitschrift* 103 (2010), 699–714.

Pontanti, F., "Scholarship in the Byzantine Empire (529–1453)", in F. Montanari (ed.), *History of Ancient Greek Scholarship. From the Beginnings to the End of the Byzantine Age*, Leiden/Boston 2020, pp. 373–529.

Previale, L., "Teoria e prassi del panegirico bizantino", *Emerita* 17 (1949), 72–105, 340–366.

Prosopographisches Lexikon der Palaiologenzeit (= PLP), 12 vols., ed. E. Trapp et al., Vienna 1976–96.

Rabe, H., "Rhetoren-Corpora", *Rheinisches Museum für Philologie* 67 (1912), 321–57.

Radošević, N., "Waiting for the End – The Byzantine Rhetoric of the First Half of the Fifteenth Century", *Zvornik Radova Vizantinoloskog Instituta* 43 (2006), 58–70.

Rhoby, A., "Die Rezeption der spätantiken Rhetorik in den spätbyzantinischen ἐκφράσεις τόπων", in W. Kofler (ed.), *Pontes III: Die Antike Rhetorik in der europäischen Geistesgeschichte* (Comparanda, 6), Innsbruck 2005, pp. 115–25.

Rhoby, A., "Hunde in Byzanz", in J. Drauschke/E. Kislinger a.o. (eds.), Lebenswelten zwischen Archäologie und Geschichte. Festschrift für Falko Daim zum 65.

Geburtstag (Monographien des Römisch-Germanischen Zentralmuseums, 150), Mainz 2018, pp. 807–20.

Rhoby, A., "Theodoros Metochites' *Byzantios* and Other City *Encomia* of the 13th and 14th Centuries", in Odorico/Messis (eds.), *Villes de toute beauté*, pp. 81–99.

Riehle, A., *Funktionen der byzantinischen Epistolographie. Studien zu den Briefen und Briefsammlungen des Nikephoros Chumnos (ca. 1260–1327)*, PhD Thesis, University of Munich 2011.

Riehle, A., "Rhetorical Practice", in S. Papaioannou (ed.), *The Oxford Handbook of Byzantine Literature*, Oxford 2021, pp. 294–315.

Rigo, A./N. Zorzi (eds.), *I libri di Bessarione. Studi sui manoscritti del Cardinale a Venezia e in Europa* (Bibliologia, 59), Turnhout 2021.

Rollo, A., "Sul destinatario della Σύγκρισις τῆς παλαιᾶς καὶ νέας Ῥώμης", in V. Fera,/ A. Guida (eds.), *Vetustatis indagator. Scritti offerti a Filippo di Benedetto*, Messina 1999, pp. 61–80.

Romano, R., *Constantino Acropolita. Epistole*, Naples 1991.

Ryder, J., *The Career and Writings of Demetrius Kydones: A Study of Fourteenth-Century Byzantine Politics, Religion and Society* (The Medieval Mediterranean, 85), Leiden/ Boston 2010.

Saradi, H., "Η ἔκφρασις τῆς Τραπεζούντας ἀπό τον Βησσαρίωνα: η αρχαιότητα και το ιστορικό μήνυμα", *Βυζαντινός Δόμος* 17–18 (2009–2010), 33–56.

Saradi, H., "The *Kallos* of the Byzantine City: The Development of a Rhetorical Topos and Historical Reality", *Gesta* 34 (1995), 37–56.

Saradi, H., "The Monuments in the Late Byzantine *Ekphraseis* of Cities", *Byzantinoslavica* 69 (2011), 179–92.

Schawcross, T., "A New Lykourgos for a New Sparta. George Gemistos Plethon and the Despotate of the Morea", in Gerstel, *Viewing the Morea*, pp. 419–52.

Schmitt, O.J., "Kaiserrede und Zeitgeschichte im späten Byzanz: Ein Panegyrikos Isidors von Kiew aus dem Jahre 1429", *Jahrbuch der Österreichischen Byzantinistik* 48 (1998), 209–42.

Ševčenko, I., "Agapetos East and West: The Fate of a Byzantine *Mirror of Princes*", *Revue des Études Sud-Est-Européennes* 16 (1978), 3–45.

Ševčenko, I., *La vie intellectuelle et politique à Byzance sous les premiers Paléologues: Études sur la polémique entre Théodore Métochite et Nicéphore Choumnos* (Corpus Bruxellense Historiae Byzantinae. Subsidia, 3), Brussels 1962.

Ševčenko, I., "Society and Intellectual Life in the Fourteenth Century", in M. Berza/ E. Stanescu (eds.), *Actes du XIVᵉ Congrès International des Études Byzantines, Bucarest, 6–12 Septembre 1971*, vol. 1, Bucharest 1974, pp. 65–92.

Ševčenko, I., "The Decline of Byzantium Seen Through the Eyes of its Intellectuals", *Dumbarton Oaks Papers* 15 (1961), 169–86.

Sideras, A., *Die byzantinischen Grabreden. Prosopographie, Datierung, Überlieferung 142 Epitaphien und Monodien aus dem byzantinischen Jahrtausend* (Wiener Byzantinistische Studien, 19), Vienna 1994.

Siniossoglou, N., *Radical Platonism in Byzantium: Illumination and Utopia in Gemistos Plethon*, Cambridge 2011.

Spingou, F., *Words and Artworks in Byzantium. Twelfth-Century Poetry from MS. Marcianus Gr. 524*, Surrey 2021.

Stamouli, A.-P., *Οι «εκφράσεις» στα αγιολογικά κείμενα της παλαιολόγειας εποχής*, PhD Thesis, University of the Peloponnese 2015.

Talbot, A.M., "Empress Theodora Palaiologina, Wife of Michael VIII", *Dumbarton Oaks Papers* 46 (1992), 295–303 (repr. in ead., *Women and Religious Life in Byzantium*, Aldershot 2001, no. V).

Tambrun-Krasker, B., *Pléthon: Le retour de Platon*, Paris 2006.

Taxidis, I., "Die Episode des Palamedes in den byzantinischen Progymnasmata", *Byzantinische Zeitschrift* 102 (2009), 731–37.

Taxidis, I., "Les monodies et les oraisons funèbres pour la mort du despote Jean Paléologue", *Medioevo Greco* 9 (2009), 267–84.

Taxidis, I./D. Nikou/I. Chrysostomidis, *The Ekphraseis in the Literature of the Palaeologan Era* (Hellenica, 99), Alessandria 2021.

Thorn-Wickert, L., *Manuel Chrysoloras, ca. 1350–1415: Eine Biographie des byzantinischen Intellektuellen von dem Hintergrund der hellenistischen Studien in der italienischen Renaissance* (Bonner romanistische Arbeiten, 92), Frankfurt am Main/Berlin/Bern 2006.

Tinnefeld, F., "Intellectuals in Late Byzantine Thessalonike", *Dumbarton Oaks Papers* 57 (2003), 153–72.

Topping, P., "Greek Manuscript 1 (the Works of Ioannes Dokeianos) of the University of Pennsylvania Library", *The Library Chronicle* 29 (1963), 1–15.

Toth, I., *Imperial Orations in Late Byzantium (1261–1453)*, PhD Thesis, University of Oxford 2003.

Toth, I., "Rhetorical *Theatron* in Late Byzantium: The Example of Palaeologan Imperial Orations", in M. Grünbart (ed.), *Theatron. Rhetorische Kultur im Spätantike und Mittelalter* (Millenium-Studien, 10), Berlin/New York 2007, pp. 427–46.

Turyn, A., *Dated Greek Manuscripts of the Thirteenth and Fourteenth Centuries in the Libraries of Great Britain*, Washington 1980.

Verpeaux, J., *Nicéphore Choumnos. Homme d'état et humaniste byzantin (ca. 1250/1255–1327)*, Paris 1959.

Voudouri, A., *Αυτοτελή εγκώμια πόλεων της ύστερης βυζαντινής περιόδου υπό το πρίσμα της προγενέστερης παράδοσής τους*, PhD Thesis, National and Kapodistrian University of Athens 2016.

Voudouri, A., "Representations of Power in the Byzantios Oration of Theodore Metochites: Illusion and Realities", *Parekbolai* 3 (2013), 107–30.

Vryonis, S. "Byzantine Cultural Self-Consciousness in the Fifteenth Century", in S. Ćurčić/D. Mouriki (eds.), *The Twilight of Byzantium. Aspects of Cultural and Religious History in the Late Byzantine Empire*, Princeton 1991, pp. 5–14.

Webb, R., "The *Progymnasmata* as Practice", in Y.L. Too (ed.), *Education in Greek and Roman Antiquity*, Leiden/Boston/Köln 2001, pp. 289–316.

Webb, R., "Describing Rome in Greek: Manuel Chrysoloras' *Comparison of Old and New Rome*", in Odorico/Messis, *Villes de toute beauté*, pp. 123–33.

Wendel, C., "Planudes Maximos", *Realenzyklopädie* 20 (1950), 2202–53.

Wilson, N.G., "A Byzantine Miscellany: Ms. Barocci 131 Described", *Jahrbuch der Österreichischen Byzantinistik* 27 (1978), 157–79.

Wilson, N.G., *From Byzantium to Italy. Greek Studies in the Italian Renaissance*, Baltimore 1992 (London ²2017).

CHAPTER 2

Intellectual Pursuits for Their Own Sake

Sophia Mergiali-Sahas

1 The Byzantine Disposition towards Knowledge

Pursuit of knowledge for its own sake was not the norm but rather a rare phenomenon in Byzantium. No matter how stable and vital Hellenic learning may have been in Byzantine education,[1] the Byzantines never ceased repeating that learning was not, and should never be, an end in itself; learning should be, rather, a means aimed at leading a person inductively from the secular to the highest form of knowledge – the knowledge of God.[2] The purpose therefore, was always to maintain harmony between secular knowledge and Christian faith.[3] For the vast majority of Byzantines education was sought primarily for its practical use and benefits. Thus, the learning process was limited to the transmission of a knowledge (grammar, poetry, rhetoric) which had a direct application to public life, served as a means of social advancement, and was meant to secure a career in the imperial service, or in the ecclesiastical hierarchy. Even for the most educated people, the major preoccupation was to preserve their ancient Greek heritage in the sciences rather, than to introduce

---

1 On Byzantine education in general see Kazhdan/Browning, "Education"; Markopoulos, "Education"; Mondrain, *Lire et écrire à Byzance*; Browning, "Church, State and Learning in Twelfth-Century Byzantium"; Ševčenko, *Society and Intellectual Life in Late Byzantium*; Constantinides, *Higher Education in Byzantium*; Mergiali, *L'enseignement et les lettrés pendant l'époque des Paléologues*; Mergiali-Sahas, "Παλαιολόγεια εκπαίδευση".

2 The Byzantines made a distinction between what they called "outer knowledge", or "the wisdom of the Hellenes" (θύραθεν σοφία), and "inner knowledge" or theology (σοφία ἡ καθ' ἡμᾶς). On this, see Inglebert, "'Inner' and 'Outer' Knowledge". See also, Katsiampoura, "Faith or Knowledge?". The dictum of John of Damascus (ca. 675–749) at the beginning of his *Capita Philosophica* has remained particularly memorable in this respect: Φιλοσοφία πάλιν ἐστὶ φιλία σοφίας. Σοφία δὲ ἀληθὴς ὁ Θεός ἐστιν· ἡ οὖν ἀγάπη ἡ πρὸς τὸν Θεόν, αὕτη ἐστὶν ἡ ἀληθὴς φιλοσοφία; see John of Damascus, *Περὶ φιλοσοφίας*, ed. Kotter, vol. 1, p. 56, lines 25–27. See also Nicol, "The Byzantine Church and Hellenic Learning", pp. 25–26; and Kaldellis, *Hellenism in Byzantium*, p. 396, who notes that "Outer wisdom was always respected and practiced professionally in Byzantium even if some feared and hated it".

3 Nicolaïdis, *Science and Eastern Christianity*, p. x.

INTELLECTUAL PURSUITS FOR THEIR OWN SAKE   77

innovations to it, as the study of sciences was mainly seen as a means of exercising intelligence.[4]

In spite of all these, during the Palaeologan era (1261–1453) certain (indeed, few) intellectuals stood above the average, opened new paths to knowledge, and emphasised worldly wisdom for its own sake. These men of higher cultural awareness seem to be motivated by a devotion to scientific or literary pursuits for their own curiosity and ideological interest, thus breaking down preconceived ideas, but also for the sake of their own satisfaction. More eager than ever before to espouse their ancient Greek legacy,[5] or even to seek new wisdom from the outside world by travelling abroad, they display a mentality and trend distinct from the traditional Byzantine values on matters of learning. For this striking minority of intellectuals, the pursuit of knowledge becomes an end in itself, that extends to even somewhat "unorthodox" fields compared to the norms of Byzantine society.

Up to at least 1204, Byzantines who were eager to seek foreign knowledge and introduce it into Byzantium, and learned a foreign language for that purpose were rather rare, as they considered their empire to be the centre of the world. However, the Latin occupation of Constantinople opened a cross-cultural conduit. There seems to have been a general reluctance on the part of the Byzantine intellectuals to travel beyond the borders of the Byzantine Empire in order to acquire knowledge. In addition to all the dangers and discomforts, the most important obstacles were cultural bias, the feeling of cultural alienation, mental unease, emotional pain and above all a sense of superiority of the Byzantine cultural milieu.[6]

Speaking about intellectual pursuits for their own sake, our attention will also be directed towards the motives that drove each of those scholars to pursue a particular kind of knowledge in parallel with his official occupation, especially under adverse conditions. Five names seem to stand out as the most typical examples in this regard: the statesman Theodore Metochites, the court

---

4 See Tannery, *Quadrivium de Georges Pachymère*, text edited by E. Stephanou, p. 6, line 1: "Ὅτι δὲ τὰ μαθήματα καὶ παίγνια τοῦ νοός εἰσιν.

5 See Kaldellis, *Hellenism in Byzantium*, p. 394: "During the Palaeologan era, Hellenism is defined not only as *paideia* but also as philosophy and national identity." Angold, "Autobiography & Identity", p. 43: "Gregory's [of Cyprus] autobiography is built around the obstacles he had to surmount to attain 'Hellenic Wisdom' ... Gregory understood in the most personal way that this was an essential ingredient of his and the Byzantine identity ... For Gregory 'Hellenic Wisdom' is an end in itself; not, ... a steppingstone to Orthodoxy". By the same, even more, "Plethon insisted that they must become Hellenes in religion as well as in culture" p. 54.

6 See Ciggaar, *Western Travelers to Constantinople*, pp. 12–13, pp. 17–18 and p. 35. Galatariotou, "Travel and Perception in Byzantium", pp. 229–30.

physician (*aktouarios*) John Zacharias, the physician Gregory Chioniades, the statesman Demetrios Kydones, and the Emperor Manuel Palaiologos. With an unprecedented zeal, they engaged themselves, respectively, in the study of astronomy, astrology, Persian astronomy, the Latin language and western philosophical theology, and literary finesse and composition.

2 Theodore Metochites: The Statesman and the Study of Astronomy

Theodore Metochites (*c.*1270–1332),[7] the most eminent and powerful of the officials at the court of Emperor Andronikos II Palaiologos (1282–1328), also emerged as a leading scholar and a prolific writer of his time. His spectacular political trajectory was paralleled by a tireless intellectual activity. Progressing steadily from one public office to the next,[8] he was further entrusted by the emperor with the office of minister of finance (*logothetes tou genikou*) and in 1305 with that of his chief minister (*mesazon*) in the imperial administration,[9] ascending to the highest office, that of prime minister (*megas logothetes*), a few years later (1321). But more than anyone else, Andronikos II honored him with his valuable personal friendship. Metochites, along with his full engagement with the affairs of public life and the imperial administration by day, would immerse himself equally intensively in intellectual endeavors in the evenings, as if he were completely estranged from political responsibilities and learning were his single preoccupation.[10] His writings reflect not only the changes in the fortunes of his life, but also his broad intellectual horizons – the latter extending to such scientific and literary genres as poetry, rhetoric, essay-writing, epistolography, philosophy and astronomy. Proud of all aspects of his work, especially his poems, he nevertheless considered the rediscovery and renewal of astronomy as his own greatest achievement.

---

7 On Metochites (*PLP* 17982) see Ševčenko, "Théodore Métochites, Chora et les courants intellectuels de l'époque", pp. 15–3; Id., *Études sur la polémique entre Théodore Métochite et Nicéphore Choumnos*; de Vries-van der Velden, *Théodore Métochite: une réévaluation*; Fryde, *The Early Palaeologan Renaissance*, pp. 322–36; Bazzani, "Theodore Metochites, a byzantine humanist"; Talbot, "Metochites, Theodore"; Bydén, "Metochites, Theodore". See also, chapter 8 in this volume.

8 See Verpeaux, "Le cursus honorum de Théodore Métochite".

9 The title "mesazon" (literally, the "intermediary") signifies the court official who plays a key role between the emperor and his subjects, as well as between the emperor himself and his diplomatic counterparts. See Guilland, "Les Logothètes", p. 18, note 61. Kazhdan, "Mesazon". Verpeaux, "Contribution à l'étude de l'administration byzantine: ὁ μεσάζων".

10 Nikephoros Gregoras, *Roman History*, ed. Schopen, vol. 1, pp. 272–73.

INTELLECTUAL PURSUITS FOR THEIR OWN SAKE

I have brought to prominence again that science, renovating it among mortal men, because it had been neglected in the past; from a few hidden sparks I managed to light the great fire of that science through my own efforts, and thus I obtained shining glory for myself both now and in the future in all ages, since I renewed the study of what has been considered the most precious of all human acquisitions from old times until now, which had disappeared from the sight of men for many years.[11]

This emerged as a result of the work he did on Ptolemy's *Megale Mathematike Syntaxis*, known in the Arabic tradition as *al-Majistī* and in the western Latin tradition as the *Almagest*.

Generally speaking, astronomy always attracted a considerable amount of interest within the Byzantine world.[12] Indeed, its connection with astrology, its use for the computation of Easter, and its very essence as a science contributed to its status as an attractive field of scholarship and intellectual training. Moreover, during the golden age of Byzantine astronomy, which coincides with the Palaeologan era,[13] the act of predicting an eclipse emerged as one of the main tasks of Byzantine astronomers who, through the computation of a lunar or solar eclipse, were able to demonstrate their high level of aptitude in astronomy. There is also another important factor in predicting an eclipse, namely the association of this phenomenon by some astronomers, with a forthcoming natural disaster or a serious calamity, usually the death or the overthrowing of a prominent political figure.[14]

Metochites' activity as a researcher and master of astronomy was, certainly, not of a professional nature. He was initially a public statesman who was

---

11   Theodore Metochites, *Advice addressed to the Wise Nikephoros Gregoras*, ed. Polemis, p. 129. Cf. Theodore Metochites, *Autobiographical preface*, ed. Bydén, p. 443, lines 784–92: ὡς αὐτός ἐστιν αἴτιος καὶ ἀρχηγὸς ταυτησὶ τῆς νέας ἀναδείξεως τῆς ἀστρονομικῆς ἐπιστήμης, καὶ ὅτι κινδυνεύουσα παντάπασιν ἀπολιπεῖν τὸν βίον πολλῶν ἤδη τῶν χρόνων ἀφανὴς ἐκ μέσου γενομένη, καλλίστη τις αὕτη καὶ πρώτη τῆς ὅλης σοφίας μοῖρα, ἐπ᾽ αὐτοῦ τοὐμοῦ βασιλέως καὶ ὑπ᾽αὐτοῦ μάλιστα ... καινίζεται καὶ σβεννυμένη καθάπαξ ἤδη νῦν γε λοιπὸν ἀνάπτειν, ὡς ἄρ᾽ ἐξ ἀρχῆς, δοκεῖ.

12   On Byzantine astronomy in general see Pingree, "Gregory Chioniades and Palaeologan Astronomy" and Cutler, "Astronomy". Tihon, *Études d'astronomie byzantine*; Ead., "L'astronomie byzantine (du Ve au XVe siècle)"; Ead., "Astronomy". Caudano "Astronomy and Astrology", pp. 202–30.

13   Tihon, "L'astronomie byzantine (du Ve au XVe s.)", pp. 612–13. Caudano, "Astronomy and Astrology", pp. 219–20.

14   Tihon, "Les sciences exactes à Byzance", p. 412. Pingree/Croke/Cutler, "Eclipses". Tihon, "Astronomical Promenade in Byzantium", pp. 268–69 and 285–87. Mavroudi, "Occult Science and Society", p. 72.

attracted by astronomy far and beyond his political endeavors and at a relatively advanced age. Indeed, infatuated by astronomy,[15] Metochites begun studying this discipline in 1313 at the age of forty-three, under the persistent instigation of the emperor. Andronikos II introduced to him to his future teacher, Manuel Bryennios, one of the few Byzantines at that time able to understand Ptolemy. As politics and public affairs absorbed the majority of his day and any leisure time was scarce, Metochites made Bryennios a resident of his own house so that he may take advantage of his knowledge. How else would he be able to assimilate the wisdom and the nuances of the *Almagest* without the help of a teacher?[16] Just four years later, around 1316/1317, Metochites proudly presented the fruit of his studies. He made public the first book of his monumental work *Stoicheiôsis astronomike (Abridged Elements of Astronomy)*, a three-part treatise on Ptolemy and a purely theoretical piece of work, although void of any observational findings.[17] Given the celestial and sublime character of astronomy, which was incomprehensible to the masses, Metochites' intention with this treatise was to offer to his contemporaries and to those who were to follow a comprehensive work that popularized and clarified the thought of the two masters of astronomy, Ptolemy and Theon:

> I collected all the marvelous teachings concerning astronomy in my relevant book. I did all this and attained my goal, inventing new methods for this science, and making everything easy for the sake of our contemporaries, so that they might learn accurately, without any pains, everything concerning the sun, the moon and the other stars.[18]

Given that Emperor Andronikos II had permitted only a few scholars – conscientious of being part of the intellectual elite of their time – to be initiated

---

15 Theodore Metochites, *To the Wise Nikephoros Xanthopoulos*, ed. Polemis, p. 235, lines 276–77: ζῆλος ἐνὶ κραδίῃ, μάλ' ἐπεὶ μέτ' ἄρα μερόπεσσι παντάπασ'ἤδε ἄιστος ἔην and for the transl. in English, Polemis, *Poems*, p. 253.
16 Theodore Metochites, *Autobiographical preface*, ed. Bydén, p. 431, lines 444–49, p. 432, lines 472–82, p. 433, lines 483–89, p. 434, lines 513–23.
17 Theodore Metochites, *Autobiographical preface*, ed. Bydén, p. 438, lines 635–50 and p. 441, lines 718–24. Fryde, *The Early Palaeologan Renaissance*, pp. 348–49. For the critical edition of the first five introductory chapters of Metochites' *Stoicheiosis Astronomike*, see Bydén, *Theodore Metochites' Stoicheiosis Astronomike and the Study of Natural Philosophy and Mathematics*; for the critical edition of chapters 5–30, see Theodore Metochites, *Stoicheiosis Astronomike 1.5–30*, eds. Paschos/Simelidis.
18 Theodore Metochites, *Advice addressed to the Wise Nikephoros Gregoras*, trans. Polemis, p. 132.

INTELLECTUAL PURSUITS FOR THEIR OWN SAKE 81

into this discipline,[19] one may wonder what Metochites' own motives would have been to assume this endeavor. One may perhaps surmise that in undertaking the study of astronomy Metochites was understandably interested in proving that, in the context of his times, the Ptolemaic tradition remained superior to all others, especially that of Persia, a country which was growing in reputation due to its many astronomical works which were circulating translated into Greek.[20] The preface of his *Stoicheiôsis astronomike* contains the following admonition: "Be a Greek and shun the theories of the Indians, the Scythians or the Persians, or any other foreign ideas."[21] A "proponent of the 'national' Ptolemaic tradition",[22] Metochites elevated astronomy to a "subject on the peak" within the learning environment of his generation, vesting it also with the unprecedented social prestige of the reign of Andronikos II. Thus, he succeeded in raising "the level of sophistication in Byzantine astronomy to a height it had not attained for centuries".[23] In fact, he professed that nothing can be known with certainty outside the field of mathematics, in which astronomy occupies the most prominent place. Metochites was not making any innovation beyond his ancient sources, but he was treating his subject with a greater clarity and a real pedagogical intention in mind.[24] He boasted of having revived astronomy, a great and useful task in itself, on behalf of all men who longed for this wisdom.[25]

Metochites' intellectual pursuits persisted into the last years of his life, even after the reversal of his fortunes in 1328 and his exile to Didymoteichon. It was there that he wrote the last four of his twenty poems, an act which comforted him, in his words, as "medicine for his aching spirit."[26] His literary works, which, as he himself says, touch upon each and every branch of culture,[27] shed light on his motives for engaging in life-long intellectual enterprises. First and foremost, Metochites' inner impulse was to attain immortality in this world:

---

19   See the excerpt from an unpublished letter of Georges Oinaiotes to John Zacharias in Kourousis, "Ὁ ἀκτουάριος Ἰωάννης ὁ Ζαχαρίας", p. 49: ... ἐπεί σε καλῶς εἰδότα οἶδα δι' ὅσης ἐπιμελείας ὁ θειότατος καὶ ἅγιος ἡμῶν βασιλεὺς πεποίηται τὸ μὴ πολλοὺς χώραν λαμβάνειν τοῦ κορυφαίου τούτου μαθήματος (sc. τῆς ἀστρονομίας).

20   Tihon, "Les sciences exactes à Byzance", p. 274.

21   Pingree, "Gregory Chioniades and Palaeologan Astronomy", p. 140.

22   Mavroudi, "Occult Science and Society in Byzantium", p. 66.

23   Pingree, "Gregory Chioniades and Palaeologan Astronomy", p. 137.

24   Tihon, "Les sciences exactes à Byzance", pp. 385–86.

25   Theodore Metochites, *To the Wise Nikephoros Xanthopoulos*, ed. Polemis, p. 235, lines 293–294: καί τε τόδ' ἀτρεκέως ἐρέειν μέγα τ'ὠφέλιμόν τε, ἔργον ἄνυσ' ὁπόσοι σοφίας τῆσδ' ἄνδρες ἔρανται.

26   Featherstone, *Theodore Metochites's Poems 'To Himself'*, p. 12 and 15.

27   Theodore Metochites, *To the Wise Nikephoros Xanthopoulos*, ed. Polemis, p. 227, line 71.

I have written books dealing with many different branches of human wisdom, which demonstrate amply my deep knowledge; no one who knows the selfishness of our common human nature would blame such a desire: all men enjoy to be or to look glorious.[28]

He expresses the hope that his literary and scientific works will serve as a bulwark against oblivion for his name:

They will probably help all future people to keep my glorious, most desired, memory alive ... that is why we wish to be glorious even after we die, taking pleasure in the shadows of future time, when we will not be able either to hear or to see anything as in the past, or when we will no longer exist.[29]

Metochites intended his voluminous collection of philosophical and historical essays, the *Semeioseis gnomikai,* to be "a picture of his mind".[30] His experiences of all kinds of contradiction and instability that shaped his life seem to be repeated in his writings. This aspect reflects the constraints under which Metochites and his contemporaries were living at the time. While for others study could be a matter of routine, for him it was a matter of survival. Thanks to his own hard work and devotion to learning, that which was otherwise impossible became a reality during his lifetime. A son of parents who were in disgrace and fully dependent on his own resources, Metochites took refuge in his intellectual gifts and intensified his love for learning in order to ameliorate, if not to reverse, his own adverse fortune. His attachment to the imperial government did not alienate him from his personal intellectual pursuits. In an unstable, volatile world and in the midst of crisis, devotion to knowledge proved to be a meaningful refuge:

Actually, if someone finds refuge in education and stays there, as in a temple that no one can defile, he feels safe and is not afraid of ... the threat and instability of the circumstances ... Everything can turn upside down and change completely. But no one can take away from someone

---

28 Theodore Metochites, *Advice addressed to the Wise Nikephoros Gregoras,* trans. Polemis, p. 131. Theodore Metochites, *To the Wise Nikephoros Gregoras,* ed. Polemis, p. 93, lines 233–238. Theodore Metochites, *To the Wise Nikephoros Xanthopoulos,* ed. Polemis, p. 233, lines 233–238.

29 Theodore Metochites, *Advice addressed to the Wise Nikephoros Gregoras,* trans. Polemis, p. 134.

30 Theodore Metochites, *To the Wise Nikephoros Xanthopoulos,* ed. Polemis, p. 234, line 256.

INTELLECTUAL PURSUITS FOR THEIR OWN SAKE 83

what is a wise mind, the ingenuity, the happiness and the pleasure, which science and education offer to their suitors' fans.[31]

He simultaneously lived two different lives, the busy life of public affairs (*vita activa*) and the quiet life of study (*vita contemplativa*). His public life as a statesman, which provided him with his fortune but also led to his downfall, is that which Metochites regrets most of all. He himself wishes he had never yielded to the lure of power:

> Although everyone thinks that I am proud of this great, far-famed glory, I wish I had never obtained it ... I believe that it would have been better for me not to have enjoyed such a supposedly happy life but to have lived free of all troubles ... If only I could return to that time, when I had not yet seen the imperial palace, a spectacle most desirable to all people, and had not yet obtained positions in the court, much sought-after by all people, being glorified to such an extent and being forced to stick to it willy-nilly.[32]

It was his intellectual pursuits that made him live a meaningful life. He maintained that knowledge is the only lasting and inalienable acquisition of a human being; the only thing that makes life worth sustaining, that which provides a secure shelter in the midst of turmoil. As he confesses, his love for wisdom gave meaning and increased the joy of his life, alleviating both public and personal grief.[33] Metochites' personality reveals a case of a mentality completely foreign to medieval norms,[34] longing for immortality in this world through his writings; a personality astonishingly similar to that of the Italian humanists, like Petrarch, "long recognized as the first humanist".[35]

---

31 Theodore Metochites, *On Morals or Concerning Education*, eds. Polemis/Kaltsogianni, ch. 26, p. 365, lines 5–12.

32 Theodore Metochites, *To the Wise Xanthopoulos*, trans. Polemis, pp. 239–240. In his eleventh poem entitled "To the scholar Theodore Xanthopoulos, and his own misfortunes" written in 1326, Metochites regrets the fact that he was lured by politics, which prevented him from devoting himself entirely to the enjoyment of the intellectual life; he expressed the same feelings in his speech, Ἠθικὸς ἤ περὶ παιδείας, written around 1305 in the midst of his political career; see Theodore Metochites, *On Morals or Concerning Education*, eds. Polemis/Kaltsogianni, p. 196, lines 14–28 and p. 198, lines 1–20.

33 Theodore Metochites, *To the Wise Nikephoros Xanthopoulos*, ed. Polemis, p. 230, lines 153–155.

34 Ševčenko/Featherstone, *Two Poems by Theodore Metochites*, p. 3.

35 Bazzani, "Theodore Metochites, a Byzantine Humanist", pp. 41 and 49.

84   MERGIALI-SAHAS

3   John Zacharias: The Court Physician and the Study of Astrology

A figure closely linked to Theodore Metochites and inspired by him as a
member of the elite of astronomers, is John Zacharias or John Aktouarios
(c.1275–c.1330). He is the last of the great Byzantine physicians, who, contrary to the established practice of writing synopses, has left a number of
full-length medical books.[36] Byzantine medicine "reached its climax with
John Aktouarios about a hundred years before the fall of Constantinople".[37]
His research and observations on urine diagnosis and treatment as well as his
reflections on many diseases are praiseworthy, revealing a highly skilled prac-
titioner and a scholarly-minded person open to new knowledge, both from the
Islamic world and the Latin West.[38] Information concerning his life is scant
and scattered. His life and the heyday of his career coincide mainly with the
reign of Andronikos II Palaiologos (1282–1328),[39] during which an unprecedented revival of astronomy took place. The highlights that illuminate the
main stages of his itinerary in life can be summarized as follows. Most likely
he belonged to the circle of Maximos Planoudes' students, and was fortunate
enough to receive a good general education, which could lead to a career as a
state or military official. Seeking to make himself useful to others, he chose to
study medicine.[40] In 1299 we find him studying medicine in Constantinople
and coming close to being officially proclaimed a doctor. Before 1307 he was
practicing medicine and had earned himself a reputation as a skilled doctor.
He was awarded the title *aktouarios*, meaning chief physician, at the imperial

---

36   On John Zacharias (Aktouarios) (*PLP* 6489) see Kourousis, "Ὁ ἀκτουάριος Ἰωάννης Ζαχα-
       ρίας παραλήπτης τῆς ἐπιστολῆς ι᾽ τοῦ Γεωργίου Λακαπηνοῦ". Id., "Ὁ ἀκτουάριος Ἰωάννης ὁ
       Ζαχαρίας". Id., "Ὁ ἀκτουάριος Ἰωάννης Ζαχαρίας συγγραφεὺς ἀποδοθέντων αὐτῷ μὴ ἰατρικῶν
       πονημάτων". Id., *Τὸ Ἐπιστολάριον*, pp. 522–25. Hohlweg, "John Actuarius", pp. 121–33. Mer-
       giali, *L'enseignement et les lettrés*, pp. 57–59. Bouras-Vallianatos, *Innovation in Byzantine
       Medicine*. Scarborough/Talbot, "John Aktouarios".
37   Cf. Temkin, "Byzantine Medicine: Tradition and Empirism", p. 114. For a brief introduction
       to Byzantine Medicine, see Touwaide, "Medicine and Pharmacy".
38   Hohlweg, "John Actuarius", p. 133. Bouras-Vallianatos, *Innovation in Byzantine Medi-
       cine*, 206.
39   On this point we disagree with A. Hohlweg ("John Actuarius", p. 121), who places "John's
       golden age in the years when the Emperor Andronikos III ruled" (sc. 1328–1341) and con-
       tradicts himself later in his article by stating that "We possess no news of him or about
       him which with certainty might be dated during the reign of Emperor Andronikos III ...
       Whether John died in 1328, or shortly thereafter, must for the moment remain an open
       question".
40   John Zacharias, *On Urines*, ed. Ideler, p. 3, lines 1–8. Cf. Bouras-Vallianatos, *Innovation in
       Byzantine Medicine*, pp. 71–103.

INTELLECTUAL PURSUITS FOR THEIR OWN SAKE

court and head doctor of the state between the years 1310 and 1323.[41] As a physician, he became the exponent of the idea that medical practice must be based on personal observation and experience on the part of the physician. This meant that he had to reach an accurate diagnosis before prescribing an appropriate treatment for the disease, something which had a tremendous impact upon the life of his contemporaries.[42] Three medical treatises bear his name: *On Urines*, *Medical Epitome* (*De methodo medendi*) and *On the Activities and Affections of the Physic Pneuma and the Corresponding Regimen*.[43] The first was written between the years 1315 and 1321, while the latter two were probably written in 1326.[44]

His written works, containing incidents from his personal life, and what can be drawn from his correspondence with his contemporaries, point to intellectual interests which go beyond medicine per se. He had access to the inner circle of astronomers at the court of Emperor Andronikos II. Zacharias asserts the value of secular knowledge, considers astronomy as the culmination of wisdom, and expresses the belief that a man can attain perfection and divine knowledge only through science;[45] anyone who wants to connect the natural and the supernatural world, or the material and the spiritual world, must go through a process of systematization of knowledge. His ideas about the usefulness of secular wisdom are explored in three dialogues of rhetorical, philosophical, astronomical and astrological nature, under the titles *Hermodotos or on beauty*, *Mousokles or on optimal life*[46] and *Hermippos or on astrology*,[47] written at the beginning of the 14th century.[48] The authorship of these three dialogues is still disputed.[49] Nevertheless, S. Kourousis has argued that these three works should be associated, in terms of content and form, with

---

41   Kourousis, *Τὸ Ἐπιστολάριον*, pp. 118–21 and p. 522. In the manuscripts he is qualified as "σοφώτατος καὶ λογιώτατος βασιλικὸς γιατρός"; Cf. Costomiris, "Études sur les écrits des médecins grecs", p. 426. Hohlweg, "John Actuarius", p. 126, n. 45.

42   Bouras-Vallianatos, *Innovation in Byzantine Medicine*, p. 206.

43   For the edition of the three medical treatises, see John Zacharias (Aktouarios), *On Urines*, ed. Ideler; John Zacharias (Aktouarios), *Medical Epitome*, ed. Ideler; John Zacharias (Aktouarios), *On the Activities and Affections of the Physic Pneuma*, ed. Ideler. For an analysis of these medical treatises, see Bouras-Vallianatos, *Innovation in Byzantine Medicine*. On the third treatise see also Kakavelaki, *Η έννοια του πνεύματος κατά την Αρχαία και Βυζαντινή Περίοδο*.

44   Kourousis, *Τὸ Ἐπιστολάριον*, p. 523.

45   Kourousis, "Ὁ ἀκτουάριος Ἰωάννης Ζαχαρίας", pp. 57–59.

46   The first two dialogues were edited as works of John Katrares (John Katrares, *Dialogues*, ed. Elter).

47   John Zacharias (Aktouarios), *Hermippos*, eds. Kroll/Viereck.

48   Kourousis, *Τὸ Ἐπιστολάριον*, pp. 38, pp. 149–50 and p. 380.

49   Papathanassiou, "The Occult Sciences in Byzantium", p. 479, note 63.

the rhetorical, medical, philosophical and astronomical education and literary preferences of Zacharias, and must be dated to his heyday. Kourousis has arrived at this conclusion due to similarities in subject matter between the aforementioned dialogues and Zacharias' medical writings.[50]

What emerges from Zacharias' posture, which is foreign to the prevalent Byzantine collective mentality, is the significance that secular wisdom has for knowledge itself, as well as being a value in itself and a path to spiritual perfection.[51] With reference to the role that ascetic life plays in attaining spirituality, Zacharias believes that asceticism serves only as a preparatory stage to perfection which, again, can be attained through knowledge of the sciences.[52] Such views point to Zacharias' independence of mind, in his path to intellectual and spiritual perfection. Particularly striking and novel in his thought is his daring exaltation of astrology as a means of attaining the knowledge of God and its necessity for the lives of people, a position that is enunciated in his dialogue *Hermippos* or *On astrology*:

> I think no one could deny the fact that astrology is the pinnacle of science and, thanks to this, one can prosper and manage his life in the best way. I would not even hesitate to argue that primarily thanks to astrology one can arrive at the knowledge of God.[53]

Given that astrology was a particularly sensitive issue during his time, his devotion to and enthusiasm for this rather debated, if not outright banned, discipline is impressive. Astrology was practiced throughout the Byzantine millennium, and numerous manuscripts containing astrological compilations were in circulation. However, the position of the mainstream Orthodox tradition, which had been expressed by the first systematic theologian of the Orthodox faith John of Damascus (*c.*675–749) in his *De fide orthodoxa*, that everything that depends on free will cannot be determined by the course and the behavior of the stars, seems to have set certain limits as to its use as

---

50 Kourousis, *Tὸ Ἐπιστολάριον*, pp. 149, pp. 232–36, p. 452, p. 524.

51 John Zacharias (Aktouarios), *Hermippos*, eds. Kroll/Viereck, p. 70, lines 187–91: ὃ δὴ διὰ τῆς τοιαύτης ἐπιστήμης ἡμῖν μάλιστα περιγίνεται. ὁ δὲ ἄνευ ταύτης ἐπὶ τὴν θεωρίαν ἐκείνην ὁρμῶν ἀτελέστερος ἂν εἴη εἰκότως καὶ ἀμαθής, οὐκ ἔχων εἰδέναι τρίβον, καθ᾽ ἣν ῥαδίως ἐπ᾽ αὐτὴν ἄνεισιν.

52 Kourousis, "*Tὸ Ἐπιστολάριον*", pp. 221–22.

53 John Zacharias (Aktouarios), *Hermippos*, eds. Kroll/Viereck, p. 4, lines 18–20: ὅτι μὲν οὖν ἐπιστήμης πάσης αὕτη κεφάλαιον καὶ δι᾽ αὐτῆς εὖ ζῆν τε καὶ διατιθέναι τὰ κατὰ τὸν βίον ἔστιν, οὐκ ἄν μοί τις ἀμφισβητήσαι δοκεῖ and p. 69, lines 23–25: ἐγὼ δὲ οὐδὲν ἐνδοιάσας εἴποιμι, ὡς ἐκ μόνων ἢ πρώτων τούτων (sc. τῶν ἀστρολογικῶν πραγμάτων) τὸν δημιουργὸν ἔστι καταμανθάνειν.

INTELLECTUAL PURSUITS FOR THEIR OWN SAKE

a scholarly discipline.[54] The stance of the emperors and even of the Church towards astrology had been quite ambiguous, ranging from firm condemnation to some degree of tolerance.[55] A similar ambiguity or contradiction appears to linger among Byzantine intellectuals of the Palaeologan era: ostensibly they rejected astrology, but on the other hand they themselves were responsible for the surge of interest in astrology which emerged from the end of the 13th century, accompanied by a voluminous astrological production. Thus, "astrology is continuously attested in the literate culture of the Byzantine world" and the "astrologers were members of the educated elite, associated with the imperial court and consulted by the rich and powerful".[56] It must be noted, however, that Theodore Metochites, the authority on matters of astronomy at the time, took pains to dissociate astronomy from astrology, considering detrimental to the Christian faith that part of astrology which deals with the prediction of anything that might happen in the future.[57] Zacharias' dialogue on astrology presents him as a profound connoisseur and even an ardent lover of astrology,[58] the defense of which he had undertaken by affirming that it is the divine power, not the stars, that is the determining *cause* of events; the stars have only been imbued with an ability to announce events. According to his theory, there exists a successive and harmonious inter-dependence within the world: the earth and the rest of creation depend on nature, nature depends on the stars, and the stars depend on the Creator.[59] Furthermore, he argues that, because of its divine substance, the soul is directly related to the Creator, and thus the stars have no power to exercise any influence on the soul. He thus removes from astrology the element of fatalism which the Christian faith denounces. On the other hand, Zacharias accepts the notion that the human body, which plays a role in the material sphere, can occasionally be influenced by the stars although the hour of one's death, for example, cannot be

54   John of Damascus, *De fide orthodoxa*, ed. Kotter, p. 59, lines 117–25. For a brief survey on astrology in the Roman Empire and in Byzantium, see now Papathanassiou, "The Occult Sciences in Byzantium" pp. 474–79.

55   Tihon, "Les sciences exactes à Byzance", p. 420.

56   Magdalino, "The Byzantine Reception of Classical Astrology", p. 38 and p. 37.

57   Theodore Metochites, *Autobiographical preface*, ed. Bydén, p. 466, lines 163–65 and p. 467, lines 172–73: ἀλλ' ἴσως ἐνίους ταράττει θάτερον τῆς ἀστρολογικῆς μέρος, ὃ περὶ τὸ προγνωστικὸν τῶν ἐσομένων καὶ ἀποτελεσματικὸν καταγίνεται, ... τοῦτό γε μὴν προδήλως πάνυ τοι καὶ ἀναντιρρήτως λυμαίνεται τῇ πίστει καὶ τῇ καθ' ἡμᾶς χριστιανικῇ θεοσεβείᾳ.

58   John Zacharias (Aktouarios), *Hermippos*, eds. Kroll/Viereck, p. 1, lines 16–17: οἶσθα δέ, ὅπως ἐρωτικῶς εἰς αὐτὴν ἔχω.

59   Kourousis, Τὸ Ἐπιστολάριον, pp. 165–66.

determined by their course.[60] It is only a waste of time, according to him, to look to the stars "for dynasties or glories or marriages and even more for wealth and victories."[61] Along with his daring defense of astrology, Zacharias in one of his medical treatises (*On Urines*) unleashed a fierce attack against those uneducated ones who slander astrological predictions on the assumption that such predictions are inspired by demons.[62]

4   Gregory Chioniades: The Physician and the Study of Persian Astrology

This very same theme brings us now to the third figure. Byzantine astronomy had its roots in Claudius Ptolemy, whose works were studied and practiced till the end of the Byzantine Empire.[63] By the end of the 13th century, however, and as a result of the Mongol invasion of Persia, the fashionable Persian astronomy began to make its appearance in the Byzantine world. The proponent of this new trend was a Byzantine physician from Constantinople, Gregory Chioniades (*c.*1240–*c.*1320),[64] whose broad scientific pursuits led him off the beaten path and resulted in an "international" career beyond Constantinople – to Tabriz, via Trebizond. As to how Chioniades succeeded in introducing Persian astronomy to Byzantium, the answer comes from another physician and astronomer, George Chrysokokkes,[65] who had learned Persian astronomy in Trebizond, probably from a student and successor of Chioniades.[66] In the preface of his astronomical treatise entitled *Persian Syntaxis in Astronomy*, written around 1347, Chrysokokkes provides us with some valuable details about Chioniades' life:

---

60   John Zacharias (Aktouarios), *Hermippos*, eds. Kroll/Viereck, p. 11, lines 4–14: τὸ δὲ σῶμα τῆς ὑλικῆς προσπαθείας μέτοχον ὂν πάθη τε παντοδαπὰ καὶ κράσεις διαφόρους ὑφίσταται εὖ τε καὶ τοὐναντίον ἐχούσας. καὶ ταύτας δή φαμεν εἰς τὴν τῶν ἀστέρων ἀνήκειν ἐνέργειαν, οὐκ αὐτὴν τὴν οὐσίαν καὶ δύναμιν τῆς ψυχῆς …

61   John Zacharias (Aktouarios), *Hermippos*, eds. Kroll/Viereck, p. 40, lines 6–8 and 12–14.

62   John Zacharias (Aktouarios), *On Urines*, ed. Ideler, p. 145, lines 1–25.

63   Tihon, "Les sciences exactes à Byzance", p. 392.

64   PLP 30814. Pingree, "Gregory Chioniades and Palaeologan Astronomy", pp. 135–60. Id., *The Astronomical Works of Gregory Chioniades, I, The Zīj al-ʿAlāʾī*, pp. 7–8 and pp. 16–18. Id., "Chioniades Gregory". Haramundanis, "Chioniades Gregor [Georges]", p. 229. Tihon, "Les tables astronomiques persanes", pp. 471–76. Mergiali, *L'enseignement et les lettrés*, pp. 39–40.

65   On George Chrysokokkes (PLP 31142), see Lampsides, "Georges Chrysococcis, le médecin et son œuvre". Tihon, "Astronomical Promenade in Byzantium", pp. 279–80.

66   Mergiali, *L'enseignement et les lettrés*, p. 40, note 135.

... a certain Chioniades, who had been raised in Constantinople and succeeded in understanding all sciences, fell also in love with another remarkable science, thanks to which he could acquire wisdom and practice medicine rigorously. When he heard that he had to go to Persia in order to satisfy his interest, leaving aside everything else, he took off as quickly as he could. When he arrived at Trebizond, he assiduously frequented the Great Komnenos [Alexios II, 1297–1330], to whom he made known his intentions and he was deemed worthy of great solicitude. Indeed, he received from him enough money and proceeded to Persia. In a short period of time, he learned the language of the Persians, met their king and found favor with him. When he tried to study astronomy, he had no teacher, as the law of Persia allowed anyone who was not Persian to learn any science, except astronomy which was only for the Persians.... After many struggles, and having served the king of the Persians, he received with some difficulty what he wanted.... After having amassed a great deal of wealth and acquired many servants, he returned to Trebizond with many astronomical books.[67]

For Chioniades astronomy and astrology were useful tools in his rigorous practice of medicine. As health is the most crucial factor in determining how an individual's life will progress, astrology could, inevitably, be used in medicine. An expert in astrology could prescribe more effective treatments and make a firmer prognosis regarding the final outcome of the patient's illness;[68] this explains Gregory Chioniades' keen interest in astrology, and his decision to leave his familiar Byzantine surroundings and expose himself to the staggering experiences of a foreign country, a new language and an unfamiliar mentality. He did not choose Tabriz, the capital of the ruling Il-Khans, casually.[69] The Mongol domination of Persia in the second half of the 13th century coincided with a remarkable expansion of studies in the sciences, and especially astronomy. Il-Khan Hūlāgū (?–1265), grandson of Genghis Khan, had already

---

67   George Chrysokokkes, *Syntaxis*, ed. Lampros. For a French translation of this passage see Tihon, "Les sciences exactes à Byzance", p. 401.

68   On this topic see Papathanassiou, "Iatromathematica (medical astrology) in Late Antiquity and the Byzantine Period".

69   Tihon, "Astronomical Promenade in Byzantium", p. 274. Based on Hippocrates and Galen, Chrysokokkes displays the ties between astronomy and medicine, justifying his own and Chioniades' astronomical pursuits: *Since by some good fortune I, too, have studied medicine and have chanced upon their treatises, I realized what great benefit it is for medicine to understand the movement of the planets* ...; see ibid., p. 279. Ptolemy in the *Tetrabiblos* explicitly mentions that the Egyptians are those who developed medical astrology the most; see Mavroudi, "Occult Science and Society", p. 48.

built an observatory in Marāgha, south of Tabriz, in 1259, which had become one of the largest in the Islamic world, also attracting researchers and students from the Western world and the Far East.[70] When Chioniades arrived in Tabriz, a new observatory had been established by Ghāzān Khān (1295–1304), which had also developed into a center of international studies. The existence of such a famous observatory, more new schools of astronomy and renowned teachers,[71] as well as rumors that the Il-Khan allocated generous pensions and stipends to scientists,[72] may have been some of the incentives that motivated scholars from faraway parts of the world to venture to Persia. Among them was Gregory Chioniades. In 1295[73] he decided to travel to northern Persia, which was ruled by Ghāzān Khān and his Prime Minister Rashīd al-Dīn. The reign of Ghāzān Khān, the greatest of the Il-Khans and a figure interested in all aspects of learning, is considered by many to be the Golden Age of the Mongol empire.[74] Chioniades made a first stop at Trebizond, where he related his decision to Emperor Alexios II Komnenos (1297–1330) and succeeded in obtaining not only his moral support but also payment of expenses for his journey to Tabriz. With the secrets of astronomy being reserved only for the subjects of the Khanate of Persia, Chioniades was able to gain the same privilege only after he had managed to become an intimate member of the Khan's court. He thus studied astronomy and astrology under Shams al-Dīn al-Bukhārī, an astronomer and teacher from Bukhārā, founder of the observatory of Maragha and author of the Persian version of the *Zīj al-'Alā 'ī*, which became the basis of Chioniades' work.[75] A small segment from the preface of Chioniades' *Persian Composition of Astronomy* is highly informative:

> This book is called an astronomical composition (*syntaxis*) according to the Greeks, but a *zīj* according to the language of the Persians. From the oral instruction of Shams Bukhārī, a man of the Persian race who has studied the entire rational curriculum to its limit, I listened to this

---

70   Tihon, "Les tables astronomiques persanes", p. 471. Tihon, "Astrological Promenade in Byzantium", p. 273.

71   Mavroudi, "Occult Science and Society", pp. 61–62.

72   Daryaee, *The Oxford Handbook of Iranian History*, p. 255 and p. 258.

73   Pingree, *The Astronomical Works of Gregory Chioniades, I, The Zīj al-'Alā'ī*, p. 21: "the notes probably go back to the fall of 1295, when his course with Shams began".

74   Lane, *Daily Life in the Mongol Empire*, p. 10. Daryaee, *The Oxford Handbook of Iranian History*, p. 258. Boyle, "Dynastic and political history of the Il-Khāns", pp. 396–97.

75   Pingree, *The astronomical works of Gregory Chioniades, vol. I: The Zīj al-'Alā ī*, p. 16. Id., "Gregory Chioniades", p. 143.

INTELLECTUAL PURSUITS FOR THEIR OWN SAKE

teaching of the science (that is) better than any others, which I reduced to writing to remember it ...[76]

Having become an expert in the field of astronomy, in 1302 Chioniades returned, again via Trebizond, to Constantinople, where he started teaching Persian astronomy and medicine. He had also acquired a significant number of books on astronomy written in Persian which he set about translating into Greek. These books were translations of those which his master Shams al-Dīn al-Bukhārī had made in Tabriz in 1296 from their original Arabic sources.[77] Chioniades dedicated his Greek translation of one of Shams al-Dīn's treatises on the astrolabe to Emperor Andronikos II.[78] In the summer of 1305 Chioniades returned to the capital of the Mongols as bishop of the Orthodox people in Tabriz – a gesture by Emperor Andronikos II possibly as part of a broader diplomatic plan of rapprochement with Il-Khan Ghāzān.[79] Chioniades remained in Tabriz as bishop until about the year 1310, when he retired to Trebizond and spent the rest of his life there as monk. Chioniades' long residence among the Persians and his interest in astrology drew accusations of heterodoxy, and towards the end of his life he was obliged to write a confession of Christian faith to defend against them.[80]

Chioniades seems to have played a key role in the dissemination of Persian scientific knowledge, as his Greek translations of Persian books on astronomy enjoyed a wide circulation throughout Western and Central Europe and made a great impression among European scholars (especially Copernicus) in the fifteenth century. The new knowledge derived from Chioniades' astronomical corpus became accessible and was utilized by the Western world when, after

76 Pingree, *The astronomical works of Gregory Chioniades*, p. 37 and the Greek text, ibid., p. 36, lines 1–9: Περσικὴ σύνταξις ἀστρονομίας. Τὸ βιβλίον τόδε καθ' Ἕλληνας μὲν σύνταξις λέγεται, κατὰ δὲ τὴν τῶν Περσῶν διάλεκτον ζῆζι. ἀπὸ φωνῆς τοίνυν τοῦ Σὰμψ Πουχάρης, ἀνδρὸς τὸ γένος Πέρσου πᾶσαν λογικὴν παιδείαν εἰς ἄκρον ἐξησκημένου, ταύτην περὶ τῆς ἐπιστήμης τῆς κρείττονος τῶν ἄλλων [ταύτης] τὴν διδασκαλίαν ἀκήκοα, ἣν καὶ εἰς μνήμην γραφῇ ἀκήκοα, ἣν καὶ εἰς μνήμην γραφῇ παρεδέδωκα ὡς ἂν μὴ τῷ χρόνῳ καὶ αὖθις ἡ θαυμασία ἐπιστήμη τοῖς τῆς λήθης βυθοῖς ἐναποκρυβῇ ...

77 Pingree, *The astronomical works of Gregory Chioniades*, p. 7.

78 Ibid., p. 17.

79 Pingree, "Gregory Chioniades and Palaeologan Astronomy", p. 143. Andronikos II, continuing the diplomatic relations of his father Michael VIII with Hulagu, the khan of Persia, decided to renew the alliance by offering one of his illegitimate daughters to Ghazan, and after Ghazan's death (1304), to his successor, Olǧäitü. These negotiations were lengthy. See George Pachymeres, *History*, ed. Failler, vol. 4, p. 441, lines 20–28. Laiou, *Constantinople and the Latins*, pp. 175–76. For the embassy to the Il-Khan Ghāzān, which took place in 1304, see Dölger, *Regesten*, p. 43, no. 2265.

80 See Westerink, "La profession de foi de Grégoire Chioniadès".

92   MERGIALI-SAHAS

the fall of Constantinople, Byzantine scholars brought his Greek manuscripts to the West.[81]

5   Demetrios Kydones: The Statesman and the Study of Western Philosophical Thought

A similar case of Chioniades' receptive attitude towards a foreign language and foreign wisdom, is Demetrios Kydones (c.1324–c.1397/98),[82] a fascinating figure of the second half of the 14th century, a distinguished scholar, proliferous writer, promising translator and remarkable statesman. He was a pioneer of a pro-Latin party in his generation which strove for a religious, cultural and political rapprochement with the West. Born into a noble family of Thessaloniki, Kydones received an excellent classical education. This was thanks to his parents, who regarded education and culture as prerequisites and guarantees for his future happiness and prosperity.[83] They wanted him to follow a career of his liking and inclinations, while also making good and wise use of the family's fortune:

> My parents were Christians, good people, who fashioned their lives according to their beliefs. They did not rear me to devote my life to some narrow-specialized trade for the mere purpose of earning a living for myself. Instead, they entrusted my education entirely to learned and wise men, obviously convinced that my future well-being would be found in the realm of the intellect and the spirit. My parents had sufficient wealth to see to the education of their children and to assure a wholesome social life as well as to take care of our needs. Therefore, they expected that if I were well raised and educated, I too would one day use that wealth wisely. When I finished preparatory school, I began to devote myself to the sciences, and to those subjects which particularly suited my intelligence

---

81   See Nicolaïdis, "Scientific exchanges between Hellenism and Europe", p. 181. Paschos/ Sotiroudis, pp. 5–11 and p. 16.

82   On Demetrios Kydones see Loenertz, "Démétrius Cydonès I: De la naissance à l'année 1373". Id., "Démétrius Cydonès II: De 1373 à 1375". Kianka, Demetrius Cydones (c. 1324–c.1397). Mergiali, L'enseignement et les lettrés, pp. 113–51. Demetrios Kydones, Letters, trans. F. Tinnefeld, vol. 1, pp. 1–74. Ryder, The Career and Writings of Demetrius Kydones. Plested, Orthodox Readings of Aquinas, pp. 63–72. Leonte, "The Letters of Demetrios Kydones".

83   Demetrios Kydones, Apology, ed. Mercati, p. 359, lines 8–13: Ἐγὼ χριστιανοῖς ἄνωθεν γονεῦσι χρησάμενος..., ἐπ' ἄνδρας δὲ μόνον λόγων καὶ σοφίας πεῖραν ἔχοντας ἐτερπόμην, νοῦ μόνου καὶ φρενῶν δεῖσθαι νομισάντων ὡς ἔοικε τὴν ἐσομένην μοι παρ'αὐτῶν εὐπορίαν.

INTELLECTUAL PURSUITS FOR THEIR OWN SAKE

and disposition. I was obviously inclined toward the deeper sciences, and I always ranked among the top students in my classes. I flourished like a healthy plant and soon began to show great promise.[84]

However, with the sudden death of his father at the end of his secondary studies, he was forced to leave the tranquility of a life devoted to studies and assume the care of his family, which had been financially ruined during the civil war (1341–47). He embarked on a government career which for the next forty years (1347–86) saw him rise to key positions in the imperial administration, initially in the service of John VI Kantakouzenos (1347–1354) and subsequently of John V Palaiologos (1355–1386). His exceptional personality and abilities, his social, political and intellectual prestige, his expertise on a number of important matters of government and his sense of duty towards his country at a time of intense crisis, made him a unique and irreplaceable servant to both emperors. His long political career as μεσάζων,[85] director of the imperial chancery and head of the imperial revenues, did not prevent Kydones from also dominating intellectual life for half a century, giving it new dimensions and venues. Political collapse, the bankruptcy of the state, and the drastic deterioration of living conditions during the second half of the 14th century resulted in the neglect of studies and a precipitous drop in the level of education.[86] At this junction Kydones undertook a personal course of action, imparting his zeal for classical learning, especially for Plato and Demosthenes, to his contemporaries. This becomes evident in his correspondence with a group of young people captivated by his advice.[87] Through his own open disposition towards Western thought, Kydones managed to broaden the

---

84 For the English translation of Kydones' *Apology* see Likoudis, *Ending the Byzantine Greek Schism*, p. 22.

85 According to Kianka, "During the reign of John VI the *mesazon* did not have the power and authority generally associated with the office of prime minister. Kydones' functions included those of master of requests and also those of chancellor or head of the imperial secretarial staff. Although his functions were limited to one or two areas of administration, his role as *mesazon* increased his influence in the government since it involved a close and continual personal contact with the emperor who chose him especially for this role"; see Kianka, "Demetrius Kydones and Italy", p. 101. During the second half of the 14th century the office of *mesazon* became important in Byzantine diplomacy and was given to those occupied mainly with external affairs along with chancellery activities. See Oikonomides, "La chancellerie impériale de Byzance du 13ᵉ au 15ᵉ siècle", pp. 169–70.

86 Demetrios Kydones, *Letters*, no. 239, ed. Loenertz, p. 141, lines 7–9: νῦν δὲ λόγοις πανταχόθεν ὁ πόλεμος καὶ τοῖς γονεῦσιν εὐχὴ μηδ' ἐπὶ νοῦν γοῦν ἐλθεῖν τοῖς υἱέσιν λόγων ἐπιθυμίαν, ὡς, ἂν αὐτῶν φροντίσωσι, προσαιτήσουσιν, ἢ τῶν ἀνδραπόδων χεῖρον βιωσομένοις.

87 See Mergiali, *L'enseignement et les lettrés*, pp. 117–21.

intellectual horizons of his time. His interest in Western thought came as a result of learning Latin, necessitated by the inadequacy of the official interpreters. To perform his duties properly, he was obliged to communicate effectively with various Western agents (ambassadors, mercenaries, merchants and prominent noblemen) engaged in official business with the emperor or flocking to the imperial court as visitors and admirers of its splendor.[88] As he himself states:

> I was forced to express my dissatisfaction with the interpreters whenever they muffed their translations and caused misunderstandings with my petitioners. It was a real nuisance to me to be unable to come to terms with some of my visitors because of the language difficulty. So, in order to solve such problems, and not to have to depend on the linguistic abilities of others, I decided to learn Latin.[89]

His teacher, a Dominican monk from Pera who taught him Latin in depth during the period 1347–1354, played a decisive role in what followed.[90] Kydones attained his goal by excelling in Latin without refraining from his main enterprise. As he states, "Having tasted the lotus, I could no longer help myself but trying to saturate my insatiable desire for the Latin language."[91] At the instigation of his teacher, he became engaged with the translation of Thomas Aquinas' *Summa contra gentiles* into classical Greek, a work that he completed in 1354, a month after Kantakouzenos' resignation from the imperial throne. The attraction which Thomas Aquinas' thought exercised upon Kydones further pushed him to proceed in 1355 with the translation of a great part of Aquinas' other *Summa*, the *Summa theologiae*, as well as of the theological works of Augustine and Anselm of Canterbury. The accuracy of the arguments displayed by the Latin writers and their profound knowledge and use of classical philosophy fascinated Kydones to such an extent that from a translator of Latin theological treatises he gradually became an adherent of the Latin

---

88   Kydones, *Apology*, ed. Mercati, p. 360, lines 41–44: ἦσαν ἐν ἐκείνοις καὶ τῶν Ἑσπερίων πολλοί, οἱ μὲν πρεσβείας τελοῦντες, οἱ δ' ἐμπορίας διατιθέντες, οἱ δ' ὡς ἔθος μισθοφοροῦντες. Πολλοὶ δὲ τούτοις καὶ τῶν καλουμένων παρ' ἑκάστοις λαμπρῶν ἐπιθυμοῦσι γίνεσθαι θεαταί. Kianka, "The Apology of Demetrius Cydones", p. 60.

89   Likoudis, *Ending the Byzantine Greek Schism*, p. 23.

90   On the Dominican presence, missionary and scholarly activities in Pera and in Constantinople and their crucial role in the East, see Loenertz, "Les établissements dominicains de Pera-Constantinople". Delacroix-Besnier, *Les Dominicains et la chrétienté grecque aux XIVᵉ et XVᵉ siècles*. Tsougarakis, *The Latin Religious Orders in Medieval Greece 1204–1500*, pp. 171, 174 and 186–89.

91   Demetrios Kydones, *Apology*, ed. Mercati, p. 363, lines 30–31.

INTELLECTUAL PURSUITS FOR THEIR OWN SAKE   95

theology itself. The impact that Kydones' translations of masterpieces of Latin
theology had upon the Byzantine intellectual elite was manifold and unprecedented. In his endeavor, Kydones was greatly encouraged by Emperor John VI
who, for his part, predicted that such an effort would offer immense benefit
to Byzantine Greek culture.[92] As an ardent admirer, Kydones wanted to make
Latin theological thought known to his contemporaries and, thus, reconcile
Western theological rationalism with the Greek Aristotelian tradition:

> Therefore, I increased my translating activity day by day, and made many
> great Latin writers accessible to our people who previously had not even
> known of them. Thus, I provided our learned scholars the opportunity to
> become even more learned. At the same time I put to shame those who
> were in the habit of finding fault out of sheer jealousy.[93]

Kydones' unusual pursuit of western theology was seen by some as a truly
worthwhile undertaking, while others criticized it sternly. He expressed his
bitterness for the myopic view among the latter of his countrymen, who considered any approach to the Latins worthless. He states:

> Do we not richly reward and highly esteem our traders who venture
> abroad and enrich our own land by transporting wares from foreign mar-
> kets? Why then should we not cherish even more someone who gathers
> the riches of other nations in order to greatly enhance our own knowl-
> edge and learning?[94]

This was the first time that the voice of Thomas Aquinas had echoed in
Byzantium due to the initiative and effort not of a Latin but of a Byzantine, and
a prominent scholar and statesman at that. After his conversion to Catholicism
(1357), Kydones expressed his desire to expand his own intellectual horizons
by visiting Italy, coming into contact with its intellectual circles, studying Latin
books and, finally, getting an experience of the kind and the level of education provided by the Western world at the time. In one of his letters written
between 1367–1368, he states that while those who took refuge in Italy aimed at

---

92   Demetrios Kydones, *Apology*, ed. Mercati, p. 363, lines 18–23: καὶ οὕτω πολλὰ τῶν ἐκεῖ κεφα-
      λαίων εἰς τὴν Ἑλλάδα μετενεγκών, ὁπότε σχολάζοιμεν παρεῖχον ἀναγινώσκειν τῷ βασιλεῖ. ὁ δ'
      ἄρα φιλήκοος ὢν ἤδετό τε τοῖς διδομένοις κἀμὲ τῶν περὶ ἐκεῖνα πόνων ἐπήνει, καὶ προῦτρεπε μὴ
      ῥαθυμεῖν ἀλλ'ὅλον ἐμαυτὸν πρὸς ἑρμηνείαν ὅλου τοῦ βιβλίου συντείνειν, πολὺ κέρδος προλέγων
      ἐντεῦθεν ἔσεσθαι τῷ κοινῷ τῶν Ἑλλήνων.

93   Likoudis, *Ending the Byzantine Greek Schism*, pp. 26–27.

94   Ibid., p. 29.

gaining riches and positions, he was interested only in delving into the science of theology that was cultivated there:

> The desire to converse with those men possessed me, even when I was very young ... because their knowledge of theology is combined with the knowledge of philosophy ... But now, since my desire has not ceased, I am looking forward to the spring voyage. I want to associate myself with them, not because I want to become rich or because I love honors (motives which draw most people to Italy and the Tiber) ... What attracts me to them is their knowledge of theology and their way of proceeding in all aspects of their dialectics with rational arguments. This, indeed, is what strikes every intelligent person ... [This] is the gist of my impulse toward them.[95]

A fact that deserves special attention is that Kydones idealized the Church of Rome, described in his own words as "a storehouse of all wisdom, bringing forth companies of philosophers, surrounded by groups of theologians, adorned by monks of manifold virtue."[96] Kydones also intended to visit France in the spring of 1371, to learn about the country, come into contact with its intellectuals and learn their language.[97] Although he was not able to bring his plans to live permanently in Italy to fruition, in the second half of the 14th century he systematically promoted the ideal of religious, political and cultural rapprochement between Byzantium and the West, thus helping to bridge the cultural gap between the Latin-speaking West and the Greek-speaking Byzantium.

6   Manuel Palaiologos: The Emperor and Literary Finesse and Composition

As far as Manuel II Palaiologos (1391–1425) is concerned, any intellectual interests and cultural evolution during his reign were profoundly influenced by the dwindling resources and political impotence of Byzantium to face the looming Ottoman presence with its eight-year long blockade of Constantinople (1394–1402). Under these circumstances, any intellectual activity was a distraction rather than an intellectual pursuit by the people who enjoyed the shelter and

---

95   Demetrios Kydones, *Letters*, no. 103, ed. Loenertz, lines 63–79.
96   Kianka, "The *Apology* of Demetrius Cydones", p. 67 and note 62.
97   Demetrios Kydones, *Letters*, no. 37, ed. Loenertz, lines 16–18, 28–34 and 41–47.

INTELLECTUAL PURSUITS FOR THEIR OWN SAKE

privacy of his court. From the very beginning of his reign, Manuel was faced with two realities: the fact that the very existence of Constantinople itself was undermined and at the same time, that he himself had to serve as a military vassal in Bayezid's army. A person of many abilities, he managed to excel equally as a statesman, diplomat, soldier, theologian and a man of letters;[98] and this, in spite of the fact that "he was often at a loose end and seldom able to exercise all his talents because of the restricted and inhibited empire that had been left to him."[99]

As the 14th century was coming to a close and the empire was dramatically shrinking, a growing widespread disposition in favor of Hellenic self-consciousness led to a stubborn effort on the part of many to regain the quality of style and the sense of Attic Greek in its former purity. This domination of Hellenism, which even led intellectuals to certain excesses, can be viewed as an effort to disguise a humiliating present by re-appropriating a glorious past.

Manuel II is praised by his contemporaries as an emperor-philosopher, in the Platonic sense of the word, for his ability to combine political activity with a philosophical drive.[100] He inspired the intellectual elite of his time and, with his literary production, exerted a great influence upon it. In his pursuit to preserve the Hellenic tradition, he promoted a particular kind of linguistic refinement in Attic Greek by adding value to the merits of literary composition: "The ability to write is clearly better than being wealthy, is sweeter also than all sweet things, and, indeed, brings the greater glory."[101] To this, he does not omit to list the elements and preconditions of a literary composition: adequate training during youth, talent of using fine words and noble ideas, a nature receptive to this kind of exercise and, above all, the existence of free time.[102] Referring to himself with excessive modesty, the emperor admits that he meets none of these conditions. However, his personal course of life allows us to understand that what he always lacked was free time:

---

98 The latest monograph on Manuel II Palaiologos is that of Leonte, *Imperial Visions of Late Byzantium*. See also Celik, *Manuel II Palaiologos (1350–1425). A Byzantine Emperor in a Time of Timult*.

99 Nicol, *The Last Centuries of Byzantium*, p. 296.

100 See Demetrios Kydones, *Letters*, no. 259, ed. Loenertz, p. 164, lines 24–26: ἐπὶ σοῦ τὸν φιλό-σοφον βασιλέα, ὃ μόνον Πλάτων λέγει τὰς πόλεις παύσειν κακῶν. Demetrios Chrysoloras, *Comparison*, ed. Lampros, p. 232, lines 7–17. Bees, *Les manuscrits des Météores*, no. 154, p. 185, fol. Ζʹa: Πρὸς σὲ δέ, οὐ βασιλέα μᾶλλον, ἢ φιλόσοφον ὄντα, λέγω ...

101 Manuel II Palaiologos, *Letters*, no. 11, ed. Dennis, p. 29, lines 2–3. I preferred Barker's translation of this letter; Barker, *Manuel II Palaeologus*, p. 415.

102 Manuel II Palaiologos, *Letters*, no. 11, ed. Dennis, p. 29, lines 5–9.

So, when I was a child, it was not possible for me to frequent only the haunts of the Muses and to make this my sole employment, so that I could overtake every man of wisdom, even those who pride themselves in their learning. But once I was out of my earliest instruction, toils followed one upon another ... And once I had passed the age of children, though before reaching manhood, a different fortune ensued with my advancing age, one filled with storm and tumults ... if therefore, I ever in my childhood reaped the fruits of my studies, I cast aside at least the bulk of this, having been transferred elsewhere from my literary pursuits.[103]

It is clear that circumstances prevented Manuel II from following the usual course of studies. According to Demetrios Kydones, Manuel managed to imitate Demosthenes and Plato fully, only by combining his passion for literature with his natural gifts, despite never having had a teacher.[104]

Animated by a sense of duty and responsibility, Manuel II devoted himself to matters of administration of an impoverished state consisting only of its capital city, the fate of which lay in the hands of the Turks. As the state was going through its crisis, the emperor, burdened with heavy and numerous tasks, regretted being deprived of his literary pursuits. In a letter to Demetrios Chrysoloras, he gives a characteristic description of his extremely busy everyday life attending to state duties:

The multitude of tasks I have to do ... forces me to keep away from those things which are essential for survival. I have lost track of the time for meals and have little thought for food, whatever might be served. I have shaken sleep from my eyes, and often my bed receives me only at dawn ... How excessively busy I have been should also be clear from this: I have shaken off my eagerness for books and every literary activity, as well as the gratification I derived from them ... But since, anxious though I am to have our affairs in the best state, obstacles arise from all sides ... For as

---

103 See the emperor's letter to one Alexios Iagoup, translated by Barker, *Manuel II Palaeologus*, p. 412.

104 Demetrios Kydones, *Letters*, no. 262, ed. Loenertz p. 167, lines 13–15: ὅς γε οὐδὲν μὲν ἐδέξω παρ' οὐδενός, σαυτῷ δὲ μόνῳ διδασκάλῳ χρησάμενος καὶ πρὸς τοὺς τῆς φύσεως ἰδὼν θησαυ-ρούς, πένητας ὄντως καὶ προσαίτας σοφίας τοὺς τῶν διδασκάλων ἤλεγξας μαθητάς, τὸ πάλαι λεγόμενον, ... λαμπρῶς ἐπὶ σαυτοῦ βεβαιώσας. See also, ibid., no. 82, p. 114, lines 11–23, p. 115, lines 30–31: καὶ ῥητορεύεις μετὰ κάλλους τῆς ἠχοῦς Δημοσθένους ἐχόμενος and no. 276, p. 194, lines 5–7: ἐπιὼν τὴν γενναίαν ἐπιστολήν. ἐν ἐκείνῃ μὲν γὰρ ἐνόμιζον ὁρᾶν τὸν πάλαι πότ' οἰχόμε-νον Πλάτωνα καὶ ζῶντα καὶ κινούμενον καὶ φθεγγόμενον ...

INTELLECTUAL PURSUITS FOR THEIR OWN SAKE

things now stand, we are a slave to the cares oppressing us rather than master of our own desires.[105]

As a matter of fact, his fervent activity in literary composition was so manifest that he often felt obliged to justify his pronounced taste for his studies:

> Once I had been ensnared by my studies, however, I was not able to put aside my desire. But, while I viewed fortune as an opponent, I regarded the aid gained from my studies as a trainer. So, I endeavored, by advancing in studies, to endure my dreadful ordeal and, at the same time, as long as I endured, to advance in studies.[106]

At times a kind of bitterness colors his reaction to those who criticize him for his literary preoccupations. He writes to Demetrios Kydones during his mandatory participation in a campaign in Asia Minor as a vassal of Bayezid in the winter of 1391: "... for those who cannot bear to see me devote my time to literary interests when I am home would be far more vociferous in their criticism if they could see me doing the same thing out here."[107]

It is obvious therefore that Manuel II never enjoyed conditions favorable to pursuing the literary skills at the center of his interests. Thus, he deliberately turned every event, every circumstance, and every activity, private or public, into an opportunity for reflection, study, and creative writing. For instance, during the dark period of his strict and harsh imprisonment in the Anemas Tower with his father and his brother (1376–79), he took great pains to continue his literary studies independently. Another crisis, the Turkish siege of Thessaloniki which brought his independent five-year (1383–1387) rule of the city to an end,[108] prompted him to compose a *Discourse of Counsel to the Thessalonians*[109] in an attempt to invigorate the Thessalonians to fight for their freedom.[110] Contrary to what one might expect, multiple current events

---

105   Manuel II Palaiologos, *Letters*, no. 44, ed. Dennis, pp. 116–18.

106   Barker, *Manuel II Palaeologus*, p. 413.

107   Manuel II Palaiologos, *Letters*, no. 19, ed. Dennis, p. 58.

108   See Dennis, *The Reign of Manuel II Palaeologus in Thessalonica*.

109   Manuel II Palaiologos, *Discourse of Counsel to the Thessalonians when they were besieged*.

110   Manuel's *Discourse of Counsel to the Thessalonians* and other letters written during the siege of Thessalonica by the Turks "demonstrate Manuel's practice of falling back on intellectual distractions amid pressure and adversity ... Kydones even felt obliged to warn Manuel against pursuing his studies to the extent of neglecting his military responsibilities in the beleaguered city"; Barker, *Manuel II Palaeologus*, p. 417. Kydones, *Letters*, no. 304, p. 224, lines 29–30: εἰ δ'ὁ χρόνος ἀμφοῖν οὐκ ἀρκεῖ, πρὸς Θεοῦ, τοῦ μὲν ῥητορεύειν ἄλλος ἔστω καιρός, ὁ δὲ πᾶς ταῖς κατὰ ἐχθρῶν ἐργασίαις διδόσθω.

or challenges throughout his life, and crucial ones at that, constituted opportunities for writing and served as an impetus for him to develop his literary skills and convey the proper messages. The most heterogeneous incidents of his life, if pieced together, seem to form an outline of Manuel's literary corpus, and unveil his state of mind. Consider, for example, the dialogue he carried on with an educated Persian about Christianity and Islam and the truth afforded by each, probably in 1391 in the winter barracks near Ankara, and this while on campaign as a military vassal of Bayezid;[111] or, the *panegyrikos* that he wrote on the occasion of the recovery of his father John V from a serious illness;[112] also in his forties, a dialogue with his mother Helen Kantakouzene on marriage, which he recorded late in 1396 and which influenced him to decide to marry.[113] Before embarking for the West, he wrote two texts for his son John VIII, heir to the throne, under the titles *Fundamentals of imperial conduct* and *Seven ethicopolitical Orations*.[114] The defeat of his old enemy Bayezid I by the Mongols at Ankara (1402) prompted him to write a fictitious dialogue between these two adversaries.[115] While in Paris on a diplomatic journey and as guest of King Charles VI (1368–1422) in the old Louvre, he did not spend his time only in contacts and negotiations regarding Western aid against the Turkish threat, but also used the opportunity to compose two works inspired by this circumstance: a small rhetorical essay, an *ekphrasis*, depicting scenes of spring on a dyed woven hanging tapestry in the royal residence, as well as a lengthy theological treatise *On the Procession of the Holy Spirit*. The latter was in response to a Latin tract presented to him by an anonymous "monk practicing his monastic life in the suburbs of Paris" and "in reclusion".[116] Even the death of his youngest brother Theodore, despot of the Morea, to whom he was very closely attached,

---

111 Manuel II Palaiologos, *Dialogue which was held with a certain Persian, the Worthy Mouterizes, in Angkyra of Galatia*, ed. Trapp. For a new edition, see Baum (ed.)/Senoner (trans.), *Kaiser Manuel II. Palaiologos. Dialog über den Islam und Erziehungsratschlage*.

112 Manuel II Palaiologos, *Panegyric on the Emperor's Health*, ed. Boissonade.

113 Manuel II Palaiologos, *Moral Dialogue or Concerning Marriage*. See also Dabrowska, "Ought one to marry?". Leonte, *Imperial Visions of Late Byzantium*, pp. 113–23.

114 Manuel II Palaiologos, *Fundamentals of imperial conduct* and Manuel II Palaiologos, *Seven ethico-political orations*. See also, Leonte, "Teaching Virtues: The Didactic Project of Emperor Manuel II Palaiologos". Id., *Imperial Visions of Late Byzantium*, pp. 124–98. Kakkoura, *An annotated critical edition of Emperor Manuel II Palaeologus*.

115 Manuel II Palaiologos, *Timur's Address to Bayezid*; ed. in Legrand, *Lettres de l'empereur Manuel Paléologue*, pp. 103–104.

116 For his well-known *ekphrasis*, see Manuel II Palaiologos, *A Representation of Spring in a Woven, Dyed Drapery*, ed. Davis. Dendrinos, "Manuel II Palaeologus in Paris (1400–1402)", pp. 401–402. For the *On the Procession of the Holy Spirit*, see Dendrinos, *An annotated critical edition (edition princeps) of Emperor Manuel II Palaeologus' treatise 'On the Procession of the Holy Spirit'*. Dendrinos, "Manuel II Palaeologus in Paris (1400–1402)", p. 410.

INTELLECTUAL PURSUITS FOR THEIR OWN SAKE

in 1407, prompted him to compose a moving funeral oration.[117] With the exception of his correspondence (68 letters in total – a priceless source of personal information about him that reflects his own attitude toward his writing), his literary production in general is deprived of personal confessions and rarely yields personal feelings and expectations about his literary pursuits.[118] All these are examples of events, occasions and incidents which offered the emperor opportunities for recording but also of literary expression, and "demonstrate Manuel's practice of falling back on intellectual distractions amid pressure and adversity."[119]

The emperor had no illusions. His eagerness to rediscover his ancestors did not interfere with his sense of reality. 1397 found him wondering about the purpose of any intellectual effort in the face of the imminent peril which the Turks represented for the very existence of the empire.[120] In spite of the political distress he often faced, he never lost his awareness of a cultural decline. The achievements of the past may have been beyond the grasp of the simple citizen of his time; but as for him, what is valid is stated in one of his letters to his friend, Gabriel of Thessaloniki, where his attitude toward his own writing is exposed:

> I would not want to rank myself at all with those possessing high reputation in the art of writing. For, I am not ignorant of the *Phaedrus* by Plato, son of Ariston. Nor, therefore, would I ever succumb to the desires of other people who encourage me to be overly proud. Nevertheless, it seems to me exceedingly stupid if, as regards the fruits of our effort that seem to be of some usefulness, we should obliterate them completely because they are not absolutely marvelous ... After all, the best course for those of us who endeavor to write at all is to regard the works of the leaders in writing as our models, so far as is possible ... Certainly if one should place the writings of the ancients beside those of the present age, he is "exchanging gold for bronze ... And yet, should we abstain

---

117   Manuel II Palaiologos, *Funeral Oration for His Brother Theodore*, ed. Chrysostomides. Leonte, *Imperial Visions of Late Byzantium*, pp. 199–236.

118   On Manuel's letters, Dennis (*The Letters of Manuel II Palaeologus*, p. xx) aptly comments: "The letters of Manuel may be difficult to understand; nonetheless they are real letters, written to communicate real messages to real people. Some are trivial, others obscure and many were subsequently edited for publication.... Still, his letters are actual letters and, written by the Emperor himself, they are historical sources of the first rank and contain a great deal more information about the man and the period than one might suspect".

119   Barker, *Manuel II Palaeologus*, p. 417.

120   Manuel II Palaiologos, *Letters*, no. 33, ed. Dennis, lines 39–40.

from the practice of writing, our education will be so undermined that it would become impossible for us to understand the dogmas from which is derived our True Faith.[121]

Literary meetings were held in the palace under his auspices, forming an expert audience consisting of scholars before which literary works were presented for evaluation. Occasionally the audience showed enthusiasm for certain works through applause. In his correspondence[122] Manuel uses the term *theater* to characterize these meetings, signifying that despite their limited and exclusive audience, their importance was paramount and their literary judgment indisputable.[123] Thus, as far as the aspect of social life during his reign is concerned, we are faced with an actual institution. The radiance of a *theater* gathered around Manuel II seems to have emanated beyond the limits of the capital, while admittance of a person to such a *theater* was considered equivalent to a certification of talent and high culture. The most astute summary of the driving force behind his literary pursuits was provided by the emperor himself:

> With these points in mind, my worthy friend, I continue writing, not as much as I ought, but as much as my time allows, so that I will serve to those under my sway as an example in the love of letters, in order that they, as they mingle so much with barbarians, may not themselves become entirely barbarized.[124]

In summary, we would say that looking at the crop of detached, pure devotees to intellectual pursuits among the intellectuals of the Palaeologan renaissance, one is faced with a contradiction: that at a time of irreversible political

---

121   Barker, *Manuel II Palaeologus*, p. 423.

122   Manuel II Palaiologos, *Letters*, no. 9, ed. Dennis, line 7: τοῦ θεάτρου σειομένου καὶ εὐφημούντων τὸν σοφιστήν; no. 27, line 2: τὰ εἰρημένα σοι ἐν μικρῷ μὲν οὐ φαύλῳ δ' ἀνεγνώσθη θεάτρῳ; no. 28, lines 18–19: ἀεὶ δὲ συρίττειν παρέχων τὸ θέατρον οἷς γενναῖος ἀθλητὴς ἅπασιν ἀναφαίνῃ.

123   Ibid., no. 27. On the meaning and role of the term *theatron* in Byzantium and its significance as a cultural phenomenon within Byzantine society, see Marciniak, "Byzantine *Theatron* – A Place of Performance?". For the *theaters* in Late Byzantium, see Toth, "Rhetorical Theatron in Late Byzantium: The example of Palaeologan imperial orations". See also, Medvedev, "The so-called θέατρα as a form of communication of the Byzantine Intellectuals in the 14th and 15th Centuries". Gaul, "Performative Reading in the Late Byzantine Theatron". Leonte, *Imperial Visions of Late Byzantium*, pp. 58–64.

124   Manuel II Palaiologos, *Letters*, no. 52, ed. Dennis, lines 33–35. The English translation is of Barker, *Manuel II Palaiologos*, p. 423.

INTELLECTUAL PURSUITS FOR THEIR OWN SAKE 103

decline and decay, a steady weakening of the imperial court and a mounting Turkish threat, an exaltation and flourishing in learning seems, *prima facie*, to be out of place, especially an exaltation of novel enterprises. These rare learning enterprises, which went against the main currents of Byzantine traditional scholarship, should be seen as neither meaningless nor aimless in any way. It rather seems that, at least for Theodore Metochites, John Zacharias, Gregory Chioniades, Demetrios Kydones, and Manuel Palaiologos, the pursuit of learning was, indeed, a way of life: a means of distraction from uneasiness; an exploration of the "foreign" and "unorthodox"; an alternative to mere survival in the midst of adversities; a comforting refuge in an unstable and volatile environment; a paved path leading to mental growth, spiritual perfection and divine knowledge; an exercise in making life worth living and attaining immortality from this world – all with an unavoidably imminent eclipse of the Byzantine empire in sight. The question of whether these five intellectual figures might constitute a glimmer of the dawning Renaissance is a matter of historical judgment.

Bibliography

Primary Sources

Demetrios Chrysoloras, *Comparison*, ed. Lampros, Σύγκρισις παλαιῶν ἀρχόντων καὶ νέου τοῦ νῦν αὐτοκράτορος Μανουὴλ Παλαιολόγου, in Lampros, Παλαιολόγεια καὶ Πελοποννησιακά, vol. 3, pp. 222–45.

Demetrios Kydones, *Apology*, ed. G. Mercati, *Notizie di Prochoro e Demetrio Cidone, Manuele Caleca e Teodoro Meliteniota ed altri appunti per la storia della teologia e della letteratura bizantina del secolo XIV* (Studi e Testi, 56), Vatican City 1931, pp. 359–403.

Demetrios Kydones, *Letters*, ed. R.-J. Loenertz, *Demetrius Cydones, Correspondance*, vol. 1 (Studi e Testi, 186), Vatican City 1956, pp. 1–182; *Demetrius Cydones, Correspondance*, vol. 2 (Studi e Testi, 208), Vatican City 1960, pp. 1–417.

Demetrios Kydones, *Letters*, trans. F. Tinnefeld, *Demetrios Kydones. Briefe* (Bibliothek der griechischen Literatur, 12, 16, 33, 50 & 60), 5 vols., Stuttgart 1981–2003.

George Chrysokokkes, *Syntaxis*, ed. S. Lampros, "Τοῦ σοφωτάτου ἰατροῦ κυροῦ Γεωργίου τοῦ Χρυσοκόκκη εἰς τὴν σύνταξιν τῶν Περσῶν ἐκτεθεῖσα πρὸς τὸν αὐτοῦ ἀδελφόν κὺρ Ἰωάννην τὸν Χαρσιανίτην", *Νέος Ἑλληνομνήμων* 15 (1921), 334–36.

George Pachymeres, *History*, ed. A. Failler, *Georges Pachymérès Relations Historiques*, (Corpus Fontium Historiae Byzantinae, 24), 5 vols., Paris 1984–2000.

John of Damascus, *On Philosophy*, ed. P.B. Kotter, *Die Schriften des Johannes von Damaskos* (Patristische Texte und Studien, 7), vol. 1, Berlin 1969.

John of Damascus, *On the Orthodox Faith*, ed. P.B. Kotter, *Die Schriften des Johannes von Damaskos* (Patristische Texte und Studien, 12), vol. 2, Berlin 1973.

John Katrares, *Dialogues*, ed. A. Elter, *Io. Katrarii Hermodotus et Musokles dialogi, Nataliacia regis augustissimi Guilelmi imperatoris germanici*, Bonn 1898, cols. 5–54.

John Zacharias (Aktouarios), *Hermippos*, eds. G. Kroll/P. Viereck, *Anonymi Christiani Hermippus de astrologia dialogus*, Leipzig 1895.

John Zacharias (Aktouarios), *Medical Epitome*, ed. Ideler, *Physici et medici Graeci minores*, vol. 2, pp. 353–463.

John Zacharias (Aktouarios), *On Urines*, ed. Ideler, *Physici et medici Graeci minores*, vol. 2, pp. 3–192.

John Zacharias (Aktouarios), *On the Activities and Affections of the Physic Pneuma*, ed. Ideler, *Physici et medici Graeci minores*, vol. 1, pp. 312–86.

Manuel II Palaiologos, *A Representation of Spring in a Woven, Dyed Drapery*, ed. J. Davis, "Manuel II Palaeologus' Depiction of Spring in a Dyed, Woven Hanging" in C. Dendrinos et al. (eds.), *Porpyrogenita. Essays on the History and Literature of Byzantium and the Latin East in Honour of Julian Chrysostomides*, London 2003, pp. 411–12.

Manuel II Palaiologos, *Dialogue which was held with a certain Persian, the Worthy Mouterizes, in Angkyra of Galatia*, ed. E. Trapp, *Manuel II Palaiologos, Dialoge mit einem "Perser"* (Wiener Byzantinistische Studien, 2), Vienna/Graz/Cologne 1966; W. Baum (ed.)/R. Senoner (trans.), *Kaiser Manuel II. Palaiologos. Dialog über den Islam und Erziehungsratschlage*, Vienna 2003.

Manuel II Palaiologos, *Discourse of Counsel to the Thessalonians when they were besieged*, ed. B. Laourdas, "Ὁ Συμβουλευτικὸς πρὸς τοὺς Θεσσαλονικεῖς τοῦ Μανουὴλ Παλαιολόγου", *Μακεδονικά* 3 (1955), 295–302.

Manuel II Palaiologos, *Fundamentals of imperial conduct*, in *Patrologia Graeca*, vol. 156, cols. 309–384.

Manuel II Palaiologos, *Funeral Oration on his Brother Theodore*, ed. J. Chrysostomides, *Manuel II Palaeologus. Funeral Oration on his Brother Theodore* (Corpus Fontium Historiae Byzantinae, 26), Thessaloniki 1985.

Manuel II Palaiologos, *Letters*, ed. & trans. G.T. Dennis, *The Letters of Manuel II Palaeologus* (Corpus Fontium Historiae Byzantinae, 8), Washington, D.C. 1977.

Manuel II Palaiologos, *Moral Dialogue or Concerning Marriage*, ed. A.D. Angelou, *Manuel Palaiologos. Dialogue with the empress-mother on marriage. Introduction, text and translation* (Byzantina Vindobonensia, 19), Vienna 1991.

Manuel II Palaiologos, *Panegyric on the Emperor's Health*, ed. J.F. Boissonade, *Anecdota nova*, Hildesheim 1962, pp. 223–38.

Manuel II Palaiologos, *Precepts of Imperial Conduct*, in *Patrologia Graeca*, vol. 156, cols. 320–84.

Manuel II Palaiologos, *Seven ethico-political orations*, in *Patrologia Graeca*, vol. 156, cols. 385–562.

Manuel II Palaiologos, *Timur's Address to Bayezid*, in *Patrologia Graeca*, vol. 156, cols. 280C–281A.

Nikephoros Gregoras, *Roman History*, eds. L. Schopen/I. Bekker, *Nicephori Gregorae Byzantina Historia* (Corpus Scriptorum Historiae Byzantinae, 19), 3 vols., Bonn 1829/55.

Physici et medici Graeci minores, ed. J.L. Ideler, 2 vols., Berlin 1841–42.

Theodore Metochites, *Advice addressed to the wise Nikephoros Gregoras, and a section concerning the author's own writings*, ed. Polemis, *Theodori Metochitae Carmina*, pp. 85–97.

Theodore Metochites, *Advice addressed to the wise Nikephoros Gregoras, and a section concerning the author's own writings*, trans. I. Polemis, *Poems*, pp. 85–135.

Theodore Metochites, *Autobiographical preface*, ed. B. Bydén, *Theodore Metochites' Stoicheiosis Astronomike and the Study of Natural Philosophy and Mathematics in Early Palaeologan Byzantium* (Acta Universitatis Gothoburgensis, 66), Gothenburg 2003, pp. 417–43.

Theodore Metochites, *Miscellanea*, ed. K. Hult, *Theodore Metochites on Ancient Authors and Philosophy, Semeioseis Gnomikai 1–26 & 71* (Studia Graeca et Latina Gothoburgensia, 65), Gothenburg 2002.

Theodore Metochites, *Miscellanea*, ed. K. Hult, *Theodore Metochites on the Human Condition and the Decline of Rome. Semeioseis Gnomikai 27–60. Critical Edition with Introduction, Translation, Notes, and Indexes* (Studia Graeca et Latina Gothoburgensia, 70), Gothenburg 2016.

Theodore Metochites, *Miscellanea*, eds. C.G. Müller/T. Kiessling, *Theodori Metochitae Miscellanea philosophica et historica*, Leipzig 1821 (repr. Amsterdam 1966).

Theodore Metochites, *Miscellanea*, ed. S. Wahlgren, *Theodore Metochites' Sententious Notes Semeioseis Gnomikai 61–70 & 72–81. A Critical Edition with Introduction, Translation, Notes, and Indexes* (Studia Graeca et Latina Gothoburgensia, 71), Gothenburg 2018.

Theodore Metochites, *On Morals or Concerning Education*, eds. I. Polemis/E. Kaltsogianni, *Theodorus Metochites, Orationes* (Bibliotheca Teubneriana, 2031), Berlin/Boston 2019, pp. 347–429.

Theodore Metochites, *Poems*, ed. I. Polemis, *Theodori Metochitae carmina* (Corpus Christianorum, Series Graeca, 83), Turnhout 2015

Theodore Metochites, *Poems*, trans. I. Polemis, *Theodore Metochites, Poems. Introduction, translation and notes* (Corpus Christianorum in Translation, 26), Turnhout 2017.

Theodore Metochites, *Stoicheiosis Astronomike 1.5–30*, eds. E.A. Paschos/C. Simelidis, *Introduction to Astronomy by Theodore Metochites (Stoicheiosis Astronomike 1.5–30)*, (World Scientific), Singapore/Kackensack, NJ, 2017.

Theodore Metochites, *To the Wise Nikephoros Xanthopoulos*, ed. Polemis, *Theodori Metochitae Carmina*, pp. 225–36.

Theodore Metochites, *To the Wise Nikephoros Xanthopoulos and a Section on His Own Writings*, trans. Polemis, *Poems*, pp. 245–55.

Theodore Metochites, *To the Wise Xanthopoulos and a Section concerning His Own Misfortunes*, trans. Polemis, *Poems*, pp. 213–44.

Secondary Literature

Angold, M.J., "Autobiography & Identity: The Case of the Later Byzantine Empire", *Byzantinoslavica* 60 (1999), 36–59.

Barker, J.W., *Manuel II Palaeologus (1391–1425). A Study in Late Byzantine Statesmanship*, New Brunswick/New Jersey 1969.

Bazzani, M., "Theodore Metochites, a byzantine humanist", *Byzantion* 76 (2006), 32–52.

Bees, N.A., *Les manuscrits des Météores*, vol. 1, Athènes 1967.

Bouras-Vallianatos, P., *Zacharias Aktouarios (c. 1275–c.1330)* (Oxford Studies in Byzantium), Oxford 2020.

Boyle, J.A., "Dynastic and political history of the Il-Khāns", in id. (ed.), *The Cambridge History of Iran, vol. 5 The Saljuq and Mongol periods*, Cambridge 1968.

Browning, R., "Church, State and Learning in Twelfth-Century Byzantium", in id., *History, Language and Literacy in the Byzantine World* (Variorum Reprints), Northampton 1989, no. VI, pp. 5–24.

Bydén, B., "Metochites, Theodore", in *Encyclopedia of Medieval Philosophy: Philosophy Between 500 and 1500*, vol. 1, London 2011, p. 1267.

Bydén, B., *Theodore Metochites' Stoicheiosis Astronomike and the Study of Natural Philosophy and Mathematics in Early Palaeologan Byzantium*, (Acta Universitatis Gothoburgensis, 66), Gothenburg 2003.

Caudano, A.-L., "Astronomy and Astrology" in Lazaris (ed.), *A Companion to Byzantine Science*, pp. 202–30.

Çelik, S., *Manuel II Palaiologos (1350–1425). A Byzantine Emperor in a Time of Timult*. Cambridge 2021.

Ciggaar, K.N., *Western Travelers to Constantinople. The West and Byzantium, 962–1204: Cultural and Political Relations*, Leiden 1996.

Costomiris, A.-G., "Études sur les écrits des médecins grecs", *Revue des Études Grecques* 10 (1897), 405–445.

Cutler, A., "Astronomy", in Kazhdan et al. (eds.), *The Oxford Dictionary of Byzantium*, vol. 1, pp. 216–17.

Dąbrowska, M., "Ought one to marry? Manuel II Palaiologos' point of view", *Byzantine and Modern Greek Studies* 31 (2007), 146–56.

Daryaee, T., *The Oxford Handbook of Iranian History*, Oxford 2012.

Delacroix-Besnier, C., *Les Dominicains et la chrétienté grecque aux XIV e et XV e siècles*, Rome 1997.

Dendrinos, C., *An annotated critical edition (edition princeps) of Emperor Manuel II Palaeologus' treatise 'On the Procession of the Holy Spirit'*, PhD thesis, Royal Holloway, University of London 1996.

Dendrinos, C., "Manuel II Palaeologus in Paris (1400–1402): Theology, Diplomacy and Politics", in M. Hintenberger/Chr. Schabel (eds.), *Greeks, Latins and Intellectual History 1204–1500*, Leuven/Paris/Walpole, MA 2011, pp. 397–422.

Dennis, G.T., *The Reign of Manuel II Palaeologus in Thessalonica, 1382–1387* (Orientalia Christiana Analecta, 159), Rome 1960.

de Vries-van der Velden, E., *Théodore Métochite: une réévaluation*, Amsterdam 1987.

Dölger, F., *Regesten der Kaiserurkunden des Oströmischen Reiches von 565–1453. (4 Teil: Regesten von 1282–1341)*, vol. 4, Munich/Berlin 1960.

Featherstone, J.M., *Theodore Metochites's Poems 'To Himself'. Introduction, Text and Translation*, Vienna 2000.

Fryde, E., *The Early Palaeologan Renaissance (1261–c. 1360)* (The Medieval Mediterranean, 27), Leiden/Boston 2000.

Galatariotou, C., "Travel and Perception in Byzantium", *Dumbarton Oaks Papers* 47 (1993), 221–41.

Gaul, N., "Performative Reading in the Late Byzantine Theatron", in T. Shawcross/I. Toth (eds.), *Reading in the Byzantine Empire and Beyond* (Cambridge University Press), Cambridge 2018, 215–33.

Grünbart, M. (ed.), *Rhetorische Kultur in Spätantike und Mittelalter / Rhetorical Culture in Late Antiquity and the Middle Ages* (Millennium-Studien, 13), Berlin 2007.

Guilland, R., "Les Logothètes. Études sur l'histoire administrative de l'Empire byzantin", *Revue des Études Byzantines* 29 (1971), 5–115.

Haramundanis, K., "Chioniades Gregor [Georges]" in Th. Hockey et al. (eds.), *Biographical Encyclopedia of Astronomers*, New York 2007.

Hohlweg, A., "John Aktouarios' *De methodo medendi* – on the new edition", *Dumbarton Oaks Papers* 38 (1984), 121–33.

Inglebert, H., "'Inner' and 'Outer' Knowledge: The Debate between Faith and Reason in Late Antiquity" in Lazaris (ed.), *A Companion to Byzantine Science*, pp. 27–52.

Kakavelaki, A., *Η έννοια του πνεύματος κατά την Αρχαία και Βυζαντινή Περίοδο. Μελέτη της αρχαίας και βυζαντινής φιλοσοφίας και ιατρικής*, Athens 2018.

Kakkoura, C., *An annotated critical edition of Emperor Manuel II Palaeologus: Seven ethico-political orations*, PhD thesis, University of London, 2013.

Kaldellis, A., *Hellenism in Byzantium. The Transformation of Greek Identity and the Reception of Classical Tradition*, Cambridge 2007.

Katsiampoura, G., "Faith or Knowledge? Normative relations between religion and science in Byzantine textbooks", *Almagest. International Journal for the History of Scientific Ideas* 1 (2010), 112–23.

Kazhdan, A.P. et al. (eds.), *The Oxford Dictionary of Byzantium*, 3 vols., New York/Oxford 1991.

Kazhdan, A.P., "Mesazon", in id. et al. (eds.), *The Oxford Dictionary of Byzantium*, vol. 2, p. 1346.

Kazhdan, A.P./R. Browning, "Education", in Kazhdan et al. (eds.), *The Oxford Dictionary of Byzantium*, vol. 1, pp. 677–78.

Kianka, F., *Demetrius Cydones (c.1324–c.1397): Intellectual and Diplomatic Relations between Byzantium and the West in the Fourteenth Century*, PhD thesis, Fordham University 1981.

Kianka, F., "Demetrius Kydones and Italy", *Dumbarton Oaks Papers* 49 (1995), 99–110.

Kianka, F., "The Apology of Demetrius Cydones: A Fourteenth-Century Autobiographical Source", *Byzantine Studies/Études Byzantines* 7/1 (1980), 57–71.

Kourousis, S.I., "Ὁ ἀκτουάριος Ἰωάννης Ζαχαρίας παραλήπτης τῆς ἐπιστολῆς ι΄ τοῦ Γεωργίου Λακαπηνοῦ. Τὰ βιογραφικά", *Ἀθηνᾶ* 78 (1980–1982), pp. 237–76.

Kourousis, S.I., "Ὁ ἀκτουάριος Ἰωάννης ὁ Ζαχαρίας (1275 ca.–1330 ca.) πρόδρομος κακοδόξιῶν Βαρλαὰμ τοῦ Καλαβροῦ (1290 ca.–1348)", *Ἀθηνᾶ* 80 (1990), 385–406.

Kourousis, S.I., "Ὁ ἀκτουάριος Ἰωάννης Ζαχαρίας συγγραφεὺς ἀποδοθέντων αὐτῷ μὴ ἰατρικῶν πονημάτων", *Ἀθηνᾶ* 82 (1997–1998), pp. 27–77.

Kourousis, S.I., *Τὸ ἐπιστολάριον Γεωργίου Λακαπηνοῦ-Ἀνδρονίκου Ζαρίδου (1299–1315 ca.) καὶ ὁ ἰατρός-ἀκτουάριος Ἰωάννης Ζαχαρίας (1275 ca.–1328/;). Μελέτη φιλολογική* (Ἀθηνᾶ. Σειρὰ διατριβῶν καὶ μελετημάτων, 23), Athens 1984.

Laiou, A.E., *Constantinople and the Latins. The Foreign Policy of Andronicus II. 1282–1328*, Cambridge, Mass. 1972.

Lampros, S., *Παλαιολόγεια καὶ Πελοποννησιακά*, 4 vols., Athens 1912–30.

Lampsides, O., "Georges Chrysococcis, le médecin et son œuvre", *Byzantinische Zeitschrift* 38 (1938), 312–22.

Lane, G., *Daily Life in the Mongol Empire*, Westport, Connecticut 2006.

Lazaris, S., (ed.), *A Companion to Byzantine Science* (Brill's Companions to the Byzantine World, 6), Leiden/Boston 2020.

Legrand, E., *Lettres de l'empereur Manuel Paléologue*, Paris 1893.

Leonte, F., *Imperial Visions of Late Byzantium. Manuel II Palaiologos and Rhetoric in Purple* (Edinburg Byzantine Studies), Edinburgh 2020.

Leonte, F., "Teaching Virtues: The Didactic Project of Emperor Manuel II Palaiologos", *Byzantinoslavica* 76 (2018), 24–44.

Leonte, F., "The Letters of Demetrios Kydones", in Riehle (ed.), *A Companion to Byzantine Epistolography*, pp. 146–73.

Likoudis, J., *Ending the Byzantine Greek Schism*, New Rochelle, NY 1992.

Loenertz, R.-J., "Démétrius Cydonès I: De la naissance à l'année 1373", *Orientalia Christiana Periodica* 36 (1970) 47–72.

Loenertz, R.-J., "Démétrius Cydonès II: De 1373 à 1375", *Orientalia Christiana Periodica* 37 (1971) 5–39.

Loenertz, R.-J., "Les établissements dominicains de Pera-Constantinople", *Echos d'Orient* 34 (1935), 332–49.

Magdalino, P., "The Byzantine Reception of Classical Astrology", in C. Holmes/J. Waring (eds.), *Literacy, Education and Manuscript Transmission in Byzantium and Beyond* (The Medieval Mediterranean, 41), Leiden/Boston/Cologne 2002, pp. 33–57.

Marciniak, P., "Byzantine *Theatron* – A Place of Performance?", in Grünbart (ed.), *Theatron*, pp. 277–85.

Markopoulos, A., "Education", in E. Jeffreys/J. Haldon/R. Cormack (eds.), *The Oxford Handbook of Byzantine Studies*, Oxford 2008, pp. 785–95.

Mavroudi, M., "Occult Science and Society in Byzantium: Considerations for Future Research", in P. Magdalino/Ead. (eds.), *Occult Sciences in Byzantium*, Geneva 2006, pp. 39–95.

Medvedev, I., "The so-called θέατρα as a form of communication of the Byzantine Intellectuals in the 14th and 15th", in N.G. Moschonas (ed.), *Η επικοινωνία στο Βυζάντιο* (Κέντρο Βυζαντινών Ερευνών / Ε.Ι.Ε), Athens 1993, pp. 227–235.

Mergiali, S., *L'enseignement et les lettrés pendant l'époque des Paléologues (1261–1453)* (Ἑταιρεία τῶν Φίλων τοῦ Λαοῦ: Κέντρον Ἐρεύνης Βυζαντίου, 5), Athens 1996.

Mergiali-Sahas, S., "Παλαιολόγεια εκπαίδευση", in T. Lounghis/E. Kislinger (eds.), *Βυζάντιο. Ιστορία και Πολιτισμός. Ερευνητικά πορίσματα*, vol. 2, Athens 2015, pp. 441–53.

Mondrain, B., (ed.), *Lire et écrire à Byzance. Actes de la table ronde tenue à Paris à l'occasion du XXe Congrès International des études byzantines, 19–25 août 2001* (Association des amis du Centre de Byzance), Paris 2006.

Nicol, D.M., "The Byzantine Church and Hellenic Learning", in id., *Byzantium: its ecclesiastical history and relations with the western worlds* (Variorum Reprints), London 1972, XII, pp. 23–57.

Nicol, D.M., *The Last Centuries of Byzantium, 1261–1453*, Cambridge ²1993.

Nicolaïdis, E., *Science and Eastern Christianity. From the Greek Fathers to the Age of Globalization*, Baltimore 2011.

Nicolaïdis, E., "Scientific exchanges between Hellenism and Europe: translations into Greek, 1400–1700", in P. Burke/R. Po-Chia Hsia, *Cultural Translation in Early Modern Europe*, Cambridge 2007.

Oikonomides, N., "La chancellerie impériale de Byzance du 13e au 15e siècle", *Revue des Études Byzantines* 43 (1985), pp. 167–95.

Papathanassiou, M.K., "Iatromathematica (medical astrology,) in Late Antiquity and the Byzantine Period", *Medicina nei Secoli* 11 (1999), 291–322.

Papathanassiou, M.K., "The Occult Sciences in Byzantium", in Lazaris (ed.), *A Companion to Byzantine Science*, pp. 464–495.

Paschos, E.A./P. Sotiroudis, *The Schemata of the Stars. Byzantine Astronomy from A.D. 1300*, London 1998.

Pingree, D., "Chioniades Gregory", in Kazhdan et al. (eds.), *The Oxford Dictionary of Byzantium*, vol. 1, pp. 422–23.

Pingree, D., "Gregory Chioniades and Palaeologan Astronomy", *Dumbarton Oaks Papers* 18 (1964), 135–160.

Pingree, D., *The Astronomical Works of Gregory Chioniades, I, The Zīj al-ʿAlāʾī, part 1, Text, translation, commentary; part 2, Tables, Corpus des astronomes byzantine II*, 2 vols., Amsterdam 1985–86.

Pingree, D./B. Croke/A. Cutler, "Eclipses", in Kazhdan et al. (eds.), *The Oxford Dictionary of Byzantium*, vol. 1, pp. 671–72.

Plested, M., *Orthodox Readings of Aquinas*, Oxford 2015.

Riehle, A. (ed.), *A Companion to Byzantine Epistolography* (Brill's Companions to the Byzantine World, 7), Leiden/Boston 2020.

Ryder, J.R., *The Career and Writings of Demetrius Kydones. A Study of Fourteenth Century Byzantine Politics, Religion and Society* (The Medieval Mediterranean, 85), Leiden/Boston 2010.

Scarborough, J./A.-M. Talbot, "John Aktouarios", in Kazhdan et al. (eds.), *Oxford Dictionary of Byzantium*, vol. 2, p. 1056.

Ševčenko, I., *Études sur la polémique entre Théodore Métochite et Nicéphore Choumnos* (Corpus Bruxellense. Historiae Byzantinae Subsidia, 3), Brussels 1962.

Ševčenko, I., *Ideology, Letters and Culture in the Byzantine World* (Variorum Reprints), London 1982.

Ševčenko, I., "Théodore Métochites, Chora et les courants intellectuels de l'époque", in id., *Ideology, Letters and Culture in the Byzantine World*, no. VIII, pp. 15–39.

Ševčenko, I./J. Featherstone, *Two Poems by Theodore Metochites*, Brookline, Mass. 1981.

Talbot, A.M., "Metochites, Theodore", in Kazhdan et al. (eds.), *The Oxford Dictionary of Byzantium*, vol. 2, pp. 1357–58.

Tannery, P., *Quadrivium de Georges Pachymère* (Studi e Testi, 94), Vatican City 1940.

Temkin, O., "Byzantine Medicine: Tradition and Empirism", *Dumbarton Oaks Papers* 16 (1962), 97–115.

Tihon, A., "Astrological Promenade in Byzantium in the Early Paleologan Period", in P. Magdalino/M. Mavroudi (eds.), *The Occult Science in Byzantium*, Geneva 2006, pp. 265–90.

Tihon, A., "Astronomy", in D.C. Lindberg/M.H. Shank (eds.), *The Cambridge History of Science. Vol. 2. Medieval Science*, Cambridge 2013, pp. 195–99.

Tihon, A., *Études d'astronomie byzantine* (Variorum Reprints), Hampshire 1994.

Tihon, A., "L'astronomie byzantine (du Ve au XVe siècle)", *Byzantion* 51 (1981), 603–24.

Tihon, A., "Les sciences exactes à Byzance", *Byzantion* 79 (2009), 380–434.

Tihon, A., "Les tables astronomiques persanes à Constantinople dans la première moitié du XIVe siècle", *Byzantion* 57 (1987), 471–87.

Toth, I., "Rhetorical Theatron in Late Byzantium: The example of Palaeologan imperial orations", in Grünbart (ed.), *Theatron*, pp. 429–48.

Touwaide, A. "Medicine and Pharmacy", in Lazaris (ed.), *A Companion to Byzantine Science*, pp. 354–403.

Tsougarakis, N., *The Latin Religious Orders in Medieval Greece 1204–1500*, Turnhout 2012.

Verpeaux, J., "Contribution à l'étude de l'administration byzantine: ὁ μεσάζων", *Byzantinoslavica* 16 (1955), 270–96.

Verpeaux, J., "Le cursus honorum de Théodore Métochite", *Revue des Études Byzantines* 18 (1960), 195–98.

CHAPTER 3

Continuity and Evolution in Autobiographical Literature

Sofia Kotzabassi

1 The Past

'Autobiography', "an account of a person's life written by that person", according to the Oxford English Dictionary, is not a word that occurs in Byzantine literature.[1] The absence of the term, and of any framework of guidelines for those wishing to write an autobiography, makes assigning texts to this category an almost entirely subjective exercise. In any case, none of the texts that have been so labelled contains a full account of the author's life. The percentage of (auto)biographical material varies, and this is what leads scholars to include or exclude some of them from the autobiographical canon.

Two works from the Early Byzantine period, Libanios' *Oration 1* (Βίος ἢ περὶ τῆς ἑαυτοῦ τύχης)[2] and the long poem (1949 iambic trimeters) of Gregory of Nazianzos titled Εἰς τὸν ἑαυτοῦ βίον (*De vita sua*),[3] display enough of the characteristics of autobiography to be assigned without difficulty to the genre, which includes both prose and metrical writings. In the span of centuries intervening before the 13th, some autobiographical elements may be traced in various Byzantine texts, among them works of history and hagiography, poems, and accounts of travels,[4] but there is no text that can be described as an autobiography.

After several centuries of silence we have the first work that can properly be called an autobiography, penned by Nikephoros Blemmydes, who lived and

---

1 For the term and its meaning see Hinterberger, *Autobiographische Traditionen*, pp. 43–8.
2 Libanios, *Autobiography (Oration 1)*, ed. Foerster.
3 Gregory of Nazianzos, *Autobiography*, ed. Jungck.
4 If one excludes certain autobiographical elements in epistolary texts, such as e.g., the letters of Theodore Stoudites, or historical writings, such as John Kaminiates' account of the sack of Thessaloniki in 904, the disposition towards autobiographical reference in the *literati* of the first millennium is rather limited. Conversely, from the beginning of the 11th–12th century elements of autobiography appear with increasing frequency both in the works of historians, especially Michael Psellos and Anna Komnene, and in the poems of John Mauropous and the writings of Nikephoros Basilakes.

© KONINKLIJKE BRILL NV, LEIDEN, 2023 | DOI:10.1163/9789004527089_005

worked in the intellectual environment of the Empire of Nicaea and who in two texts describes his life and spiritual progress.[5] In the first text the writer declares that he wishes to recount some details of his life, since he is neither willing nor able to describe it all, while in the second he adds some further events that he wishes to include, explaining the reasons for that decision.

Blemmydes' two-part autobiography seems to have sparked the writing of the autobiographical texts that followed in the Palaeologan period, making him a pioneer among the *literati* of the age in that genre as well.

This period was, besides, a less introverted age, which probably encouraged its *literati* to express their personal views on life in autobiographical texts that are frequently an explanation of their spiritual journey or a defence of their choices in life.

These autobiographies are sometimes self-contained pieces and sometimes parts of a larger work, usually in an introductory text intended to paint for the reader a picture of the writer and his life, with its choices.

There are, of course, works in which personal information about the writer is included, but without the coherence and structure that would justify describing them as autobiography.[6] In other cases, spurred by a specific occasion, men of letters choose to recount a particular period of their life, often relating to an official mission they undertook or to some historically critical juncture; such descriptions are found intercalated into historical texts of the period or take the form of journals or memoirs, which, as one might expect, contain a good deal of autobiographical detail.

2   The Autobiographer

The writer decides on each occasion whether he wishes to tell the story of his life as an external narrator (third-person narrative) or as the protagonist of the events he is relating. In the latter case, he sometimes uses the first-person singular, which makes the narrative wholly personal and places the writer squarely at centre stage in his narrative, and sometimes the first-person plural, which distances him somewhat from the narrator-protagonist. Even in the second case, however, the writer-narrator and the protagonist are not entirely one and the same, for the passage of time has left the protagonist of the narrative

---

5   See Nikephoros Blemmydes, *Autobiography*, ed. Munitiz.
6   Historical works in which the writer is also a protagonist, such as those of George Pachymeres, John Kantakouzenos, and George Sphrantzes, fall into this category.

in the past while the writer and narrator, the one outside the text and the other within it, belong to the present.[7]

Some writers use more than one manner; others may reveal their identity at the end of the narrative, or not at all.[8] Nikephoros Blemmydes sometimes speaks of himself in the singular and sometimes in the plural, Demetrios Kydones uses the singular, with the exception of the preamble to his autobiography, where he also uses the plural, while Gregory II of Cyprus and John VI Kantakouzenos prefer the third-person narrative,[9] but while the Patriarch reveals his identity at the end of his autobiography, the Emperor never does.

3 Titles of Autobiographies and Their Evolution

Blemmydes' autobiography is titled *Περὶ τῶν κατ' αὐτὸν διήγησις μερική*, a formulation that has led to difficulties of interpretation. The most recent editor, Munitiz, renders the term "διήγησις μερική" as "partial account", deeming the phrase to indicate that the work is not a full account of the author's life, while Hinterberger, in his study on *Autobiography in Byzantium*, interprets it quite differently: in his view, διήγησις μερική means a detailed account.[10]

The debate is not without interest, because there is a similar title to one of the manuscripts of the brief autobiography of Patriarch Gregory II of Cyprus, a text that, as he says, was intended to serve as the introduction to an edition of his works.[11] The content of the autobiography penned by Gregory of Cyprus does not confirm Hinterberger's proposed interpretation of the phrase διήγησις μερική, which in any case is found only on a single manuscript in the codex Leiden, Bibliotheek der Rijksuniversiteit, Leidensis B.P.G. 49, unlike the title of the older manuscript, in the codex Modena, Biblioteca Estense, Mutinensis α.R.6.19: Γρηγορίου τοῦ ἁγιωτάτου καὶ μακαριωτάτου οἰκουμενικοῦ πατριάρχου περὶ τοῦ καθ' ἑαυτὸν βίου ὡς ἀπ' ἄλλου προσώπου (on his life as if recounted

---

7   See Hinterberger, *Autobiographische Traditionen*, pp. 116–121.

8   See e.g. Nikephoros Blemmydes, Demetrios Kydones.

9   John Kantakouzenos' *History* has an autobiographical element in that the author is also a protagonist in many of the events he describes.

10   See Hinterberger, *Autobiographische Traditionen*, p. 116.

11   Gregory of Cyprus, *Autobiography*, ed. Lameere, pp. 189 lines 30–32: Διὰ τοῦτο καὶ τῶν ὑποκειμένων ὅσα μὲν σπουδαῖα, τῇ ἀκμῇ λογιστέα, ἃ δὲ μὴ τοιαῦτα, τῇ νεότητι προσνεμητέα καὶ τῷ ἀτελεῖ τῆς ἀσκήσεως. (English translation by Pelendridis) In the same way, those of the author's works which are considered important, are connected to the period of his maturity; and those which are not so, are ascribed to his youth and lack of practice. (Gregory of Cyprus, *Autobiography*, trans. Pelendrides, p. 43).

CONTINUITY AND EVOLUTION IN AUTOBIOGRAPHICAL LITERATURE 115

by another),[12] which better befits the third-person narrative style Gregory adopts, revealing his identity only at the end.[13]

The terms διήγησις and περὶ τῶν καθ᾿ ἑαυτόν are also found in the preamble to Theodore Metochites' *Stoicheiosis astronomike*, which is a kind of intercalated autobiography.[14]

The sense of "partial account" that Munitiz gives the phrase διήγησις μερική in the title of Blemmydes' autobiography is indirectly corroborated by the title of Joseph Rhakendytes' autobiography, Σύνοψις ἐν ἐπιτομῇ εἰς τὰ κατ᾿ αὐτόν (A general view/ summary with regard to what concerns himself), which, in common with the titles of other autobiographies, contains a statement of the subject of the work, namely, τὰ κατ᾿ αὐτόν.[15]

4 Self-Contained Autobiographies

If we wish to discuss self-contained autobiographies in the age of the Palaeologans, then we must focus on the brief account penned by Patriarch Gregory II of Cyprus and the longer one written by the scholar and high-ranking officer of the Byzantine court Demetrios Kydones.

4.1 *Gregory II of Cyprus*

George-Gregory of Cyprus (1241–1290) was one of the most important *literati* of the early Palaeologan period. Although his writings are not particularly extensive,[16] he earned the esteem of his contemporaries and later men of letters alike both for his contribution to the revival of the "Attic" style and for his work as a philologist and copyist, an activity that, as he states in his autobiography, was one of the reasons for his modest creative output.

---

12   See Kotzabassi, "'Περὶ τοῦ καθ᾿ ἑαυτὸν βίου ὡς ἀπ᾿ ἄλλου προσώπου'", pp. 281–85.

13   Gregory of Cyprus, *Autobiography*, ed. Lameere, pp. 191, lines 10–12: Ἡ δέ που πυκτίς, ὅπερ καὶ ἄνωθεν ἔφην, καλῶς τὸν πατέρα τοῖς ἀναγινώσκουσι δείξει. (English translation by Pelendridis) The book will to some degree, as mentioned earlier, reveal the author favourably to its readers. (Gregory of Cyprus, *Autobiography*, trans. Pelendrides, p. 45).

14   Theodore Metochites, *Stoicheiosis Astronomike*, ed. Bydén, p. 417: Προοίμιον, ἐν ᾧ καὶ διήγησις τοῦ συγγραφέως περὶ τῶν καθ᾿ ἑαυτόν (Preface, which also contains an account by the writer of himself); see also, below, p. 19.

15   See edition below, p. 121.

16   It comprises six encomia for saints, two encomiastic orations, for the Emperors Michael VIII Palaiologos and Andronikos II, a few short rhetorical treatises, and five theological works on the procession of the Holy Spirit, which were written in the context of theological controversies during the period of his prelacy. His collected Letters, 250 in total, are of exceptional importance.

Gregory of Cyprus decided to write an account of his life as a preamble to the edition of the works that he was preparing, as so many Byzantine scholars did. Utilizing a very personal and emotional style, he describes his desire for education and the hurdles he had to overcome in order to achieve his goal.[17]

Born in Cyprus, most probably in 1241, he was not satisfied with the Latin schooling of his then Frankish-ruled birthplace and sought teachers with whom he could continue his education. With disarming frankness, he describes how he managed to deceive his parents, who did not want him to leave Cyprus, and boarded a ship sailing for Palestine, and all the adventures and difficulties he encountered as he made his way to Ephesos, where he hoped to study with Nikephoros Blemmydes, of whom he had heard. This intention, however, was never realised, for he was advised by people who knew the scholar not to approach him, since Blemmydes, like his pupils, disliked company and would almost certainly refuse even to admit George to the monastery, because he was young, poor and a stranger.

And so the young George elected to go to Nicaea, hoping to find suitable teachers there. But once again he was disappointed, for those he found taught only grammar and poetry, and he would even have contemplated returning home had that not been so dauntingly difficult.

Fortunately, the situation changed, for shortly afterwards the Byzantines recaptured Constantinople from the Crusaders and the Emperor Michael VIII appointed the *megas logothetes* George Akropolites to teach the young man. Gregory of Cyprus gives an enthusiastic description of his studies with George Akropolites – Aristotelian Logic, Arithmetic, Geometry and Rhetoric – and reports that he eventually outshone all his fellow students in rhetoric, although at first they mocked him as unskilled, and invites the readers of the works included in the edition headed by his autobiography to judge for themselves whether they were not as exemplary in style as those of the ancient orators.

His account of the ecclesiastical events of the age, of the efforts of Michael VIII Palaiologos to unite the Churches, of his unwilling election to the patriarchal throne of Constantinople, and of the difficulties he faced as Patriarch, is exceptionally brief and intended mainly to justify the limited extent of his writings. Like many other scholars before him, Patriarch Gregory declares that he would have preferred to devote his life to study and writing, far from ecclesiastical strife and the responsibilities of office, which leave him no time for writing. He also adds another two reasons for his limited literary

---

17   See Hinterberger, *Autobiographische Traditionen*, pp. 354–58 (with previous bibliography).

CONTINUITY AND EVOLUTION IN AUTOBIOGRAPHICAL LITERATURE

output, one being the poor health that plagued him[18] and the other the copying of manuscripts of earlier writers, an occupation to which he devoted himself systematically, as much because he had some skill as a copyist as because he loved books and as a poor youth had no other means of acquiring them.

Patriarch Gregory does not hesitate to assess his own work, ascribing the imperfections of certain works to the inexperience of youth, and leaves the final judgement to the reader, lest he be accused of subjective appraisal and of flattering himself.

4.2   Demetrios Kydones

The second self-contained autobiography of the Palaeologan period was written by the scholarly Byzantine courtier Demetrios Kydones, whose life and work fall mainly within the second half of the 14th century (*c*.1324–*c*.1397/8).[19] He followed a political career as *mesazon* of three Byzantine emperors, John VI Kantakouzenos, John V Palaiologos and his son, Manuel II Palaiologos.

According to his autobiography Kydones, who was born into a wealthy family in Thessaloniki, displayed an appetite for learning from a very early age. However, the death of his father made it necessary for him to interrupt his studies and approach John Kantakouzenos, who had succeeded to the imperial throne, for a place at court. The emperor's love of learning and letters caused him to regard Kydones with an interest and affection that soon developed into friendship and hastened the young Thessalonian's rise through the ranks of the imperial hierarchy. The offices he held and the obligations associated with them, especially the discussions with Western envoys, spurred Kydones to find someone to teach him Latin, so that he would be able to dispense with the services of an interpreter.

Kydones eventually found a teacher who more than met his requirements, for not only could he teach Latin, but he could also lead a willing disciple into the furthest reaches of philosophy. This teacher, whose name Kydones does not reveal, was a clergyman, a priest or monk with whom he had been acquainted for some time. When he learned that Kydones wished to learn Latin he commended this resolve and offered to instruct him, even leaving his monastic brethren for a time for this purpose.

---

18   He mentions his illnesses in his letters as well; see e.g. Gregory of Cyprus, *Letters*, nos. 12, 15, ed. Eustratiades, pp. 11, 13; also P. Timplalexi, *Medizinisches in der byzantinischen Epistolographie*, passim.

19   Demetrios Kydones, *Apology*, ed. Mercati, pp. 359–403. See also, Kianka, "The Apology of Demetrios Cydones" and Hinterberger, *Autobiographische Traditionen*, pp. 367–71.

Kydones' desire to learn Latin caused talk in the palace, with some contending that he was too old to succeed in such an endeavour and others that the emperor would not tolerate it and would transfer him elsewhere. The result, however, was remarkable, for Kydones learned to speak and read Latin as if it were his mother tongue.

His teacher was so pleased with his progress in the language that he gave him Thomas Aquinas' treatise *Summa contra gentiles* for further reading practice. Kydones read it avidly and began to translate it into Greek; when he had time, he would pass his translation on to the emperor. When Kantakouzenos read his work, he urged Kydones to finish it, and thus, as he says, his translation is now in the hands of many who praise the author and profit from its reading.

This occupation afforded him so much pleasure that he continued to translate, while the emperor, who loved books and preferred to accumulate a great library instead of other possessions, kept the copyists' purses filled.

This account of his translation of Aquinas' works leads Kydones into a description of relations between Byzantium and the West and their theological differences, allowing him to express his own opinion in the matter through the text.

5 Autobiographical Prefaces

5.1 *Theodore Metochites*

Theodore Metochites (1270–1332), son of George Metochites, Archdeacon to Patriarch John Bekkos, the principal champion of Michael VIII's promotion of Church Union, faced considerable difficulties in the early years of his life since his father was sentenced to prison by the Council of Blachernae (1285) after Andronikos II ascended the throne and reversed his predecessor's ecclesiastical policy. He managed to study, however, and even to rise to prominence, thanks to his love of letters and the support of Andronikos II, to whom he remained faithful until his death.

This prominent scholar and statesman, who served as *logothetes tou genikou* and *megas logothetes* under Andronikos II, is the only Byzantine man of letters who includes autobiographical material in a number of his works. Writing on autobiographical texts in Byzantium, Hunger tentatively includes the Ἠθικός ἢ περὶ παιδείας as a kind of autobiography;[20] the (subsequent) edition of the work, however, shows that it does not merit this label.

---

20 Hunger, *Die hochsprachliche profane Literatur der Byzantiner*, vol. 1, p. 169. The text had not then been edited. See now Theodore Metochites, *Orations*, eds. I. Polemis/E. Kaltsogianni, pp. 347–429.

CONTINUITY AND EVOLUTION IN AUTOBIOGRAPHICAL LITERATURE 119

What can, by contrast, be described as an autobiography of Theodore Metochites is the preface to the *Stoicheiosis astronomike*, in which he traces his path to the acquisition of knowledge and the mastery of science.[21]

The very title of the first chapter both recalls the autobiographies of earlier scholars[22] and points to what follows: προοίμιον, ἐν ᾧ διήγησις τοῦ συγγραφέως περὶ τῶν καθ᾽ ἑαυτόν (preface containing the writer's account of himself).

Metochites begins by evoking his love for and interest in learning even as child, which his parents encouraged, and continues with an outline of the stages of his education. At the age of thirteen, he says, having completed his grounding in grammar and poetry, he turned to rhetoric, studying the ancient orators and avoiding the modern practitioners who had destroyed the art with their infelicitous use of words and rhetorical figures.

He continued, as was normal, with Aristotle's *Logic*, before turning to mathematics. Metochites complains that they had been abandoned and that for years no one, teacher or student, had worked systematically with mathematics beyond Nicomachus' *Arithmetic* and to a point Euclid's *Elements*, that is, the theory of plane figures but not the more complex topics of irrational numbers and conical figures, nor the works of Apollonius of Perga, Serenus, and Theodosius of Bithynia on the other solid figures; in fact, when he mentioned or asked questions about those topics he received only ironic responses, mocking him for attempting the impossible.

Discouraged by his inability to advance in the study of mathematics, he turned on the one hand to *sacred literature* and on the other to collecting the works that had long guided the conduct of human life, devoting himself to Aristotle's works on the natural sciences, logic, and moral philosophy, and to exercises in rhetoric until he reached the age of twenty, when Andronikos II admitted him to the archives (ἐν τοῖς ἀρχείοις καλέσας).[23]

Mention of Andronikos II leads Metochites into a long digression in praise of the emperor (§ 11–21), which concludes with a repetition of his appointment to the archives, a position that would bring him into the emperor's circle. Despite his youth (ἀτὰρ νέον ἔτ᾽ ὄντα) and short tenure (just one year) in the imperial service, Andronikos II made him a member of the Senate. This promotion further increased his interest in education and letters, which he constantly pursued and which, more than anything else, was the subject of his inquiries.

---

21   Theodore Metochites, *Stoicheiosis Astronomike*, ed. Bydén, pp. 417–43; see also, Hinterberger, *Autobiographische Traditionen*, pp. 360–61.

22   See above Nikephoros Blemmydes and Gregory of Cyprus.

23   See Theodore Metochites, *Stoicheiosis Astronomike*, I 173, ed. Bydén, p. 423; cf. Gregory of Cyprus, *Letters*, no. 20 (to John Staurakios), ed. Eustratiades, pp. 15–16.

At this stage he was occupied, as he tells us, with the various embassies to which he was appointed and the composition of such works as the two encomia for Andronikos II. These court duties did not, however, prevent him from continuing his studies, focusing primarily on rhetoric and philosophy rather than astronomy; he considered the latter science beyond his reach and believed his time better spent on something useful and not something unobtainable, however worthwhile.

Everything changed in an instant, however, when Manuel Bryennios, a scholar from Constantinople, demonstrated that he knew more about mathematics and astronomy than anyone else. He had learned the basic principles of mathematics from a kinsman and then devoted his natural ability, through study and hard work, to mastering the science of Astronomy. He won the emperor's enthusiastic admiration in a single meeting.

When Andronikos revealed to Metochites this new treasure-trove of wisdom that had so long remained hidden in the darkness of ignorance, his love for science was immediately re-awakened. Thus, disregarding the likelihood that he would be mocked for wishing to learn something new at his advanced age (he was 43), he threw himself into this new pursuit, taking Bryennios into his household so that, as an eager audience, he could devote any time that could be spared from his other occupations to studying with him.

Bryennios taught him about the heavenly bodies and their movements, Theon's *Commentaries* on Ptolemy's *Handy Tables*, which he later worked on himself, and all the other mathematical sciences. This brought him to the study of Ptolemy's *Almagest*, seeking to understand its meaning and purpose, although many, including Bryennios, thought it foolish to even try to grapple with things so exceedingly complex and abstruse. Metochites, however, persisted, reading the work through not just once but twice, as well as a number of other related works; he intended to supplement his study of Ptolemy by completing his study of Euclid's *Geometry*, the solid as well as the plane figures, and then his other works (*Optics, Catoptrics, Data* and *Phaenomena*), as an introduction to Astronomy, plus Theodosius of Bithynia's *Sphaerics* and all the other books mentioned earlier, Apollonius of Perga's *Conics* and Serenus' *On the section of a cylinder*.

After four years of study, he demonstrated his knowledge of astronomy by predicting solar and lunar eclipses. That was when he had the idea of writing his *Stoicheiosis astronomike*, based on Ptolemy's *Almagest* but simplified so as to be accessible to those with no knowledge or experience of the subject. In this treatise, he also attempts to explain the *Handy Tables* compiled by Ptolemy and amplified by Theon, made abstruse by their succinctness and lack

CONTINUITY AND EVOLUTION IN AUTOBIOGRAPHICAL LITERATURE

of explication, his aim being to produce an introductory handbook for readers interested in astronomy.

The preface to the *Stoicheiosis astronomike* is not the only text in which Metochites includes information about himself. Apart from his poetry,[24] autobiographical details may also be found in the Ὑπομνηματισμοὶ καὶ σημειώσεις γνωμικαὶ (*Miscellanea philosophica et historica*), particularly in Chapter 28, where he describes the difficulties he faced with his early schooling and his struggle to educate himself and carve out a career from the age of twenty. He also speaks of the sympathetic understanding and assistance he received from Emperor Andronikos II Palaiologos, and extols his love of letters. While it was, he says, by God's grace that he found favour with the emperor, he also refers to the difficulties and problems confronting the empire at that time and the dangers he himself incurred.[25]

5.2 *Joseph Rhakendytes*

Joseph Rhakendytes prefaces his *Synopsis variarum disciplinarum* with a brief autobiography under the title Σύνοψις ἐν ἐπιτομῇ εἰς τὰ κατ' αὐτόν and a 140-line poem, in which he sketches the contents of his book.[26] He begins by expressing his preference for the contemplative life over a life of action, and then mentions that he comes from a middle-class family in Ithaca, without dwelling on the subject lest his comments be taken as praise or censure. From early childhood he tried to discern what was right for him, and chose to follow the inclination of his soul towards God, to whom he entrusted himself and for whose guidance he prays throughout his life. He thus left his home and his family and, having donned the monk's habit, passed through many places (like Odysseus), seeking to swell his initial desire for God. Thus, he arrived at last at Constantinople, the place of letters, and there met wise and spiritual men.

With them he obtained every kind of education, but being, as he says, not well suited to that benefit he retained nothing of what he learned (neither virtue nor letters). This notwithstanding, he remained firm in his intention and hopes that God would at last grant him his desire.

---

24   Theodore Metochites, *Poems*, ed. Polemis, pp. 5–73 (Theodore Metochites, *Poems*, trans Polemis pp 47–111)· see also, Vassis, Spirituality and emotion: Poetic trends in the Palaeologan Period, in this volume chapter 5, pp. 180–181: Theodore Metochites: Autobiography or Introspection?

25   Theodore Metochites, *Miscellanea*, eds. Müller/Kiessling, pp. 185–95.

26   *Rhetores graeci*, ed. Walz, vol. 3, pp. 467–77; Treu, "Der Philosoph Joseph", pp. 34–38. See also, Hinterberger, *Autobiographische Traditionen*, pp. 358–60.

In the end, he decided to compose a handbook of rhetoric, a short-cut to spare the reader the study of too many volumes. And so, he himself studied the works of many wise men, some dealing with rhetoric, some with logic and natural philosophy but mainly apodeictic and dialectic logic, others with the subjects of the quadrivium, others with the human body and the soul. After systematically studying all these, he compiled this work using passages from different sources so as not to labour in vain over the composition of an original work, so that each reader may find what he needs without having to run hither and thither. The object of the book, he says, is his desire, as a monk who sought the perfection of the soul in virtue and did not want to follow a life of action, to study analytical treatises that he had loved from the beginning of his life, but wished that anyone might readily find what they needed in his work.

He ends by urging those who benefited from it to give glory to God and to pray for him.

6   In Search of a Master

The title that H.-G. Beck gave his translation of the *Autobiography* of Gregory of Cyprus[27] could just as well be applied to those of Theodore Metochites and Demetrios Kydones. Just as the young George of Cyprus sought a teacher of rhetoric and found him in the person of the *megas logothetes* George Akropolites, so Theodore Metochites sought a teacher of astronomy and found him in Manuel Bryennios, and Demetrios Kydones a teacher of Latin, whom he found in the person of a Dominican monk.

All three found their teachers in Constantinople, having gone there to continue their studies with no family support: Gregory from Cyprus, running away from home and surviving many reverses before achieving his goal; Metochites, returning to Constantinople, which he had left in 1285, following his father George Metochites into exile for his collaboration with the deposed Patriarch John Bekkos and his part in the Council of Lyon and the Union of the Churches; and Demetrios Kydones from Thessaloniki, which he left after the death of his father.

All three say that they completed their grammatical studies quickly thanks to their natural propensity for learning.[28]

---

27   Beck, *Byzantinisches Lesebuch*, pp. 147–52 (Auf der Suche nach Meistern).

28   See Gregory of Cyprus, *Autobiography*, ed. Lameere, pp. 173, lines 13–15: ὡς δὲ τῆς τούτων (sc. γραμματιστῶν) ἐπιστήμης παρῆλθε τὴν χρείαν, παρῆλθε δ᾽ ἐν πάνυ νέᾳ τῇ ἡλικίᾳ,
δοκῶν εὖ πεφυκέναι τὴν ψυχὴν πρὸς μαθήματα (Gregory of Cyprus, *Autobiography*, trans.

CONTINUITY AND EVOLUTION IN AUTOBIOGRAPHICAL LITERATURE 123

Metochites describes, in similar terms as Gregory although at much greater length, the teaching of grammar, rhetoric, philosophy and mathematics. Both speak negatively of the fashion for Asianism in rhetoric and its followers, and refer to the twists and turns in Aristotle's logic.[29] It may be that Metochites had the autobiography of Gregory of Cyprus in mind, since one of the manuscripts preserving it was owned by Nikephoros Gregoras, who had a number of Metochites' books.

Although none of the three says so explicitly, each of them was, in his own particular field, a model for those coming afterwards, Gregory in rhetoric, Metochites in astronomy and Kydones in Latin theological texts.

7 Autobiographical Confessions

Kydones' autobiography is the first of a group of texts that contain autobiographical material but were written primarily to defend a choice made by the author. And while Kydones may be the first to defend his attachment to Latin literature, he is certainly not the only one to do so. The same is true of the first *Apologia* of Gennadios Scholarios,[30] probably written either just before the Council of Ferrara/Florence (1438–1439) or upon his return from it, although it contains very little biographical information. There is far more

---

Pelendrides, p. 21: When he no longer needed these teachers' knowledge, this really had been achieved at a very tender age, and since it seemed that he had a natural aptitude for learning); Theodore Metochites, *Stoicheiosis Astronomike*, ed. Bydén, p. 428, lines 28–35: καί τοίνυν ἔτη γεγονὼς τρία ἐπὶ τοῖς δέκα, τῶν μὲν τῆς γραμματικῆς ἐκλογισμῶν ... εἰς τὴν ἑξῆς χρῆσιν ἀπαλλάττομαι, τάχιστα μὲν, οὐκ ἔξω δ᾽ ἴσως τοῦ καιροῦ, οὐδ᾽ ἀνικάνως ἔχων, ἀπαλλάττομαι δ᾽ οὖν; Demetrios Kydones, *Apology*, ed. Mercati, p. 359, lines 15–19: τὰ παιδιὰ τοίνυν μαθήματα διελθὼν ἠρχόμην καὶ τῶν ἀκριβεστέρων ἅπτεσθαι λόγων καὶ ὅσα διανοίας δεῖται καὶ νοῦ, καὶ ἔδοξα προσήκουσαν φύσιν τῇ σεμνότητι τῶν μαθημάτων εἰσφέρεσθαι, ὥσθ᾽ ὁπότ᾽ ἐχρῆν τοὺς ἐπὶ λόγους εὐδοκιμοῦντας τῶν ἡλικιωτῶν ἀριθμεῖσθαι, ἐμοῦ πρὸ τῶν ἄλλων παρὰ πᾶσιν ἐγένετο μνήμη.

29   See Gregory of Cyprus, *Autobiography*, ed. Lameere, p. 185, lines 12–14: ἐξηγητὴν μὲν τῶν λαβυρίνθων Ἀριστοτέλους – οὕτω γὰρ ἐγὼ καλῶ τὰς ἐκείνου στροφὰς καὶ πλοκὰς (Gregory of Cyprus, *Autobiography*, trans. Pelendrides, p. 35: as an interpreter of Aristotle's labyrinths – this is what I call his twists and knots); Metochites, *Stoicheiosis Astronomike*, ed. Bydén, p. 429, lines 54–55: ἐντεῦθεν λοιπὸν τὰς τῆς Ἀριστοτέλους λογικῆς ποικίλας στρο φάς καὶ δρόμους καὶ πάντα παλαίσματα. Metochites uses a similar turn of phrase for Ptolemy (p. 435, lines 549–550): πρὸς τὰς ἐκεῖσε δυσδιεξόδους καὶ λαβυρινθώδεις στροφὰς καὶ πλοκὰς. Kydones (Demetrios Kydones, *Apology*, ed. Mercati, p. 366, lines 95–96) also refers to the labyrinths of Aristotelian (and Platonic) philosophy, and praises the achievements of the Latin philosophers.

30   Gennadios II Scholarios, *Apology*, eds. Petit/Siderides/Jugie.

124   KOTZABASSI

personal detail in works like his pastoral letters, written after 1454,[31] but they
still do not provide a complete account of his life. Other works that fall into
the category of autobiography are two homilies by Scholarios' friend Theodore
Agallianos,[32] and Paul Tagaris' address to the patriarch in 1394, in which he
attempted to prove that he could perfectly well be both the Catholic Patriarch
of Constantinople and the Orthodox Patriarch of Jerusalem.[33]

8   Autobiographical Poems

A number of Byzantine poets frequently used their work to express personal
feelings about life. Thus, titles such as *On Himself, On Life* or *On the Vanity of
Life* are common in Byzantine poetry. One must not forget, indeed, that one
of the oldest autobiographies, that of Gregory of Nanzianzos, is written in
iambic trimeter.

His autobiography certainly served as a model for later men of letters who
wanted to compose autobiographical poems. Of the oldest of these, written by
the historian and patriarchal official George Pachymeres, there survive only
small fragments in hexameter, with the title τὰ καθ' ἑαυτόν (*On himself*), which
are insufficient to provide a clear picture of the content of the work.[34]

Following in the same tradition, Theodore Metochites includes among his
twenty long hexameter poems, which treat a variety of subjects, two (numbers 1
and 2) that contain extensive autobiographical sections although their theme
is the renovation of the Chora Monastery, which Metochites funded, while

---

31   See Angold, "The Autobiographies of Patriarch Gennadios II Scholarios", pp. 68–89.

32   See Angold, "Theodore Agallianos: The Last Byzantine Autobiography". In his first Oration
      (Περὶ τῶν κατ' αὐτὸν ἢ κατὰ τῶν κατ' αὐτοῦ) Theodore Agallianos gives a brief description
      of his early years and his studies with the future Metropolitan of Ephesos Mark Eugenikos
      and Patriarch Joseph. He then speaks of his ordination to the priesthood and the prepara-
      tions for the Council of Ferrara, and of the sudden illness that struck him as he was on
      his way to the Patriarchal Mass that preceded the delegation's departure and obliged him
      to remain behind; he describes this as an instance of Divine Providence, an intervention
      that prevented him from attending the Council, the results of which, as well as other
      ecclesiastical developments, are described in the remainder of the Oration.

33   See Nicol, "The Confessions of a Bogus Patriarch: Paul Tagaris Palaiologos".

34   George Pachymeres, *Autobiographical poem*, ed. Detorakis; see also, Vassis, Spirituality
      and emotion: Poetic trends in the Palaeologan Period, in this volume chapter 5, pp.
      180–81.

CONTINUITY AND EVOLUTION IN AUTOBIOGRAPHICAL LITERATURE 125

seven other poems show an autobiographical intention but without any narration of specific elements of his life.[35]

9 Autobiographical Prefaces in Testaments and *Typika*

Like the edition of an author's works, the drafting of a testament or a *Typikon* for a monastery often provides a good opportunity for a review of the life and works of the author and founder. The relation of his life that usually forms the prologue to such a document allows the author to give an account of himself to his readers. This self-presentation serves his purposes, whether in explanation of his acts and choices or of his position on crucial issues of the period, or of his writings, as we have seen in other autobiographies (e.g., Gregory of Cyprus).

Michael VIII Palaiologos' presentation of himself in the *Typikon* he composed for the Kellibara Monastery continues a tradition known from similar texts by St. Christodoulos, founder of the Monastery of St. John the Theologian in Patmos, St. Neophytos the Recluse in Cyprus, and John Xenos. Theodora Synadene follows Michael VIII's example in her *Typikon* for the *Bebaia Elpis* convent in Constantinople, which she prefaces with a lengthy account of her life, while at roughly the same time Theodore Sarantenos includes a diagram of his life in his testament, as does Matthew I, Patriarch of Constantinople, a few decades later.

The limited autobiographical information found in other testaments, such as, for example, those of John Bekkos and Patriarch Athanasios or the two testaments of Constantine Akropolites, does not give a complete picture of their lives. Akropolites, however, often included autobiographical details in other works, such as letters and hagiographical works.

9.1 *Michael VIII Palaiologos and the Typikon of Kellibara Monastery*

When the Kellibara Monastery (Latros) was amalgamated with the Monastery of St. Demetrios in Constantinople, Michael VIII Palaiologos wrote a new *Typikon* for the unified foundation, which he prefaced with an autobiographical account of himself written before 1282.[36] Michael begins his prologue by thanking God for His benefactions to mankind and to himself and declares

---

35 Theodore Metochites, *Poems*, ed. Polemis, pp. 5–73 (Theodore Metochites, *Poems*, trans. Polemis, pp. 47–111); see also, Vassis, Spirituality and emotion: Poetic trends in the Palaeologan Period, in this volume Chapter 3: Theodore Metochites: autobiography or introspection?

36 Grégoire, "Imperatoris Michaelis Palaeologi de vita sua".

that his recital of his life is not done boastfully but from an obligation to proclaim the goodness of God and to express his gratitude for all he has received from Him.

This is followed by a lengthy passage devoted to his parents, whom he does not name. He stresses the valour and piety of his paternal forebears, probably as a counterweight to the criticism his own ecclesiastical policy received (strife with Patriarch Arsenios Autoreianos, union with the Catholic Church) and his mother's imperial lineage. He then mentions his ties to John III Vatatzes, in whose court he was raised, his skill at arms and in warfare, and the confidence the emperor demonstrated in him by appointing him to command the army, which gave him an opportunity to gain distinction and become even dearer to John III, who betrothed him to his niece Theodora.

A large part of the autobiography is devoted to an extensive account of the successful wars he conducted against the enemies of the empire. He mentions his delivery from the dangers in store for him in the empire after the death of John III, through his voluntary exile to the Seljuks, where he continued to fight against the Mongols, his reconciliation with John's successor, Theodore II Laskaris, his return to Nicaea, and his elevation to the imperial throne after the latter's death, all the while stressing that these things were not of his doing but the work of God.

Michael's narrative continues with a recital of his victory against the Despot of Epiros Michael II Angelos in the battle of Pelagonia (1259), the extension of Byzantine rule in the Peloponnese, his successes against the Turks, making, naturally, special mention of the recovery of Constantinople in 1261, and ends with a description of his campaigns against the Turks in Western Asia Minor, the Mongols and Bulgarians in Thrace, the pirates in the Aegean, the occupation of Euboea and the destruction of the Venetian navy, and, finally, his confrontation with Charles of Anjou, in whose crushing defeat in the war of the Sicilian Vespers (30/31 March 1282) Michael was, he claimed, the instrument through which God liberated Sicily.

Michael VIII closes the autobiographical part of his *Typikon* for the Monastery of St. Demetrios-Kellibara by giving thanks to God for his son and co-emperor, Andronikos II.

9.2   *Theodora Synadene (Typikon for the Convent of Bebaia Elpis)*

An attitude similar to that expressed by Michael VIII in the *Typikon* of the Monastery of St. Demetrios-Kellibara concerning God's great blessings is seen in the introduction to the *Typikon* of the Convent of *Bebaia Elpis* founded by his niece, Theodora Palaiologina Synadene (before 1270–ca. 1332, PLP 21381).[37]

---

37   Theodora Synadene, *Typikon*; Hinterberger, *Autobiographische Traditionen*, pp. 276–77.

The reason Theodora gives for founding the convent is her love of God, which she speaks of at length in the preamble. Her purpose is twofold: to provide a secure refuge for women who have chosen the ascetic way of life, and to create a peaceful harbour, sheltered from the storms of the world, for herself and her beloved daughter, whom she had consecrated from birth to the Blessed Virgin, thus in some small measure repaying her great debt of gratitude for all the blessings she had received.

The principal autobiographical part of the preface, which is written in the first-person singular, begins with a brief account of her parents and their lineage. Her father, a brother of Michael VIII Palaiologos, held the rank of *sebastokrator* and earned a reputation for valour in the wars against the empire's foes. Theodora does not allow herself to extol his virtues, this being unbefitting of her position as a close relative and her nun's habit, both of which, rather, impose silence, but moves on to her mother, a daughter of the Branas family, as renowned a lineage as her father's.

After her parents' early death, she became a ward of her uncle, Michael VIII, who betrothed her to a man distinguished equally for fineness of physique and of character. He was a descendant of the Komnenoi and the Synadenoi, who before his marriage was exalted with the rank of *stratopedarches* and was as successful in his commission as her father had been.

She then refers briefly to the death of her husband and in this context, mentions her daughter Euphrosyne and her two young sons, in whom lay her hopes.

Her husband's death led to her decision to abandon the pleasures and delights of the world and, with her daughter, devote herself to the Blessed Virgin, taking with her a few young like-minded maidens. This venture, and her orphaned children, she entrusted to God.

With this she concludes the autobiographical part of the *Typikon* and the founding of the convent and moves on to her primary purpose, the composition of a Rule for its organisation and operation.

9.3   *Patriarch Matthew I*

The testament of Patriarch Matthew I (1397–1410), written in September 1407, is composed in the form of a spiritual autobiography. The patriarch writes in the first-person singular,[38] and begins with the thought and intention of becoming a monk which had possessed him since he was just 12 years old. To this end he strove endlessly to turn his mind from the world and to live the life of those blessed men who dedicated themselves to God, praying constantly that God would lead him to such a person, who could guide him to salvation.

---

38   Hunger, "Das Testament des Patriarchen Matthaios I".

These thoughts continuing to occupy his mind and soul, he resolved to tell his parents of his intention to abandon the world and his desire to become a monk, begging them to help him fulfil his most ardent wish. Their love for him, however, made them unable to understand his desire and they endeavoured to turn him from his purpose, describing the hardships of the monastic life. But the more they sought to dissuade him, the stronger his desire and resolve grew.[39]

Three years passed in this way and, rather than flagging, his desire to attain his goal burned more fiercely than ever, and his parents came to realise that he truly did not wish to live any longer in the world. When they finally accepted his decision, they themselves took him to Mark, a monk famous for his virtue and revered by the emperor, and asked him to accept their son. At first Mark hesitated, because the boy was still so young, but at last he agreed, admitted him to the monastery, and instructed him in the coenobitic life.

Matthew then mentions his obedience to the orders of his spiritual father and those who succeeded him after his death. The first of these was Neilos, who subsequently became Patriarch of Constantinople, with whom he enjoyed an exceptionally close relationship, both when Neilos was superior of the monastery and later when he became Patriarch. Matthew expresses his gratitude to Neilos for all he did for him and for naming him as his successor.

At this point Matthew digresses from his narrative to give a brief history of the monastery and its founder, John Charsianeites, who took the name of Job when he assumed the monastic habit, having resolved to abandon the world and the honour and esteem in which he was held by the emperor and officials, and to found the monastery that bears his name, upon which he bestowed all his wealth. The land on which it was built belonged to a man called Ampar, and at the time was vacant save for some ruins. Having purchased the property, Charsianeites first built the church and then the cells, bestowed lands and vineyards and dwellings upon the foundation, and searched for a devout man whom he could entrust with its governance, freeing himself from all ties with it.

In those days, a monk called Mark had arrived in Constantinople, who by order of the emperor became superior of the Monastery of Kosmidion. John Charsianeites approached him and through his own entreaties and those of

---

39   The description of his parents' opposition to his departure from their house and his becoming a monk is reminiscent of Gregory of Cyprus' parents' opposition to his desire to leave home to study at Nicaea.

CONTINUITY AND EVOLUTION IN AUTOBIOGRAPHICAL LITERATURE

other distinguished persons persuaded him to become the superior of the Charsianeites Monastery, where he would enjoy greater tranquillity.

And so it came to pass, although things did not turn out exactly as had been hoped, for when John Palaiologos entered Constantinople, Mark did not escape the fury of the populace, being considered a partisan of John Kantakouzenos. When, therefore, a mob attacked his house, he only managed to escape by seeking refuge in the church of Hagia Sophia. In this way he was saved, but lost everything he possessed, while John Palaiologos took away from the monastery the village of Palatitzia and gave it to the monastery of Stoudios.

After this Matthew speaks of how the monastery of Charsianeites acquired new estates, and of the donations made by John Kantakouzenos, who took up residence there, and in the end returns to the disarray prevailing in the monastery through the indifference of the monks, left without a leader after Mark had died and his successor, Neilos, had become patriarch. When Matthew returned to the monastery after Neilos' death, he strove to reverse the decline, restore order and make it prosperous again.

His narrative continues with a brief account of the disasters caused by Turkish aggression, the two Patriarchs (Antony and Kallistos) who reigned during those dark days, and his own eventual election to the Patriarchy.

He then describes Manuel II's journey to Italy to seek help and the agitation stirred up against himself, which led to his deposition from the patriarchal throne (1402). Matthew reiterates his forgiveness of those who spoke unjustly against him, which he had expressed earlier and is now putting in writing, since the emperor has returned to Constantinople and he himself has set about restoring the monastery, which had been partially destroyed by the Turkish besiegers. And he concludes with the efforts he made, with the emperor's assistance, to improve the organisation of the institution. To this end he appends the Rule issued by Mark, which was written by Patriarch Neilos and describes how the monks in the monastery should live, and concludes by entrusting its leadership after his death to an ordained monk, who is not named, and with prayers for the successful continuation of the work of the monks so that they may gain eternal life.

Although elements of autobiography appear in texts of earlier periods, it is incontestable that such material increases in the Palaeologan age, both in the form of separate or embedded passages in various literary genres and in that of isolated personal references in, for example, letters or hagiological works, as is the case with the *Grand Logothetes* Constantine Akropolites, who often includes details of his personal or family life in letters, as he does as well in several of his encomia for saints, in which he does not confine himself to the

130   KOTZABASSI

miracles performed by the saint for himself or members of his family but also recalls earlier incidents in his life, as in the case of the encomium for St. Euplos, where he speaks of the days when he was a pupil at the school of the Church of Sts. Peter and Paul.[40]

This extroversion evident in the Palaeologan age is also expressed in the greater number of copyists' names we find on Byzantine manuscripts, whether in bibliographical annotations or in invocations to sacred figures penned by copyists in the margins of the manuscripts they were copying.[41]

Whether this reflects a change of mentality or merely a contemporary trend remains to be demonstrated.

Bibliography

Primary Sources

Demetrios Kydones, *Apology*, ed. G. Mercati, *Notizie di Prochoro e Demetrio Cidone, Manuele Caleca e Teodoro Meliteniota ed altri appunti per la storia della teologia e della letteratura bizantina del secolo XIV* (Studi e Testi, 56), Vatican City 1931, pp. 359–403.

Gennadios II Scholarios, *Apology*, eds. L. Petit/X.A. Sidéridès/M. Jugie, *Oeuvres complètes de Gennade Scholarios*, vol. 1, Paris 1928, pp. 376–89.

George Pachymeres, *Autobiographical poem* (fragments), ed. T. Detorakis, "Ἀνέκδοτα ποιήματα τοῦ Γεωργίου Παχυμέρη", in B. Kremmydas/Ch. Maltezou/N.M. Panagiotakis (eds.), Ἀφιέρωμα στὸν Νίκο Σβορῶνο, 2 vols., Rethymno 1986, vol. 1, pp. 299–307.

Gregory of Cyprus, *Autobiography*, ed. W. Lameere, *La tradition manuscrite de la correspondance de Grégoire de Chypre Patriarche de Constantinople*, Brussels 1937, pp. 173–91.

Gregory of Cyprus, *Autobiography*, trans. A. Pelendrides, *The autobiography of George of Cyprus (Ecumenical Patriarch Gregory II)*, London 1993.

Gregory of Cyprus, *Letters*, ed. S. Eustratiades, Γρηγορίου Κυπρίου οἰκουμενικοῦ Πατριάρχου ἐπιστολαὶ καὶ μῦθοι, Alexandria 1910.

Gregory of Nazianzos, *Autobiography*, ed. C. Jungck, *Gregor von Nazianz. De vita sua*, Heidelberg 1974, pp. 54–148.

---

40   Constantinides, *Higher Education in Byzantium in the Thirteenth and Early Fourteenth Centuries*, p. 39, no. 39.

41   See in this regard the manuscripts of Gregory of Cyprus and the manuscripts Vatican City, Biblioteca Apostolica Vaticana, Vat. gr. 2207, Vienna, Österreichische Nationalbibliothek, Vind. hist. 3 etc.

John VI Kantakouzenos, *History*, ed. L. Schopen, *Ioannis Cantacuzeni ex Imperatoris Historiarum libri IV graece et latine*, 3 vols., (Corpus Scriptorum Historiae Byzantinae, 41), Bonn 1828–32.

Libanios, *Autobiography (Oration 1)*, ed. R. Foerster, *Libanii opera*, vol. 1, Leipzig 1903 (repr. Hildesheim 1997), pp. 79–206.

Nikephoros Blemmydes, *Autobiography*, ed. J.A. Munitiz, *Nicephori Blemmydae Autobiographia sive Curriculum vitae necnon Epistula universalior* (Corpus Christianorum. Series Graeca, 13), Turnhout/Louvain 1984.

Rhetores Graeci, ed. C. Walz, 9 vols., Stuttgart 1832–36 (repr. Osnabrück 1968).

Theodora Synadene, *Typikon*, ed. H. Delehaye, *Deux typica byzantins de l'époque des Paléologues*, Brussels 1921, pp. 18–96.

Theodore Metochites, *Miscellanea*, eds. C.G. Müller/T. Kiessling, *Theodori Metochitae Miscellanea philosophica et historica*, Leipzig 1821 (repr. Amsterdam 1966).

Theodore Metochites, *Orations*, eds. I. Polemis/E. Kaltsogianni, *Theodorus Metochites, Orationes* (Bibliotheca Teubneriana, 2031), Berlin/Boston 2019.

Theodore Metochites, *Poems*, ed. I. Polemis, *Theodori Metochitae carmina* (Corpus Christianorum, Series Graeca, 83), Turnhout 2015.

Theodore Metochites, *Poems*, trans. I. Polemis, *Theodore Metochites, Poems. Introduction, translation and notes* (Corpus Christianorum in Translation, 26), Turnhout 2017.

Theodore Metochites, *Stoicheiosis Astronomike*, ed. B. Bydén, *Theodore Metochites' Stoicheiosis Astronomike and the Study of Natural Philosophy and Mathematics in Early Palaiologan Byzantium* (Studia Graeca et Latina Gothoburgensia, 66), Gothenburg 2003.

Secondary Literature

Angold, M.J., "The Autobiographies of Patriarch Gennadios II Scholarios", in T. Shawcross/I. Toth (eds.), *Reading in the Byzantine Empire and Beyond*, Cambridge 2018, pp. 68–90.

Angold, M.J., "Theodore Agallianos: The Last Byzantine Autobiography", in E. Motos Guirao/M. Morphakidis Philaktós (eds.), *Constantinopla: 550 ãnos de su caída*. Granada 2006, pp. 35–44.

Beck, H.-G., *Byzantinisches Lesebuch*, Munich 1982.

Constantinides, C.N., *Higher Education in Byzantium in the Thirteenth and Early Fourteenth Centuries (1204–ca. 1310)* (Texts and Studies of the History of Cyprus, 11), Nicosia 1982.

Grégoire, H., "Imperatoris Michaelis Palaeologi de vita sua", *Byzantion* 29/30 (1959/60), 447–76.

Hinterberger, M., *Autobiographische Traditionen in Byzanz* (Wiener Byzantinistische Studien, 22), Vienna 1999.

Hunger, H., "Das Testament des Patriarchen Matthaios I. (1397–1410)", *Byzantinische Zeitschrift* 51 (1958), 288–309.

Hunger, H., *Die hochsprachliche profane Literatur der Byzantiner* (Byzantinisches Handbuch: Handbuch der Altertumswissenschaft, 12.5), 2 vols., Munich 1978.

Kianka, F., "The Apology of Demetrius Cydones: A Fourteenth-Century Autobiographical Source", *Byzantine Studies/Études Byzantines* 7/1 (1980), 57–71.

Kotzabassi, S., "'Περὶ τοῦ καθ᾽ ἑαυτὸν βίου ὡς ἀπ᾽ ἄλλου προσώπου'. Παρατηρήσεις στην αυτοβιογραφία του πατριάρχη Γρηγορίου Β΄ ´Κυπρίου", *Ἑλληνικά* 58 (2008), 279–91.

Nicol, D.M., "The Confessions of a Bogus Patriarch: Paul Tagaris Palaiologos, Orthodox Patriarch of Jerusalem and Catholic Patriarch of Constantinople in the Fourteenth Century", *Journal of Ecclesiastical History* 21 (1970), 289–99.

Timplalexi, P., *Medizinisches in der byzantinischen Epistolographie (1110–1453)* (Europäische Hochschulschriften. Reihe VII. Abt. B Geschichte der Medizin, 9) Frankfurt am Main 2002.

Treu, M., "Der Philosoph Joseph", *Byzantinische Zeitschrift* 8 (1899) 1–64.

CHAPTER 4

Writing the History of Decline

Apostolos Karpozilos

1   Historiography from Nicaea to Constantinople

Under the rule of the Latin emperors, Byzantine education, traditions, court etiquette and the basic elements of the machinery of state, the administration and the bureaucracy, were forced into exile, or rather were uprooted and transplanted. Naturally enough, subjugation to the Franks aroused the national sentiments of those living within the Empire and those in the free zones of the Byzantine East alike. The crimes committed by the Crusaders against the civilian population and their spoliation of churches and holy places further deepened the breach between the two halves of Christendom. Reconstruction of the Empire would thenceforth direct the policy of the independent statelets formed after 1204. While it may be an exaggeration to say that the *Megali Idea* took root in the period of the Latin Empire, although solid arguments have been advanced in support of that opinion, this time of political and social upheaval was marked by a revival of interest in Greek Antiquity. This was not, of course, the first time that classical literature had become the object of systematic study. This time, however, the words *Hellenes*, *Hellas* and *Hellenism* were associated directly with the inhabitants of the traditionally Greek provinces, their language, their religion and their traditions, at least in the mind of certain scholars who evidently wanted to sever all ties with the elder Rome. The corollary was that there emerged from the exiled government in Nicaea a new ruling class, a new intellectual and political elite, exemplified by such outstanding personalities as George Akropolites, the historian of the Empire of Nicaea, who chronicled the struggles of the Laskarids against the Latin conquerors. The intellectual activity that characterised the court of Nicaea is to some degree reflected in the historiography of George Akropolites, the letters of Theodore II, the biography and the theological and philosophical writings of Nikephoros Blemmydes, and some other representative texts of that period Another source of information, revealing the interests and preoccupations of the intellectual class and shedding light on their reading, is found in the codices that were compiled at Nicaea during this period. We know that Nikephoros Blemmydes travelled beyond the boundaries of the Laskarid state, to various

© KONINKLIJKE BRILL NV, LEIDEN, 2023 | DOI:10.1163/9789004527089_006

parts of the Greek world, in search of books;[1] his passionate pursuit cannot be considered an isolated case. Nor was it accidentally that at this time a parchment codex of hymns was erased and re-used for Pindar and commentaries on his work: this is the codex Vienna, Österreichische Nationalbibliothek, Vind. suppl. gr. 64, written in 1275. The catalogue of thirty or so manuscripts from this period published by Herbert Hunger is also of particular interest for their content.[2]

2 George Akropolites: The Historian of the Laskarids of Nicaea

While Nicaea produced, in George Akropolites, an historian who dedicated his work to the Laskarids, the same was not true of Epiros, which could boast neither historians nor other scholars born and bred on its soil. Thus, the only valid historian of the period 1204–1261 is George Akropolites, whose *Chronike Syngraphe* attempted to give a concise history of the empire of Nicaea from 1203–1261. The chronicle compiled by Theodore Skoutariotes some years later is not of the same value, although his additions to Akropolites' text are interesting for the different picture they sometimes paint, especially in relation to Theodore II Laskaris.

In assessing the *Chronike Syngraphe*, which gives an account of the background to the founding of the empire of Nicaea and the struggles of its princes for survival in the days of the Latin Empire, one must bear in mind that, apart from the chronicles of the crusaders, we have no other historical sources against which to cross-check its account and evaluate its contribution to historiography. In other words, the absence of an historian from the opposite camp, that is, from the Angeloi of Epiros, is sorely felt. The Chronicles of Joel and Ephraim, finally, written respectively during the 13th century and at the turn of the 14th, are of little worth as historical sources for contemporary events. Joel ended his account with the Fall of Constantinople in 1204, and Ephraim stopped at 1261. We know nothing about the lives of these two chroniclers, nor even about where and in what circumstances they compiled their accounts. Akropolites and Skoutariotes lived in Nicaea, of course, as did George Pachymeres, but their work was written in Constantinople. The opinions of these last three do not concur, because both Skoutariotes and Pachymeres, unlike Akropolites, became apologists for the Laskarids and attacked, the one directly and the

---

1 Nikephoros Blemmydes, *Autobiography*, I, 64,1–4, ed. Munitiz.
2 Hunger, "Von Wissenschaft und Kunst der frühen Palaiologenzeit", pp. 124–25.

WRITING THE HISTORY OF DECLINE

other indirectly, the policy followed by Michael VIII Palaiologos which resulted in the abandonment of the Asian provinces to their fate.

The historiography of the 13th century introduced nothing new in the way of narrative technique or in the thinking or mentality of its authors and the way they dealt with their subject matter. The only innovation occurs in the work of the chroniclers, for alongside the traditional genre describing world history from Creation there now appeared a new kind of chronicle, different from its predecessors in both language and style. This kind of chronicle made its appearance in the Frankish-ruled Peloponnese (*Chronicle of the Morea*), in Western-held Epiros (*Chronicle of the Tocco*), and in distant Cyprus (*Chronicle* of Leontios Machairas). One of the features that distinguishes these chronicles from the traditional sort is their use of the vernacular of the day, with the concomitant elements of local speech forms, the glaring absence of Constantinopolitan scholarly tradition, at least in the western-style texts, and their blatantly propagandistic nature, with their pro-Latin bias and the like. Thus alongside the comprehensive traditional chronicles (Joel, Skoutariotes, Ephraim) there now appear western-influenced narratives (*Chronicle of the Morea, Chronicle of the Tocco*), and local histories (*Chronicles* of Panaretos, Ioannina).

The works and days of the Laskarids are traced by Akropolites either condescendingly, as with Theodore I Laskaris and John III Vatatzes, or with open prejudice, as in the case of Theodore II and his counsellors, especially the Mouzalon brothers, whom he ridiculed, describing them contemptuously as ἀνδράρια μηδενὸς ἢ τριῶν ὀβολῶν ἄξια, παιδιαῖς ἀνατεθραμμένα καὶ κυμβάλων μέλεσί τε καὶ ᾄσμασι (ed. Heisenberg, I, 124,10–12). His main aim was to present Michael Palaiologos as the only person capable of taking the helm of the tempest-tossed ship of state and bringing it safely into harbour, and thereby justifying his seizure of the throne, by casting slurs on the Laskarid emperors. John Vatatzes, for example, not only took a maidservant from the women's quarters as his mistress but fully intended to bestow a high position on her: ἐς τοσοῦτον τῆς ἀγάπης αὐτῆς ἐξεκρέματο, ὡς καὶ πέδιλα ὑποδεδέσθαι δοῦναι ταύτην κοκκοβαφῆ ... (ed. Heisenberg, I, 104,6–7). As for Theodore Laskaris, he had entrusted τὴν τῶν Ῥωμαίων ἀρχὴν καὶ τὰ αὐτῆς πράγματα ἀνδραρίοις βδελυροῖς καὶ ἀνθρωπίσκοις οὐτιδανοῖς, passing over brilliant and valiant generals (I, 156,10–12). Akropolites served Michael Palaiologos as Grand Logothete for more than twenty years (1259–1282), and was hated in Constantinople for the harshness with which, in implementing the decision of the Council of Lyon (1274), he persecuted the anti-unionists. His negative opinion of the emperor is patent in his comment that his former pupil was a disappointment to his subjects, who had been deceived by his youth, his mildness and his affability: ἃ δὴ πάντα φενάκη ἦν καὶ ὑποκριτικὸν προσωπεῖον (1, 105,9–10). What is chiefly worth noting, however, is that his generalisations are not backed by any specific criticism in support of his judgement. He simply attempts to dissociate himself as much as possible from his former benefactors, downplaying his personal involvement in political matters and modestly highlighting the virtues of the emperor-in-the-making, Michael Palaiologos. On the other hand, the constant theme of his accusations is confined to the contemptible counsellors with whom Theodore II had surrounded himself (1, 123,5–15, 124,10–17, 156,8–17, 160,13–15), who patently did not belong to that part of the aristocracy that assumed power at the end of his reign. Akropolites, whose history was of course commissioned, deliberately omitted the blinding of the young John and the turmoil caused by Michael Palaiologos' coup d'etat. His narrative ends, rather abruptly, with the recapture of Constantinople in 1261, an unquestionably auspicious moment at the commencement of his patron's reign. Continued beyond this point, his account could not have ignored the disunion, the social unrest, the military reverses of the period, and the constant religious strife. Akropolites did not want to record these things, for obvious reasons. What he left unsaid so as not to sully the memory of Michael VIII was set down by Pachymeres in a fierce historical denunciation. The weakening of central authority left, I think, a certain margin for freedom of expression, which is apparent in the criticisms boldly levelled by the historian against the first two Palaeologan emperors, father and son.

3 George Pachymeres: How Asia Minor Was Lost

Pachymeres plainly disliked Michael VIII Palaiologos, whom he considered a greedy, scheming hypocrite (I 26, ed. Failler, 105,9–12. 141,24–25), and one, moreover, whose blood-stained accession to the throne had doomed his reign to failure. His heir, Andronikos II, he thought weak and acquiescent, particularly towards the autocratic and arrogant Patriarch Athanasios (VII 21, 71,25–73,4. 73,22–23. XIII 23, 679,17 et seq.). By the time he had finished writing his history, in the early 14th century, Pachymeres had come to the conclusion that there was no hope that the empire could recover. His pessimism is expressed in the first words of his Preface (I 1, 25,12–20). He ascribes the beginning of the decline to Michael's fatal decision to abandon Asia Minor to its fate by moving his troops to the West (I 5, 31,21–33,11). In order to weaken the forces in Asia Minor, who had turned against him because of his usurpation of the throne, Michael Palaiologos cut the pay and the privileges enjoyed by frontier troops, and especially the tax-free status of military estates, the result being the

WRITING THE HISTORY OF DECLINE

collapse of the defensive system that had for decades been maintained by the economic policy of the Laskarids, resting on institutions that had contributed to the peace and relative prosperity of Asia Minor (III 22, 291,25–293,29. IV 27, 407,4–21). Those whose lands were held in *pronoia* were forced to abandon them and turn to the Turks (III 22, 293,13–29), leaving the borders undefended and Caria and the regions of the Maeander and the Sangarius open to invasion (IV 27, 403,19–407,3. VI 20, 591,30–593,4).

The same critical spirit is evident in Pachymeres' account of the reign of Andronikos II, who would have laid down his life to heal the ecclesiastical schism and restore peace to the empire. This pious emperor attempted to reconcile the two warring factions, even paying a visit to the Anatolian provinces in pursuit of that goal, but was unsuccessful in this endeavour. Although the Council of Blachernai (1285) condemned the arguments of the pro-union Patriarch John Bekkos and by extension the decisions that had been signed at the Council of Lyon in 1274, which thereafter remained a dead letter (VII 34, 103,6 et seq.), the battle with the Arsenists continued to rage as fiercely as ever, despite the efforts of the moderate clerics. Andronikos' acquiescence to the demands of the zealots may have worsened the tension, but in any case, as Pachymeres tellingly points out, they were seeking their own vindication (VII 35, 117,5–7).

The reign of Andronikos II, however, was disturbed by more than the religious disputes that were the legacy of his father's ecclesiastical policy. Empty coffers forced him to devalue the hyperpyron by one half, thus driving market prices up and the populace into poverty. In a bid to reduce military expenditure he dismantled his fleet, whose eighty-some ships he had been struggling to maintain, relying thenceforth on his Genoese allies. This, however, left the Greek seas at the mercy of pirates, whose ranks were promptly swelled by many of his now unemployed sailors (VII 26, 81,20–83,28). The economic crisis, compounded by poor administration and corrupt officials, had serious consequences for the defences of the provinces in Asia Minor. The troops on the Seljuq frontier, Pachymeres notes, went unpaid because their officers kept the money for themselves, and consequently abandoned their posts (IX 8, 235,10–237,8). The emperor, for his part, did nothing to reorganise the army, but instead hired Alan and Catalan mercenaries as supposedly more experienced and more effective than his own subjects, and in the case of the Catalans without even agreeing on the number required and the rate of pay (X 16, 337,32 et seq. 19, 345,15 et seq. XI 12, 431,2 et seq.). These decisions proved disastrous not only for the economy but for the defence of the realm as well. The Anatolian provinces essentially remained totally unprotected, with the result that the Turkish forces marched unhindered to the coast of Bithynia, directly opposite the imperial capital, ... ὥσπερ ὑπνώττοντος βασιλέως ἢ μὴ ζῶντος (XI 21, 453,26–27). In the absence of other contemporary sources, Pachymeres' account of what happened to the Greek population of Anatolia and how, heart in mouth, they abandoned their homes, their belongings and their property solely to save themselves from slavery, acquires particular significance (X.26, 369,3–10).

4 Nikephoros Gregoras: On Civil Wars, Social Strife and Hesychasm

With Asia Minor lost for good, the end of Byzantium was fore-ordained. The state squandered its energy in largely sterile domestic wranglings that inevitably had political repercussions, as was the case with the hesychast controversy.[3] The civil wars – which were purely power struggles with no ideological content – continued throughout the 14th and 15th centuries, until the subjugation of the Peloponnese. The population of this shrunken empire declined dramatically, as tens of thousands were killed in the endless fighting, felled by the Black Death, or impelled to flee for safety to Turkish-held territories.

The political crisis that plagued the reign of Andronikos II continued under his successors. When Nikephoros Gregoras began to write his *History* in the 1340s there had already been two bloody civil wars, one that pitted Andronikos II against his grandson, Andronikos III (1321–1328), and one between Anne of Savoy and John Kantakouzenos (1341–1347). Gregoras painted a graphic picture of the devastation wrought by these civil wars in Macedonia and Thrace. The responsibility for the decline of the empire lay solely, he believed, with those in power, who corrupted the truth, which was all that could save the nation. Gregoras, too, rooted the crisis in the reign of Michael VIII, accepting Pachymeres' account. But for the damage caused by the second civil war (1341–1347) he laid the blame solely on John Kantakouzenos, with whom he had come into open conflict over the hesychast question. Gregoras explicitly accused him of using the hesychasts to seize power, of intervening improperly in ecclesiastical affairs, and in his own case of persecuting and attempting to get rid of him; Gregoras was in fact imprisoned in the Chora Monastery for four years by order of Kantakouzenos, where, however, he continued to write.[4]

Gregoras also described in the blackest of colours the period of the civil war (XV 3, 753,20–754,22) when Kantakouzenos sought Turkish allies, applying first

---

3 On the hesychast controversy see Polemis (chapter 10) in this volume.
4 On Gregoras' stay there see Taxidis (chapter 12, pp. 463–464) in this volume.

WRITING THE HISTORY OF DECLINE

to Umur, Emir of Aydin, for reinforcements, and later to the Ottoman Sultan Orhan, to whom he offered the hand of his daughter Theodora. With their help he succeeded in gaining power; but, having arrived on European soil, they remained. In 1352 his erstwhile allies seized the fortress of Tzympe, and in 1354 Kallipolis, a city of strategic importance that became their base of operations for further conquests. The ambitious Kantakouzenos had been unable to foresee the disastrous consequences of his Turkish alliance.[5]

This *History* is for the most part an opposition account, a denunciation of Kantakouzenos and his supporter Gregory Palamas, a *manifesto* of the author's views on the nature – created or uncreated – of the Taborian Light, an uneven work with dull, lengthy discursions on theological matters and an endless quotations from classical literature.

The period in which Nikephoros Gregoras lived and worked was one of theological discussion and dispute, reflecting the different philosophical, theological and political currents of the day. It was also a period of dynastic struggle and civil war. Specifically, the death of Andronikos III (1341) kindled a harsh and bloody battle for power. Gregoras initially stayed out of this dynastic conflict, but the fight for the throne between John Kantakouzenos and the widowed Empress, Anne of Savoy, drew in religious figures who wrangled over the mystic theology of the hesychasts of Mount Athos, and especially the teachings of Gregory Palamas. Gregoras' involvement in this politico-religious strife, which was to prove fatal for him and his historical work, began with the presence, and the teachings, of Barlaam of Calabria in Constantinople circa 1330, the same year which saw the return of Theodore Metochites to the capital from his exile.

Gregoras took no interest or part in the discussions Barlaam somewhat later instigated on hesychasm and the teachings of Gregory Palamas on the essence and energy of God, namely that while the Taborian light was uncreated and eternal it was nonetheless attainable by the hesychasts. He held himself aloof from these discussions, and for a time remained away from the imperial court, devoting himself solely to his work (XVI 8, 720,10 et seq.). Later, in late 1346 and following the condemnation of Gregory Akindynos (1347), Barlaam's chief opponent after Gregory Palamas, and ordered by the Empress Anna to set down his opinions in writing (XV 7, 769,1–5. 770,4–5), he became involved willy-nilly in the hesychast controversy, as he explains at length in his *Antirrhetika*,[6] which brought him into conflict with the emperor John Kantakouzenos, a strong supporter of Gregory Palamas and the Athonite monks. There had, however, been

---

5 Ostrogorsky, *History*, pp. 519, 530.
6 Beyer, *Nikephoros Gregoras Antirrhetika I*, pp. 169–73.

a breach with Kantakouzenos, although the emperor never ceased to hope that it would be mended, and indeed, after the death of Patriarch Isidore in 1349, he offered Gregoras the patriarchal throne in an attempt at reconciliation that was, however, refused (XVIII 1, 871,22–872, 8).

Gregoras' open criticism of Kantakouzenos (XXVI 37–39, 105,5 et seq.) could not be allowed to continue, and so by order of the emperor he was confined to the Monastery of Chora and forbidden any communication with the outside world, as he records (XXI 4, 1013,8–11). His release came four years later, with the fall of Kantakouzenos and the entry of John V Palaiologos into Constantinople in November 1354. The last years of his life are not fully known to us. He devoted himself exclusively to writing theological diatribes against the opinions of Palamas, provoking the wrath of the hesychasts and particularly John Kantakouzenos, who despite his abdication had remained the leader of the movement. Relations between the two men were never re-established, and even after his death Gregoras apparently continued to arouse the hatred of his opponents. His writings were falsified in an attempt to discredit him, while Kantakouzenos labelled his *History* unreliable (*History*, IV 24, 172,16–173,12. IV 25, 183,16–184,1). Even after his death, which occurred *circa* 1360, his opponents continued to revile him. According to his pupil and supporter John Kyparissiotes, his body was dragged through the streets of Constantinople by his adversaries for several days in mock procession,[7] and his name remained on the Church's list of heretics until the end of the century.[8]

Everyday life is described in Gregoras' *Roman History* in the blackest of shades. The desolation of the countryside from continual attacks and the ravages of civil war had destroyed the economy. The Turks were moving into Thrace, at times as invaders and at others as allies of Kantakouzenos or Anne of Savoy. In their wake – whatever the reason for their coming – they left devastation (XIII 12, 683,5–16. XV 1, 747,14–748,9), for even as allies they returned to Asia with rich spoils and accompanied by prisoners whom they deliberately whipped before the walls so as to sell them at a high price to the citizens watching the gruesome scene in fear and trepidation from their vantage point (XV 5, 764,2–18). For Gregoras the civil war between Kantakouzenos and the regency in Constantinople had all the elements of the absurd: the two adversaries sought an unachievable goal, while the cities were stripped of gold and glory (XII 15, 622,5–10). The fields remained untilled, and goods and money

---

7   *Patrologia Graeca*, vol. 152, cols. 733C–736A. Dentakis, Ἰωάννης Κυπαρισσιώτης, pp. 14–15, 18.

8   van Dieten, *Nikephoros Gregoras Rhomäische Geschichte*, I, 30–35. Beyer, "Eine Chronologie der Lebensgeschichte des Nikephoros Gregoras", pp. 151–55. Mercati, *Notizie di Procoro e Demetrio Cidone*, p. 56.

WRITING THE HISTORY OF DECLINE

alike became rare. Transit trade had passed entirely into the hands of the Genoese in Galata, who collected 200,000 coins annually in export tax, while barely 30,000 trickled into the coffers of the customs house in Constantinople (XVII 1, 841,6–842,4). The wealth of the state had been squandered on civil war and through the reckless spending of the Empress Anne, who sought to empty the treasury so that Kantakouzenos would not be able to remain in power (XV 11, 789,17–790,4). In ordinary life chaos reigned supreme. The once splendid buildings of the city fell into squalid ruins, passers-by could use the imperial palaces as places to relieve themselves (XI 11, 568,8–11), and the imperial court had become a public washhouse, where the laundresses went unhindered to wash their *clothes in the running water in the palace courtyard* (IX 8, 431,22–24). Gregoras saw the decline of the state from the point of view of the ruling class. He had little sympathy for the common people, the vulgar mob, the plebs, as he characteristically called them (VI 1, 162,23–163,3. VI 2, 171,12–16. XII 12, 614,5. XIII 8, 663,15. XIII 10, 675,13), so that social problems and their real causes left him indifferent, if not unconcerned. The social uprisings and civil strife that shook the age he attributed not to social inequality, bad government and injustice, but to the will of God and His judgment, which he believed was beyond human understanding (VIII 6, 316,1–317,2. XIV 7, 714,3–15), adding simply that through that judgement order and justice might with the grace of God in the end prevail (XIII 13, 687,10–23).

Gregoras has little to say about the revolt of the Zealots in Thessaloniki (1342), though some of his observations are interesting. In the autumn of 1343 the city was blockaded by Kantakouzenos' Turkish allies and, confronted with the spectre of famine, the people were on the verge of insurrection (XIII 10, 673,14–19). Among the citizens he distinguished the farmers/shepherds and the day-labourers as ready to rise against the rich (XIII 10, 673,19–674,4). In those difficult days a third group had appeared, emerging from the riff-raff (συρφετώδης), a mob knowing neither right nor wrong and obedient to no law, old or new. Like the savage surf that carries the ship to the bottom of the sea with all hands aboard, so they reduced the houses of the rich to rubble and without reason turned their swords upon the unfortunate (XIII 10, 673,4–674,17). These were the Zealots,[9] who stood up against Kantakouzenos and his protégé Gregory Palamas. At another point in his narrative he describes the regime instituted by the Zealots as mob rule, which is led and goes wherever chance takes it. ἀλλ' ὀχλοκρατία ξένη τις καὶ οἵαν φέροι ἂν καὶ ἄγοι τὸ αὐτόματον

---

9   For the Zealots and their movement, see Matschke, *Fortschritt und Reaktion in Byzanz*, pp. 175–79. Werner, "Gesellschaft und Kultur im XIV. Jahrhundert", pp. 104–10. Cf. also Charanis, "Internal Strife in Byzantium".

(XVI 1, 796,11–12). The responsibility for this degeneration lay solely with those in power, who corrupted the truth, which was all that could save the nation. Finally, Gregoras placed the preservation of Orthodoxy above secular authority, as decreed by the political ideology of the day, and as is clear from his criticism of the religious policy of John Kantakouzenos. For ultimately the prosperity of the empire depended on the godliness of the emperor.

5 John Kantakouzenos: A Reluctant Emperor and His History

In the eleventh century Michael Psellos had introduced a new kind of historiography, which eschewed the 'objectivity' of traditional chronicling and history writing, thus lending a strong personal element to the narration of events. The historian would thereafter no longer simply record facts, emotionally detached from the subject of his account, but would write as a person who thinks and acts independently. Classic examples of this new kind of history are Michael Psellos' *Chronographia* and Niketas Choniates' *History*. In the *History* of John Kantakouzenos we have the culmination of the personal element, for the work is no more than an account and a defence of his political life. This, indeed, is something he had to do, given his fall from power, in order to justify himself to his contemporaries.

In stark contrast to the emotionally charged narrative penned by Gregoras, John Kantakouzenos' *History* reads like a dull novel. It tells the story of two friends, the young prince Andronikos III, who was persecuted by his grandfather Andronikos II, and the narrator, Kantakouzenos himself, who helps the young Andronikos regain his throne. The friendship between the two is the dominant topic in the first part of the narrative (I 2, 19,7–10. I 7, 34,5–22), and it is sometimes taken to extravagant lengths, particularly when the author is talking of private moments: Kantakouzenos, for example, shared the emperor's bed – παρόντος καὶ ἀπόντος τοῦ βασιλέως – and slippers and the like (II 9, 369,17–370,2);[10] and when Andronikos thought he was at death's door and wished to take his leave of him, he invited him to climb onto the bed with him – ἐπὶ τῆς κλίνης ἀνακλίθητε τῆς ἐμῆς καὶ τὴν σοὶ φιλτάτην κεφαλὴν τοῖς γόνασιν ἐπίθες καὶ χεῖρας ἐπίβαλε τοῖς ὀφθαλμοῖς (II 17, 408,2–4). The account continues with the events of the civil war and the assuming of power by Kantakouzenos – against his will, as he maintains. This is the message he wants to leave with the reader: that he ascended the throne without aspiring to. It is an account of his rise and fall from power in which he presents himself as a martyr who

---

10   Cf. F. Tinnefeld, "Idealizing Self-centered Power Politics", pp. 397–415.

WRITING THE HISTORY OF DECLINE

fought against the forces of evil, just like the Biblical fathers, Joseph and the prophet-king David. God, indeed, intended him for the kingdom, revealing His will to the Metropolitan of Didymoteichon, who proclaimed it.[11] Gregoras and Kantakouzenos were poles apart, the former writing his account as the events unfolded, so that his aims changed with the changing circumstances, while the latter intended from the outset to secure his own personal vindication and posthumous fame.

This *History* is clearly more of a memoir, despite being presented as an historical account with the customary linear chronology in its narration of the events of the period 1320–1356. What makes it unique is the fact that it was the first time that an emperor had assumed the role of historian, albeit under a pseudonym (as Brother Christodoulos), in order to justify the actions of his political rise and seven-year reign. It is thus a work of history of an intensely personal character. This alone is enough to cast doubt on the author's reliability as an historian and on his objectivity in general, as regards the interpretation of the facts and events he discusses. Despite all the misgivings and reservations one may have, his work is still a basic source for the period of the civil wars that engulfed the waning empire of the first half of the 14th century, for the simple reason that it is a personal testimony, if not the political appraisal of one of the leading actors of the period 1320–1556.

From this point of view, the narration of events in the form of a traditional historical account merits a unique place in Byzantine literature. For the first time we have the hero of the story who is also the author of the work. Prior to this the author of a work of history, whether as historian or chronicler, found himself by virtue of his position alone at a certain distance from the events he was describing; that is, in no case did the writer play an organic role in shaping situations or political developments. At best, he was an observer who recorded events based on what he himself saw, observed and noted, or on the information he could gather from those around him, as in the case of Nikephoros Bryennios and Anna Komnene. Even when he took an active part in political life or experienced important events first-hand as an eyewitness, like Michael Psellos or Niketas Choniates, in composing his history he would try to distance himself as author from himself as eye-witness, in order to be as objective as possible.

John Kantakouzenos was dealing with a difficult period, because in the age in which he was writing memories of the civil wars were still fresh. He was well aware that his actions had divided the Byzantine world into two camps, the supporters of the Palaeologans, who came from the lower classes, farmers,

---

11   Kazhdan, "L'Histoire de Cantacuzène", pp. 279–327.

labourers, seamen, and the upper classes, who sided with the Cantacuzenist party (II, 180,19–181,2. III, 255,9–11. 284,23 et seq. 290,6–291,2. 304,17–305,3). These dreadful events are presented in simple language with no rhetorical flourishes or verbal excesses, solely for the sake of giving an appearance of sincerity and credibility to his account.[12] The writer's tone is calm and dispassionate even when referring to his adversaries. All these elements are used artfully, so that in the end the reader is convinced of the historian's honesty and objectivity. It is, nonetheless, methodologically unsound to rely solely on his account, disregarding other contemporary sources.

6   The Historiographic Gap

From the middle of the 14th century to the time of the historians of the Fall there is a period of nearly one hundred years with no serious historiography. There are chronicles, mainly local, and short treatises dealing with the conquest of the Balkan Peninsula and the Ottoman blockade of Constantinople. There was no decline in literary production in other genres, which might have explained the neglect of comprehensive historical works. But history is usually written by the victor, and perhaps that reality may explain the period of silence. Whatever the reason, even the historians who wrote about the Fall of Constantinople and who referred in their texts to earlier events (Doukas, Chalkokondyles) paid more attention to the works and days of the conquerors than to the history of their own side. Presumably they had nothing to write about – the Turks had monopolised the political and military stage for decades, while the struggle for power and the religious and political in-fighting had tarnished domestic politics until the very eve of the final disaster. On the other hand, the Turkish advance had almost reached the gates of the city, which repeatedly repelled the enemy forces from such close quarters.

Constantinople ought, normally, to have fallen during Bayezid's eight-year siege of the city (1395–1402), but he unexpectedly withdrew his army to confront the Mongol general Timur in the Battle of Ankara (28 July 1402). Earlier, the Turkish sultan had inflicted a crushing defeat on the crusaders, under Sigismond of Hungary, at Nicopolis (25 September 1396), sealing his control over most of the Balkan region. His backing assured Manuel II Palaiologos' accession to the throne (1390), but with the obligation to take part in the sultan's campaigns in Asia Minor for the next two years. The emperor's impressions of the now abandoned Greek cities, whose very names had been wiped

---

12   Tinnefeld, "Idealizing Self-centered Power Politics", pp. 407–11.

WRITING THE HISTORY OF DECLINE

from the memory of those who remained behind, are recorded in his letters to his friend Demetrios Kydones.[13] After Bayezid's defeat at Ankara, his state was weakened by the civil wars between the heirs to the throne. Conditions were favourable for the reconstruction of Byzantium; but this opportunity, too, was lost.

Constantinople's unexpected delivery from the eight-year Turkish siege was attributed to the miraculous intervention of the Theotokos, according to a narrative of the miraculous event (Διήγησις περὶ τοῦ γεγονότος θαύματος), which is thought to have been based on a chronicle – now lost – by John Chortasmenos.[14] During the tumultuous interregnum in the Ottoman Empire the Byzantines did manage to recover some territory temporarily, but were unable to organise a battle-worthy army to stand against the aggressive expansionism of Murad II (1421–1451). Plainly, the leadership and the dynamism that could have imposed changes on old mindsets and rigidities were lacking.

In 1422 Murad II laid siege to Constantinople from June 10 to August 24, and the city was miraculously saved, as we are told by John Kananos, author of the narrative Περὶ τοῦ ἐν Κωνσταντινουπόλει γεγονότος πολέμου describing the occurrence, by what seemed to be the intervention of the Theotokos. The information he gives about the beleaguered city, however, is fairly general and of little significance. What is worth noting is the absence from his account of the representatives of authority, unlike the lower classes which seem to have taken charge of the city's defence. The fact of the siege was recorded by the historians of the 15th century – very briefly by Sphrantzes (X. Grecu, 14,10–18) and at somewhat greater length by Doukas (XXVIII, 1–6, Grecu, 229,10–237,6) and Chalkokondyles (II, 7,14–22, ed. Darkó).

The Turkish armies then turned their sights on Thessaloniki, but having been thwarted of their object headed south, razing the Hexamilion fortification and laying waste to the Morea. John VIII was finally forced to capitulate in 1426 on humiliating terms, including payment of an annual tribute. Thessaloniki was, consequently, the next target of Turkish expansionism. Earlier, during a four-year siege (1383–1387), Manuel Palaiologos had fought with every means at his

---

13   Manuel II Palaiologos, *Letters*, nos. 14, 16, 19–21, 29, ed. & trans. Dennis, pp. 36–39, 46–50, 57–63.

14   The editor of the text, P. Gautier ("Un récit inédit du siège de Constantinople"), questioned its ascription to Chortasmenos, while the opposite view was argued by D. Nastase, "La chronique de Jean Chortasménos". Cf. Hunger, *Hochsprachliche Literatur*, vol. 2, p. 335. The observations of the author of the narrative are of exceptional interest, including among other things the information that much of the city's beleaguered population was driven by hunger to defect to the Turks, leaving the city empty (Gautier, "Un récit inédit du siège de Constantinople", p. 106, lines 13–14 and 23–24).

disposal to keep it free, despite the objections of a segment of the population who were against the idea of fighting with no prospect of victory and would have preferred to lay down their arms. In the end Manuel was forced to abandon the city with his companions, leaving the citizens to open the gates to the besieger and surrender. The Turkish occupation lasted from 1387 till the summer of 1402.[15] The new regime was not, it seems, terribly oppressive, nor did it leave traumatic memories – in any case, Thessaloniki did not on that occasion suffer the devastation of a city reduced by force of arms and abandoned to looting.[16]

As in the case of John Kananos, the account written by John Anagnostes of the final fall of Thessaloniki in 1430 (Διήγησις περὶ τῆς τελευταίας ἁλώσεως τῆς Θεσσαλονίκης) is neither a history nor a chronicle in our familiar sense of those literary genres. It is, rather, an on the whole successful recital of the events that marked the fate of Thessaloniki, with all the dramatic consequences these had for its citizens. This record, undertaken, we assume, at the urging of some scholar, was an eye-witness description set down for future generations by John Anagnostes, who was fortunately aware of the importance that his testimony would have for them. This perception of the necessity of preserving the historical memory of a momentous event presupposes not only a certain level of education but also familiarity with similar historical works. His text does not, however, appear to follow a specific model. The only possible candidate would be the account left by John Kaminiates, but comparison of the two texts suggests no such link, barring the occasional interchangeable phrase. Anagnostes may have been familiar with Kaminiates' narrative, but was perhaps not enough of a scholar to make use of it as a model for his own account. The phrase ἡ χειροποίητος τοῦ λίθου βροντή (ed. Böhlig 27,57–58), which A. Kazhdan apparently mistakenly interprets as referring to the thunder of cannon, is a typical lexical borrowing – unless it is mere coincidence, which given the infrequency of its use seems unlikely.[17]

7 Byzantium on the Eve of the Fall. Stories of Defeat and Discord

In the 15th century the Byzantine Empire was confined to Constantinople and a few provincial cities in Asia Minor and continental Greece. The emperor no

---

15 Dennis, "The second Turkish Capture of Thessalonica".
16 Nicol, *The Last Centuries of Byzantium*, pp. 449–453.
17 Kazhdan, "Some questions addressed to the scholars". See also Karpozilos, *Βυζαντινοὶ ἱστορικοὶ καὶ χρονογράφοι*, pp. 270–71.

WRITING THE HISTORY OF DECLINE

longer exercised central authority, since each province had its own governor who only nominally recognised the emperor's authority. The Turkish forces had advanced almost to the gates of the capital, which was repeatedly threatened from its own doorstep. Insecurity and fear reigned everywhere, inside and outside the city. The future looked black, and there was nowhere to look for help except from the Christian West, and there only at a price, as those who conducted the negotiations with Rome knew full well. The ideological clashes between the pro-unionists and the anti-unionists had begun in the days of Michael VIII, with the Council of Lyon and the enactment of the unification of the Churches (1274), a union which, however, remained on paper. Now the confrontation had taken on much greater dimensions, perhaps because it expressed the desires and the fears of the Greek world.[18]

Helen Glykatzi-Ahrweiler has argued that the Greek Church's hostility to Rome combined with belief in a fatalistic eschatology regarding the end of Byzantium and the world served to weaken the city's will to defend itself and essentially favoured submission to the Turks.[19] The supporters of Church union were not necessarily representing the interests of the Catholic Church; on the contrary, they could see that the West offered the only economic and political escape route for the bankrupt state, for there was no hope that a flame of regeneration could be rekindled from the ashes of its ruins. The renaissance of the Hellenic world – from pagan Sparta, as if in proof of the bankruptcy of Christian thinking – envisioned by philosopher George Gemistos Plethon was wholly utopian. Earlier, the realism of Demetrios Kydones had collided with the intransigence of the ultra-Orthodox, who looked not to the terrestrial kingdom which was dying before their eyes but saw unsullied faith in Orthodoxy as the road to salvation.

Michael Kritoboulos saw the end of the empire as a natural corollary of its rise and decline, as happens with every organism that is born and later dies (A 3, ed. Reinsch, 14,18–29). In this particular case, the Byzantine state was no exception to the rule nor differed from other states that fell into decline. At its

---

18   Cf. Dölger, "Politische und geistliche Strömungen".

19   "The criminal passivity displayed by the Byzantines in the face of the Turkish threat betrays above all the inability of the Byzantine nation, blinded by its passionate hostility to Rome, to do what was necessary for its survival and indispensable for the preservation of the State in transition". (Glykatzi-Ahrweiler, L'idéologie politique de l'Empire byzantin, p. 144). Glykatzi-Ahrweiler's opinion that the Byzantines preferred barbarianisation to Romanisation and that the intellectual return to classicism was a utopia or a flight from grim reality were countered by van Dieten ("Politische Ideologie und Niedergang"), who wrote that hostility to Rome neither promoted pro-Turkish sentiment nor led to passiveness, since both parties fought together on the walls of the city against the conqueror, and added that her opinion had no basis in source evidence.

height the empire was identified with the *oikoumene*, the one universal society, and these two concepts were considered inseparable, so that the dissolution of the state meant the end of the world. The only *basileus*, the natural ruler of the world, was the Byzantine emperor, wrote Patriarch Antony IV to Grand Prince Basil I of Moscow in the 1390s, replying to his assertion that "we have a Church but not an emperor" with the words "It is not possible for Christians to have a Church without an emperor" (eds. Miklosich/Müller, II, 191,16–18). The tsar of Moscow was refusing to recognise the universal sovereignty of the Byzantine emperor, the heir of Constantine the Great, who had become a vassal of the sultan. At that point the patriarch of necessity stepped in, since the roles had been reversed and the Church was now the defender of the tottering kingdom, as G. Ostrogorsky insightfully observed.[20] Meanwhile, the theologians were endeavouring to explain the triumph of Islam and the delivery of the faithful into the hands of the infidel in eschatological terms. These ideas passed into various apocalyptic texts each time a great danger loomed. In this spirit, Gennadios Scholarios thought that resistance to the last siege was useless, for he was convinced that God had delivered Constantinople to the infidel because of the multitude of its sins (Doukas, XXXVI 3, 317,9). He expected the end of the world to come with the end of the empire, and even calculated the date after the fall of the city.[21]

The idea of the universality of the empire and of the emperor as the anointed of God to kingship, like the prophet-king David, concepts that had been promoted for centuries by politicians and clerics, no longer had any political content. Ideologically, there was a void. What was missing was quite simply the political ideology that could rally the people combatively at a critical moment in their history. Bessarion and Plethon had, each from his own perspective, proposed reform measures, rescue programmes to redress the economy and raise a militia exempt from taxation, in a bid to avoid disaster.[22] But it was too late. Byzantium no longer existed; at best, it had become a city-state. Manuel II Palaiologos understood this sorrowful reality perfectly well, much better than his son John, who had not fully comprehended the dramatic condition into which the state had declined fifteen years before the end finally came. In a confidential discussion with his counsellor George Sphrantzes on the political impasse facing them, the aged emperor said, "But today, with our troubles

---

20   Ostrogorsky, *History*, p. 553.

21   Gennadios II Scholarios, *Works*, eds. Petit/Sidéridès/Jugie, vol. 3, p. 287; vol. 4, pp. xxix and 511–12.

22   See Lampros, *Παλαιολόγεια καὶ Πελοποννησιακά*, vol. 3, pp. 309–312; vol. 4, pp. 38, 115–16, 131, 135.

closing in upon us from every side, our Empire needs not a great *basileus*, but a good manager" (ἀμὴ σήμερον, ὡς ἂν παρακολουθοῦσιν εἰς ἡμᾶς τὰ πράγματα, οὐ βασιλέα θέλει ἡ ἡμῶν ἀρχή, ἀλλ' οἰκονόμον, XXIII, 7, ed. Maisano, 82,21–22).[23] At least three emperors (John V, Manuel II, John VIII) had travelled to the West seeking financial help or hoping that they could stir the Western Christians to a new crusade against the infidel, John V even converting to Catholicism in Rome (1369) to secure the support of the Pope.

The bankrupt *basileis* all returned empty-handed. They had pledged everything they had to Western banks, and indeed in the case of John V the Venetian authorities would not permit him to leave until he had paid his debts or, in lieu of cash, ceded Tenedos to them. And as if the troubles caused by Turkish expansionism were not enough, Bayezid's blockade of the capital itself for eight straight years (1394–1402), during which time thousands died of hunger, fled or were taken prisoner, the city was further beleaguered by dynastic and domestic strife, with one side turning alternately to the Turks or the Western nations against the other. Returning from Venice in 1391, Demetrios Kydones found the capital in total disarray, as he wrote to a correspondent. Outside the walls the Turks held sway, and the spectre of famine loomed constantly over the people. The victorious Turks imposed swingeing taxes, which even the penniless had to pay. Their greed knew no bounds, making it impossible to meet their demands. The people looked to servitude as a solution to their woes. The quarrelling of the emperors over the shadow of power, which was the root cause of the collapse of the state, continued as before (ἡ τῶν βασιλέων περὶ τοῦ τῆς ἀρχῆς ταύτης εἰδώλου διχόνοια), and for its sake they served the barbarian, because it was he who decided who should prevail. Thus the emperors were the first to submit to the barbarian, and after them their subjects (ὥστ' ἀνάγκη πρὸ τῶν πολιτῶν τοὺς βασιλέας αὐτοὺς ἐκείνῳ δουλεύειν καὶ ζῆν πρὸς τὰς ἐκείνου παραγγελίας), even campaigning with him in Phrygia and Pontus with what troops were left to them, leaving the city undefended. On the domestic front the city was torn by rivalries and struggles for primacy, particularly among the upper ranks, with each one seeking to grasp everything for himself (καὶ ὡς ἑκάστῳ σπουδὴ εἰ δύναιτο μόνῳ πάντα καταφαγεῖν) and, when he could not, threatening to go over to the enemy and with his help fight against his own country and his friends.[24]

The political situation in Constantinople was now determined by external factors. The importance of the city itself was of course geopolitical, for it

---

23   For a closer analysis of the passage, see Kiousopoulou, *Βασιλεύς ἢ οικονόμος*, 186–89.
24   Demetrios Kydones, *Letters*, no. 442, ed. Loenertz, vol. 1, pp. 406–08. Charanis, "Internal Strife in Byzantium", pp. 308–09.

was the place where Europe and Asia met. The Turks had made Adrianople their capital in 1365, and their passage from one continent to the other was impeded by the Byzantine city, the only fortified place still standing in the way of their conquest of the whole of Asia Minor. Besides, in order to neutralise Constantinople as a naval and commercial base and to gain control over shipping in the straits, no sooner had the young Mehmed II seized power than he built the famous Rumeli Hisar fortress (1452) on the west bank of the Bosporos (A 6, ed. Reinsch, 18,27–19,24).

The written sources available to us give only a fragmentary picture of Byzantine society before the disaster. Popular feeling revolted against the pro-Roman propaganda of the court and a segment of the intelligentsia. Memories of the crusader capture of the city and the Latin Empire had not entirely faded. Moreover, recognition of papal supremacy and doctrinal compromise would bring upon them the wrath of God, and the disaster that all were awaiting would, naturally, be the punishment for the betrayal of their faith. On the other hand, there were many who, seeing that the West had progressed in all fields of knowledge and science, had learned Latin, discovered Western writers contemporary and ancient, and translated them into Greek. With the looming crisis many of these had sought refuge in the West, and as it drew closer still the trickle of refugees became a flood. The politico-religious disputes between unionists and anti-unionists were an extension of the clash between State and Church. John VIII, who signed the proclamation of Union (July 1439), saw that after the conquest of Thessaloniki in 1430 he had no other choice than to appeal to the West for help. He believed that in this way συναιρομένου Θεοῦ, ἐπακολουθήσῃ τῇ πατρίδι τι ἀγαθόν.[25] Patriarch Joseph II did not want the council to convene in Italy and particularly the Greek delegation as guests of the papal court: εἰ ἐκεῖσε γένηται, οὐκ ἔσται καλὸν τὸ συμπέρασμα τῆς συνόδου, for this would make them financially dependent on the Western side and in the end they would be obliged to do as it wished: ἐν γοῦν τῷ ἀπελεθεῖν οὕτω καὶ ἐκδέχεσθαι καὶ τὴν ἡμερησίαν τροφὴν ἐξ ἐκείνων, ἤδη γίνονται δοῦλοι καὶ μισθωτοί, ἐκεῖνοι δὲ κύριοι.[26] And, of course, he was right – his fears were realised. The

---

25 Sylvester Syropoulos, *Memoirs*, ed. Laurent, pp. 412, lines 34–35. Kiousopoulou, "Ἡ κοινωνικὴ διάσταση τῆς σύγκρουσης ἀνάμεσα στοὺς ἐνωτικοὺς καὶ τοὺς ἀνθενωτικούς". According to this author, the two sides clashed over political choices that would affect the future. One faction spoke for the powerful merchants, who had commercial links with the West, and who for that reason supported Union. On the other side were the churchmen and the common people, who wanted an agreement with the Turks that would secure the survival of the nation and the Orthodox Church. See also, and especially, Necipoğlu, "Constantinopolitan Merchants and the Question of their Attitudes".

26 Sylvester Syropoulos, *Memoirs*, ed. Laurent, p. 120, lines 13–14 and 18–19.

WRITING THE HISTORY OF DECLINE

Emperor, however, was determined to press on with the unification, and his only fear was lest someone disrupt the negotiations: δειλιῶ μήποτε εὑρεθῇ τι καλογέριν καὶ φωνήν τινα ῥίψῃ ἐκεῖσε, ἥτις μεγάλην ἡμῖν προξενήσει βλάβην.[27]

The Palaeologan period has been described as the 'last Byzantine Renaissance'.[28] And the curious thing is that at the end of the Byzantine millennium there was indeed a vigorous resurgence of intellectual and artistic activity, the hallmark of which was the systematic study of Ancient Greek literature, copying and commenting on the ancient texts. This was an irrepressible movement, which oriented the Byzantine world more closely than ever before towards the ancient Greek. And at this stage, at this time of collapse, Hellenism as an intellectual notion acquires a whole different dimension, not merely philological and historical, since the new ideals sought in the world of the ancients stimulated the idea of Hellenism, the cultivation of a Hellenic consciousness, and converted it into a *vademecum* for the nation, for the historical past truly becomes a point of reference for the present.

The intellectual elite is represented by a small group of scholars, which in the 14th century numbered some one hundred and seventy persons, who were economically dependent on the court, the patriarchate or some patron.[29] Cultural activity was, naturally, supported by the aristocracy, that is, the imperial family, the secular and ecclesiastical office-holders, and the wealthy landowners. In turn, the intelligentsia expressed the choices and the interests of a closed caste that held the reins of power. The landed aristocracy had been financially ruined by the two civil wars and the Ottoman expansionism that had brought the Turks to the very gates of Constantinople. The few who survived the crisis invested in commercial enterprises with Western merchants. The resulting impact on intellectual life is not recorded in the sources, but it is possible nonetheless to form an idea: presumably, the shrinking of the aristocracy and the penury of the court caused many to seek their fortune in the West or take refuge in the Church. Years ago I. Ševčenko spoke of a regression in letters on the eve of the Fall, a unilateral turning to theology, particularly in and following the period of the hesychast movement, a shift of interest and intellectual goals at the expense of classical learning and philosophy. However this may be, the general decline is to a degree reflected in the texts of the period,

---

27 Ibid., p. 172, lines 2–3.

28 See also Runciman, *The Last Byzantine Renaissance*. There are, however, differences of opinion concerning the intellectual movement of the period, to what extent it can be compared to the Italian Renaissance or whether it was simply a revival of classicism. See more generally on this question Kyritses, "Η άλωση της Κωνσταντινούπολης και το τέλος του βυζαντινού πολιτισμού".

29 Ševčenko, "Society and Intellectual Life in the Fourteenth Century".

although social inequality, the corruption of the ruling class and the political impasse were of little interest to the intelligentsia as a whole, despite the fact that they were well aware of the political situation, and indeed some of them dealt with it in a very specific way.[30]

8   Michael Kritoboulos: The Sultan's Historian

Perhaps inevitably, given the material available to him, Michael Doukas devoted the bulk of his *History* to the Turks; but it nonetheless bothered him that he was writing about the period after the Fall, and especially about the victories and the prowesses of Mehmed II (XLII 14, 399,19–21). Michael Kritoboulos, however, had no such qualms. His decision to write about the victorious wars of Mehmed II was deliberate, and his object was personal gain. He submitted his book to Mehmed for his approval, in the hope that it would prove highly acceptable and thus reach the widest possible readership. He also promised a second treatise that would describe the further successes that he hoped the Sultan would, with God's aid, achieve in the future (A 2,1, ed. Reinsch, 13,11–14). Whatever the Sultan's decision, he for his part thanked God for permitting him to recount the triumphs of his master. For in the past others had penned Turkish history – one wonders here whom he had in mind – but without success (A 2,2, 13,14–18). He knew, of course, that his work would cause a stir among Greek readers. In anticipation of their possible rejection, he set out his reasons for writing what he wrote. He was not writing out of malice, which was not in his nature, nor was he criticising his people for failing to remain powerful forever. If there were those who were incompetent, that was not the fault of the nation, but of ill government (A 3,1–7, 13,29–15,3). Finally, he was following the example of the historian Josephus, who had dedicated his work to the Roman conquerors of Palestine (A 3, 8, 15,7–14) and, in similar fashion, was dedicating his own composition to Mehmed the Conqueror.

He came to terms, nonetheless, with the new order of things, abandoning any thought of a revival of the Greek world, the fate of which was in any case of little concern to him. His interest was now focused on the conquests of Mehmed II and the new political power that had risen to supremacy in Asia Minor and the Balkans. He promoted the Greek language and Greek culture, of course, but as a means of propaganda to reveal the magnificence of the Turkish

---

30   Ševčenko, "The Decline of Byzantium Seen through the Eyes of its Intellectuals". Kyritses, "Ἡ ἅλωση τῆς Κωνσταντινούπολης καὶ τὸ τέλος τοῦ βυζαντινοῦ πολιτισμοῦ", pp. 164–72.

WRITING THE HISTORY OF DECLINE

sultan to the Western nations, since Arabic and Turkish were less well known in the world at large (Kritoboulos, *Letter*, ed. Reinsch, 4,33–5,5).

Kritoboulos accepted the new state of affairs, and came to terms with it. He also went one step further, seeing in the Sultan the heir to the throne of Byzantium – θεοῦ θελήματι κυρίῳ γῆς καὶ θαλάττης – who exercised his power just as his Byzantine predecessors had done, and acclaiming him as generous, humane and fond of building – in other words, praising him for the virtues and qualities that were customarily lauded in the Emperors of Rome at the Byzantine court (Α 73, 1–24. Β 1, 90,14–28. Γ 17, 140,6–21. Δ 9, 166,9–18). Nor did Kritoboulos content himself with these – in any case false – flattering epithets for the Conqueror: he further described him as a philhellene, and traced his ancestry to the Greek court. The supposed philhellenism of the Ottoman conqueror, inspired by similar old-fashioned narratives and in imitation of Alexander the Great, manifested itself in a visit to the Acropolis in Athens (Γ 9,4, 128,11–129,3) and another to Troy (Δ 11,5, 170,3–17). This kind of exaggeration was customary in propaganda writing, in encomia and, to a lesser degree, in histories such as those of the *Continuators of Theophanes* and Joseph Genesios. In his attempt to Hellenise the Turkish oppressor, Kritoboulos did not hesitate to place in his mouth exhortations in the style of Thucydides that Mehmed was supposed to have uttered to the assembled Turks before bloody battles, or to mention his philosophical musings with George Amiroutzes (Δ 9,2 165,21–166,18. Ε 10,5, 195,3–33).

A primitive realism does, it must be confessed, emerge from the pages of his *History*, the result, I suppose, of a coming to terms with the Turkish oppressors that certain circles had accepted from the beginning.[31] Acquiescence towards the conqueror, whether Christian or Muslim, was not something new. The siege of 1430 divided the citizens of Thessaloniki, with part of the population in favour of surrendering the city to Murad II rather than continuing to resist. Earlier, in another Turkish siege, which lasted for four years (1383–1387), Manuel Palaiologos eventually abandoned the city, because the people no longer had the will to endure the Turkish blockade.[32] Kritoboulos himself thought voluntary submission to the conqueror, with all the corollaries of surrender, preferable to armed resistance, which usually meant a bloodbath. His pro-Turkish stance was probably aimed at personal gain, which for a time he reaped as governor of Imbros. But it also reflected the views of a world that from religious conviction alone was averse to the West. We do not know whether there

---

31   See also P. Bádenas, "Τα συμφιλιωτικά ρεύματα Ελλήνων λογίων στην αυλή του Μεγάλου Τούρκου".

32   Manuel II Palaiologos, *Letters*, no. 67, ed. Dennis, p. 187, lines 19–30.

was any theological foundation underlying his anti-unionist attitude, since the nature of his work meant that he avoided any reference to Christian concepts, or whether, as we suppose, it was purely a matter of financial interest. In the end, his attempt to attract the Sultan's attention and interest proved to have been in vain. His *History* was not widely read, was never translated, nor was it ever used by his Turkish contemporaries or later historians, and remained totally unknown to research scholarship until it came to light in the middle of the nineteenth century. His intended second volume, which would have been dedicated exclusively to the military achievements of Mehmed II, evidently found no supporters and was apparently never written.

9   Michael Doukas: A Dispassionate Critic

Unlike Kritoboulos, the pragmatist, Michael Doukas interprets the political decline of the empire and the undoing of the nation in theological terms: ... καὶ τὰ πάντα κακά, τί καὶ πῶς καὶ διὰ τί; διὰ τὰς ἁμαρτίας ἡμῶν (XXIX 5, 251,8–9). He links its causes to the civil wars between Andronikos II and his grandson and, later, the wars waged by John Kantakouzenos to secure the throne for himself. In addition, he saw the crime that placed Michael VIII on the throne as a turning point, for since that date the Lord's grace was no longer with the Byzantine kings, just as had happened with the perfidious Jews at the time of Christ's Passion. In a word, he considered the Palaeologans to be usurpers (VI 2, 49,5–19). Moral depravity inevitably led to political ignobility, making the end of the empire a foregone conclusion (III 5, 47,12–13). The Byzantine monarchs are presented in his work as wholly inert and unable to withstand the onslaught of the Turkish forces. In any case, none of the emperors stands out for his ability, with perhaps the sole exception of Manuel II: ὄντως σοφώτατος καὶ ἐνάρετος ἔν τε σωφροσύνῃ καὶ κοσμιότητι (XXVIII 7, 237,8–9). The Turkish armies constantly threatened the capital and the despairing emperors, like their subjects, could find nothing better to do than lift their hands in supplication to God, pleading the rightness of their cause (XV 7, 91,23–28), or, like Constantine XI to Mehmed II, declare their impotence and leave the fate of their people in the hands of the Lord: Ἐγὼ γὰρ πρὸς τὸν Θεὸν καταφεύγω καί, εἰ θελητὸν αὐτῷ ἐστι τοῦ δοῦναι καὶ τὴν πόλιν ταύτην εἰς χεῖρας σου, τίς ὁ ἀντιπεῖν δυνάμενος; (XXXIV 11, 305,29–30). In other cases they are portrayed as entertaining false hopes, as if totally out of touch with reality, or taking hasty and foolish decisions (XXXIV 2, 293,7 et seq.). The Turks maintained the initiative of action and naturally play the leading role throughout his narrative. The fact

WRITING THE HISTORY OF DECLINE

that they were destined to rule over East and West is declared at the outset of the historian's account, as foretold by his grandfather, who had found asylum with the Turks (v 5, 47,11–16).

The prophecies and predictions of all sorts in his text concerning the fall of the empire and the future of the Christian nation are perplexing. Not, of course, the Biblical framework Doukas had in mind and within which he placed Constantinople, likening it to a New Jerusalem, so that its fall is foreshadowed in the words of the Old Testament prophets. This is a very old approach to historical developments, which ultimately are directed by the will of God. Doukas does not appear to be superstitious in his views; as a rule he records facts and events honestly and soberly, save for the very few cases in which he allows an emotional element to penetrate his account, as for example in his description of the fall of the city and the attitude of the ultra-Orthodox towards the pro-unionists. He believes, or more accurately he wants to believe, that the Turkish oppression will also disappear with the final collapse of the Byzantine state. This thought occasionally surfaces in his text, in various contexts, such as the prophetic dream of Murad II (XXXIII 8, 287,5–11) and the oracle vouchsafed to Michael VIII, with the keyword μαμάϊμι, indicating, by their initials, the series of emperors who would follow him after his death (XLII 14, 401,7–14).[33] Doukas expected these prophecies to be fulfilled and the nation to rise again: ... ὀνειροπολοῦντες ἐκδεχόμεθα τὴν ἀνάρρυσιν ... καὶ τὰ προρρηθέντα παρά τινων εὐλαβῶν ἀνδρῶν εἰς ἐκδοχὴν ἐλπίζοντες (XLII 14, 401,1618). But it is unclear when he expects this momentous reversal to occur or how he envisions the rebirth of the Greek nation once the Byzantine Empire has gone: Ἴσθι τέκνον, εἰ μὴ παντελὴς φθορὰ τοῖς Ῥωμαίοις ἐπέλθοι, οὐκ ἐπιγελάσει τοῖς χριστιανοῖς ἡ τύχη· δεῖ γὰρ τὴν Πόλιν ὑπὸ τῶν Τούρκων φθαρεῖναι καὶ οὕτω τὰ τῶν χριστιανῶν δυστυχήματα τέλος ἕξουσι (XXXVIII 13, 343,18–20). Also, his declaration that he began to write his history because he believed that the Ottoman supremacy would come to an end is both vague and tentative: Ἀλλὰ τὸ πεῖσάν μοι γράφει ἐστὶ τοῦτο, ὃ λέξων ἔρχομαι. Ἔμαθον παρά τινων γερόντων τιμίων ἀνδρῶν, ἔτι νέος ὤν, ὅτι τὸ τέλος τῆς τυραννίδος τῶν Ὀτμάνων ἔσται ὁμοῦ φθάσαν σὺν τῷ τέλει τῆς βασιλείας τῶν Παλαιολόγων. Ὁμοῦ γὰρ ἤρξαντο ὁ Ὀτμὰν ἐν τυραννίδι καὶ Μιχαὴλ Παλαιολόγος ἐν βασιλείᾳ ... (XLII 14, 399,21–401,3). However the case may be, while he rejects out of hand several of these beliefs concerning the end of the empire, he does have a somewhat vague conviction that the nation will rise

---

33 There is also a reference to the oracle in the *Chronicon Minus*: καὶ οὕτως ἀπώλετο ἡ βασιλεία τῶν Ῥωμαίων ἐν τῷ δυστυχεῖ Δράγασι ... ἐπληρώθη δ᾽ ὁ χρησμὸς τὸ μαμάϊμι (*Chronicle* 22, 53, ed. Schreiner, p. 188).

156   KARPOZILOS

again from the ashes of its destruction, since the Turkish tyranny will also meet a similar fate.[34]

10   George Sphrantzes: A Diary in the Form of a Chronicle

Doukas was a supporter of Church union, but did not display the blinkered fanaticism typical of so many of his contemporaries. In any case, as far as he was concerned, there could be no question of choice between the tiara and the turban, however the matter might be seen by Loukas Notaras, whose opinion, like that of Scholarios, he found inadmissible. The circumstances required a rapprochement with Rome in exchange for the military assistance so urgently needed. For his part, although he understood why it was necessary to negotiate with the Latins, Sphrantzes thought it was a mistake to proceed with unification at the time, because that would provoke a Turkish invasion (XXIII,4, ed. Maisano, 80,26–29). His *Chronicon Minus*, which is strongly autobiographical and was written in journal form, left out a great deal, including the popular opposition to the scheme. Sphrantzes seems to have kept a personal diary, in which, whether from habit or from clerical conscientiousness, he recorded the most important current events of the day. His work, in other words, was intended neither for a particular readership nor to serve some specific end.

As a member of many diplomatic missions however, and through the various government posts he held as a reward for his services, he was perfectly familiar with the events of the final decades before the end of the empire. He is, of course, the only historian to have experienced first-hand the siege of Constantinople and the tragic moment of its submission to Mehmed II and his army. He took part in the defence of the capital, fighting alongside Constantine Palaiologos as a close friend and associate. He knew so much and yet, whether because he lacked the necessary training for such an enterprise, or more likely the incentive, or merely the ambition, he did not write a history. He is, of course, reckoned among the historians of the Fall, although he devoted no more than a brief note to this tragic event, in the manner of a chronicler. He confined himself to the minimum of what he knew, witnessed and experienced, but however fragmentary his personal testimony must always be of interest.

The notes he kept in diary form for the period 1413–1477, which he worked on in Corfu after 1468 and before the serious illness that befell him in October 1476, form the main body of his *Chronicon Minus*. There is no indication in these

---

34   B. Flusin, "Prédictions et prophéties dans l'oeuvre de Doucas". Cf. also Krasavina, "Mirovozzrenie i social'no-političeskie vzgliady vizantijskogo istorika Duki", pp. 106–07.

WRITING THE HISTORY OF DECLINE

notes that the material was selected according to any particular plan. He begins with the death of Bayezid (1412) and the succession of Turkish sultans, simply recording them without comment (I 1, ed. Maisano, 4,8–14). He then moves on to happenings in the Byzantine court, the installation of patriarchs, births, deaths and marriages, arrivals of notable figures in the capital, and the like (II–VI, 4,8–14,11). His narration of events becomes more cohesive, one may say, after 1421, that is, after the death of Mehmed I (VII 1, 14,12 et seq.). From this point on, Sphrantzes begins to keep a concise record of political developments in the Ottoman world, to the degree, of course, that they affected the domestic front (IX 1–XI 1, 20,1–22,13). A fair amount of his material is nonetheless still devoted to his own family circle and his personal experiences as an imperial official. He discloses secret conversations that he had with the emperors (XVII 1, 40,13–22) and occasionally expresses some indirect criticism, as for example of John VIII Palaiologos' ill-judged decision to oppose Murad's accession to the throne, despite his father's reservations (VIII 3, 18,15–26),[35] and his insistence on pressing forward with the negotiations with Rome (XXIII 2–7). He also expresses objections to the mooted Council (XXIII 1, 80,4–5), for he believed that from the political point of view the Council of 1438 was wholly inopportune and indeed, since it provoked Turkish aggression, brought about the end of the empire (XXIII 4, 80,26–29).

Clearly, what Sphrantzes recorded in his journal were things of which he had personal knowledge from his several capacities: diplomatic missions, confidential discussions, facts and dates directly connected with court circles. His *Chronicon* is imbued with the profoundly religious attitude that shaped his character and directed his life.[36] If there is a message in his text it can be summarised in a single sentence – the last of the Palaiologoi did everything he could to save Constantinople: ὁ δὲ μακαρίτης καὶ αὐθέντης μου ὁ βασιλεὺς τί οὐκ ἔπραξε κρυφίως καὶ φανερῶς πρὸς βοήθειαν τοῦ ὁσπιτίου αὐτοῦ καὶ τῶν Χριστιανῶν ἢ τῆς ζωῆς αὐτοῦ; ἢ ἐνεθυμεῖτο ὅτι, ἐὰν ἐπισυμβῇ τίποτε, νὰ φύγῃ δυνατοῦ καὶ εὐκόλου ὄντος; (XXXVI 10, 140,20–23). He himself was fully aware that the Byzantine state had collapsed irreversibly and that the idea of empire was outmoded. What remained of the ancient grandeur of the Romans was but a tiny spark – καὶ τοῦ τῶν Ῥωμαίων μικροῦ τούτου σπινθῆρος (XXXV 5, 132,2–3). Manuel II had already acknowledged this sad reality in a conversation with Sphrantzes: οὐ βασιλέα θέλει ἡ ἡμῶν ἀρχή, ἀλλ' οἰκονόμον (XXIII 7, 82,22). The chronicler's use of informal language was perfectly apposite to an empire on its last legs and the

---

35 Προεῖδον γὰρ καὶ τὰς ἐνθυμήσεις αὐτοῦ καὶ τὰ ἐδόξαζε κατορθῶσαι μὲ τὸν Μουσταφᾶν, καὶ εἶδον καὶ τὰ τέλη τῶν κατορθωμάτων εἰς τί κίνδυνον μᾶς ἔφερον (XXIII,7, 82,24–26).

36 See also George Sphrantzes, *Chronicon*, ed. Maisano, pp. 17*–20*.

provincialism that in some ways characterised his thinking. The imperial idea required a different, more scholarly style of writing, but this was not, apparently, something that greatly concerned him.[37]

11 Laonikos Chalkokondyles: The Rise and Expansion of the Ottoman State

Unlike Kritoboulos' *History*, which was delivered as a single manuscript, the Turkish history written by Laonikos Chalkokondyles was evidently intended for a much wider readership, for it was produced in thirty manuscript copies, translated into Latin as early as 1556, and the original edited a few decades later (1615). Chalkokondyles strove for objectivity in his treatment of the Turks, and his writing is without prejudice. His thinking is free of the religiosity characteristic of his contemporaries, and he shuns any mention of God or divine providence. He calls the Byzantine emperors *basileis Hellenon* and the people of the Byzantine Empire and their contemporary descendants Hellenes, not *Rhomaioi*, apparently coming to terms with the new order of things in thus making a clear break with the past (1, 4,10–16 ed. Darkó), and plainly following the teachings of his Hellenist tutor, George Plethon. The bulk of his treatise was devoted to the rise and expansion of the Ottoman state; his interest in Byzantium was limited, and his opinion of the Greek emperors was not particularly flattering, his criticism of them often agreeing with that of Doukas. The Romans linked fortune with virtue, that is, nobility with boldness, while the fortune of the Greeks was not commensurate even with the limits of their virtue (1, 3,10–11). There is no indication in the text that he was a man of faith, nor any evidence to the contrary. He believed in the renascence of the nation, not, of course, on a metaphysical basis, but somewhat indefinitely and with no indication as to when the renaissance he envisioned might take place (1, 2,15–19). Like his fellow historians, he did not seek to identify the root causes of the decline – social inequality, bad government and the corruption of the ruling class.

The collapse of the Byzantine state required Chalkokondyles to adopt certain basic principles, in keeping with both the new state of affairs and his personal perceptions of the Greek nation. He removed the word Constantinople from his vocabulary, without explanation, using instead the city's earlier appellation of Byzantium; similarly, he called the emperors of the New Rome *basileis*

---

37   Reinsch, "Αυτοκρατορία και γλώσσα μετά την Άλωση".

WRITING THE HISTORY OF DECLINE 159

Hellenon, and their subjects Hellenes rather than *Rhomaioi*.[38] In his preface, which gives a basic outline of the founding of the Eastern Roman Empire, he neglected even to mention Constantine the Great or recognise the links between the Byzantine emperors and the Roman state. Essentially, he refused any link, and saw only religious and political differences between Greeks and Romans. Consequently, any correlation between the Greek world and the Roman imperium is immaterial.[39] In his view, in fact, it was a mistake for the Greeks to accept the Roman appellation (1, 6,15–16). The Westerners tried to paper over the religious differences that separated them from the Greeks, but they, however, preserved their traditional customs (1, 5,5–6). Over this rapid historical review hung the shadow of the mutual hostility and mistrust that proved too powerful even for the Western Pontiff, who led the Fourth Crusade against Constantinople: καὶ ἀπὸ ταύτης δὴ τῆς διαφορᾶς συχνούς τε τῶν ἐσπερίων καὶ δὴ τοὺς Ἐνετούς, ἐνάγοντος ἐπὶ τάδε τοῦ Ῥωμαίων ἀρχιερέως, στόλῳ στρατεύεσθαι μεγάλῳ ἐπὶ τοὺς Ἕλληνας ... καὶ Βυζαντίου τὴν πόλιν κατὰ κράτος ἑλεῖν (1, 5,6–10). And later, when John VIII appealed to the Pope for help, his demarche did not have the desired effect (1, 5,19–6,7).

But what precisely was Chalkokondyles aiming at with his decision to shake off the Roman past of the empire now lost forever? The concept of the New Rome, with all that ensued from its ecumenical character, was rooted in the Orthodox world, but Chalkokondyles did not identify with ecclesiastical tradition, on the evidence of his text, at least. The question is whether his *Greekness* expressed a deeper ideological stance and not just a style. In any case, the world of antiquity does not permeate his history, as it does, for example, the *Byzantine History* of Nikephoros Gregoras. This may have been deliberate, as ill-suited to the Turkish expansionism he was discussing. His choices, however, recall Herodotus and reflect a secular spirit in many ways alien to traditional historiography. The way in which he interprets the rise and fall of the

---

38   Gemistos Plethon had expressed a similar opinion in his report to Manuel II: Ἐσμὲν γὰρ οὖν, ὧν ἡγεῖσθέ τε καὶ βασιλεύετε, Ἕλληνες τὸ γένος, ὡς ἥ τε φωνὴ καὶ ἡ πάτριος παιδεία μαρτυρεῖ. *Patrologia Graeca*, vol. 160, col. 821B.

39   Nonetheless, at the time of the talks on Church union during the reign of Michael VIII, in which George Akropolites played an active role, the Byzantine party attempted to trace the common roots of the two halves of Christendom. In this spirit Akropolites reminded the Italians of the harmony and accord that existed between the two peoples, who had shed their old appellations and were now called simply Rhomaioi, sharers of a single faith and a common name: κἀντεῦθεν ἵνα μὴ τοῖς ἐθνικοῖς τούτοις ὀνόμασι περιγράφωνται, τῇ πρεσβυτέρᾳ Ῥώμῃ ἑτέρα νέα ἀντῳκοδόμηται, ἵνα ἐξ οὕτω μεγίστων πόλεων κοινὸν ἐχουσῶν τοὔνομα Ῥωμαῖοι πάντες κατονομάζοιντο καὶ ὡς τὸ τῆς πίστεως κοινὸν οὕτως ἔχοιεν καὶ τὸ τῆς κλήσεως (George Akropolites, *Works*, ed. Heisenberg, vol. 2, p. 64, lines 15–19. See Kaldellis, "Historicism in Byzantine Thought and Literature", pp. 15–16.

Byzantine Empire in his preface, where he speaks of virtue (meaning soldierly courage and decisiveness) in conjunction with fortune, goes beyond the traditional perceptions of the plans of divine providence and is more reminiscent of secular models. Like Kritoboulos, he justified choosing to write in Greek, because it was a universal language (I, 2,12–14). It ultimately remained the only solid value after the great catastrophe. And in it he placed his hopes for the future, envisioning the rebirth of the Greek nation (I, 2,15–19).

The information that Chalkokondyles provides fills in several of the gaps in historiography from the second half of the 14th century to the historians of the Fall. Fragmentary and incomplete though they may be, these accounts nonetheless paint a vivid picture of the storm-tossed state, for the Turks had become the moderators of the domestic political scene, even in questions of succession to the throne. Manuel Palaiologos took power with the support of Bayezid, but only after paying a tribute of thirty thousand gold coins and promising to follow the sultan in his future campaigns. In fulfilment of this engagement he took part in the siege of Philadelphia in 1390 and was one of the first to scale the walls of the beleaguered city (ed. Darkó, II, 58,16–20). Chalkokondyles repeats the apparently widespread view that Bayezid would have taken Constantinople if he had not been attacked by Timur (II, 78,6–11; see Kritoboulos, A 16,10, ed. Reinsch, 32,33–33,3). Over the ten-year siege of the city (in reality it was eight years – 1394–1402) thousands died of hunger or fell into enemy hands, he tells us (II, 77,12–18). He also includes a detail that can only come from a Turksh source and that illustrates Bayezid's human side: when he learned that his son Ertogrul had been killed at Sebasteia, he was seized by profound grief, and upon hearing a shepherd playing his pipes exclaimed αὐλεῖ δὴ ᾠδήν, οὔτε Σεβάστειαν ἀπώλεσεν, οὔτε παῖδα Ὀρθογρούλην (III, 138,1–2).

He writes of the fate of the Greek nation without emotion, although he does not pass over the Turkish atrocities in silence (IX, 230,4–12). Only once, in recounting the massacre of the population of Leontarion, does he appear to lose the self-control he had imposed as a measure of objectivity in his narration, when he compares the victors to wolves (IX, 234,8–11). On the other hand, he praises their military skills and the impeccable organisation of their armies (VII, 114,11–115,21. VIII, 149,12–150,9). His opinion of most of the emperors is fairly negative, and to a degree coincides with Doukas' criticisms. He condemns the civil wars between Andronikos II and Andronikos III and their ill-conceived policy of neglecting the army and hiring mercenaries, which hastened the collapse of the state, for it emptied the imperial coffers and benefited only the aristocracy (I, 15,4–9. 17,13–19). In less than two pages he describes the

WRITING THE HISTORY OF DECLINE

fruitless endeavours of John v to save his state, by appealing to the leaders of the Western nations for help, which, naturally, was not forthcoming. He also mentions his imprisonment for debt in Venice, the refusal of his son Andronikos IV to provide the necessary funds, and his rescue by his second son, Manuel, who secured his release with money brought from Thessaloniki (I, 46,3–47,18). He is, however, less harshly judgemental of John v than Doukas, particularly as regards his supposed immorality and incompetence as ruler (X, 4. XI, 2. XII,2, Grecu, 65,9–12. 67,8–12. 71,22–25). In his view, John VIII was equally ineffective, since instead of preventing Murad II from crossing into Thrace he ἐσχόλαζέ τε περὶ γυναικὸς ἔρωτα, ἧς ἐρῶν ἐτύγχανεν (V, 6,13–14). After this point his account frequently echoes those of Doukas and Kritoboulos, though this does not necessarily indicate interdependence.

In writing his history Chalkokondyles relied primarily on Turkish sources. In fact, according to Hungarian Byzantinologist Gyula Moravcsik, Laonikos Chalkokondyles knew Turkish, and was able to make use of both written and oral testimonies of Ottoman expansionism.[40] His chief contribution lies in his exploitation of those sources, but what precisely they were we can only conjecture. He does indeed demonstrate a certain familiarity with the Turkish language, often embellishing his account with Turkish words (ἀλοφατζίδες, ζύχιδες, καρίπιδες, σαραπτάριοι, σιλικτάριος, τάμπεζιν, etc.).[41] When speaking of the tax system and national revenues in the days of Mehmed II, he cites the Turkish secretaries of the Sultan's court (VIII, 201,10).[42] He also knows, evidently from Turkish sources, the Greeks who obtained office and pursued careers in the service of Mehmed II (VIII, 196,7–197,6). That said, no systematic comparison between the *Historiarum demonstrationes* and the surviving Turkish sources has as yet been attempted, to ascertain whether he did in fact use written documents and to what extent.

The most curious thing, however, is that Chalkokondyles made no use of known historical works of the 13th and 14th centuries, but apparently made do with oral evidence.[43] This is comprehensible and to be expected for contemporary events. His history, however, goes back at least a century before his time, and covers a wide range of topics. One wonders, then, who his informants were, who knew so much about Turkish and Byzantine history, the geography and

---

40   Moravcsik, *Byzantinoturcica*, vol. 1, pp. 391–97.
41   Moravcsik, *Byzantinoturcica*, vol. 2, pp. 65, 131, 154, 274, 276, 298.
42   Vryonis, "Laonicus Chalkokondyles and the Ottoman Budget".
43   Ἐπυθόμην δὲ μετὰ ταῦτα τῶν περιοίκων γενέσθαι τὰ σώματα ἀμφὶ τὰ ἑξακισχίλια, ὑποζύγια δὲ πολλαπλάσια (IX, 230,13–14) (for the number of victims slaughtered in Leontarion in the Peloponnese).

ethnology of the two great continents, and in what circumstances he recorded all the material which he worked into a comprehensive and cohesive account. That he based his work on oral testimony is confirmed by his own statement in his account of the administrative system implemented by Mehmed II (VIII, 197,20–201,18), and he intimated that he was relying on oral tradition in several other instances as well (I, 126,8. Cf. also I, 11,15. 19,4. II, 56,9, III, 110,10. XI, 230,13 etc.). He was, of course, an eye witness to important military events, including Murad's Peloponnesian campaign and the destruction of the Hexamilion (VII, 115,4–6). It may well be that the final word on the subject of his sources remains to be said. Kritoboulos, in his preface, criticises certain historians who dealt with Turkish history carelessly and unmethodically, who recorded events from memory or from their own experience without bothering to verify their accuracy (A 2, ed. Reinsch, 13,14–18). On this point, Kritoboulos may well have had Chalkokondyles in mind, although as far as we know no one has yet attempted to collate their works to see how far each was familiar with the work of the other.

12 But What Can We Say by Way of Conclusion?

There has to be some truth in the saying that history is written by the victor. But sometimes the histories of defeat and destruction prove to be truer than those extolling the winner. At least in the second case the writers do not indulge in fulsome praise, but tend to deal critically with the leading players on their stage. The historiography of the Palaeologan period belongs to the latter category – it records terrible military defeats and catastrophic civil wars resulting in a shrinking state, political unrest in the cities and provinces, and the dissolution of the system of defence. Each in his own way, the historians recorded all the consequences of the general collapse. At first glance their accounts seem to be governed by ideas and stereotypes familiar from older works: fatal political decisions and disasters are ascribed as a rule to divine providence and the like. They put forward no new ideas, and from the literary point of view their writing is neither creative nor fresh.

But what precisely impelled these scholars to write their histories? In some cases, they may have had political aims on the government side: Akropolites and Kantakouzenos fall into this category, as does, although in totally different circumstances, Kritoboulos. In the case of Pachymeres and Gregoras, we find a predisposition towards the opposing camp, expressing not only the

WRITING THE HISTORY OF DECLINE

writer but also specific political-ecclesiastical circles, in Gregoras primarily the hesychasts. Gregoras took an active part in the hesychast controversy, and his text is thus to some extent autobiographical. In the case of his adversary, John Kantakouzenos, we have for the first time a protagonist who is also the author. Previously, his position alone distanced the writer of a work of history, whether historian or chronicler, from the events he described. That is, the author played no part in political developments or the shaping of situations; at most, he was an observer who recorded events based on his own personal observations or information supplied by those around him. The historians wrote for a specific, scholarly readership, which served as a spur to their efforts. In the case of Michael Doukas it is hard to determine either the circumstances in which he wrote his book or the audience for whom it was intended, for his life was spent in Frankish merchant circles in coastal Asia Minor; but apart from his connection with the Gattilusio family we know virtually nothing about his circumstances. Questions that are of particular interest to the modern historian, notably the underlying causes of events, seem to have been of no consequence to them. The information they record can occasionally be correlated to other texts, chiefly letters and speeches, allowing possible gaps in their accounts to be filled in. Their classicism did not help them in their writing, for they transposed the present into the remote past with outmoded expressions ill-suited to the reality they were relating: for example, the two great plagues of the 14th and 15th centuries are described by Kantakouzenos and Kritoboulos in the style of Thucydides. This raises the question, even in the case of the pestilence described by Prokopios, of how faithful their account of the symptoms and spread of the disease can have been if they were copying, or even writing in the manner of, an ancient text. Other classicizing features of their works, for example their dating system and the names they used for foreign peoples, need scarcely be mentioned. Their intellectual dependence on the ancient world, coupled with their conviction that the current of history was directed by divine providence, were in the end impediments to any inquiry into the root causes of the events they were describing. Pessimism pervades their pages – everything has passed into the hands of the enemy, on both sides of the Bosporos, because fate, or rather divine providence, has decreed it so. Their perception of history is wholly traditional, and naturally the concept of fate, of fortune, of divine providence in their accounts acquires a fatalistic cast proportional to the circumstances.

Bibliography

Primary Sources

Chronicle, ed. P. Schreiner, *Die byzantinischen Kleinchroniken* (Corpus Fontium Historiae Byzantinae, 12/1), Vienna 1975.

Demetrios Kydones, *Letters*, ed. R.-J. Loenertz, *Démétrius Cydonès. Correspondance* (Studi e Testi, 186 & 208), 2 vols., Vatican City 1956–60.

Documents, eds. F. Miklosich/I. Müller, *Acta et diplomata graeca medii aevi sacra et profana*, 6 vols., Vienna 1860–90.

Doukas, *History*, ed. V. Grecu, *Ducas, Historia Turco – Byzantina (1341–1462)* (Scriptores Bizantini, 1), Bucharest 1958.

Gennadios II Scholarios, *Works*, eds. L. Petit/X.A. Sidéridès/M. Jugie, *Oeuvres complètes de Gennade Scholarios*, vol. 3, Paris 1930; vol. 4. Paris 1935.

George Akropolites, *History/Works*, ed. A. Heisenberg, *Georgii Acropolitae opera*, 2 vols., Leipzig 1903.

George Acropolites, *History*, trans. R. Macrides, *George Akropolites, the History. Introduction, Translation and Commentary*, Oxford 2007.

George Pachymeres, *History*, ed. A. Failler, *Georges Pachymérès. Relations Historiques* (Corpus Fontium Historiae Byzantinae, 24), 5 vols., Paris 1984–2000.

George Sphrantzes, *Chronicle*, ed. R. Maisano, *Giorgio Sfranze, Cronaca* (Corpus Fontium Historiae Byzantinae, 29), Rome 1990.

John Anagnostes, *Diegesis*, ed. I. Tsaras, *Διήγησις περὶ τῆς τελευταίας ἁλώσεως τῆς Θεσσαλονίκης*, Thessaloniki 1958.

John Kananos, *Diegesis*, ed. A. Cuomo, *Ioannis Canani de Constantinopolitana obsidione relatio* (Byzantinisches Archiv, 30), Berlin/Boston 2016.

John VI Kantakouzenos, *History*, ed. L. Schopen, *Ioannis Cantacuzeni ex Imperatoris Historiarum libri IV graece et latine* (Corpus Scriptorum Historiae Byzantinae, 41), 3 vols., Bonn 1828–32.

Laonikos Chalkokondyles, *History*, ed. E. Darkó, *Laonici Chalcocondylae Historiarum Demonstrationes*, 2 vols., Budapest 1922–23.

Manuel II Palaiologos, *Letters*, ed. & trans. G.T. Dennis, *The Letters of Manuel II Palaeologus* (Corpus Fontium Historiae Byzantinae, 8), Washington, D.C. 1977.

Michael Kritoboulos, *History*, ed. D.R. Reinsch, *Critobuli Imbriotae Historiae*, (Corpus Fontium Historiae Byzantinae, 22), Berlin/New York 1983.

Nikephoros Blemmydes, *Autobiography*, ed. J.A. Munitiz, *Nicephori Blemmydae Autobiographia sive Curriculum Vitae necnon Epistula universalior* (Corpus Christianorum. Series Graeca, 13), Turnhout/Louvain 1984.

Nikephoros Gregoras, *Roman History*, eds. L. Schopen/I. Bekker, *Nicephori Gregorae Byzantina Historia* (Corpus Scriptorum Historiae Byzantinae, 19), 3 vols., Bonn 1829–55.

WRITING THE HISTORY OF DECLINE 165

Sylvester Syropoulos, *Memoirs*, ed. V. Laurent, *Les "mémoires" de Sylvestre Syropoulos sur le concile de Florence (1438–1439)*, Rome 1971.

Theodore Skoutariotes, *History*, ed. K.N. Sathas, Μεσαιωνικὴ Βιβλιοθήκη, vol. 7, Venice 1894.

Secondary Literature

Andriotes, N.P., "Κριτόβουλος ὁ Ἴμβριος καὶ τὸ ἱστορικό του ἔργο", Ἑλληνικά 2 (1929), 167–200.

Arnakis, G., "The Names of the Months in the History of Georgios Pachymeres", *Byzantinisch-neugriechische Jahrbücher* 18 (1945–1949), 144–53.

Bádenas, P., "Τα συμφιλιωτικά ρεύματα Ελλήνων λογίων στην αυλή του Μεγάλου Τούρκου", *Ο ελληνικός κόσμος ανάμεσα στην Ανατολή και τη Δύση, 1453–1981, Proceedings of the 1st European Conference on Modern Greek Studies, Berlin, 2–4 October 1998*, vol. 2, Athens 1999, pp. 409–19.

Baştav, S., "Die türkische Quellen des Laonikos Chalkokondyles", in F. Dölger/ H.-G. Beck, *Akten des XI. internationalen Byzantinistenkongresses München 1958*, Munich 1960, pp. 34–42.

Baştav, S., "Valeur de l' oeuvre de Doukas au point de vue de l' histoire des Turcs", *Cultura Turcica* 2 (1965), 213–35.

Bees, N.A., "Zum Bericht des L. Chalkokondylis über den Feldzug Murads II. Gegen Morea", *Byzantinisch-neugriechische Jahrbücher* 17 (1939–43), 234–41.

Beyer, H.-V., "Eine Chronologie der Lebensgeschichte des Nikephoros Gregoras", *Jahrbuch der Österreichischen Byzantinistik* 27 (1978), 127–55.

Beyer, H.-V., "Nikephoros Gregoras als Theologe und sein erstes Auftreten gegen die Hesychasten", *Jahrbuch der Österreichischen Byzantinistik* 20 (1971), 171–88.

Beyer, H.-V., *Nikephoros Gregoras Antirrhetika I. Einleitung, Textausgabe, Übersetzung und Anmerkungen* (Wiener Byzantinistische Studien, 12), Vienna 1976.

Beyer, H.-V., "Über die wahrscheinliche Identität des Autors der Version brève des Relations historiques de Georges Pachymérès mit Manuel Philes", *Anticnaja drevnost' i srednie veka* 27 (2006), 269–306.

Blum, W. "L'historiographie et le personnage de Georges Acropolites (1217–1282)", *Byzantinische Forschungen* 22 (1996), 213–20.

Charanis, P., "Internal Strife in Byzantium during the Fourteenth Century", *Byzantion* 15 (1940–1941), 208–30.

Darkó, E., "Neue Beiträge zur Biographie des Laonikos Chalkokandyles", *Byzantinische Zeitschrift* 27 (1927), 276–85.

Darkó, E., "Neue Emendationsvorschläge zu Laonikos Chalkokondyles", *Byzantinische Zeitschrift* 32 (1932), 2–12.

Darkó, E., "Zum Leben de Laonikos Chalkodyles", *Byzantinische Zeitschrift* 24 (1923–24), 29–39.

Dennis G.T., "The second Turkish Capture of Thessalonica 1391, 1394 or 1430?", *Byzantinische Zeitschrift* 57 (1964), 53–61.

Dentakis, V.L., Ἰωάννης Κυπαρισσιώτης, ὁ σοφὸς καὶ φιλόσοφος, Athens 1965.

van Dieten, J.L., *Entstehung und Uberlieferun der Historia Rhomaike des Nikephoros Gregoras, insbesondere des ersten Teiles: Lib. I–XI*, Cologne 1975.

van Dieten, J.L., *Nikephoros Gregoras Rhomäische Geschichte* (Bibliothek der griechischen Literatur), 6 vols., Stuttgart 1973–2003.

van Dieten, J.L., "Politische Ideologie und Niedergang im Byzanz der Palaiologen", *Zeitschrift für Historische Forschung* 6 (1979), 1–35.

Ditten, H., "Bemerkungen zu Laonikos Chalkokondyles' Deutschland-Exkurs", *Byzantinische Forschungen* 1 (1966), 49–75.

Ditten, H., "Bemerkungen zu Laonikos Chalkokondyles' Nachrichten über die Länder und Völker an der europäischen Küsten des Schwarzen Meeres (15. Jahrhundert u. Z.)", *Klio* 43–45 (1965), 185–246.

Ditten, H., "Der byzantinische Historiker Laonikos Chalkokondyles über die slawischen und baltischen Völker Osteuropas", *Zeitschrift für Slawistik* 11 (1966), 594–608.

Ditten, H., *Der Russland Exkurs des Laonikos Chalkokondyles*, Berlin 1968.

Ditten, H., "Spanien und die Spanier im Spiegel der Geschichtsschreibung des byzantinischen Historikers Laonikos Chalkokondyles (15. Jahrhundert)", *Helikon* 3 (1963), 170–95.

Dölger F., "Politische und geistliche Strömungen im Sterbenden Byzanz", *Jahrbuch der Österreichischen Byzantinischen Gesellschaft* 3 (1954), 1–18.

Dräseke, J., "Kaiser Kantakuzenos' Geschichtswerk", *Neue Jahrbücher für das classische Altertum* 33 (1914), 489–506.

Dräseke, J., "Kantakuzenos' Urteil über Gregoras", *Byzantinische Zeitschrift* 10 (1901), 106–27.

Dräseke, J., "Zu Johannes Kantakuzenos", *Byzantinische Zeitschrift* 9 (1900), 72–84.

Efthymiadis, S./A. Mazarakis, "Questions de chronologie sur Ramon Muntaner (Ch. 234) et Georges Pachymérès (XIII, 27–38): La prise de Phocée et de Thasos en 1307", *Nea Rhome* 5 (2008), 303–21.

Emrich, G., "Michael Kritobulos, der byzantinische Geschichtsschreiber Mehmeds II", *Materialia Turcica* 1 (1975), 35–43.

Failler, A., "Chronologie et composition dans l' Histoire de Georges Pachymère", *Revue des Études Byzantines* 38 (1980), 5–103; 39 (1981), 145–249.

Failler, A., "Chronologie et composition dans l' Histoire de Georges Pachymérès (Livres VII–XIII)", *Revue des Études Byzantines* 48 (1990), 5–87.

Failler, A., "Citations et réminiscences dans l' Histoire de Georges Pachymérès", *Revue des Études Byzantines* 62 (2004), 159–80.

Failler, A., "La tradition manuscrite de l' Histoire de Georges Pachymère (Livres I–VI)", *Revue des Études Byzantines* 37 (1979), 123–220.

Failler, A., "La tradition manuscrite de l' Histoire de Georges Pachymère (Livres VII–XIII)", *Revue des Études Byzantines* 47 (1989), 91–181.

Failler, A., "Le principe de l' économie ecclesiastique vu par Pachymère", *Jahrbuch der Österreichischen Byzantinistik* 32.4 (1982), 287–95.

Failler, A., «Nouvelle note sur la chronologie du règne de Jean Cantacuzène», *Revue des Études Byzantines* 34 (1976), 118–24.

Fatouros, G., "Ein Testimonienapparat zu Nikephoros Gregoras' Byzantina Historia", *Byzantine Studies/Études Byzantines* 1 (1974), 107–46.

Fatouros, G., "Textkritische Beobachtungen zu Johannes Kantakuzenos", *Byzantinoslavica* 37 (1976), 191–93.

Flusin, B., "Predictions et propheties dans l' oeuvre de Doucas", in P. Odorico/P. Agapitos (eds.), *L' ecriture de la memoire. La litterarite de l' historiographie, Actes du IIIe colloque international philologique EPMHNEIA. Nicosie, 6–7–8 Mai 2004* (Dossiers Byzantins, 6), Paris 2006, pp. 353–73.

Gautier, P., "Un récit inédit du siège de Constantinople par les Turcs, 1394–1402", *Revue des Études Byzantines* 23 (1965), 100–17.

Glykatzi-Ahrweiler, H., *L'idéologie politique de l'Empire byzantin*, Paris 1975.

Golitsis, P., "La date de composition de la *Philosophia* de Georges Pachymère et quelques précisisons sur la vie de l' auteur", *Revue des Études Byzantines* 67 (2009), 209–15.

Grecu, V., "Georgios Sphrantzes. Leben und Werk. Makarios Melissenos und sein Werk. Die Ausgabe", *Byzantinoslavica* 26 (1965), 62–73.

Grecu, V., "Kritobulos aus Imbros. Sein wahrer Name. Die Widmungsbriefe. – Die Ausgabe. – Das Geschichstswerk", *Byzantinoslavica* 18 (1957), 1–17.

Grecu, V., "L' épitre dédicatrice de l' historien Critobule à Mohammed II le Vainqueur", *Mélanges d'histoire littéraire et de littératures comparée offerts à Charles Drouhet par ses amis, ses collègues et ses anciens élèves à l'occasion du 30e anniversaire de son enseignement à l'université*, Bucharest 1940, pp. 197–202.

Grecu, V., "Pour une meilleure connaissance de l' historien Doukas", *Mémorial Louis Petit: mélanges d'histoire et d'archéologie byzantines*, Bucharest 1948, pp. 128–41.

Grecu, V., "Zu den Interpolationen im Geschichtswerk des Laonikos Chalkokondyles", *Bulletin de la section historique de l' Académie roumaine* 27 (1946), 92–94.

Guilland, R., *Essai sur Nicephore Grégoras, l' homme et l' oeuvre*, Paris 1926.

Harris, J., "Laonikos Chalkokondyles and the rise of the Ottoman Turks", *Byzantine and Modern Greek Studies* 27 (2003), 153–70.

Heisenberg, A., "Studien zur Textgeschichte des Georgios Akropolites", *Programm des Kgl. Humanistischen Gymnasiums zu Landau*, Landau 1894, 5–55.

Hohlweg, A., "Astronomie und Geschichtsbetrachtung bei Nikephoros Gregoras", in W. Seibt (ed.), *Geschichte und Kultur der Palaiologenzeit. Referate des Internationalen*

Symposions zu Ehren von Herbert Hunger (Wien, 30. November bis 3. Dezember 1994) (Philosophisch-Historische Klasse Denkschriften, 241), Vienna 1996, 51–63.

Hunger, H., *Die hochsprachliche profane Literatur der Byzantiner*, vol. 1, Munich 1978.

Hunger, H., "Thukydides bei Johannes Kantakuzenos. Beobachtungen zur Mimesis", *Jahrbuch der Österreichischen Byzantinistik* 25 (1976), 181–93.

Hunger, H., "Von Wissenschaft und Kunst der frühen Palaiologenzeit", *Jahrbuch der Österreichischen Byzantinischen Gesellschaft* 8 (1959), 123–55.

Ivánka, E., "Der Fall Konstantinopels und das byzantinische Geschichtsdenken", *Jahrbuch der Österreichischen byzantinischen Gesellschaft* 3 (1954), 19–34.

Kaldellis, A., "Historicism in Byzantine Thought and Literature", *Dumbarton Oaks Papers* 61 (2008), 1–24.

Kaldellis, A., "The Date of Laonikos Chalkokondyles' *Histories*", *Greek, Roman and Byzantine Studies* 52 (2012), 111–36.

Kaldellis, A., "The Greek Sources of Laonikos Chalkokondyles' *Histories*", *Greek, Roman and Byzantine Studies* 52 (2012), 738–65.

Kaldellis, A., "The Interpolations in the Histories of Laonikos Chalkokondyles", *Greek, Roman and Byzantine Studies* 52 (2012), 259–83.

Karpozilos A., *Βυζαντινοί ἱστορικοί καὶ χρονογράφοι, Τόμος Β': 8ος–10ος αἰώνας*, Athens 2002.

Kazhdan, A.P., "L' Histoire de Cantacuzène en tant qu' oeuvre littéraire", *Byzantion* 50 (1980), 279–335.

Kazhdan, A.P., "Some questions addressed to the scholars, who believe in the authenticity of Kaminiate's capture of Thessaloniki", *Byzantinische Zeitschrift* 71 (1978), 301–14.

Kiousopoulou, T., *Βασιλεύς ἢ οικονόμος. Πολιτική εξουσία και ιδεολογία πριν την Άλωση*, Athens 2007 (trans. P. Magdalino, *Emperor or Manager: Power and Political Ideology in Byzantium before 1453*, Geneva 2011).

Kiousopoulou, T., "'Η κοινωνικὴ διάσταση τῆς σύγκρουσης ἀνάμεσα στοὺς ἑνωτικοὺς καὶ τοὺς ἀνθενωτικοὺς τὸν 15ο αἰώνα", *Μνήμων* 23 (2001), 25–36.

Kotzabassi, S., "Der Kopist des Geschichtswerkes von Dukas", in F. Berger/C. Bockmann/G. de Gregorio/M.I. Ghisu/ead./B. Noack/ (eds.), *Symbolae Berolinenses. Festschrift für Dieter Harlfinger*, Amsterdam 1993, pp. 307–23.

Kotzabassi, S., "Ist der Kopist des Geschichtswerk von Dukas Dukas selbst?", *Byzantinische Zeitschrift* 96 (2003), 679–83.

Krasavina K., "Mirovozzrenie i social'no-političeskie vzgliady vizantijskogo istorika Duki", *Vizantijskij Vremennik* 34 (1973), 97–111.

Kyritses, D.S., "Η άλωση της Κωνσταντινούπολης και το τέλος του βυζαντινού πολιτισμού", in T. Kiousopoulou (ed.), *1453. Η άλωση της Κωνσταντινούπολης και η μετάβαση από τους μεσαιωνικούς στους νεώτερους χρόνους*, Heraklio 2011, pp. 161–72.

WRITING THE HISTORY OF DECLINE 169

Laiou, A.E., "On political geography: the Black Sea of Pachymeres", in R. Beaton/ C. Roueché (eds.), *The Making of Byzantine History: Studies dedicated to Donald M. Nicol*, Aldershot 1993, pp. 94–121.

Lambakis, S., Γεώργιος Παχυμέρης, πρωτέκδικος καὶ δικααιοφύλαξ: Εἰσαγωγικὸ δοκίμιο, (Ἐθνικὸ Ἵδρυμα Ἐρευνῶν – Μονογραφίες, 5), Athens 2004.

Lambakis, S., "'Ὑπερφυσικὲς δυνάμεις, φυσικὰ φαινόμενα καὶ δεισιδαιμονίες στὴν Ἱστορία τοῦ Γεωργίου Παχυμέρη", Σύμμεικτα 7 (1987), 77–101.

Lampros, S., Παλαιολόγεια καὶ Πελοποννησιακά, vol. 3, Athens 1926; vol. 4, Athens 1930.

Laurent, V., "Les manuscrits de l' Histoire Byzantine de Georges Pachymère", *Byzantion* 5 (1929/30), 129–205.

Loenertz, R., "Ordre et désordre dans les Mémoires de Jean Cantacuzène", *Revue des Études Byzantines* 22 (1964), 222–37.

Macrides, R., "George Akropolites' rhetoric", in E. Jeffreys (ed.), *Rhetoric in Byzantium*, Aldershot 2003, pp. 201–209.

Maisano, R., "Il contributo della tradizione indiretta al testo delle Memorie di Giorgio Sfranze", *Miscellanea filologica*, vol. 1, Salerno 1986, pp. 179–91.

Maisano, R., "Lo storico Giorgio Sfranze dentro e fuori i confini della storia", *Italoellenika: Rivista di cultura greco-moderna* 1 (1988), 111–22.

Maisano, R., "Riconsiderazioni sul testo delle Memorie di Giorgio Sfranze", in U. Criscuolo (ed.), Ταλαρίσκος. *Studia Graeca Antonio Garzya sexagenario a discipulis oblata*, Napoli 1987, pp. 363–401.

Markopoulos, A., "Das Bild des anderen bei Laonikos Chalkokondyles und das Vorbild Herodot", *Jahrbuch der Österreichischen Byzantinistik* 50 (2000), 205–16.

Matschke, K.-P., *Fortschritt und Reaktion in Byzanz. Konstantinopel in der Bürgerkriegsperiode von 1341 bis 1354* (Berliner Byzantinistische Arbeiten, 42), Berlin 1971.

Mavromatis, L., "Les historiens à Byzance: Jean Cantacuzène", *Bulletin Association G. Budè* 33 (1981), 80–88.

Mercati, G., *Notizie di Procoro e Demetrio Cidone, Manuele Caleca e Teodoro Meliteniota ed altri appunti per la storia della teologia e della letteratura bizantina del secolo XIV* (Studi e Testi, 56), Rome 1931.

Miller, T.S., "The Plague in John VI Cantacuzenus and Thucydides", *Greek, Roman and Byzantine Studies* 18 (1976), 385–95.

Miller, W., "The Historians Doukas and Phrantzes", *Journal of Hellenic Studies* 46 (1926), 63–71.

Miller, W., "The Last Athenian Historian: Laonikos Chalkokondyles", *Journal of Hellenic Studies* 42 (1922), 36–49.

Moravcsik, G., *Byzantinoturcica*, 2 vols., Berlin 1958.

Moravcsik, G., "Zur Laonikos-Ausgabe von Darkó", *Byzantinische Zeitschrift* 32 (1932), 478–79.

Nastase D., "La chronique de Jean Chortasménos et le dernier siècle d' historiographie byzantine", *Σύμμεικτα* 8 (1989), 389–404.

Necipoğlu, N., "Constantinopolitan Merchants and the Question of their Attitudes towards Italians and Ottomans in the late Palaeologan Period", in C. Scholz/ G. Makris (eds.), *ΠΟΛΥΠΛΕΥΡΟΣ ΝΟΥΣ, Miscellanea für Peter Schreiner zu seinem 60. Geburtstag* (Byzantinisches Archiv, 19), Munich/Leipzig 2000, pp. 251–63.

Nicol, D.M., *The Last Centuries of Byzantium (1261–1453)*, Cambridge ²1993.

Nicoloudis, N., "Observations on the Possible Sources of Laonikos Chalkokondyles' Demonstrations of Histories", *Βυζαντινά* 17 (1994), 75–82.

Odorico, P., *Jean Caminiatès – Eustathe de Thessalonique – Jean Anagonostès. Thessalonique: chroniques d' une ville prise, textes traduits du grec et présentès*, Toulouse 2005.

Ostrogorsky, G., *History of the Byzantine State*, trans. J. Hussey, Oxford 1968.

Panaino, A., "Gambling with names and games. A curious episode in the Historia Turcobyzantina by Michael Doucas", *Bizantinistica. Rivista di Studi Bizantini e Slavi* 10 (2008), 215–24.

Papadopoulos, I., "Über Maius und Minus des Georgios Sphrantzes", *Byzantinische Zeitschrift* 38 (1938), 323–31.

Papadrianos, J.A., "L' historien byzantin Doukas et les Serbes", *Cyrillomethodianum* 1 (1971), 113–20.

Parisot, V., *Cantacuzène, homme d' état et historien*, Paris 1845.

Petrides, A.K., "Georgios Pachymeres between Ethnography and Narrative: *Συγγραφικαί Ἱστορίαι* 3.3–5", *Greek, Roman and Byzantine Studies* 49 (2009), 295–318.

Reinsch, D.R., "Αὐτοκρατορία καὶ γλῶσσα μετὰ τὴν Ἅλωση: Γεώργιος Ἀμοιρούτζης καὶ Γεώργιος Σφραντζής", in E. Motos Guirao/M. Morfakidis Filactós (eds.), *Κωνσταντινούπολη. 550 χρόνια μετά τήν ἅλωση*, Granada 2006, pp. 121–26.

Reinsch, D.R., "Kritoboulos of Imbros. Learned historian, Ottoman raya and Byzantine patriot", *Zbornik radova Vizantološkog Instituta* 40 (2003), 297–311.

Rödel, B., "Zur Sprache des Laonikos Chalkokondyles und des Kritobulos aus Imbros", in *Programm des kőniglichen humanistischen Gymnasiums Ingolstadt 1904–1905*, Munich 1905, pp. 9–36.

Runciman, S., *The Last Byzantine Renaissance*, Cambridge 1970 (repr. 2008).

Ševčenko, I., "Society and Intellectual Life in the Fourteenth Century", in M. Berza/ E. Stanescu (eds.), *Actes du XIVᵉ Congrès International des Études Byzantines*, vol. 1, Bucharest 1974, pp. 65–92.

Ševčenko, I., "The Decline of Byzantium Seen through the Eyes of its Intellectuals", *Dumbarton Oaks Papers* 15 (1961), 169–86.

Teoteoi, T., "La conception de Jean VI Cantacuzène sur l' État byzantin vue principalement à lumière de son Histoire", *Revue des Études Sud-Est Européennes* 13 (1975), 167–85.

Tinnefeld, F., "Idealizing Self-centered Power Politics in the Memoirs of Emperor John VI Kantakouzenos", in J. Langdon/S.W. Reinert/J. Stanojevich Allen/C.P. Ioannides (eds.), *TO ΕΛΛΗΝΙΚΟΝ: Studies in Honor of Speros Vryonis, Jr.*, vol. 1: *Hellenic Antiquity and Byzantium*, New Rochelle, NY 1993, pp. 397–415.

Vryonis, S., "Laonicus Chalkokondyles and the Ottoman Budget", *International Journal of Middle Eastern Studies* 7 (1976), 423–32.

Weiss, G., *Joannes Kantakuzenos – Aristocrat, Staatsmann, Kaiser und Mönch – in der Gesellschaftsentwicklung von Byzanz im 14. Jahrhundert* (Studien zur Geistesgeschichte des östlichen Europa, 4), Wiesbaden 1969.

Werner, E., "Gesellschaft und Kultur im XIV. Jahrhundert: sozial-ökonomische Fragen", in *Actes du XIVe congrès international des études Byzantines. Bucarest, 6–12 Septembre 1971*, Bucharest 1974, pp. 93–110.

Wifstrand, A., "Laonikos Chalkokondyles, der letzte Athener", *Scripta Minora Regiae Societatis Humaniorum Litterarum Lundensis* 2 (1971–1972), 5–20.

Wurm, H., "Der Codex Monacensis gr. 307a. Ein Beitrag zur Überlieferungsgeschichte des Laonikos Chalkokondyles", *Jahrbuch der Österreichischen Byzantinistik* 44 (1994), 455–62.

Wurm, H., "Die handschriftliche Überlieferung der Ἀποδείξεις Ἱστοριῶν des Laonikos Chalkokondyles", *Jahrbuch der Österreichischen Byzantinistik* 45 (1995), 223–32.

Wurm, H./E. Gamillscheg, "Bemerkungen zu Laonikos Chalkokondyles", *Jahrbuch der Österreichischen Byzantinistik* 42 (1992), 213–19.

Zachariadou, E.A., "Pachymeres on the 'Amourioi' of Kastamonu", *Byzantine and Modern Greek Studies* 3 (1977), 57–70.

CHAPTER 5

Spirituality and Emotion: Poetic Trends in the Palaeologan Period

Ioannis Vassis

1   Poetry and Rhetoric

Byzantine poetry was written on much the same terms as the other literary genres, and, naturally, within the same cultural environment. It has in fact frequently been claimed that the only significant element differentiating poetry from prose is the use of metre, while poetry has been described – admittedly with a fair measure of exaggeration – as versified rhetoric. The Byzantine literati who commonly tried their hand at the composition of poetical texts as well as prose works naturally made use of the rules of rhetoric and figures of speech that they had been taught, in order to praise the emperor and the influential, to lament the death of a distinguished person or to interpret the message of an icon. As well as the use of specific rhythmic and prosodic patterns, however, the choice of the poetic form also entails the employment of other devices, which dictate both a particular mode of syntactic structure and discursive focus and also a manner of handling the subject that is quite different from that of prose composition. In an epigram, for example, the meaning must be compressed in a way that is generally incompatible with the norms of prose rhetoric. By the same token, the use of Homeric language for an encomium or elegy written in hexameters is imposed both by the metre and by the tradition of the genre, and even when the poet is creating new words, he will have to imitate the epic modes of expression. A didactic poem, finally, requires the use of a clearly accentual metre, such as the fifteen-syllable, the so-called political verse, and a relatively simple, occasionally playful, vocabulary, since the aim is to make a lesson or a series of moral precepts as easy and pleasant as possible to understand and commit to memory.[1]

Most Byzantine poems are occasional works, written for a specific circumstance and intended to be used in a specific environment and for a particular purpose. And it is precisely that purpose that in most cases dictated the use of a specific poetic form and linguistic register. Literature in the Byzantine age

---

1   See Lauxtermann, "Byzantine Didactic Poetry", pp. 41–46.

© KONINKLIJKE BRILL NV, LEIDEN, 2023 | DOI:10.1163/9789004527089_007

SPIRITUALITY AND EMOTION   173

plainly had a functional nature far removed from the modern romantic conception of poetry written solely as an expression of personal emotion.

In the Palaeologan period, as indeed was for the most part the case in earlier periods as well, 'learned' poetry (and literature in general) was the product of a small, highly educated élite, closely connected despite the occasional fluctuations within that circle. The public to which this literature was addressed comprised the members of that élite and their powerful patrons, that is, the emperor and his court, the magnates and high-ranking officers of Church and state who had the necessary education.[2]

Literati and intellectuals had the opportunity to show off their skill in the art of oration and to present their literary works *viva voce* before an audience both at public court ceremonies and at what were known as *theatra*, assemblies of confrères that usually took the form of reading circles with common aesthetic and ideological aspirations. In these cases the poetic texts, which are what concern us here, gave the public attending the performance an aural and visual experience that must often have been akin to that of a theatrical performance as we understand it today.[3]

2   Poetry for the Court and the Powerful Aristocracy

Some court poems were clearly composed to be performed at an imperial ceremony. One such case was the *prokypsis*, a ceremony of the later Byzantine period that took place twice a year, on Christmas Eve and at Epiphany.[4] The emperor, often accompanied by his son, the co-emperor, and other relatives, stood on a high wooden platform, concealed by a curtain, which was suddenly and dramatically drawn aside to reveal him in a blaze of artificial light. The court, the people and the army greeted him with acclamations accompanied by musical instruments, while hymns of praise written especially for the occasion were sung, likening the appearance of the monarch to the rising of

---

2 See Ševčenko, "The Palaeologan Renaissance", pp. 144–71; Matschke/Tinnefeld, *Die Gesellschaft im späten Byzanz*, pp. 221–385.

3 Cf. Medvedev, "The So-called θέατρα as a Form of Communication"; Marciniak, "Byzantine Theatron – A Place of Performance?"; Toth, "Rhetorical Theatron in Late Byzantium"; Gaul, *Thomas Magistros und die spätbyzantinische Sophistik*, pp. 17–61; idem, "Performative Reading".

4 See Heisenberg, "Aus der Geschichte und Literatur der Palaiologenzeit", pp. 85–132; Angelov, *Imperial Ideology and Political Thought in Byzantium*, pp. 41–45. The *prokypsis* may have evolved from the impressive ceremonial appearance of the emperor in the imperial lodge at the Hippodrome; the roots of the ceremony probably date back to the late 12th century and the reign of Manuel I Komnenos, see Jeffreys, M., "The Comnenian Prokypsis".

the sun. The scholar-monk and teacher Manuel-Maximos Holobolos (*c.*1245–1310/14) is the best known of the poets who composed panegyrics to be sung at this ceremony. Twenty of his poems praising the emperors Michael VIII and Andronikos II Palaiologos have survived, written in a highbrow linguistic register in fifteen-syllable verse, a metre traditionally used from at least the 10th century for hymns sung at court ceremonies.[5] These poems have a fairly standard structure and develop familiar ideological motifs, centring on the theme of the emperor-as-sun, whose benevolent activity fills his subjects with light and showers them with blessings while that same fiery splendour scorches and crushes the enemies of the state. The poet skilfully combines the stereotypical sun or light motifs, familiar from earlier court poetry and particularly from that of the Comnenian period (when its principal exponent was Theodore Prodromos), with the theme of the feast day's celebration, that is, the birth and the epiphany of Christ, whose earthly imitation and representative the emperor was considered to be.[6]

A great number of poems were written to celebrate important events in the life of the emperor and his family: births, coronations, nuptials, expeditions, military triumphs, deaths. These occasional works, encomiastic or elegiac, are usually written in fifteen-syllable verse, and were not necessarily intended to be sung. Most of them must have been intended for public performance and may have been presented in written form to the person they celebrated. Examples include a panegyric in 13 quatrains on the birth of John V Palaiologos (1332), son of Andronikos III,[7] composed by Manuel Philes, the most prolific poet of the Palaeologan period.[8] Circa 1366 this same John, who by then had ascended the throne, became the subject of a long panegyric by John Katakalon, deacon of Adrianople.[9] Some political verses on the feasts of Christmas and the Epiphany, probably written for performance during the ceremony of the *prokypsis*, are also the work of Manuel Philes, although it is not clear which emperor they praise.[10] Philes also wrote a poem celebrating the entry of Andronikos III (1328–1341) into Constantinople and his assumption of power after the fall of his grandfather in May 1328, imitating the style and

---

5   Boissonade, *Anecdota graeca*, vol. 5, pp. 159–82 (19 poems); Treu, "Manuel Holobolos", pp. 546–47 (1 poem).

6   See Hörandner, *Theodoros Prodromos*, pp. 89–108 and idem, "Court poetry: questions of motifs", pp. 78–79.

7   Manuel Philes, *Panegyrikos*, ed. Holzinger, pp. 385–86.

8   See Kubina, *Die enkomiastische Dichtung des Manuel Philes*.

9   *Patrologia Graeca*, vol. 158, cols. 961–70 (414 lines).

10   Manuel Philes, *Poems*, F 210, ed. Miller, vol. 1, pp. 379–80 (16 lines).

SPIRITUALITY AND EMOTION 175

metre of Theodore Prodromos,[11] and, sometime in the 1320s, a long (roughly a thousand lines) dramatic composition on his patron and protector the *megas domestikos* (and later emperor) John Kantakouzenos.[12] On the fringes of the empire, Stephen Sgouropoulos, *protonotarios* at the court of Trebizond, dedicated two panegyrics to the Emperors John II (1280–1297) and Alexios II (1297–1330),[13] following the tradition of the imperial heartland. Finally, it is striking that even after the Fall of Constantinople George Amiroutzes (*c.*1400–after 1469) should remain faithful to the same tradition and compose encomiastic verses for Sultan Mehmed the Conqueror, whom he saw as continuing the long and glorious line of Byzantine emperors.[14]

Laments for the deaths of emperors and members of the imperial family are the subject of numerous elegies, written to be declaimed either at the funeral (epitaphs) or at a memorial service honouring the memory of the deceased and offering words of consolation to the family (monodies). In these poems the predominant theme, apart from the expected praises for the virtues of the deceased, is the uncertainty of human life; they frequently observe that the grave is the inevitable end even for those who had the good fortune, albeit fleeting, to enjoy wealth and high office. Worthy of mention here are also the poems composed in a variety of metres by prominent state officials like Nikephoros Choumnos and Theodore Metochites, and court poet Manuel Philes.

Nikephoros Choumnos (*c.*1250/55–1327), *mesazon*, *mystikos* and head of the imperial secretariat, statesman and prolific writer, composed three simple and unaffected poems in fifteen-syllable verse on the death of Michael IX Palaiologos († 12 October 1320), son and co-emperor of Andronikos II.[15]

His political and literary adversary Theodore Metochites also wrote epitaphs, but in pretentious archaic hexameters, for Michael IX, for the empress Irene-Yolanda of Montferrat († 1317), the second wife of Andronikos II, and for the caesar John Palaiologos († 1326), nephew of Andronikos II and husband

---

11   Manuel Philes, *Historical Poems*, ed. Gedeon, pp. 219–20 (173 lines).
12   Manuel Philes, *Poems*, F 1, ed. Miller, vol. 1, pp. 143–84.
13   Stephen Sgouropoulos, *Poems*, ed. Papadopoulos-Kerameus, vol. 1, pp. 434–37. His other six poems are written in Anacreontic verse (trochaic octasyllable). Two of them offer advice to the emperor, while in the other four the poet formulates personal requests (ibid., ed. Papadopoulos-Kerameus, pp. 431–34, and Papatheodorides, "Ἀνέκδοτοι στίχοι", pp. 264–82).
14   George Amiroutzes, *Poems*, ed. Janssens/Van Deun, pp. 314–18.
15   Nikephoros Choumnos, *Poems*, ed. Martini, pp. 124–29. By contrast, an anonymous monody on the same emperor, also in fifteen-syllable verse but written in a much more elevated style, is evidently the work of a person perfectly familiar with both poetic diction and the Byzantine tradition in this genre. *Poem for the death of Michael IX Palaiologos*, ed. Reinsch, pp. 373–75.

of Metochites' daughter Irene.[16] The tone of this last work is very personal, for it is far more a tragic narration of the poet's own woes and his daughter's fate than a celebration of the virtues of the deceased. Manuel Philes dedicated a monody to the caesar John Palaiologos,[17] and also wrote a much longer poem, of 607 dodecasyllables, on the death of the Despot John Palaiologos († 1307), firstborn son of Andronikos II and Irene-Yolanda of Montferrat.[18] John died without issue at the age of 21, four years after his marriage to Irene-Eulogia Choumnaina, the daughter of Nikephoros Choumnos. Rejecting the standard format, Philes gave this monody a theatrical character with roles assigned to four *dramatis personae*, the bereaved father, mother, brother and widow, who do not speak among themselves but take up the thread in turn, addressing the deceased and lamenting his death. The poet appears at the beginning of the poem as attendant, speaking a prologue to the 'drama'. This unconventional monody concludes with an epigram appropriate for use as an epitaph on the Despot's grave.

John Chortasmenos (c.1370–1431), notary in the patriarchal chancery, bibliophile, teacher, and eventually Metropolitan of Selybria (1425–1430), composed a long three-part monody (a prose passage between a section in dodecasyllable and one in fifteen-syllable verse) on the death of Andrew Asan and his son Manuel,[19] incorporating lines from poems by Theodore Prodromos almost word-for-word.[20] This work shares certain morphological features with Philes' monody, save that here Manuel's mother speaks with her son, while the poet remains absent until the final brief conclusion.

Remarkably, in addition to the monodies for the loss of a prominent member of the court or the aristocracy, there have also survived two anonymous verse laments for the fall of Thessaloniki, the empire's second most important city, to the Turks in 1430. Although clearly aspiring to emulate the classicizing trend of the age, they are written in clumsy hexameters and give the impression of being mere exercises.[21]

---

16 Theodore Metochites, *Poems*, ed. Polemis, pp. 139–75 (Theodore Metochites, *Poems*, trans. Polemis, pp. 171–201).

17 Manuel Philes, *Poems*, 96, ed. Martini, pp. 137–41.

18 Manuel Philes, *Poems*, F 213, ed. Miller, vol. 1, pp. 388–414; see Gaul, "Embedded dialogues and dialogical voices", pp. 191–93; Kubina, *Die enkomiastische Dichtung des Manuel Philes*, pp. 271–84. For Philes' epitaphs generally see Papadogiannakis, *Studien zu den Epitaphien des Manuel Philes*. For the prose epitaphs and monodies for John Palaiologos see Taxidis, "Les monodies et les oraisons funèbres" (for the monody by Philes see ibid., p. 273).

19 Ed. Hunger, *Johannes Chortasmenos*, pp. 227–37.

20 See Hörandner, "Musterautoren und ihre Nachahmer", p. 212.

21 Ed. Lampros, "Τρεῖς ἀνέκδοτοι μονῳδίαι", pp. 372–90.

SPIRITUALITY AND EMOTION

3   Manuel Philes and the Art of the Epigram

The Byzantines were particularly fond of the epigram, the relatively brief and compact form that in antiquity was chiefly intended for use in inscriptions, and they systematically cultivated it in all its varieties (funerary, votive, satirical, etc.), without constraints of length and with the religious epigram as the predominant type.[22] Manuel Philes (*c.*1270–*c.*1335) is the most representative and certainly the most prolific poet of the Palaeologan period, both for the extent and for the variety of his work. About 25,000 lines[23] are preserved, in about 150 manuscripts, in which he is frequently described as 'most wise and most learned', an indication of the impact of his work and of the esteem in which he was held as a poet, both by his contemporaries and long afterwards.

Manuel Philes came from Asia Minor. He had married, although his wife had died young, and was the father of two children. He took part as imperial envoy in three embassies, to southern Russia (1297), to Persia (1304) and to Georgia (1305/6), but does not appear ever to have had a permanent civil service position.[24] He was thus almost always dependent for the necessities of life on the favour of the emperor, the support of prosperous friends, and commissions from wealthy patrons. Apart from the encomiastic works he addressed to them, they were also the recipients of innumerable petitions,[25] often in the form of laconic verse letters[26] asking them to supply some need (e.g., food for himself, hay for his animals, a coat)[27] or thanking them for a generous gift he had received in return for his offerings of complimentary verse.

Philes composed an astonishing number of epigrams, of remarkable diversity: on works of art and architecture (icons and monumental paintings,

---

22   See e.g. Rhoby, *Byzantinische Epigramme auf Fresken und Mosaiken*, pp. 37–47 ("Das byzantinische Epigramm") and id., "The Epigram in Byzantium".

23   Most of his poems have been edited by Miller, *Manuelis Philae carmina*, 2 vols., and Martini, *Manuelis Philae carmina inedita* (for the other editions see Stickler, *Manuel Philes und seine Psalmenmetaphrase*, pp. 6–9). A more recent (critical) edition of 119 epigrams: Braounou-Pietsch, *Beseelte Bilder*, pp. 57–199. It is estimated that some 5,000 lines still remain unpublished.

24   About the life of Philes see Stickler, *Manuel Philes und seine Psalmenmetaphrase*, pp. 10–36.

25   See Kubina, "Manuel Philes – A Begging Poet?"; Bazzani, "The Art of Requesting". The phenomenon of the so-called beggar poets, who depended for their existence on the support of powerful patrons, is seen mainly in the 12th century with John Tzetzes, Theodore Prodromos and 'Manganeios' Prodromos, Michael Glycas, Ptochoprodromos, and others, see Kulhánková, "Die byzantinische Betteldichtung".

26   Cf. Kubina, "Functions of Letters in Verse and Prose", pp. 80–88.

27   For the recurrent motif of the coat, which in Philes appears quite often, see Kulhánková, "Ich bin auch eines schicken Mantels wert", pp. 196–99.

reliquary caskets, palaces, churches, monasteries, funerary chapels, gravestones, fountains), textiles of every sort, and liturgical vessels.[28] While some of these epigrams can fairly certainly be seen as simply describing a scene in an icon[29] or meditating upon its religious content,[30] most of them are votive verses, intended to be engraved or painted on an object and composed at the behest of distinguished members of the court and the aristocracy, to express the personal devotion of the donor, to declare their social status and perpetuate their name, or to honour the memory of a relative in grand style.[31] One such epigram is carved on the cornice running around the exterior wall of the chapel Maria-Martha built in the Pammakaristos Monastery in Constantinople to house the tomb of her husband, the military governor Michael Glabas Tarchaneiotes.[32] Epigrams of this sort were also written by many other poets of the period, among them Nikephoros Kallistou Xanthopoulos and the scholar-monk Manuel-Maximos Planoudes, who in 1299/1301 compiled an important collection of Greek epigrams in 7 books, selected from the collection of Constantine Kephalas (9th c.). Planoudes' *Anthology* revived interest in the tradition of the genre and served as a source of inspiration for many epigrammatists.[33]

Some of Philes' finest epigrams are those on the supernatural dimension of the icon of a holy figure. More than any other, the poet makes use of the motif of the 'living image', which is of course familiar from the epigrams of Hellenistic and Late Antiquity, but he views the icon first and foremost as a devotional object and secondarily as a work of art. He is less interested in praising the skill of the artist than in exalting the religious function of the icon, which gives form to the transcendental, suggesting to the person who sees it and reads the accompanying inscription a particular manner of conceiving the

---

28   See Rhoby, "Poetry on commission", pp. 276–84.

29   One characteristic example is a poem (Manuel Philes, *Poems*, E 106, ed. Miller, vol. 1, pp. 46–50) describing an icon of the Prophet Elijah which Philes offered to a cleric or monk (see Baseu-Barabas, "Die Speisung des Elias durch den Raben").

30   See for example an epigram on an icon of the Virgin Mary (Manuel Philes, *Poems*, ed. Martini, pp. 31–32) and the analysis by Takács, "Manuel Philes' Meditation on an Icon".

31   For the votive epigrams of Philes see Talbot, "Epigrams of Manuel Philes on the Theotokos tes Peges", and ead., "Epigrams in Context".

32   Manuel Philes, *Poems*, E 223, ed. Miller, vol. 1, pp. 117–18; see Talbot, "Epigrams in Context", pp. 77–79.

33   See Cameron, *The Greek Anthology*, pp. 75–77; Pietsch-Braounou, "Ein Aspekt der Rezeption der *Anthologia Planudea*".

SPIRITUALITY AND EMOTION

unseen and responding emotionally to the seen.[34] For example, in an epigram on an icon of the Archangel Michael the poet stresses that art is worthy of admiration not when it represents, but when it has the power to conjure up the immaterial substance of the figure depicted:

Εἰ σωμάτων μίμησιν ἡ τέχνη γράφει,
τοῦτο γραφική, τοῦτο καὶ φύσιν ἔχον·
καινὸν γὰρ οὐδὲν ζωγραφεῖν ὕλην ὕλῃ·
ὅταν δὲ καὶ νοῦν καὶ πυρὸς φλόγα γράφῃ
καὶ πνεῦμα καὶ φῶς ἐν βραχεῖ περιγράφῃ,
τέρας βλέπων θαύμαζε τὴν τέχνην, ξένε.

If art represents the likeness of bodies,
this is painting, this is a natural thing;
there is nothing extraordinary in representing matter with another [kind
    of] matter.
But when the art shows the mind, and the flame,
and includes the spirit and the light in a close image,
then admire the art, stranger, because you see something supernatural.[35]

The epigrams Philes composed for use as a frontispiece before the title of a book or to introduce several chapters of a work also constitute a substantial part of his œuvre: examples include the epigrams he wrote for the 45 orations of Gregory of Nazianzos and for the 30 chapters of St. John Climacus's ascetic work.[36] He also composed a number of metrical prefaces for orations to be given in an ecclesiastical setting, which will be discussed later, as well as a host of commissioned epitaphs.[37]

Apart from the occasional deliberate recycling of a poem, adapted as necessary to the new requirements in such an extensive body of work as Philes', one would not be surprised to find a fair number of repetitions. As the epigrams

---

34   See Manuel Philes, *Poems*, ed. Braounou-Pietsch, pp. 33–52. The motif of the 'living image' also appears at this time in 22 epigrams of Nikephoros Kallistou Xanthopoulos, who may have been influenced by Philes. See ibid., ed. Braounou-Pietsch, pp. 229–34.

35   Manuel Philes, *Poems*, ed. Braounou-Pietsch, p. 66; trans. Oikonomides "The Holy Icon as an Asset", p. 37 (adapted).

36   Manuel Philes, *Poems*, App. 7.1–45, ed. Miller, vol. 2, pp. 340–52; ibid., F 211, vol. 1, pp. 380–88.

37   See Brooks, "Poetry and female patronage", and Papadogiannakis, *Studien zu den Epitaphien des Manuel Philes*.

treating the same subject in a variety of ways clearly show, however, he lacks neither invention nor skill; indeed, a demonstration of proficiency may perhaps be one of the characteristic features of his poetry, as he seeks to show that he is a master of the models of each genre and can imitate them expertly, while at the same time introducing small but significant variations. Philes nonetheless sometimes gives the impression that he is copying himself, when he resorts to familiar images, standard motifs and, more commonly, ready-made expressions, standard lines and half-lines,[38] either drawn from his own poetic idiolect or borrowed from the long Byzantine tradition of poetry in dodecasyllable,[39] with which he was certainly thoroughly acquainted. His style is over-elaborate, which may be why he is sometimes obscure. This notwithstanding, no one can deny that Philes, a poet conscious and proud of his intellectual achievements, had not only an incomparable mastery of metre and rhythm but also a creative spirit,[40] a lyrical voice and an elegance that are particularly evident in the relatively short form of the votive or ekphrastic epigram.[41] When the entire body of his work has been critically edited and studied in depth, it will reveal all the different facets of a poet who at the very least is interesting and worthy of attention.

4 Theodore Metochites: Autobiography or Introspection?

This was an age in which a number of emperors, patriarchs and men of letters, among them Michael VIII Palaiologos, Patriarch Gregory II of Cyprus and the teacher-monk Joseph Rhakendytes,[42] wrote prose accounts of their lives. There were, however, others who turned to poetic forms and, particularly, to the time-tested hexameter to speak of important moments in their lives or to express thoughts and feelings about a critical turn of events, in an attempt to ponder the uncertainty of human affairs and the reasons for it.

---

38 See Papadogiannakis, *Studien zu den Epitaphien des Manuel Philes*, pp. 60–69.
39 The dodecasyllable gradually evolved from the ancient iambic trimeter. It received its final form in the hands of George Pisides (7th c.), and thereafter dominated Byzantine poetry almost exclusively, especially for epigrams. See Maas, "Der byzantinische Zwölfsilber"; Rhoby, "Vom jambischen Trimeter zum byzantinischen Zwölfsilber"; Lauxtermann, *Byzantine Poetry*, 338–42 and 357–59; Bernard, "Rhythm in the Byzantine Dodecasyllable".
40 On Philes' sophisticated poetic technique see e.g. Bazzani, "A Poem of Philes", pp. 68–69.
41 For example, a 19-line epigram (Manuel Philes, *Poems*, ed. Miller, vol. 1, pp. 65–66) describing an icon of the Virgin and Child in a heavenly garden has been fairly called a "minor lyrical pearl", see Tinnefeld, "Die Ikone in Textzeugnissen des späten Byzanz", pp. 301–02.
42 See chapter 3 in this volume.

SPIRITUALITY AND EMOTION 181

In his old age George Pachymeres (1242–c.1310), historian and patriarchal official, wrote a long autobiographical poem in 9 parts[43] called "τὰ καθ' ἑαυτόν" ("on himself"), of which only a few brief sententious passages survive. The length and nature of these fragments, however, which include the inevitable lament over the vanity of human existence, is such that no safe conclusions can be drawn as to the character of the work as a whole.

A similar tactic was used by Theodore Metochites (1270–1332), one of the most distinguished political and intellectual figures of the early Palaeologan revival under Andronikos II.[44] Among the finest works of his rich and diverse literary œuvre are twenty long poems (totalling 9,000 lines) in hexameters, covering a variety of genres: funerary verses, panegyrics for saints, epistles to friends and relatives, etc. Two of these, despite being of a religious nature and concerning the Chora Monastery, which he restored and rebuilt magnificently (1315/16), contain long autobiographical passages, in which he recalls his literary career, his rise to the highest office and his role in the administration of the empire,[45] and reflects on his perpetual endeavour to combine the active life of the statesman with the contemplative life of the devoted scholar – a condition not easily achieved but which, if attained, says Metochites, assures moral satisfaction and mental equilibrium. Seven other poems,[46] addressed to himself in imitation of Gregory of Nazianzos, at least as regards the choice of form and the tendency towards self-introspection, are clearly autobiographical in intent although they do not narrate his life in an historical perspective. Four of these were written following his return to Constantinople after a two-year exile (1330) to relieve and assuage the pain of his fall from high office: he had been *megas logothetes* but was exiled when Andronikos II Palaiologos was forced to yield his throne to his grandson Andronikos III (1328). The envy that menaces human happiness, the uncertainty of life, the unexpected shifts of fortune and the attempt of the enlightened mind to come to terms with inescapable destiny are some of the principal themes of these poems.

Metochites uses a sophisticated and highly personal diction that, in addition to the various Ionian and Doric types echoing Homer and Pindar, also

---

43 Ed. Detorakis, "Ἀνέκδοτα ποιήματα τοῦ Γεωργίου Παχυμέρη", pp. 299–307.

44 For Metochites see generally Ševčenko, "Theodore Metochites, the Chora, and the Intellectual Trends of his Time"; de Vries-van der Velden, *Théodore Métochite*.

45 Theodore Metochites, *Poems*, ed. Polemis, pp. 5–73 (Theodore Metochites, *Poems*, trans. Polemis, pp. 47–111); see Hinterberger, "Studien zu Theodoros Metochites", pp. 289–92, 302–19.

46 Theodore Metochites, *Poems*, 14–20, ed. Polemis, pp. 249–335 (Theodore Metochites, *Poems*, trans. Polemis, pp. 265–336); see Hinterberger, *Autobiographische Traditionen*, pp. 72–73, and idem, "Studien zu Theodoros Metochites", passim.

contains a wealth of neologisms. His linguistic and stylistic peculiarities and creative handling of classical models are largely a consequence of his desire to differentiate himself from the pack and create something new. From this point of view Metochites was an innovative poet, although his verses won no approval from his peers, perhaps in part because of the well-known Byzantine aversion to any innovation, to anything that diverged perceptibly from the traditional. Nor, however, has modern scholarship considered his poems as a worthy artistic achievement: his writing has been described as "cerebral" and "devoid of feeling",[47] and his hexameters "clumsy" because they do not adhere rigorously to the rules of prosody.

In Venetian-ruled Crete, two poets – Stephen Sachlikes (c.1331/32–after 1391)[48] and Leonardos Dellaportas (c.1330–1419/20)[49] – would also insert autobiographical elements into poems composed for another reason, written in the vernacular in fifteen-syllable verse, the former, in fact, using rhyme for the first time in Greek poetry.[50] Prosperous townsmen both, they each spent a period in prison, where they wrote their autobiographical works. Sachlikes is the bolder and more obviously influenced by the Italian literature of the early Renaissance, while Dellaportas is more conservative and retains closer ties with Byzantine tradition.

5 Poetry in the Service of the Church

5.1 Hymnography

Poetry served the liturgy of the Church from its early days, as original verse and new musical forms were invented to strengthen and exalt the religious sentiment of the faithful.[51] The hymnography of the Palaeologan period, however, was dominated by convention, conformity, and imitation of the great models of the past: the age of the composers of the great canons (8th–9th c.) was long gone and the Church had all the hymns it needed, its liturgical books having been more or less fully codified by the 11th–12th century. Monks, churchmen

---

47 Ševčenko, "The Palaeologan Renaissance", p. 147. For the language and metre of Metochites' poems see now, Theodore Metochites, *Poems*, ed. Polemis, pp. LX–LXXV.

48 Stephen Sachlikes, *Poems*, eds. Mavromatis/Panayotakis. See Holton, *Literature and society*, pp. 51–55.

49 Leonardos Dellaportas, *Poems*, ed. Manoussakas. See Holton, *Literature and society*, pp. 56–58.

50 See Luciani, "Autobiografismo e tradizione"; Hinterberger, *Autobiographische Traditionen*, pp. 73–74.

51 See e.g., Giannouli, "Hymn Writing in Byzantium".

SPIRITUALITY AND EMOTION   183

and literati nonetheless continued throughout the Palaeologan period to compose hymns to honour the memory of various saints or eminent hierarchs of
their day. Manuel Philes, for example, wrote a canon to thank St. Nicholas for
his help at a difficult juncture in his life,[52] and Theoktistos Stoudites composed
eleven canons praising Patriarch Athanasios I (1289–1293 and 1303–1309),[53]
two of them in a (prosodically imperfect) iambic metre imitating St. John
of Damascus. Texts for hymns were also written by Ignatios Vatopedinos,
Manuel-Maximos Holobolos (second half of the 13th c.), Maximos Planoudes
(c.1255–c.1305), Nikephoros Kallistou Xanthopoulos (c.1268/74–post 1328) and
Matthew Blastares (d. post 1348).[54]

5.2   Metrical Prefaces for Public Performance

Liturgical practice was also served by other types of poetry, usually written in
dodecasyllable, that was not intended to be sung. The first half of the 14th century witnessed the blossoming of a particular category of poems that had first
appeared in the middle of the 12th century. These were metrical prefaces to
be recited before the reading of homilies and hagiographical texts, especially
panegyrics for saints, in the context of a mass.[55] The recital of such a poem
was evidently intended to attract the attention of the audience and to introduce it somewhat more formally into the theme and content of the homily or
Vita it was about to hear, taking care at the same time to lavish due praise on
the author of the text and the saint to whom it was dedicated. Such prefaces
were written by a considerable number of poets and men of letters, some well-
known and others less so, among them first and foremost Manuel Philes,[56]
but also including Manuel-Maximos Holobolos and Nikephoros Kallistou
Xanthopoulos in Constantinople and Andrew Libadenos in Trebizond.

5.3   Metrical Calendars

Following a tradition introduced by Christophoros Mytilenaios (11th c.) and
successfully continued by Theodore Prodromos (12th c.), metrical calendars[57]
in classical metres, that is, iambic couplets and/or single-line epigrams in hexameters on the saints and feasts for the whole Church year were written in

---

52   Manuel Philes, *Kanon on Saint Nicholas*, ed. Antonopoulou, pp. 206–13.
53   Theoktistos Stoudites, *Kanons*, ed. Afentoulidou-Leitgob, pp. 165–227.
54   Paschos, Ὁ Ματθαῖος Βλάσταρης καὶ τὸ ὑμνογραφικὸν ἔργον του, and idem, Ἅπαντα τὰ ὑμνογρα-
      φικὰ τοῦ Ματθαίου Βλάσταρη.
55   See Antonopoulou, "On the Reception of Homilies".
56   See Antonopoulou, ibid., pp. 68–74.
57   See Darrouzès, "Les calendriers byzantins en vers"; Efthymiadis, "Greek Byzantine
      Hagiography in Verse", pp. 163–64.

this period by a number of learned churchmen and scholars, such as Manuel-Matthew Gabalas, Metropolitan of Ephesos (1271/2–1355/60),[58] the Metropolitan of Crete Nikephoros Moschopoulos (1285–1311/12),[59] John Chortasmenos, notary in the patriarchal chancery and later Metropolitan of Selymbria (c.1370–1431),[60] and, finally, the Cretan scholar and prolific copyist Michael Apostoles (c.1420–1478).[61] These late Byzantine calendars are usually not complete (or at least no complete ones have survived), and therefore may have been, like the one composed by Mytilenaios and incorporated into the liturgical books (*menaia*) of the Church, written to supplement existing collections or enrich them with new variations, possibly to meet the needs of a specific bishopric. Among the finest of these are the 133 five-line epigrams composed by Michael Apostoles, which depart from tradition in that they contain, in addition to a pair of dodecasyllables, a hexameter and an elegiac couplet and are clearly addressed to a well-educated public with interests differing from those of the average church-goer. Another work usually assigned to the genre of metrical calendars is an unusual synaxarion by Nikephoros Kallistou Xanthopoulos,[62] in which 14–17 dodecasyllables are dedicated to the principal saints of each month. Although presumably composed as an aide-memoire for feast days, its succinctness led to its being used to accompany miniatures of saints on (two surviving) illuminated manuscripts.

5.4   *Poetry in the Service of Polemic Theology*

As has been so astutely observed, "the really passionate writing of the fourteenth century was still reserved for the religious controversies, especially that between the Palamites and the anti-Palamites".[63] The Hesychast controversy, a cultural and religious crisis which shook Byzantine society in the 1340s, arose over the divine light of the Transfiguration of Christ.[64] Gregory Palamas and the hesychast monks held that this light was uncreated, while the monk Barlaam of Seminara, in Calabria, and his followers insisted that it was created, arguing that the only uncreated energies of the Father are the Son and the Holy Spirit.

---

58   Matthew of Ephesos (Manuel Gabalas), *Epigrams*, ed. Reinsch, pp. 53–54 (only 8 epigrams survive, on saints commemorated in the month of October).

59   Nikephoros Moschopoulos, *Metrical calendar*, ed. Papaeliopoulou-Photopoulou, pp. 199–228 (couplets for the saints commemorated in October, November and part of December).

60   John Chortasmenos, *Poems*, ed. Hunger, pp. 183–213.

61   Michael Apostoles, *Metrical calendar*, ed. Laourdas, pp. 174–202.

62   Ed. Stefec, "Die Synaxarverse des Nikephoros Xanthopoulos", pp. 154–59.

63   Ševčenko, "The Palaeologan Renaissance", p. 165.

64   See e.g. Russell, "The Hesychast controversy" and chapter 9 in this volume.

SPIRITUALITY AND EMOTION

Two learned monks used verse as well as prose to argue their positions in the matter, one in support of the Palamite doctrine and the other against it. The first volley came from Gregory Akindynos (*c*.1300–*c*.1348), who in 1342 wrote a 509-line poem[65] attacking Palamas and his 'heretical' teachings on the divine energies. He was encouraged in his anti-Palamite polemics by Patriarch John XIV Kalekas, who sought to equate Hesychasm with a political movement in favour of John VI Kantakouzenos during the civil war (1341–47) between the latter and John V Palaiologos.

Akindynos' polemic was swiftly answered by his erstwhile friend, the monk David Dishypatos, with a 600-line poem[66] composed at the urging of an acquaintance and before – by his own avowal – he had even read the work in question or fully grasped his adversary's theological positions. In it he charged Akindynos with couching his pamphlet in an agreeable verse form, the better to influence his young followers. Using exactly the same weapon (and possibly addressing the same audience) Dishypatos presented the basic positions of the Hesychasts, who, he emphasised, conceived of the uncreated light as a divine energy that is not identical with its substance but through contemplation can lead to a mystic communion with God.

One final group of works that may be included in this category are three short poems on the light of the Transfiguration, written by Alexios Lampenos after the victorious end of the Hesychast conflict (1351) in praise of Gregory Palamas, then Archbishop of Thessaloniki, whom he hails as a new St. John Chrysostom.[67]

6 Poetry for Teaching Purposes

6.1 *Didactic and Admonitory Poems*

The poetic form had been used for teaching purposes since the time of Hesiod. The tradition was maintained through Late Antiquity (Dionysius Periegetes, Oppian) and descended to the Byzantines, who preferred other metres to the hexameter, and especially the political verse. The supreme representative of the genre was Michael Psellos, who in the 11th century treated a variety of subjects in verse, from grammar and rhetoric to law and medicine, usually at the bidding of the emperor for the education of the young heir to the

---

65   *Patrologia Graeca*, vol. 150, cols. 843–62.

66   David Dishypatos, *Poem on Akindynos*, ed. Browning, pp. 723–39; see Beyer, "David Disypatos", pp. 124–25.

67   Alexios Lampenos, *Poem on the Thaborian Light*, ed. Gedeon.

throne.[68] The chief continuator of this tradition in the 12th century was John Tzetzes. The Palaeologan age produced a considerable body of didactic and admonitory verse, in poems of varying length. The most characteristic exponent of the genre was Manuel Philes, who wrote a long poem on the properties of animals[69] (drawing his material chiefly from Aelian's *De natura animalium*),[70] in which he discussed different species of birds, land animals and fish, from the greatest to the least (from the eagle to the bee, from the lion to the spider, from the whale to the anchovy), highlighting each one's most curious features. In another four shorter poems he dealt with certain kinds of plants (wheat, grape, rose, pomegranate),[71] while in yet another he described an elephant.[72] In all likelihood these poems were all addressed to the young co-emperor Michael IX Palaiologos; indeed, in the shorter ones he is quite clearly seeking to stress the properties of the elephant and the plants that suggest the qualities of the ideal prince.[73]

Another poet who seems to have pursued didactic aims was Nikephoros Kallistou Xanthopoulos, who composed in dodecasyllable concise accounts of a multitude of topics, primarily religious, presumably so they could be more easily committed to memory by his young students or anyone else who was interested. He devoted three poems to a synopsis of the historical books of the Old Testament, from *Genesis* to the Fourth Book of *Maccabees*, and then completed the history of the Jews, up to Titus' conquest of Jerusalem, using Flavius Josephus and John Zonaras as his source.[74] He also attempted a somewhat odd verse summary of the New Testament, recounting the genealogy, the miracles and the parables of Christ and enumerating memorable persons

---

68 See Hörandner, "The Byzantine Didactic Poem"; Lauxtermann, "Byzantine Didactic Poetry"; Hörandner, "Teaching with verse in Byzantium".

69 Manuel Philes, *On the Properties of Animals*, eds. Lehrs/Dübner, pp. 1–48 (1,692 dodecasyllables). Another 323 somewhat clumsily composed lines were later added to the poem by the highly prolific copyist Angelos Vergikios (16th c.). These interpolations are indicated in the above edition by square brackets.

70 See Kindstrand, "Manuel Philes' Use of Aelian's *De natura animalium*"; Capponi, "Eliano fonte di Phile".

71 Manuel Philes, *On Plants*, eds. Lehrs/Dübner, pp. 57–64 (365 lines).

72 Manuel Philes, *On the Elephant*, eds. Lehrs/Dübner, pp. 49–56 (381 lines). Two more of his poems (ibid., 65–67), on the subject of the silkworm, appear at first glance to be didactic works but are really a request to some powerful friend for a silk garment.

73 On the sociocultural background and the representations of imperial power in Philes' poem on animals, see Leonte, "... For I have brought to you the fugitive animals of the desert".

74 *Patrologia Graeca*, vol. 147, cols. 605–24 (1,016 lines), 623–32 (484 lines), and 601–06 (158 lines). See Berger, "Nikephoros Kallistu Xanthopulos und die jüdische Geschichte", pp. 11–15.

SPIRITUALITY AND EMOTION

and events: the disciples, their miracles, the women bearing spices, and so on.[75] Xanthopoulos organises his material in small units, each introduced by a brief metrical heading, thus making these synoptic lists easy to memorise independently of one another. Another group of works in this category are the short poems itemising, in similar fashion, the Twelve Great Feasts, the Evangelists, the Fathers and Hymnographers of the Church, the books of the Bible, the Ten Commandments, etc. He used the same system again for a synopsis of the Triodion, the synaxarion of the saints for the whole year, and a concise verse chronicle that begins with Adam and in 452 dodecasyllables catalogs, in brief units, the names of the patriarchs, judges and kings of the Israelites and the leaders of every nation (Assyrians, Persians, Macedonians, Greeks, Romans), concluding with the Christian emperors and the patriarchs of Constantinople.[76]

Another example of didactic verse is the poem Manuel II Palaiologos (1395–1421) composed to demonstrate an effective way of proselytizing persons of another religion and initiating them into the Christian faith, at a time when the Islamization of Asia Minor had assumed disquieting dimensions. It is interesting to note that this learned emperor, who had a thorough grounding in theology, did not describe the strategy of initiation in a theoretical treatise but instead chose the form of a dramatic verse monologue (*ethopoiia*), in which he himself plays the role of the catechist addressing an unbeliever.[77]

From the fringes of the empire, from Cyprus and Crete, which had fallen into the hands of the French (Cyprus, in 1192) and the Venetians (Crete, 1211–1669), come three admonitory poems. In addition to works on philosophy and astronomy, George Lapithes (*fl. c.*1340–1349) also wrote a fairly long moralistic poem,[78] in which he addresses his young audience or readers in a kindly, quasi-paternal, tone, offering advice on how to behave properly in public and private life and outlining the duties of a citizen towards his family, the state, and society. The poem is clearly influenced by the *Spaneas*, the widely known 12th-century admonitory poem in the vernacular, which appeared in several

---

75   Ed. Guntius, *Cyri Theodori Prodromi epigrammata*, pp. τ 8r–υ 6r.

76   Ed. Guntius, *Cyri Theodori Prodromi epigrammata*, pp. σ 7r–τ 8r; Colonna, *Un ἀνέκδοτον*, pp. 6–19 (452 lines). For the lists of emperors and patriarchs of New Rome see Kotzabassi, "Die Kaiser- und Patriarchenlisten", pp. 132–40.

77   Manuel II Palaiologos, *Verses to an Atheist*, ed. Vassis, pp. 55–78 (809 fifteen-syllable lines).

78   George Lapithes, *Didactic poem*, ed. Chatzisavvas, pp. 77–141 (1,491 fifteen-syllable lines).

188   VASSIS

versions (one of them from Cyprus),[79] which shows that Lapithes was one of those who kept Greek learning and Byzantine tradition alive in Cyprus.[80]

In Crete, Stephen Sachlikes[81] and the Venetian-Cretan nobleman Marinos Falieros wrote short admonitory poems to their sons, but these can scarcely be classed as belonging to the Palaeologan revival. For example, the *Logoi didaktikoi* that Marinos Phalieros[82] wrote (sometime between 1421 and 1430) for his firstborn son are primarily concerned with the young nobleman's position in society, his relations with women and his role as the head of the family, and are plainly influenced by a Western model, although from other works of his it is clear that the poet was acquainted both with the *Spaneas* and with vernacular Byzantine romances.

6.2   *Alphabets and Ascetic* Kephalaia

Two didactic poems addressed to a monastic audience exemplify the character of two genres with a long tradition in ascetic literature, the admonitory alphabet[83] and the monastic *Kephalaia*,[84] while significantly modernising their form and structure. In 1282 or thereabouts Meletios Galesiotes, called The Confessor for his fierce resistance to the union of the Churches agreed by Michael VIII Palaiologos in 1274 through the Council of Lyons, composed while in exile on the island of Skyros an extremely long work in seven parts (of which only four survive) containing approximately 20,000 fifteen-syllable lines. Part Four, which is the longest of them all, is titled 'Alphabetalphabetos'[85] and is arranged in 24 alphabetical sections, each containing 24 alphabetical parts. This is the longest and most complex alphabet of its kind ever written in Byzantium. From the point of view of content, the work is organised into 199 chapters detailing the virtues that a monk must acquire and the passions that he must subdue. Meletios drew his material largely from such sources as sacro-profane *gnomologia* on moral topics, like the work of Pseudo-Maximos,

---

79   See Danezis, "Ο Σπανέας και οι πολιτικοί στίχοι του Γεωργίου Λαπίθη".

80   Characteristically, he both enjoyed the protection of the Frankish prince Hugues IV de Lusignan (1324–1359) and maintained close, friendly relations with the chief anti-Palamists in Constantinople (Nikephoros Gregoras, Gregory Akindynos and Barlaam the Calabrian).

81   *Precepts to Frantziskes*: Stephen Sachlikes, *Poems*, eds. Mavromatis/Panayotakis, pp. 158–74 (461 fifteen-syllable lines).

82   Marinos Phalieros, *Didactic poem to his son*, eds. Bakker/van Gemert, pp. 65–75 (326 fifteen-syllable lines). See Holton, *Literature and society*, pp. 58–61.

83   For admonitory alphabets, see Anastasijević, *Die paränetischen Alphabete*.

84   On this genre see Géhin, "Les collections de *kephalaia* monastiques".

85   Meletios Galesiotes, *Alphabetalphabetos*, ed. Simopoulos, *Μελέτιος ὁ Γαλησιώτης*, pp. 115–528. A critical edition is in preparation by the author of this chapter.

SPIRITUALITY AND EMOTION

the writings of the great ascetic monks, like St. John Climacus, and the sayings of the Desert Fathers. His work is addressed to his spiritual children, and while the learned diction he uses is clear and easy to understand, the style is not always simple, being patently influenced by the sources, which are generally paraphrased. It is worth noting, however, that although the work is a kind of versified *florilegium* it is more than a mere compilation of maxims and apophthegms, for Meletios has skilfully woven together material from diverse sources into a smoothly unified edifying text appropriate for monastic reading.

A little later, in the early part of the 14th century, Andronikos Komnenos Doukas Palaiologos, cousin of Emperor Andronikos II, composed 100 iambic quatrains on the virtues that one must pursue and the vices that one must avoid.[86] Of these only 86 still survive, incorporated into a curious (as yet not fully edited) anthology of moral *kephalaia* in verse and prose, of an ascetic nature. The diction of these quatrains is learned and the prosody careful, but no one could argue that they are distinguished for their originality or their poetic feeling, being brief but ornately expressed formulations of moral precepts in the form of banal aphorisms on the monastic life and the duties of those who profess it.

6.3   *Allegorical Poems*

Two poems of a moralizing nature expound on spiritual values in an allegorical fashion. The lengthy anti-romance that (Theodore?) Meliteniotes titled *On Chastity (Εἰς τὴν Σωφροσύνην),*[87] its fifteen-syllable lines couched in a learned diction, was written in roughly the middle of the 14th century.[88] In the course of a country walk in springtime the narrator meets a woman, whose name is Chastity, who offers to help him overcome the seven dangerous obstacles on the way to her marvellous castle. As the narrator explains, step by step, the path leading to the castle is an allegorical journey to heaven, which however is possible only for those who eschew earthly pleasures and with self-discipline take care to safeguard their purity of soul. The poem is described as a love story, but a chaste one, since the theme is abstinence. It was written, the poet says, for the delectation of those who are fond of literature which does not resort to false myths. In this curious and original tale, which seems to have inspired no

---

86   Constantinides, "Ἀνδρονίκου Παλαιολόγου Κεφάλαια", pp. 194–206.

87   Meliteniotes, *On Chastity*, ed. Miller, pp. 11–138 (3,060 lines). Only a small fragment of the poem (lines 1107–1247) has been critically edited: Schönauer, *Untersuchungen zum Steinkatalog*, pp. 5–20. A critical edition in preparation by A. Kambylis/I. Vassis.

88   For the date of composition (after 1336?) see Schönauer, *Untersuchungen zum Steinkatalog*, pp. 13*–14*.

imitators, motifs like that of the castle[89] and themes familiar from vernacular romances are combined with a wealth of information about historical and mythological figures, precious stones, metals, plants and animals, encyclopaedic information that the poet inserts wherever he can, sometimes in the form of lengthy lists.[90]

An anonymous poem entitled *Λόγος παρηγορητικὸς περὶ δυστυχίας καὶ εὐτυχίας* (*Consolation concerning Ill Fortune and Good Fortune*),[91] written before 1350 and composed in everyday language, is based on fairy-tale themes, and primarily the motif of searching for the road to good fortune. Here too we have a journey undertaken by a misfortunate man, who is seeking the Castle of Ill-Fortune in order to understand the cause of his woes, but who in the end attains the mysterious and inaccessible Castle of Good-Fortune. Both appear in the poem as women, while the road to the castle shows the traveller the personification of Time. Like Meliteniotes, this poet too has composed an allegorical poem employing the means and tropes of a romance.[92]

7 Rewriting the Past

In the first half of the 14th century there arose a fashion for rewriting certain texts, particularly those of a religious nature, in verse. In the same period there also appeared prose translations of two historical works and a rhetorical essay on the behaviour of kings, reworked in a simpler register of Greek and obviously intended to be accessible to a broader public, untrained in the atticising style.[93] As we shall see, however, most verse 'translations' do not seem to have had this purpose.

Nikephoros Kallistou Xanthopoulos 'translated' the prose *Life and Miracles of St. Nicholas*, as recounted by Symeon Metaphrastes, into approximately 2,700 dodecasyllables, drawing as well on various other sources so as to add to his account the miracles performed after the saint's death.[94] Since he also rewrote

---

89 See Cupane, "Il motivo del castello", pp. 246–60.

90 Cupane, "Una passeggiata", pp. 84–90, sees in this work an interesting literary dialogue between Byzantium and the West.

91 *Consolation concerning Ill Fortune and Good Fortune*, ed. Cupane, pp. 646–90 (769 lines).

92 See Cupane, "Κατέλαβες τ' ἀμφίβολα τῆς τυφλῆς δαίμονος πρόσωπα".

93 For a consideration of the circles to which these translations were addressed, see Davis, "Anna Komnene and Niketas Choniates 'translated'"; Efthymiadis, "Déclassiciser pour édifier?".

94 This *Vita* has not yet been fully edited. Nikephoros Kallistou Xanthopoulos, *Life and Miracles of St. Nicholas*, ed. Papadopoulos-Kerameus, pp. 357–66 published only the second part (with 9 of the saint's 13 miracles).

SPIRITUALITY AND EMOTION 191

several other lives of saints in prose, as did many other literati of the early Palaeologan period,[95] it is not clear why he chose a metrical form for the life of St. Nicholas, unless it was intended as a didactic work, like those discussed earlier, although it lacks their synoptic character.

Manuel Philes translated 98 of the Psalms of David into roughly 3,600 fifteen-syllable lines.[96] He chose the dodecasyllable for his translations of other ecclesiastical songs, such as the Akathist Hymn[97] and sundry troparia,[98] presumably seeking to adapt familiar, important hymns to the tastes of the age.

The *Dioptra*, a long didactic theological poem written circa 1095 in very simple language with numerous vernacular features by the Athonite monk Philip Monotropos, was rewritten early in the 14th century by (Theodore) Phialites.[99] The title 'Correction' (Διόρθωσις) applied to the poem suggests that the revision was made with the intent to elevate the linguistic register and normalize the fifteen-syllable verse structure of a work that was already widely read.[100] While Philip was addressing a moderately well-educated monastic and ecclesiastical public, Phialites was seeking to adapt the original text to the taste of a more cultivated readership, perhaps the senior clergy of the day, with higher literary expectations.

Similar efforts are seen in the periphery of the Empire, and especially in Greek areas under western rule, but in the opposite direction: the rewriting of long-established texts in a simpler register and style. Clearly, we are looking at entirely different preferences, bearing no relation to the intellectual climate prevailing in the capital.

Clumsy is perhaps the best that can be said of the rewriting of the *Iliad* in trochaic octasyllable (8,799 lines) by Constantine Hermoniakos, who between 1323 and 1335, at the behest of the Italian Despot of Epiros John II Orsini and his wife Anna Palaiologina, wrote a motley and very mediocre history of the

---

95 See Talbot, "Old Wine in New Bottles"; Hinterberger, "Hagiographische Metaphrasen"; idem, "Hagiographical Enkomia as Metaphrasis".

96 Manuel Philes, Translation of the Psalms, ed. (partially) Stickler, pp. 169–194 (these translations are preserved in two versions). See Ricceri, "Two Metrical Rewritings of the Greek Psalms"; Gioffreda/Rhoby, "Die metrische Psalmenmetaphrase des Manuel Philes".

97 Manuel Philes, *Poems*, App. 1, ed. Miller, vol. 2, pp. 317–33 (294 lines).

98 Ed. Tsululin, "Τὸ χειρόγραφο ἀρ. 31", pp. 335–36; cf. Kotzabassi, "Ἔμμετρες μεταφράσεις", pp. 359–60.

99 On him see *PLP* 29715.

100 Theodore Phialites, *Diorthosis*, ed. Auvray, pp. 19–108 (the edition includes only the *Klauthmoi*, a poem of contrition addressed to the Soul; the other four parts of Phialites' 'translation' have not yet been edited). On the *Dioptra* of Philippos see E. Afentoulidou-Leitgeb, "The Dioptra of Philippos Monotropos", pp. 181–91 (who is preparing a critical edition of the whole work).

Trojan War, including events preceding and following those narrated by Homer. Demonstrating little imagination or creative boldness, the author based his work primarily on John Tzetzes' allegorical synopsis of the *Iliad* and the very popular verse chronicle by Constantine Manasses, with occasional reference to the Homeric text.[101] There is no mention of the ancient gods, but frequent bursts of moralizing, while the author's chief interest seems to be in weaponry and the art of its manufacture, which he analyses on the basis of their contemporary forms. His linguistic deficiencies may reflect the mediocrity of the education available in provincial centres in the first half of the 14th century.

Much later, towards the end of the 15th century, in Venetian-ruled Crete, George Choumnos would rewrite the first two books of the Old Testament (*Genesis* and *Exodus*) in 2,832 fifteen-syllable lines (1,416 rhyming couplets), in a vernacular register mixed with elements of Cretan dialect and phrases from ecclesiastical texts.[102] In addition to the Bible he drew on a prose paraphrase known as the *Palaia* (9th c.?), incorporating elements of popular religious tradition. Although his poem is merely a rewriting of prose texts, it does contain some genuinely lyrical passages.

8   Verse Chronicles

A series of verse chronicles shows that the example of Constantine Manasses, who first composed such a work in the 12th century, continued to affect the way in which summaries of world history or accounts of important historical events were approached in the Palaeologan period, although some chroniclers writing far from Constantinople clearly reflect a Western influence.

In the 1320s Ephraim Ainios composed a chronicle in dodecasyllable.[103] Although his choice of form and archaic diction or rare poetic turns of phrase (usually imposed by the metre) betray a classical bent, his language also includes elements of common speech. His chronicle, which is preserved in a single acephalous manuscript, covers the history of the Roman emperors from Caligula to Michael VIII Palaiologos. The narrative is more detailed in its account of the Comnenian period, and deals far more thoroughly with the events of the Nicaean Empire (1204–1261). The chronicler's interest focuses

---

101   Constantine Hermoniakos, *Iliad*, ed. Legrand. For the author's sources see Jeffreys, "Constantine Hermoniakos and Byzantine Education", pp. 81–109; Lavagnini, "Tales of the Troian War", pp. 239–40.

102   George Choumnos, *Kosmogennisis*, ed. Megas, pp. 41–169.

103   Ephraim Ainios, *Chronicle*, ed. Lampsides, pp. 3–337 (9,588 dodecasyllables). See Nilsson, "The Past as Poetry: Two Byzantine World Chronicles in Verse", pp. 524–30.

primarily on the religious policy of the emperors and each one's attitude towards Orthodox doctrine. His sources are on the whole well known, and he was clearly selective in his – often summary – use of them. Nonetheless, the author does here and there give free rein to his literary imagination to develop, for example, the characters of the figures in a more lyrical manner, abandoning from time to time the dry recital of names and events.

An anonymous chronicle, written in 1392, recounts in 759 fifteen-syllable lines the events of the period from 1180 to 1282, with particular emphasis on the Crusaders' seizure of Constantinople (1204) and its reconquest by Michael VIII Palaiologos (1261), and on the religious policy followed by that emperor and his successor Andronikos II on the thorny issue of union between the Eastern and the Western Church.[104] The language is elegant without being pretentious, but the work itself is of little historical value, being based on the histories of Niketas Choniates, George Akropolites and George Pachymeres, although it does furnish certain details relating chiefly to the fall and recovery of the Byzantine capital.

From the Latin-ruled territories of the empire come two verse chronicles, products of an elite (Latin or Byzantine) faithful to its new rulers, although written in the vernacular. *The Chronicle of Morea*[105] is a kind of founding epic of the Frankish kingdoms created in the Peloponnese after 1204. This anonymous work exists in 4 versions (Greek, French, Italian and Spanish), which likely derive from a lost common original composed around 1320. The Greek version is the only one in verse form and is thought to be the oldest; it is preserved essentially in two forms, dating from the 1380s. A brief reference to the First Crusade and a detailed description of the Fourth and the Fall of Constantinople (1204) are followed by a thorough account of the Frankish conquest and rule of the Peloponnese up to 1292.

The *Chronicle of the Tocco* (of Cephallonia) is a kind of family epic that must have been written in the third decade of the 15th century (1429). It covers the years 1375–1425, when Count Carlo I Tocco ruled over Epiros and the Ionian Islands.[106] The anonymous author appears to have been familiar with the *Chronicle of Morea* and to have used it as a model, at least for line structure and language, which is informal and sprinkled with Latin and Italian words.

---

104 *The Fall of Constantinople*, ed. Matzukis, pp. 91–155.

105 *Chronicle of Morea*, ed. Egea, pp. 2–456. See Shawcross, *The Chronicle of Morea*.

106 *Chronicle of the Tocco*, ed. Schirò, pp. 220–508 (3,923 fifteen-syllable lines; the text as preserved lacks both beginning and end: roughly 800 lines have been lost). See Ilieva, "Images of Towns in Frankish Morea".

194 VASSIS

9 Pamphlets and Satirical Poems

Byzantine humour in the middle and late periods often took the form of lampooning specific persons rather than situations. Around 1335–1340 John Katrares composed a pamphlet in octasyllable lines against a monk named Neophytos who aspired to the patriarchate. Probably moved by personal interest, the well-known copyist and scholar, who belonged to the circle of Demetrios Triklinios of Thessaloniki, attacked Neophytos in a manner both crude and harsh as a vainglorious and poorly educated person who could barely speak Greek (probably because he was of Bulgarian origin).[107] Another characteristic example of the genre is a scabrous poem by Philes,[108] coarsely ridiculing the impotence of an old man whom the poet or his circle regarded with enmity. In another of his poems,[109] Philes used delicate irony to poke fun at a tavern-keeper who had turned his establishment into a brothel, pandering his wife to customers.

One sub-category of this genre is the animal fable, written for both satirical and educational ends. In three such tales of the 14th century, written in vernacular idiom in fifteen-syllable verse, the characters are animals or birds with human virtues and weaknesses. Despite certain similarities with Aesop's fables, these poems differ markedly in length and organisation of the narrative, which is composite and complex. From the aspect of form, two of these belong to the genre of *Rangstreitdichtung*, or disputes: that is, they are dialogues in which two opposing parties argue their superiority over each other, mocking and casting slurs on one another, often in a comic or grotesque manner. Since later readers would have difficulty identifying the figures and situations referred to, the satiric thrust of these poems is subsumed in a broader divertive and didactic function that they may not originally have had, and in later manuscripts these works are frequently recommended, particularly to the young, for entertainment and instruction. In the *Book of Birds* (*Πουλολόγος*),[110] the eagle, the king of the feathered kingdom, invites his subjects to his son's wedding. There ensues a fierce argument, in which each bird defends his right to attend the wedding feast rather than another, based on how useful each is to mankind and especially to the royal court and the aristocracy surrounding it. In the end the intervention of the eagle is required to put a stop to the disputes.

---

107 John Katrares, *Verses against Neophytos*, ed. Romano, pp. 445–65 (222 lines).

108 Manuel Philes, *Poems*, ed. Miller, vol. 1, pp. 371–76.

109 Manuel Philes, *Poems*, ed. Miller, vol. 1, pp. 330–31; see Lauxtermann, *La poesia*, pp. 338–39.

110 *Book of Birds*, ed. Tsavari, pp. 247–99; Eideneier, *Μεσαιωνικές ιστορίες ζώων*; see Prinzing, "Zur byzantinischen Rangstreitliteratur", pp. 261–71. For the possible satirical references in the poem see Makris, "Zum literarischen Genus des Pulologos".

SPIRITUALITY AND EMOTION

The anonymous *Tale of Quadrupeds* (Διήγησις τῶν τετραπόδων ζώων)[111] describes, in a similar but more sophisticated fashion, a meeting between the carnivores and the herbivores, convened by the lion as king of the animals. Each wild beast boasts of his prowess, while deriding the others. When their king is false to the oath of peace among his subjects, the assembly degenerates into a fierce battle, during which the gentle animals manage to defeat the savage. The moral of the tale is clear and is spelled out at the end: when the powerful rely solely on their superior strength, they can be defeated by a weaker opponent.

In the *Tale of the Hero Donkey* (Συναξάριον τοῦ τιμημένου γαδάρου),[112] the humble, harmless donkey proves to be wilier than the fox and the wolf, who for a trifle and with treacherous cunning threaten his life, and in the end gets the better of them; the hero is presented virtually as a saint, hence the title *Synaxarion*. In this mixed narrative genre the brief *mythos*, as we know it from the rhetorical exercises known as *progymnasmata*, is combined with traditional elements of the romance.

10   Vernacular Romances

After a silence of nearly eight centuries the late antique novel was reborn in 12th-century Byzantium, in four works written in a 'learned' idiom and – for the most part – in verse. Their action unfolds against the backdrop of an ancient city, and their primary model was the late antique prose romance (particularly the *Leucippe and Clitophon* by Achilles Tatius and the *Aethiopica* by Heliodorus).[113] This tradition was continued and renewed in the 13th–14th century by three original romances of love: *Livistros and Rodamne*,[114] *Velthandros*

---

111   *Tale of the Quadrupeds*, eds. & trans. Nicholas/Baloglou, 160–219; Eideneier, *Μεσαιωνικές ιστορίες ζώων*; see Prinzing, "Zur byzantinischen Rangstreitliteratur", pp. 272–84; Moennig, "Ρητορική καὶ διήγησις των τετραπόδων ζώων"; Stewart, "An Entertaining Tale of Quadrupeds".

112   *Tale of the Hero Donkey*, ed. Moennig, pp. 138–48 (393 fifteen-syllable lines); see Lauxtermann/Janssen, "Asinine tales east and west".

113   For an overview of Byzantine fiction see Beaton, *The Medieval Greek Romance*; idem, "Byzantine Verse Romances"; Cupane, "Il romanzo"; Cupane/Krönung, *Fictional Storytelling*; Goldwyn/Nilsson, *Reading the Late Byzantine Romance*. On the 'learned' novels of the 12th century see also Nilsson, "Romantic Love in Rhetorical Guise".

114   *Livistros and Rodamne, Redaction α*, ed. Agapitos, pp. 257–432 (4,601 lines); *Livistros and Rodamne, Redaction V*, ed. Lendari, pp. 143–255 (4,013 lines). See Cupane, "In the Realm of Eros", pp. 101–10.

and Chrysantza,[115] *Kallimachos and Chrysorrhoe*.[116] These works differ significantly from their predecessors, however, both in diction and metre and, in part, in the models from which they derive morphological and thematic elements. Although they use the same rhetorical means (descriptions of people, gardens and buildings; letters, songs and monologues), they introduce innovations in relation to the Comnenian novels with regard to subject matter, metre (fifteen-syllable verse instead of dodecasyllable) and language, which is not learned but rather a mixed idiom in which the vernacular predominates. This, however, does not make them "folk literature": their elaborate rhetorical form and complex narrative structure suggest that, initially at least, they were intended to satisfy the sophisticated tastes and expectations of the cultivated, aristocratic reader rather than the general public.[117] Although each one takes place in a different setting, which does not match any specific historic context, numerous elements reflect the Byzantine courtly way of life.[118]

One particularly striking aspect of the Palaeologan romances is the appearance in them of certain basic features of the Old French romances and *fabliaux* of the 12th century, such as witches, magic rings, horses enchanted by demons, mysterious flaming rivers, and remote lonely castles inhabited by dragons or by Eros, the powerful king, and his court. Apart from the selective adoption of certain elements of Western romances,[119] which lend a rather superficial effect, new motifs and narrative formats, and especially a new perception of adventure and sensuality, enrich and renew the traditional structure and imagery of the tale of star-crossed lovers and give it a whole new dynamic. The romances follow a standard narrative plot with assorted variations. They usually begin with the hero, generally a prince, wandering in foreign lands, where in mysterious circumstances he meets the love of his life in a marvellous castle.[120] Unforeseen situations separate the lovers, sometimes forever, sometimes to be reunited after various reversals of fortune. Daring love scenes that are either described or merely intimated (providing an occasion for allegorical interpretations on the part of the reader or listener), love letters and lyrical

---

115   *Velthandros and Chrysantza*, ed. & trans. Cupane, pp. 228–304 (1,348 lines). See eadem, "In the Realm of Eros", pp. 110–14.

116   *Kallimachos and Chrysorrhoe*, ed. & trans. Pichard, pp. 1–92; *Kallimachos and Chrysorrhoe*, ed. & trans. Cupane, pp. 58–212; *Kallimachos and Chrysorrhoe*, ed. & trans. Polemis, pp. 92–270 (2,605 lines). See id., pp. 9–77 and Cupane, "In the Realm of Eros", pp. 114–18.

117   See Cupane, "In the Realm of Eros", and eadem, "Let me tell you a wonderful tale".

118   On the Byzantine atmosphere of the Palaiologan romances see Hunger, "Un roman byzantin", and Agapitos, "The Court of Amorous Dominion".

119   See Cupane, "Intercultural Encounters".

120   See Cupane, "Il motivo del castello".

SPIRITUALITY AND EMOTION

songs exchanged between the pair, motifs such the apparent death of one of the lovers, and recognition scenes, are among the basic elements used to create a thrilling and colourful plot.

Apart from these so-called 'original'[121] romances of late Byzantine fiction there are another six that are adaptations of Western templates: *The War of Troy*,[122] *The Old Knight*,[123] *Apollonius of Tyre*,[124] *Theseid*,[125] *Florios and Platziaflora*,[126] and *Imperios and Margarona*.[127] These are generally assumed to have been written in the Latin-ruled territories or possibly in Constantinople, and their original versions composed between the 14th and the end of the 15th century. It should be noted that all the romances are usually preserved in later manuscripts and often in several versions, making it impossible to reconstitute an original text.

Other compositions on the fringes of this genre contain material drawn from Homeric and post-Homeric Troy.[128] The *Achilleid*[129] and the *Byzantine Iliad* or the *Tale of Troy*[130] recount the love affairs of two Homeric heroes, Achilles and Paris, combining pseudo-historical and erotic elements. Another figure, finally, who is the stuff of legend, is the hero of the *Byzantine Alexander Poem*, one of the many reworkings of the fictional biography of the Macedonian

---

121 See Yiavis, "The Categories of 'Originals' and 'Adaptations'".

122 *The War of Troy*, eds. Papathomopoulos/Jeffreys, pp. 1–710 (14,401 lines). On this 13th-century adaptation of the French *Roman de Troie* by Benoît de St Maure see Yiavis, "The Adaptations of Western Sources", pp. 129–34; Jeffreys, "From Herakles to Erkoulios".

123 *Old Knight*, ed. Rizzo Nervo, pp. 40–54 (307 lines). For the French romance of the Arthurian cycle on which this fragmentarily preserved text is based see Yiavis, ibid., pp. 134–38.

124 *Apollonius of Tyre*, ed. Kechagioglou, vol. 1, pp. 429–69 (869 lines). For the Tuscan *Storia d'Apollonio di Tiro*, which is thought to have served as its model, see Yiavis, ibid., pp. 138–41.

125 Partial edition by Follieri, *Il Teseida Neogreco* (Book 1), and Olsen, "The Greek Translation" (Book VI). For this Greek adaptation of Giovanni Boccaccio's *Teseida, delle nozze d'Emilia* (c.1340) see Yiavis, ibid., pp. 142–44.

126 *Florios and Platziaflora*, ed. Cupane, pp. 464–565 (1,795 lines). For his probable Tuscan exemplar (*Cantare di Fiorio e Biancifiore*) see Yiavis, ibid., pp. 144–48.

127 *Imperios and Margarona*, ed. Kriaras, pp. 215–49 (unrhymed version). For the basic, but not sole, French template (*Pierre de Provence et la belle Maguelone*) see Yiavis, ibid., pp. 148–50.

128 For the use of Troy material see Goldwyn/Nilsson, "Troy in Byzantine Romances".

129 *Achilleid, Naples version*, ed. Smith/co-eds. Agapitos/Hult, pp. 15–74 (1,820 lines), and *Achilleid, Oxford version*, ed. Smith, pp. 155–76 (763 lines); *Achilleid, Naples version*, ed. & trans. Cupane pp. 324–442. See Lavagnini, "Tales of the Troian War", pp. 240–46.

130 *Byzantine Iliad*, eds. Nørgaard/Smith, pp. 23–62 (1,166 lines). See Lavagnini, "Tales of the Troian War", pp. 246–55; Moennig, "Intertextuality in the Late Byzantine Romance *Tale of Troy*".

commander.[131] It is characteristic of these works that their ancient heroes are disguised as Byzantines in terms of their mentality, behaviour, mode of life, and the environment within which they act.

In concluding this overview of late Byzantine poetry, one might say that in the Palaeologan period the literati continued to cultivate with enthusiasm all the familiar poetic genres inherited from the Comnenian age, enriching and renewing the tradition on the levels of both form and subject matter, but drawing as well on the Western literature that inescapably entered their lives after the fall of Constantinople in 1204. As was to be expected, the ancient capital remained the most faithful repository of tradition in this area, while the literature that was cultivated in the new centres created on the periphery of the empire, most of them under Latin rule, bore certain marks, albeit as yet faint, that would slowly and steadily lead to the dawn of a new age.

Bibliography

Primary Sources

Achilleid, Naples version, ed. O.L. Smith/co-eds. P.A. Agapitos/K. Hult, *The Byzantine Achilleid. The Naples Version* (Wiener Byzantinistische Studien, 21), Vienna 1999, pp. 15–74.

Achilleid, Naples version, ed. & trans. Cupane, *Romanzi cavallereschi bizantini*, pp. 324–442.

Achilleid, Oxford version, ed. Smith, *The Byzantine Achilleid*, pp. 155–76.

Alexios Lampenos, *Poem on the Thaborian Light*, ed. M.I. Gedeon, "Τοῦ Λαμπηνοῦ ὕμνοι εἰς τὸ Θαβώριον φῶς", *Ἐκκλησιαστικὴ Ἀλήθεια* 3 (1882–1883), 190–91.

Apollonius of Tyre, ed. G. Kechagioglou, *Ἀπολλώνιος της Τύρου. Ὑστερομεσαιωνικές και νεότερες ελληνικές μορφές*, 2 vols., Thessaloniki 2004, vol. 1, pp. 429–69.

Book of Birds, ed. I. Tsavari, *Ὁ Πουλολόγος. Κριτικὴ ἔκδοση μὲ εἰσαγωγή, σχόλια καὶ λεξιλόγιο* (Βυζαντινὴ καὶ Νεοελληνικὴ Βιβλιοθήκη, 5), Athens 1987.

Byzantine Alexander Poem, ed. W.J. Aerts, *The Byzantine Alexander Poem* (Byzantinisches Archiv, 26), 2 vols., Boston/Berlin 2014, vol. 1, pp. 33–232.

Byzantine Iliad, ed. L. Nørgaard/O.L. Smith, *A Byzantine Iliad* (Opuscula Graecolatina, 5), Copenhagen 1975.

Chronicle of Morea, ed. J.M. Egea, *La crónica de Morea* (Nueva Roma, 2), Madrid 1996.

Chronicle of the Tocco, ed. G. Schirò, *Cronaca dei Tocco di Cefalonia di anonimo. Prolegomeni, testo critico e traduzione* (Corpus Fontium Historiae Byzantinae, 10), Rome 1975.

---

131   *Byzantine Alexander Poem*, ed. Aerts vol. 1, pp. 33–232 (6,130 lines). See Moennig, "A Hero Without Borders", pp. 178–80.

SPIRITUALITY AND EMOTION

Consolation concerning Ill Fortune and Good Fortune, ed. Cupane, *Romanzi cavallereschi bizantini*, pp. 646–90.

Constantine Hermoniakos, *Iliad*, ed. E. Legrand, *La guerre de Troie. Poème du XIVe siècle en vers octosyllabes par Constantin Hermoniacos, publié d'après les manuscrits de Leyde et de Paris* (Bibliothèque Grecque Vulgaire, 5), Paris 1890 (repr. Athens 1974).

David Dishypatos, *Poem on Akindynos*, ed. R. Browning, "David Dishypatos' Poem on Akindynos", *Byzantion* 25–27 (1955–57), 713–45.

Ephraim Ainios, *Chronicle*, ed. O. Lampsides, *Ephraem Aenii Historia Chronica* (Corpus Fontium Historiae Byzantinae, 27), Athens 1990.

Florios and Platziaflora, ed. Cupane, *Romanzi cavallereschi bizantini*, pp. 464–565.

George Amiroutzes, *Poems*, eds. B. Janssens/P. Van Deun, "George Amiroutzes and his poetical oeuvre", in B. Janssens/B. Roosen/P. Van Deun (eds.), *Philomathestatos. Studies in Greek and Byzantine Texts Presented to Jacques Noret for his Sixty-Fifth Birthday* (Orientalia Lovaniensia Analecta, 137), Leuven 2004, pp. 297–324.

George Choumnos, *Kosmogennisis*, ed. G.A. Megas, Γεωργίου Χούμνου, Ἡ κοσμογέννησις. Ἀνέκδοτον στιχούργημα τοῦ ΙΕ΄ αἰῶνος. Ἔμμετρος παράφρασις τῆς Γενέσεως καὶ Ἐξόδου τῆς Παλαιᾶς Διαθήκης. Κριτικὴ ἔκδοσις, Athens 1975.

George Lapithes, *Didactic poem*, ed. A. Chatzisavvas, Στίχοι πολιτικοὶ αὐτοσχέδιοι εἰς κοινὴν ἀκοὴν τοῦ σοφωτάτου κυρίου Γεωργίου Λαπίθου τοῦ Κυπρίου (Lapithos, 15), Besançon 2001, pp. 77–141.

George Pachymeres, *Autobiographical poem* (fragments), ed. T. Detorakis, "Ἀνέκδοτα ποιήματα τοῦ Γεωργίου Παχυμέρη", in B. Kremmydas/C. Maltezou/N.M. Panayotakis (eds.), Ἀφιέρωμα στὸν Νίκο Σβορῶνο, 2 vols., Rethymno 1986, vol. 1, pp. 299–307.

Gregory Akindynos, *Poem against Gregory Palamas*, in *Patrologia Graeca*, vol. 150, cols. 843–62.

Imperios and Margarona, ed. E. Kriaras, Βυζαντινὰ ἱπποτικὰ μυθιστορήματα (Βασικὴ Βιβλιοθήκη, 2), Athens 1955, pp. 197–249.

John Chortasmenos, *Metrical Calendar*, ed. H. Hunger, "Aus den letzten Lebensjahren des Johannes Chortasmenos. Das Synaxarion im cod. Christ Church gr. 56 und der Metropolit Ignatios von Selybria", *Jahrbuch der Österreichischen Byzantinistik* 45 (1995), 159–218.

John Chortasmenos, *Poems*, ed. H. Hunger, *Johannes Chortasmenos (ca. 1370–ca. 1436/37). Briefe, Gedichte und kleine Schriften. Einleitung, Regesten, Prosopographie, Text* (Wiener Byzantinistische Studien, 7), Vienna 1969.

John Katakalon, *Poem in Praise of John V Palaiologos*, in *Patrologia Graeca*, vol. 158, cols. 961–70.

John Katrares, *Verses against Neophytos*, ed. & trans. R. Romano, *La satira bizantina dei secoli XI–XV*, Torino 1999, pp. 445–65.

Kallimachos and Chrysorrhoe, ed. & trans. M. Pichard, *Le roman de Callimaque et Chrysorrhoe*, Paris 1956.

200 VASSIS

Kallimachos and Chrysorrhoe, ed. & trans. Cupane, *Romanzi cavallereschi bizantini*, pp. 58–212.

Kallimachos and Chrysorrhoe, ed. & trans. I. Polemis, Καλλίμαχος και Χρυσορρόη (Παλιότερα κείμενα της Νεοελληνικής Λογοτεχνίας, 14), Thessaloniki 2021.

Leonardos Dellaportas, *Poems*, ed. M.I. Manoussakas, Λεονάρδου Ντελλαπόρτα ποιήματα (1403/1411). Έκδοση κριτική. Εἰσαγωγή, σχόλια καὶ εὑρετήρια (Ἀκαδημία Ἀθηνῶν. Κέντρο Ἐρεύνης τοῦ Μεσαιωνικοῦ καὶ Νέου Ἑλληνισμοῦ), Athens 1995.

Livistros and Rodamne, Redaction α, ed. P.A. Agapitos, Ἀφήγησις Λιβίστρου καὶ Ροδάμνης. Κριτικὴ ἔκδοση τῆς διασκευῆς α (Βυζαντινὴ καὶ Νεοελληνικὴ Βιβλιοθήκη, 9), Athens 2006.

Livistros and Rodamne, Redaction V, ed. T. Lendari, Ἀφήγησις Λιβίστρου καὶ Ροδάμνης (*Livistros and Rodamne*). *The Vatican Version* (Βυζαντινὴ καὶ Νεοελληνικὴ Βιβλιοθήκη, 10), Athens 2007.

Manuel Holobolos, *Poems*, ed. J.F. Boissonade, *Anecdota graeca e codicibus regiis*, 5 vols., Paris 1829–33 (repr. Hildesheim 1962), vol. 5, pp. 159–82.

Manuel Holobolos, *Poem*, ed. M. Treu, "Manuel Holobolos", *Byzantinische Zeitschrift* 5 (1896), 538–59.

Manuel II Palaiologos, *Verses to an Atheist*, ed. I. Vassis, "Ἀνέκδοτοι στίχοι προς ἄθεον ἄνδρα του Μανουὴλ Β´ Παλαιολόγου", *Βυζαντινά* 32 (2012), 37–100.

Manuel Philes, *Historical Poems*, ed. M.I. Gedeon, "Μανουὴλ τοῦ Φιλῆ ἱστορικὰ ποιήματα", Ἐκκλησιαστικὴ Ἀλήθεια 3 (1882–83), 215–20; 244–50; 652–59.

Manuel Philes, *Kanon on Saint Nicholas*, ed. Th. Antonopoulou, "A Kanon on Saint Nicholas by Manuel Philes", *Revue des Études Byzantines* 62 (2004), 197–213.

Manuel Philes, *On Plants*, eds. F.S. Lehrs/F. Dübner, *Manuelis Philae versus iambici de proprietate animalium*, in C.F. Ameis (ed.), *Poetae bucolici et didactici*, Paris 1862, pp. 57–64.

Manuel Philes, *On the Elephant*, eds. F.S. Lehrs/F. Dübner, *Manuelis Philae versus iambici*, ibid., pp. 49–56.

Manuel Philes, *On the Properties of Animals*, eds. F.S. Lehrs/F. Dübner, *Manuelis Philae versus iambici*, ibid., pp. 1–48.

Manuel Philes, *On the silkworm*, eds. F.S. Lehrs/F. Dübner, *Manuelis Philae versus iambici*, ibid., pp. 65–67.

Manuel Philes, *Panegyrikos*, ed. C. von Holzinger, "Ein Panegyrikus des Manuel Philes", *Byzantinische Zeitschrift* 20 (1911), 385–86.

Manuel Philes, *Poems*, ed. E. Miller, *Manuelis Philae carmina*, 2 vols., Paris 1855–57 (repr. Amsterdam 1967).

Manuel Philes, *Poems*, ed. A. Martini, *Manuelis Philae carmina inedita ex cod. C.VII.7 Bibliothecae Nationalis Taurinensis et cod. 160 Bibliothecae Publicae Cremonensis* (Atti della R. Accademia di Archeologia, Lettere e Belle Arti, 20/Supplemento), Naples 1900.

SPIRITUALITY AND EMOTION 201

Manuel Philes, *Poems*, ed. E. Braounou-Pietsch, *Beseelte Bilder. Epigramme des Manuel Philes auf bildliche Darstellungen* (Veröffentlichungen zur Byzanzforschung, 26), Vienna 2010, pp. 57–199.

Manuel Philes, *Translation of the Psalms*, ed. Stickler, *Manuel Philes und seine Psalmenmetaphrase*, pp. 169–94.

Marinos Phalieros, *Didactic poem to his son*, eds. W.F. Bakker/A.F. van Gemert, *The Λόγοι διδακτικοί of Marinos Phalieros. A critical edition with introduction, notes and index verborum* (Byzantina Neerlandica, 7), Leiden 1977.

Matthew of Ephesos (Manuel Gabalas), *Epigrams*, ed. D. Reinsch, *Die Briefe des Matthaios von Ephesos im Codex Vindobonensis Theol. gr. 174*, Berlin 1974, pp. 53–54.

Meletios Galesiotes, *Alphabetalphabetos*, ed. T.N. Simopoulos, *Μελέτιος ὁ Γαλησιώτης (1230–1307). Ὁ ἄγνωστος θεολόγος, ὅσιος, ὁμολογητής, λόγιος, συγγραφεύς*, Athens 1978.

Meliteniotes, *On Chastity*, ed. E. Miller, "Poëme allégorique de Meliténiote, publié d'après un manuscrit de la Bibliothèque Impériale", *Notices et extraits des manuscrits de la Bibliothèque Impériale et autres bibliothèques* 19/2 (1858), 11–138.

Meliteniotes, ed. S. Schönauer, *Untersuchungen zum Steinkatalog des Sophrosyne-Gedichtes des Meliteniotes mit kritischer Edition der Verse 1107–1247* (Meletemata, 6), Wiesbaden 1996.

Michael Apostoles, *Metrical calendar*, ed. B. Laourdas, "Μιχαὴλ Ἀποστόλη ἀνέκδοτα ἐπιγράμματα", *Ἐπετηρὶς Ἑταιρείας Βυζαντινῶν Σπουδῶν* 20 (1950), 172–208.

Monodies for the Sack of Thessaloniki, ed. S.P. Lampros, "Τρεῖς ἀνέκδοτοι μονῳδίαι εἰς τὴν ὑπὸ τῶν Τούρκων ἅλωσιν τῆς Θεσσαλονίκης", *Νέος Ἑλληνομνήμων* 5 (1908), 369–91.

Nikephoros Choumnos, *Poems*, ed. E. Martini, "Spigolature bizantine I. Versi inediti di Niceforo Chumnos", *Società Reale di Napoli. Rendiconto delle tornate e dei lavori della Reale Accademia di Archeologia, Lettere e Belle Arti* n.s. 14 (1900), 121–29.

Nikephoros Moschopoulos, *Metrical calendar*, ed. E. Papaeliopoulou-Photopoulou, *Νικηφόρος Μοσχόπουλος καὶ τὸ ἀνέκδοτο ποιητικὸ ἔργο του*, PhD thesis, National and Kapodistrian University of Athens 1991, pp. 199–228.

Nikephoros Xanthopoulos, *Chronography*, ed. Guntius, *Cyri Theodori Prodromi epigrammata*, pp. σ 7r–τ 8r; M.E. Colonna, *Un Ἀνέκδοτον del ms. Monacensis graecus 551*, Naples [1959], pp. 6–19.

Nikephoros Xanthopoulos, *Life and Miracles of St. Nicholas*, ed. A. Papadopoulos-Kerameus, *Ἀνάλεκτα Ἱεροσολυμιτικῆς σταχυολογίας*, 4 vols., Saint Petersburg 1891–97, vol. 4, pp. 357–66.

Nikephoros Xanthopoulos, *List of Byzantine Emperors and Patriarchs of Constantinople*, ed. S. Kotzabassi, "Die Kaiser- und Patriarchenlisten des Nikephoros Xanthopoulos", in C. Gastgeber/S. Panteghini (eds.), *Ecclesiastical History and Nikephoros Kallistou Xanthopoulos* (Veröffentlichungen zur Byzanzforschung, 37), Vienna 2015, pp. 125–40.

202 VASSIS

Nikephoros Xanthopoulos, *Metrical synaxarion*, ed. R.S. Stefec, "Die Synaxarverse des Nikephoros Xanthopulos", *Jahrbuch der Österreichischen Byzantinistik* 62 (2012), 145–61.

Nikephoros Xanthopoulos, *Synopsis of the Jewish History according to Flavius Josephus*, in *Patrologia Graeca*, vol. 147, cols. 601–06, 623–32.

Nikephoros Xanthopoulos, *Synopsis of the Jewish History according to the Bible*, in *Patrologia Graeca*, vol. 147, cols. 605–24.

Nikephoros Xanthopoulos, *Synopsis of the New Testament*, ed. Guntius, *Cyri Theodori Prodromi epigrammata*, pp. τ 8r–υ 6r.

Old Knight, ed. F. Rizzo Nervo, *Il Vecchio Cavaliere* (Medioevo Romanzo e Orientale. Testi, 6), Soveria Mannelli 2000.

Poem for the death of Michael IX Palaiologos, ed. D.R. Reinsch, "Ein unediertes Gedicht anläßlich des Todes Michaels IX.", *Revue des Études Sud-Est Européennes* 31 (1993), 371–80.

Stephen Sachlikes, *Poems*, eds. G.K. Mavromatis/N.M. Panayotakis, *Στέφανος Σαχλίκης, Τὰ ποιήματα. Χρηστικὴ ἔκδοση μὲ βάση καὶ τὰ τρία χειρόγραφα*, Athens 2015.

Stephen Sgouropoulos, *Poems*, ed. A. Papadopoulos-Kerameus, *Ἀνάλεκτα Ἱεροσολυμιτικῆς σταχυολογίας*, 4 vols., Saint Petersburg 1891–97, vol. 1, pp. 431–37.

Stephen Sgouropoulos, *Poems*, ed. Tr. Papatheodorides, "Ἀνέκδοτοι στίχοι Στεφάνου τοῦ Σγουροπούλου", *Ἀρχεῖον Πόντου* 19 (1954), 262–82.

Tale of the Hero Donkey, ed. U. Moennig, "Das Συναξάριον τοῦ τιμημένου γαδάρου. Analyse, Ausgabe, Wörterverzeichnis", *Byzantinische Zeitschrift* 102 (2009), 109–66.

Tale of the Quadrupeds, eds. & trans. N. Nicholas/G. Baloglou, *An Entertaining Tale of Quadrupeds. Translation and Commentary*, New York 2003.

The Fall of Constantinople, ed. C. Matzukis, *The Fall of Constantinople, Fourth Crusade. A Critical Edition with Translation, Grammatical and Historical Commentary of the Codex 408 Marcianus Graecus (ff. 1–13v) in the Library of St. Mark, Venice*, Athens 2004.

Theodore Metochites, *Poems*, ed. I. Polemis, *Theodori Metochitae carmina* (Corpus Christianorum. Series Graeca, 83), Turnhout 2015.

Theodore Metochites, *Poems*, trans. I. Polemis, *Theodore Metochites, Poems. Introduction, translation and notes* (Corpus Christianorum in Translation, 26), Turnhout 2017.

Theodore Phialites, *Diorthosis*, ed. E. Auvray, *Les pleurs de Philippe. Poëme en vers politiques de Philippe le Solitaire* (Bibliothèque de l'École des Hautes Études. Sciences philologiques et historiques, 22), Paris 1875, pp. 19–108.

Theoktistos Stoudites, *Kanons*, ed. E. Afentoulidou-Leitgeb, *Die Hymnen des Theoktistos Studites auf Athanasios I. von Konstantinopel. Einleitung, Edition, Kommentar* (Wiener Byzantinistische Studien, 27), Vienna 2008.

SPIRITUALITY AND EMOTION 203

Theseid, Book I, ed. E. Follieri, *Il Teseida Neogreco. Libro I. Saggio di edizione*, Athens/
Rome 1959.

Theseid, Book VI, ed. B. Olsen, "The Greek Translation of Boccaccio's *Theseid*, Book 6",
Classica et Mediaevalia 41 (1990), 275–301.

The War of Troy, eds. M. Papathomopoulos/E.M. Jeffreys, Ὁ πόλεμος τῆς Τρωάδος (*The
War of Troy*). Κριτικὴ ἔκδοση (Βυζαντινὴ καὶ Νεοελληνικὴ Βιβλιοθήκη, 7), Athens 1996.

Velthandros and Chrysantza, ed. & trans. C. Cupane, *Romanzi cavallereschi bizantini*,
pp. 228–304.

Secondary Literature

Afentoulidou-Leitgeb, E., "The Dioptra of Philippos Monotropos: Didactic Verses or
Poetry?", in Bernard/Demoen (eds.), *Poetry and its Contexts in Eleventh-century
Byzantium*, pp. 181–91.

Anastasijewič, D.N., *Die paränetischen Alphabete in der griechischen Literatur*, Munich
1905.

Angelov, D., *Imperial Ideology and Political Thought in Byzantium, 1204–1330*, Cambridge
2007.

Antonopoulou, T., "On the Reception of Homilies and Hagiography in Byzantium. The
Recited Metrical Prefaces", in Rhoby/Schiffer (eds.), *Imitatio – Aemulatio – Variatio*,
pp. 57–79.

Baseu-Barabas, T., "Die Speisung des Elias durch den Raben. Ein Epigramm des Manuel
Philes als Zeugnis für ein verschollenes Kunstwerk", *Jahrbuch der Österreichischen
Byzantinistik* 43 (1993), 233–40.

Bazzani, M., "A Poem of Philes to Makarios Chrysokephalos? The case of Poem
Florentinus 58", *Byzantinische Zeitschrift* 104 (2011), 55–69.

Bazzani, M., "The Art of Requesting in the Poetry of Manuel Philes", in Rhoby/Zagklas
(eds.), *Middle and Late Byzantine Poetry*, pp. 183–207.

Beaton, R., "Byzantine Verse Romances", in Hörandner/Rhoby/Zagklas (eds.), *A Companion to Byzantine Poetry*, pp. 539–55.

Beaton, R., *The Medieval Greek Romance*, 2nd ed., London 1996.

Berger, A., "Nikephoros Kallistu Xanthopulos und die jüdische Geschichte", in
A. Berger/S. Mariev/G. Prinzing/A. Riehle (eds.), *Koinotaton Doron. Das späte Byzanz
zwischen Machtlosigkeit und kultureller Blüte (1204–1461)* (Byzantinisches Archiv, 31),
Berlin/Boston 2016, pp. 1–15.

Bernard, F., "Rhythm in the Byzantine Dodecasyllable: Practices and Perceptions", in
Rhoby/Zagklas (eds.), *Middle and Late Byzantine Poetry*, pp. 13–41.

Bernard, F./K. Demoen (eds.), *Poetry and its Contexts in Eleventh-century Byzantium*,
Farnham 2012.

Beyer, H.-V., "David Disypatos als Theologe und Vorkämpfer für die Sache des Hesychasmus (ca. 1337–ca. 1350)", *Jahrbuch der Österreichischen Byzantinistik* 24 (1975), 107–28.

Boissonade, J.F., *Anecdota graeca e codicibus regiis*, 5 vols., Paris 1829–33 (repr. Hildesheim 1962).

Brooks, S.T., "Poetry and Female Patronage in Late Byzantine Tomb Decoration: Two Epigrams by Manuel Philes", *Dumbarton Oaks Papers* 60 (2006), 223–48.

Cameron, A.D.E., *The Greek Anthology from Meleager to Planudes*, Oxford 1993.

Capponi, F., "Eliano fonte di Phile", *Rivista di cultura classica e medioevale* 34 (1992), 222–61.

Cavallo, G. (ed.), *Lo spazio letterario del Medioevo, 3. Le culture circostanti, vol. I: La cultura bizantina*, Rome 2004.

Colonna, M.E., *Un Ἀνέκδοτον del ms. Monacensis graecus 551*, Naples [1959].

Constantinides, D.K., "Ἀνδρονίκου Παλαιολόγου Κεφάλαια περὶ ἀρετῆς καὶ κακίας", *Βυζαντινά* 15 (1989), 179–236.

Cupane, C., "Il motivo del castello nella narrativa tardobizantina. Evoluzione di un'allegoria", *Jahrbuch der Österreichischen Byzantinistik* 27 (1978), 229–67.

Cupane, C., "Il romanzo", in Cavallo (ed.), *Lo spazio letterario del Medioevo, 3. Le culture circostanti, vol. I: La cultura bizantina*, pp. 407–53.

Cupane, C., "Κατέλαβες τ' ἀμφίβολα τῆς τυφλῆς δαίμονος πρόσωπα. Il λόγος παρηγορητικὸς περὶ Δυστυχίας καὶ Εὐτυχίας e la figura di Fortuna nella letteratura greca medievale", in Panayotakis (ed.), *Origini della Letteratura neogreca*, vol. 1, pp. 413–37.

Cupane, C., "In the Realm of Eros: The Late Byzantine Vernacular Romance – Original Texts", in ead./Krönung (eds.), *Fictional Storytelling*, pp. 95–126.

Cupane, C., "Intercultural Encounters in the Late Byzantine Vernacular Romance", in Goldwyn/Nilsson (eds.), *Reading the Late Byzantine Romance*, pp. 40–68.

Cupane, C., "'Let me tell you a wonderful tale': Audience and Reception of the Vernacular Romances", in ead./Krönung (eds.), *Fictional Storytelling*, pp. 479–94.

Cupane, C., *Romanzi cavallereschi bizantini* (Classici Greci. Autori della tarda antichità e dell'età bizantina), Torino 1995.

Cupane, C., "Una passeggiata nei boschi narrativi. Lo statuto della finzione nel 'Medioevo Romanzo e Orientale'. In margine a un contributo recente", *Jahrbuch der Österreichischen Byzantinistik* 63 (2013), 61–90.

Cupane, C./B. Krönung (eds.), *Fictional Storytelling in the Medieval Eastern Mediterranean and Beyond* (Brill's Companions to the Byzantine World, 1), Leiden/Boston 2016.

Danezis, G., "Ὁ Σπανέας καὶ οἱ πολιτικοί στίχοι τοῦ Γεωργίου Λαπίθη", *Δίπτυχα* 4 (1986–1987), 413–25.

Darrouzès, J., "Les calendriers byzantins en vers", *Revue des Études Byzantines* 16 (1958), 59–84 (repr. in id., *Littérature et histoire des textes byzantins*, London 1972, no. IV).

Davis, J., "Anna Komnene and Niketas Choniates 'translated': The fourteenth-century Byzantine metaphrases", in R. Macrides (ed.), *History as Literature in Byzantium* (Society for the Promotion of Byzantine Studies, 15), Farnham 2010, pp. 55–70.

de Vries-van der Velden, E., *Théodore Métochite: Une réévaluation*, Amsterdam 1987.

Efthymiadis, S., "Déclassiciser pour édifier ? Remarques et réflexions à propos de la métaphrase de l'*Alexiade* d'Anne Comnène", *Travaux et Mémoires* 21/1 (2017), 139–50.

Efthymiadis, S., "Greek Byzantine Hagiography in Verse", in id. (ed.), *The Ashgate Research Companion to Byzantine Hagiography*, 2 vols., Farnham 2014, vol. 2, pp. 161–79.

Eideneier, H., *Μεσαιωνικές ιστορίες ζώων. Διήγησις των τετραπόδων ζώων και Πουλολόγος*, Heraklio 2016.

Gaul, N., "Embedded dialogues and dialogical voices in Palaiologan prose and verse", in A. Cameron/id. (eds.), *Dialogues and Debates from Late Antiquity to Late Byzantium*, Abingdon/New York 2017, pp. 184–202.

Gaul, N., "Performative Reading in the Late Byzantine Theatron", in Shawcross/Toth (eds.), *Reading in the Byzantine Empire and Beyond*, pp. 215–33.

Gaul, N., *Thomas Magistros und die spätbyzantinische Sophistik. Studien zum Humanismus urbaner Eliten in der frühen Palaiologenzeit* (Mainzer Veröffentlichungen zur Byzantinistik, 10), Wiesbaden 2011.

Géhin, P., "Les collections de *kephalaia* monastiques. Naissance et succès d'un genre entre création originale, plagiat et florilège", in A. Rigo (ed.), *Theologica minora. The Minor Genres of Byzantine Theological Literature* (Byzantioς. Studies in Byzantine History and Civilization, 8), Turnhout 2013, pp. 1–50.

Giannouli, A., "Hymn Writing in Byzantium: Forms and Writers", in Hörandner/Rhoby/Zagklas (eds.), *A Companion to Byzantine Poetry*, pp. 487–516.

Gioffreda, A./A. Rhoby, "Die metrische Psalmenmetaphrase des Manuel Philes. Präliminarien zu einer kritischen Edition", *Medioevo Greco* 20 (2020), 119–41.

Goldwyn, A.J./I. Nilsson (eds.), *Reading the Late Byzantine Romance. A Handbook*, Cambridge 2019.

Goldwyn, A.J./I. Nilsson, "Troy in Byzantine Romances. Homeric Reception in *Digenis Akritis*, the *Tale of Achilles* and the *Tale of Troy*", in id./ead. (eds.), *Reading the Late Byzantine Romance*, pp. 188–210.

Grünbart, M. (ed.), *Theatron. Rhetorische Kultur in Spätantike und Mittelalter* (Millennium-Studien, 13), Berlin/New York 2007.

Guntius, H., *Cyri Theodori Prodromi epigrammata ut uetustissima, ita pijssima, quibus omnia utriusque testamenti capita felicissime comprehenduntur: cum alijs nonnullis, quae Index uersa pagella singillatim explicat*, Basel 1536.

Heinseberg, A., "Aus der Geschichte und Literatur der Palaiologenzeit", *Sitzungsberichte der Bayerischen Akademie der Wissenschaften, Philosophisch-philologische und historische Klasse* 10 (1920), 1–144 (repr. in id., *Quellen und Studien zur spätbyzantinischen Geschichte*, London 1973, no. I).

Hinterberger, M., *Autobiographische Traditionen in Byzanz* (Wiener Byzantinistische Studien, 22), Vienna 1999.

Hinterberger, M., "Hagiographical Enkomia as *Metaphrasis* in the 14th Century. Some Preliminary Observations", in S. Constantinou/C. Høgel/A. Andreou (eds.), *Metaphrasis: A Byzantine Concept of Rewriting and its Hagiographical Products* (The Medieval Mediterranean, 125), Leiden/Boston 2020, pp. 285–323.

Hinterberger, M., "Hagiographische Metaphrasen: Ein möglicher Weg der Annäherung an die Literaturästhetik der frühen Palaiologenzeit", in Rhoby/Schiffer (eds.), *Imitatio – Aemulatio – Variatio*, pp. 137–52.

Hinterberger, M., "Studien zu Theodoros Metochites. Gedicht I – Des Meeres und des Lebens Wellen – Die Angst vor dem Neid – Die autobiographischen Texte – Sprache", *Jahrbuch der Österreichischen Byzantinistik* 51 (2001), 285–319.

Holton, D. (ed.), *Literature and society in Renaissance Crete*, Cambridge 1991.

Hörandner, W., "Court poetry: questions of motifs, structure and function", in E. Jeffreys (ed.), *Rhetoric in Byzantium. Papers from the Thirty-fifth Spring Symposium of Byzantine Studies, Exeter College, University of Oxford, March 2001* (Society for the Promotion of Byzantine Studies, Publications, 11), Aldershot 2003, pp. 75–85.

Hörandner, W., "Musterautoren und ihre Nachahmer: Indizien für Elemente einer byzantinischen Poetik", in P. Odorico/P.A. Agapitos/M. Hinterberger (eds.), *«Doux remède ...» Poésie et poètique à Byzance* (Dossiers byzantins, 9), Paris 2009, pp. 201–17.

Hörandner, W., "Teaching with verse in Byzantium", in id./Rhoby/Zagklas (eds.), *A Companion to Byzantine Poetry*, pp. 459–86.

Hörandner, W., "The Byzantine Didactic Poem: A Neglected Literary Genre? A Survey with Special Reference to the Eleventh Century", in Bernard/Demoen (eds.), *Poetry and its Contexts in Eleventh-century Byzantium*, pp. 55–67.

Hörandner, W., *Theodoros Prodromos, Historische Gedichte* (Wiener Byzantinistische Studien, 11), Vienna 1974.

Hörandner, W./A. Rhoby/N. Zagklas (eds.), *A Companion to Byzantine Poetry* (Brill's Companions to the Byzantine World, 4), Leiden/Boston 2019.

Hunger, H., "Un roman byzantin et son atmosphère: Callimaque et Chrysorrhoè", *Travaux et Mémoires* 3 (1968), 405–22 (repr. in id., *Byzantinistische Grundlagenforschung. Gesammelte Aufsätze*, London 1973, no. XIX).

Ilieva, A., "Images of Towns in Frankish Morea: The Evidence of the 'Chronicles' of the Morea and of the Tocco", *Byzantine and Modern Greek Studies* 19 (1995), 94–119.

Jeffreys, E., "Constantine Hermoniakos and Byzantine Education", *Δωδώνη. Ἐπιστημονικὴ Ἐπετηρὶς τῆς Φιλοσοφικῆς Σχολῆς τοῦ Πανεπιστημίου Ἰωαννίνων* 4 (1975), 81–109 (repr. in ead./M.J. Jeffreys, *Popular Literature in Late Byzantium* [Variorum Reprints], London 1983, no. IX).

Jeffreys, E., "From Herakles to Erkoulios, or the Place of the *War of Troy* in the Late Byzantine Romance Movement", in Goldwyn/Nilsson (eds.), *Reading the Late Byzantine Romance*, pp. 166–87.

Jeffreys, M., "The Comnenian Prokypsis", *Parergon. Bulletin of the Australian and New Zealand Association for Medieval and Renaissance Studies* n.s. 5 (1987), 38–53.

Kindstrand, F., "Manuel Philes' Use of Aelian's *De natura animalium* in his *De animalium proprietate*", *Studi italiani di filologia classica* ser. III, 4 (1986), 119–39.

Kotzabassi, S., "Ἔμμετρες μεταφράσεις του Μανουὴλ Φιλῆ", *Ἑλληνικά* 45 (1995), 359–62.

Kubina, K., "Manuel Philes – A Begging Poet? Requests, Letters and Problems of Genre Definition", in Rhoby/Zagklas (eds.), *Middle and Late Byzantine Poetry*, pp. 147–81.

Kubina, K., *Die enkomiastische Dichtung des Manuel Philes. Form und Funktion des literarischen Lobes in der frühen Palaiologenzeit* (Byzantinisches Archiv, 38), Berlin/Boston 2020.

Kubina, K., "Functions of Letters in Verse and Prose: A Comparison of Manuel Philes and Theodore Hyrtakenos", in K. Kubina/A. Riehle (eds.), *Epistolary Poetry in Byzantium and Beyond. An Anthology with Critical Essays*, New York/London 2021, pp. 78–90.

Kulhánková, M., "Die byzantinische Betteldichtung. Verbindung des Klassischen mit dem Volkstümlichen", in Rhoby/Schiffer (eds.), *Imitatio – Aemulatio – Variatio*, pp. 175–80.

Kulhánková, M., "Ich bin auch eines schicken Mantels wert. Zum Manteltopos in der griechischen Dichtung", in M. Kulhánková/K. Loudová (eds.), *Ἔπεα πτερόεντα. Růženě Dostálové k narozeninám*, Brno 2009, pp. 191–200.

Lauxtermann, M., "Byzantine Didactic Poetry and the Question of Poeticality", in P. Odorico/P.A. Agapitos/M. Hinterberger (eds.), *"Doux remède ..." Poésie et poétique à Byzance* (Dossiers Byzantins, 9), Paris 2009, pp. 37–46.

Lauxtermann, M., *Byzantine Poetry from Pisides to Geometres. Texts and Contexts*, vol. 2 (Wiener Byzantinistische Studien, 24/2), Vienna 2019.

Lauxtermann, M., "La poesia", in Cavallo (ed.), *Lo spazio letterario del Medioevo. 3. Le culture circostanti, vol. I: La cultura bizantina*, pp. 301–43.

Lauxtermann, M./M.C. Janssen, "Asinine tales east and west: the Ass's Confession and the Mule's Hoof", *Byzantinische Zeitschrift* 112.1 (2019), 105–22.

Lavagnini, R., "Tales of the Trojan War: Achilles and Paris in Medieval Greek Literature", in Cupane/Krönung (eds.), *Fictional Storytelling*, pp. 234–59.

Leonte, F., "'... For I have brought to you the fugitive animals of the desert': Animals and Representations of the Constantinopolitan Imperial Authority in Two Poems by Manuel Philes", in A.M. Choyke/G. Jaritz (eds.), *Animaltown: Beasts in medieval urban space*, Oxford 2017, pp. 179–87.

Luciani, C., "Autobiografismo e tradizione nell'opera di Sachlikis e Dellaportas", *Rivista di Studi Bizantini e Neoellenici* n.s. 34 (1997), 155–81.

Maas, P., "Der byzantinische Zwölfsilber", *Byzantinische Zeitschrift* 12 (1903), 278–323 (repr. in id., *Kleine Schriften*, ed. W. Buchwald, Munich 1973, pp. 242–88).

Makris, G., "Zum literarischen Genus des Pulologos", in Panayotakis (ed.), *Origini della Letteratura neogreca*, vol. 1, pp. 391–412.

Marciniak, P., "Byzantine Theatron – A Place of Performance?", in Grünbart (ed.), *Theatron*, pp. 277–85.

Matschke, K.-P./F. Tinnefeld, *Die Gesellschaft im späten Byzanz. Gruppen, Strukturen und Lebensformen*, Cologne/Weimar/Vienna 2001.

Medvedev, P., "The So-called θέατρα as a Form of Communication of the Byzantine Intellectuals in the 14th and 15th Centuries", in N.G. Moschonas (ed.), *Επικοινωνία στο Βυζάντιο. 4–6 Οκτωβρίου 1990 (Πρακτικά του Β΄ διεθνούς συμποσίου)*, Athens 1993, pp. 227–35.

Moennig, U., "A Hero Without Borders: 1 Alexander the Great in Ancient, Byzantine and Modern Greek Tradition", in Cupane/Krönung (eds.), *Fictional Storytelling*, pp. 159–89.

Moennig, U., "Intertextuality in the Late Byzantine Romance *Tale of Troy*", in Shawcross/Toth (eds.), *Reading in the Byzantine Empire and Beyond*, pp. 351–72.

Moennig, U., "Ρητορική και διήγησις των τετραπόδων ζώων", in G.K. Mavromatis/N. Agiotis (eds.), *Πρώιμη Νεοελληνική Δημώδης Γραμματεία (Πρακτικά του 6ου Διεθνούς Συνεδρίου Neograeca Medii Aevi)*, Heraklio 2012, pp. 573–90.

Nicholas, N./G. Baloglou, *An Entertaining Tale of Quadrupeds. Translation and Commentary*, New York 2003.

Nilsson, I., "Romantic Love in Rhetorical Guise: The Byzantine Revival of the Twelfth Century", in Cupane/Krönung (eds.), *Fictional Storytelling*, pp. 39–66.

Nilsson, I., "The Past as Poetry: Two Byzantine World Chronicles in Verse", in Hörandner/Rhoby/Zagklas (eds.), *A Companion to Byzantine Poetry*, pp. 517–38.

Oikonomides, N., "The Holy Icon as an Asset", *Dumbarton Oaks Papers* 45 (1991), 35–44.

Panayotakis, N.M. (ed.), *Origini della Letteratura neogreca. Atti del II Congresso Internazionale «Neograeca Medii Aevi»*, 2 vols., Venice 1993.

Papadogiannakis, N., *Studien zu den Epitaphien des Manuel Philes. Inaugural-Dissertation zur Erlangung des Grades eines Doktors der Philosophie des Fachbereichs Altertumswissenschaften der Freien Universität Berlin*, Heraklio 1984.

Paschos, P.B., Ἅπαντα τὰ ὑμνογραφικὰ τοῦ Ματθαίου Βλάσταρη, Athens 1980.

Paschos, P.B., Ὁ Ματθαῖος Βλάσταρης καὶ τὸ ὑμνογραφικὸν ἔργον του, Thessaloniki 1978.

Pietsch-Braounou, E., "Ein Aspekt der Rezeption der *Anthologia Planudea* in Epigrammen des Manuel Philes auf Bilder", in Rhoby/Schiffer (eds.), *Imitatio – Aemulatio – Variatio*, pp. 217–30.

Prinzing, G., "Zur byzantinischen Rangstreitliteratur in Prosa und Dichtung", *Römische Historische Mitteilungen* 45 (2003), 241–86.

Rhoby, A., *Byzantinische Epigramme auf Fresken und Mosaiken* (Byzantinische Epigramme in inschriftlicher Überlieferung, hrgg. von W. Hörandner/Id./A. Paul, Bd. 1) (Veröffentlichungen zur Byzanzforschung, 15), Vienna 2009.

Rhoby, A., "Poetry on Commission in Late Byzantium (13th–15th Century)", in Hörandner/Id./Zagklas (eds.), *A Companion to Byzantine Poetry*, pp. 264–304.

Rhoby, A., "The Epigram in Byzantium and Beyond", in C. Henriksén (ed.), *A Companion to Ancient Epigram*, Hoboken 2019, pp. 679–93.

Rhoby, A., "Vom jambischen Trimeter zum byzantinischen Zwölfsilber. Beobachtungen zur Metrik des spätantiken und byzantinischen Epigramms", *Wiener Studien* 124 (2011), 117–42.

Rhoby, A./E. Schiffer (eds.), *Imitatio – Aemulatio – Variatio*. Akten des internationalen wissenschaftlichen Symposions zur byzantinischen Sprache und Literatur (Wien, 22.–25. Oktober 2008) (Veröffentlichungen zur Byzanzforschung, 21), Vienna 2010.

Rhoby, A./N. Zagklas (eds.), *Middle and Late Byzantine Poetry: Texts and Contexts* (Βyzantιος. Studies in Byzantine History and Civilization, 14), Turnhout 2019.

Ricceri, R. "Two Metrical Rewritings of the Greek Psalms. Pseudo-Apollinaris of Laodicea and Manuel Philes", in M. Cutino (ed.), *Poetry, Bible and Theology from Late Antiquity to the Middle Ages* (Millennium-Studien, 86), Berlin/Boston 2020, pp. 223–36.

Russell, N., "The Hesychast Controversy", in A. Kaldellis/N. Siniossoglou (eds.), *The Cambridge Intellectual History of Byzantium*, Cambridge 2017, pp. 494–508.

Schönauer, S., *Untersuchungen zum Steinkatalog des Sophrosyne-Gedichtes des Meliteniotes mit kritischer Edition der Verse 1107–1247* (Meletemata, 6), Wiesbaden 1996.

Ševčenko, I., "Theodore Metochites, the Chora, and the Intellectual Trends of His Time", in P.A. Underwood (ed.), *The Kariye Djami, vol. 4: Studies in the Art of the Kariye Djami and Its Intellectual Background* (Bollingen series, 70), Princeton 1975, pp. 17–91.

Ševčenko, I., "The Palaeologan Renaissance", in W. Treadgold (ed.), *Renaissances before the Renaissance: cultural revivals of late antiquity and the Middle Ages*, Stanford 1984, pp. 144–71.

Shawcross, T., *The Chronicle of Morea: Historiography in Crusader Greece* (Oxford Studies in Byzantium), Oxford 2009.

Shawcross, T./I. Toth (eds.), *Reading in the Byzantine Empire and Beyond*, Cambridge 2018.

Stewart, K., "'An Entertaining Tale of Quadrupeds'. Animals and Insults in a Late Byzantine Poem", in T. Schmidt/J. Pahlitzsch (eds.), *Impious Dogs, Haughty Foxes and Exquisite Fish. Evaluative Perception and Interpretation of Animals in Ancient and Medieval Mediterranean Thought*, Berlin/Boston 2019, pp. 165–83.

Stickler, G., *Manuel Philes und seine Psalmenmetaphrase* (Dissertationen der Universität Wien, 229), Vienna 1992.

Takács, S.A., "Manuel Philes' Meditation on an Icon of the Virgin Mary", *Byzantinische Forschungen* 15 (1990), 277–88.

Talbot, A.-M., "Epigrams in Context: Metrical Inscriptions on Art and Architecture of the Palaiologan Era", *Dumbarton Oaks Papers* 53 (1999), 75–90.

Talbot, A.-M., "Epigrams of Manuel Philes on the Theotokos tes Peges and Its Art", *Dumbarton Oaks Papers* 48 (1994), 135–65.

Talbot, A.-M., "Old Wine in New Bottles: The Rewriting of Saints' Lives in the Palaeologan Period", in S. Ćurčić/D. Mouriki (eds.), *The Twilight of Byzantium. Aspects of Cultural and Religious History in the Late Byzantine Empire*, Princeton 1991, pp. 15–26 (repr. in ead., *Women and Religious Life in Byzantium* [Variorum Reprints], Aldershot 2001, no. x).

Taxidis, I., "Les monodies et les oraisons funèbres pour la mort du despote Jean Paléologue", *Medioevo Greco* 9 (2009), 267–84.

Toth, I., "Rhetorical Theatron in Late Byzantium: The Example of Palaiologan Imperial Orations", in Grünbart (ed.), *Theatron*, pp. 429–48.

Treu, M., "Manuel Holobolos", *Byzantinische Zeitschrift* 5 (1896), 538–59.

Tsolakis, E., "Τὸ χειρόγραφο ἀρ. 31 τῆς Δημοτικῆς Βιβλιοθήκης Κοζάνης. Κωδικολογικά – Τὸ περιεχόμενο – Ἀνέκδοτα ποιήματα τοῦ Μανουὴλ Φιλῆ", *Ἑλληνικά* 24 (1971), 321–36.

Yiavis, K., "The Adaptations of Western Sources by Byzantine Vernacular Romances", in Cupane/Krönung (eds.), *Fictional Storytelling*, pp. 127–56.

Yiavis, K., "The Categories of 'Originals' and 'Adaptations' in Late Byzantine Romance. A Reassessment", in Goldwyn/Nilsson (eds.), *Reading the Late Byzantine Romance*, pp. 19–39.

CHAPTER 6

Epistolography, Social Exchange and Intellectual Discourse (1261–1453)

Alexander Riehle

1 Byzantine Epistolography: Forms, Functions, and Transmission

With the term "epistolography" we commonly refer to letter-writing as a multifunctional cultural practice. Letters have a long history in the Euro-Mediterranean region as a medium of communication through which practical affairs are negotiated (e.g., business, administrative procedures, requests) and social relationships are established, fostered and transformed (e.g., "friendship letters," letters of consolation).[1] In this function, the text of the letter usually was only one element of a complex communicative act. The role of the letter-bearer was often not confined to delivering the missive to the recipient but could involve oral messages that conveyed the actual concern of the letter-exchange or the performance of ritualized gestures complementing the message. The sending of gifts regularly formed part of letter-exchanges. Foodstuffs, textiles or books could accompany the letter or be the actual incentive for writing one. In such cases, the message and the gift, which could carry also a symbolic meaning, were often interrelated. Finally, the letter as a material object should be taken into account when attempting a holistic interpretation of a multi-media letter-exchange, although in the case of Byzantine epistolography our conclusions have to remain purely hypothetical, since no original letters have come down to us save for the early papyri that have been preserved in the dry climate of Egypt, a few imperial and patriarchal letters, and a rather peculiar epistolary poem from the 15th century.[2]

---

1 For Ancient Greek letter-writing, see Ceccarelli, *Ancient Greek Letter Writing*, Sarri, *Material Aspects*, Bauer, "Letter Writing in Antiquity"; for Medieval Western Europe see the classic study by Constable, *Letters and Letter Collections* and Wahlgren-Smith, "Letter Collections in the Latin West"; for general introductions to Byzantine epistolography, see Mullett, "Epistolography", Papaioannou, "Letter-Writing", Grünbart, "L'epistolografia", Riehle, "Byzantine Epistolography". In particular on the various functions of letter-writing, see Littlewood, "An 'Ikon of the Soul'".

2 On these aspects of Byzantine epistolography, see Bernard, "Epistolary Communication" (with further bibliography). For imperial letters see Beihammer, "Epistolography and

---

© KONINKLIJKE BRILL NV, LEIDEN, 2023 | DOI:10.1163/9789004527089_008

While this socio-communicative and pragmatic dimension of letter-writing is present in all letter-exchanges – from private letters of common people who were either sufficiently educated to write a letter themselves or could afford to hire a professional scribe, to official correspondence – since at least the 4th century BC epistolary writing had also entered learned discourse. Philosophical and political treatises were framed as letters (e.g., the letters of or attributed to Plato, Isocrates and Epicurus), the epistolary mode was fictionalized (e.g., the pseudo-historical, rustic and erotic letters of the Hellenistic, Roman and late antique periods), and the private correspondence of educated elites became markedly rhetorical. Thus, from a medium of communication the letter developed also into a literary genre.

As a genre, letters present certain formal and functional features that render them distinguishable from other genres such as orations or treatises. According to ancient theorists, a letter was "a conversation halved" that compensated for direct interpersonal exchange, when such interaction was hampered by spatial separation. It ought to be brief and in a conversational, albeit slightly elevated, style.[3] In terms of structure, after a prescript – most commonly ὁ δεῖνα τῷ δεῖνι χαίρειν: "So-and-so to so-and-so, greetings!" – the text proper was usually introduced by a prologue, which could include a wish, such as an expression of joy or thanksgiving for having received a letter from the recipient. The body of the letter was more flexible and less formalized than other sections of the letter, as it had to be adapted to the specific occasion of the given exchange. In the opening of the body, the writer laid the groundwork for the purpose of the letter, for instance by informing the addressee about an incident that had led them to writing a letter, by praising or reproaching the addressee or by pondering over the values of friendship, thus segueing to the presentation of the actual objective of the letter (e.g., a request or a recommendation of another person). The letter usually ended with a concluding exhortation (epilogue), wishes for the addressee, greetings to other persons and a valediction such as ἔρρωσο ("farewell!"; postscript).[4] Moreover, a set of conventional

---

Diplomatics"; for the epistolary poem, penned by Gerardos, see Kubina/Riehle, *Epistolary Poetry*, no. 48.

3 See the various texts anthologized in Malherbe, *Ancient Epistolary Theorists*.

4 For a good overview of the structure of papyrus and New Testament letters see Klauck, *Ancient Letters*, pp. 9–42. In the case of learned letters, which survive exclusively as manuscript copies, some of the formal features were altered for the purpose of publication. For example, the prescript was usually replaced by a heading providing solely the name of the addressee in the dative, and the concluding valediction was commonly omitted. With the exception of forms of address (see Grünbart, *Formen der Anrede*), a systematic survey of formal und structural aspects of learned letters is still lacking. For recent case studies see Riehle,

motifs existed – e.g., the presence (παρουσία) of the writer in his letter, the friend as *alter ego* – from which the writer could draw for the specific purpose and addressee.[5] The perpetuation of such distinctive formal patterns was granted by handbooks of letter-writing providing sample letters for different occasions along with instructions (Ps-Demetrios, Ps-Libanios/Ps-Proklos), but even more so by letter-collections of authors who were regarded as exemplary models of epistolary style (for Byzantium chiefly writers of late antiquity, such as Libanios, Synesios and the Church Fathers). Direct reference or allusion to the ancient and Christian classics was another device regularly employed by learned letter-writers.[6]

For educated epistolographers such devices were much more than a means of embellishing a letter for aesthetic reasons. Letter-writing was part of an intellectual exchange through which authors could present their literary skills and make a claim to belonging to the educated elite. Composing letters that adhered to established stylistic ideals and included intertextual references that could only be appreciated by a small circle of highly educated men (and, rarely, women) formed part of the self-understanding of intellectuals as an exclusive group of *pepaideumenoi* who belonged or were closely attached to the political elites and shared common ideals.

This also becomes evident in the transmission of letters. With the few exceptions mentioned above, all surviving letters from Byzantium are preserved as manuscript copies only. Authors, or their disciples or admirers, regularly "published" their letters – usually a selection of their original correspondence that included those pieces that where regarded as the best or most suitable for the purpose of publication – as part of their literary oeuvre.[7] The aim of such a publication was usually the presentation of a specific persona of the author (e.g., as an intellectual, influential politician, ecclesiastical leader) – in other words, letter-collections could constitute the author's (auto)biography.[8] For this purpose, the redactors selected some letters, arranged them in a way that suited their needs (usually not strictly chronologically) and revised the text of the letters, sometimes significantly as the case of Demetrios Kydones demonstrates. Before dispatching his letters, Kydones transcribed them into loose quires in order to save a copy for himself; these quires are today preserved as

---

Funktionen der byzantinischen Epistolographie, pp. 217–42 and Taxidis, *Μάξιμος Πλανούδης*, pp. 287–303.

5   See Karlsson, *Idéologie* and Thraede, *Grundzüge*.

6   See Littlewood, "A Statistical Survey".

7   On the transmission of letters and the formation of letter-collections, see Riehle, "Letters and New Philology", pp. 477–90 with further references at p. 483 n. 72.

8   See Riehle, "Epistolography as Autobiography" and id., "Letters and New Philology", pp. 483–84.

codex Vat. gr. 101. For the purpose of publication, he revised his transcriptions, adding or deleting single words or whole sentences, changing the wording, etc., sometimes to the point that the new text bore little resemblance to the original letter. Kydones then passed on his revised transcriptions to a scribe – the scholar Manuel Kalekas, himself known as a prolific letter-writer – adding marginal notes in which he instructs Kalekas on how to proceed in producing a clean copy of his collection. This copy, too, survives today as codex Urb. gr. 133.[9] Kydones' collection is certainly the most striking and best documented example of the entire Byzantine period, since, to my knowledge, no other dossier of authorial copies survives that subsequently formed the basis for the "published" clean copy. There is evidence, however, that other epistolographers, especially of the Palaeologan period, proceeded in similar ways.[10] In providing a vehicle for authorial self-representation and for establishing and maintaining social relationships, epistolography thus fulfilled multiple socio-pragmatic functions for Byzantine literati.

2 Social Exchange and Intellectual Discourse: Notes on Theory and Terminology

Interest in and research on social dynamics in Byzantium has grown continuously over the past decades. Notions and practices of different forms of interpersonal relationships such as kinship, friendship and patronage are being explored, social networks detected and analyzed. The scrutiny of epistolography as part of such dynamics has greatly benefitted from the integration of relevant sociological theories and methods.

In her pioneering 1988 article "Byzantium: A Friendly Society?," Margaret Mullett contested the until then prevailing view that the Byzantines were generally skeptical towards friendship and relied almost exclusively on family ties, observing that "relationships we would normally define as friendship or patronage either may be multiplex and include blood relationship or may be described in terms of blood tie. But that does not mean that extra-kin relationships did not exist and were not as important a social glue as kinship itself" (p. 9). The best evidence for this can be found in intellectual, and in particular epistolary, discourse, for which the acknowledgement and praise of friendship

---

9   See Loenertz, *Les recueils*, pp. 1–18 and Hatlie, "Life and Artistry", pp. 81–102.

10   See, e.g., Riehle, *Funktionen der byzantinischen Epistolographie*, pp. 47–85 and id., "Epistolography as Autobiography" on Nikephoros Choumnos; on Manuel II Palaiologos see the introduction to the edition of his *Letters* by George Dennis, pp. xxi–xxii.

was a vital element (pp. 9–10). Mullett further asserted that the Byzantines "took a very practical view of friendship ... A friendship was a failure if it failed to serve its purpose" (p. 13). In other words, friends were mostly regarded and framed as interest groups, even if the vocabulary used in this context might point to the opposite: the idea of reciprocity was crucial among *philoi*. In such cases of instrumental social ties, it is hard to draw a line between friendship and patronage: the term *philoi* is regularly applied to both in the sources, and the defining criteria of reciprocity and duration are met by both of them as well. However, the concept of symmetry might help to distinguish between the two: while friendship presupposes equality of status, patronage involves an asymmetrical (i.e., unequal) relationship between two people, meaning that they do not have the same social status and that they provide different kinds of goods and services in their interpersonal exchange (pp. 16–18). In later studies, Mullett elaborated on her view that the literary treatment of friendship drawing on ancient and Christian ideals – including the use of traditional "topoi" – did not constitute an indiscriminate repetition of earlier writing, but on the contrary was heavily tied to social practices.[11]

In recent years, Byzantinists dealing with aspects of social exchange among educated elites have followed the threads teased apart by Mullett. Of particular interest for the present chapter are Floris Bernard's and Niels Gaul's interpretations of Byzantine literary culture in the 11th and early 14th centuries respectively, both of which draw on theories of the French sociologist Pierre Bourdieu. In his examination of "intellectual friendship" in 11th-century Byzantium, Bernard argues that gift-giving and concomitant textual practices – such as the refusal of gifts in letters and the offering of "gifts of words" – functioned as representations through which the intellectual elite of the 11th century constituted and reaffirmed itself as a distinctive social group tied by bonds of friendship and shared intellectual values.[12] Similarly, Gaul has pointed out the dynamic interplay between *paideia* ("education, learning") and power among urban elites in the early 14th century. These elites used their learning as "symbolic capital" in order to advance their personal or socio-political interests. The cornerstone of this *paideia*, expressing shared ideals, was the classicizing sociolect developed by the literati of the so-called Second Sophistic of the late Roman period. The most important literary space for the investment of symbolic capital through learning was the *theatron*: a gathering of intellectuals, in which mostly orations but also texts belonging to other genres such as letters were

---

11   See especially her "Friendship in Byzantium" (with references to her earlier work).
12   Bernard, "'Greet Me with Words'".

performed.[13] Finally, in my own "Rhetorik, Ritual und Repräsentation" I have pointed to the important role that epistolary discourse – including friendship language, exchange of gifts, humor and reproach – and concomitant ritualized acts of communication and representation played for Constantinopolitan educated elites of the early Palaeologan period in the context of social integration and distinction.

Seminal also has been Mullett's contribution to the introduction of social network analysis to Byzantine studies. In her reading of the letter-collection of the metropolitan Theophylaktos of Ohrid she employed a methodology and terminology borrowed from the Manchester school of anthropologists of the late 1960s and 1970s. Analytical categories such as role relation, transactional content, directional flow and duration of interaction helped her define the nature of each relationship in Theophylaktos' network. She could then reconstruct and analyze this network structurally (e.g., its size and density, clusters within the network) and examine how Theophylaktos made use of the relationships entangled in his network.[14] Recently, more complex quantitative methods of network analysis have been applied to social groupings in Byzantium, many of which with letters as their main source material.[15]

In Byzantium, the fabric of such networks naturally shifted over the centuries due to changes in the political, social and cultural realms. In the following, I will present some facets of networks of intellectual elites in the different phases of the colorful history of the late Byzantine empire and examine the role that epistolography played in various forms of exchange within these networks, without adhering too strictly to the methods of social network analysis. It would be beyond the scope and limits of the present chapter to attempt a reconstruction of entire networks with the help of quantitative methods, which would require evaluating an enormous volume of source material. I will instead confine myself to outlining the general parameters of the composition, functioning, and uses of networks of intellectuals in each period, while focusing on social conceptions and practices within such networks – including role relations such as friendship and patronage, patterns of and motifs for epistolary communication, transactional contents (goods and services) exchanged in this framework, and rituals involved in such interactions – and their relation to intellectual discourse. By "intellectual discourse" I mean on the one hand acts of communication aiming at affirming, or negotiating, intellectual ideals (e.g., through the very exchange of literary letters and books), and actual intellectual

---

13   Gaul, *Thomas Magistros*; see also id., "The Letter in the *Theatron*".
14   Mullett, *Theophylact of Ochrid*, pp. 163–222.
15   See the overview in Preiser-Kapeller, "Letters and Network Analysis".

EPISTOLOGRAPHY, SOCIAL EXCHANGE AND INTELLECTUAL DISCOURSE   217

exchange (discussions of scholarly matters, theological debates, etc.) on the other.[16]

I have divided my discussion into three sections, each dealing with one period of the late Byzantine Empire, followed by a glance at the fate of learned Greek letter-writing after the fall of Constantinople. This periodization is guided by developments in the political and social history of the empire, which had a forceful impact on the constitution and behavior of its intellectual elites.[17] The early Palaeologan period, which is particularly rich in surviving material, will be treated in more detail and with more examples, while the discussion of the period between c.1360 and 1453 will be necessarily more cursory.

3   A Microcosm: Letters within the Constantinopolitan Intellectual Elite (1261–1321)

The restoration of Byzantine rule over Constantinople in 1261 ushered in a period of ideological and cultural renovation. The first emperors of the new dynasty of the Palaiologoi, Michael VIII (1259–1282) and Andronikos II (1282–1328), were keen on promoting educated men to official posts and rewarding them with court titles so that they could contribute to the propagation of imperial ideology by evoking traditional ideals in highly elaborate prose and verse texts. According to Niels Gaul, these men functioned as '"switchboards,' or fuses, between Constantinopolitan and urban or local literati on the one hand and the Palaiologoi or the aristocratic elite on the other."[18] While some of them belonged to the old families of the empire, others were parvenus from the lower-ranking bureaucracy who managed to ascend because of their education.[19] These aristocrats and court officials of a lowlier background formed the core of an intellectual elite that was centered in and around Constantinople, strongly tied to each other and engaged in a permanent struggle between isolation and openness towards newcomers.[20] The core of

---

16   For such an approach see, in addition to the work discussed above, the comparative volume Steckel/Gaul/Grünbart, *Networks of Learning*, and in particular the concluding chapters by Steckel ("Networks of Learning") and Gaul ("Rising Elites and Institutionalization"). In the recent *Cambridge Intellectual History of Byzantium* (eds. Kaldellis/Siniossoglou) neither networks nor epistolography receive substantive discussion.

17   Cf. Matschke/Tinnefeld, *Die Gesellschaft im späten Byzanz*, pp. 367–71.

18   Gaul, "All the Emperor's Men", p. 263.

19   For a few striking examples from Thomas Magistros' circle in Thessaloniki see Gaul, *Thomas Magistros*, pp. 237–39.

20   On the early Palaeologan aristocracy see Kyritses, *The Byzantine Aristocracy* and Matschke/Tinnefeld, *Die Gesellschaft im späten Byzanz*, pp. 18–54.

this group comprised renowned men such as Theodore Mouzalon, Nikephoros Choumnos, Theodore Metochites, Leo Bardales, Constantine Akropolites and also a woman of high rank and esteem, namely Theodora Raoulaina. This core was joined by other figures of different profiles: high-ranking Church officials such as the patriarchs Gregory of Cyprus and John Glykys;[21] educated monks who maintained strong ties with the Constantinopolitan aristocracy and in some cases advanced to, or were at least offered, higher ecclesiastical offices, for instance, Joseph the Philosopher, Theoleptos of Philadelphia and Matthew of Ephesos; and intellectuals with no or a low-ranking official position who hoped to benefit from their learning and connection to the political elites, for instance, Theodore Hyrtakenos, Michael Gabras and Maximos Neamonites.[22] A key element of their ideology and identity was a higher learning based on the principles of Atticism as it had been developed during the so-called Second Sophistic. This ideal included the composition, commissioning and performance of orations and the exchange of rhetorically elaborate letters, which involved textual and non-textual rituals and were often accompanied by gifts and, in particular, books.[23]

The following discussion focuses on examples from the reign of Andronikos II, as intellectual discourse reached its peak under this emperor, who had a stronger personal penchant for learning than did his father Michael VIII, and epistolary exchange is best documented for this period.[24] Arguably the most influential person within the intellectual elite of the capital of this period was Gregory of Cyprus (c.1240–1289/90), monk and from 1283 to 1289 Patriarch of Constantinople, who was acknowledged by contemporaries as the leading scholar of his time: the historian Nikephoros Gregoras even claims that it was Gregory who was responsible for the revival of classical learning after a period during which "the noble harmony of Greek in literature and the Atticizing

---

21 Patriarch Athanasios I (c.1230–1320), from whom a substantial corpus of letters survives (*Letters to the Emperor*, ed. & trans. Talbot; his letters to various ecclesiastics remain unpublished), did not belong to this intellectual elite. In fact, he vehemently reproached educated statesmen like Choumnos for their vanity (see no. 37, ed. Talbot, p. 78, lines 33–36 with translation at p. 79 and commentary at p. 347). On his outsider status see also Nikephoros Gregoras, *Roman History* VI 5, ed. Schopen, vol. 1, p. 180, lines 18–19: "He was ignorant of learning in the letters and of civic manners" (ἦν δὲ ὁ ἀνὴρ ἀδαὴς μὲν τῆς τῶν γραμμάτων παιδείας καὶ τῶν πολιτικῶν ἠθῶν).

22 See Ševčenko, "Society and Intellectual Life", pp. 69–76, who in this part of his study, however, offers too monolithic a view of the entire 14th century.

23 See Laiou, "The Correspondence of Gregorios Kyprios", esp. pp. 94–97 for a case study on Gregory of Cyprus.

24 For Andronikos' policy of systematically tying middling-stratum intellectuals to the imperial family, see Gaul, "All the Emperor's Men".

EPISTOLOGRAPHY, SOCIAL EXCHANGE AND INTELLECTUAL DISCOURSE

language" (τὸν ἐν ταῖς γραφαῖς εὐγενῆ τῆς Ἑλλάδος ῥυθμὸν καὶ τὴν Ἀττικίζουσαν γλῶσσαν ἐκείνην) had been forgotten.[25] Himself a student of the renowned scholar and politician George Akropolites, Gregory became the teacher of several young men who were to advance to the highest civil and ecclesiastical offices:[26] Theodore Mouzalon (1256/58–1294), *megas logothetes* and *mesazon* ("prime minister") of Andronikos II;[27] Theodore's successor as the right-hand man of the emperor, Nikephoros Choumnos (c.1260–1327); the *protoasekretis* Manuel Neokaisareites (born c.1250/60); and John Glykys, first a high-ranking civil servant and later Patriarch of Constantinople (1315–19). Further members of his circle included Gregory's former fellow-student John Pediasimos (c.1240–1310/14) and the widowed noblewoman Theodora Raoulaina (c.1240–1300). One of the most outstanding scholars of late Byzantium, Maximos Planoudes (c.1255–1305), may have been his student for a while and had strong ties to Gregory's circle, as one can infer, for instance, from his letters to Mouzalon, Choumnos, Raoulaina and Glykys.

What bound these people together and rendered them a close-knit group was a set of shared values that found expression in various ways and realms. The well-documented exchange of books, usually involving also the dispatch of accompanying letters, provides the best evidence for their eagerness to share their knowledge and benefit intellectually from their peers.[28] Nikephoros Choumnos lent Theodora Raoulaina his copy of Aristotle's *Meteorology*, which included the commentary of Alexander of Aphrodisias, and encouraged her to amend the text, as it was rife with scribal mistakes.[29] Maximos Planoudes restored a miscellaneous codex containing various ancient treatises on mathematics and harmonics, which Theodore Mouzalon had sent him and Planoudes

---

25   Nikephoros Gregoras, *Roman History* VI 1, ed. Schopen, vol. 1, p. 163, lines 9–15.

26   For the teaching and students of George Akropolites and Gregory of Cyprus see Constantinides, *Higher Education*, pp. 31–49 and Mergiali, *L'enseignement*, pp. 15–25.

27   The inference that Mouzalon was Gregory's student hinges on the interpretation of a letter in which Mouzalon states to Gregory that "I am pleased to be both your student and child, my great father-teacher" (Gregory of Cyprus, *Letters*, no. 118, ed. Eustratiades, pp. 95–96 = Theodore Mouzalon, *Letters*, no. 3, ed. Samara, p. 217, lines 5–6: ἀγαπῶ καὶ μαθητὴς εἶναι καὶ παῖς σοῦ τοῦ μεγάλου διδασκάλου πατρός). While Constantinides (*Higher Education*, p. 36) understands this to refer to Mouzalon personally, Samara (Θεόδωρος Μουζάλων, p. 189; see also pp. 24–25) seems to favor a generic interpretation. Samara further suggests that Mouzalon was the son of Theodora Raoulaina from her first marriage to George Mouzalon and that he grew up together with the future emperor Andronikos II at the imperial court (ibid., pp. 22–24).

28   On the availability and circulation of books in this period see Constantinides, *Higher Education*, pp. 133–58 and Karpozilos, "Books and Bookmen".

29   Nikephoros Choumnos, *Letters*, no. 76, ed. Boissonade, pp. 91–93.

had found to be in a poor condition.[30] Gregory of Cyprus beseeched the deacon Kallistos to send him his manuscript of Aristotle's *Ethics* because his search for a good copy had been to no avail[31] and praised John Glykys for the beauty of his handwriting in a copy of Gregory of Nazianzos' letters.[32] Michael Gabras (born c.1290) was particularly interested in manuscripts of one of the most important representatives of the Second Sophistic, Aelius Aristides, and asked various educated men in his network to send him their copies.[33]

Texts of contemporary authors were likewise in high demand. In fact, Apostolos Karpozilos observed that epistolographers of the early Palaeologan period seem to be more concerned with the circulation of their own writings (orations, philosophical or scientific treatises, etc.) than with the exchange of manuscripts containing ancient or earlier religious texts.[34] In a letter to an anonymous addressee, Nikephoros Choumnos asks that Theodore Metochites' recently composed speech, which was on everyone's lips, be sent to him.[35] It is possible that Choumnos at that time did not yet know Metochites well enough to contact him directly and instead approached someone closer to Metochites – maybe his nephew Leo Bardales who was also a close associate of Choumnos'. Frequently authors themselves took the initiative and dispatched their compositions to their peers asking them to review and evaluate them. Choumnos, for instance, asked the Gabras brothers to assess one of his writings by using the ancient authors as a touchstone. Michael Gabras responded with a letter full of praise and admiration.[36] That this mutual critique and, usually, praise of their literary compositions had a strong social component is explicitly stated in a letter of Theodore Hyrtakenos: Theodore had sent one of his poetic compositions (ἔπη) to the well-known scholar George Galesiotes and now asks for a just verdict. If George judges that the composition is flawed,

---

30 Maximos Planoudes, *Letters*, no. 67, ed. Leone, p. 99, line 24 – p. 100, line 5 and p. 102, lines 7–15, with Wendel, "Planudes als Bücherfreund", pp. 80–81.

31 Gregory of Cyprus, *Letters*, no. 47, ed. Eustratiades, p. 34.

32 Gregory of Cyprus, *Letters*, no. 98, ed. Eustratiades, p. 75, with Kourousis, "Ὁ λόγιος οἰκου-μενικὸς Πατριάρχης", pp. 306–08.

33 Michael Gabras, *Letters*, nos. 259, 260, 266, 269, 270, 326, 449, ed. Fatouros, vol. 2, pp. 415–17, 423–24, 427–28, 518–19, 690–91, with Karpozilos, "Books and Bookmen", pp. 267–68.

34 Karpozilos, "Books and Bookmen", p. 271.

35 Nikephoros Choumnos, *Letters*, no. 91, ed. Boissonade, pp. 126–27.

36 Nikephoros Choumnos, *Letters*, no. 30, ed. Boissonade, pp. 35–36; Michael Gabras, *Letters*, no. 99, ed. Fatouros, vol. 2, pp. 161–62. For examples from the letters of Gregory of Cyprus see Kotzabassi, "Gregorios Kyprios as Reader and Critic", pp. 76–81.

EPISTOLOGRAPHY, SOCIAL EXCHANGE AND INTELLECTUAL DISCOURSE   221

he encourages him to amend it and send it back, since this would be the "proof of absolute friendship" (ἀκράτου φιλίας τεκμήριον).[37]

In this framework, letters were not only the medium through which the request and delivery were accomplished but functioned as essays of literary criticism. One such case is Nikephoros Choumnos' Letter 78, in which on the basis of the Hermogenian system of *ideai* he assesses and lauds a letter from Leo Bardales, which he had previously asked to be sent to him (Letter 75).[38] This mutual critique and praise conducted through the medium of letter-writing was part of an affirmative ritual, consisting of a set sequence of staged actions: the sending of a text accompanied by the request of evaluation was followed by exuberant praise and compliments, which in turn stipulated expressions of joy and thankfulness.[39]

Praise was frequent, but not by default. Failure to comply with the accepted linguistic ideals could engender harsh criticism, as in the case of Theodora Raoulaina who reproached her protégé Gregory of Cyprus for having written her "a naïve and all too priestly letter".[40] Connected to this rather unexpected frankness is another phenomenon that can be regularly observed in correspondence of this period. While the sending of gifts usually gave rise to thanksgiving and praise of the sender's generosity, letter-writers of the early Palaeologan period frequently made humorous or even ironic comments about gifts they had received, sometimes resulting in the recipient's blatant rejection of them.[41] The roots of this seemingly rude behavior are probably to be sought in the intellectual milieu of the 10th century, in which according to Alexander Kazhdan humor and mockery played a communicative role.[42] By late Byzantine times it had become an accepted code of playful social exchange.

---

37   Theodore Hyrtakenos, *Letters*, no. 52, ed. & trans. Karpozilos/Fatouros, pp. 200–01 (= ed. la Porte-du Theil (1860), pp. 16–17).

38   Nikephoros Choumnos, *Letters*, no. 75 and 78, ed. Boissonade, pp. 88–91 and 94–96. For examples from the corpus of Gregory of Cyprus see Kotzabassi, "Gregorios Kyprios as Reader and Critic", esp. pp. 83–86.

39   See, for instance, the correspondence between Nikephoros Choumnos and Theodore Metochites: Nikephoros Choumnos, *Letters*, nos. 37–40 and 133–134, ed. Boissonade, pp. 45–51 and 155–59.

40   Gregory of Cyprus, *Letters to Theodora Raoulaina*, no. 18, ed. Kotzabassi, p. 158 with Laiou, "The Correspondence of Gregorios Kyprios", p. 96. For further examples from Gregory's correspondence see Kotzabassi, "Gregorios Kyprios as Reader and Critic", pp. 86–87.

41   Examples in Riehle, "Rhetorik, Ritual und Repräsentation", pp. 270–72 with n. 43.

42   Kazhdan, *A History of Byzantine Literature (850–1000)*, pp. 331–33. See also Chernoglazov, "Was bedeuten drei Fische?", Bernard, "'Greet Me with Words'" and id., "Humor in Byzantine Letters".

Another important factor in the literati networks and intellectual discourse of this period was teaching and teacher-student relationships. Several of the intellectuals mentioned above are known to have been involved in some sort of teaching activities, be it as "professors" with an official appointment or as private tutors. The teacher's importance for the young men's intellectual and moral formation was deemed so high that kinship vocabulary was regularly used to describe their relationship.[43]

Gregory of Cyprus took great care for his students not only during their studies under him, but also later on, and the medium of letter-writing played an important role as a vehicle for instruction, admonition and intellectual discourse (exchange of books, evaluation of their compositions), as attested, for instance, in his numerous letters to his (former) students Theodore Mouzalon and Manuel Neokaisarites, who may have owed their careers to their influential teacher.[44] Likewise Constantine Akropolites (c.1250–1323/24) held his teacher, who might be identified with Manuel Holobolos, in high regard and continued to exchange letters with him concerning intellectual matters.[45]

As the classroom was one of the spaces where the established cultural and social values were imparted to adolescent scholars-to-be, fellow-students often maintained close relationships even after leaving school. Gregory of Cyprus and John Pediasimos had studied together under George Akropolites and remained friends also after Pediasimos' departure from Constantinople to Ohrid where he had been appointed as *chartophylax*. On one occasion, Pediasimos sent a young man by the name of Doukopoulos to his former fellow student asking Gregory to instruct him so that he may perfect his knowledge. Gregory's response opens as follows: "I know how to honor friendship and how to appreciate love of learning. Thus I was delighted to see the good Doukopoulos both for his own sake, as he possess love of learning along with

---

43   See, for instance, Constantine Akropolites, *Letters*, no. 66, ed. Romano, p. 159, lines 3–4: "a teacher is, indeed, also a father, since, as we have learned, he is the cause of well-being" (ὁ γὰρ διδάσκαλος καὶ πατὴρ πάντως, ἅτε δὴ τοῦ εὖ εἶναι, ὡς μεμαθήκαμεν, αἴτιος); Maximos Planoudes, *Letters*, no. 8, ed. Leone, p. 20, lines 6–9: "How much do you think I long for the time when, deo volente, I will instruct him [i.e. the addressee's son] as a father in matters of learning, just as I am now his spiritual father!" (ἐγὼ δ' ἐκείνου τοῦ χρόνου πῶς οἴει γλίχομαι, ὅταν, ὥσπερ νῦν εἰμὶ πατὴρ αὐτῷ τὰ πνευματικά, οὕτως (εἴη δὲ σὺν θεῷ φάναι) καὶ τὰ ἐς λόγους πατὴρ προκαθέζεσθαι μέλλω).

44   See in general Laiou, "The Correspondence of Gregorios Kyprios", p. 95. For Gregory's letters to Neokaisarites see the examples discussed in Matschke/Tinnefeld, *Die Gesellschaft im späten Byzanz*, p. 294; some of Mouzalon's responses to Gregory's letters are preserved in the latter's collection (Theodore Mouzalon, *Letters*, ed. Samara).

45   Constantine Akropolites, *Letters* nos. 66, 71 and 73, ed. Romano, pp. 159, 163 and 164 with Constantinides, *Higher Education* 39.

EPISTOLOGRAPHY, SOCIAL EXCHANGE AND INTELLECTUAL DISCOURSE 223

natural talent, and because you, who hold the first rank among my friends, recommended him to me, and – shall I say the third reason? – because he delivered to me a beautiful and most dear letter." Gregory then praises his addressee for his learning, emphasizing that there is nothing that he could teach the young man that Pediasimos himself could not, and finally reproaches him for not writing more frequently.[46] It is thus their commitment to the ideals of friendship (φιλία) and love for learning (φιλομάθεια) that dominated their relationship and governed interactions between them. Especially since their separation epistolography provided them with a means of reaffirming these values and of effecting transactions.

Maximos Planoudes' students, all of whom expressed deep admiration and indebtedness towards their teacher, continued to be tied by bonds of friendship after leaving school despite being dispersed to different regions of the empire. Again, it was the medium of letter-writing that helped them maintain and reaffirm their relationship and common intellectual ideals.[47]

Although there is little direct evidence for the inclusion of epistolography in the school curriculum, the examples above suggest that the art of letter-writing was taught to advanced students as part of their rhetorical training. The eight brief letters of Theodore Modenos, who flourished around 1300, possibly in the Macedonian city of Serres, are in all likelihood an example of the first attempts of an adolescent to write friendship letters adhering to the rules of the genre.[48]

Finally, the question of patronage and its relation to friendship must be addressed in this context. As becomes evident already in some of the examples discussed above, the discourse of intellectual friendship was not exclusively driven by pure love of learning and altruistic interest for the preservation and perpetuation of literary culture. The acquisition of a higher education was rather a form of capital that could be invested and exploited in various contexts. In letters of request addressed to the highly educated political elite – who acted as "brokers" mediating between less influential subjects (including middling-stratum intellectuals) and the imperial court[49] – writers most commonly first

---

46   Gregory of Cyprus, *Letters*, no. 35, ed. Eustratiades, pp. 24–26, quotation at p. 24: Καὶ φιλίαν οἶδα τιμᾶν ἐγὼ καὶ φιλομάθειαν ἀγαπᾶν. Οὐκοῦν τὸν καλὸν Δουκόπουλον καὶ δι᾿ αὐτόν, αὐτὸν εἶδον ἡδέως ὄντα μετὰ τοῦ εὖ πεφυκέναι φιλομαθῆ, καὶ διὰ τὸν τοῦτον ἡμῖν συστήσαντά σε, τὰ πρῶτα παρ᾿ ἡμῖν ὄντα τῶν φίλων – εἴπω καὶ τὸ τρίτον; – εἶδον αὐτὸν ἡδέως καὶ ὅτι μοι καλῆς καὶ φιλτάτης διάκονος γέγονεν ἐπιστολῆς.

47   See the evidence discussed in Constantinides, *Higher Education*, pp. 83–88.

48   Theodore Modenos, *Letters*, ed. Treu.

49   See Gaul, "All the Emperor's Men", esp. pp. 265–67 and the case studies in Laiou, "The Correspondence of Gregorios Kyprios", pp. 97–106 and Riehle, "Theodoros Xanthopoulos", esp. pp. 167–68 and 171–75.

224 RIEHLE

stressed shared intellectual ideals before proceeding to address their cause. For instance, Michael Gabras' letter *To one of the powerful*, whose recipient can be identified with Theodore Metochites (1270–1332), consists of a lengthy praise of Metochites' *Encomiun of Gregory of Nazianzos* followed by a plea to intervene with the emperor on his behalf. Similarly, Theodore Hyrtakenos (c.1260–1327) addressed a letter to Metochites in which, after a prologue rife with references to ancient literature, he highlights Theodore Mouzalon's and Nikephoros Choumnos' efforts in favor of needy teachers and finally begs his addressee to follow in the footsteps of his predecessors by providing him with a salary from imperial funds.[50] Thus, education and participation in intellectual discourse was a promising basis for receiving all kinds of support.

The notion of reciprocity was the guiding principle for all such social transactions. When, for instance, John Glykys recommended a young man to Maximos Planoudes asking him to become his teacher and Planoudes could not meet his request, Planoudes felt the need to apologize with the following words: "I am aware that I have benefitted from your great and good friendship and wish that I could always and also now do you the greatest of all favors, but the circumstances do not allow me to do so for the time being [...]. Therefore I ask you now to accept my apologies and not to blame me, one who is willing but not able [to fulfill your request], but to blame along with me the circumstances which do not want me to be able [to do so]."[51] In this and other cases Planoudes evokes friendship. There are, however, some instances in Planoudes' correspondence in which we can glimpse more clearly an asymmetrical relationship that points to patronage rather than to friendship. When, for example, he asked the right-hand-man of the emperor, Theodore Mouzalon, for support for the library of the "imperial monastery" in which he dwelled, he repeatedly addresses him as "my lord" (ὁ κύριός μου/κύριέ μου), evidently avoiding friendship language.[52] Similarly, he calls Theodora Raoulaina his lady (ἡ κυρία μου). Raoulaina seems to have functioned as Planoudes' patron. When she re-founded the Monastery of St. Andrew *en te Krisei* in Constantinople, she

---

50 Michael Gabras, *Letters*, no. 84, ed. Fatouros, vol. 2, pp. 135–36; Theodore Hyrtakenos, *Letters*, no. 74, ed. & trans. Karpozilos/Fatouros, pp. 264–67 (= ed. la Porte-du Theil (1860), p. 35).

51 Maximos Planoudes, *Letters*, no. 23, ed. Leone, p. 50, lines 4–14: καὶ γὰρ σύνοιδα πολλῆς σοι καὶ καλῆς φιλίας ὢν ὀφειλέτης, καὶ βουλοίμην ἂν ἀεί τε καὶ νῦν τὴν μεγίστην σοι πασῶν καταθέσθαι χαρίτων· ἀλλ' ὁ καιρὸς συγχωρεῖν τό γε νῦν ἔχον οὐ βούλεται [...] νυνὶ μέντοι συγγνώμην εἴπερ τις ἔχειν αἰτοῦμαί σε καὶ μὴ μέμφεσθαι τὸν βουλόμενον ἐμέ, μὴ δυνάμενον δέ· μέμφεσθαι δὲ σὺν ἐμοὶ τὸν μὴ βουλόμενον δύνασθαί με καιρόν.

52 Maximos Planoudes, *Letters*, no. 67, ed. Leone, pp. 98–102 with Constantinides, *Higher Education*, pp. 70–71 and Taxidis, *Μάξιμος Πλανούδης*, pp. 80–83.

EPISTOLOGRAPHY, SOCIAL EXCHANGE AND INTELLECTUAL DISCOURSE   225

commissioned him to compose epigrams for her founder's portrait. Moreover, codex Monac. gr. 430 (Thucydides) may have been a gift from her to Planoudes.[53]

Raoulaina is an exceptional case of a Byzantine female bibliophile, author and scribe, who was also a patroness of other intellectuals.[54] We know of several female patrons of the arts and letters in this period, but only few seem to have been directly involved in intellectual discourse. Of Raoulaina's correspondence with her closest protégé Gregory of Cyprus, 29 of Gregory's letters survive that attest to the high esteem Raoulaina was held in both as a patron and as a scholar.[55] It is a regrettable, and telling, fact that Raoulaina's part of their letter-exchange has not come down to us, as it would be interesting to observe whether – and if so, how – a woman deployed the established language and imagery of the male-dominated friendship discourse. The only surviving letters penned by a Byzantine woman are those of Irene-Eulogia Choumnaina Palaiologina – daughter of Nikephoros Choumnos and, after being widowed, abbess of the Monastery of Christ Philanthropos Soter – and show a deep sense of moral and intellectual inferiority towards the male correspondent, an anonymous, highly educated monk, who can be identified with Gregory Akindynos.[56] However, with her correspondence Irene sought not only spiritual guidance, as scholars today usually claim, but also intellectual stimulus.[57]

To conclude this section, within the closely tied Constantinopolitan elite under the first two Palaeologan emperors, learning functioned as symbolic capital which could be invested in various ways and on different occasions for the benefit of oneself or one's circle of relatives and friends. In this dynamic, letter-writing was an important vehicle both on the level of the creation and affirmation of symbolic capital – e.g., through rhetorical composition, the performance and circulation of letters, literary criticism and the concomitant exchange of books – and of its subsequent transformation into actual leverage or power, as seen, for instance, in requests and recommendations. The fact that such numerous and voluminous letter-collections from this period survive is, therefore, perhaps not a mere coincidence owing to the vagaries of textual

---

53 For Planoudes and Raoulaina see the evidence discussed in Riehle, "Theodora Raulaina", pp. 310–11.

54 Riehle, "Theodora Raulaina"; see now also Zorzi, "Una copista".

55 Gregory of Cyprus, *Letters to Theodora Raoulaina*, ed. Kotzabassi.

56 On this identification see the forthcoming edition of Gregory's *Opera minora* by Juan Nadal Cañellas and Dionysios Benetos (personal communication).

57 Irene Choumnaina, *Correspondence with an Anonymous Monk*, esp. no. 7, ed. & trans. Hero, pp. 40–43.

transmission but may well point to a particular importance of epistolography as communicative medium for the intellectual elite of that time.[58]

4 The Dynamics of Crisis and Change: Epistolography and Intellectual Discourse during the Period of Civil Wars (1321–1391)

Although Byzantine intellectuals of the Palaeologan period have long been regarded as escapist ivory-tower scholars, it seems on the contrary that they were well aware of and responded to the political, ideological and cultural crisis that their empire underwent in the last two centuries of its millennial history.[59] In a world full of insecurity and anxieties, learning and intellectual friendship were not a means to escape reality, but to cope with it. Thus, Nikephoros Gregoras states in a letter to Andronikos II from the period of the first civil war that "learning [οἱ λόγοι] by its very nature strives against all worldly affairs that time brings forth, since it is superior to and higher than things mortal" and encourages him to continue in his efforts for the promotion of learning in times of crisis.[60] In the last quarter of the 14th century the rhetorician Theodore Potamios frequently addresses companions from the past in a quest to "renew their friendship" (ἀνανεοῦν/ἀνανεώσασθαι τὴν φιλίαν), since the demise of the state and civil wars between competing emperors, whom he bluntly criticizes, had hampered social and intellectual intercourse.[61] This tendency of literati to foster existing ties and to forge new ones with political and intellectual elites in order to adapt to a new and insecure reality can be observed from the very beginning of the crisis in the 1320s. This crisis was triggered by the ongoing loss of territory in Asia Minor to Turkish tribes and in the Balkans first to the Serbs and Bulgarians, then to the Ottomans. By the middle of the 14th century all that was left of an empire formerly stretching from Italy and North Africa to Mesopotamia amounted to Constantinople and its Thracian and Eastern Macedonian hinterland, Thessaloniki and its environs, a semi-independent dominion in the Peloponnese, and a few islands in the Northern Aegean. This development of course had a devastating effect on

---

58   See the chart in Riehle, "Rhetorik, Ritual und Repräsentation", p. 276.

59   Ihor Ševčenko pointed to this as early as 1961 (Ševčenko, "The Decline of Byzantium"), but his account has, until very recently, not always been heeded.

60   Nikephoros Gregoras, *Letters*, no. 118, ed. Leone, vol. 2, pp. 308–10 (quotation at lines 26–28: οἱ δὲ λόγοι φύσιν ἔχοντες ἀντιστρατευομένην τοῖς ἐν βίῳ πράγμασιν ἅπασιν, ὅσα βόσκει χρόνος, ἅτε κρείττους τε ὄντες καὶ ἀνώτεροι τοῦ θνητοῦ).

61   Theodore Potamios, *Letters*, esp. nos. 2 and 12, ed. & trans. Dennis, pp. 6–7 and 18–19 (translations at 21–22 and 32–33).

EPISTOLOGRAPHY, SOCIAL EXCHANGE AND INTELLECTUAL DISCOURSE   227

the economy of the empire, as imperial revenues were dramatically reduced. The inhabitants of the empire did not have to wait long to witness severe internal struggles, beginning with the conflict between Andronikos II and his grandson Andronikos III, the first of a series of civil wars.

This period of external and internal struggles entailed a fundamental reformation of society, and in particular of the aristocracy, which eventually would develop into a loosely-tied group of entrepreneurs.[62] Concurrently, from the mid-14th century onwards learning and education lost the pivotal role for aristocratic identity that it had played in the first half of that century. The old intellectual elite, whose unity was based on common personal, political and intellectual interests, showed its first symptoms of dissolution in the 1320s with the feud between the two Andronikoi. In this transitional period certain changes can be observed in some of the collections discussed above. A few examples may suffice to illustrate this observation.

Around 1321/22, Andronikos II's former right-hand man Nikephoros Choumnos – who had retired due to health issues but was still an influential counselor to the emperor in crucial affairs – addressed two letters to the most important supporters of the younger Andronikos, namely John Kantakouzenos (c.1295–1383), to whom he had recently been introduced, and Alexios Apokaukos (d. 1345). Although Choumnos did not know the two upstarts well, the letters abound in the traditional vocabulary and imagery of friendship, which suggests that he attempted to forge an alliance with them through the medium of letter-writing.[63] In a similar fashion, Nikephoros Gregoras (1290/94–1358/61) – a disciple of Andronikos II's "prime minister" Theodore Metochites – sent a letter to Alexios Apokaukos in which he praises his addressee for his wisdom and his efforts to promote learning and encourages him to keep on doing so. This may be interpreted as an attempt to integrate one of the most prominent representatives of Andronikos III's circle into the old aristocracy surrounding Andronikos II with its strong intellectual values.[64]

If these letters are to be regarded as pieces of diplomacy, other epistolographers approached the new political elites for more personal and mundane motives. Theodore Hyrtakenos, for instance, sent a letter to Alexios Apokaukos in the 1320s in which he reminded him of the time when Alexios had been his student, praised him for his virtue and concluded: "Since you are

---

62   See Matschke/Tinnefeld, *Die Gesellschaft im späten Byzanz*, pp. 158–220; Kiousopoulou, *Βασιλεύς ή Οικονόμος*, pp. 54–57 and 81–116 (= *Emperor or Manager*, pp. 36–38 and 55–80).

63   Nikephoros Choumnos, *Letters*, nos. 129 and 132, ed. Boissonade, pp. 150–51 and 154–55 with Riehle, *Funktionen der byzantinischen Epistolographie*, pp. 309–10.

64   Nikephoros Gregoras, *Letters*, no. 119 (transmitted in two versions), ed. Leone, vol. 2, pp. 310–12.

a philosopher, do not ever forget me, your teacher – and I might dare say your friend – who happens to be in need."[65] Another good example is Matthew of Ephesos (1270/71–1359/60), whose correspondence covers the years from 1310 to *c.*1341. In his quest to acquire the see of Philadelphia after Theoleptos' death in 1322, Matthew tried, without success, to obtain the support of the ruling elite in Constantinople through the intervention of the learned and well-connected monk Joseph the Philosopher (*c.*1260/80–1330). Matthew pleaded that Joseph use his wisdom and rhetorical skills to persuade Andronikos II. In addition, he asked him to approach Theodore Metochites, who had great influence over the emperor and could convince him with his compelling power of speech.[66] A few years after this failed attempt, in 1329, he received the bishopric of Ephesos with the help of the upstart and supporter of Andronikos III, Syrgiannes, whom he, obviously in an attempt to strengthen his ties to his new benefactor, thanks in a highly rhetorical letter that praises particularly the addressee's learning and appreciation of friendship.[67]

Although a supporter of the old regime, Nikephoros Gregoras, whose correspondence spans the period from around 1320 to 1360, eventually also adapted to the changing political circumstances. His (pre-)civil-war network consisted mostly of members of the old aristocracy. Apart from one letter to Andronikos II himself, which constitutes a eulogy of his energetic support of learning (λόγοι),[68] he corresponded with Andronikos' "prime minister", his former teacher Theodore Metochites, with the previous right-hand man of the emperor Nikephoros Choumnos, as well as with Joseph the Philosopher, Theoleptos of Philadelphia and Theodore Xanthopoulos, all of whom were highly educated and lived, permanently or temporarily, in Constantinople, with strong ties to the imperial court. These letters are primarily concerned with intellectual matters, most importantly the exchange and critique of their own works and praise of their wisdom, which once again proves the paramount importance of learning as a unifying bond between the members of

---

65   Theodore Hyrtakenos, *Letters*, no. 69, ed. & trans. Karpozilos/Fatouros, pp. 248–53, quotation at p. 252, l. 45–47 (translation modified) (= ed. la Porte-du Theil (1860), pp. 30–31, quotation at p. 30): φιλόσοφος ὢν αὐτός, οὐκ ἐπιλήσαιτ' ἄν μου ποτέ· τοῦτο μὲν παιδευτοῦ, τοῦτο δ' ἐρεῖν καὶ φίλου θαρρῶ, καὶ δεομένου τυγχάνοντος.

66   Matthew of Ephesos (Manuel Gabalas), *Letters*, no. B3, ed. & trans. Reinsch, pp. 84–85 (translation at 227–29). See also nos. B4, B10 and B17, ibid., pp. 86–87, 95 and 110 (230–31, 240 and 260).

67   Matthew of Ephesos (Manuel Gabalas), *Letters*, no. B34, ed. & trans. Reinsch, pp. 141–42 (translation at 299–301).

68   See above, p. 226 at n. 60.

EPISTOLOGRAPHY, SOCIAL EXCHANGE AND INTELLECTUAL DISCOURSE 229

the ruling elite and people associated with them.[69] There are, however, also letters of request showing that the purpose of such networks was the mutual benefit of its members.[70] With Andronikos II's abdication and Metochites' exile, Gregoras' fate naturally changed for the worse. In his *Roman History* he would write: "If we, too, who sided with the old emperor as was reasonable, got entangled in the turbulences of that storm, this should not surprise anyone. For it would not have been right if we had not taken someone's side, as Solon advises [us to do]. And it was only reasonable that, when the shepherd was hit hard, the entire flock would equally suffer."[71] However, he seems to have reconciled with the new emperor, and when Andronikos III was on the battlefield, he sent him an encouraging letter in which he describes the emperor as the protector of the people of Constantinople.[72] Furthermore, Gregoras became closely attached to the younger Andronikos' supporter and later emperor John Kantakouzenos, who himself was a distinguished man of letters. 22 missives of Gregoras' corpus are addressed to him, which make John, at least quantitatively, his most important correspondent. Despite their close contact and mutual interest in literature, to which their correspondence amply testifies, their relationship seems to have been an asymmetrical one. In his letters to Kantakouzenos, Gregoras notably avoids friendship language even where one would expect such language.[73] Instead, he frequently praises him as benefactor – both due to his military deeds for the Byzantines in general and due to his personal philanthropy – and, particularly, as patron of the letters, describing him as the one who "watches over and nourishes our words" and "animates and spearheads learning,"[74] while comparing him favorably

---

69   Nikephoros Gregoras, *Letters*, e.g., nos. 22–26, 46 and 62, ed. Leone, vol. 2, pp. 71–91, 157–60 and 187–88.

70   Nikephoros Gregoras, *Letters*, e.g., nos. 27, 38 and 64, ed. Leone, vol. 2, pp. 91–92, 132–33 and 191.

71   Nikephoros Gregoras, *Roman History* IX 6, ed. Schopen, vol. 1, p. 427, lines 4–9: Εἰ δὲ καὶ ἡμεῖς τῷ γηραιῷ κατὰ τὸ εἰκὸς προσκείμενοι βασιλεῖ ῥοθίοις τισὶν ἐνετύχομεν τοῦ χειμῶνος ἐκείνου, καινὸν οὐδέν. οὔτε γὰρ δίκαιον ἦν, ἡμᾶς μηδεμιᾷ προσκεῖσθαι μερίδι, τοῦ Σόλωνος τοῦτο προτρέποντος· καὶ πρός γε τῶν εἰκότων αὖ, τοῦ ποιμένος παταχθέντος δεινὰ παθεῖν κατὰ τὸ ἀνάλογον ἅπαν τὸ ποίμνιον.

72   Nikephoros Gregoras, *Letters*, no. 89, ed. Leone, vol. 2, p. 240. See also no. 130 to John Kantakouzenos, ibid., pp. 330–32.

73   E.g. no. 86 (ed. Leone, vol. 2, pp. 234–35, at lines 1–21) in which Gregoras, employing traditional epistolary motifs, complains about the distance that separates them.

74   Nikephoros Gregoras, *Letters*, no. 120, ed. Leone, vol. 2, pp. 312–14, at lines 17–18 and 28–29: τῷ τῶν ἡμετέρων λόγων ἐπόπτῃ καὶ προμηθεῖ ... τὸν τῆς τῶν λόγων ζωῆς παροχέα καὶ πρύτανιν. Further references to Kantakouzenos' support of learning: no. 11, ibid., pp. 43–48, at lines 57–74; no. 19, ibid., pp. 61–62; no. 41, ibid., pp. 140–44: Gregoras links the success (or failure) of rulers and military commanders of the past to their interest in learning (or

with rulers from antiquity.[75] Thus not surprisingly, a good deal of Gregoras' letters to Kantakouzenos are requests, either for himself or for people associated with him.[76]

In sum, the examples discussed in the previous paragraphs point to shifting patronage and friendship networks in which intellectuals invested their learning as capital, often with the help of letter-writing.

The political crisis that Byzantium witnessed around the mid-14th century gave birth to another development also reflected in patterns of epistolary communication. Interestingly, and somewhat paradoxically, the shrinking of the empire did not further reinforce the exclusive status of Constantinople as the sole center of higher learning, but on the contrary triggered a process of decentralization. The few remaining urban centers of the empire during this period, in particular Thessaloniki and Mistra, developed into hubs of intellectual life.[77] This development might in part be explained by the waning financial capabilities of the imperial court at Constantinople, which had lost its role as the supreme patron of the arts.[78]

While within the networks of the Constantinopolitan epistolographers of the late 13th and first decades of the 14th century Thessalonians play only a minor role, the increasing political and cultural importance of this city is clearly echoed in correspondence from the 1330s onwards.[79] A good example is again Gregoras, many of whose letters are addressed to Thessalonians,

---

      lack thereof); no. 57, ibid., pp. 175–77; no. 122, ibid., pp. 315–18: people praise him for his philanthropy and for "the revival of letters, which he re-erected after they had fallen" (τὴν τῶν λόγων ἀναβίωσιν, οὓς πεπτωκότας ἀνέστησας); no. 126, ibid., pp. 323–25; no. 130, ibid., pp. 130–32, at lines 36–39.

75   E.g., Kyros (no. 57, ed. Leone, vol. 2, pp. 175–77, at lines 45–50 and no. 106, ibid., pp. 277–78), Menestheus (no. 122, ibid., pp. 315–18, at lines 78–93), Antigonos I (no. 125, ibid., p. 323).

76   E.g., no. 18, ed. Leone, vol. 2, pp. 60–61 (help for a relative who had suffered wrong); no. 86, ibid., pp. 234–35, at lines 22–36 (intervention in the affairs of a monastery); no. 92, ibid., pp. 247–48 (help for someone "in danger" who has benefitted before from Kantakouzenos' philanthropy); no. 106, ibid., pp. 277–78 (support for the bearer of the letter and his mother); no. 149, ibid., pp. 369–70 (Gregoras acts as mediator for other people because he is known for his close ties to Kantakouzenos; help for a friend of his); no. 156, ibid., p. 375 (protection of a certain Daniel who is persecuted by his opponents despite a court order forbidding this).

77   For Thessaloniki see Matschke/Tinnefeld, *Die Gesellschaft im späten Byzanz*, pp. 321–23; Tinnefeld, "Intellectuals in Late Byzantine Thessalonike"; Bianconi, *Tessalonica nell'età dei Paleologi*. For Mistra see Mergiali, *L'enseignement*, pp. 142–51 and 193–220; Matschke/Tinnefeld, *Die Gesellschaft im späten Byzanz*, pp. 324–25.

78   Ševčenko, "Society and Intellectual Life", pp. 79–83; Kalopissi-Verti, "Patronage and Artistic Production", pp. 76–85.

79   See Tinnefeld, "Intellectuals in Late Byzantine Thessalonike", pp. 158–60.

EPISTOLOGRAPHY, SOCIAL EXCHANGE AND INTELLECTUAL DISCOURSE 231

among them the metropolitan of Thessaloniki, Ignatios; the *sakellios* (Gregory or John?) Bryennios, who belonged to Thomas Magistros' circle; and the *protonotarios* Niketas Soteriotes. These letters abound in traditional epistolary motifs, such as the nature and values of friendship; the distance between the two corresponding friends, which can only be overcome by writing letters; the silence of the correspondent; etc.[80] Gregoras apparently sought to get and keep in touch with the political, ecclesiastical and intellectual elites of the city, using letters as his primary means of communication. This becomes particularly evident from a letter addressed to the eminent intellectual and philologist Thomas Magistros (*c.*1280–1347/48), a native of Thessaloniki and outspoken advocate of the political interests of his hometown and its people. With this letter, dating from shortly before 1332, Gregoras tried to establish a relationship with Magistros, whom he had not yet met, stating that "I shall converse with you from afar, as if we were familiar and friends, aiming at nothing but sharing learning. For while the saying 'friends share all things' implies that friendship is the cause of the sharing of things, I, on the contrary, contend that the sharing of things is the cause of friendship. For, as [human] nature is equally given to rich and poor [...], so also wisdom [...] distributes intellectual qualities to all people in equal share and wants them to be brothers in spirit."[81] Gregoras thus subverts one of the most common epistolary motifs concerning friendship, arguing that the sense of community precedes and establishes friendship, even among people who never met. In their case, it was intellectual pursuits that were to be the basis for a friendly relationship. When Magistros responded, Gregoras thanked and praised him as follows: "[When I received your letter] numerous learned men happened to be with me marveling, while they listened to the letter, at the nobility of its thoughts, the beauty of its composition, the grace and elegance attached to its character, and they greatly blessed the city of the Thessalonians for its possession. For you, they said, are its sole intellectual eye and the best whetstone for its well-trained tongues in [the art of] speaking. I was also greatly delighted to see that you did not deceive my hopes,

---

80 Nikephoros Gregoras, *Letters*, nos. 129, 133, 134, 141, 158 and 159, ed. Leone, vol. 2, pp. 329–30, 334–339, 347 and 378–79.

81 Nikephoros Gregoras, *Letters*, no. 91, ed. Leone, vol. 2, pp. 243–47 (quotation at lines 15–26: ὁμιλήσω σοι καὶ πόρρωθεν ἤδη καθάπερ συνήθει καὶ φίλῳ, πρὸς μόνην αὐτὴν ἀποβλέψας τὴν κοινωνίαν τοῦ λόγου. Ἡ μὲν γὰρ παροιμία 'κοινὰ τὰ τῶν φίλων' εἶναι φάσκουσα δεῖν τὴν φιλίαν αἴτιον τῆς κοινωνίας προτίθησι τῶν πραγμάτων. ἐγὼ δὲ τοὐναντίον τὴν κοινωνίαν τοῦ πράγματος αἰτίαν γίνεσθαι ἀξιῶ τῆς φιλίας. ὥσπερ γὰρ κοινὰ τὰ τῆς φύσεως δίδοται καὶ πλουσίοις καὶ πένησι [...], οὕτω καὶ ἡ σοφία [...] ὅμοια τὰ τῆς παιδείας ἅπασι διανέμει, καὶ ἀδελφὰ φρονεῖν ἀλλήλοις [...] ἀξιοῖ).

but that you granted [me] to win a friend – a good friend in every respect and a better one than I could have hoped for."[82]

In this correspondence we can observe how, after the old Constantinopolitan elite had fallen from power, one of its supporters attempted to establish bonds between his circle and the most prominent representative of the elite of the second most important city of the empire. Epistolography, in its dual function as a literary genre that reflected shared intellectual values and as a medium of communication substituting for oral communication when personal encounters were not possible, was of paramount importance for achieving this goal.

With the upheaval that the Zealot rising (1342–49) caused to the city, Thessaloniki's intellectual life seems to have waned. The continuing presence and activities of intellectuals in the city until at least its first conquest by the Ottomans in 1387 is, however, well attested in several letter-collections of writers who were either Thessalonians or closely attached to the city's intellectual and political life: for instance, Demetrios Kydones, Nicholas Kabasilas Chamaetos, Isidore Glabas and Theodore Potamios.

Another important urban center emerged in the Peloponnese, when in 1348 Emperor John VI Kantakouzenos established the Despotate of Morea and installed his son Manuel Kantakouzenos as its ruler. This new hegemony with its capital at Mistra soon attracted the attention of intellectuals. After Manuel's appointment as Despot of Morea, Gregoras sent him a letter in which he stresses that neither the passing of time nor physical separation can harm the friendship to which they had committed a long time ago.[83] More importantly, a small collection of twelve letters by a bureaucrat from the Peloponnese survives that sheds an interesting light on the formation of a new center of political and intellectual life. Its author is Manuel Raoul, who originated from Lakonia, was educated in Thessaloniki, spent a short time in the closest proximity to Emperor John VI Kantakouzenos and was apparently a highly educated rhetorician. After John Kanzoukenos' abdication in December of 1354, Raoul sent him a long encomiastic letter, praising him for his decision to leave the

---

82   Nikephoros Gregoras, *Letters*, no. 142, ed. Leone, vol. 2, p. 348 (quotation at lines 10–18: Ἔτυχον γὰρ ἡμῖν καὶ τῶν ἐλλογίμων τηνικαῦτα παρακαθήμενοι πλεῖστοι, οἳ δὴ καὶ τεθαυμάκασιν ἀκηκοότες τὴν τοῖς γράμμασιν ἐγκειμένην τῆς διανοίας εὐγένειαν, τό τε τῆς συνθήκης κάλλος καὶ τὴν τῷ ἤθει ἐφέρπουσαν χάριν καὶ ἀστειότητα, καὶ ἐμακάρισαν οὐ μετρίως τὴν Θεσσαλονικέων τοῦ κτήματος· σὲ γὰρ εἶναι καὶ μόνον τὸν λογικὸν αὐτῆς ὀφθαλμὸν καὶ τὴν πρὸς τὸ λέγειν ἀρίστην ἀκόνην τῶν ἐλλογίμων ταύτης γλωσσῶν. ἤσθημεν δὲ καὶ ἡμεῖς οὐ μετρίως ὅτι τῶν ἐλπίδων ἡμᾶς οὐκ ἔψευσας, ἀλλ' ἔδωκας φίλου τυχεῖν ἀγαθοῦ τὰ πάντα καὶ κρείττονος ἢ κατὰ τὰς ἐλπίδας). For this exchange of letters between Gregoras and Magistros see also Gaul, *Thomas Magistros*, pp. 43–46.

83   Nikephoros Gregoras, *Letters*, no. 96, ed. Leone, vol. 2, 251–53.

EPISTOLOGRAPHY, SOCIAL EXCHANGE AND INTELLECTUAL DISCOURSE   233

worldly affairs behind and reminding him of the time when they were together and conversed with one another. As a result of this letter, John recommended Raoul to his son Manuel Kantakouzenos, who then invited Raoul to join him in Mistra and rewarded him with a court office. This conclusion can be drawn from another letter sent by Raoul from the Peloponnese to John, in which he blesses his addressee for "having entreated your son, our Great Despot, to take care of us."[84] In Mistra, Raoul established and maintained the kind of intellectual relationships that we know from the Constantinopolitan elite, exchanging letters with local secular and ecclesiastical magnates. For instance, in a typical example of learned epistolary discourse, Raoul reproached the *parakoimomenos* Angelos Kalothetos for failing to write him with the following words: "That you were attached to learning from your childhood and practiced it for a long time [...], and then you choose not to write letters, but hesitate for so long, embracing silence – who would not be incited by this to blame you?"[85] Over the next century, the Morea with its center at Mistra was to produce and attract more distinguished intellectuals – George Gemistos (Plethon) being the most famous example in the 15th century.

Finally, one should at least mention that regions not under the rule of the Byzantine emperor during this period could boast the presence of renowned scholars with contacts to the Constantinopolitan elites, among them Venetian Crete, Lusignan Cyprus and the Empire of Trebizond ruled by the Grand Komnenoi.[86]

The mid-14th was not only a period of political and social crisis and change, but also witnessed a fierce theological controversy. Although letters were used also in earlier decades as medium, and sometimes weapons, for theological dispute, particularly in the course of the struggle over the union of the Greek and Roman Churches,[87] epistolography had a more vital presence within the hesychast controversy around Gregory Palamas (1294–1357) and his followers on the one hand and the anti-Palamite circles led by Barlaam of Calabria (*c.*1290–1348), Gregory Akindynos (ca. 1300–1348) and Nikephoros Gregoras on

---

84   Manuel Raoul, *Letters*, nos. 1 and 2, ed. Loenertz, pp. 130–42, quotation at p. 141, lines 37–38: τὸν σὸν υἱὸν τὸν ἡμέτερον τουτονὶ καὶ μέγαν δεσπότην ἐπὶ τὴν ἡμετέραν κηδεμονίαν παρακαλῶν.

85   Manuel Raoul, *Letters*, no. 4, ed, Loenertz, p. 146, lines 11–16: τὸ δὲ σὲ λόγοις παιδόθεν προσκείμενον κἄν **τούτοις** οὕτως ἐπὶ μακρὸν ἀσκήσαντα [   ], ἔπειτα μὴ ἐπιστέλλειν ἐθέλειν, ἀλλ᾿ ἐπὶ τοσοῦτον κατοκνεῖν, σιωπὴν ἀσπαζόμενον, τίν᾿ οὐκ ἂν πρὸς κατηγορίαν σὴν ἤγειρεν;

86   See Matschke/Tinnefeld, *Die Gesellschaft im späten Byzanz*, pp. 325–29.

87   See, e.g., the *Letter to Andronikos II* by the Dominican Simon of Constantinople (ed. Anagnostou) on the issue of the procession of the Holy Spirit and the response to Simon's arguments by Matthew Blastares in his *Letter to Guy de Lusignan* (ed. Arsenij). See Paschos, *Ματθαῖος Βλάσταρης*, pp. 95–98.

234 RIEHLE

the other.[88] In this context, letter-writing served simultaneously as a vehicle of mediation between the conflicting parties and as a medium for disputing theological matters. Thus Gregory Akindynos, who was at first a close associate of Palamas' but later became one of the leading anti-Palamites, introduced Barlaam to Palamas through letters. Palamas' first surviving letter to Akindynos comments at length on one of Barlaam's anti-Latin treatises and expresses his wish to meet its author. Notably, in the manuscripts it bears the rubric "[this letter] was written to Akindynos, when he was still numbered among the orthodox and friends," suggesting that theological like-mindedness and friendship were understood as inseparable within ecclesiastical circles.[89] This interpretation is corroborated by Palamas' second letter to Akindynos, in which the author admits his still friendly disposition towards Barlaam, but stresses that the love of God is superior to any worldly friendship.[90] It is this series of letter-exchanges between Palamas, Barlaam and Akindynos, dating from the years 1336–41, that stands at the very beginning of the hesychast controversy.[91] Even after the definitive ruling of Palamas' teaching as orthodox (1351), anti-Palamism remained firmly rooted in some intellectual circles.

This section examined the ways in which the crises that Byzantium witnessed in the 14th century affected intellectual discourse and prompted responses from educated elites. Remaining a fundamental medium of cultural and social reaffirmation, epistolography provided intellectuals with a means to compensate for the ever-increasing instability of the world in which they lived. While in the first decades of the Palaeologan period letter-writing had primarily served to strengthen the coherence of a small elite, it now became increasingly used as a medium of approaching and maintaining contacts with new elites across the empire and of addressing and negotiating controversial matters. In this, the example of learned epistolography shows the flexibility of Byzantine intellectual discourse, whose transformative force is, paradoxically, rooted in its strict adherence to tradition.

---

88   See also the contribution of Ioannis Polemis in this volume.

89   Gregory Palamas, *Letters to Akindynos and Barlaam*, no. 1, ed. Meyendorff, pp. 203–19, quotation at p. 203: ἐγράφη δὲ πρὸς Ἀκίνδυνον, ἔτι τοῖς εὐσεβέσι καὶ φίλοις ἐναριθμούμενον.

90   Gregory Palamas, *Letters to Akindynos and Barlaam*, no. 2, ed. Meyendorff, p. 221, lines 8–22.

91   Gregory Palamas, *Letters to Akindynos and Barlaam*, ed. Meyendorff with the introductory remarks by P.K. Chrestou at pp. 179–99; Barlaam of Calabria, *Greek Letters*, nos. 1 and 3, ed. & trans. Fyrigos, pp. 194–273 and 299–369 with the introductory remarks at pp. 67–97; Gregory Akindynos, *Letters*, nos. 7–11, ed. & trans. Hero, pp. 20–57 with the introductory remarks at pp. xi–xv and the commentary at pp. 319–30.

5 Caught in the Middle: Epistolography and Intellectual Discourse in the Last Decades of the Byzantine Empire (1391–1453)

With Manuel II Palaiologos' (1350–1425) definitive assumption of power in 1391 Constantinople's intellectual life seems to have experienced a certain revival.[92] Since the emperor himself was highly educated in the classics and a prolific author of rhetorical and theological writings, he enjoyed the company of literati and organized *theatra* just as the emperors and high aristocrats of the early Palaeologan period had done. To be sure, during Manuel's reign the empire's fate was already sealed: Constantinople was an isolated island surrounded by Ottoman territory and besieged for eight years early in his reign (1394–1402). Nevertheless, Manuel's court – and to a lesser degree also the courts of his successors – provided a stimulus to intellectual discourse in the last decades of Byzantium's long history, and epistolary writing naturally loomed large in his circle. The emperor's own letters, many of which were composed and dispatched during his frequent and extensive journeys, are the most vivid testimony to his preoccupation with matters of literature and his inclination to surround himself with men of letters.[93] To his circle belonged the retired statesman Demetrios Kydones (*c*.1324–1397), 80 of whose letters have Manuel as their recipient; the teacher-diplomat Manuel Chrysoloras (*c*.1350–1415); and Demetrios Chrysoloras (*c*.1360–1416), who couched an apologetic text to the emperor in the form of *One hundred letters on one and the same subject* ('Ἐπιστολαὶ ἑκατὸν ἐφ᾽ ἑνὶ πράγματι).[94] Kydones' student Manuel Kalekas (d. 1410) worked as teacher of grammar in Constantinople in the first years of Manuel's reign.[95] Another intellectual attached to Manuel's court was John Chortasmenos (*c*.1370–1436), who was to become the teacher of several renowned scholars of the last generation of Byzantine literati (Mark Eugenikos, Gennadios/George Scholarios, Bessarion). His correspondence with the political and intellectual elite of Constantinople and Thessaloniki constitutes a prototypical learned epistolary collection, including letters asking for or responding to critiques of his writings, letters concerning his teaching,

---

92   Mergiali, *L'enseignement*, pp. 165–91.

93   Manuel II Palaiologos, *Letters*, ed. & trans. Dennis.

94   Demetrios Chrysoloras, *One Hundred Letters*, ed. & trans. Conti Bizzarro. On Kydones' and Manuel Chrysoloras' letters see below, pp. 239–40.

95   Manuel Kalekas, *Letters*, nos. 1–12, ed. Loenertz, pp. 167–84 with introductory remarks at pp. 17–23.

236   RIEHLE

and epistolary encomia and requests addressed to the emperor and other men
in power.[96]

In a report about the reading of a speech of Eustathios of Berroia in the
presence of the emperor, Chortasmenos claimed that "now more than ever
good things receive the opportunity to be showcased, now wisdom along
with virtue is rewarded and learning occupies an important place in the
imperial palace."[97] Yet the chances of educated men to enter imperial service
because of their education seem to have diminished somewhat in the final
two decades of Byzantium's history. Thus in the early 1430s Gennadios/George
Scholarios (c.1400–1472) – frustrated with his situation in Constantinople
because the emperor refused to provide him with a salary – approached the
Despot of Morea Theodore II Palaiologos in an attempt to acquire a paid post
at his court at Mistra.[98] Around twenty years later, shortly before the fall of
Constantinople, Scholarios called Loukas Notaras (c.1390/1400–1453) "the only
worshipper of learning among those in charge of the state affairs" (σὺ μόνος ἐκ
τῶν ἐφεστώτων τοῖς πράγμασι λόγων γεγονὼς θιασώτης), deeming "your virtue to
be a bliss for ourselves" (τὴν ὑμῶν ἀρετὴν εὐδαιμονίαν οἰκείαν κρίνομεν εἶναι), for
two reasons: "If those attached to learning can hope to receive something good
from you, how much more will you grant them your favor when you participate
in the best of all pursuits on the same level, if not on a superior one! If, on the
other hand, we will only be rescued if reason guides us, then we wish that you,
who are in charge of the state affairs, might surpass your subjects in wisdom,
because you will know better how to rescue [us]."[99] In the eyes of a scholar,
the education of an aristocrat-statesman thus had a twofold significance: it

---

96   John Chortasmenos, *Letters*, ed. Hunger with introductory remarks at pp. 35–37 and sum-
     maries and prosopographical notes at pp. 71–110, 113–20, 123–24 and 127–29. Critique of
     his writings: nos. 1, 4, 5, 6, 7, 9, 15, 20, 39, 40; teaching: nos. 27, 36, 37; letters of praise and
     request: nos. 8, 24, 26, 35, 38, 42, 45, 49, 53, 55, 56.

97   John Chortasmenos, *Letters*, no. 10, ed. Hunger, pp. 160–61, quotation at p. 160, lines 16–17:
     νῦν γάρ, εἴπερ ἄλλοτέ ποτε, καιρὸν ἔχει τὰ καλὰ πρὸς ἐπίδειξιν ἰέναι, νῦν ἡ σοφία τιμᾶται μετὰ
     τῆς ἀρετῆς, καὶ λόγοι χώραν πολλὴν ἐν βασιλείοις ἔχουσι.

98   Gennadios II Scholarios, *Letters*, No.6–7, eds. Petit/Sidéridès/Jugie, pp. 417–19 with
     Blanchet, *Georges-Gennadios Scholarios*, pp. 300–01.

99   Loukas Notaras, *Correspondence*, no. 13, ed. Lampros, pp. 202–12, at pp. 202–05 with
     quotations at p. 203, lines 19–28 (= Gennadios II Scholarios, *Letters*, no. 52, eds. Petit/
     Sidéridès/Jugie, pp. 494–500, at pp. 494–96 with quotations at p. 494, lines 26–34): Εἴτε
     γὰρ δέοι τοὺς περὶ λόγους ἔχοντας ἐλπίζειν τι παρ' ὑμῶν ἀγαθόν, πότε μᾶλλον αὐτοῖς χαριεῖσθε
     ἢ τοῦ καλλίστου τῶν ἐπιτηδευμάτων ἐκ τῶν ἴσων αὐτοῖς συμμετέχοντες, ἔστι δ' οὗ καὶ νικῶντες,
     εἴτε μέλλοιμεν ὑπὸ λόγου κυβερνώμενοι σῴζεσθαι, τοὺς ἐπὶ τῶν πραγμάτων ὑμᾶς εὐξαίμεθ' ἂν
     ὑπερβάλλειν σοφίᾳ τοὺς ἀρχομένους, ὡς ἂν καὶ σῴζειν μᾶλλον εἰδείητε.

EPISTOLOGRAPHY, SOCIAL EXCHANGE AND INTELLECTUAL DISCOURSE 237

enabled him to appreciate the value of learning and therefore take care of less well-off literati, and to govern the state wisely, particularly in times of crisis.

Yet Notaras, who rose from the new group of powerful entrepreneurs to become "prime minister" (*mesazon*) of the last two Byzantine emperors, John VIII (1425–1448) and Constantine XI (1449–1453), was certainly not as steeped in the classics as earlier aristocrats of the Palaeologan period had been. He is not known to have authored any literary texts besides a small corpus of letters, chiefly made up of a correspondence with Gennadios/George Scholarios. Interestingly, almost the entire correspondence focuses on the theme of Notaras' lack of learning. In one letter Notaras regrets that on account of the "anomaly of state affairs and frequent travels" (ἡ δὲ τῶν πραγμάτων ἀνωμαλία καὶ τὸ ἄλλοτε ἄλλους ἀμείβειν τόπους) he has "not learned to write Attic and Ionic" (οὐδὲν γὰρ ἀττικίζειν καὶ ἰωνίζειν μεμάθηκα) and therefore has to avail himself of the "common [language]" (κοινή) even in written discourse.[100] On another occasion, Notaras asks Scholarios to review his draft of a missive to "the rulers of the Turks" (τὰ πρὸς τοὺς ἄρχοντας τῶν Τούρκων γραφέντα μοι γράμματα) commissioned by the emperor, and readily offers 200 gold coins for this service.[101] This and other passages of their letter-exchange reveal that the wealthy Notaras acted as Scholarios' patron. While the statesman Notaras benefitted from Scholarios' learning, Scholarios in turn could hope for Notaras' material and political support. For this reason, Scholarios thought he had enough leverage and influence over Notaras to gain his support for the cause of the anti-unionists (i.e., those who opposed the union of the Greek and Roman Churches). Notaras, however, being a pragmatist who apparently sought to mediate between the two conflicting parties while concealing his own sentiments on the issue, advised Scholarios to put an end to his opposition because it would be to no avail.[102] Similarly, John Eugenikos (*c.*1394–1453/54), another outspoken opponent of the union of the Churches, tried to persuade Notaras to openly join the orthodox party in two highly rhetorical, parenetical letters,

---

100   Loukas Notaras, *Correspondence*, no. 7, ed. Lampros, p. 194.
101   Loukas Notaras, *Correspondence*, no. 11, ed. Lampros, pp. 198–99. See also Scholarios' response, ibid., no. 12, pp. 200–02.
102   See Scholarios' letter in Loukas Notaras, *Correspondence*, no. 13, ed. Lampros, pp. 202–12, at pp. 205–12 (= Gennadios II Scholarios, *Letters*, no. 52, eds. Petit/Sidéridès/Jugie, pp. 494–500, at pp. 496–500); his lengthy letter to Notaras on the issue of the union (*Polemics against the Union of the Churches*, no. 12, eds. Petit/Sidéridès/Jugie, pp. 136–51, esp. at p. 145, lines 22–29 and p. 151, lines 16–34); and the quotations in his letter to Silbestros and Agallianos from a now-lost letter-exchange with Notaras (ibid., no. 15, pp. 166–70, at p. 170, lines 16–25) with Kiousopoulou, "Λουκάς Νοταράς", pp. 169–71 and Blanchet, *Georges-Gennadios Scholarios*, pp. 440–41.

while evoking their mutual friendship with traditional motifs.[103] Another letter by Eugenikos suggests that Notaras' response contained the same advice to yield to the official position on the union as did his letters to Scholarios.[104] These and other pieces of correspondence show that theological strife again began to permeate learned epistolary discourse from the 1430s onwards, as the question of the union of the Churches once more became increasingly pressing because of the dire political situation.[105]

While Byzantine identity had been increasingly Hellenized and political ideology secularized since the 13th century, the opponents of the union – a close-knit group of ecclesiastical officials of the Patriarchate of Constantinople – tried to resuscitate the traditional Christian take on the self-understanding of the Eastern Roman Empire.[106] In one of the letters to Notaras already mentioned, John Eugenikos gave a precise definition of this re-discovered identity: "We ..., Christ's people, the holy nation, the royal priesthood [cf. Ex 19:6 and 23:22; 1 Pt 9], who not only are the most orthodox on earth, but also have a share in reason and learning, are adorned with intelligence, distinguished from every barbarian nation and take pride in belonging to the admirable race of the Romans."[107] With this appeal to return to the traditional Byzantine self-understanding based on the orthodox faith as defined by the Church Fathers and the Ecumenical Councils, Greek learning and Roman citizenship, the highly educated members of the anti-unionist party tried to convince the political elites of the necessity to abide by orthodoxy rather than paying for their (vain) hope for papal help against the Turks with the denial of the right faith.

This call to reversion was of course a reaction to shifting (self-)perceptions that emerged from the period of transformation in late Byzantium,

---

103 John Eugenikos, *Letters*, no. 13, ed. Lampros, pp. 170–73; *Letter to Notaras concerning the Union of Churches*, ed. Lampros.

104 John Eugenikos, *Letters*, no. 15, ed. Lampros, pp. 175–76, e.g. at p. 176, lines 6–7: "Do not expect me ever to renounce the right dogma!" (Μὴ οὖν με τῶν καλῶς δεδογμένων ἀποστῆναί ποτε προσδόκα).

105 In addition to Scholarios and John Eugenikos, see particularly the *Letters* of John's brother Mark Eugenikos (ed. Petit), in which the metropolitan of Ephesos encouraged various ecclesiastics (especially in the provinces) to resist "Latinism" (λατινισμός).

106 See Kiousopoulou, *Βασιλεύς ἤ Οἰκονόμος*, pp. 58–77 and 201–44 (= *Emperor or Manager*, pp. 38–52 and 141–73).

107 John Eugenikos, *Letter to Notaras concerning the Union of Churches*, ed. Lampros, p. 142, lines 14–19: Ἡμεῖς ..., ὁ τοῦ Χριστοῦ λαός, τὸ ἅγιον ἔθνος, τὸ βασίλειον ἱεράτευμα, οἱ μὴ μόνον ὀρθόδοξοι τῶν ἐπὶ γῆς μάλιστα, ἀλλὰ καὶ λόγου καὶ παιδείας μετεσχηκότες καὶ συνέσει κεκοσμημένοι καὶ παντὸς ἔθνους βαρβάρων ἀπηλλοτριωμένοι καὶ τοῦ θαυμαστοῦ τῶν Ῥωμαίων γένους εἶναι φιλοτιμούμενοι.

EPISTOLOGRAPHY, SOCIAL EXCHANGE AND INTELLECTUAL DISCOURSE 239

which included an increasing political and cultural openness toward the Latin west. By the 7th century, when Greek was definitively established as the official language of the *kratos ton Rhomaion*, knowledge of Latin had waned in the Greek speaking east. It was only in the late 13th century that scholars like Manuel Holobolos and Maximos Planoudes started engaging in the study of ancient and medieval Latin literature. In the field of vernacular literature, western models played an important role for the composition of narrative texts. Commercial relations and the growing diplomatic contacts between Byzantium and western powers necessitated by the bleak political situation of the empire further boosted exchange in various realms. While these contacts regularly prompted negative responses among certain factions, as seen in the pamphlets of the anti-unionists, a significant portion of late 14th and 15th century scholars showed a deep admiration for western European culture and even embraced Catholicism.[108] Demetrios Kydones, who converted to the Roman Church as early as 1357, can be regarded as the pioneer of this movement. Kydones had served already under John VI Kantakouzenos as *mesazon* and after a short period of exile following the latter's abdication – during which he devoted himself to translating Thomas Aquinas – returned to the court of Constantinople to continue his services under John V Palaiologos. In 1369 he traveled with the emperor to Rome and convinced him to follow his example in embracing the catholic faith. Ever since, Kydones entertained the idea of taking up residence in Italy. Interestingly, however, his vast surviving correspondence, which amounts to 450 letters, does not include any missives to Italian scholars or politicians.[109] Another intellectual in civil service, Manuel Chrysoloras, followed in Kydones' footsteps. In 1397, he accepted Palla Strozzi's invitation to teach Greek in Florence, responding to the increasing interest in ancient Greek culture that was triggered by the movement today known as the Renaissance.[110] Among Chrysoloras' students were such renowned humanists as Leonardo Bruni, Ambrogio Traversari and Guarino Veronese. After his return to Constantinople, Chrysoloras continued his activities as an imperial diplomat with extensive travels to the west (Italy, France, Spain, England). From Rome

---

108 Emperor Manuel himself sent Guarino Veronese his funeral oration on his brother Theodore and asked him to have it translated into Latin if he deemed it worthy of being presented to a wider public: Manuel II Palaiologon, *Letters*, no. 60, ed. & trans. Dennis, pp. 166–69.

109 Demetrios Kydones, *Letters*, ed. Loenertz; trans. Tinnefeld. The most recent contributions to Kydones' epistolary oeuvre are Tinnefeld, *Die Briefe des Demetrios Kydones* and Leonte, "The Letters of Demetrios Kydones". On the geographical distribution of his addressees see also Matschke/Tinnefeld, *Die Gesellschaft im späten Byzanz*, p. 57.

110 See the classic study by Wilson, *From Byzantium to Italy*.

he sent a long letter to the Emperor Manuel, in which he compared the "old Rome" with the "new one" (i.e., Constantinople), stressing their resemblance, while conceding a slight superiority of Constantinople over her "mother" Rome.[111] In another letter dispatched from the same place to his nephew John Chrysoloras, he draws similar comparisons and expresses regret over the fact that Greeks and Italians now ignore their common past and like-mindedness.[112] Further letters in Greek and Latin he addressed to Italian humanists, some of whom had studied with him (e.g., Guarino Veronese, Leonardo Bruni, Umberto Decembrio), as well as to Pope Innocent VII.[113] Manuel Kalekas was introduced to this circle of scholars by his teacher Kydones in the early 1390s and learned Latin from Jacopo Angeli during the humanist's stay in Constantinople. Due to his insistence on anti-Palamism, he went into exile with sojourns in Pera, the Peloponnese, Crete, Italy and finally Mytilene, where he became a Dominican monk. The correspondence of this nomadic phase of his life – including letters sent home and to like-minded Greeks and Latins in Italy and Cyprus – provides a particularly interesting testimony to the mobility of this new generation of scholars.[114] Before his turning to the anti-unionist party, Gennadios/ George Scholarios showed Pope Eugenius IV his reverence in an encomiastic letter, apparently in an attempt to establish himself at the Curia (1434). In a letter sent to Milan, Scholarios reports that he had recited a letter by Francesco Filelfo before the emperor and reassures his addressee of the emperor's sympathy and his own friendly feelings for him (1442). In another missive to an Italian humanist which constitutes an example of a typical friendship letter, Scholarios apologized to Ambrogio Traversari for not being able to visit him, on account of his illness, during his sojourn in Ferrara in 1438 and asks him to provide him and his entourage shelter in his monastery, after the decision had been taken to transfer the council to Florence.[115]

Conversely, western humanists such as Guarino Veronese (1374–1460), Jacopo Angeli (c.1360–1410/11) and Francesco Filelfo (1398–1481) came to Byzantium in order to look for manuscripts and to learn Greek. Filelfo's is a particularly interesting case. To his literary legacy belongs a collection of 110 Greek letters

---

111 Manuel Chrysoloras, *Comparison between the Old and the New Rome* (= *Letters*, no. 1), ed. Billò.

112 Manuel Chrysoloras, *Letters*, no. 2, *Patrologia Graeca*, vol. 156, pp. 53–58.

113 See the brief survey in Thorn, "Das Briefcorpus des Manuel Chrysoloras".

114 Manuel Kalekas, *Letters*, nos. 13–89, ed. Loenertz, pp. 184–307 with introductory remarks at pp. 23–46.

115 Gennadios II Scholarios, *Letters*, nos. 15–16 and 21, eds. Petit/Sidéridès/Jugie, pp. 432–35 and 440–41 with Blanchet, *Georges-Gennadios Scholarios*, pp. 296–97, 302–04 and 348.

EPISTOLOGRAPHY, SOCIAL EXCHANGE AND INTELLECTUAL DISCOURSE 241

from the period after his return to Italy (1427), which reveal an astonishingly profound acquaintance with the conventions of Byzantine letter-writing and, remarkably, preserve also the full standard formula at the beginning and end of each letter, which were usually omitted in the manuscript copies.[116] His addressees include mainly Greek scholars resident in Italy (Theodore Gazes, Bessarion, John Argyropoulos, Andronikos Kallistos, George Trapezountios, Demetrios Kastrenos, Demetrios Chalkokondyles), but also Italian humanists who had mastered Greek (e.g., Guarino, Ambrogio Traversari, Giovanni Aurispa, Ermolao Barbaro, Marsilio Ficino).[117]

Compared to the relative coherence and solidity of the group of *pepaideumenoi* in the early Palaeologan period, the examples briefly discussed in this section demonstrate the diversity and complexity of intellectual networks in the decades preceding the fall of Constantinople – a trend looming already in the 14th century (see the previous subchapter). Not only does it appear that the geographical space in which intellectuals acted and interacted has grown significantly, but also mental horizons seem to have widened, while "conservative" forces attempted to counteract these seeming innovations. These developments underline the struggle between the forces of transformation and reversion into which Byzantium was forced by the advance of the Ottomans.[118] Letter-writing was firmly entwined in these dynamics, as it offered the possibility of long-distance communication between intellectuals in the wider Mediterranean, while at the same time preserving and spreading accepted cultural codes through the perpetuation of established social and linguistic conventions.

6   The End? Afterword on the Fate of Greek Letter-Writing after 1453

The capture of Constantinople on May 29, 1453 marked the end of the political and cultural entity we call Byzantium. But this political event did of course not obliterate Greek letter-writing as a medium of social and intellectual exchange. Some men of the last generation of Byzantine literati fled to different parts of the collapsing empire, to regions under Latin dominion or to Italy. The Constantinopolitans Michael Apostoles (*c*.1430–1478) and Constantine

---

116   See above, p. 112 at n. 4. On Filelfo's sojourn in Constantinople see Ganchou, "Les *ultimate voluntates*". On his interest in ancient Greek epistolography see De Keyser/Speranzi, "Gli *epistolographi graeci*".

117   Francesco Filelfo, *Greek Letters*, ed. & trans. Legrand; *Collected Letters*, ed. & trans. De Keyser (for the Greek letters in this edition see the list of incipits in vol. 4, pp. 1982–84).

118   On this see Necipoğlu, *Byzantium between the Ottomans and the Latins*.

Laskaris (1434–1501) made their ways westwards after their release from Turkish imprisonment. Apostoles found a new home as teacher and scribe in Candia, from where he corresponded with peers and patrons on Crete itself as well as in various other regions of the Mediterranean (Italy, Cyprus, Chios, Rhodes, Beirut).[119] Laskaris taught Greek in Milan and Naples before settling as a teacher in Messina. He was in contact with Greek émigrés and western scholars alike (among others Bessarion, Theodore Gazes, Giorgio Valla, and Juan Pardo), with whom he exchanged manuscripts and shared his own writings.[120] Others had settled in Italy already before the fall of Constantinople. Bessarion (c.1408–1472), who had received his education in Constantinople under Chortasmenos and completed his studies with George Gemistos at Mistra, settled in Italy after the council of Ferrara-Florence to become a cardinal and aspirant to the papal throne. He was undoubtedly the most renowned and influential of all Greek émigrés, acting as a patron of the letters, a collector of Greek and Latin manuscripts and the author of philosophical and theological treatises.[121] Theodore Gazes (c.1410–1476), a native of Thessaloniki who received a higher education in Constantinople, migrated to Italy around 1440, where he acquired a reputation as a translator of Greek literature into Latin, an Aristotelian philosopher and a grammarian. His Greek and Latin letters testify to his ties and intellectual exchange (and controversies) with Italian and Greek émigré humanists like Bessarion, Andronikos Kallistos, Antonio Beccadelli, and particularly Francesco Filelfo.[122]

Many of these Greek émigrés feared that with the collapse of the Byzantine Empire, Greek literary culture might come to an end. Bessarion thus envisioned, and eventually laid the foundation for, a library where after the fall of Constantinople the remaining Greeks would have access to the classical and Christian Greek literary legacy;[123] Laskaris urged Giovanni Gatto, Bishop of Catania, to restore the study of Greek letters in his city[124] and compiled an abridged grammar specifically for western students "because the Latins are no

---

119 Michael Apostoles, *Letters*, ed. Stefec with Riehle, "Kreta: ein 'melting pot' der frühen Neuzeit?".
120 Constantine Laskaris, *Letters*, esp. nos. 1, 4, 7, 8, 13, 14, ed. Martínez Manzano.
121 Bessarion, *Letters*, ed. Mohler. On Bessarion an ample bibliography exists. See most recently Monfasani, *Bessarion Scholasticus* and the essays in Märtl/Kaiser/Ricklin, "*Inter latinos graecissimus, inter graecos latinissimus*".
122 Theodore Gazes, *Letters*, ed. Leone with Leone, "Le lettere di Teodoro Gaza".
123 Bessarion, *Letters*, no. 30, ed. Mohler, pp. 378–79, at p. 379, lines 10–30.
124 Constantine Laskaris, *Letters*, no. 1, ed. Martínez Manzano, pp. 158–59.

EPISTOLOGRAPHY, SOCIAL EXCHANGE AND INTELLECTUAL DISCOURSE   243

native speakers [...] and cannot learn our language easily;"[125] Apostoles proposed to Italian authorities a reformation of the method of language instruction for foreigners;[126] and Gazes reprimanded a young compatriot in Italy for having sent him a letter in Latin (ῥωμαϊστί) although he knew very well how to use their native language (ἡ πάτριος φωνή) adding that "I, however, gladly send you letters using our native tongue, since the Greek language is rarely used among Italians who, out of ignorance and bigotry, neglect Greek learning."[127]

These and other emigrant literati made an important contribution to the preservation of Greek culture within the humanist movement of Renaissance Europe. Yet, the Byzantine tradition of epistolography as a medium of social exchange and intellectual discourse was to live on much more persistently and vividly on the territory of the former Byzantine Empire now under Ottoman rule. It was learned men such as the officials of the Patriarchate of Constantinople John and Theodosios Zygomalas (1498–1581/1544–1614), the Athenian philosopher and schoolmaster Theophilos Korydaleus (1560–1646) and his student Eugenios Giannoulis (1590/97–1682), the *Phanariotes* Alexandros and Nicholas Maurokordatos (1641–1709/1680–1730), and the scholar-teachers of the Greek Enlightenment Neophytos Doukas (*c.*1760–1845) and Constantine Koumas (1777–1836) who, within new socio-political contexts, carried on, and transformed, the Byzantine tradition of letter-writing well into the 19th century.[128]

Acknowledgments

My thanks go to Divna Manolova, Florin Leonte, Matthew Briel and John Kee for their helpful remarks and edits.

---

125   Constantine Laskaris, *Prologue to the Third Book on Nouns and Verbs*, ed. Martínez Manzano, p. 207, lines 6–8: διά τε τὸ τῶν Λατίνων ἀλλόφωνον [...] καὶ μὴ δύνασθαι εὐχερῶς τὰ ἡμέτερα μανθάνειν.

126   Michael Apostoles, *Parenetical Oration*, ed. & trans. Riehle with Riehle, "Fremdsprachen-didaktik zwischen Ost und West".

127   Theodore Gazes, *Letters*, no. 6, ed. Leone, p. 52, lines 7–9: ἔγωγε μέντοι πρὸς σὲ τῇ πατρίῳ χρώμενος ἐπιστέλλω ἄσμενος, διὰ τὸ σπανίως συμβαίνειν ἑλληνίζειν τὴν φωνὴν ἐν Ἰταλιώταις λόγων ἀμελοῦσιν Ἑλληνικῶν ὑπ' ἀπειροκαλίας τε καὶ μικροψυχίας.

128   See the collected essays in Academy of Athens, Πρακτικὰ τοῦ ἐπιστημονικοῦ συμποσίου: Νεοελληνικὴ ἐπιστολογραφία. For the letters of the Zygomalades see Rhoby, "The Letter Network of Ioannes and Theodosios Zygomalas" and Toufexis, "Οι Θεματοεπιστολαί του Θεοδόσιου Ζυγομαλά". For Koumas see Ransmayr, "Ὑγίαινε, φίλον ἦτορ!".

244 RIEHLE

Bibliography

Primary Sources

Athanasios I, *Letters to the Emperor*, ed. & trans. A.-M. Maffry Talbot, *The Correspondence of Athanasius I, Patriarch of Constantinople. Letters to the Emperor Andronicus II, Members of the Imperial Family, and Officials* (Corpus Fontium Historiae Byzantinae, 7), Washington, D.C. 1975.

Barlaam of Calabria, *Greek Letters*, ed. & trans. A. Fyrigos, *Dalla controversia palamitica alla polemica esicastica (con un'edizione critica delle "Epistole greche" di Barlaam Calabro)* (Medioevo, 11), Rome 2005, pp. 194–400.

Bessarion, *Letters*, ed. L. Mohler, *Kardinal Bessarion als Theologe, Humanist und Staatsmann*, vol. 3 (Quellen und Forschungen aus dem Gebiete der Geschichte, 24), Paderborn 1942, pp. 415–571.

Constantine Akropolites, *Letters*, ed. R. Romano, *Constantino Acropolita. Epistole*, Naples 1991.

Constantine Laskaris, *Letters*, ed. T. Martínez Manzano, *Konstantinos Laskaris: Humanist – Philologe – Lehrer – Kopist* (Meletemata, 4), Hamburg 1994, pp. 156–74.

Constantine Laskaris, *Prologue to the Third Book on Nouns and Verbs*, ibid., pp. 207–08.

Demetrios Chrysoloras, *One Hundred Letters*, ed. F. Conti Bizzarro, *Demetrio Crisolora. Cento epistole a Manuele II Paleologo*, Napels 1984.

Demetrios Kydones, *Letters*, ed. R.-J. Loenertz, *Démétrius Cydonès. Correspondance* (Studi e Testi, 186 & 208), 2 vols., Vatican City 1956–60.

Demetrios Kydones, *Letters*, trans. F. Tinnefeld, *Demetrios Kydones. Briefe* (Bibliothek der griechischen Literatur, 12, 16, 33, 50 & 60), 5 vols., Stuttgart 1981/2003.

Francesco Filelfo, *Collected Letters*, ed. & trans. J. De Keyser, *Francesco Filelfo. Collected Letters*: Epistolarum Libri XLVIII (Hellenica, 54), 4 vols., Alessandria 2015.

Francesco Filelfo, *Greek Letters*, ed. & trans. É. Legrand, *Cent-dix lettres grecques de François Filelfe*, Paris 1892.

Gennadios II Scholarios, *Letters*, eds. L. Petit/X.A. Sidéridès/M. Jugie, *Oeuvres complètes de Gennade Scholarios*, vol. 4, Paris 1935, pp. 398–503.

Gennadios II Scholarios, *Polemics against the Union of the Churches*, eds. L. Petit/X.A. Sidéridès/M. Jugie, *Oeuvres complètes de Gennade Scholarios*, vol. 3, Paris 1930, pp. 1–204.

Gregory Akindynos, *Letters*, ed. & trans. A.C. Hero, *Letters of Gregory Akindynos* (Dumbarton Oaks Texts, 7 / Corpus Fontium Historiae Byzantinae, 21), Washington, D.C. 1983.

Gregory of Cyprus, *Letters*, ed. S. Eustratiades, *Γρηγορίου Κυπρίου οἰκουμενικοῦ Πατριάρχου ἐπιστολαὶ καὶ μῦθοι*, Alexandria 1910.

EPISTOLOGRAPHY, SOCIAL EXCHANGE AND INTELLECTUAL DISCOURSE 245

Gregory of Cyprus, *Letters to Theodora Raoulaina*, ed. S. Kotzabassi, "Scholarly Friendship in the Thirteenth Century: Patriarch Gregorios II Kyprios and Theodora Raoulaina", *Parekbolai* 1 (2011), 115–70.

Gregory Palamas, *Letters to Akindynos and Barlaam*, ed. J. Meyendorff, in P.K. Chrestou, *Γρηγορίου τοῦ Παλαμᾶ συγγράμματα*, vol. 1, Thessaloniki 1962, pp. 179–312.

Irene Choumnaina, *Correspondence with an Anonymous Monk*, ed. & trans. A.C. Hero, *A Woman's Quest for Spiritual Guidance: The Correspondence of Princess Irene Eulogia Choumnaina Palaiologina* (The Archbishop Iakovos Library of Ecclesiastical and Historical Sources, 11), Brookline, Mass. 1986.

John Chortasmenos, *Letters*, ed. H. Hunger, *Johannes Chortasmenos (ca. 1370–ca. 1436/37): Briefe, Gedichte und kleine Schriften* (Wiener Byzantinistische Studien, 7), Vienna 1969, pp. 153–89, 198–209, 215–16 and 225–26.

John Eugenikos, *Letters*, ed. S.P. Lampros, *Παλαιολόγεια καὶ Πελοποννησιακά*, vol. 1, Athens 1912–23, pp. 154–210 and 315–23.

John Eugenikos, *Letter to Notaras concerning the Union of Churches*, ibid., pp. 137–46.

Loukas Notaras, *Correspondence*, ed. S.P. Lampros, *Παλαιολόγεια καὶ Πελοποννησιακά*, vol. 2, Athens 1912–24, pp. 182–212.

Manuel Chrysoloras, *Comparison between the Old and the New Rome* (= *Letters*, no. 1), ed. C. Billò, "Manuele Crisolora, *Confronto tra l'Antica e la Nuova Roma*", *Medioevo greco* 0 (2000), 1–26.

Manuel Chrysoloras, *Letters*, in *Patrologia Graeca*, vol. 156, pp. 23–60.

Manuel Kalekas, *Letters*, ed. R.-J. Loenertz, *Correspondance de Manuel Calecas* (Studi e Testi, 152), Vatican City 1950.

Manuel II Palaiologos, *Letters*, ed. & trans. G.T. Dennis, *The Letters of Manuel II Palaeologus* (Corpus Fontium Historiae Byzantinae, 8), Washington, D.C. 1977.

Manuel Raoul, *Letters*, ed. R.J. Loenertz, "Emmanuelis Raul epistulae XII", *Ἐπετηρὶς Ἑταιρείας Βυζαντινῶν Σπουδῶν* 26 (1956), 130–63.

Mark Eugenikos, *Letters*, ed. L. Petit, *Documents relatifs au Concile de Florence II: Œvres anticonciliaires de Marc d'Éphèse* (Patrologia Orientalis, 17,2 = no. 83), Paris 1923 (repr. Turnhout 1974), pp. 311–45 = 449–83.

Matthew Blastares, *Letter to Guy de Lusignan*, ed. Arsenij, *Pismo Matthija Vlastarja*, Moscow 1891.

Matthew of Ephesos (Manuel Gabalas), *Letters*, ed. & trans. D. Reinsch, *Die Briefe des Matthaios von Ephesos im Codex Vindobonensis Theol. Gr. 174*, Berlin 1974.

Maximos Planoudes, *Letters*, ed. P.L.M. Leone, *Maximi monachi Planudis epistulae* (Classical and Byzantine Monographs, 18), Amsterdam 1991.

Michael Apostoles, *Letters*, ed. R. Stefec, *Die Briefe des Michael Apostoles* (Schriften zur Kulturgeschichte, 29), Hamburg 2013.

246 RIEHLE

Michael Apostoles, *Parenetical Oration*, ed. & trans. A. Riehle, "Der Λόγος παραινετικός des Michaelos Apostoles. Edition und Übersetzung", *Βυζαντινά* 31 (2011), 45–82.

Michael Gabras, *Letters*, ed. G. Fatouros, *Die Briefe des Michael Gabras* (*ca. 1290–nach 1350*) (Wiener Byzantinistische Studien, 10), 2 vols., Vienna 1973.

Nikephoros Choumnos, *Letters*, ed. J.F. Boissonade, *Anecdota Nova*, Paris 1844 (repr. Hildesheim 1962), pp. 1–190.

Nikephoros Gregoras, *Letters*, ed. P.A.M. Leone, *Nicephori Gregorae Epistulae*, 2 vols., Matino 1982–83.

Nikephoros Gregoras, *Roman History*, eds. L. Schopen/I. Bekker, *Nicephori Gregorae Byzantina Historia* (Corpus Scriptorum Historiae Byzantinae, 19), 3 vols., Bonn 1829–55.

Simon of Constantinople, *Letter to Andronikos II*, ed. M.S. Anagnostou, "Ἀνέκδοτη ἐπιστολὴ τοῦ Σίμωνος τοῦ Κωνσταντινουπολίτου πρὸς τὸν αὐτοκράτορα Ἀνδρόνικο Βʹ τὸν Παλαιολόγο", *Ἐπιστημονικὴ Ἐπετηρὶς τῆς Φιλοσοφικῆς Σχολῆς τοῦ Πανεπιστημίου Ἀθηνῶν* 43 (2011/12), 55–71.

Theodore Gazes, *Letters*, ed. P.M.A. Leone, *Theodori Gazae Epistolae*, Naples 1990.

Theodore Hyrtakenos, *Letters*, eds. & trans. A. Karpozilos/G. Fatouros, *The Letters of Theodoros Hyrtakenos*, Athens 2017.

Theodore Hyrtakenos, *Letters*, ed. F.J.G. la Porte-du Theil, "Notice et extraits d'un volume de la Bibliothèque nationale, coté MCCIX parmi les Manuscrits Grecs, et contenant les *Opuscules* et *les Lettres* anecdotes *de Théodôre l'Hyrtacènien*", *Notices et extraits des Manuscrits de la Bibliothèque nationale* 5 (1798), 709–44; 6 (1800), 1–48.

Theodore Modenos, *Letters*, ed. M. Treu, *Theodori Pediasimi euisque amicorum quae exstant*, Potsdam 1899, 41–43.

Theodore Mouzalon, *Letters*, ed. Samara, *Θεόδωρος Μουζάλων*, pp. 175–224.

Theodore Potamios, *Letters*, ed. & trans. G.T. Dennis, "The Letters of Theodore Potamios", in id., *Byzantium and the Franks, 1350–1420*, London 1982, no. XII.

Secondary Literature

Academy of Athens, *Πρακτικὰ τοῦ ἐπιστημονικοῦ συμποσίου: Νεοελληνικὴ ἐπιστολογραφία* (*16ος–19ος αἰ.*), *Ἀθήνα, 20–21 Μαρτίου 2003* (= *Μεσαιωνικὰ καὶ Νέα Ἑλληνικά* 8), Athens 2006.

Bauer, Th.J., "Letter Writing in Antiquity and Early Christianity", in Riehle (ed.), *Companion*, pp. 33–67.

Beihammer, A., "Epistolography and Diplomatics", in Riehle (ed.), *Companion*, pp. 200–26.

Bernard, F., "Epistolary Communication: Rituals and Codes", in Riehle (ed.), *Companion*, pp. 307–32.

Bernard, F., "'Greet Me with Words'. Gifts and Intellectual Friendship in Eleventh-Century Byzantium", in Grünbart (ed.), *Geschenke erhalten die Freundschaft*, pp. 1–11.

Bernard, F., "Humor in Byzantine Letters of the Tenth to Twelfth Centuries. Some Preliminary Remarks", *Dumbarton Oaks Papers* 69 (2015), 179–96.

Bianconi, D., *Tessalonica nell'età dei Paleologi. Le pratiche intellettuali nel riflesso della cultura scritta* (Dossiers Byzantins, 5), Paris 2005.

Blanchet, M.-H., *Georges-Gennadios Scholarios (vers 1400–vers 1472). Un intellectuel orthodoxe face à la disparition de l'Empire byzantin* (Archives de l'Orient Chrétien, 20), Paris 2008.

Ceccarelli, P., *Ancient Greek Letter Writing. A Cultural History (600 BC–150 BC)*, Oxford 2013.

Chernoglazov, D., "Was bedeuten drei Fische? Betrachtung von Geschenken in byzantinischen Briefen (IV.–XII. Jh.)", in Grünbart (ed.), *Geschenke erhalten die Freundschaft*, pp. 56–69.

Constable, G., *Letters and Letter Collections* (Typologie des Sources du Moyen Age Occidental, 17), Turnhout 1976.

Constantinides, C.N., *Higher Education in Byzantium in the Thirteenth and Early Fourteenth Centuries (1204–ca. 1310)* (Texts and Studies of the History of Cyprus, 11), Nicosia 1982.

De Keyser, J./D. Speranzi, "Gli *epistolographi graeci* di Francesco Filelfo", *Byzantion* 81 (2011), 177–206.

Ganchou, Th., "Les *ultimate voluntates* de Manuel et Iôannès Chrysolôras et le séjour de Francesco Filelfo à Constantinople", *Bizantinistica*, serie seconda 7 (2005), 195–285.

Gaul, N., "All the Emperor's Men (and His Nephews). *Paideia* and Networking Strategies at the Court of Andronikos II Palaiologos, 1290–1320", *Dumbarton Oaks Papers* 70 (2016), 245–70.

Gaul, N., "Rising Elites and Institutionalization – *Ēthos/Mores* – 'Debts' and Drafts. Three Concluding Steps towards Comparing Networks of Learning in Byzantium and the 'Latin' West, c.1000–1200", in Steckel/Gaul/Grünbart (eds.), *Networks of Learning*, pp. 235–80.

Gaul, N., "The Letter in the *Theatron*: Epistolary Voice, Character, and Soul (and Their Audience)", in Riehle (ed.), *Companion*, pp. 353–73.

Gaul, N., *Thomas Magistros und die spätbyzantische Sophistik: Studien zum Humanismus urbaner Eliten der frühen Palaiologenzeit* (Mainzer Veröffentlichungen zur Byzantinistik, 10), Wiesbaden 2011.

Grünbart, M., *Formen der Anrede im byzantinischen Brief vom 6. bis zum 12. Jahrhundert* (Wiener Byzantinistische Studien, 25), Vienna 2005.

Grünbart, M. (ed.), *Geschenke erhalten die Freundschaft. Gabentausch und Netzwerkpflege im europäischen Mittelalter* (Byzantinistische Studien und Texte, 1), Münster 2011.

Grünbart, M., "L'epistolografia", in G. Cavallo (ed.), *Lo spazio letterario del medioevo. 3: Le culture circostanti*, vol. 1: *La cultura bizantina*, Rome 2004, pp. 345–78.

Hatlie, P., "Life and Artistry in the 'Publication' of Demetrios Kydones' Letter Collection", *Greek, Roman and Byzantine Studies* 37 (1996), 75–102.

Kaldellis, A./N. Siniossoglou (eds.), *The Cambridge Intellectual History of Byzantium*, Cambridge 2017.

Kalopissi-Verti, S., "Patronage and Artistic Production in Byzantium during the Palaiologan Period", in S.T. Brooks (ed.), *Byzantium: Faith and Power (1261–1557). Perspectives on Late Byzantine Art and Culture*, New Haven/London 2006, pp. 76–97.

Karlsson, G., *Idéologie et cérémonial dans l'épistolographie byzantine. Textes du Xe siècle analysés et commentés* (Studia Graeca Upsaliensia, 3), 2nd ed., Uppsala 1962.

Karpozilos, A., "Books and Bookmen in the 14th C. The Epistolographical Evidence", *Jahrbuch der Österreichischen Byzantinistik* 41 (1991), 255–76.

Kazhdan, A., *A History of Byzantine Literature (850–1000)* (Institute for Byzantine Research – Research Series, 4), Athens 2006.

Kiousopoulou, T., *Βασιλεύς ἡ Οικονόμος. Πολιτική εξουσία και ιδεολογία πριν την Ἅλωση*, Athens 2007 (trans. P. Magdalino, *Emperor or Manager: Power and Political Ideology in Byzantium before 1453*, Genoa 2011).

Kiousopoulou, T., "Λουκάς Νοταράς: Ψήγματα μιας βιογραφίας", in Ph. Evangelatou-Notara/T. Maniate-Kokkine (eds.), *Κλητόριον εἰς μνήμην Νίκου Οἰκονομίδη*, Athens 2005, pp. 161–76.

Klauck, H.-J., *Ancient Letters and the New Testament. A Guide to Context and Exegesis*, trans. D.P. Bailey, Waco 2006.

Kotzabassi, S., "Gregorios Kyprios as Reader and Critic", in ead./G. Mavromatis (eds.), *Realia Byzantina* (Byzantinisches Archiv, 22), Berlin 2009, pp. 76–88.

Kourousis, S.I., "Ὁ λόγιος οἰκουμενικὸς Πατριάρχης Ἰωάννης ΙΓ΄ ὁ Γλυκύς", *Ἐπετηρὶς Ἑταιρείας Βυζαντινῶν Σπουδῶν* 41 (1974), 297–405.

Kubina, K./A. Riehle (eds.), *Epistolary Poetry in Byzantium and Beyond. An Anthology with Critical Essays*, London 2021.

Kyritses, D.S., *The Byzantine Aristocracy in the Thirteenth and Early Fourteenth Centuries*, PhD thesis, Harvard University 1997.

Laiou, A., "The Correspondence of Gregorios Kyprios as a Source for the History of Social and Political Behaviour in Byzantium or, on Government by Rhetoric", in W. Seibt (ed.), *Geschichte und Kultur der Palaiologenzeit. Referate des Internationalen Symposions zu Ehren von Herbert Hunger (Wien, 30. November bis 3. Dezember 1994)* (Österreichische Akademie der Wissenschaften: Philosophisch-Historische Klasse. Denkschriften, 241 / Veröffentlichungen der Kommission für Byzantinistik, 8), Vienna 1996, pp. 91–108.

Leone, P.L.M., "Le lettere di Teodoro Gaza", in M. Cortesi/E.V. Maltese (eds.), *Dotti bizantini e libri greci nell'Italia del secolo XV. Atti del Convegno internazionale, Trento 22–23 ottobre 1990*, Naples 1992, pp. 201–18.

Leonte, F., "The Letters of Demetrios Kydones", in Riehle (ed.), *Companion*, pp. 146–73.

Littlewood, A.R., "An 'Ikon of the Soul': the Byzantine Letter", *Visible Language* 10 (1976), 197–226.

Littlewood, A.R., "A Statistical Survey of the Incidence of Repeated Quotations in Selected Byzantine Letter-Writers", in J. Duffy/J. Peradotto (eds.), *Gonimos. Neoplatonic and Byzantine Studies Presented to Leendert G. Westerink at 75*, Buffalo 1988, pp. 137–54.

Loenertz, R.-J., *Les recueils de lettres de Démétrius Cydonès* (Studi e Testi, 131), Vatican City 1947.

Malherbe, A.J., *Ancient Epistolary Theorists* (SBL Sources for Biblical Study, 19), Atlanta 1988.

Märtl, C./C. Kaiser/T. Ricklin (eds.), *"Inter latinos graecissimus, inter graecos latinissimus". Bessarion zwischen den Kulturen* (Pluralisierung & Autorität, 39), Berlin/ Boston 2013.

Matschke, K.-P./Tinnefeld, F., *Die Gesellschaft im späten Byzanz. Gruppen, Strukturen und Lebensformen*, Cologne/Weimar/Vienna 2001.

Mergiali, S., *L'enseignement et les lettrés pendant l'époque des Paléologues (1261–1453)* (Ἑταιρεία τῶν Φίλων τοῦ Λαοῦ: Κέντρον Ἐρεύνης Βυζαντίου, 5), Athens 1996.

Monfasani, J., *Bessarion Scholasticus. A Study of Cardinal Bessarion's Latin Library* (Byzantios: Studies in Byzantine History and Civilization, 3), Turnhout 2011.

Mullett, M., "Byzantium: A Friendly Society?", *Past and Present* 118 (1988), 3–24.

Mullett, M., "Epistolography", in E. Jeffreys (ed.), *The Oxford Handbook of Byzantine Studies*, Oxford 2008, pp. 882–93.

Mullett, M., "Friendship in Byzantium: Genre, Topos and Network", in J. Haseldine (ed.), *Friendship in Medieval Europe*, Stroud 1999, pp. 166–84.

Mullett, M., *Theophylact of Ochrid. Reading the Letters of a Byzantine Archbishop* (Birmingham Byzantine and Ottoman Monographs, 2), Aldershot 1997.

Necipoğlu, N., *Byzantium between the Ottomans and the Latins. Politics and Society in the Late Empire*, Cambridge 2009.

Papaioannou, S., "Letter-Writing", in P. Stephenson (ed.), *The Byzantine World*, London/ New York 2010, pp. 188–99.

Paschos, P.B., *Ὁ Ματθαῖος Βλάσταρης καὶ τὸ ὑμνογραφικὸν ἔργον του*, Thessaloniki 1978.

Perentidis, S. (ed.), *Ο Ιωάννης και ο Θεοδόσιος Ζυγομαλάς και η εποχή τους*, Athens 2009.

Preiser-Kapeller, J., "Letters and Networks Analysis", in Riehle (ed.), *Companion*, pp. 431–65.

Ransmayr, A., *'Ὑγίαινε, φίλον ἦτορ!' Stilistische Untersuchungen zur neugriechischen Epistolographie anhand der Briefe von Konstantinos M. Koumas*, MA thesis, University of Vienna 2008.

Rhoby, A., "The Letter Network of Ioannes and Theodosios Zygomalas", in Perentidis (ed.), *Ο Ιωάννης και ο Θεοδόσιος Ζυγομαλάς*, pp. 125–52.

Riehle, A. (ed.), *A Companion to Byzantine Epistolography* (Brill's Companions to the Byzantine World, 7), Leiden 2020.

Riehle, A., "Byzantine Epistolography: A Historical and Historiographical Sketch", in id. (ed.), *Companion*, pp. 1–30.

Riehle, A., "Epistolography as Autobiography. Remarks on the Letter-collections of Nikephoros Choumnos", *Parekbolai* 2 (2012), 1–22.

Riehle, A., "Fremdsprachendidaktik zwischen Ost und West. Michaelos Apostoles und der Griechischunterricht im Quattrocento", in M. Altripp (ed.), *Byzanz in Europa. Europas östliches Erbe* (Βyzantiος. Studies in Byzantine History and Civilization, 2), Turnhout 2011, pp. 25–49.

Riehle, A., *Funktionen der byzantinischen Epistolographie. Studien zu den Briefen und Briefsammlungen des Nikephoros Chumnos (ca. 1260–1327)*, PhD thesis, University of Munich 2011.

Riehle, A., "Kreta: ein 'melting pot' der frühen Neuzeit? Bemerkungen zum Briefnetzwerk des Michaelos Apostoles", in Märtl/Kaiser/Ricklin, *"Inter latinos graecissimus, inter graecos latinissimus"*, pp. 167–86.

Riehle, A., "Letters and New Philology", in id. (ed.), *Companion*, pp. 466–501.

Riehle, A., "Rhetorik, Ritual und Repräsentation. Zur Briefliteratur gebildeter Eliten im spätbyzantinischen Konstantinopel (1261–1328)", *Frühmittelalterliche Studien* 45 (2011), 259–76.

Riehle, A., "*Καί σε προστάτιν ἐν αὐτοῖς τῆς αὐτῶν ἐπιγράψομεν σωτηρίας*. Theodora Raulaina als Stifterin und Patronin", in L. Theis/M. Mullett/M. Grünbart (eds.), *Female Founders in Byzantium and Beyond*, Vienna 2014 = *Wiener Jahrbuch für Kunstgeschichte* 60/61 (2011/12), pp. 299–315.

Riehle, A., "Theodoros Xanthopulos, Theodoros Metochites und die spätbyzantinische Gelehrtenkultur. Zu einem unbeachteten Brief im Codex Laur. Plut. 59.35 und den Xanthopulos-Briefen im Codex Vat. gr. 112", in A. Berger/S. Mariev/G. Prinzing/ A. Riehle (eds.), *Koinotaton Doron. Das späte Byzanz zwischen Machtlosigkeit und kultureller Blüte (1204–1461)* (Byzantinisches Archiv, 31), Boston 2016, pp. 161–83.

Samara, D., *Θεόδωρος Μουζάλων. Ἡ ζωὴ καὶ τὸ συγγραφικὸ ἔργο ἑνὸς λογίου τοῦ 13ου αἰώνα* (Βυζαντινὰ Κείμενα καὶ Μελέτες, 64), Thessaloniki 2018.

Sarri, A., *Material Aspects of Letter Writing in the Graeco-Roman World* (Materiale Textkulturen, 12), Berlin 2018.

Ševčenko, I., "Society and Intellectual Life in the Fourteenth Century", in M. Berza/ E. Stanescu (eds.), *Actes du XIVᵉ Congrès International des Études Byzantines, Bucarest, 6–12 Septembre 1971*, vol. 1, Bucharest 1974, pp. 65–92.

Ševčenko, I., "The Decline of Byzantium Seen through the Eyes of its Intellectuals", *Dumbarton Oaks Papers* 15 (1961), 169–86.

Steckel, S., "Networks of Learning in Byzantine East and Latin West: Methodological Considerations and Starting Points for Further Work", in Steckel/Gaul/Grünbart (eds.), *Networks of Learning*, pp. 185–233.

Steckel, S./N. Gaul/M. Grünbart (eds.), *Networks of Learning. Perspectives on Scholars in Byzantine East and Latin West, c. 1000–1200*, Zurich 2014.

Taxidis, E., *Μάξιμος Πλανούδης. Συμβολή στη μελέτη του corpus των επιστολών του* (Βυζαντινά Κείμενα και Μελέτες, 58), Thessaloniki 2012.

Thorn, L., "Das Briefcorpus des Manuel Chrysoloras: eine Blütenlese", in E. Konstantinou (ed.), *Der Beitrag der byzantinischen Gelehrten zur abendländischen Renaissance des 14. und 15. Jahrhunderts* (Philhellenische Studien, 12), Frankfurt am Main 2006, pp. 17–28.

Thraede, K., *Grundzüge griechisch-römischer Brieftopik* (Zetemata, 48), Munich 1970.

Tinnefeld, F., *Die Briefe des Demetrios Kydones. Themen und literarische Formen* (Mainzer Veröffentlichungen zur Byzantinistik, 11), Wiesbaden 2010.

Tinnefeld, F., "Intellectuals in Late Byzantine Thessalonike", *Dumbarton Oaks Papers* 57 (2003), 153–72.

Toufexis, N., "Οι *Θεματοεπιστολαί* του Θεοδόσιου Ζυγομαλά και η μετάβαση από τη βυζαντινή στην πρώιμη νεοελληνική παράδοση", in Perentidis, *Ο Ιωάννης και ο Θεοδόσιος Ζυγομαλάς*, pp. 305–40.

Wahlgren-Smith, L., "Letter Collections in the Latin West", in Riehle (ed.), *Companion*, pp. 92–122.

Wendel, C., "Planudes als Bücherfreund", *Zentralblatt für Bibliothekswesen* 58 (1941), 77–87.

Wilson, N.G., *From Byzantium to Italy: Greek Studies in the Italian Renaissance*, Baltimore 1992 (London ²2017).

Zorzi, N., "Una copista, due copisti, nessuna copista? Teodora Raulena e i due codici attribute alla sua mano", *Medioevo greco* 19 (2019), 259–82.

CHAPTER 7

The Reappropriation of Philosophy in the Palaeologan Period

Pantelis Golitsis

1 Introduction: Philosophy 'Re-Hellenised'

Compared to other periods of Byzantine history, the Palaeologan era presents us with a philosophy that is mostly characterized by two related features: autonomy and high sophistication. We can easily grasp the autonomy of Palaeologan philosophy by noticing a change in the field of semantics: whereas in earlier Byzantium the word 'philosophy' did not only refer to the study of philosophical topics as these were defined by ancient thinkers, but also (if not primarily) to monks and the ascetic way of life,[1] throughout the Palaeologan era monks gradually ceased to be called philosophers. Philosophy seemed, henceforth, to regain its Hellenic origins.

---

1 It suffices for our purpose to quote a characteristic passage of Michael Psellos' *Chronicle*, ed. Reinsch, book 4, 34, p. 68, lines 1–7: "I know that this man (i.e. the Emperor Michael IV) displayed absolute piety after he gained the throne. Not only did he regularly attend Church but he was also devoted to *philosophers* and honoured them with great enthusiasm. By 'philosophers' I do not here mean those who investigate the essences of beings and seek the principles of the universe, while they neglect the principles of their own salvation; I mean those who despise the world and live in the company of supramundane things", transl. Kaldellis (see n. 27) modified. (Οἶδα δὲ καὶ τὸν ἄνδρα εὐσέβειαν πᾶσαν μετὰ τὴν βασιλείαν ἐπιδειξάμενον, καὶ οὐ θείοις ναοῖς μόνον προσκείμενον, ἀλλὰ καὶ φιλοσόφοις ἀνδράσι προσανακείμενον καὶ ὑπερφυῶς θεραπεύοντα· φιλοσόφους δέ φημι οὐ τοὺς τὰς οὐσίας τῶν ὄντων διερευνησαμένους, οὐδὲ τὰς ἀρχὰς μὲν τοῦ κόσμου ζητήσαντας, τῶν δὲ ἀρχῶν τῆς οἰκείας σωτηρίας καταμελήσαντας, ἀλλὰ τοὺς κόσμου καταφρονήσαντας καὶ μετὰ τῶν ὑπερκοσμίων ζήσαντας.) For the two senses of philosophy in Byzantium, see the classic studies by Dölger, "Zur Bedeutung von φιλόσοφος und φιλοσοφία in byzantinischer Zeit" and Ševčenko, "The definition of philosophy in the *Life of Saint Constantine*". Before Psellos, John of Damascus (died *c*.743) gave Christian content to a traditional definition of philosophy through a syllogism in the first figure; cf. John of Damascus, *Philosophical chapters*, ed. Kotter, proem, lines 25–27 (I have modified the punctuation): "Again, philosophy is the love of wisdom; the true wisdom is God; in consequence, the love toward God is the true philosophy." (Φιλοσοφία πάλιν ἐστὶ φιλία σοφίας· σοφία δὲ ἀληθὴς ὁ θεός ἐστιν· ἡ οὖν ἀγάπη ἡ πρὸς τὸν θεὸν αὕτη ἐστὶν ἡ ἀληθὴς φιλοσοφία.) "Love toward God" is what mostly, if not exclusively, characterizes the life of the monk.

© KONINKLIJKE BRILL NV, LEIDEN, 2023 | DOI:10.1163/9789004527089_009

THE REAPPROPRIATION OF PHILOSOPHY IN THE PALAEOLOGAN ERA   253

Palaeologan monks or theologians who wished to promote the value of ascetic life and diminish the value of the study of ancient philosophy, related the word 'philosophy' to the Hellenic *paideia* and the inappropriate assimilation of ideas transmitted through ancient philosophical texts. We can readily detect this attitude in the words addressed by the Patriarch of Constantinople (1353–1354) Philotheos Kokkinos (*c*.1300–1379), a Palamite who had been a monk at the Great Lavra on Mount Athos, to the Byzantine man of letters and sciences Nikephoros Gregoras (*c*.1292–*c*.1361):

> You now look to me, o Gregoras, like that scourge-bearing Ajax, who is recounted by your Sophocles. I call 'yours' the poets and the philosophers of the Greeks, because *you too* have received from them the teachings of their abolished wisdom but you did not judge that they have been abolished and ceased. Nor did you listen to the wise teacher of the Church Paul, who says 'that God made the wisdom of this world look foolish' and that 'because in God's wisdom the world failed to know God through wisdom, God chose to save all who believe through the simple-mindedness of preaching'.[2]

The fideistic thesis expressed by Kokkinos might recall the unsophisticated apologetics of early Christian writers.[3] This is denied, however, by a close

---

2   Philotheos Kokkinos, *Fourth Antirrhetic against Gregoras*, ed. Kaimakis, lines 367–75: "Ἔοικάς μοι νῦν, ὦ Γρηγορά, τῷ παρὰ τῷ σῷ Σοφοκλεῖ μαστιγοφόρῳ ἐκείνῳ Αἴαντι. Σοὺς δὲ λέγω τοὺς τῶν Ἑλλήνων τουτουσὶ ποιητάς τε καὶ φιλοσόφους, ἐπειδὴ παρ' ἐκείνων τὰ τῆς καταργουμένης ἐκείνων σοφίας μαθήματα δεξάμενος καὶ αὐτός, οὐχ ὡς περὶ καταργουμένων καὶ παυομένων ἐκείνων ἐφρόνησας. Οὐδὲ τοῦ σοφοῦ διδασκάλου τῆς Ἐκκλησίας ἤκουσας Παύλου λέγοντος 'ὅτι ἐμώρανεν ὁ Θεὸς τὴν σοφίαν τοῦ κόσμου τούτου', καὶ ὅτι, 'ἐπειδὴ ἐν τῇ σοφίᾳ τοῦ Θεοῦ οὐκ ἔγνω ὁ κόσμος διὰ τῆς σοφίας τὸν Θεόν, εὐδόκησεν ὁ Θεὸς διὰ τῆς μωρίας τοῦ κηρύγματος σῶσαι τοὺς πιστεύοντας' (1 Cor. 1:20–21). Kokkinos later speaks qualifiedly of the "philosophers according to the Church, who are really wise" (ibid., line 379: τοὺς τῆς Ἐκκλησίας φιλοσόφους καὶ σοφοὺς ὄντως τούτους), wanting to contrast the Church Fathers to the (Greek) philosophers, followed by Gregoras. See also n. 38.
3   Compare, for instance, Neilos of Ancyra's *Ascetic discourse*, in *Patrologia Graeca*, vol. 79, p. 721B: "Philosophy is correct moral practice combined with a true doctrine of knowledge about What Is. Of this both the Jews and the Greeks have fallen short, because they have asked for the wisdom which descended from the heavens and have attempted to philosophize without Christ, the one who exemplified with his words and deeds the true philosophy." (Φιλοσοφία γάρ ἐστιν ἠθῶν κατόρθωσις μετὰ δόξης τῆς περὶ τοῦ ὄντος γνώσεως ἀληθοῦς. Ταύτης δὲ ἀπεσφάλησαν ἄμφω καὶ Ἰουδαῖοι καὶ Ἕλληνες, τὴν ἀπ' οὐρανοῦ παραγενομένην σοφίαν παραιτησάμενοι καὶ χωρὶς Χριστοῦ φιλοσοφεῖν ἐπιχειρήσαντες, τοῦ μόνου παραδείξαντος ἔργῳ καὶ λόγῳ τὴν ἀληθῆ φιλοσοφίαν.) Neilos' definition of philosophy later became canonical through its inclusion to the Lexicon of *Suda*; cf. *Suda*, ed. A. Adler, vol. 4, p. 733, lines 6–8.

reading of the text itself; not only Gregoras but *also* Kokkinos ("you too", he says speaking of Gregoras) had received the teachings of the Greek poets and philosophers.[4] Contrary to Gregoras, however, Kokkinos judged (φρονεῖν) those teachings to be untrue. His criticism of the Greek philosophers is not dictated by a general and received negative stance towards the Hellenes, as was mostly the case in earlier centuries, but is rather based on his personal assessment of ancient philosophical literature. His criticism of Gregoras is harsh and somewhat sophisticated: not only was the Byzantine philosopher unable to grasp the fallacies of Hellenic wisdom but he also failed to save himself by simply believing in the teaching of Saint Paul; he is thus shown to fall short even of the simple-minded people to whom the message of the Gospel is addressed. We have already reached the second of the features named at the beginning of our chapter, sophistication.

Byzantine philosophy attained its peak of sophistication at the very end of Byzantium, or even afterwards. Bessarion's (1403–1472) *Against Plato's Calumniator*, written in Greek in 1459 and printed in Latin in 1469,[5] where George Trapezountios' (1395–c.1472) anti-Platonic and pro-Aristotelian theses are refuted, subsumed under its lengthy and detailed expositions the controversial discussions about the value of the philosophies of Plato and Aristotle,[6] which had begun in 1439, when George Gemistos Plethon (c.1355–1452) published his pamphlet *On Aristotle's Departures from Plato*.[7] Similarly, George Scholarios'

---

4 Note that, as has been pointed out by Podskalsky, *Theologie und Philosophie in Byzanz*, p. 1, Kokkinos makes in the immediately following lines a hidden reference to Plato's *Phaedrus*; compare *Fourth Antirrhetic against Gregoras*, lines 376–377 (μηδὲ συνεὶς μηδὲ τοῖς ποτίμοις τῶν λόγων τοὺς ἁλμυροὺς ἀποκλύσας) with *Phaedrus*, 243d4–5 (ἐπιθυμῶ ποτίμῳ λόγῳ οἷον ἁλμυρὰν ἀκοὴν ἀποκλύσασθαι). This was meant to show to Gregoras Kokkinos' own familiarity with Greek 'wisdom'.

5 For some of the Greek sources of Bessarion's work, to which Latin Scholastic sources were later added in view of the Latin printed edition, see, most recently, Monfasani, "Cardinal Bessarion's Greek and Latin Sources".

6 On Bessarion's intellectual stance, appealing to sound philological criticism and to an unbiased understanding of the teachings of ancient philosophers, see Hankins, *Plato in the Italian Renaissance*, vol. 1, pp. 217–32. The point of the controversy between Byzantine 'Platonists' and 'Aristotelians', namely which one of the two ancient philosophical authorities comes closer to the Christian doctrine, is helpfully elucidated by Karamanolis, "Plethon and Scholarios on Aristotle".

7 George Gemistos Plethon, *On Aristotle's Departures from Plato*, ed. Lagarde. A new edition of the first part of Plethon's opuscule, prepared by Börje Bydén, is available (George Gemistos Plethon, *On Aristotle's Departures from Plato*, ed. Bydén). Plethon, who does not hesitate to call Aristotle an 'ignorant' (ἀμαθής) more than once, aimed at showing to the Westerners, contrary to their own common assumption, how much inferior to Plato Aristotle was.

(*c.*1400–*c.*1472) self-understanding as an exegete of Aristotle, as it appears in his *Letter to Constantine Palaiologos*, depends on an impressive acquaintance with a great variety of sources, including not only Greek and Byzantine commentators on Aristotle but also Thomas Aquinas and other Latin authors, as well as Arab and Persian thinkers such as Averroes and Avicenna.[8] Scholarios utters a verdict that was wholly unthinkable before his time, when he says of the Arab commentator that "no one is ignorant of the fact that Averroes is the most excellent among Aristotle's commentators."[9]

We may say, therefore, that the main activity of philosophers during the Palaeologan period was the reappropriation of philosophy: it consisted primarily in exploring the meaning of ancient philosophical texts and concluding, either positively or negatively, as to the value of philosophical knowledge. This was reflected on the type of philosophical writing adopted by Palaeologan thinkers: running commentaries (which enable a detailed engagement with the ancient philosophical texts) superseded the genre of the epitome (which promoted a selective reading of ancient philosophy). At the same time both the admirers and the repudiators of ancient philosophers wrote polemical treatises against each other. Although a critical attitude towards philosophy is observed in earlier Byzantine thinkers (e.g., in Michael Psellos and in John Italos in the eleventh century), their criticisms did not occur within the lively dialectics that characterize the Palaeologan era. As we shall see, philosophy had a specific role to play with regard to the actual concerns of Palaeologan society, the most prominent of which were the challenge posited by the rise of Hesychasm and the interaction with the Western Church and Scholasticism. However, in order to be actual, philosophy had first to be accessible.

2 Making Philosophy Accessible: Ancient Texts and Byzantine Commentaries

The reappropriation of philosophy during the Palaeologan era is reflected in the abundant production of running commentaries on ancient philosophical texts. Such commentaries contrasted with the abridged forms of philosophical

---

8 See Ierodiakonou, "The Byzantine commentator's task: Transmitting, transforming or transcending Aristotle's Text".

9 Gennadios II/George Scholarios, *Opera: Dedicatory Letter to Constantine Palaiologos*, eds. Petit/Jugie/Siderides, vol. 7, p. 3, lines 20–21: Ἀβερόην δὲ οὐδείς, οἶμαι, ἀγνοεῖ τῶν ἐξηγητῶν Ἀριστοτέλους ὄντα τὸν κράτιστον. Of course, Scholarios was familiar with Arabic philosophy through Latin sources; see Steiris, "Pletho, Scholarios and the Arabic philosophy".

writing that had been preferred in earlier periods of Byzantine history. George Pachymeres (1242–after 1310) produced running commentaries on the six treatises of Aristotle's *Organon*, as well as on Aristotle's *Physics*, *Metaphysics* and *Nicomachean Ethics*; he also completed the mutilated commentary of Proclus on Plato's *Parmenides* by providing an exegesis that contrasts sharply with its Neoplatonic interpretation.[10] Pachymeres' contemporary, the hieromonk Sophonias (died after 1307), possibly a Catholic convert, composed paraphrastic commentaries on Aristotle's *De anima* and *Parva naturalia*, and possibly on the *Categories*, on the first book of the *Prior Analytics* and on the *Sophistici elenchi*.[11] John Pediasimos (*c*.1250–early 14th cent.), who held the teaching office of the 'consul of the philosophers' (ὕπατος τῶν φιλοσόφων), composed scholia on Aristotle's *Prior* and *Posterior Analytics*.[12] Theodore Metochites (1270–1332) wrote selectively a *Paraphrase on all the physical treatises of Aristotle* (including the *De anima*),[13] expressing in one of his *Essays* (*semeiosis* 21) his intellectual disappointment with regard to Aristotle's *Metaphysics*.[14] John Chortasmenos (*c*.1370–*c*.1436/37), who was the teacher of Bessarion and Scholarios, composed a commentary on Aristotle's *Posterior Analytics*.[15] George Scholarios produced extensive commentaries, based on

---

10   On Pachymeres' commentaries see the overview provided by Golitsis, "Georges Pachymère comme didascale"; they are unedited except for Pachymeres' commentary on the *Nicomachean Ethics*, recently published by Xenophontos, *Georgios Pachymeres, Commentary on Aristotle, Nicomachean Ethics*, and his commentary on Aristotle's *Physics*, which has been inadequately edited and wrongly attributed to Michael Psellos by Benakis, *Michael Psellos: Kommentar zur Physik des Aristoteles*. On the authorship of this commentary and the forgery related to its supposed Psellan authorship see Golitsis, "Un commentaire perpétuel à la *Physique* d'Aristote" and id., "Nicéphore Calliste Xanthopoulos, élève de Georges Pachymère". Pachymeres' commentary on the *Parmenides* is edited by Westerink, *Commentary on Plato's Parmenides*.

11   Respectively edited as *Sophoniae in libros Aristotelis De anima paraphrasis*, ed. Hayduck; *Themistii (Sophoniae) In Parva naturalia commentarium*, ed. Wendland; *Anonymi Categoriarum paraphrasis*, ed. Hayduck; *Themistii quae fertur in Aristotelis Analyticorum priorum librum I paraphrasis*, ed. Wallies; and *Anonymi in Sophisticos elenchos paraphrasis*, ed. Wallies.

12   See John Pediasimos, *Selected commentary on Analytics*, ed. de Falco; John Pediasimos, *Other commentary on Analytics*, ed. de Falco. On Pediasimos see lately Pérez Martín, "L'écriture de Jean Pothos Pédiasimos d'après ses scholies aux *Elementa* d'Euclide".

13   Παράφρασις εἰς πάντα τὰ φυσικὰ Ἀριστοτέλους; an edition of this work is being prepared by the Berlin-Brandenburgische Akademie der Wissenschaften (Commentaria in Aristotelem Graeca et Byzantina).

14   See Theodore Metochites, *Miscellanea*, ed. Hult, p. 190, lines 13–22.

15   See Cacouros, "Un commentaire byzantin inédit".

THE REAPPROPRIATION OF PHILOSOPHY IN THE PALAEOLOGAN ERA   257

the *Logica vetus* of the Scholastics,[16] on Porphyry's *Eisagoge* and on Aristotle's *Categories* and *On the interpretation*.[17]

These new commentaries, which purported to satisfy actual intellectual needs and pedagogical demands, were added to new copies of ancient commentaries, which abound throughout the Palaeologan era. The mss. Athens, National Library of Greece, Metochiou Panagiou Taphou 106, fol. 7v, Vatican City, Biblioteca Apostolica Vaticana, Vat. gr. 241, fol. 6r, and Venice, Biblioteca Marciana, Marc. gr. 203, fol. 230r,[18] which are datable to the end of the 13th century and to the beginning of the 14th century, provide lists of the ancient commentaries that were available in Constantinople for further studying the work of the Stagirite.

Circles of Palaeologan scholars, churchmen and laymen alike, were keen on collecting every text that was available in ancient philosophy and making new and better (often through collation of different manuscripts) copies of them. We can aptly visualize such enterprises in a monumental manuscript, namely the ms. Florence, Biblioteca Medicea Laurenziana, Laur. plut. 85.1, which has been labeled 'Oceanus' due to its thickness and big size. The 'Oceanus', which was made to form a single codex at a later time, was possibly produced in the 1280s by several copyists related to George of Cyprus during his patriarchate (1241–1289, Patriarch Gregory II, 1283–1289). At any rate, it has come to life by the wish to collect and to copy, so as to preserve, all the Aristotelian commentaries that were available to this erudite circle.[19] It includes: Leo Magentenos' and John Philoponos' commentaries on Porphyry's *Eisagoge*; David's, Magentenos' and Simplikios' commentaries on the *Categories*; Ammonios', Magentenos' and Michael Psellos' commentaries on *On the interpretation*; Magentenos', Philoponos' and an anonymous commentary on the *Prior Analytics*; Philoponos' commentary, an anonymous commentary and Theodore Prodromos' commentary on the *Posterior Analytics*; Alexander of Aphrodisias' commentary on the *Topics*; pseudo-Alexander of Aphrodisias' commentary on the *Sophistici elenchi*; Eustratios', Aspasios' and Michael of

---

16   See Ebbesen/Pinborg, "Gennadios and Western Scholasticism: Radulphus Brito's *Ars Vetus* in Greek Translation".

17   Gennadios II/George Scholarios, *Opera*, eds. Petit/Siderides/Jugie, vol. 7. See now Balcoγαννοπούλου, *Τὸ διδακτικό ἐγχειρίδιο λογικῆς τοῦ Γεωργίου Σχολαρίου*.

18   They have been published respectively in *Alexandri Aphrodisiensis in librum Aristotelis De sensu commentarium*, ed. Wendland, p. XVII; *Stephani in librum Aristotelis De interpretatione commentarium*, ed. Hayduck, p. V; and Usener, "Interpreten des Aristoteles".

19   On Laur. 85.1 see lately Golitsis, "Quelques remarques sur les copistes et le contexte d'apparition du ms. *Laurentianus plut.* 85.1, dit l'« Océan »"; Acerbi/Gioffreda, "Manoscritti scientifici della prima età paleologa in scrittura arcaizzante".

Ephesos' composite commentary on the *Nicomachean Ethics*; Philoponos' commentary on the *De anima*; Philoponos' and Olympiodoros' commentaries on the *Meteorology*; Philoponos' commentary on *On coming-to-be and perishing*; Simplikios' commentary on the *Physics*; Michael of Ephesos' commentaries on the *Parts of Animals* and on the *Progression of animals*; Michael of Ephesos' commentary on the *Parva naturalia* (including the treatise *On the motion of animals*); Alexander's commentary on *Metaphysics* A-Δ and pseudo-Alexander's (that is, Michael of Ephesos') commentary on *Metaphysics* I-N. The fact that Simplikios' commentary on *De caelo*, as well as pseudo-Alexander's commentary on books E, Z, H and Θ of the *Metaphysics*, were not included in this new manuscript, suggests that in the first decades of the Palaeologan era the quest for manuscripts containing ancient commentaries on Aristotle was more difficult and slower than is usually assumed. The 'Oceanus' is just a part, albeit the most notable one, of a greater editorial enterprise that occurred during the first decades of the Palaeologan era. One of its scribes also took part in the copying of the ms. Florence, Biblioteca Medicea Laurenziana, Laur. plut. 85.6, which is a manuscript of Plato.[20]

Similar activities of producing new copies of ancient philosophical texts are attested throughout the entire Palaeologan era. George Pachymeres and his collaborators produced new copies not only of Aristotle (Florence, Biblioteca Medicea Laurenziana, Laur. plut. 87.5; Vatican City, Biblioteca Apostolica Vaticana, Vat. gr. 261), but also of Plato and of his Neoplatonic commentators (Naples, Biblioteca Nazionale, Neap. gr. III. E. 17; Paris, Bibliothèque nationale de France, Par. gr. 1810).[21] Nikephoros Gregoras, who was responsible for the organization of Theodore Metochites' library in the re-founded monastery of Chora, restored older manuscripts and supervised the copying of new ones.[22] In one of them, namely the ms. Rome, Biblioteca Angelica, Angelicus gr. 42 (C. 3. 13), fol. 1v, which contains Aristotle's *Organon*, Gregoras points to the possessor of the manuscript with the words κυροῦ Θεοδώρου ἐντελεχείᾳ σώματος ὀργανικοῦ ("[this book] belongs to Sir Theodore, a body endowed with organs in actuality"), thus referring to Aristotle's definition of soul as "the first actuality of a natural body endowed with organs",[23] and suggesting that the book represented not merely a material but primarily an intellectual possession

---

20   See Menchelli, "Cerchie aristoteliche e letture platoniche", p. 495.

21   See Golitsis, "La production de manuscrits philosophiques autour de Georges Pachymère".

22   See, more recently, Bianconi, "Eracle e Iolao. Aspetti della collaborazione tra copisti nell'età dei paleologi", pp. 536–54.

23   Aristotle, *On the Soul*, II 1, 412b4–6: Εἰ δή τι κοινὸν ἐπὶ πάσης ψυχῆς δεῖ λέγειν, εἴη ἂν ἐντελέχεια ἡ πρώτη σώματος φυσικοῦ ὀργανικοῦ.

of (the soul of) Metochites. The priest Malachias,[24] who was working for Philotheos Kokkinos and the pro-Palamite Emperor John VI Kantakouzenos (1347–1354),[25] accomplished the monumental task of producing several new copies of Aristotelian treatises along with commentaries added around the Aristotelian text in multiple layers. Similar examples can be multiplied.[26] The Palaeologan period attests through its manuscripts an extensive interest in (teaching) ancient philosophy. This cannot be properly explained unless related to actual intellectual needs.

3   The Actuality of Philosophy

The efflorescence of philosophy observed throughout the Palaeologan period is closely related to the importance that good knowledge of ancient philosophy gradually acquired for Byzantine intellectuals. These intellectuals had real philosophical commitments and, contrary to what is sometimes assumed, did not merely display an antiquarian or paideutic interest in ancient philosophy.[27] To be sure, Hellenic *paideia* was always a mark of distinction for

---

24   Previously known as *Anonymus aristotelicus*; see Harlfinger, *Die Textgeschichte der pseudo-aristotelischen Schrift Περὶ ἀτόμων γραμμῶν*, pp. 55–57.

25   See Mondrain, "L'ancien empereur Jean VI Cantacuzène et ses copistes", pp. 278–90, who suggests a connection of Malachias with Gregoras too. Martínez Manzano, "Malaquías Mónaco, alias *Anonymus Aristotelicus*", now suggests with plausibility that Malachias was the monachal name of Matthew Kantakouzenos, joint emperor of Byzantium from 1353 to 1357, and son of John VI.

26   For a selective overview see Kotzabassi, "Kopieren und Exzerpieren in der Palaiologenzeit".

27   The legitimacy of such an approach in Byzantium seems to be implied by an addition to the *Synodicon of Orthodoxy* made in the late 11th century as a consequence of John Italos' (1025–after 1082) condemnation; cf. *The Synodicon of Orthodoxy*, ed. Gouillard, lines 214–18: "Anathema upon those who go through the Hellenic teachings and are taught not simply for the sake of education but follow those doctrines of them which are vain, and believe in those doctrines as true, and insist on their certainty to such an extent that they teach them without fear and lead others to them, sometimes secretly, sometimes openly." (Τοῖς τὰ ἑλληνικὰ διεξιοῦσι μαθήματα καὶ μὴ διὰ παίδευσιν μόνον ταῦτα παιδευομένοις, ἀλλὰ καὶ δόξαις αὐτῶν ταῖς ματαίαις ἑπομένοις καὶ ὡς ἀληθέσι πιστεύουσι, καὶ οὕτως αὐταῖς ὡς τὸ βέβαιον ἐχούσαις ἐγκειμένοις, ὥστε καὶ ἑτέρους ποτὲ μὲν λάθρᾳ, ποτὲ δὲ φανερῶς ἐνάγειν αὐταῖς καὶ διδάσκειν ἀνενδοιάστως, ἀνάθεμα) It is difficult, however, to dissociate education from judgment (this is also suggested by Kokkinos' passage that we quoted earlier, p. 253) and, indeed, the passage does not really make this dissociation: it opposes those who adhere to some Hellenic doctrines (as is made clear in what follows, Plato's doctrine of Ideas is one of them) *with certainty* (αὐταῖς ὡς τὸ βέβαιον ἐχούσαις ἐγκειμένοις), that is, in a religious-like manner. This passage of the *Synodicon* has been quite often misunderstood, e.g. lately by Kaldellis, "Byzantine Philosophy Inside and Out: Orthodoxy and dissidence in counterpoint", p. 141.

cultivated Byzantines; knowledge of Platonic dialogues, for example, could certainly make an impression on the social elites of Byzantium. Nonetheless, Palaeologan churchmen and laymen *vindicated or rejected* Plato or Aristotle, or both philosophers,[28] because their teachings, or at least some of them, were important for their own activities and personal concerns. Barlaam of Calabria (*c.*1290–1348), for instance, wished to support the unintelligibility and indemonstrability of God's essence by appealing not only to the Church Fathers but also to Plato's *Parmenides* and *Republic*.[29] Barlaam's adherence to the Greek philosophers provoked the criticism of Gregory Palamas (1296–1359), to whom Barlaam responded with the following words:

> But 'you praise', you say, 'the Greeks and call them admirable'. But if, my dearest, I praised them for their differences with the Fathers, you would be justified in reproaching me; but since I praise them for those matters in which they think the same as our own <authorities>, excerpting from the Hellenic writings, too, the exceeding holiness of our doctrines, how have you not been unjust to me, when you accuse me for the opposite? For, surely, it is not even possible to say how many times our Fathers, when they discourse on the incomprehensible and, above all, when they turn their writings against Eunomius, proclaim that the doctrines of the Christians cannot be demonstrated.[30]

Aristotle was equally, if not more, relevant to actual religious concerns. To what extent, for instance, should one trust Aristotelian syllogistic was a question that occupied a great deal of the Palamite or Hesychast controversy and

---

28 I refer to Plato and Aristotle because these two philosophers retained almost exclusively the interest of Palaeologian scholars. Note, however, that Nikephoros Choumnos (*c.*1250/55–1327) wrote a treatise against Plotinus (Ἀντιθετικὸς πρὸς Πλωτῖνον, *Patrologia Graeca*, vol. 140, cols. 1404–1438) and that Nicholas Kabasilas Chamaetos (*c.*1319/23–after 1391) composed a short refutation of sceptical arguments, edited by Demetracopoulos (Nicholas Kabasilas, *Against Pyrrho*). That there was no Sceptical movement in early 14th-century Byzantium, as it was once believed, has been convincingly shown by Bydén, "'To every argument there is a counter-argument'".

29 See Fyrigos, "Barlaam Calabro tra umanesimo italiano e antiumanesimo bizantino", pp. 36–37.

30 Barlaam of Calabria, *Greek Letters*, no. 3, ed. Schirò, lines 677–85: Ἀλλ' ἐπαινεῖς, φής (scripsi: φησί Schirò), τοὺς Ἕλληνας καὶ θαυμασίους ἀποκαλεῖς. ἀλλ' εἰ μέν, ὦ βέλτιστε, ἐν οἷς τοῖς πατράσι διαφέρονται τούτους ἐπήνουν εἰκότως ἄν μοι ἐμέμφου· εἰ δ' ἐν τούτοις αὐτοὺς ἐπαινῶ ἐν οἷς ταὐτὰ τοῖς ἡμετέροις φρονοῦντας ὁρῶ, ἐρανιζόμενος καὶ ἐκ τῶν ἐκείνων τὸ ὑπέρσεμνον τῶν καθ' ἡμᾶς δογμάτων, πῶς οὐκ ἀδικεῖς, εἰ ταῦτά μοι ἐγκαλεῖς; καὶ μὴν οὐκ ἔστιν εἰπεῖν ὁσάκις αὐτὸ τοῦτο οἱ πατέρες ἡμῶν διαμαρτύρονται, ὡς οὐκ ἀποδεικτά ἐστι τὰ χριστιανῶν δόγματα, ἐν οἷς τε περὶ ἀκαταλήπτου διαλέγονται καὶ πρὸς Εὐνόμιον μάλιστα ἀποτείνονται.

THE REAPPROPRIATION OF PHILOSOPHY IN THE PALAEOLOGAN ERA 261

its extensions, an event of major importance in late Byzantine history.[31] Should the Byzantines determine the content of Christian faith and settle questions of theophany with the help of Aristotle's syllogistic, as the Latins did? Such was Prochoros Kydones' (1333–1370/71) contention, who famously wrote:

> I believe that every truth (i.e. even a religious one) is either a beginning of a syllogism or a syllogism.[32]

Should the Byzantines enter into discussions with the Latins about Trinitarian issues, which separated the Eastern from the Western Church, and let logic and ancient dialectics decide the outcome of the controversy? A negative response to this question was given by Neilos Kabasilas (died 1363), who wrote a treatise entitled *That is not possible for the Latins, by using syllogisms, to prove that the Holy Spirit proceeds from the Son*.[33] If, however, the Byzantines entered into such discussions, would they fall short of true Christian faith, as this had been defined by the Church Fathers? Prochoros Kydones was condemned by the ecclesiastical Synod of 1368, because he substituted the Holy Scriptures with rational thinking based on Aristotelian syllogistic:

> And going on with his writing, he (*sc.* Kydones) puts in between the following chapter titles: 'That the intellective energy of God is the essence of God'; 'That the intellective power of God is the essence of God'; 'That the wisdom of God is the essence of God'; 'That the truth of God is the essence of God'; 'That the will of God is the essence of God'.[34] And *he proves all these theses not from the divine scriptures, nor by putting forward the sayings of the Saints, but through his own reasonings and using forsooth as proofs the Aristotelian syllogisms.* And when he speaks about God – or, to say it better, when he battles against God – speaking about

---

31 For a discussion of Palamas', Barlaam's and Gregoras' attitude to Aristotle's logic see Ierodiakonou, "The anti-logical movement in the fourteenth century".

32 Tinnefeld, "Ein Text des Prochoros Kydones in Vat. gr. 609", lines 3–4: Οἶμαι γὰρ ὅτι πᾶσα ἀλήθεια ἢ ἀρχὴ συλλογισμοῦ ἐστιν ἢ συλλογισμός. This thesis distinguishes Prochoros from earlier anti-Palamites, such as Gregoras, Gregory Akindynos (c.1300–1348) and Barlaam, who opposed the ignorance of the Latins who used "apodictic syllogisms" to clarify theological matters.

33 'Ὅτι οὐκ ἔστι Λατίνοις, συλλογισμοῖς χρωμένοις, ἀποδεῖξαι τὸ Πνεῦμα τὸ Ἅγιον ἐκ τοῦ Υἱοῦ ἐκπορευόμενον". A part of this treatise has been edited by Candal, *Nilus Cabasilas et theologia S. Thomae de processione Spiritus Sancti*, pp. 188–385.

34 Kydones' chapter titles derive from Thomas Aquinas' *Summa contra Gentiles*, I, 73, as has been pointed out by Triantafyllopoulos, "The Thomist basis of Prochoros Kydones' anti-Palamite treatise 'De essentia et operatione Dei'", p. 424.

the most divine light that shone from Christ on the Mount, he puts the following title: 'That the Tabor light is created'; [...] and he proves this through many syllogisms of Aristotle, and he says and syllogizes many blasphematory and impious things.[35]

The controversy between the pro-Palamites and anti-Palamites in its two phases,[36] along with its ramifications for the political question of the union of the Churches, which constantly occupied Byzantine society before and after the Council of Lyons of 1274, is the most prominent example of interference between religious (and political) reality and the teachings of ancient philosophy in Byzantine history. In his so-called *Triads*,[37] Palamas basically attempted to point out the importance of philosophy in explaining and defending to the non-mystic how the mystic can indeed have a direct experience of God. Barlaam, on the contrary, believed that philosophy itself exhausts the indirect experience that man can have of God in this life, in the sense of understanding His attributes through His works and thanks to the divine grace. The final victory of Palamism, however, established that any person who approached theological truths, as revealed to the Prophets, the Holy Apostles and the Evangelists, and as subsequently explained by the Holy Fathers, through the lenses of Hellenic philosophy was a false Christian and, tacitly, a Latinophile: "*O philosopher, you who badly worship the syllogisms and not the Gospel*", says Kokkinos again of Gregoras.[38] The experience of the Saint superseded the

---

35 *Tome of 1368 (against the monk Prochoros Kydones)*, ed. Rigo, lines 236–54: Μεταξὺ δὲ προϊὼν ἐπιγραφὰς τίθησι τοῖς κεφαλαίοις τοιαύτας· "Ὅτι ἡ νοερὰ τοῦ Θεοῦ ἐνέργειά ἐστιν ἡ οὐσία αὐτοῦ. "Ὅτι ἡ νοερὰ τοῦ Θεοῦ δύναμίς ἐστιν ἡ οὐσία αὐτοῦ. "Ὅτι ἡ σοφία τοῦ Θεοῦ ἐστιν ἡ οὐσία αὐτοῦ. "Ὅτι ἡ ἀλήθεια τοῦ Θεοῦ ἐστιν ἡ οὐσία αὐτοῦ. "Ὅτι ἡ τοῦ Θεοῦ θέλησίς ἐστιν ἡ οὐσία αὐτοῦ. Καὶ ταῦτα ἀποδείκνυσιν οὐκ ἀπὸ τῶν θείων γραφῶν, οὐ ῥητὰ προφέρων ἁγίων, ἀλλὰ τοῖς ἰδίοις λογισμοῖς καὶ ταῖς ἀποδείξεσι χρώμενος δῆθεν τοῖς ἀριστοτελικοῖς συλλογισμοῖς. Περὶ δὲ τοῦ λάμψαντος ἀπὸ τοῦ Χριστοῦ ἐν τῷ ὄρει θειοτάτου φωτὸς θεολογῶν, μᾶλλον δὲ θεομαχῶν, ἐπιγραφὴν μὲν τίθησιν· "Ὅτι τὸ ἐν Θαβορίῳ φῶς κτιστόν· [...] καὶ τοῦτο διὰ πολλῶν ἀποδείκνυσι τῶν τοῦ Ἀριστοτέλους συλλογισμῶν, καὶ πολλὰ ἕτερα βλάσφημα καὶ δυσσεβῆ λέγει καὶ συλλογίζεται.

36 The two phases of the Hesychast controversy are distinguished through the sanction of Palamite theology by the Synod of 1351. The second phase of the controversy is characterized by the use of works by Thomas Aquinas, which started circulating in Byzantium from 1354 onwards in translations made by the brothers Demetrios and Prochoros Kydones. On the reception of Thomas in Byzantium see Papadopoulos, Ἑλληνικαὶ μεταφράσεις θωμιστικῶν ἔργων and, more recently, Fyrigos, "Tomismo e anti-Tomismo a Bisanzio" and Dendrinos/Demetracopoulos, *Thomas Latinus – Thomas Graecus*.

37 Gregory Palamas, *Defence of the Holy Hesychasts*, ed. Meyendorff.

38 Philotheos Kokkinos, *Sixth Antirrhetic against Gregoras*, ed. Kaimakis, lines 308–309: ὦ φιλόσοφε, ὁ τοὺς συλλογισμοὺς ἀντὶ τοῦ Εὐαγγελίου κακῶς προσκυνῶν.

THE REAPPROPRIATION OF PHILOSOPHY IN THE PALAEOLOGAN ERA 263

arguments of the theologian: it was not the scholastic but the truly pious (εὐσεβής) monk who could experience in this world, through his prayer and his self-transformation, a union with God's uncreated energy, that is, the manifestation of His essence. This was the outcome of a larger dispute on the relation between Christianity and philosophy, which had started several decades earlier.

4   The Rehabilitation(s) of Plato and Aristotle

When Michael VIII Palaiologos regained control of Constantinople from the Latins in 1261, Byzantine scholars and men of letters coming from Nicaea became gradually more and more acquainted with the western religious orders, especially the Dominicans, which had been established in the city.[39] Towards the end of the 13th century, the Dominicans had already translated into Greek some works of their *frater* Thomas Aquinas (1225–1274) and showed to Byzantine Greeks their own good knowledge of Greek philosophy, especially of Aristotle; the 'wise and prudent' Sophonias, as he is called by Pachymeres,[40] was probably one of them. The Latins even possessed Aristotelian works of Aristotle that were considered lost for the Byzantines,[41] and they had integrated Aristotle's philosophy into their theological method for the benefit of their faith.[42] Byzantinists traditionally associate the Palaeologan efflorescence of letters with the intellectual fermentations that occurred earlier in the Empire of Nicaea.[43] The case of philosophy, however, suggests that it was rather the striking encounter with an Aristotle actualized by the Latins that provoked a massive interest in the work of the Stagirite during the first decades of the Palaeologan dynasty. As we shall presently see, if there is a connection to be made with earlier Byzantine thinking, this is not so much with the Empire of Nicaea but with earlier centuries.

---

39   On the prosperity of the Dominicans in Constantinople, see Congourdeau, "Notes sur les Dominicains de Constantinople au début du 14e siècle", et Violante, *La provincia domenicana in Grecia.*

40   George Pachymeres, *History*, ed. Failler, vol. 3, p. 227, line 23: τὸν ἱερομόναχον Σοφονίαν, ἄνδρα σοφόν τε καὶ συνετόν.

41   Consider Manuel Holobolos' (*c.*1245–1310/14) enthusiasm, when 'a certain Italian, a man of considerable education and learning' brought him a copy of the Latin version of (pseudo-) Aristotle's *De plantis*; the incident is discussed by Fischer, "Manuel Holobolos and the role of bilinguals in relations between the West and Byzantium".

42   See Bydén, "'Strangle Them with These Meshes of Syllogisms'".

43   See the classic study by Hunger, "Von Wissenschaft und Kunst der frühen Palaiologenzeit".

264 GOLITSIS

The most important philosopher of the Empire of Nicaea was undoubtedly Nikephoros Blemmydes (1197–1269), a man who, as Gregory II/George of Cyprus (1241–1289) reports with some exaggeration, was considered by his contemporaries as "the wisest not merely among us Greeks but among all men".[44] His most influential work was his *Epitome Eisagogica*, a compendium of logic and physics that Blemmydes originally conceived for the teaching that he dispensed in the monastery he founded near Ephesos, dedicated to "God-Who-Is" (Θεοῦ τοῦ ὄντος). The *Epitome* is mainly a derivative work and is tacitly based on those late antique commentaries on Aristotle's logical and physical treatises that were available to the wise monk.[45] Blemmydes does not reveal any interest in making accessible the text of the Aristotelian treatises themselves and, quite tellingly, he does not even mention the name of Aristotle or the names of his commentators. It is plain that his aim was not to promote the study of Aristotle but to gather from Aristotle and his commentators whatever he thought was useful for his monastic students to know: "*those topics that are not remote from usefulness*", he later recalls in his *Autobiography*.[46] Selectivity with regard to ancient philosophy was a profoundly traditional attitude on the part of a Christian thinker: it lies in the heart of St. John of Damascus' *Philosophical chapters*, and, by extension, of his authoritative *Fount of knowledge*.[47]

---

44 Gregory of Cyprus, *Autobiography*, ed. Lameere, p. 181, lines 12–14: ἀνὴρ ὡς ἐλέγετο οὐ μόνον Ἑλλήνων τῶν ἐφ' ἡμῶν ἀλλὰ καὶ πάντων ἀνθρώπων σοφώτατος. In his *Praise of Nicaea*, the Emperor Theodore II Doukas Laskaris (1254–1258) says that "the inhabitants of Nicaea philosophize according to the science of Aristotle, Plato and Socrates" (Theodore II Doukas Laskaris, *Praise of Nicaea*, ed. Tartaglia, p. 72, lines 114–116: φιλοσοφοῦσι μὲν καὶ ταῖς Ἀριστοτελικαῖς καὶ Πλατωνικαῖς καὶ Σωκράτους ἐπιστήμαις οἱ ταύτης οἰκήτορες); but this is clearly a rhetorical exaggeration necessary to a *laus orbis*.

45 On Blemmydes' sources see Lackner, "Zum Lehrbuch der Physik des Nikephoros Blemmydes" and Golitsis, "Nicéphore Blemmyde lecteur du Commentaire de Simplicius à la *Physique* d'Aristote".

46 Nikephoros Blemmydes, *Autobiography*, ed. Munitiz, II, p. 75, line 8: ὅσα μὴ πόρρω τοῦ χρησίμου.

47 Cf. John of Damascus, *The Fount of Knowledge*, ed. Kotter, proem, lines 43–48: "First of all I shall set forth the best contributions of the wise men of the Greeks, because I know that whatever there is of good has been given to men from above by God, since 'every best giving and every perfect gift is from above, coming down from the Father of lights' (James 1:17). If, however, there is anything that is contrary to the truth, then it is 'a dark invention of the deceit of Satan and a fiction of the mind of an evil spirit', as the eminent theologian Gregory once said (*Sermon* 39, 3)." Transl. Chase, slightly modified. (Καὶ πρότερον μὲν τῶν παρ' Ἕλλησι σοφῶν τὰ κάλλιστα παραθήσομαι εἰδώς, ὡς, εἴ τι μὲν ἀγαθόν, ἄνωθεν παρὰ θεοῦ τοῖς ἀνθρώποις δεδώρηται, ἐπειδὴ «πᾶσα δόσις ἀγαθὴ καὶ πᾶν δώρημα τέλειον ἄνωθέν ἐστι καταβαῖνον παρὰ τοῦ πατρὸς τῶν φώτων». Εἴ τι δὲ τῆς ἀληθείας ἀντίπαλον, τῆς σατανικῆς πλάνης «εὕρημα σκοτεινὸν καὶ διανοίας ἀνάπλασμα κακοδαίμονος», ὡς ὁ πολὺς ἐν θεολογίᾳ Γρηγόριος.) An echo of John of Damascus' approach can also be detected in Barlaam's

THE REAPPROPRIATION OF PHILOSOPHY IN THE PALAEOLOGAN ERA   265

One of Blemmydes' monastic students, namely George Akropolites (1217–1282), to whom Michael VIII later entrusted the restoration of the imperial school of higher studies in the regained Constantinople,[48] reveals in the most eloquent way the limitations of the traditional approach to philosophy:

> I spoke about these <two passages of Gregory of Nazianzos> to Blemmydes – this marvellous man who was most learned in philosophy – when I was still young and studied with him. But he had nothing clear to say to me; he repeated, all in all, what the other exegetes (I mean the great author Maximos [sc. the Confessor] and those who followed him) had said on the Father, explaining <his text> either in a general context or in the form of a commentary. But when I grasped by myself the mysteries of philosophy and *joined the most divine Plato, the Muse-inspired Proklos and other most inspired men, such as Iamblichos, Plotinos and others* whom it is not the right time to enumerate, I was guided to the comprehension of that passage.[49]

Not only does Akropolites attest to Blemmydes' limited acquaintance with Plato and the Platonic tradition[50] but, most significantly, he promotes a different approach to ancient philosophy, an approach which is subversive of

---

    response to Palamas; cf. Barlaam of Calabria, *Greek Letters*, no. 3, ed. Schirò, lines 696–97: "<Of what do you accuse me?> Of claiming that, if the Greeks said something which is in accordance with our doctrines, it has been made manifest to them by God?" (ὅτι εἴ τι καὶ Ἕλληνες εἶπον τοιοῦτον οἷον τοῖς ἡμετέροις συμφωνεῖν, παρὰ θεοῦ ἰσχυρίζομαι πεφανερῶσθαι αὐτοῖς;)

48   On Akropolites' teaching see Golitsis, "Georges Pachymère comme didascale", pp. 61–62.

49   George Akropolites, *Opera: On some sentences by Gregory of Nazianzos*, ed. Heisenberg, vol. 2, p. 71, lines 1–13: Περὶ τούτων καὶ γὰρ ἐν μείραξιν ἔτι τελῶν καὶ τῷ θεσπεσίῳ ἐκείνῳ ἀνδρὶ τῷ φιλοσοφοτάτῳ Βλεμμύδῃ, ἡνίκα παρ' αὐτῷ ἐφοίτων, ἐκοινολογησάμην, ἀλλ' οὐδέν τί μοι εἶχεν εἰρηκέναι σαφῶς, ἀλλ' ἅπερ καὶ ἄλλοι τὰ τοῦ πατρὸς ἐξηγούμενοι (λέγω δὲ τὸν μέγαν ἐν τοῖς λόγοις Μάξιμον καὶ τοὺς μετ' αὐτὸν) εἰς πλάτος ἢ καὶ κατὰ σχολὴν διασαφοῦντες εἰρήκεσαν, ἐκεῖνά μοι καὶ αὐτὸς πρὸς τὴν ἀπορίαν ἐφθέγγετο. ἀλλ' ἐπείπερ αὐτὸς τῶν τῆς φιλοσοφίας ἡψάμην ὀργίων τῷ τε θειοτάτῳ συνῆλθον Πλάτωνι καὶ τῷ μουσολήπτῳ Πρόκλῳ, ἔτι τε μὴν τοῖς ἐνθεαστικωτάτοις ἀνδράσιν Ἰαμβλίχῳ τε καὶ Πλωτίνῳ καὶ τοῖς λοιποῖς, οὓς οὐ καιρὸς καταλέγειν, ἐποδηγήθην πρὸς τὴν διάγνωσιν τοῦ ῥητοῦ.

50   Note, however, that in his *Epitome of logic* Blemmydes calls Plato, without naming him, 'some great philosopher'; *Patrologia Graeca*, vol. 142, col. 689B: καθώς που καί τις μέγας φιλόσοφος ἐγνωμάτευσεν ἄριστα, τότε τοὺς ὑπηκόους εὖ ἔχειν ἀποφηνάμενος, ὅτε βασιλεύει φιλόσοφος ἢ φιλοσοφεῖ βασιλεύς (cf. *Republic*, x, 689a–b); see Angelov, "Classifications of political philosophy and the concept of royal science in Byzantium". Blemmydes' knowledge of Plato seems to have been derivative.

his teacher's.[51] The Church Fathers do not merely legitimize the selective reading of Greek philosophers, according to the compatibility of the latter to the former, but, quite on the contrary, Greek philosophers are now deemed necessary to any person who wishes to properly understand the sayings of the Church Fathers; even "the great Maximos" the Confessor, who was in all probability an unrivalled authority for both Blemmydes and John of Damascus, seemed to Akropolites an insufficient exegete of Gregory of Nazianzos.

In rehabilitating the study of Plato and the Neoplatonists as useful for the *understanding* of (and not the *faith* to) Christian doctrine, Akropolites revived an earlier approach of similar scope, promoted by Michael Psellos (1018–after 1076).[52] Psellos, before explaining John of Damascus' sentence "substance is a self-existing thing" (οὐσία πρᾶγμα αὐθύπαρκτον),[53] points out for his students the usefulness of Hellenic doctrines:

> If, in the following expositions, I make also use of some Hellenic <divine> names as well as of some of the doctrines of the best philosophers, you should not blame me for that. For not every Hellenic doctrine has been disproved of by us <Christians>; on the contrary, some of them can help us towards our own belief.[54]

And concluding his commentary, Psellos invites his students to make use of the Hellenic doctrines, if they judge that these could help them to intellectually approach the Christian truth, named here ὁ ἀληθὴς λόγος:

---

51 For a brief assessment of Blemmydes' and Akropolites' approach to philosophy, see Golitsis, "A Byzantine philosopher's devoutness to God", pp. 121–23.

52 Blemmydes restricted the usefulness of ancient philosophy to ancient logic (and physics); cf. Nikephoros Blemmydes, *Epitome of logic*, col. 688C: "Since the science of logic is not of insignificant usefulness to <the comprehension of> the Holy Scripture and of all the Words of Truth, we judged it necessary to leave for the students of the Word of <God> Who Is and for those initiated to the Truth some small comments that we have made on this science of logic" ('Επειδήπερ ἡ λογικὴ ἐπιστήμη πρὸς τὴν ἱερὰν Γραφὴν καὶ πάντας τοὺς τῆς ἀληθείας λόγους οὐκ ὀλίγον φέρει τὸ χρήσιμον, δέον ἐκρίναμεν τοῖς τοῦ λόγου φοιτηταῖς τοῦ ὄντος καὶ τῆς ἀληθείας μύσταις μικρούς τινας ἐν ταύτῃ τῇ λογικῇ λιπεῖν ἡμετέρους ὑπομνηματισμούς.)

53 Cf. John of Damascus, *Philosophical chapters*, ed. Kotter, § 40, line 2.

54 Michael Psellos, *Comment on the sentence "Substance is a self-existing thing"*, ed. Duffy, opusculum 7, lines 51–54: Εἰ δέ τισι καὶ τῶν Ἑλληνικῶν ὀνομάτων καὶ τῶν παρὰ τοῖς φιλοσοφωτέροις δόξῶν ἐπὶ τοὺς ἡμετέρους λόγους συγκαταχρησόμεθα, κακίζειν οὐ χρή· οὐ γὰρ πᾶσα Ἑλληνὶς δόξα διαβέβληται πρὸς ἡμῶν, τινὲς δὲ καὶ συνεργοὶ τοῦ ἡμετέρου τυγχάνουσι δόγματος.

THE REAPPROPRIATION OF PHILOSOPHY IN THE PALAEOLOGAN ERA   267

I have classified all these <teachings> for you, because I wanted to guide you into erudition and to acquaint you with the Hellenic doctrines. And I know that at least some of them are contrary to our beliefs. I, of course, have not been zealous to teach you all these because I want you to replace your Christian beliefs with the Hellenic doctrines – I would be mad if I were to do that – but because I want you to stay committed to the former and simply have knowledge of the latter. If, however, the Hellenic doctrines can somehow help your attempts towards <understanding> the true logos, then use them.[55]

Apart from his direct disciple John Italos, it seems that George Akropolites too followed Psellos' path some two centuries later. The Psellan reading of ancient philosophy, with its extensions into the early 12th century,[56] might be the channel through which the revival of the study of Plato and the Neoplatonists in Palaeologan Constantinople passed.

A similar rehabilitation of Aristotle might be detected in the work of Pachymeres, who was possibly a disciple of Akropolites. In his commentary on Aristotle's *Physics*, Pachymeres assimilates Aristotle's first unmoved mover to Apostle Paul's 'blessed and only sovereign':

From this point on, <Aristotle> philosophizes about how it can be that something unmoved and exempt from all change, both absolutely and accidentally, which moves something else, really exists; that is the divine, which is primarily and by itself, unlike and unmixed with regard to all moving things. And this is 'the blessed and only Sovereign';[57] it has in fact an absolute power over all things, because it surpasses all things in so far as it is not subject to any kind of movement.[58]

---

55   Ibid., lines 117–23: Ταῦτα δὲ πάντα διηριθμησάμην ὁμοῦ μὲν ὑμᾶς εἰς πολυμάθειαν ἄγων, ὁμοῦ δὲ καὶ ταῖς Ἑλληνικαῖς δόξαις ποιούμενος ἐντριβεῖς. καὶ οἶδα ὡς ἐνίαις γε τούτων ἀντιπεσεῖται τὰ ἡμέτερα δόγματα. ἐγὼ γὰρ οὐχ ὥστε τούτων ἐκεῖνα ἀνταλλάξασθαι διεσπούδασα πρὸς ὑμᾶς – μαινοίμην γὰρ ἄν –, ἀλλ' ἵνα τούτοις μὲν ἦτε προσκείμενοι, ἐκείνων δὲ μόνον τὴν εἴδησιν ἔχητε. εἰ δέ πῃ καὶ συνεργοῖεν ὑμῖν πρὸς τὸν ἀληθῆ λόγον διακινδυνεύοντα, καὶ χρήσασθε.

56   See the commentaries on Aristotle, of rather Neoplatonic allure, by Eustratios Metropolitan of Nicaea and Michael of Ephesos, who were related as disciples to Italos and to Psellos. On Eustratios' Neoplatonic sources, see Trizio, "Neoplatonic source-material in Eustratios of Nicaea's commentary on book VI of the *Nicomachean Ethics*".

57   Cf. 1 Tim. 6:13–16.

58   Cod. Florence, Biblioteca Medicea Laurenziana, Laur. 87.5, fol. 137v, lines 1–4: Ἐντεῦθεν φιλοσοφεῖ πῶς ἔσται τι ἀκίνητον καὶ ἐκτὸς ἁπάσης μεταβολῆς καὶ ἁπλῶς καὶ κατὰ συμβεβηκός, κινητικὸν δὲ ἑτέρου, ὅπερ ἐστὶ τὸ θεῖον καὶ μόνως καὶ πρώτως καὶ ἀσυγκρίτως καὶ ἀμιγῶς ἐκ

Pachymeres' philosophical work is related to concerns of his own day. It introduces the topic that was to become dominant in later discussions, namely the limits of philosophy and the relation between reason and faith. Opposing the monastic ideals of the Patriarch of Constantinople Athanasios I (1303–1309),[59] who was earlier a monk on Mount Athos and was later declared a saint, Pachymeres wrote a synopsis of Aristotle's philosophy, divided in twelve books, which he entitled *Philosophia*. In the general prooemium of the work, Pachymeres denounces 'the despisers of philosophy' (οἱ τῆς φιλοσοφίας καταφρονηταί), that is, the monks, whose inhumanity has made them 'hate the first of the goods <for man>, that is, the senses',[60] a phrase that is reminiscent of Aristotle's opening of the *Metaphysics*.[61] In the prooemium of the first book of the *Philosophia*, the humanist value of philosophy is linked to its divine provenance with the (tacit) help of Plato's *Timaeus*:

> Philosophy has been sent through a divine fate, as a divine gift of a sort that has never arrived nor will arrive again from God to man; it is a sort of blessed activity of the mind and a pursuit superior to all corporal pursuits.[62]

For Pachymeres, philosophy (that is, ancient philosophy) was capable not only of generating knowledge about the human soul and the natural world that surrounds the senses, but also of instilling the right convictions about the knowledge that man can have of God. In the poetic epilogue that closes his running commentary on the *Physics*, Pachymeres praises Aristotle for his intellectual findings and transforms him into a forerunner of Christian truth. More specifically, Aristotle is praised for "having found" a providential pole, i.e. God, who

---

πάντων τῶν κινουμένων. καὶ τοῦτό ἐστι τὸ "ὁ μακάριος καὶ μόνος δυνάστης"· δύναται γὰρ κατὰ πάντων ὡς ὑπερφέρον πάντων κατὰ τὸ μὴ ὑποκεῖσθαι κινήσει ἡτινιοῦν.

59 See Golitsis, "La date de composition de la *Philosophia* de Georges Pachymère".

60 Cf. cod. Paris, Bibliothèque nationale de France, Par. gr. 1930, fol. 4v, lines 26–28: … ἐκείνοις (*sc.* τοῖς τῆς φιλοσοφίας καταφρονηταῖς) δ' ἀπεναντίας τούτων ἐξ ἀναλγησίας ἡ πρόθεσις, ὡς μισῆσαι καὶ αὐτὴν μίαν τῶν ἀγαθῶν οὖσαν καὶ πρωτίστην, τὴν αἴσθησιν. I am preparing an edition of the *prooimion* of the work and of the first book, which abridges the *Organon*, for the series *Commentaria in Aristotelem Byzantina* of the Academy of Athens.

61 Cf. Aristotle, *Metaphysics*, A 1, 980a21–22: Πάντες ἄνθρωποι τοῦ εἰδέναι ὀρέγονται φύσει· σημεῖον δ' ἡ τῶν αἰσθήσεων ἀγάπησις.

62 Ἡ φιλοσοφία, ὥσπερ τι θεῖον δῶρον καὶ οἷον οὔθ' ἧκεν οὔθ' ἥξει παρὰ θεοῦ τοῖς ἀνθρώποις, ἔν τινι θείᾳ κατεπέμφθη μοίρᾳ νοός τις μακαρία ἐνέργεια οὖσα καὶ ἀσχολία πασῶν σωματικῶν ἀσχολιῶν ὑπερτέρα; inspired by Plato's *Timaeus*, 47b1–2: ἐπορισάμεθα φιλοσοφίας γένος, οὗ μεῖζον ἀγαθὸν οὔτ' ἦλθεν οὔτε ἥξει ποτὲ τῷ θνητῷ γένει δωρηθὲν ἐκ θεῶν.

THE REAPPROPRIATION OF PHILOSOPHY IN THE PALAEOLOGAN ERA 269

is nameless, eternal, powerful, partless and unmoved,[63] and "having stopped" there. To put it differently, Pachymeres praises Aristotle for having determined God's properties and not having committed himself to a vain pursuit of knowledge of God's essence. The attitude of the wise Aristotle towards divinity, says Pachymeres, should be an example to all men.[64] One can hardly dissociate Pachymeres' poem from a concern against contemporary claims of union with God, which predated the official Hesychast doctrine.[65] Pachymeres seems to have inaugurated the opposition of Christian intellectuals to ascetic fundamentalism, which was starting to preoccupy the Constantinopolitan society at the end of the 13th century and was to be later subsumed into the Hesychast controversy. Theodore Metochites also set out to show in essays 73–76 of his *Semeioseis Gnomikai* that a true Christian life is possible outside monasticism.

Palaeologan philosophy exhibited a remarkable continuity in its development mainly through its reflections on the sort of experience that man can have of God in this world. In their simplified form, contradictory reflections on this topic took the outlook of a conflict between Eastern mysticism and Western rationality and became a matter of faith. In its essence, however, the conflict was an exchange of arguments, at times vehement, about the legitimacy of mystical experience of God, mostly promoted by sophisticated monks, *vs* the predominance of rational knowledge in determining matters of theophany, mostly promoted by erudite clerics and laymen. The conflict quickly involved a questioning about the use of ancient philosophy in Christian theology, denied by the Orthodox tradionalists, and the avowed subordination of the former to the latter. In its extreme form, the subordination of philosophy to theology turned into militant Thomism, which we can exemplify in the following letter, addressed by the brother of Prochoros Kydones, Demetrios (*c.*1324–*c.*1397) to George the Philosopher:

---

63   George Pachymeres, *Poetic epilogue to the commentary on Aristotle's Physics*, ed. Golitsis, lines 13–15: εὗρες καὶ πόλον, οὔτι γ' ἔρημον ἐόντα προνοίης / εὗρες νώνυμον ἀίδιον κράτος ἀμερὲς αἰὲν / ὡσαύτως ἔχον, ἠδ' ἀκίνητον ὑπ' οὐδενὸς ἄλκαρ. Pachymeres' reasoning might be compared to Thomas' first of the "five ways" (*quinque viae*) that prove the existence of God, that is, the argument from motion (*Summa theologiae* I, q. 2, a. 3).

64   Cf. ibid., lines 19–21: "Vain is he who wishes to seek further / since you, who are wise, who know the measures of human wisdom / and have reached what on account of no many fortifications is unconquerable, have stopped." (κενὸς ὅς γεμαστεύσοι / ἠύτε σύ δε σοφὸς σοφίης μέτρα οἶσθα βροτείης / καὶ οἱ προσκύρσας ὅσ' ἐρύματ' ἀδηρίτῳ, ἔστης.)

65   The *Vita* of Athanasios, who was Pachymeres' main opponent, was written by a Palamite, John Kalothetos. Note also that Nikephoros the Hesychast, whom later Hesychasts recognized as their forefather, was Pachymeres' contemporary. On Nikephoros and early Hesychasm see Rigo, "Niceforo l'esicasta (XIII sec.)".

Do not mock me, if I rejoice at the man (sc. Thomas) and put his views before the views of our (sc. Orthodox) <teachers>. First of all, you should think here of Plato, who said that we should take little care of Socrates and great care of the truth. Secondly, in virtue of what you have written, you should consider that this is also your opinion. For a person who thinks that the contemporary among our <Orthodox teachers> are of no value whatsoever, and who does not even deem them worthy to be compared with those in Italy, in what way does he not share with me the same view on Thomas? So, you too will be rightly judged badly by those who, as you say, calumniate me, those of course who according to you are unworthy, and who are vexed by the goods that belong to their neighbours; whose boorishness if I refuted, I would be highly esteemed both by you and by Plato, pushing those people to philosophize with the bites of my refutations. This is the service that Socrates says he himself contributed to the Athenians, a service of which he predicted that no one else would be able to contribute any more, if he died. And if you claim that I deprive Plato and his disciple (sc. Aristotle), who are Hellenes, of the chief rank and that I transmit my hybris to the "common of the Hellenes", I have no memory of me wanting to compare those men to Thomas. As I have already said to many and as I will frankly repeat now: if Plato and all the Peripatetic philosophers were present and Thomas ought to argue against them about the hope that exists in us (sc. Christian salvation), these men would have been defeated in their arguments, so that Plato and the rest would have chosen the Church instead of the Academy.[66]

---

66   Demetrios Kydones, *Letters*, no. 33, ed. Loenertz, lines 58–76: Μὴ σκῶπτε τοίνυν εἰ χαίρω τἀνδρί, καὶ πρὸ τῶν ἡμετέρων ἄγω τἀκείνου. πρῶτον μὲν γὰρ κἀνταῦθα τοῦ Πλάτωνος μέμνησο, Σωκράτους ἐπ' ὀλίγον μὲν φροντιστέον εἰπόντος, τῆς δ' ἀληθείας ἐπὶ πολύ (cf. *Crito*, 48a5–7). ἔπειτ' ἐν οἷς ἔγραφες καὶ σαυτοῦ νόμιζε ταύτην εἶναι τὴν ψῆφον. ὁ γὰρ τῶν ἡμετέρων τοὺς νῦν μηδ' εἶναι τὸ παράπαν οἰόμενος, μηδὲ παραβάλλειν αὐτοὺς ἀξιῶν τοῖς ἐν Ἰταλίᾳ, πῶς οὐ τῆς περὶ τὸν Θωμᾶν δόξης μοι κοινωνεῖ; ὥστε καὶ σὺ δικαίως κακῶς ἀκούσῃ ὑφ' ὧν κἀμὲ φῇς διασύρεσθαι, τούτων δὴ τῶν κατὰ σὲ μηκέτ' ὄντων καὶ τῶν τοῖς ἀγαθοῖς τῶν πέλας ἀνιωμένων· ὧν εἰ τὴν ἀγροικίαν ἐλέγχοιμι καὶ παρὰ σοὶ δικαίως ἂν εὐδοκιμοίην καὶ Πλάτωνι, τοῖς τῶν ἐλέγχων δήγμασιν ἐπὶ φιλοσοφίαν κινῶν. ταύτην γὰρ ἑαυτόν φησι Σωκράτης Ἀθηναίοις εἰσφέρειν τὴν λειτουργίαν, ἣν οὐδένα ἄλλον ἐκεῖνος εἰσοίσειν αὐτοῦ τελευτήσαντος προὔλεγεν. εἰ δέ με Πλάτωνα καὶ τὸν ἐκείνου μαθητὴν φῇς τῶν πρωτείων ἀποστερεῖν Ἕλληνας ὄντας, καὶ δι' ἐκείνων ἐπὶ τὸ κοινὸν τῶν Ἑλλήνων τὴν ὕβριν [διὰ] διαβιβάζειν, ἐγὼ μὲν οὐδεπώποτε μέμνημαι Θωμᾷ βουληθεὶς παραθεῖναι τοὺς ἄνδρας· ὅπερ δὲ πολλοῖς εἶπον καὶ νῦν ἐρῶ μετὰ παρρησίας, ὡς εἰ Πλάτων καὶ οἱ ἐκ τοῦ Περιπάτου πάντες παρῆσαν, καὶ ἔδει Θωμᾶν πρὸς αὐτοὺς περὶ τῆς ἐν ἡμῖν ἐλπίδος διαγωνίζεσθαι, οὕτως ἂν καὶ κατ' αὐτοὺς τοὺς λόγους ἡττήθησαν ὡς Πλάτωνα ἂν κἀκείνους εὐθὺς τὴν Ἐκκλησίαν ἀντὶ τῆς Ἀκαδημίας ἑλέσθαι.

THE REAPPROPRIATION OF PHILOSOPHY IN THE PALAEOLOGAN ERA   271

The subsequent triumph of Palamism brought about not only the condemnation of Byzantine Thomists but also the condemnation of Aristotle, who was henceforth considered an ally of the Latins.[67] It is indicative of the richness of Palaeologan philosophy that at the very end of Byzantium George Scholarios, a defender of the doctrine of the Hesychasts, who, contrary to his fellow Bessarion, eventually opposed the Union of the Churches and became the first Patriarch of Constantinople under Ottoman rule (as Gennadios II, 1454–1464).[68] Vindicated not only Aristotle but also Thomas. In a praise that is reminiscent of Pachymeres' poetic epilogue to his commentary on the *Physics*, Scholarios presents Aristotle, on the basis of his *Metaphysics*, as the only ancient monotheist, a tacit enemy of paganism and a real forerunner of Christianity, who possessed the truth about God before God's revelation through Christ:

> In what follows, Aristotle posits even more brilliantly the unity of the divine essence, arguing both from the intellection [of itself] and from the order of beings with regard to the First as their common good and useful, although here too he does so sparingly out of fear, as we have said, of the many. It is in the end of book *Lambda* [cf. Λ 10, 1076a3–4] that he rejects in a more lucid manner the multiplicity of principles and gods, and that he posits that there is a unique king of the universe and a unique God. You, Aristotle, have come to be the only real philosopher in Hellas and have been rightly called 'the philosopher par excellence', you who are the last in time among the great philosophers of Hellas, those who started from a faint point and progressed through time in wisdom, the one succeeding the other; but you are the summit above all philosophers, so that those who lived shortly before you (*sc.* Plato) are with regard to you what [all] previous philosophers were with regard to them. And, for the time being, I leave aside the part of your philosophy (*sc.* logic) that has been studied with great care and has been admired in every language of the world and by every nation. For you are the unique, the first and the last inventor of philosophy, and the author and teacher of the race of men. But it is your most lucid doctrine about the one God and your repugnance against the irrational polytheism that I now timely make the unique cause of the miracle surrounding you (for I believe that you are the only one among those [*sc.* Greek] philosophers, or the first among few, who has done that); for the divine Logos together with the soul,

---

67   Before the Palamites, Gregoras himself had condemned Aristotle within his traditional anti-Latin polemics; see Bydén, "The criticism of Aristotle in Nikephoros Gregoras' *Florentius*".

68   On Scholarios' life and works see Blanchet, *Georges-Gennadios Scholarios (vers 1400-vers 1472)*.

which the Logos [i.e. Christ] received in dispensing the salvation of men, was directly known by you. You were the wise above all Hellenes; this is why you received the truth about divine things from above, according to what the time allowed, being pure in nature and in zeal and life, both of which are required in faith. This is what I think; our Lord Jesus Christ knows what has become of you.[69]

Scholarios' genuine admiration for Aristotle and his firm belief that Aristotle's allegedly monotheistic philosophy was close to Christianity are the two main reasons for which he eagerly responded to Plethon's downgrading of the Stagirite. The last episode of Byzantine intellectual history, that is, the controversy between 'Platonists' and 'Aristotelians' shortly before and after the fall of Byzantium, can be thus seen as a remote consequence of the Hesychast controversy.

Scholarios' admiration for Aristotle was linked to his overt admiration for Thomas Aquinas, whom he considered equal in wisdom to the wisest of men. While introducing to his readers his epitome of Thomas' *Summa contra Gentiles*, Scholarios, now Patriarch Gennadios II, states that the differences between the Eastern and the Western Church were in reality only a few. He links his translations of Thomas' theological writings to the general Byzantine

---

69 Gennadios II/George Scholarios, *Opera: Praise of Aristotle*, eds. Petit/Jugie/Siderides, vol. 8, p. 506, line 28 – p. 507, line 11: Ἐφεξῆς δὲ καὶ λαμπρότερον τὴν ἑνότητα τῆς θείας οὐσίας ἔκ τε τῆς νοήσεως ἔκ τε τῆς τῶν ὄντων πρὸς αὐτὸ (*sc.* τὸ πρῶτον) τάξεως ὡς κοινὸν ἀγαθὸν καὶ εὔχρηστον, εἰ κἀνταῦθα φειδομένως τῷ δέει τῶν πολλῶν, ὡς εἴρηται, τίθησιν. Ἐν δὲ τῷ τέλει τοῦ Λ καὶ φανερώτερον τὴν πολυαρχίαν ἀναιρεῖ καὶ πολυθεΐαν, καὶ ἕνα μόνον βασιλέα τοῦ παντὸς καὶ Θεὸν εἶναι τίθησιν. Ὄντως φιλόσοφος σὺ μόνος ἐν Ἑλλάδι καὶ γέγονας καὶ δικαίως οὕτως ἐκλήθης κατ᾽ ἐξοχήν, Ἀριστότελες, ὕστατος μὲν τῷ χρόνῳ τῶν μεγάλων παρ᾽ Ἑλλάδι φιλοσόφων κατὰ καιρὸν προβαινόντων ἐξ ἀμυδροτάτης πρώτης ἀρχῆς καὶ προκοπτόντων ἐπὶ σοφίας, ἄλλου μετ᾽ ἄλλον εὐθὺς ἐκ διαδοχῆς· κορυφαῖος δὲ ἐπὶ πᾶσιν αὐτός, ὥστ᾽ εἶναι τοὺς μικρῷ πρὸ σοῦ παραβαλλομένους σοι ὅπερ ἦσαν οἱ πρότεροι πρὸς ἐκείνους. Καὶ τὴν μὲν ἄλλην σου φιλοσοφίαν παρίημι νῦν ὑπὸ πάσης γλώττης ἐν κόσμῳ καὶ γένους παντὸς πολλῇ σπουδῇ γνωρισθεῖσαν καὶ θαυμασθεῖσαν· σὺ γὰρ μόνος καὶ πρῶτος καὶ τελευταῖος τῆς φιλοσοφίας εὑρετὴς καὶ συγγραφεὺς καὶ διδάσκαλος τῷ τῶν ἀνθρώπων ὑπῆρξας γένει· ἀλλὰ τὴν περὶ τοῦ ἑνὸς Θεοῦ καθαρωτάτην σου δόξαν καὶ τὴν τῆς ἀλόγου πολυθεΐας ἀποστροφὴν αἰτίαν μόνην ποιοῦμαι νῦν ἐγκαίρως τοῦ περὶ σὲ θαύματος (οἶμαι δέ σε καὶ μόνον τῶν ἄλλων φιλοσόφων ἐκείνων, ἢ πρῶτον ἐν ὀλίγοις, πεποιη-κέναι) τῷ θείῳ Λόγῳ μετὰ ψυχῆς, ἣν οἰκονομῶν τὴν τῶν ἀνθρώπων σωτηρίαν προσείληφεν, ὑπὸ σοῦ εὐθὺς γνωρισθέντι· σοφός τε γὰρ ὑπὲρ πάντας ἦσθα τοὺς Ἕλληνας· διὸ καὶ τὴν περὶ τῶν θείων ἀλήθειαν ἐντεῦθεν ἔσχες, ὡς ὁ καιρὸς ἐδίδου, φύσει τε καὶ σπουδῇ καὶ βίῳ καθάρειος, ἃ πρὸς τὴν πίστιν ἄμφω ζητοῦνται. Οὕτω μὲν ἐγὼ νομίζω· ὁ δὲ δεσπότης ἡμῶν Ἰησοῦς Χριστὸς οἶδε τί σοι γέγονε. As Cacouros, Ὁ Γεώργιος Σχολάριος ἐξηγητὴς τοῦ Ἀριστοτέλους, p. 280, points out, this *elogium* is in reality a comment on Aristotle, *Metaphysics*, Λ 7, 1073a3–11.

THE REAPPROPRIATION OF PHILOSOPHY IN THE PALAEOLOGAN ERA   273

effort towards the union of the Churches. But when the union failed and Byzantium fell, Scholarios burnt his translations:

> The writer of these books is Latin in descent; and for this reason he was bound to the doctrine of the Latin Church as his paternal; for *this is the custom of men*. He was wise and was not lacking any of the perfections in wisdom that are possible for men. He wrote many commentaries on Aristotle's philosophy and many commentaries on the Old and the New Testament, and was seen as the author of many subjects in self-standing books, some of which relate to the sacred theology, and some others to the Aristotelian philosophy. I have read almost all of these books, some of them (those that had been previously translated by others) in the language of the Greeks – the books that I abridge here are among them – and all of them in the Latin originals, some of which I myself translated in our language. But, alas, all this effort was vain, since it was doomed to be destroyed together with our homeland and was destroyed indeed for the sake of the burning of our badness, since the mercy of God was not any more able to withstand His justice. This wise man should be therefore studied in everything, since he is an excellent exegete and abridger of Christian theology in those matters in which his Church is in accordance with our Church. The matters in which he and his Church differ from us are just a few, that is, the procession of the Holy Spirit, and the divine essence and the divine energy, how they unite with each other and how they differ; with regard to these matters not only do I subscribe to our paternal doctrine but I have battled for it through many books.[70]

---

70 Gennadios II/George Scholarios, *Opera: Epitome of Thomas Aquinas' 'Summa contra Gentiles'*, eds. Petit/Jugie/Siderides, vol. 5, p. 1, lines 15 – p. 2, line 16: Ὁ δὲ τῶν βίβλων συγγραφεὺς Λατῖνος μὲν ἦν τῷ γένει· διὸ καὶ τῇ δόξῃ τῆς ἐκκλησίας ἐκείνης ὡς πατρίῳ κατείληπτο· τοῦτο δὴ τὸ ἀνθρώπειον ἔθος· σοφὸς δὲ καὶ τῶν ἐν σοφίᾳ τελείων ἐν ἀνθρώποις οὐδενὸς ἐνδεής· καὶ πλεῖστα μὲν εἰς τὴν Ἀριστοτελικὴν φιλοσοφίαν, πλεῖστα δὲ εἰς τὴν παλαιὰν καὶ νέαν Γραφὴν συνεγράψατο ἐξηγούμενος· πλείστων δὲ ὑποθέσεων ἡγεμὼν ἐν ἰδίοις ὤφθη βιβλίοις, τῶν μὲν εἰς τὴν ἱερὰν θεολογίαν, τῶν δὲ εἰς τὴν ἀριστοτελικὴν φιλοσοφίαν ἀναγομένων· οἷς πᾶσι σχεδὸν ἡμεῖς ἐνετύχομεν, ὀλίγοις μὲν τοῖς ἑρμηνευθεῖσιν ὑπ' ἄλλων πρότερον εἰς τὴν τῶν Ἑλλήνων φωνήν, ἐν οἷς καὶ τὰ ἐνταῦθα ἐπιτετμημένα βιβλία εἰσί, τοῖς σύμπασι δὲ ἐν τοῖς λατινικοῖς πρωτοτύποις, ὧν ἔνια καὶ ἡμεῖς εἰς τὴν ἡμετέραν φωνὴν ἡρμηνεύσαμεν. Ἀλλ' ἅπας ἡμῖν, φεῦ, ὁ περὶ τὰ τοιαῦτα πόνος μάταιος ἦν, τῇ πατρίδι συναπολεῖσθαι μέλλων καὶ συναπολωλεκὼς διὰ τὴν ἔκκαυσιν τῆς ἡμετέρας κακίας, οὐκέτι δυναμένης τῆς θείας ἐλεημοσύνης πρὸς τὴν αὐτοῦ δικαιοσύνην ἀντέχειν. Ἐν πᾶσι μὲν οὖν σπουδαστέος ὁ σοφὸς οὗτος ἀνήρ, ὡς ἄριστος τῆς χριστιανικῆς θεολογίας ἐξηγητὴς καὶ συνόπτης, ἐν οἷς καὶ ἡ ἐκκλησία αὐτοῦ τῇ ἡμετέρᾳ ἐκκλησίᾳ συνάδει· ἐν οἷς δὲ ἐκείνη τε καὶ αὐτὸς πρὸς ἡμᾶς διαφέρετον, ὀλίγα δ' εἰσίν, περί τε τῆς τοῦ Πνεύματος ἐκπορεύσεως δηλονότι καὶ τῆς θείας οὐσίας καὶ ἐνεργείας, ὅπως τε ἐνοῦνται καὶ πῶς διαφέρουσιν,

According to Gennadios II, it is part of the human ethos to defend the doctrines of one's ancestors. Under the present human condition, he implies, the union of the Churches was doomed to fail and Byzantium was doomed to fall. Still, Thomas' writings, especially his theological writings, like the *Summa contra Gentiles* that he epitomizes here, are worthy of study for their excellence and the services that they are henceforth to provide to Orthodox Christians under Muslim rule. This rather sad prologue to the epitome of *Summa contra Gentiles* by the traditionalist Patriarch, who, somewhat ironically, underscores the paucity of differences between the two Churches, announces in a way the centuries to come in Ottoman Greece, in which philosophy and theology parted company anew.

Through their respective defence of Aristotle and Plato, Scholarios and Bessarion, the traditional Orthodox and the Catholic convert, give us a picture of Byzantine philosophy at its best. This picture was the final product of a long reappropriation of philosophy, both in terms of collecting and in terms of interpreting ancient philosophical texts, which started in the first decades of the Palaeologan era thanks to the efforts of George Akropolites, Gregory II/George of Cyprus and George Pachymeres and continued with Theodore Metochites, Nikephoros Gregoras and many others.

Bibliography

Primary Sources

Alexandri Aphrodisiensis in librum Aristotelis De sensu commentarium (Commentaria in Aristotelem Graeca, 3.1), ed. P. Wendland, Berlin 1901.

Anonymi Categoriarum paraphrasis (Commentaria in Aristotelem Graeca, 23.2), ed. M. Hayduck, Berlin 1883.

Anonymi in Sophisticos elenchos paraphrasis (Commentaria in Aristotelem Graeca, 23.4), ed. M. Wallies, Berlin 1884.

Barlaam of Calabria, *Greek Letters*, ed. G. Schirò, *Barlaam Calabro. Epistole Greche* (Istituto Siciliano di Studi Bizantini e Neogreci. Testi e Monumenti, 1), Palermo 1954.

Demetrios Kydones, *Letters*, ed. R.-J. Loenertz, *Démétrius Cydonès, Correspondance* (Studi e Testi, 186 & 208), 2 vols., Vatican City 1956–60.

Scholarios, *Opera*, eds. M. Jugie/L. Petit/X.A. Siderides, *Oeuvres complètes de Gennade Scholarios*, 8 vols., Paris 1928–36.

περὶ τούτων οὐχ ἁπλῶς μόνον ἡμεῖς τῇ πατρίῳ δόξῃ μᾶλλον τιθέμεθα, ἀλλὰ καὶ ταύτης πολλοῖς βιβλίοις ὑπερηγωνισάμεθα.

THE REAPPROPRIATION OF PHILOSOPHY IN THE PALAEOLOGAN ERA 275

George Akropolites, *On some sentences by Gregory of Nazianzos*, ed. A. Heisenberg, *Georgii Acropolitae opera*, vol. 2, Leipzig 1903, pp. 70–80.

George Gemistos Plethon, *On Aristotle's Departures from Plato*, ed. B. Lagarde, "Le *De differentiis* de Pléthon d' après l' autographe de la Marcienne", *Byzantion* 43 (1973), 321–343; ed. B. Bydén, "*On Aristotle's Departures from Plato 0–19: Greek Text and English Translation*", in id./C. Thomsen Thörnqvist (eds.), *The Aristotelian Tradition. Aristotle's Works on Logic and Metaphysics and Their Reception in the Middle Ages*, Turnhout 2017.

George Pachymeres, *Commentary on Plato's Parmenides*, eds. L.G. Westerink et al., *George Pachymeres. Commentary on Plato's Parmenides* [*Anonymous Sequel to Proclus' Commentary*] (Philosophi Byzantini, 4), Athens 1989.

George Pachymeres, *History*, ed. A. Failler, *Georges Pachymérès. Relations historiques* (Corpus Fontium Historiae Byzantinae, 24), 5 vols., Paris 1984–2000.

George Pachymeres, *Poetic epilogue to the commentary on Aristotle's Physics*, ed. P. Golitsis, "A Byzantine philosopher's devoutness to God: George Pachymeres' poetic epilogue to his commentary on Aristotle's *Physics*", in Bydén/Ierodiakonou (eds.), *The Many Faces of Byzantine Philosophers*, pp. 109–27.

George Pachymeres, *Commentary on Aristotle, Nicomachean Ethics*, ed. S. Xenophontos, *Georgios Pachymeres. Commentary on Aristotle, ›Nicomachean Ethics‹. Critical Edition with Introduction and Translation* (Commentaria in Aristotelem Graeca et Byzantina – Series academica, 7), Berlin 2022.

Gregory of Cyprus, *Autobiography*, ed. W. Lameere, *La tradition manuscrite de la correspondance de Grégoire de Chypre Patriarche de Constantinople*, Brussels 1937, pp. 173–91.

Gregory Palamas, *Defence of the Holy Hesychasts*, ed. J. Meyendorff, *Grégoire Palamas. Défense des saints hésychastes* (Spicilegium Sacrum Lovaniense. Études et documents, 30), Louvain 1973.

John of Damascus, *Philosophical chapters*, ed. P.B. Kotter, *Die Schriften des Johannes von Damaskos* (Patristische Texte und Studien, 7), vol. 1, Berlin 1969.

John Pediasimos, *Other commentary on Analytics*, ed. V. de Falco, "Altri Scolii di Giovanni Pediasimo agli Analitici", *Byzantinische Zeitschrift* 28 (1928), 251–69.

John Pediasimos, *Selected commentary on Analytics*, ed. V. de Falco, *Joannis Pediasimi in Aristotelis Analytica scholia selecta*, Naples 1926.

Michael Psellos, *Chronicle*, ed. D.R. Reinsch, *Michaelis Pselli Chronographia*, 2 vols., (Millenium-Studien, 51), Berlin/Boston 2014.

Michael Psellos, *Philosophical works*, ed. J. Duffy, *Michaelis Pselli Philosophica minora*, vol. 1, Leipzig 1992.

Nicholas Kabasilas, *Against Pyrrho*, ed. J.A. Demetrakopoulos, Νικολάου Καβάσιλα Κατὰ Πύρρωνος. Πλατωνικὸς φιλοσκεπτικισμὸς καὶ ἀριστοτελικὸς ἀντισκεπτικισμὸς στὴ βυζαντινὴ διανόηση τοῦ 14ου αἰῶνα, Athens 1999.

Nikephoros Blemmydes, *Autobiography*, ed. J.A. Munitiz, *Nicephori Blemmydae Autobiographia sive Curriculum vitae necnon Epistula universalior* (Corpus Christianorum. Series Graeca, 13), Turnhout/Louvain 1984.

Nikephoros Blemmydes, *Epitome of logic*, in *Patrologia Graeca*, vol. 142, cols. 685–1004.

Philotheos Kokkinos, *Fourth Antirrhetic against Gregoras*, ed. D.B. Kaimakis, *Φιλοθέου Κοκκίνου δογματικὰ ἔργα* (Θεσσαλονικεῖς Βυζαντινοὶ Συγγραφεῖς, 3), Thessaloniki 1983, pp. 83–122.

Philotheos Kokkinos, *Sixth Antirrhetic against Gregoras*, ed. D.B. Kaimakis, *Φιλοθέου Κοκκίνου δογματικὰ ἔργα* (Θεσσαλονικεῖς Βυζαντινοὶ Συγγραφεῖς, 3), Thessaloniki 1983, pp. 167–221.

Sophoniae in libros Aristotelis De anima paraphrasis (Commentaria in Aristotelem Graeca, 23.1), ed. M. Hayduck, Berlin 1883.

Stephani in librum Aristotelis De interpretatione commentarium (Commentaria in Aristotelem Graeca, 18.3), ed. M. Hayduck, Berlin 1885.

Suda, ed. A. Adler, *Suidae Lexicon*, 5 vols., Stuttgart 1971.

Themistii quae fertur in Aristotelis Analyticorum priorum librum I paraphrasis (Commentaria in Aristotelem Graeca, 23.3), ed. M. Wallies, Berlin 1884.

Themistii (Sophoniae) In Parva naturalia commentarium (Commentaria in Aristotelem Graeca, 5.6), ed. P. Wendland, Berlin 1903.

Theodore II Doukas Laskaris, *Praise of Nicaea*, ed. A. Tartaglia, *Theodorus II Ducas Lascaris Opuscula rhetorica*, Munich/Leipzig 2000, pp. 68–84.

Theodore Metochites, *Miscellanea*, ed. K. Hult, *Theodore Metochites on Ancient Authors and Philosophy. Semeioseis Gnomikai 1–26 & 71* (Studia Graeca et Latina Gothoburgensia, 65), Gothenburg 2002.

The Synodicon of Orthodoxy, ed. J. Gouillard, "Le Synodikon de l'Orthodoxie", *Travaux et mémoires* 2 (1967), 45–107.

Tome of 1368, ed. A. Rigo, "Il Monte Athos e la controversia palamitica dal Concilio del 1351 al 'Tomo Sinodale' del 1368 (Giacomo Trikanas, Procoro Cidone e Filoteo Kokkinos)", in id. (ed.), *Gregorio Palamas e oltre*, pp. 55–134.

Secondary Literature

Acerbi, F./A. Gioffreda, "Manoscritti scientifici della prima età paleologa in scrittura arcaizzante", *Scripta* 12 (2019), 9–52.

Angelov, D., "Classifications of political philosophy and the concept of royal science in Byzantium", in Bydén/Ierodiakonou (eds.), *The Many Faces of Byzantine Philosophers*, pp. 23–49.

Balcoyannopoulou, E., *Το διδακτικό εγχειρίδιο λογικής του Γεωργίου Σχολαρίου: Δομή, πηγές και καινοτομίες*, PhD thesis, University of Patras 2018.

Benakis, L., *Michael Psellos: Kommentar zur Physik des Aristoteles* (Commentaria in Aristotelem Byzantina, 5), Athens 2008.

Bianconi, D., "Eracle e Iolao. Aspetti della collaborazione tra copisti nell'età dei paleologi", *Byzantinische Zeitschrift* 96 (2003), 521–58.

Blanchet, M.-H., *Georges-Gennadios Scholarios (vers 1400-vers 1472). Un intellectuel orthodoxe face à la disparition de l'empire byzantin* (Archives de l'Orient chrétien, 20), Paris 2008.

Bravo García, A./I. Pérez Martín (eds.), *The Legacy of Bernard de Montfaucon: Three Hundred Years of Studies on Greek Handwriting* (Bibliologia, 31), Turnhout 2010.

Bydén, B., "'Strangle Them with These Meshes of Syllogisms': Latin Philosophy in Greek Translations of the Thirteenth Century", in J.O. Rosenqvist (ed.), *Interaction and Isolation in Late Byzantine Culture* (Swedish Research Institute in Istanbul Transactions, 13), Stockholm 2004, pp. 133–57.

Bydén, B., "The Criticism of Aristotle in Nikephoros Gregoras' *Florentius*", in D. Searby/E. Balicka-Witakowska/J. Heldt (eds.), *Dōron Rodopoikilon: Studies in Honour of Jan Olof Rosenqvist*, Uppsala 2012, pp. 107–22.

Bydén, B., "'To every argument there is a counter-argument': Theodore Metochites' defence of scepticism (*Semeiosis* 61)", in K. Ierodiakonou (ed.), *Byzantine Philosophy and its Ancient Sources*, Oxford 2002, pp. 183–217.

Bydén, B./K. Ierodiakonou (eds.), *The Many Faces of Byzantine Philosophers*, Athens 2012.

Cacouros, M., *Ὁ Γεώργιος Σχολάριος ἐξηγητὴς τοῦ Ἀριστοτέλους, ἐρανιστὴς τοῦ Μετοχίτου καὶ μεταφραστὴς λατινικῶν ἔργων στο Corpus aristotelicum. Πρώτη προσέγγιση* (Aristoteles Byzantinus atque Postbyzantinus, 1), Athens 2015.

Cacouros, M., "Un commentaire byzantin inédit au second livre des *Analytiques postérieurs*, attribuable à Jean Chortasmenos", *Revue d'Histoire des Textes* 24 (1994), 149–98.

Candal, M., *Nilus Cabasilas et theologia S. Thomae de processione Spiritus Sancti* (Studi e Testi, 116), Vatican City 1945.

Chase, Jr., F.H., *St. John of Damascus. Writings* (The Fathers of the Church, 37), Boston 1958.

Congourdeau, M.-H., "Notes sur les Dominicains de Constantinople au début du 14e siècle", *Revue des Études Byzantines* 45 (1987), 175–81.

Dendrinos, C./J. Demetracopoulos, *Thomas Latinus – Thomas Graecus. Proceedings of International Conference on Thomas Aquinas and his Reception in Byzantium held in the National Library of Greece, Athens on 15–16 December 2017*, Athens 2022.

Dölger, F., "Zur Bedeutung von φιλόσοφος und φιλοσοφία in byzantinischer Zeit", in F. Dölger, *Byzanz und die europäische Staatenwelt: Ausgewählte Vorträge und Aufsätze*, Darmstadt 1964, pp. 197–208.

Ebbesen, S./J. Pinborg, "Gennadios and Western Scholasticism: Radulphus Brito's *Ars Vetus* in Greek Translation", *Classica et Mediaevalia* 33 (1981–82), 263–319.

Fischer, E., "Manuel Holobolos and the role of bilinguals in relations between the West and Byzantium", in Speer/Steinkrüger (eds.), *Knotenpunkt Byzanz*, pp. 210–22.

Fyrigos, A., "Barlaam Calabro tra umanesimo italiano e antiumanesimo bizantino", in C. Sabbione (ed.), *Calabria Bizantina. Civiltà bizantina nei territori di Gerace e Stilo*, Soveria Mannelli 1998, pp. 31–41.

Fyrigos, A., "Tomismo e antitomismo a Bisanzio (con una nota sulla "Defensio S. Thomae ad versus Nilum Cabasilam" di Demetrio Cidone)", in A. Molle (ed.), *Tommaso d'Aquino e il mondo bizantino*, Venafro 2004, pp. 27–72.

Golitsis, P., "A Byzantine philosopher's devoutness to God: George Pachymeres' poetic epilogue to his commentary on Aristotle's *Physics*", in Bydén/Ierodiakonou (eds.), *The Many Faces of Byzantine Philosophers*, pp. 109–27.

Golitsis, P., "Georges Pachymère comme didascale. Essai pour une reconstitution de sa carrière et de son enseignement philosophique", *Jahrbuch der Österreichischen Byzantinistik* 58 (2008), 53–68.

Golitsis, P., "La date de composition de la *Philosophia* de Georges Pachymère et quelques précisions sur la vie de l'auteur", *Revue des Études Byzantines* 67 (2009), 209–15.

Golitsis, P., "Nicéphore Blemmyde lecteur du Commentaire de Simplicius à la *Physique* d'Aristote", in C. D'Ancona Costa (ed.), *The Libraries of the Neoplatonists* (Philosophia Antiqua, 107), Leiden 2007, pp. 243–56.

Golitsis, P., "Nicéphore Calliste Xanthopoulos, élève de Georges Pachymère", in M. Cronier/B. Mondrain (eds.), *Le livre manuscrit grec : écritures, matériaux, histoire* (Travaux et mémoires, 24), Paris 2020, pp. 305–315.

Golitsis, P., "Quelques remarques sur les copistes et le contexte d'apparition du ms. *Laurentianus plut.* 85.1, dit l' « Océan »", in C. Brockmann/D. Deckers/D. Harlfinger/ S. Valente (eds.), *Griechisch-byzantinische Handschriftenforschung. Traditionen, Entwicklungen, neue Wege*, Berlin 2020, pp. 463–69.

Golitsis, P., "Un commentaire perpétuel à la *Physique* d'Aristote, faussement attribué à Michel Psellos", *Byzantinische Zeitschrift* 100 (2007), 637–76.

Hankins, J., *Plato in the Italian Renaissance* (Columbia Studies in the Classical Tradition, 17), 2 vols., Leiden 1990.

Harlfinger, D., *Die Textgeschichte der pseudo-aristotelischen Schrift Περὶ ἀτόμων γραμμῶν. Ein kodikologisch-kulturgeschichtlicher Beitrag zur Klärung der Überlieferungsverhältnisse im Corpus aristotelicum*, Amsterdam 1971.

Hunger, H., "Von Wissenschaft und Kunst der frühen Palaiologenzeit", *Jahrbuch der Österreichischen Byzantinischen Gesellschaft* 8 (1953), 123–55.

Ierodiakonou, K., (ed.), *Byzantine Philosophy and its Ancient Sources*, Oxford 2002.

Ierodiakonou, K., "The anti-logical movement in the fourteenth century", in ead. (ed.), *Byzantine Philosophy and its Ancient Sources*, pp. 219–36.

Ierodiakonou, K., "The Byzantine commentator's task: Transmitting, transforming or transcending Aristotle's Text", in Speer/Steinkrüger (eds.), *Knotenpunkt Byzanz*, pp. 199–209.

Kaldellis, A., "Byzantine Philosophy Inside and Out: Orthodoxy and dissidence in counterpoint", in Bydén/Ierodiakonou (eds.), *The Many Faces of Byzantine Philosophers*, pp. 129–51.

Karamanolis, G., "Plethon and Scholarios on Aristotle", in Ierodiakonou (ed.), *Byzantine Philosophy and its Ancient Sources*, pp. 253–82.

Kotzabassi, S., "Kopieren und Exzerpieren in der Palaiologenzeit", in Bravo García/ Pérez Martín (eds.), *The Legacy of Bernard de Montfaucon*, pp. 473–82.

Lackner, W., "Zum Lehrbuch der Physik des Nikephoros Blemmydes", *Byzantinische Forschungen* 4 (1972), 157–69.

Martínez Manzano, T., "Malaquías Mónaco, alias *Anonymus Aristotelicus*: filosofía, ciencias y exégesis bíblica en la Constantinopla de la controversia palamita", *Aevum* 93 (2019), 495–558.

Menchelli, M., "Cerchie aristoteliche e letture platoniche (manoscritti di Platone, Aristotele e commentatori)", in Bravo García/Pérez Martín (eds.), *The Legacy of Bernard de Montfaucon*, pp. 493–502.

Mondrain, B., "L'ancien empereur Jean VI Cantacuzène et ses copistes", in Rigo (ed.), *Gregorio Palamas e oltre*, pp. 249–96.

Monfasani, J., "Cardinal Bessarion's Greek and Latin Sources in the Plato-Aristotle Controversy of the 15th Century and Nicholas of Cusa's relation to the controversy", in Speer/Steinkrüger (eds.), *Knotenpunkt Byzanz*, pp. 469–80.

Papadopoulos, S.G., Ἑλληνικαὶ μεταφράσεις θωμιστικῶν ἔργων. Φιλοθωμισταὶ καὶ ἀντιθωμισταὶ ἐν Βυζαντίῳ. Συμβολὴ εἰς τὴν ἱστορίαν τῆς Βυζαντινῆς θεολογίας, Athens 1967.

Pérez Martín, I., "L'écriture de Jean Pothos Pédiasimos d'après ses scholies aux *Elementa* d'Euclide", *Scriptorium* 64 (2010), 109–19.

Podskalsky, G., *Theologie und Philosophie in Byzanz. Der Streit um die theologische Methodik in der spätbyzantinischen Geistesgeschichte (14./15. Jh.), seine systematischen Grundlagen und seine historische Entwicklung* (Byzantinisches Archiv, 15), Munich 1977.

Rigo, A. (ed.), *Gregorio Palamas e oltre: studi e documenti sulle controversie teologiche del XIV secolo bizantino* (Orientalia Venetiana, 16), Florence 2004.

Rigo, A., "Niceforo l'esicasta (XIII sec.): alcune considerazioni sulla vita e sull'opera", in T. Špidlík (ed.), *Amore del bello, studi sulla Filocalia. Atti del "Simposio Internazionale sulla Filocalia", Pontificio Collegio Greco, Roma, Novembre 1989* (Spiritualità orientale), Magnano 1991, pp. 79–119.

Ševčenko, I., "The definition of philosophy in the *Life of Saint Constantine*", in M. Halle (ed.), *For Roman Jakobson. Essays On the Occasion of His Sixtieth Birthday*, 11 October 1956, The Hague 1956, pp. 449–57.

Speer, A./P. Steinkrüger (eds.), *Knotenpunkt Byzanz. Wissensformen und kulturelle Wechselbeziehungen*, Berlin 2012.

Steiris, G., "Pletho, Scholarios and the Arabic philosophy", in D. Searby (ed.), *Never the Twain Shall Meet: Latins and Greeks Learning from Each Other in Byzantium*, (Byzantinisches Archiv. Series Philosophica, 2), Berlin 2017, pp. 309–34.

Tinnefeld, F., "Ein Text des Prochoros Kydones in Vat. gr. 609 über die Bedeutung der Syllogismen für die theologische Erkenntnis", in A. Schoors/P. van Deun (eds.), *Philohistôr: Miscellanea in honorem Caroli Laga septuagenarii*, Louvain 1994, pp. 520–23.

Triantafyllopoulos, C., "The Thomist basis of Prochoros Kydones' anti-Palamite treatise 'De essentia et operatione Dei' and the reaction of the Byzantine Church", in Speer/ Steinkrüger (eds.), *Knotenpunkt Byzanz*, pp. 411–30.

Trizio, M., "Neoplatonic source-material in Eustratios of Nicaea's commentary on book VI of the *Nicomachean Ethics*", in C. Barber/D. Jenkins (eds.), *Medieval Greek Commentaries on the Nicomachean Ethics* (Studien und Texte zur Geistesgeschichte des Mittelalters, 101), Leiden 2009, pp. 71–109.

Usener, H., "Interpreten des Aristoteles", *Rheinisches Museum für Philologie* 20 (1865), 133–36.

Violante, T.M., *La provincia domenicana in Grecia* (Dissertationes historicae, 25), Rome 1999.

CHAPTER 8

Κόσμου θεωρία: Cosmic Vision and Its Significance in the Works of Theodore Metochites and Other Contemporary Intellectuals

Ioannis Polemis

1 Introduction

According to the testimony of ancient authorities, Anaxagoras, when asked for what reason he had been born, replied: "in order to contemplate the sun, the moon and the sky".[1] This attitude was shared by almost all other Greek philosophers.[2] The Greeks understood their philosophy as a child of astronomy. As Arendt puts it, "philosophy begins with an awareness of this invisible harmonious order of the *kosmos*, which is manifest in the midst of the familiar visibilities ... Another early world for the invisible in the midst of the appearances is *physis*, nature, which according to the Greeks is the totality of all things".[3] The answer to the question put to Anaxagoras involved man's whole attitude towards nature and life on earth. The position of the early-14th c. politician, scholar and polymath Theodore Metochites on these matters was seemingly the same as that of Anaxagoras. In an essay of his *Miscellanea*, Metochites puts to himself the question whether existence is better than non-existence.[4] One of the reasons Metochites invokes for justifying existence over non-existence is the ancient cosmological argument:

> Furthermore, it is immediately clear even to the blind, as they say, that it is really a great gift for those who have prayed for an existence governed by reason and have received, in addition to all else, such a great treasure and supplement to life and being, the rational and contemplative activity and life, that they partake of being and have been given the ability to observe closely and enjoy such a great thing, the contemplation of being

---

1 Presocratics, *Fragments*, Fragm. A1, ed. Diels, 376, pp. 10–11. This very *dictum* of Anaxagoras was quoted by Metochites' student Nikephoros Gregoras, *Letters*, no. 119a, ed. Leone, p. 310, lines 1–4.

2 Arendt, *The Life of the Mind*, pp. 133–34.

3 Ibid., p. 143.

4 Theodore Metochites, *Miscellanea*, no. 58, ed. Hult, pp. 184–204: Πότερον ἄμεινον ἀνθρώπῳ τὸ γενέσθαι ἢ τὸ μὴ γενέσθαι, καὶ ὅτι ἄμεινον τὸ γενέσθαι.

© KONINKLIJKE BRILL NV, LEIDEN, 2023 | DOI:10.1163/9789004527089_010

282 POLEMIS

things, and to celebrate the fact that they enjoy such an exceedingly beautiful spectacle, which creates ineffable delight for the heart.[5]

This answer is far from innovative. Metochites simply repeats a traditional argument for the justification of being: the contemplation of the world, the cosmic vision may help man to understand that the world is good, being the creation of a benevolent creator. To quote Arendt once more, "the affirmation of being, clearly corresponding to the element of admiration in Plato's wonder, needs faith in a Creator-God to save human reason from its speechless dizzy glance into the abyss of nothingness."[6] We shall return to this essay of Metochites at the end of the present chapter, after examining in some detail the function and development of the cosmological argument in his works. My contention will be that Metochites' answer to the question on the value of being is somewhat ambivalent. In reality Metochites was far from being absolutely convinced of the ancient argument concerning the necessity of human life, supposedly because the whole world was the artifice of a perfect artist, God Himself.

I hope that the present essay will help the reader understand a crucial problem of Byzantine intellectual history: that of the meaning and the significance of nature. We shall not concern ourselves with the earlier discussions of that term in Byzantium,[7] but we shall try to investigate the views of just one intellectual of late Byzantium, Theodore Metochites, who, however, is representative of a broader intellectual milieu, which had a new conception of the universe as a unity. Any study of Metochites is in fact a study of a whole trend of the Byzantine intellectual tradition as it was moulded and developed in the Paleologan period. That vision of the world went far beyond the theological cliches and commonplaces of earlier centuries and gave birth to a new rationalism. According to Chenu, who investigated a similar phenomenon in Western Europe in the 13th c., that rationalism "afforded a vision of man's place in the world capable of giving birth alike to science and contemplation".[8] Therefore,

5 Ibid. no. 58, 10, ed. Hult, p. 200, lines 22–202, line 3: Χωρὶς δὲ τούτων αὐτόθεν δῆλον καὶ τυφλοῖς, ὅ φασιν, ὡς μέγας ὄντως ἄρα πλοῦτος ἀνθρώποις τοῖς ἐπηυξημένοις τὸ εἶναι κατὰ τὸ λογικὸν καὶ τοσοῦτον προσλαβοῦσιν ἐπὶ πᾶσιν τοῖς οὖσι θησαυρὸν καὶ προσθήκην τῆς ζωῆς καὶ τοῦ εἶναι τὴν λογικὴν καὶ θεωρητικὴν ἐνέργειαν καὶ ζωήν, ὅτι μετέσχον δὴ τοῦ εἶναι καὶ δέδοται σφίσι κατοπτεύ-ειν ἔχειν καὶ ἐντρυφᾶν τοσούτῳ πράγματι, τῇ θεωρίᾳ τῶν ὄντων, καὶ θεάματος οὕτω καλλίστου καὶ ἄρρητον ἐμποιοῦντος γλυκυθυμίαν ἑορτάζειν τῇ ἀπολαύσει. The translation is that of Hult.
6 Arendt, The Life of the Mind, p. 147. Arendt quotes a question of M. Heidegger: "Why is there anything at all and not, rather, nothing?".
7 On the discussions on nature in the Empire of Nicaea, half a century before Metochites, see Richter, Theodoros Dukas Lascaris, pp. 9–56.
8 Chenu, Nature, Man and Society, p. 33.

COSMIC VISION AND ITS SIGNIFICANCE 283

I hope that this investigation, though limited, will stimulate the curiosity of the readers and help them appreciate some of the peculiarities and the intricacies of the intellectual discussions in late Byzantium, and their innovative character. But before coming to the investigation of the real views of Metochites concerning the value of being human, it is necessary to examine his views on the value of the contemplation of the world. This subject is touched upon in several of his works, *Ethikos* being most prominent among them.

2 The Motif of Nature in the Works of Metochites: The Well-Ordained Universe and Its Contemplation

The basic idea of *Ethikos*, one of the early treatises of Metochites, is that the entire world is a harmonic whole, governed by the laws put into it by its creator. The task of the learned man is to investigate the mysteries of creation; such an investigation will help him to attain a state of constant happiness; such is the quintessence of the *vita contemplativa*. An important presupposition for the attainment of this ideal is the study of the four mathematical sciences, which help man understand the wisdom of his creator. Drawing upon the works of Philo Judaeus, Metochites reproduces the basic tenets of the cosmic religion of late antiquity in the following way:

> There could thus be nothing more pleasant among human beings than the moment when a person turns to himself and to the acceptance of pleasure in, and discourse with books and wisdom, and focuses his mind, as far as possible, away from all other preoccupations onto a stable, utterly independent, unswerving, and undivided permanence that is also free and undisturbed. Afterward, as in a solo pipe performance, he allows his mind to be completely unfettered, and as if from a high vantage point becomes a careful overseer who observes the entire world and its boundless essence. When he opens his eyes, he can see everything in a sequence, easily and with no effort. He can see the countless harmonies of everything that exists, with which he engages; he comes into contact with something that is truly blessed and profoundly divine, with no fear or slackening, I think, without feeling fatigue or hesitation once he embarks upon this endless course. Every time he sets forth, it is as if this were an untroubled celebratory procession of the Muses, and a journey; never ending but not tiring; without a destination but quite pleasant, free of external distractions. This person has relieved the vessel of his mind from everything else and unfurled the sails of contemplation, and he

284   POLEMIS

throws it into the matter of the entire universe, as if onto a calm, serene sea. He sails all over, he enjoys many places that he fancies and considers the best, and he embraces the countless beauties of what exists. Then, because he grows extremely beautiful himself, due to his association with what is most beautiful, as they say, he returns home as he chooses, and begins pondering and examining what he has seen, and seeks refuge in the meeting place and council chamber of his thought in order to seek out and discover the truth in what he has seen. When he retrieves the meaning and reason mingled together in every single thing and finishes his examination, he is astonished and admires the inventor and craftsman, that is God, with a truly ineffable sentiment that suddenly makes him feel ineffable pleasure.[9]

The passage I have quoted is of prime importance for the study of the spirituality of Metochites. In it he repeats the old argument about the utility of the study of nature, which can lead to knowledge of God. A reader familiar with the language of Byzantine mysticism might tend to regard this text as an expression of the ordinary spirituality of the pious Byzantine man. It is true that Metochites speaks about the touch of something divine, employing mystical terminology (ἐπόπτην, θειοτάτην ἐπαφὴν ἐφαπτόμενος, ἄπλετον οὐσίαν). However, it should be pointed out that our author is dealing exclusively with

---

9   The translation is that of Xenophontos (Theodore Metochites, *On Morals*), pp. 119–21. See also the relevant passage of Theodore Metochites, *Orations*, no. 10, 54, eds. Polemis/Kaltsogianni, pp. 387–88, lines 6–33: οὐδὲν τί ποτ' ἄλλο γένοιτ' ἂν, κατ' ἀνθρώπους ἥδιον, ὅταν τις ἑαυτοῦ γενόμενος ὅλος, καὶ τῆς ἐν ταῖς βίβλοις καὶ σοφίᾳ νεύσεως καὶ τρυφῆς καὶ συνουσίας καὶ συναγαγὼν ὡς οἷόν τέ ἐστι τῶν ἄλλων ἁπάντων· εἰς ἀκλόνητον καὶ ἄσχετον καθάπαξ ἁπάντων· καὶ ἀνέκδημον· καὶ ἀμέριστον ἑδρασμὸν καὶ μονὴν ἐλευθέραν τὲ καὶ ἀτύρβαστον, ἔπειθ' οὕτω παντάπασιν ἄδετον καθάπερ ἐν μοναυλίᾳ, ὥσπερ ἀφ' ὑψηλῆς τινος σκοπιᾶς ἀπόλυτον ἐπόπτην ἀφήσῃ πρὸς ξύμπαντα τὸν κόσμον· καὶ τὴν ἄπλετον οὐσίαν, τὸν νοῦν· καὶ περισκοποῖτο, διαίρων ὁμαλῶς καὶ ἀλύπως τῷ ὀφθαλμῷ πάντα ἑξῆς· καταθεώμενος· τὰς ἀμυθήτους ἁρμονίας τῶν ὄντων· καὶ συμπλεκόμενος· καὶ μακαρίαν ὄντως καὶ θειοτάτην ἐπαφὴν ἐφαπτόμενος· μὴ κατορρωδῶν ἀμέλει, μὴ κατοκλάζων οἶμαι· μὴ κάμνων· μὴ ξυμπίπτων μὴ καθάπαξ πρὸς τὸν ἀπέραντον δίαυλον· ἀλλ' οἷόν τινα πομπὴν ἀκύμονά τε καὶ ἔμμουσον ταύτην καὶ πορείαν ἐκδημῶν ἀείποτε· ἀνήνυτον μὲν, ἄπονον δὲ· καὶ ἀόριστον μὲν, ἡδίστην δὲ, καὶ μετὰ γαλήνης τῶν ἔξωθεν, καθάπερ ἐν ἀστασιάστῳ τινί, καὶ ἠρεμαίῳ πελάγει τῇ τοῦ κόσμου παντὸς οὐσίᾳ, κουφίσας τῶν ἄλλων ἁπάντων καὶ τὰ τῆς θεωρίας ἀναπετάσας λαίφη, τὸ τῆς διανοίας σκάφος ἐφίησι, περιπλέων πάνθ' ἕκαστα, καὶ ἐπιξενούμενος καὶ κατατρυφῶν, ἅττα ἂν, δοκῇ καὶ ἃ βέλτιστα· καὶ τὰς ἀμυθήτους τῶν ὄντων ἀσπαζόμενος καλλονάς· κἄπειθ' οὕτω καθ'αἵρεσιν πᾶσαν, ἐν ἑαυτοῦ κάλλιστος ἀπὸ καλλίστων φασὶν, ἐπανιὼν οἴκαδε, ζητῇ καὶ σκέπτηται· κἂν τῷ ἑαυτοῦ συνεδρίῳ, καὶ βουλευτηρίῳ τῆς διανοίας γιγνόμενος, τἀληθὲς ἐν αὐτοῖς ἰχνηλατῇ· καὶ ἀνορύττῃ καὶ τὸν ἐφ' ἑκάστοις σύγκρατον νοῦν τε καὶ λόγον ἀναλαμβάνων τελευτῶν ἄρα καταπλήττηται, καὶ θαυμάζῃ τὸν εὑρετὴν καὶ τεχνίτην, ἐν ὄντως ἀρρήτῳ τῇ συναισθήσει· ἄρρητον αὐτίκα αὐτόθεν γλυκυθυμίαν ἀποφερόμενος. For a more detailed analysis of this passage, see Polemis, Θεόδωρος Μετοχίτης Ἠθικός, pp. 43*–89*.

COSMIC VISION AND ITS SIGNIFICANCE

the study of the universe (θεωρία τῶν ὄντων) and of the laws governing it by the industrious mind of a philosopher. The term ἄπλετος οὐσία clearly refers not to divine nature but to the essence of creation. Metochites speaks also about the discovery of the inner meaning of everything (τὸν ἐφ' ἑκάστοις σύγκρατον νοῦν τε καὶ λόγον). The use of the term λόγος in such a context was certainly not alien to any learned contemporary of Metochites. Certain Church Fathers, Maximos the Confessor most prominent among them, had even used the term *logoi ton onton*, referring to the inner meaning, the predestined purpose of each creature,[10] which one had to discover with the help of divine illumination. The study of nature is a legitimate way of approaching God according to most Church Fathers. However, Metochites is not willing to proceed any further, in contrast to those mystic Byzantine authors who speak about the *physike theoria* and hasten to stress that the search for the mysteries of creation is not enough to approach God, but must be accompanied by divine illumination, which comes from the grace of God. However, no mention of anything else except for the study of the *onta*, of creatures, is to be found either in the passage of Metochites quoted above or anywhere else in the *Ethikos*. One might argue that Metochites is not a spiritual writer, and that it is futile to seek such matters in his works, but such an argument loses something of its force, if we consider the fact that according to the official position of the Byzantine Church the contemplation of nature *had* to be accompanied by an affirmation of its inadequacy, of its limited value, and of the need to be combined with the divine illumination, which far surpasses it. This is almost a doctrinal matter if we may use the term. Such an affirmation, however, is lacking in the text of Metochites.

Accordingly, one may conclude that Metochites employs the term *theoria*, which is conspicuous in the passage we have just quoted, in the ancient sense of the study of nature and the universe, and not in a mystical sense.[11]

---

10   Völker, *Maximos Confessor*, pp. 296–318.

11   On this distinction in the 14th c., see Medvedev, *Vizantijskij Gumanizm*, pp. 118–19. It is a pity that a recent study on Metochites, by applying in an almost unintelligible-esoteric manner some recent models of textual interpretation (diagrammatology, indexicality), attempts to deny the value of trying to interpret Metochites' text as an apology for his own life, or as an effort to reevaluate the Byzantine spiritual tradition on the basis of his late antique sources (Kermanidis, *Episteme*, p. 153), insisting instead on a rather dubious attempt to underline the literary-aesthetic aspects of this treatise, on the basis of a totally misleading comparison of the text with the *Gnomikai Semeioseis*, as well as the aesthetic principles that supposedly governed the restoration of the Chora monastery. The result is a highly abstract and arbitrary picture of Metochites as an intellectual totally immersed in his literary-aesthetic preoccupations, who was neither a true philosopher nor interested in being one. This, besides being a rather a-historical interpretation of a

Metochites, as it were, secularises the Christian, mystical *theoria*. Festugière has thoroughly examined the religious aspect of the scientific study of the universe in antiquity in the second volume of his monumental work *La Révélation d'Hermès Trismégiste*, which bears the eloquent title *Le Dieu cosmique*.[12] The origins of the view that the study of the universe may lead the human mind to a better grasp of the divinity can be traced back to Diogenes of Apollonia,[13] Plato, Xenophon, and the young Aristotle. One should remember that in antiquity the stars of the sky were considered to be divine beings, which even had or ought to have their own cult, as is explicitly stated in the pseudo-platonic *Epinomis*. Stoicism made use of this theory and successfully disseminated it throughout the Graeco-Roman world, presenting it as an argument in favor of the divine providence.[14] Many Christian theologians made use of this theory as well.[15] *La réligion cosmique*, as Festugière aptly describes this phenomenon, is a powerful trend in the spirituality of late antiquity, which was very slow to die out.[16] Most creative thinkers of the time, such as Cicero or Philo Judaeus,[17] were influenced by it.

In the passage under discussion, which generally speaking is a free adaptation of the theme of the journey of the soul in Plato's *Phaedrus*,[18] Metochites copies two extracts of Philo Judaeus, one from the third book of his treatise *De specialibus legibus*, and the other from his well-known essay on the Therapeutai of Egypt, entitled *De vita contemplativa*. The first runs as follows:

> There was a time when I had leisure for philosophy and for the contemplation of the universe and its contents, when I made its spirit my own in all its beauty.... And then I gazed down from the upper sky, and straining

---

major figure of the Paleologan renaissance, comes close to a denial of the real value of the Byzantine intellectual tradition, its philosophic aspects and the historical-literary study of these aspects as well. Xenophontos (Theodore Metochites, *On Morals*, p. xx), recognizing the intrinsic value of the treatise, rightly points out that *Ethikos* "was expected to function as an ethical *vade mecum*, a manual of proper behavior in leading the good life".

12 See mainly Festugière, *La Révélation*, pp. 153–95, where the intellectual background of this trend of Hellenistic spirituality is explained.

13 Theiler, *Zur Geschichte der teleologischen Naturbetrachtung*, pp. 21 and 33.

14 See Pfeiffer, *Contemplatio Caeli*, pp. 27–69.

15 Spanneut, *Le Stoicisme*, pp. 273–85.

16 Festugière, *La Révélation*, pp. 441–56. See also Joly, *La thème*, pp. 28–39.

17 On him, see Festugière, *La Révélation*, pp. 425–33, Pfeiffer, *Contemplatio Caeli*, pp. 70–84, and Runia, *Philo of Alexandria*, pp. 458–61, where the motif of "admiration of the cosmos, praise for the creator" is discussed.

18 See Courcelle, *Connais-toi toi-même*, pp. 562–624. On the use of this image by the early Fathers see Daniélou, *Message évangelique*, pp. 115–18.

COSMIC VISION AND ITS SIGNIFICANCE

the mind's eye beheld, as from some commanding peak, the multitudinous world-wide spectacles of earthly things (καὶ τείνων ὥσπερ ἀπὸ σκοπιᾶς τὸ τῆς διανοίας ὄμμα κατεθεώμην τὰς ἀμυθήτους θεωρίας τῶν ἐπὶ γῆς ἁπάντων), and blessed my lot in that I had escaped by main force from the plagues of mortal life.[19]

Here is the second one:

At sunset they (the Therapeutai) ask that the soul may be wholly relieved from the pressure of the senses and the objects of sense and sitting where she is, consistory and council-chamber to herself, pursue the quest of truth (ἐν τῷ ἑαυτῆς συνεδρίῳ καὶ βουλευτηρίῳ γενομένην ἀλήθειαν ἰχνηλατεῖν).[20]

On the other hand, the impressive sentence of Metochites concerning the boat of the mind may have been inspired by a passage in the well-known treatise of Plutarch *De genio Socratis*,[21] where an otherworldly voyage of the soul, after temporarily escaping from the body, is described.[22] A similar image also occurs in Plutarch's *De sera numinis vindicta*.[23]

At the end of the *Ethikos* Metochites presents his vision of the wise man, whose soul is governed by reason; but this reason is a universal power governing the whole world as well. Here is a translation of this passage:

The genuine grace of rationality, however, is human beings' only exceptional advantage and the best there is. It is the supervisor and teacher of true bliss and proper behaviour throughout the world and indeed in every human being individually, foreseeing and regulating every situation; as Aeschylus aptly says, it is seated alone on the stern of the city and directs all things, governing them all efficiently, so that they are made serviceable. By "city" one could refer to anything one likes, be it the entirety of life and the world as a whole taken as a true unity, or each person

---

19 Philo Judaeus, *Opera*, III, 2, eds. Cohn/Wendland, vol. 5, p. 150, lines 13–16. See also Festugière, *La Révélation*, pp. 551–53. The translation is that of F.H. Colson (Philo Judaeus, *Works*, 475).

20 Philo Judaeus, *Opera*, 27, eds. Cohn/Wendland, vol. 6, p. 37, lines 11–17.

21 Plutarch, *Moralia* 590BC.

22 On the motif of the *Himmelsreise* encountered in this text, see the remarks of Bousset, *Die Himmelreise*, pp. 60–61, and of Culianu, *Psychanodia*, pp. 43–47.

23 Plutarch, *Moralia* 563F. On the comparison of the human soul to a ship on the sea, see Betz, *Plutarch's Theological Writings*, p. 222.

288   POLEMIS

individually, in whom rationality and the mind preside authoritatively as noble guardians and kings of nature.[24]

In all probability, this passage is once more modelled upon Philo Judaeus.[25] Metochites does not lose the opportunity to employ the image of the world as a well-ordained city, the order of which may be reflected in the soul of the wise man, in his other works as well, but in rather different contexts than that of *Ethikos*. There is a passage from his *Oration to St. Demetrios*, where he speaks of the perfume emanating from the saint's tomb, taking advantage of the same passage of Philo. Here is a free rendering of it into English:

> The fountain is inexhaustible, it is never emptied, the aromatic oil is never lacking, never hidden; it is perpetually sufficient for the whole world; it gushes springs and streams of remedy instead of blood, or rather a great river flows from there, the rapid movements of which give pleasure to the city of God (Ps. 45, 5). I do not refer only to Thessaloniki, which you govern; I consider and call the whole world a city of the great king; the architect and founder of that city is the first and unrestrained mind; your river, being a cataclysm destroying sin, irrigates that city; it cleanses all wounds and illnesses.[26]

---

24   The translation is that of Xenophontos (Theodore Metochites, *On Morals*, pp. 229–31). Here is the relevant passage of Theodore Metochites, *Orations*, no. 10, 96, eds. Polemis/ Kaltsogianni, p. 424, lines 5–20: ἡ δ' ὄντως τοῦ λόγου χάρις μόνον ἐξαίρετον ἀνθρώποις ἀγαθὸν καὶ πάντων κάλλιστον· ἐπιστάτης καὶ διδάσκαλος ἀληθοῦς εὐδαιμονίας· καὶ χρήσεως ὀρθῆς ἐν ἅπαντί τε καθάπαξ τῷ κόσμῳ· καὶ ἐν αὐτῷ ὁτῳοῦν μάλιστα· προορωμένη τε καὶ καταρρυθμίζουσα πάνθ' ἕκαστα· ἀτεχνῶς κατὰ τὸν Αἰσχύλου λόγον· μόνη ἐν τῇ πρύμνῃ καθημένη τῆς πόλεως· πάντα κυβερνῶσα καὶ πάντων ἄρχουσα εὖ γ' ὡς ἄν, χρήσιμα ποιεῖν· ἥντινα δὴ βούλεταί τις πόλιν καλεῖν· εἴτε τὸν βίον ἅπαντα καὶ τὴν τοῦ κόσμου καθάπερ ἑνὸς ἀληθῶς ὄντος, ἅπαντος θεωρίαν, εἴτ' αὐτὸν ὁντιναοῦν ἄνθρωπον ἕκαστον· ἐν ᾧ καθάπερ εὐγενὴς προστάτης καὶ τῆς φύσεως βασιλεὺς ἡγεμονικῶς ὁ λόγος τὲ καὶ νοῦς προκάθηται. The beginning of this passage is borrowed from a letter of Iamblichos preserved by Stobaios ΙΙ, 2, 6, 40: καὶ λόγῳ προέχοντες τῶν ἄλλων ζῴων καὶ τοῦτο ἐξαίρετον ἀγαθὸν κεκτημένοι τῆς ἀνθρωπίνης φύσεως.

25   Philo Judaeus, *Opera, On Dreams*, ΙΙ, 248, eds. Cohn/Wendland, vol. 3, p. 281, lines 22–26: πόλιν γὰρ Θεοῦ καθ' ἕνα μὲν τρόπον τὸν κόσμον καλεῖ ..., καθ' ἕτερον δὲ τὴν ψυχὴν τοῦ σοφοῦ.

26   Theodore Metochites, *Orations*, no. 4, 26, eds. Polemis/Kaltsogianni, pp. 145–46, lines 36–47: ἀλλ' ἀνεξάντλητος, οὐ κενοῦται, οὐδ' ἐλλείπει μετρίως· οὐδ' ὑποχωρεῖ· οὐδὲ κρύπτεται· ἀλλὰ κατὰ παντὸς ἐξαρκεῖ συνάμα τοῦ κόσμου τὲ καὶ τοῦ χρόνου· καὶ κρούνους ἰαμάτων, ἀνθ' αἱμάτων ἀεὶ πάντοθεν ἀναβλύζει καὶ ῥύακας· μᾶλλον δ' οὐδ' ἄμφω· ἀλλὰ ποταμὸς μέγιστος ὄντως ἐκεῖθεν ἕλκει καὶ ἄλλεται· οὗ τὰ ὁρμήματα τὴν πόλιν εὐφραίνουσι τοῦ Θεοῦ. καὶ οὐ ταύτην λέγω δὴ ταύτην μόνην, τὴν ὑπὸ σοὶ πολιτάρχῃ καὶ ἡγεμόνι, ἀλλ' ὄντως ἄρα, πόλιν τοῦ μεγάλου βασιλέως ἔγωγε καὶ οἴομαι καὶ καλῶ, τὸν ἅπαντα κόσμον, ἧς ὁ πρῶτος καὶ ἄσχετος νοῦς ἀρχιτέκτων καὶ πολιστής, καὶ εἰς ἣν ὁ σὸς ποταμὸς ἀρδεύει κατακλυσμὸς ἁμαρτίας, καὶ πληγῆς· καὶ πάσης νόσου καθάρσιον. The translation is my own.

COSMIC VISION AND ITS SIGNIFICANCE 289

The image employed in *Ethikos* appears once more here, adapted, admittedly in a rather embarrassing way, to a very different context. A similar passage to the one quoted above occurs in Metochites' *Poem* 10, an *encomium* of the harmonic science. After giving a concise description of the technical aspects of this science, Metochites proceeds to an analysis of the role of music in the world:

> Everything remains in perfect condition, both what is created by nature and what is constructed by human hands, through the wise mind of men imitating nature, as long as their harmonic bonds, which safeguard their existence in a reasonable and measured manner, remain indissoluble. These bonds belong to the great science of harmonics, which makes beautiful all the creatures of this world, pervading them all; the form brings to perfection the essence of all material things, bringing into action their natural habits, and giving to each one its existence; the same happens with the harmonic principles: they pervade our world in its entirety, putting into it a form that brings everything to perfection. They also resemble the nerves of our body which contribute to the good health of the human organism, giving it the permanent gift of existence; matter, lacking these harmonic principles, is useless; only those fulfilment-bringing principles safeguard our permanent existence.[27]

What one must observe is that this image appears near the end of the poem; the same occurs in both *Ethikos* and the *Oration for St. Demetrios*, where the image of the well-ordained universe comes near the end of the relevant texts. This may not be accidental. Metochites seems to want to impress upon the minds of his readers a holistic view of the world as a well-ordained structure, inside which the subject of his texts (reason, music, or St. Demetrios himself) plays an important role. Reason in *Ethikos* is a cosmic force, keeping the world in order; the same applies to the science of harmonics: it is through its laws that God created the universe. In the case of the *Oration for St. Demetrios*

---

27 The translation is my own, see Theodore Metochites, *Poems. Translation*, pp. 230–31. The text is taken from the recent edition Theodore Metochites, *Poems*, no. 10, ed. Polemis, p. 208, lines 900–913: Τόφρα γὰρ ἐσταότ' εἰσὶν ἔχοντ' εὐφυέα καλά,/ πάντα γεγαότα ἠμὲν πρήγματα φύσιος ἔργα/ ἠδέ τε τεχνήεντ' ἐπίτηδες εἰσκόμενά σφιν/ χειροπόητα διδακτὰ διὰ πραπίδεσι σουφῶν,/ ὄφρα κεν ἄλυτ' ἔασι νύ θ' ἁρμονίης δέσμια/ νούμιμα, τοῖσιν ἔκαστ' ἄραρ' ἔμμεν' ἀριπρεπέεσσι/ μέτροισί τε λόγοισί τε τῇσδ' ἐπεεικόσι κάρτα/ δὴ μεγάλης σοφίης, ἢ πρήγματα πάντ' ἐρίηρα/ θήκατο κόσμου, δι' ἄρα πάντεσσ' ἰοῦσ' αὐτή·/ ἠύτε δ' ὑλήεσσης αἰτίας εἴδε' ἔπειτα/ οὐσιάων γίνεται τελέοντα φύσιος αὐτῶν/ ἕξιν ἅπασαν ἔκαστ' ἂρ ἔμμεν', ἅπερ νύ τ' ἔασι,/ τὼς οἶδ' ἁρμονίης πεφύκαντι λόγοι περὶ πάντα/ κόσμον ἄμαδις ἕνα τελέθοντα, εἶδος τελεουργόν.

290 POLEMIS

Metochites does not abandon his effort. The aromatic oil emanating from the tomb of the saint acquires cosmic dimensions. Its aroma seems to embrace the whole world which, once more, is referred to as a city of God. This is a clear indication of Metochites' insistence on the value of the cosmic laws, as these may be discovered in various aspects of human life and of the entirety of creation. However, the cases we examined previously are not the only ones in the writings of Metochites.

In his *Second Imperial Oration* (second *Basilikos*) for the Emperor Andronikos II Palaiologos, composed around the year 1295, Metochites dedicates a large part of his oration to the description of the fortification works in Asia Minor undertaken by the emperor during his long sojourn in that area in the years 1290–1293. Metochites points out that now the eastern provinces of the Byzantine Empire are a well-fortified area, inside which all good things can be found. The image of the city of God appears once more near the end of this particular oration. Here is the translation of the passage in question:

> I think that the barriers, both those created by nature and those newly built, are well-adapted to the whole; as a result, the whole structure has an inner concord, being a great city of the great king, inside which all good things are to be found.[28]

It is significant that for Metochites the laws of nature also govern the state. What is beyond the Byzantine state, i.e. the world of the barbarians, lacks any rational order, since it functions contrary to the laws of nature; it cannot be considered "a city of the great God". Comparing the realm of the barbarians to the Byzantine state of the time of the Emperor Andronikos II, Metochites underlines this point, arguing that the barbarians have no justice at all.[29] This is an example of the classic natural right, as presupposed by the Greek authors, who required that the law should follow the order established by nature.[30] A provisional result of our investigation so far is that the theory of the well-ordained universe functions, so to speak, as both a stylistic and a structural principle of some of Metochites' works: coming almost at the end of them,

---

28 Theodore Metochites, *Orations*, no. 7, eds. Polemis/Kaltsogianni, p. 282, lines 11–22: καὶ τό γε μὴν ἔγωγε οἶμαι, διαφερόντως ἡρμόσθαι πρὸς σύμπασαν τὴν κατασκευήν· καὶ τοὺς ἀποδοθέντας, ἐγκλεισμοὺς τῇ χώρᾳ· τοῦτο μὲν παρὰ τῆς φύσεως· τοῦτο δὲ παρὰ τῆς νέας δημιουργίας, συνεχῶς ἀλλήλοις ὡς ἅπασαν ἑαυτῆς ἀναγκαίως ἠρτῆσθαι, καὶ συνεῖναι· καὶ συμπαθεῖν· καὶ πόλιν οὖσαν μίαν τὲ καὶ μεγίστην, ἑνὸς καὶ μεγίστου βασιλέως, ἐν ᾗ ξύμπαντα ὁμοῦ συνῆλθε καλῶν εἴδη.

29 Ibid., no. 22, eds. Polemis/Kaltsogianni, p. 283, lines 20–22.

30 Strauss, *Natural Right*, p. 121.

COSMIC VISION AND ITS SIGNIFICANCE

it underlines the importance of the subject praised by Metochites, which is elevated to a cosmic principle.

3 Metochites' Byzantios: A Defence of the Contemplation of Nature

Another work of Metochites in which the cosmological image is constantly employed both at the stylistic level and as a structural principle is *Byzantios*, an extensive praise of the city of Constantinople. Further developing the idea of his *Second Imperial Oration*, that the Roman state was governed by the laws of nature, Metochites describes the capital of the Byzantine Empire as the city *par excellence* governed by the same laws. The theory of nature appears at the point in the oration where Metochites speaks of the eternal renewal of the imperial city. Metochites explicitly invokes the natural philosophers:

> The city follows the pattern of the universe, as described by the naturalists: the parts of the universe are constantly perishing and constantly regenerating; there is a continuous existence and an uninterrupted renewal, which safeguards the subsistence of those various parts.[31]

The idea that the universe is constantly changing and renewing itself is rather old,[32] but it also appears in other Byzantine authors contemporary with Metochites.[33] The comparison of Constantinople with the universe reappears in the middle of the oration, where the constant circulation of the waters of the universe is employed by the author as a pattern for explaining the uninterrupted activity of Constantinople:

> Our city, seemingly imitating all these, presents herself as a reflection of the essence of the universe, being a great and perfect copy of that excellent pattern, the world.[34]

---

31 Theodore Metochites, *Orations*, no. 11, 75, eds. Polemis/Kaltsogianni, p. 496, lines 38–41: καὶ ὅπερ ἐπὶ τοῦ παντὸς τοῦδε τοῖς φυσικοῖς λόγος, ὡς ἡ τοῦ παντὸς αὐτοῦ φθορὰ συνεχὴς καθ' ἕκαστον κατὰ μέρη δηλαδή, τοῦ παντὸς ἐστὶν ἀεὶ, καὶ συνεχὴς οὐσία καὶ γένεσις· καὶ ἄπαυστος φυλακὴ· καὶ μονὴ κατὰ μέρη δηλαδή.

32 Spanneut, *Le Stoicisme*, pp. 360–62. See also Wolfson, *Philo*, p. 312. The idea appears in Aristotle's *Physics* 208a9–10 and *Metaphysics* 995b5–6; Metochites was familiar with both treatises.

33 See the treatise of Metochites' friend and later adversary Nikephoros Choumnos, *On matter and species* p. 379, lines 309–12.

34 Theodore Metochites, *Orations*, no. 11, 80, eds. Polemis/Kaltsogianni, p. 501, lines 33–36: ἡ πόλις ἔοικε, μιμησαμένη τὴν τοῦ παντὸς οὐσίαν, δείκνυσιν ἐφ' ἑαυτῆς ἀρχετύπου τὲ καλλίστου

The theory of the eternal circulation of the waters was explained by Aristotle[35] and extensively discussed by Metochites' contemporary, Nikephoros Choumnos, who wrote an entire treatise on the subject.[36] The comparison of the city with the world, or rather the cosmological significance of Constantinople, is also prominent in the following passage of *Byzantios*, where the city is described as:

> A link of the whole life ... and the necessary condition for the coherence of one world or rather for the stability of the whole world.[37]

The word σύνδεσμος is employed in cosmological contexts by ancient authors.[38] Therefore, the city, being such a σύνδεσμος, functions like the Stoic λόγος, which safeguards the unity of the whole world. One is reminded of "the city of the great king" employed in other works of Metochites as an image of the whole world. One may say that Constantinople is identified with the city of the great king, functioning as a mirror of nature as a whole.

Metochites, describing the city of Constantinople, employs another old cosmological image: that of the theatre[39] or of the great feast, which appears in its earliest form in a parable ascribed to Pythagoras and reported by Diogenes Laertius: "Life ... is like a festival; just as some come to the festival to compete, some to ply their trade, but the best people come as spectators, so in life the slavish men go hunting for fame or gain, the philosophers for truth."[40] Metochites also compares the city to a common feast and an international market.[41]

The place of the men devoted to the life of the mind is inside the city, and they are in a position to contemplate the world by carefully examining Constantinople, which is a sort of microcosm. The city of Constantinople, which is identified with the world, provides this marvelous spectacle. The use of the image of the universal feast (or rather a variation of it) is also prominent in the following passage of *Byzantios*:

καὶ μεγίστου κάλλιστον αὐτὴ καὶ μέγιστον ἐκτύπωμα καὶ κάτοπτρον τῆς ἀριστουργίας τῶν ὄντων.

35   See Solmsen, *Aristotle's System*, pp. 407–12.

36   Polemis, "Theodore Metochites' *Byzantios*", 241–46.

37   Theodore Metochites, *Orations*, no. 11, 96, eds. Polemis/Kaltsogianni, p. 516, lines 5–11: σύνδεσμος βίου ... καὶ συνεχείας ἑνὸς κόσμου, μᾶλλον δὲ τοῦ παντὸς κόσμου μονῆς ἀφορμή.

38   Pépin, *Théologie cosmique*, pp. 432–33.

39   See Fenster, *Laudes Constantinopolitanae*, pp. 185–226.

40   I quote the translation of Arendt, *The Life of the Mind*, p. 93. See also Jaeger, *Aristotle*, p. 432, and n.1.

41   Theodore Metochites, *Orations*, no. 11, 136, eds. Polemis/Kaltsogianni, p. 551, line 22.

COSMIC VISION AND ITS SIGNIFICANCE 293

I have heard some people say, and it is my own considered opinion too, that it is much better for a man to live for a few years and come into contact with numerous people and affairs than to live for many years and come into contact with very few men; this is a way of enjoying a long life. This is the profit of this life, to conclude it quickly after gathering as many experiences as possible, after seeing many things and coming into contact and conversing with many people. This is far more profitable than a long life devoid of any content and the long years of a life without any important events and deeds and without any marvelous spectacles: it resembles a man spending his life in a long detestable darkness, or someone imprisoned deep in the earth, being condemned (I do not know for what reason) to lead a detestable life without any beauty at all; such a man is blind, being devoid of the most beautiful spectacles, of all the grace of human life; he has to cover a long distance, but he has no power at all. He resembles a living corpse. If this view is correct, as every prudent man will agree, those living in Constantinople live a much longer life than those living in other cities; the citizens of Constantinople take a much greater profit of their life than the inhabitants of any other city and country. The wealth of life in Constantinople, the multitude of those men living in it, whether native or foreigners, all those things gathered in it, that universal community, and that market of the whole world which takes place here always, without any interruption, cannot be compared to the wealth of any other city.[42]

---

42   Ibid., 99, eds. Polemis/Kaltsogianni, pp. 518–19, lines 1–100, line 10: Καὶ μὴν ἐνίων ἤκουσα λεγόντων, καὶ αὐτὸς ἔγωγ' ἔδοξα πολλάκις, ἄμεινον εἶναι πολλῷ κατ' ὀλίγα πάνυ τοι βιοῦν ἔτη πλείστοις ὅσον οἷόν τ' ἄν, εἴη ξυνόντα· καὶ συνανακοινούμενον, ἀνθρώποις καὶ πράγμασιν, ἢ κατὰ πλείω μάλιστα μετ' ὀλίγων αὐτὸν συνεξεταζόμενον· καὶ τὸν τρόπον δὴ τοῦτον ἀπαντλοῦντα βίοτον μακραίωνα· καὶ τοῦτ' ἄν, εἴη κέρδος μάλιστα τοῦ βίου, καὶ πολὺ κέρδιον, τό τ' ἐπὶ μείοσι τοῖς χρόνοις, τὸν βίον οὕτως ἀφ' ἀνύτοντ' ἐκμετρῆσαι· καὶ ξυμπεράναι τάχιον, πολλοῖς ξυντετυχηκότα πράγμασι, πολλὰ μάλ' ἰδόντα· πολλῶν ἀμέλει, πεπειραμένον καὶ κοινωνήσαντα, ἢ μακρά τις ζωῆς ἐρημία· καὶ πολὺς ἐτῶν ἀριθμὸς, μετ' ὀλίγης ἔργων τὲ καὶ πραγμάτων τῆς τύχης ἐκτήκων καὶ δαπανώμενος· καὶ τῶν καλλίστων, οἶμαι, θεαμάτων χηρεύων· ὥσπερ ἀηδεῖ σκότῳ τινὶ καὶ νυκτὶ πολυμήκει ξυλλαχόντα τινὰ καὶ κατατεινόμενον τὴν ζωήν· ἢ κατάκλειστον ὑπὸ γῆς καταστενούμενον· καὶ κατάκριτον οὐκ οἶδ' ὅπως, ἐρεῖν ἀβίωτον· καὶ ὡς ἀληθῶς ἄχαριν τὸν βίον ἕλκοντα· καὶ πονήρως ἔχοντα· καὶ τυφλώττοντα τῶν βελτίστων τῆς ἐποπτείας καὶ ξυντυχίας· καὶ πάσης εὐκολίας βιοτικῆς καὶ χρήσεως, ἐρραστωνευμένης διαστηχοῦντα· καὶ ὀλιγοπνοοῦντα μακρὸν δρόμον· καὶ ὥσπερ ἐν νεκροῖς βιοῦντα καὶ πολιτευόμενον. Ἀλλ' εἰ τοῦτ' ἄρα, καὶ πᾶς ἂν, οὕτως οἶμαι συνετῶς ἐπιστατῶν τε καὶ κρίνων δόξαι, μακροβιώτατοι τῶν ἄλλων ἂν, εἶεν οἱ τῇδε συζῶντες, τῇ πόλει τόν γε τρόπον τοῦτον, ὄντως καὶ πολυολβώτατοι τῆς ζωῆς, ὑπὲρ ἑκάστους ἑκάστης καὶ χώρας καὶ πόλεως. καὶ παραβάλλειν οὐκ ἔστιν, ἅττα δὴ τῶν ἄλλων, τῇ περιουσίᾳ τῇδε· καὶ τῷ πλούτῳ τῷδε τοῦ βίου· καὶ τοῖς ἐγχωρίοις καὶ ξένοις ἐπιδήμοις τῇ πόλει πράγμασι καὶ ἀνθρώποις· καὶ τῇ πάντοθεν ἐνταῦθα εὐπορίστῳ ξυμβιώσει· καὶ παμπληθεῖ κοινωνίᾳ

The pair of opposites "light-darkness", which is employed in the above quoted passage, often occurs in the works of Metochites.[43] The Platonic background of the antithesis is more than evident. The Stoic image of the city of the world, which was very common in late antiquity and employed by two of Metochites' favorite authors, Dio of Prousa and Aelius Aristeides,[44] is also used here. But there is something more in this passage: the city is the source of the existence of the men who look upon it. We recall that Metochites points out that the contemplation of the world gives meaning to human life. The same happens with the contemplation of Constantinople, which is a value of human life itself. I think that Metochites' train of thought becomes clearer if (and here I hazard what could be taken as a somewhat a-historical approach) we take into account a key tenet of Heidegger's thought: man's existence is associated with the surrounding world, and there is a very close, existential connection between them. According to Heidegger "the essence of the human mode of existence is found in our always existing in a world."[45] This interdependence of our being with the world becomes most evident in the passage of Metochites under discussion. Man lives in communion (συνανακοινούμενον) with his fellow human beings (ἀνθρώποις) and with all things (πράγμασι) of this world. The city lends itself to use readily and easily (τῇ πόλει χρῆσθαι). And this communion (κοινωνία καὶ ξυντυχία) is the basis of life. Life outside the world and the concomitant disregard for the possibilities that the world (or Constantinople) offers, is equivalent to the absence of true life (ζωῆς ἐρημία), i.e., it is a life lacking authenticity. This phrase of Metochites is in all probability borrowed from Plotinus.[46] The world (or Constantinople) is thus the real source of our life, our existence. As Heidegger has pointed out, social relations play a tremendous role in constituting who we are.[47] "We are (to a significant degree) constituted as the beings that we are by the fact that we always inhabit a shared world, and the way we exist in this world is always essentially structured by

---

καὶ ξυντυχία· καὶ κοινῇ τῶν τῆς οἰκουμένης καὶ ἀνθρώπων τὲ καὶ πραγμάτων, ἐνθάδ' ἀγορᾷ, πληθούσῃ τὸν ἀεὶ χρόνον. The same idea appears in the *Imperial oration for the emperor Andronikos*, written by Nicholas Lampenos, a contemporary of Metochites, who probably took advantage of Metochites' *Byzantios*, see Nicholas Lampenos, *Imperial oration for the emperor Andronikos*, ed. Polemis, p. 33, lines 16–20: Ὥστε εἴ τις ὥσπερ ἐξ ἀπόπτου τινὸς σκοπιᾶς τὴν οἰκουμένην ἀπονητὶ διαθεάσασθαι βούλοιτο, οὐχ οἷός τ' ὢν διὰ πάσης ἰέναι, ἐπὶ τῆς πόλεως στήτω.

43 See, e.g., Theodore Metochites, *Orations*, no. 10, 7, eds. Polemis/Kaltsogianni, pp. 350–51, lines 15–18.

44 Richter, *Cosmopolis*, pp. 114–34.

45 Dreyfus/Wrathall (eds.), *A Companion to Heidegger*, p. 3.

46 Plotinus, *Enneads* III, 2, 15, eds. Henry/Schwyzer, p. 290, lines 29–33.

47 Dreyfus/Wrathall (eds.), *A Companion to Heidegger*, p. 6.

COSMIC VISION AND ITS SIGNIFICANCE   295

others."[48] Constantinople is described as an ἀγορὰ πλήθουσα once more at the end of our passage. This is a variation of the already familiar image of the festival of the world. One should not rush to say that Constantinople (or the world itself, which is compared with Constantinople) is described in this way because it safeguards merely its citizens' biological existence. It is described thus, because the familiarity of its inhabitants with the world (through Constantinople) makes it possible for them to interact with it, to discover the available range of ways to be, it shows them their can-be or ability-to-be.[49] In this way Metochites, who in other works seems to be suspicious of life in cities in general,[50] which is connected with the *vita activa*, manages to offer an apology for his own life in the world: living in Constantinople, which is a true copy of the greater world, does not prohibit him from pursuing his scientific interests and leading a *vita contemplativa*; on the contrary, such a life offers him the possibility to live as a sage contemplating the universe, since Constantinople is a universe in miniature. We may argue that Metochites, employing the image of the life-giving Constantinople, secularizes one of the basic tenets of the Byzantine world view: true life does not come through the Church anymore, but is distributed through Constantinople to all those who are able to appreciate its virtues, being willing to have an experience of the authentic life inside its walls!

Therefore, Metochites seems to believe that Constantinople guarantees an authentic life to the insiders like himself. We have no reason to doubt his sincerity. But does such a life have an absolute value for our author? Let us consider another passage of *Byzantios*, which may help us form an answer to that question. Describing the natural evolution and the development of the ancient city of Byzantium into the Roman capital of Constantinople, Metochites even uses the image of the expanding and developing nature: all plants and animals develop according to the laws of nature:

---

48   Ibid., p. 7. On certain social aspects of the vocabulary concerning the city in the early Paleologan period, see Gaul, *Thomas Magistros*, pp. 144–59. However, I do not adopt the general viewpoint of Gaul, who insists on interpreting the treatises of Metochites, Magistros and other authors of the same period primarily as attempts by some members of the intellectual elite to promote themselves.

49   Ibid., p. 6.

50   See, e.g., Theodore Metochites, *Orationes*, no. 10, 21, eds. Polemis/Kaltsogianni, p. 262, lines 8–10, and Theodore Metochites, *Miscellanea*, 94, eds. Müller/Kiessling, pp. 596–99. That Metochites is quite serious in his endeavor to vindicate the contemplative life is proved by his anxiousness to present the active life inside Constantinople as another form of the contemplation of nature. The recent attempt to deny this (by Kermanidis, *Episteme*, p. 134, who speaks instead about an "Harmonisierungsversuch" of these two ways of life by Metochites) is totally misleading.

Likewise, our city proceeded according to the laws governing the development of nature: initially she was small, but she became very big; from what was proper at the beginning, the city reached the point that was proper at the end; she became what was proper for her to become because of her own nature and fortune, so to speak.[51]

In my view the term προχώρησις employed in this passage is similar if not identical to the ancient term ἀκολουθία, which denotes both coherence and development of natural entities according to a certain plan.[52] One also needs to bear in mind the ancient idea of the *scala naturae*, most prominent in Aristotle, which is present in this passage as well.[53] But what we should note in particular here is the conjunction of nature and fortune; the two forces appear to be working together in total harmony. However, in some of his works Metochites is very careful to point out that nature and fortune oppose one another. To give an example, in his *Ethikos* Metochites argues that man should not believe that fortune is greater than nature:

They think that fortune is the blessing, and that nature is of secondary importance, or otherwise that fortune presumably leads the way, and that nature is of secondary importance, or otherwise that fortune presumably leads the way and nature merely consents to it. They believe that where fortune is situated, everything else follows and is assembled there, including the whole of virtue and the harmony of nature. Fortune, which is truly the most unstable and unpredictable thing there is, they regard as the only genuine, most stable thing of all, and they think that with fortune by their side they alone will be able to have everything, they alone will be able to know everything, present, future, and past events.[54]

---

51 Theodore Metochites, *Orations*, no. 11, 47, eds. Polemis/Kaltsogianni, p. 471, lines 7–14: οὕτω δὴ καὶ ἡ πόλις ἔοικε προελθεῖν κατὰ τὴν τάξιν καὶ τὴν προχώρησιν τῆς φύσεως ἐκ μικροῦ τινος τὴν ἀρχὴν εἰς τὸ μέγιστον κἀκ τοῦ προσήκοντος τῇ ἀρχῇ, πρὸς τὸ προσῆκον τῷ τέλει καὶ τὸ γιγνόμενον τῆς φύσεως καὶ τῆς τύχης ὡς εἰπεῖν.

52 Polemis, Θεόδωρος Μετοχίτης Ἠθικός, pp. 109*–10*. See also Spanneut, *Le Stoicisme*, n. 17 p. 401.

53 Lovejoy, *The Great Chain of Being*, pp. 24–66.

54 The translation is by Xenophontos in Theodore Metochites, *On Morals*, 193. See the relevant text of Theodore Metochites, *Orations*, no. 10, 81, eds. Polemis/Kaltsogianni, pp. 411–12, lines 4–12: νομίζουσί τε τὴν μὲν τύχην ἀμέλει τἀγαθόν· τὴν δὲ φύσιν ἔλαττον· ἢ τὸ μέν, ἴσως ἡγεῖσθαι· τὴν δὲ φύσιν σύμψηφον, ὡς ἄρ' ὅπου δὴ τὴν τύχην οὖσαν, ἐκεῖ λοιπὸν ἔπεσθαι καὶ ξυνεῖναι, πάνθ' ὁμοῦ, πράγματα καὶ πᾶσαν ἀρετὴν φύσεως καὶ εὐαρμοστίαν. καὶ τὸ πάντων μάλισθ' ὡς ἀληθῶς πλάνον καὶ πάντων ἀσταθμητότατον αὐτήν, μόνον εἶναι, δοκοῦσι τἀληθέστατον· καὶ πάντων ἀσφαλέστατον· καὶ σὺν αὐτῇ δὴ μόνοι τὰ πάντα ἔχειν· μόνοι τὰ πάντ' εἰδέναι, τά τ'

COSMIC VISION AND ITS SIGNIFICANCE

In Metochites' system of thought the concepts of nature and fortune play a central role, as we shall have the opportunity to see further on. However more often than not, fortune as a term does not have positive connotations. Therefore, his view that in the case of Constantinople nature and fortune work together is to be considered a deliberate exaggeration. In any case the relationship between nature and fortune in the works of Metochites seems to me worth investigating. Such an investigation may help us to determine his actual views about the true value and the meaning of human existence.

4 Nature and Fortune: Two Opposite Powers Determining Man's Life

In most cases nature is presented as a positive force in the works of Metochites, its opposite being "fortune". Fortune and its constant changes terrified Metochites, who in his works gives us vivid descriptions of the disasters caused by the caprices of this power that is beyond human control.[55] Metochites especially deplores the turn for the worse of the affairs of the Byzantine state, which fell prey to its enemies. For him, this is irrefutable proof of the power of fortune, which is in a position to destroy everything. The constant use of the image of nature, or of the well-ordered universe in the works of Metochites seems to be the outcome of his effort to resist the power of fortune, of his desire to find something stable in the midst of the constant fickleness of the affairs of this world. His existential agony can be relieved only through the contemplation of nature, of the whole world, which is governed by the laws of God. As we read in the first passage of *Ethikos* we quoted, the *vita contemplativa* safeguards the inner tranquility of the soul, which reflects the calmness and tranquility of nature itself. Metochites' work is an expression of his constant desire to find an explanation for the events of the surrounding world. This is reflected in his care to construct many of his works on the basis of the motif of the contemplation of the world, a principle of universal orderliness, as we had the opportunity to see above. The case of *Byzantios* is highly suggestive: there, contrary to his true opinions, Metochites regards the city of Constantinople as the perfect example of the concord of nature with fortune. All the other cities

---

ἐόντα τά τ᾽ ἐσσόμενα· πρό τ᾽ ἐόντα. The passage has been borrowed from Philo Judaeus, *Opera, On the Embassy* 1, eds. Cohn/Wendland, vol. 6, p. 121, lines 7–9: νομίζοντες τὸ μὲν ἀσταθμητότατον, τὴν τύχην, ἀκλινέστατον, τὸ δὲ παγιώτατον, τὴν φύσιν, ἀβεβαιότατον.

55   See the remarks of Gigante, *Scritti*, pp. 217–44.

298   POLEMIS

of the Christian world have lost their former glory, but Constantinople remains perpetually prosperous and powerful.[56]

It was probably obligatory for an orator like Metochites to praise the stability of the imperial city in one of his public speeches at the beginning of the 14th c. However, Metochites is very far from repeating these views in his more esoteric writings, which were addressed to a more exclusive audience; in these works, the perfect concord of nature with fortune gives way to an image of universal instability and constant destruction. Let us see how he describes the state and its capital city in his *Miscellanea*:

> For we exist in merely a few remnants and limbs of the life and body of our realm, so great and beautiful, almost like people who have had most, and the most essential, of their limbs amputated, and we continue to live in shame, ridicule, completely helpless regarding opportunities for existence and life, vulnerable and liable to perish easily from any small blow and assault; we who – alas! – had whatever was most beautiful, every grace, the most splendid strength, and were most prominent among all other peoples of the whole world as in a common theatre, looked up to from all directions and admired in every way. Now we live all the more miserably and dishonourably, as our state shows us up to everybody, as does the former ceremony and splendor of the glory from which we have fallen; and we live all the more dangerously now, since we have been deprived of so much in the sight of all.[57]

The place of the past triumphs and glory of the Romans is evidently Constantinople itself. It seems possible that Metochites composed this passage of the *Miscellanea* with the passage of *Byzantios* we quoted earlier in mind. The stylistic similarities are apparent: the image of the theatre of the world has now

---

56   Theodore Metochites, *Orations*, no. 11, 109, eds. Polemis/Kaltsogianni, p. 530, lines 4–110, line 7.

57   Theodore Metochites, *Miscellanea*, 38, 3, ed. Hult, p. 74, lines 4–16: καὶ ζῶμεν γὰρ ἐν ὀλίγοις κομιδῇ τοῖς λειψάνοις καὶ μέλεσι τῆς ζωῆς καὶ τοῦ σώματος οὕτω μεγίστου τε καὶ καλλίστου τῆς ἀρχῆς, ὥσπερ οἱ τὰ πλεῖστα καὶ καιριώτατα μᾶλλον ἀποκεκομμένοι, καὶ ξὺν αἰσχύνῃ καὶ γέλωτι βιοῦντες ἔτι καὶ παντάπασιν ἀνικάνως ἔχοντες πρὸς τὰς τοῦ εἶναι καὶ τοῦ ζῆν ἀφορμὰς καὶ βραχείας τινὸς προσβολῆς καὶ ἐπηρείας παρανάλωμα ῥᾷστ' εὐεπιχειρήτως λειφθέντες, οἱ πάντ', οἴμοι, πρότερον κάλλιστα πᾶσαν ὥραν καὶ κράτιστα πᾶσαν εὐτονίαν ἔχοντες καὶ ὥσπερ ἐν κοινῷ θεάτρῳ τῷ παντὶ κόσμῳ, πάντως ἡμεῖς τῶν ἄλλων ἐπίσημοι καὶ περιβλεπόμενοι πάντοθεν καὶ πάντα θαυμαζόμενοι, καὶ τοσούτῳ νῦν αἴσχιστα καὶ ἀτίμως πράττοντες, ὅσῳ καὶ μάλιστα προδείκνυσιν ἡμᾶς ἅπασιν ὁ τόπος ἐφ' οὗ καὶ τὰ φθάσαντα πομπικὰ καὶ περίοπτα τῆς δόξης, ἧς ἐκπεπτώκαμεν, καὶ τοσούτῳ μάλιστ' ἐπικινδυνότατα μένοντες ἔτι πω, ὅσῳ περ μέγιστ' ἀπεβαλόμεθα πᾶσιν εἰς τοὐμφανές. The translation is that of Hult.

COSMIC VISION AND ITS SIGNIFICANCE 299

acquired very negative connotations. Metochites seems to contradict himself on purpose. There is no doubt that in the *Miscellanea* Metochites is speaking more sincerely than in *Byzantios*. But even in *Ethikos* Metochites severely castigates his contemporary cities, which are full of impediments for any man who wishes to devote himself to the *vita contemplativa*. Metochites underlines the fact that most wise men abandon contacts with the multitudes in the cities, considering such contacts destructive of any good thoughts they may have.[58] Accordingly, the concept of the city as the ideal place where the forces of nature and fortune governing human fate are in accord with one another, so much praised in *Byzantios*, is not devoid of a certain ambiguity: Metochites is eager to undermine this concept, focusing on its sinister aspects, especially in his more "esoteric" works.

Metochites ventures yet further. Sometimes even the term "nature" has negative connotations. It is significant that in *Ethikos*, the very treatise where the concept of nature as a unity governed by the power of God is most prominent, there are some passages where nature is presented as a dangerous force, which has to be overcome through man's efforts: "Human nature is so inconsistent, always full of countless reversals and changes that derive from the body and from anything related to it."[59] Here nature resembles fortune, but the resemblance is rather negative: the negative aspects of fortune prevail over nature. Metochites points out that only those men who are devoted to the contemplative life are in a position to fight against nature: "Full of pride, they rise very high and triumph over nature to which they did not yield at all or succumb or flee in shame. I would say instead that these people are the fairest prizes of nature and its admired statues".[60] Nature is a vaguely negative force which has to be subdued by the wise man who wishes to safeguard his inner tranquility, although at the end one might become the glory of nature.

The same negative attitude towards nature is to be found in his *Poem* 10, which deals with the harmonic science. In the preface to this poem Metochites argues that the mathematical sciences deal with the immaterial, immutable mathematical entities, and, accordingly, are nobler than the physical sciences,

---

58   Theodore Metochites, *Orations*, no. 11, eds. Polemis/Kaltsogianni p. 362, lines 8–10.

59   The translation is of Xenophontos in Theodore Metochites, *On Morals*, p. 45. The relevant text of Theodore Metochites, *Orations*, no. 10, 19, eds. Polemis/Kaltsogianni p. 361, lines 9–11, is the following: Οὕτως ἐστὶν ἀνώμαλον ἡ φύσις· καὶ μυρίων ἀεὶ μεταβολῶν καὶ τροπῶν ὑπὸ τοῦ σώματος, καὶ τῶν τοῦ σώματος πλέως.

60   The translation is by Xenophontos in Theodore Metochites, *On Morals*, p. 51. The relevant text of Theodore Metochites, *Orations*, no. 10, 22, eds. Polemis/Kaltsogianni p. 363, lines 1–7, is the following: ἀριστεῖς κατὰ τῆς φύσεως, πρὸς ἣν οὐκ ἔκλιναν ὅλως οὔτ' ἐνέδοσαν οὔτ' ἐνετράπησαν, μᾶλλον δ' εἰπεῖν καλλιστεῖα καὶ ἀγάλματα ταύτης.

300 POLEMIS

which try to explain the unstable and constantly changing nature of this world: the science of mathematics "has well-defined, immaterial and invincible limits; these have nothing to do with the nature of this world, which is so mixed, being constantly in a state of flux."[61] Here it is evident that under the generic term "nature" Metochites understands not only human affairs, but also the natural environment, which in his other works is presented as most stable and well-ordained. This attitude towards nature can be attributed to the influence of Aristotle, who made a distinction between the orderliness of the movement of the stars in heaven and the confusion prevailing in the world which is under the moon, and of Iamblichos.[62]

We can give another example of Metochites' tendency to undermine his own position concerning nature expounded in his more official texts through the ideas he expresses in his, so to speak, esoteric treatises. As we have seen, Metochites compares Constantinople with a living body that reaches completeness after passing through all the stages prescribed by nature.[63] This is evaluated as a positive characteristic of the imperial city which proceeded triumphantly through the centuries to its present leading position. But in his *Miscellanea* he employs this very example in order to point out that all nations and cities are condemned to an ignominious death after passing through a process of constant growth. That is, they proceed from zenith to nadir. According to Metochites the lives of the various nations and cities resemble the life of an individual man or of one particular body: it is ordained by nature that after coming into life it functions according to certain prescribed rules, reaching its acme and thereafter ending its life.[64]

Bearing in mind what Metochites writes in *Byzantios*, one is led to the inevitable conclusion that Constantinople, the perfect example of the collaboration of nature with fortune, is doomed to disappear in the end, if what the author says in his *Miscellanea* is valid. This ambiguity in the use of the term "nature" should not be overlooked and is certainly not accidental. Metochites' attitude is not unique among ancient and medieval scholars, who are eager to hide their opinions under a cloud of ambiguities and contradictions that are

---

61 The translation is taken from Theodore Metochites, *Poems*, trans. Polemis, p. 203. See also the text, Theodore Metochites, *Poems*, ed. Polemis, p. 177, lines 36–38: τοῦδε μὲν εἴδεος ἐντὶ περάσματ' ἄυλα τ' ἄαπτα,/ φύσιος ἐνθάδ' ἀεὶ συμμιγέος εὖ μάλ' ἄτερθε, φύσιος ἥ κε πολύπλανα ῥειάουσ' ἀεὶ ἐντί. The same negative attitude towards nature appears in Metochites' Introduction to his *Stoicheiosis astronomike*, 1, 3, ed. Bydén, pp. 450–451, lines 28–31.

62 Ševčenko, *Études sur la polémique*, p. 245, and Metochites, *Ethikos*, ed. Polemis, pp. *62–*64.

63 See n. 50, above.

64 Theodore Metochites, *Miscellanea*, 112, eds. Müller/Kiessling, p. 751.

COSMIC VISION AND ITS SIGNIFICANCE

left to initiated readers to detect. This peculiarity of the ancient and medieval authors has been thoroughly examined by Leo Strauss, who has concluded that this is the usual way for these authors to proceed.[65] Constrained as they were by the prejudices of their societies, and by written or unwritten laws that strictly prohibited them from publicly expressing any doubts concerning established doctrines, they were compelled to take refuge in these half-truths: by contradicting themselves in certain crucial passages of their works, they hinted at their disagreement with established doctrines, letting the readers draw their own conclusions. But what was the true position of Metochites on the nature of this world? Did he really believe in the existence of the unbreakable laws of the divine providence governing nature as a whole and human life, or did he consider nature as a power functioning without any laws, constantly threatening the existence of human beings with her capricious changes and upheavals? By posing this question we are led back to Metochites' essay on the value of beings with which we started our enquiry.

5   "To Be or Not to Be": The Somewhat Ambiguous Answer
     of Metochites

In my view the answer Metochites gave to the question on the value of being is not easily discernible. No one would deny that Metochites believed in the existence of universal laws governing the world (mainly the world above us); accordingly, Metochites was a fervent proponent of the life of the mind, of the *vita contemplativa*,[66] which consists in the perpetual contemplation of the harmonious laws of nature governing the world. The possibility of such a life is based on the assumption of a well-ordained world which functions under the constant supervision of God, who safeguards its continuous existence. We previously demonstrated this to be a traditional motif that derives from ancient philosophy, and Metochites makes ample use of it in most of his works. Man allows himself to become absorbed in the marvelous spectacle of this world, the contemplation of which leads him to a life of tranquility and calmness. Inner calmness is nothing less than a reflection of the tranquility and calmness of the external world, contemplated by the sage. This theme is encountered so regularly in the various works of Metochites, that we can hardly doubt his sincerity. However, we have seen that another oft-occurring theme in the works

---

65   Strauss, *Persecution*, pp. 30–31. See also Melzer, *Philosophy Between the Lines*, pp. 11–52.
66   de Vries-Van der Velden, *Théodore Métochite*, p. 174, n. 115, believes that Metochites has a low esteem of the *vita contemplativa*; however, her arguments are of dubious value.

of Metochites is that of the instability of human affairs, which fall prey to capricious and malevolent fortune. Nobody can justifiably doubt his sincerity concerning this theme as well. But it is significant that sometimes, as we have already had the opportunity to see, Metochites does not hesitate to employ the most sacred and holy name of "nature" in order to describe the constant flux of human affairs. One is forced to admit that the term "nature" as used by Metochites is rather ambiguous. In most cases it refers to the whole ordained world contemplated by the sage; but in some other cases it refers to the world of human beings which is constantly changing, causing only pain and distress.

The passage of the *Miscellanea* I quoted at the beginning of this article is crucial. There Metochites, deploring the human condition, goes as far as to ask himself whether it would be better for a man not to have lived at all. Being aware of the precariousness of such a position, Metochites rushes to conclude that despite appearances existence is better than non-existence, since God Himself is the font of being: we become living entities by participating in existence as it emanates from the divinity.[67] One of the most important arguments employed by Metochites for justifying our existence on earth is our potential to contemplate the marvels of the world. But did Metochites sincerely adopt this solution? Was he truly persuaded that life in this world was something good? The pessimistic tone of most of his works allows us to entertain some doubts concerning his sincerity. In *Poem* 14, one of his most pessimistic texts, Metochites confirms our suspicions in two instances: "How many times have I cursed myself, saying that it would have been preferable for me not to have led that prestigious life"[68] and tells us that "it would better for me to abandon this life and go to the kingdom of Hades before seeing our glorious state, which was most prestigious among all the states that have existed on earth from the time men were created, become extinct."[69] His position fluctuates between the two extremes: the graceful affirmation of the importance of human existence, which provides us with the opportunity to contemplate the world, and the negation of the meaning of human life, which is full of contradictions, causing the immense suffering of human beings. This permits us to underline once again the distinction between the "exoteric" works of Metochites, and those

---

67   See Theodore Metochites, *Miscellanea* 58, 7, ed. Hult, p. 196, lines 9–15.

68   Theodore Metochites, *Poems*, trans. Polemis, p. 267. See also the text, Theodore Metochites, *Poems*, no. 14, ed. Polemis, p. 251, lines 80–81: ὢ ποσάκι μάλ᾽ ἐγὼν κατ᾽ ἄρ᾽ ἠρασάμην ἑωυτοῦ/ μήποτε τῇδε λελαχέμεναι περιφάντῳ ζωᾷ. See also de Vries-van der Velden, *Théodore Metochite*, p. 24.

69   Ibid., pp. 270–71. See also the text, Metochites, *Poems*, no. 14, ed. Polemis, p. 256, lines 206–208: Ἦ γὰρ ἄμεινον ἐνὶ φθιμένοισι γενέσθ᾽ ἠὲ πρίν,/ ἐξ ἄρ᾽ ἰδέσθαι τήνδ᾽ ἁρπασθεῖσαν βιότοιο/ παντὸς ἀρίτιμον ἀρχὴν ἔξοχον ὑπερτάταν.

COSMIC VISION AND ITS SIGNIFICANCE

texts which can be considered "esoteric", like his poems, most of which are addressed "To himself".

As Beck, who offered a short but incisive analysis of this essay of Metochites,[70] rightly observed long ago, the work of Metochites is an eloquent testimony to the disintegration of the official Byzantine ideology.[71] Beck is the only scholar who has realized the contradictory nature of Metochites' *Weltanschauung*. Even the old traditional image of the world as a theatre, which is contemplated by those men devoted to the intellectual life, is transformed into an image of anxiety and insecurity in several passages of Metochites' work.[72] Metochites' defense of divine providence is not so convincing: the author does not deal with the mystery of the divine government of the world; he does not attempt to explain human suffering in a coherent theological manner.[73] The way Metochites refers to fortune is significant: fortune is a power independent of the providence of God. This proves that Metochites, without explicitly denying the official doctrines of his Church (which was not permissible), had departed from them internally. The world had lost its meaning for Metochites. His constant anxiety to reaffirm the value of the *vita contemplativa* was nothing more than his effort to persuade himself that, at least for the philosopher, a safe place was still to be found in a world that was in constant flux, threatening the existence of what he valued more than anything else: the Byzantine state, to the service of which he had devoted his life. Metochites took refuge in a world of illusions: the contemplation of nature is a haven of stability and calmness in the midst of the disasters threatening the state as well as his own existence. He drew upon the ancient sources that stressed the value of the contemplation of the universe as a source of spiritual tranquility and inner calm. He even applied the motif of cosmic contemplation as a stylistic principle: some of his works are even structured according to this principle: the state as reinvigorated by Andronikos II, the city of Constantinople, the entire life of St. Demetrios are mere reflections of that universal order which safeguards the coherence of the world as created by God. On the other hand, Metochites could not suppress his inner doubts: in some passages of his work even nature appears under a negative light, as a force beyond human control, malevolent and even threatening to us all.

One is reminded Hamlet's famous verse: "To be or not to be, that is the question". As Dreyfus and Kelly point out, commenting on this verse, "the

---

70   Beck, *Theodoros Metochites*, pp. 113–14.
71   Ibid., pp. 115–16.
72   Ibid., pp. 106–07.
73   Ibid., pp. 109–10.

very idea that he understands this as a choice open to him indicates that his culture no longer takes it for granted that God determines these fundamental facts of our existence."[74] *Mutatis mutandis* the same applies to the case of Theodore Metochites. One should be aware that there are certain ancient testimonies which could have strengthened Metochites' belief that the problem of existence was worth investigating. A relevant passage from Sophocles, who openly declared that death was better than life, is well-known.[75] In it there are echoes of some verses of Theognis.[76] Euripides, also, in his lost tragedy *Cresphontes* deplored the human life, blessing those who died.[77] In all probability Euripides had in mind a relevant story of Herodotus.[78] In its turn, this passage of Euripides was quoted by the writer of the pseudo-Platonic *Axiochus* (368a), where several passages of Greek poets considering death better than life were adduced as well (supposedly Socrates was repeating the teaching of Prodicus). This pessimistic view of human life recurs in post-classical literature quite often. Dion Chrysostomus, a favorite author of Metochites, dealt with the subject in his *Oration* 23, where the initial question is whether any happy man may exist. *Ecclesiastes* is another example of this *contemptus mundi*.[79]

There are several other authors of the 14th c. who share Metochites' pessimism. Beck has given the example of Demetrios Kydones.[80] The examples may be multiplied.[81] What is unique to Metochites is his ambivalent attitude toward nature. On the one hand, the cosmic vision, the contemplation of nature is praised as the highest ideal of human life. Several of his contemporaries, such as Maximos Planoudes and Joseph the Philosopher, would have agreed with him as far as the importance of the study of nature as a path leading to God was

---

74 Dreyfus-Kelly, *All Things Shining*, p. 18.

75 *Oedipus Coloneus*, lines 1225–1228 (μὴ φῦναι τὸν ἅπαντα νικᾷ λόγον./ τὸ δ', ἐπεὶ φανῇ,/ βῆναι κεῖθεν, ὅθεν περ ἥκει/ πολὺ δεύτερον ὡς τάχιστα).

76 See, e.g., the relevant note of R. Jebb (ed. & transl.) in, Sophocles, *The Oedipus Coloneus*, p. 194.

77 Euripides, *Fragments*, no. 449, ed. Kannicht, p. 487, lines 4–6: τὸν φύντα θρηνεῖν εἰς ὅσ' ἔρχεται κακά,/ τὸν δ' αὖ θανόντα καὶ πόνων πεπαυμένον/ χαίροντας εὐφημοῦντας ἐκπέμπειν δόμων.

78 A. Harder (ed.), *Euripides' Kresphontes and Archelaos*, Leiden 1985, pp. 93–94, where several passages of Greek authors sharing this pessimistic view of human life are adduced.

79 See de Vries-van der Velden, *Théodore Métochite*, p. 140, n. 43, who recognized the importance of essay 37 of *Miscellanea*, identifying one of its most obscure quotations (Ps.-Plato, *Epinomis* 974a). She also believes that the source of the title of that essay is *Eccl.* 4, 2–3 (ibid., p. 181, n. 124). This is more than doubtful. That passage belongs to the common *topoi* of the pessimistic evaluation of human affairs.

80 Beck, *Theodoros Metochites*, pp. 117–21. See also Ševčenko, "The Decline of Byzantium", 172–73.

81 Medvedev, *Vizantijskij Gumanizm*, pp. 127–37.

COSMIC VISION AND ITS SIGNIFICANCE   305

concerned.[82] But we must also bear in mind that Metochites' willingness to see the sinister aspects of fate, its instability and capriciousness, which is reflected in the affairs of men as well, is not an uncommon attitude among Byzantine authors of his time either,[83] as we shall have the opportunity to see in the next section of the present chapter. What seems to me remarkable in Metochites' case is the application of the hallowed name of "nature" to all those sinister phenomena of human life. This is an expression of Metochites' inner agony. Metochites was convinced that the *vita contemplativa* was the best way of life. Throughout his life Metochites yearned for the years of his youth, when he was devoted to his studies, not caring about anything else. According to Metochites, the calm contemplation of the world, of its nature, could offer man a degree of protection from the trials and tribulations of everyday life. He had no doubts about this. But Metochites was not so certain about the value of life in general. "To be or not to be" – this was his constant anxiety. That he dared to ask this question explicitly is a testimony to his intellectual honesty. I suspect that he never found the answer to it. However, the answer was given unequivocally by George Sphrantzes in the next century, after the fall of Constantinople, in his *Chronicle*: "It would have been better for me not to be born at all; or rather, it would have been better for me to die as a child."[84] The same idea was also expressed by other scholars who had experienced the end of the Byzantine Empire, such as Bessarion of Nicaea and John Argyropoulos.[85] One cannot claim a direct dependence of Sphrantzes on Metochites; however, there is a trajectory of a pessimistic approach to human life in late Byzantium which, as time passes and the situation deteriorates, becomes much more visible.

The case of Metochites is quite telling: the sacred symbols of nature and the imperial city acquire certain ambiguous connotations in his works. Sometimes they are brought together. The imperial city is almost identified with nature as a whole, guiding man on the paths of knowledge. The contemplation of nature and of the imperial city of Constantinople gives meaning to the life of the author and every man willing to follow his instructions. This is the case of *Byzantios*, where Metochites presents his active life and his involvement in the affairs of the state as a further case of the contemplation of the inner order of beings, which gives to the Roman state its coherence; thus he tries to apologize for his abandoning the contemplative life of his youth, insisting that

---

82   See Kottoúsis, *Τὸ ἐπιστολάριον Γεωργίου Λακαπηνοῦ-Ἀνδρονίκου Ζαρίδου*, pp. 206–08, and
       483–92.
83   See de Vries-van der Velden, *Théodore Métochite*, pp. 159–63.
84   George Sphranzes, *Chronicle*, ed. Maisano, p. 4, line 4: Καλὸν ἦν μοι εἰ οὐκ ἐγεννήθην, ἢ παι-
       δίον ἀποθανεῖν.
85   Medvedev, "Neue philosophische Ansätze", p. 539.

his active life is a kind of a spiritual contemplation of the inner order of the Roman state. However, in certain other cases both nature and the city in general are considered as negative phenomena, as obstacles which the sage must overcome, if he is to proceed towards the ideal of the *vita contemplativa*. This ambiguity was a constant hallmark of the spiritual development of Theodore Metochites.

6   The Value of the Contemplation of the World according to Metochites' Contemporaries

Metochites' enthusiasm for the scientific investigation of the mysteries of creation through the so-called mathematical sciences, especially astronomy, was shared by most of his contemporaries.[86] Earlier, in the 13th c., before Metochites' birth, the Emperor Theodore II Laskaris had underlined the importance of the scientific study of creatures, as a way of praising the great wisdom of the creator.[87] He seems to maintain some distance towards the traditional treatment of the natural and mathematical sciences as mere instruments of theology.[88] This is not the place to present a full list of the works of those scholars, where the contemplation of the world is presented as the highest human ideal, as the culmination of the philosophical endeavours of a learned man in the late 13th and early 14th centuries. Maximos Planoudes,[89] George Pachymeres,[90] Manuel Gabalas,[91] and Michael Gabras[92] are some of the scholars who insist on the importance of the contemplation of nature and the world, stressing the contribution of the four mathematical sciences. Such assertions are scattered throughout the literary monuments of this period. Some examples will suffice to show that Metochites' interest in the *theoria* of the created world was not an isolated phenomenon.

A close friend of Metochites, Joseph the Philosopher (Rhakendytes), in a poem on the usefulness of secular knowledge, underlines the auxiliary role

---

86   See Cacouros, "La philosophie et les sciences", pp. 1–51.

87   Richter, *Theodoros Dukas Laskaris*, pp. 226–27.

88   Ibid., pp. 217–23.

89   See Maximos Planoudes, *Letters*, no. 2, ed. Leone, p. 6, lines 11–7, line 2, who employs the passage of the Platonic *Timaeus* 90a, where man is called "a heavenly plant", as a proof of man's proclivity for searching the heavens.

90   George Pachymeres, *Quadrivium*, eds. Tannery/Stéphanou, p. 6, line 10: ὅτι δὲ τελείωσις ψυχῆς λογικῆς τὰ μαθήματα ἐμαρτύρησε Πλάτων.

91   Manuel Gabalas, *Letters*, no. B 35, ed. Reinsch, p. 144, lines 37–45.

92   Michael Gabras, *Letters*, no. 179, ed. Fatouros, vol. 2, p. 300, lines 58–65. It is significant that this letter is in all probability addressed to Metochites.

COSMIC VISION AND ITS SIGNIFICANCE 307

that knowledge of the natural world might have for a man wishing to proceed towards God:

> O spectator, behold the reason of the things belonging to nature, which shine forth, proceeding out of the sanctuary of the wise, powerful and great cause of all things; that cause reaches everything: the earth, fire and everything in between; this takes place in accordance with the commands of God who creates everything ... Nature is the instrument of the supreme cause that brings everything into light.[93]

Another important testimony to those intellectual trends of the early 14th c. is a somewhat mysterious dialogue entitled *Mousokles*. *Mousokles* forms part of a series of three anonymous dialogues of the early 14th c. (*Hermodotos, Mousokles* and *Hermippos*) that are preserved in MS Vaticanus graecus 175.[94] All the other MSS preserving the three texts are copies of the Vatican MS. The *terminus ante quem* for the date of the three dialogues' composition is 1322, when the Vatican MS was copied.[95] The various stylistic and lexical correspondences displayed by all three texts suggest that they were written by the same author, whose identity has not been securely established as of yet. Kourousis argued for the attribution of these texts to the *aktouarios* John Zacharias,[96] a contemporary of Theodore Metochites, while Hohlweg attributed them, though with reservations, to Nikephoros Gregoras,[97] Metochites' student. Other scholars believed that their author was John Katrones, an otherwise unknown Byzantine author, whose name was allegedly preserved in the *inscriptio* of MS Turin, Biblioteca nazionale, Taurinensis C VI 26,[98] which was afterwards destroyed by a fire. Below we shall try to identify some signs of Metochites' influence on *Mousokles*.

In the dialogue two persons, a certain Mousokles and his anonymous friend, discuss which way of life may be considered the best; *Mousokles* deals with the perennial question of the happy life. The pseudo-classical setting of the dialogue is enhanced by several loans from the dialogues of Lucian. The theme

---

93 Treu, "Der Philosoph Joseph", p. 40, lines 38–53: Ἄθρει, θεατά, καὶ φυσικῶν τοὺς λόγους/ ἄνωθεν ἐκλάμποντας ἐκ τῶν ἀδύτων/ τῆς πανσθενουργοῦ καὶ σοφῆς πανταιτίας καὶ μέχρι γῆς πυρός τε καὶ τῶν ἐν μέσῳ/ ἱκνουμένης νεύματι τοῦ παντεργάτου/ ... φύσις γὰρ ἐστιν ὄργανον τεχνουργίας/ τῆς παραγωγοῦ τῶν ἁπάντων αἰτίας.

94 Vatican City, Biblioteca Apostolica Vaticana, Vaticanus gr. 175.

95 *Mousokles*, ed. Schönberger, p. 8.

96 Kourousis, Τὸ ἐπιστολάριον Γεωργίου Λακαπηνοῦ-Ἀνδρονίκου Ζαρίδου, pp. 258–330.

97 Hohlweg, "Drei anonyme Texte", 15–45 and Kourousis, "Ὁ ἀκτουάριος Ἰωάννης Ζαχαρίας", 44–60.

98 *Mousokles*, ed. Schönberger, p. 9.

308　　　　　　　　　　　　　　　　　　　　　　　　　　　　　　POLEMIS

of the dialogue is explicitly stated by the initial phrase of Mousokles' friend: "Which life is perfect and how should one describe the man leading such a life?"[99] Mousokles points out that no way of life is devoid of tribulations; all the various human lives, even if happy, are mixed with a certain portion of unhappiness: "Is there any life devoid of suffering, offering to men only pleasures? ... All human affairs are full of tribulations; no human thing can be perfect in every respect; everything has a certain portion of suffering within it."[100] This passage may be compared with several corresponding extracts from the works of Theodore Metochites, where the same pessimistic view of human life is expressed. One of the most characteristic may be found in his *Poem* 17, where Metochites argues that no good thing which is not mixed with a certain bad thing exists in human life.[101] In the same section of the dialogue the author of *Mousokles* does not fail to point out that even Homer is of the same view:

> The divine Homer was not unaware of this, but very wisely realized it in advance of us. He seems to hint at it through the parable of the two jars. It is very difficult to find someone who was able to draw a portion of good things unmixed with any evil. Most people drew just what was bad. Almost all men are placed among those who have a mixture of good and bad things; therefore, sometimes they suffer, sometimes they rejoice. No good thing is stable; no good thing that is not accompanied by something bad is to be found.[102]

It is noteworthy that in *Poem* 15, Metochites quotes the same Homeric verses in order to support his pessimistic view of human life.[103] The verses in ques-

---

99　　*Mousokles*, ed. Schönberger, p. 102, lines 1–2: Τί ποτ' ἂν, ὦ Μουσόκλεις, εἴη τὸ τοῦ ἀρίστου βίου, καὶ τίνα χρὴ τὸν οὕτω βιοῦντα καλεῖν.

100　　*Mousokles*, ed. Schönberger, p. 104, lines 64–70: ποία γὰρ αὐτῶν τὸ ἡδὺ ἀμιγὲς τοῦ λυποῦντος παρέχεται; ... τῶν γὰρ ἀνθρωπείων, εἴ τις ἀκριβῶς ἐθέλει σκοπεῖν, οὐδὲν ἀκήρατον οὐδὲ ἀγαθὸν οὐδὲ τέλειον πεφυκός ἐστι, μικτὴν δέ τινα καὶ ἴσην ἐφ' ἑκάτερα δύναμιν ἐπεσπάσαντο.

101　　Theodore Metochites, *Poems*, no. 17, ed. Polemis, p. 298, lines 369–371: πολέες δ' ἕτεροι γ' ἔασ' οὐμοῖα/ ἐσθλά τε πολλὰ ξὺν θ' ἅμα λευγαλέα λαχόντες,/ παλαιοί τε νέοι τ' οὔτις ἀμιγέ' ἐς τέλος ἐσθλά.

102　　*Mousokles*, ed. Schönberger, p. 106, lines 93–102: ἀλλ' οὐδὲ ὁ θεῖος "Ομηρος ἀγνοῶν τοῦτ' ἐτύγχανεν, ἀλλὰ σοφῶς ἄγαν καὶ πρότερος ἡμῶν τοῦτο κατεῖδε. Τῷ γὰρ ἀπορρήτῳ τοῖν δυοῖν πίθοιν τοῦτ' αἰνιττόμενος φαίνεται. καὶ ἔστι μὲν ἔργον εὑρεῖν ὅστις ἀμιγὲς ἔσπασε τἀγαθόν, τοῦ δὲ χείρονος καὶ πλείους ὡς εἰπεῖν ἔτυχον, πᾶς δέ τις σχεδὸν τῆς μικτῆς μοίρας λαχὼν ἄλλοτε μέν τε κακῷ ὅ γε τείρεται, ἄλλοτε δ' ἐσθλῷ. Οὕτως οὐδὲν μόνιμον οὐδὲ ἄπειρον κακῶν τῷ βίῳ συμπλέκεται.

103　　Theodore Metochites, *Poems*, no. 15, ed. Polemis, pp. 262–63, lines 74–80: καί θ' ὁπόσοισι μακάρτατα δῶκε ῥὰ θεὸς πρήγματ' ἐνὶ βιότοιο παλινστροφέουσι κελεύθοις/ κεδνά τ' ἀρίτιμα, ὄλβιά τε πλεῦν ἠὲ κατ' ἄλλους,/ ἀλλά τ' ἀναμὶξ δὴ πέλεθ' ἀπάντεσσιν ἀγαθά,/ σὺν δέ τε χερείω,

COSMIC VISION AND ITS SIGNIFICANCE   309

tion come from *Iliad* 24, 527–30. In *Ethikos*, Metochites repeats his view that
all human beings are unstable in terms rather similar to those used by the
anonymous author of *Mousokles*: "everything in this life is fluid, and we can
trust nothing at all".[104] The result of the investigation of the best way of life
undertaken by Mousokles and his friend is self-evident: only the sage is happy.
Proceeding further, *Mousokles*' interlocutor asks his wise mentor whether it is
possible for the man who practices justice and prudence, those virtues necessary for the practical life, to be considered happy. Mousokles almost denies this
possibility, arguing that these virtues are mere names; no one has found such
virtues exemplified perfectly in any man:

> Only the life devoted to the knowledge of real things is perfect, only that
> life is accompanied by virtue. – But if somebody is prudent or just, is he
> not to be placed among virtuous men? – I don't know if anyone, after
> making copious investigations, may find such a man ... those virtues are
> mere names, we cannot see them put into practice, so as to be in a posi-
> tion to understand their true nature. We are not able to accomplish them;
> therefore, we ignore even their definition. I leave aside those who argue
> that the purpose of human life is the acquisition of pleasure.[105]

The conclusion of the author of *Mousokles* is that "I do not deny their existence, but I do not know where on earth they are to be found, although I am
sure that they are to be found somewhere."[106] Metochites' view is almost identical: the virtues considered necessary for the happy conduct of a life in this

---

τάδε τ' ἀεὶ πέλεται πλεῦν' ἐσθλῶν,/ ἀτὰρ ὁ μέν γε ποιητὴς φάτο δύο πάρ' ἐσθλῷ/ δῆθ' ἐνὶ πήμαθ'
ἕπεσθ' ἄμαδις κράματ' οὐλέθρια. The same is written by Theodore Metochites, *Miscellanea*,
119, eds. Müller/Kiessling, pp. 813–20. The Homeric image was quite widespread in the
literature of the period, see, e.g., Manuel Gabalas, *Letters*, no. B 24, ed. Reinsch, p. 125, lines
39–40: ἐπὶ τὴν καθαρὰν καὶ ἀμιγῆ κακῶν καὶ τοὺς διπλοῦς πίθους τῶν παρόντων διεκφεύγουσαν.

104   Theodore Metochites, *Orations*, no. 10, 16, eds. Polemis/Kaltsogianni, p. 359, lines 15–17: τὰ
πάνθ' ἡμῖν κατὰ τὸν βίοτον τόνδε ῥεῖ, καὶ οὐδὲν πιστὸν παντάπασιν· οὐδὲ μόνιμον, οὔθ' ἵσταται.

105   *Mousokles*, ed. Schönberger, p. 114, lines 226–42: Μόνον οὖν τοῦτον ἄριστον βίον λέγομεν,
τὸν περὶ τὴν τῶν ὄντων γνῶσιν ἔχοντα καὶ τοῦτον μεθ' ἑαυτοῦ συμπεριφέρειν τὴν ἀρετήν; εἰ δὲ
σωφροσύνην τις ἢ δικαιοσύνην ἀσκεῖ, οὐ καὶ τοῦτον πρὸς ἀρετὴν εὖ πεφυκέναι φήσομεν; Οὐδέπω
οἶδα, εἴ τινα τοῦτον ἀνερευνώμενος δύναι' ἂν ἐξευρεῖν ... ταύτας δὲ ὀνόματα ἄλλως οὔσας ἔργοις
οὐκ ἂν σαφῶς ὁποῖαί τινές εἰσιν εὑρεῖν ἔχοιμεν, ἀλλὰ τοσοῦτ' ἀπέχομεν ταύτας ἀσκεῖν, ὥστ' οὐδ'
ἴσμεν, ὅ,τι εἰσὶ τὴν ἀρχήν. Παρεὶς γὰρ τοὺς τὴν ἡδονὴν μᾶλλον διατεινομένους τέλος εἶναι τὸ
ἄριστον.

106   *Mousokles*, ed. Schönberger, p. 116, lines 260–62: οὐ μὴν οὐδ' ἀπαγορεύω ταύτας ὅλως συνί-
στασθαι, ἀλλ' εἰσὶ μέν, οὐκ οἶδα δὲ οἷς τῶν ἐν γῇ ληπταί.

310 POLEMIS

world are not to be encountered among men, at least not in their perfect form. This is what Metochites writes:

> I often drew inferences and examined carefully within myself this political virtue and the extent to which it reforms the soul. Everyone honors it with great praise, and they elaborate and describe it with detailed words, even though until today it is truly impossible to discern it in anyone in its entirety, nor from the beginning of time did anyone succeed in employing it perfectly, possessing it fully.[107]

Further on he adds that there is a danger that one may consider any quest for virtue futile.[108] The author of Mousokles is full of praise for the man who devotes himself to the scientific study of the world, i.e. the sage, who turns his undivided attention to the *vita contemplativa*; this is the only happy man, since he is concerned with unearthing the treasure hidden within him, i.e. the spark of the spirit:

> Only the man choosing such a life may be considered wise and happy; he is a true man, who has not concealed his spark of reason, but has transformed it into a great fire which he caused to rise up high, becoming similar to God as far as possible. He is transformed into an eye looking at the decorous disposition of the whole creation. Those who have failed to do this resemble a flock of sheep according to the comic poet, living limited by their senses, which need a measure of knowledge without reason.[109]

---

107 The translation is by Xenophontos in, Theodore Metochites, *On Morals*, p. 135. The relevant text of Theodore Metochites, *Orations*, no. 10, 59, eds. Polemis/Kaltsogianni, p. 392, lines 21–27, is the following: πολλάκις δὲ αὐτὸς εἴκασα, κατασκοπούμενος ἐν ἐμαυτῷ τὴν πολιτικὴν ταύτην ἀρετήν· καὶ ὅση ψυχῆς κατόρθωσις, εὐφημίᾳ μὲν ἁπάσῃ πάντων τιμώντων· καὶ λόγοις μὲν ἐντελῶς ἀποδεδειγμένην τὲ καὶ ἀνευρημένην· οὐδέπω δὲ ὡς ἀληθῶς καὶ τήμερον, παντάπασιν ἔν τισιν ἐγνωσμένην, μηδ' ὅντινα ἄρα τῶν ἐξ ἀρχῆς· ἄνθρωπον παντελῆ κατειργασμένον ταύτην καὶ κτησάμενον. See also Metochites, *Miscellanea*, 81, 2, ed. Wahlgren, p. 198, lines 13–17: Τὸ δὲ παντὸς μᾶλλον ἀδύνατον τῇ φύσει καὶ κατ' ἀνθρώπους, ὅπου γε μηδ' ἄνθρωπον ἕνα, μηδένα μάλιστα δὴ καὶ σωφρονικὸν ἐκ φύσεως οἴκοθεν καὶ λόγου παιδείᾳ καὶ ἀσκήσει κατορθούμενον, ῥᾴδιόν ἐστιν ἑαυτῷ σύμφωνον εἶναι καὶ διὰ πάντων εἰς τὴν τοῦ ἀγαθοῦ σπουδὴν ὅμοιον ἑαυτῷ καὶ τέλειον.

108 Metochites, *Orations*, no. 10, 61, eds. Polemis/Kaltsogianni, p. 394, lines 29–31: ἀλλά τινα πλάνην οὖσαν τὴν εὐφημίαν καὶ ζήτησιν τἀγαθοῦ· καὶ σύνθημα ἀνθρώπων· καὶ λόγον ἄλλως.

109 *Mousokles*, ed. Schönberger, p. 116, lines 284–118, line 288: καὶ δικαίως ἂν καλοῖτο μόνος σοφός, μόνος εὐδαίμων ὁ τοῦτον ἑλόμενος, τὸ τοῦ ἀνθρώπου φέρων ἀξίωμα, καὶ τὸ ἐνὸν ζώπυρον οὐ καταχωννύς, ἀλλ' αἴρων ὑψοῦ, θεῷ μὲν κατὰ τὸ δυνατὸν ὁμοιούμενος, ὀφθαλμὸς ὢν τῆς τῶν ὄντων διακοσμήσεως. Οἱ δὲ μὴ τὴν ἀρχὴν πρὸς αὐτὸν ὁρμήσαντες οὐδὲν ἀλλ' ἢ κατὰ τὸν κωμικὸν πρόβατα ἄλλως περινοστοῦσιν αἰσθήσει ζῶντες ἀλόγων τινῶν δεομένῃ γνώσεως.

COSMIC VISION AND ITS SIGNIFICANCE 311

The same view is expounded by Metochites in *Ethikos*: wise men uncover on purpose the spark of reason which is hidden inside our body, resembling a drift of ash, and they make it visible.[110] The same view is expounded by Metochites' Introduction to the *Stoicheiosis Astronomike*.[111] As we see, both the anonymous author of *Mousokles* and Metochites consider the man who reveals his hidden spiritual treasure as the only true man; he is able to attain true happiness.

These correspondences between the text of *Mousokles* and the various works of Metochites are rather striking. One may justifiably argue that the author of *Mousokles* deliberately presented Mousokles as a spokesman for the main views of Metochites. We may even assume that the main interlocutor of *Mousokles* is a literary *persona* of Metochites himself. The anonymous author taking advantage of the key theories of Metochites presents a convincing picture of that author, who supposedly defended his main philosophical tenets in front of a friend during a discussion. This is also reminiscent of a similar instance in Nikephoros Gregoras' dialogue *Phlorentios*. In this dialogue all the main protagonists of the Byzantine literary scene of the second quarter of the 14th c. take part under pseudonyms. For example, Gregoras himself takes the name of Nikostratos, Barlaam of Calabria is disguised under the name of Xenophanes, and Metochites takes the name of Metrodoros.[112] The case of *Mousokles* seems to be rather similar. The anonymous author of this dialogue recasts the main theories of Metochites in dialogue form, giving us a vivid picture of the intellectual discussions held among various scholars in the early Palaeologan period. If our interpretation of the text is correct, then *Mousokles* may be read as the dialogue counterpart of Metochites' *Ethikos*, the main (and only) text of that period where the problems of the happy life and of the contemplation of the world are discussed so extensively. We are not in a position to identify the reasons that led the anonymous author of *Mousokles*

---

110 Theodore Metochites, *Orations*, no. 10, 98, eds. Polemis/Kaltsogianni p. 426, lines 4–8.

111 Theodore Metochites, *Stoicheiosis Astronomike*, 1, 2, 1, ed. Bydén, p. 443, lines 2–9: Φιλοσοφία τοίνυν κάλλιστόν ἐστιν … καὶ τὴν ἐκ Θεοῦ μεγαλοδωρεὰν αὐτῆς τῆς λογικῆς περιουσίας καὶ χρήσεως, καθ' ἣν καὶ ὑπὲρ τἄλλα πάντα ζῷα προδήλως εὐδαιμονοῦμεν, ὑπανοίξασα καὶ ἀναδειξάσασα καὶ ὥσπερ κρυπτόμενον θεῖον πῦρ τῇ σαρκικῇ σποδιᾷ καὶ ταῖς ὑλικαῖς τοῦ σώματος ἐπιχώσεσιν ἀνορύξασα καὶ ἀνάψασα.

112 It is noteworthy that several ideas of Metochites recur in the texts of his student, see for example Nikephoros Gregoras, *Florentius*, ed. Leone, p. 84, lines 628–31: οὐδὲν γὰρ ἐν ἀνθρώποις ἀληθὲς οὐδὲ βέβαιον, ἀλλ' ὥσπερ ἐν ἀδήλοις πελάγεσι κυκᾶται καὶ ναυαγεῖ τὰ ἀνθρώπινα καὶ βαθύς τις πλάνος καταχορεύει τῆς ἀνθρωπίνης σπουδῆς ἄνω καὶ κάτω σοβῶν καὶ ταράττων πᾶσαν βουλευτηρίων ἰσχὺν καὶ κύβων δίκην ἀνατρέπων τὰ δόγμασιν ἰσχυροῖς κυρούμενα σκέμματα. One has the impression of reading Metochites himself speaking through the mouth of Gregoras.

312   POLEMIS

to give such a prominent place to the defense of Metochites' theories about the contemplative life in his text. Did he want to erect a literary monument to the erudition and the dialectic skill of the powerful minister of the Emperor Andronikos II Palaiologos in order to flatter him? Was he really convinced and impressed by Metochites' arguments in favour of the so-called *vita contemplativa*? These questions cannot be definitively answered; however, the case of *Mousokles* may be regarded as an eloquent proof of Metochites' influence upon his contemporary *literati*, who were eager to imitate him and propagate his main theoretical positions. What must be noted, is the insistence of *Mousokles*' author on two points: the value of the contemplation of the world and the instability of human life. Those two points were central in Metochites' thought as well.

Another exponent of Metochites' ideas concerning the importance of the contemplation of nature in the 14th c. was his student Nikephoros Gregoras. In the Prologue to his *Roman History* Gregoras points out that the main function of history is to impress upon human minds the idea that the heavenly bodies exist forever, moving in the same way throughout all time:

> How were men in a position to know that heaven had moved in the same direction since its creation always, winding the ways of the sun, the moon and all the stars without any pause, creating a variety of decorous movements, replete with proper rhythm; these heavenly bodies declare the glory of God, night and day forever.[113]

The same view is repeated in the preface to book XII of Gregoras' *Roman History*, where the historian attempts to make a new start in his narrative:

> History permits us to read the eternal circles of the creatures as a book; through history men long since dead are able to speak with us who live and with all future generations.[114]

---

113   Nikephoros Gregoras, *Roman History*, ed. Schopen, vol. 1, pp. 4–5: Ποῦ γὰρ ἂν ᾔδεσαν ἄνθρωποι, τῆς ἱστορίας οὐκ οὔσης, ὡς ὁ μὲν οὐρανὸς τὴν αὐτὴν ταύτην ἀρχῆθεν ἀεὶ καὶ ἀεικίνητον κινούμενος κίνησιν, ἥλιον καὶ σελήνην καὶ πάντας ἀστέρας διηνεκῶς ἐξελίττει πρὸς ποικιλίαν ὁμοίως εὔτακτόν τε καὶ εὔρυθμον καὶ ὁμοίως τὴν τοῦ Θεοῦ διηγεῖται δόξαν ἐφ' ἡμέρᾳ καὶ νυκτὶ δι' αἰῶνος. On the Roman History of Gregoras see chapter 4 in this volume.

114   Nikephoros Gregoras, *Roman History*, ed. Schopen, vol. 2, p. 573: Αὕτη γὰρ ἀναγινώσκειν διδάσκει καθάπερ βιβλίον τῶν αἰωνίων ἔργων τοὺς κύκλους καὶ διὰ ταύτης οἱ πάλαι θανόντες ὁμιλοῦσι τοῖς ζῶσί τε καὶ ἀεὶ γιγνομένοις ὡς ἀεὶ παρόντες.

COSMIC VISION AND ITS SIGNIFICANCE

This argument, which perhaps appears somewhat naïve, is unusual in the *prooemia* of Byzantine historians. Hohlweg has made valuable comments on the above quoted texts of Gregoras, arriving at the conclusion that the author took advantage of a variety of sources, Diodorus Siculus most prominent among them.[115] There are two points of contact between Gregoras' second prooemium and the thought of Metochites, who devoted an entire essay of his *Miscellanea* to the theme of the usefulness of history. There Metochites, like Gregoras, points out that through history man is able to come into contact with the men of old and to take advantage of their advice. He states that history is a crucial pursuit; through history men are able to come into contact not only with mere old people who are experienced due to their age, but with the best old men of all ages, the most prudent and experienced; thus, we have the opportunity to learn everything and how we must lead our life.[116]

The second point of contact with Gregoras is Metochites' view, expounded in the same essay, that history may help those who are studying the nature of things. According to Metochites, the man who occupies himself with history will be helped in every respect and may be aided as far as the study of beings is concerned.[117]

The insistence of Metochites on the close relations between history and the so-called *theoria ton onton* may be explained if we recall the fact that Metochites was not only a fervent partisan of the *vita contemplativa*, but also an innovator of astronomy. In all his works Metochites underlined the importance of this science; he believes that astronomy, leading man to the discovery of the harmonic laws governing the universe, helps him appreciate the magnitude of creation and the benevolence of its creator. In his *Poem* 10, dealing with the harmonic science, Metochites once more expresses the same idea with that expounded by Gregoras in the preface to his historical work. Here is a characteristic extract from that poem:

> I can speak sincerely: I still preserve in my ears the powerful sound created by that science in our world; its sound is easily recognized through the ears of the mind; it sings through all creatures melodious songs,

---

115   Hohlweg, "Astronomie und Geschichtsbetrachtung bei Nikephoros Gregoras", pp. 51–63.
116   Theodore Metochites, *Miscellanea*, 111, eds. Müller/Kiessling, p. 747. One is reminded of Metochites' insistence in *Ethikos* that young men must come into contact with the wise men of old times through the books they have left us, see Theodore Metochites, *Orations*, no. 10, 32, eds. Polemis/Kaltsogianni, p. 370, lines 2–6.
117   Theodore Metochites, *Miscellanea*, 111, eds. Müller/Kiessling, p. 737.

easily perceptible by all prudent men; these songs declare the glory of our immortal, most powerful, and wise Lord.[118]

Gregoras does not fail to eulogize his deceased teacher Metochites for glorifying God by reviving the venerable science of astronomy. That is how he laments the loss of his teacher in *Roman History*: "How is it possible that this man is now dead, who, after finding heaven mute, managed to make him proclaim God's glory once more after so many years."[119] Accordingly, it may be useful to take a closer look at the text of the *Roman History* of Nikephoros Gregoras, in order to discover other traces of his teacher's influence, especially as far as the contemplation of the world is concerned.

There are several ideas of Metochites scattered throughout Gregoras' *Roman History*. According to Gregoras the world is a great theatre. This ancient philosophical idea is quite common in the works of Metochites and has been studied in depth by Beck;[120] we came across it previously, while discussing the basic tenets of Metochites' theory on the contemplation of the world. This is how Gregoras describes the theatre of the world:

> What happens in the human body is repeated in the case of the world. The whole world resembles a perfect human body, which has its own limbs. If something happens to our head or to our neck, the pain is much heavier in the legs and the ankles; the same occurs in the body of this world: the passions of the heavenly bodies move towards the earth and their effects are evident here.[121]

---

118 Theodore Metochites, *Poems*, trans. Polemis, p. 233. See also the text, Theodore Metochites, *Poems*, no. 10, ed. Polemis, pp. 210–11, lines 971–976: ὅττι κεν ἀτρεκέως ἐρέειν νύ τ' ἔχοιμι τόδε πλεῖν ἔμμεν' ἀν' οὔασι νουὸς ἀρίγνωτον πολυηχὲς τῆσδε σοφίης ἐμμελὲς εἰν κόσμοιο κράτος πρήγμασ' ἄπασι βοάον ἐχέφροσιν ἱμερόεντα σύμφων' ᾄσματα δόξαν ἀνακράγοντ' ἄνακτος παμμεδέοντος ἀθανάτοιο σοφοῦ δαμιουργοῦ.

119 Nikephoros Gregoras, *Roman History*, ed. Schopen, vol. 2, p. 479: "Ὦ πῶς ὁ σιγῶντας τοὺς οὐρανοὺς εὑρηκὼς ἐκ πολλοῦ, ἔπειτα τὴν τοῦ Θεοῦ διηγεῖσθαι δόξαν αὐτὸς παρεσκευακώς, νῦν ἐν τάφῳ σιγᾷ; Gregoras stresses the same point earlier in his address to Metochites (ibid., 1, p. 326: Ποῦ δ' οὐκ ἂν ἐλαύνοι σχετλιότητος, οὐρανοὺς μὲν διηγεῖσθαι δόξαν Θεοῦ περιηχοῦντας πᾶσαν γῆν, ἡμᾶς δὲ κωφεύειν οὐκ ἐπαΐοντας ἄττα φασίν, ἀλλ' ἄστροις τὸ θρυλούμενον τεκμαίρεσθαι τὴν τούτων ἐπιστήμην;).

120 Beck, *Theodoros Metochites*, pp. 96–114.

121 Nikephoros Gregoras, *Roman History*, ed. Schopen, vol. 1, pp. 108–109: "Ὁ γὰρ ἐν ἑνὸς ἀνθρώπου σώματι, τοῦτο κἂν τῷ τοῦ κόσμου σώματι παντὶ γίγνοιτ' ἄν. Ἐν γὰρ ὁ κόσμος σῶμα συμφυὲς ἐκ μερῶν καὶ μελῶν ὡς ὁ ἄνθρωπος φάναι συγκείμενος, καὶ ὥσπερ ἐνταῦθα τῆς κεφαλῆς ἢ τοῦ τραχήλου τὸ πάθος ἐνεργεστέραν πρὸς τὴν κνήμην καὶ τὸν ἀστράγαλον τὴν κάκωσιν ἐξετόξευσεν, οὕτω κἂν τῷ τοῦ κόσμου σώματι τὰ τῶν οὐρανίων φωστήρων παθήματα κινούμενα πρὸς τὴν γῆν ἀπερείδονται κἀνταῦθα δημοσιεύουσι τὴν ἐνέργειαν.

COSMIC VISION AND ITS SIGNIFICANCE   315

Another idea common to Metochites and Gregoras is that no happiness is perfect. Metochites stresses that no happiness is unadulterated. Good things are mixed with bad. We have already quoted some relevant verses of Metochites clarifying his positions, while discussing *Mousokles*.[122] The pessimistic approach to human life of his teacher helps Gregoras interpret various events of his contemporary life. This is how Gregoras describes certain events that took place in the Bulgarian kingdom: "In most cases great successes are followed by misfortune, which is like a sword cutting and destroying that happiness; and that law did not fail to make its appearance in our case too."[123] Narrating the story of the unfortunate general Alexios Philanthropenos, who was involved in a conspiracy against the Emperor Andronikos II Palaiologos and was blinded after having defeated the Turks, Gregoras once more expounds the pessimistic principle of his teacher we came across before: "Happiness must be mixed with sadness. Greeks say that the third jar must be full of unhappiness. Fortune was kind towards him at the beginning and gave him great pleasure, but afterwards she attacked him with all her force."[124] Many years later the blind Philanthropenos was restored to the emperor's favour thanks to the intervention of the ecumenical patriarch. This development led Gregoras to make the following comment: "I wondered how human affairs are full of disasters and lack any stability. Fortune always changes and destroys them, transforming human life into a tragic stage as if playing with it. In spite of this, the virtue of his knowledge remained unchanged".[125] Narrating the story of the Caesar Alexios Strategopoulos, who after liberating Constantinople from the Latin yoke was made prisoner by the soldiers of the despot of Epiros, Gregoras does not miss the opportunity to repeat the main teaching of Metochites: "Nothing is true and certain. Human affairs resemble a ship that is wrecked. Human experience and knowledge are led astray. Things and the decisions of

---

122   See note 103 above.

123   Nikephoros Gregoras, *Roman History*, ed. Schopen, vol. 1, pp. 132–33: Ἐπεὶ δ' ὡς τὰ πολλὰ ταῖς μεγάλαις εὐφροσύναις ἐπιφύονται λῦπαι, καθάπερ τινὰ ξίφη πολέμια τὴν τῆς εὐθυμίας ἐκείνης κατάστασιν ἐπιταράττοντα καὶ συγχέοντα, οὐδ' ἐνταῦθα τὸ ἔθος ἐπιλελοίπει.

124   Nikephoros Gregoras, *Roman History*, ed. Schopen, vol. 1, p. 196: Ἀλλ' ἐπειδὴ ἔδει ἀνακεκρᾶσθαι τοῖς λυπηροῖς τὰ ἡδέα καὶ τρίτον πίθον ἥκιστά φασιν Ἑλλήνων παῖδες ἐν Διὸς εἶναι κακῶν ἀμιγῆ, ἱλαρὰ μὲν καὶ τούτῳ δείκνυσιν ἡ τύχη τὰ πρόθυρα καὶ πλήρη χαρᾶς, μεστὸν δ' ὅλον τὸν οἶκον κακῶν ἀναρρήγνυσι κατ' αὐτοῦ. The same is repeated ibid., 1, pp. 122–23, and p. 456 and in Nikephoros Gregoras, *Letters*, no. 107, ed. Leone, p. 278, lines 6–9.

125   Nikephoros Gregoras, *Roman History*, ed. Schopen, vol. 1, p. 361: Καὶ μέντοι καὶ ἐθαύμαζον, πῶς τῶν ἀνθρωπίνων πραγμάτων οὐδὲν κεκτημένων ἀκήρατον, οὐδὲ μόνιμον, ἀλλὰ τῆς τύχης διηνεκῶς ἀκμαζούσης ἐν τῇ τούτων μεταβολῇ καὶ φθορᾷ καὶ παιζούσης τὸν βίον ταῖς ἀμοιβαῖς καθάπερ σκηνὴν τραγικὴν ἀκήρατος ἡ τῆς τούτου γνώσεως ἔμεινεν ἀρετὴ καὶ στερροτέρα τῆς τύχης. This is repeated in Nikephoros Gregoras, *Letters*, no. 9, ed. Leone, p. 40, lines 20–24.

316 POLEMIS

men who try to think over the situation are turned upside down; it resembles
what happens with those who play dice."[126] History's usefulness is that she
teaches men that all human affairs lack stability: "Man is taught by history that
no human thing is stable and fortune has no stable foundations; therefore,
he is afraid even of the slightest change of the situation, which can destroy
everything, like those who play dice".[127] One has the impression that Gregoras
shares his teacher's fear for the constant changes in human fortune, as we discussed above.

One of the reasons for Metochites' pessimistic attitude towards human life
is his realization that in this world very often immoral and uneducated men
manage to overcome and surpass those men who are perfect in most respects,
being prominent because of the exceeding qualities of their learning and character. In *Ethikos* he points out that the unscrupulous castigate the perfect and
they leave nothing undisturbed.[128]

This opinion is shared by Gregoras. This is how he introduces his narrative
about the outbreak of the civil war in 1321:

> Those men who took care to lead a virtuous life and are well-educated,
> obeying the strict Dorian laws, are unlucky; they do not succeed in their
> endeavours and the end of their actions is contrary to the initial purpose
> of the actors. This is due to God's decision high up. On the other hand,
> those men devoid of any natural qualities, being inconspicuous, ill and
> servants of the evil spirits, are in a position to surpass those prudent
> men, although they are most imprudent. Men who are prone to ridiculing
> their fellows, having the disposition of a slave, defeat those serious and
> good men.[129]

---

126 Nikephoros Gregoras, *Roman History*, ed. Schopen, vol. 1, pp. 90–91: Οὕτως οὐδὲν ἐν ἀνθρώποις ἀληθές, οὐδὲ βέβαιον, ἀλλ ἐν ἀδήλοις ὥσπερ πελάγεσι συγκυκᾶται καὶ ναυαγεῖ τὰ ἀνθρώπινα καὶ βαθύς τις πλάνος καταχορεύει τῆς ἀνθρωπίνης ἐμπειρίας καὶ γνώσεως, ἄνω καὶ κάτω
σοβῶν καὶ ταράττων πᾶσαν βουλευτηρίων σπουδὴν καὶ δίκην κύβων ἀνατρέπων τὰ δόγμασιν
ἰσχυροῖς κυρούμενα σκέμματα. It might not be a mere coincidence that Gregoras compares
Strategopoulos with Hannibal and Pompeius (ibid., 1, p. 91). The example of Pompeius
was adduced by Metochites, *Miscellanea*, 11–12, ed. Wahlgren, pp. 84, line 1–86, line 19 and
ibid., 105, eds. Müller/Kiessling, pp. 690–96.

127 Nikephoros Gregoras, *Roman History*, ed. Schopen, vol. 1, p. 575: Μηδὲν γὰρ τῶν ἐν βίῳ μόνιμον εἶναι καὶ βέβαιον, μηδὲ τὰς κρηπῖδας ἐπ' ἀσφαλοῦς ἑστάναι τῆς τύχης παιδευόμενος ἐκ τῆς
ἱστορίας, δέδιε καὶ βραχεῖαν καιροῦ ῥοπὴν ῥᾷστα δυναμένην ἀνατρέπειν ἅπαντα, καθάπερ οἱ
τοὺς κύβους ἐν τῷ παίζειν ἀναρρίπτοντες.

128 Theodore Metochites, *Orations*, no. 10, 62, eds. Polemis/Kaltsogianni, p. 394, lines 1–2.

129 Nikephoros Gregoras, *Roman History*, ed. Schopen, vol. 1, pp. 316–17: καὶ κακοδαιμονοῦσι
μὲν ὅσοι πρὸς ἀρετὴν καὶ παιδείαν ἐρρύθμισαν ἑαυτούς, καὶ τὸ ἑαυτῶν πρὸς τὴν Δώριον ὡς εἰπεῖν,

COSMIC VISION AND ITS SIGNIFICANCE 317

To give a last example of Gregoras' dependence on his teacher: Gregoras believes that the choice of the best life is a process that becomes easier as soon as a man gets accustomed to the new habits: "Custom is something easy, having no pains at all. If somebody decides to lead a perfect life because of his good intentions, (becoming accustomed to it), he will be able to live without any pains and enjoy an immortal pleasure living in his mortal body."[130] This idea is rather prominent in Metochites' *Ethikos*.[131]

There is no doubt that the ideas of Metochites' contemporaries concerning the value of the contemplation of the world around us were developed under the (direct or indirect) influence of, or in dialogue with, Metochites. The case of Nikephoros Gregoras speaks volumes for his dependence on his teacher. But as that very case indicates, the evaluation of the contemplation of the world by Metochites' contemporaries is very often coupled with a certain awareness of the trials and tribulations of man's life here on Earth. This pessimistic approach to human life was probably the most enduring result of the teaching of Theodore Metochites. His attitude rendered the whole concept of the contemplation of the world rather problematic.

Bibliography

Primary Sources

Euripides, *Fragments*, ed. R. Kannicht, *Tragicorum veterum fragmenta*, vol. 5, *Euripides*, Pars prior, Göttingen 2004.

Euripides, *Kresphontes and Archelaos*, ed. A. Harder, *Euripides' Kresphontes and Archelaos*, Leiden 1985.

George Pachymeres, *Quadrivium*, eds. P. Tannery/P.E. Stéphanou, *Quadrivium de Georges Pachymère* (Studi e Testi, 94), Vatican City 1945.

ἁρμονίαν ἀπέξεσαν ἦθος, καὶ πᾶν ὅ,τι πράξαιεν πέρας εὑρίσκει σφαλερὸν καὶ μάλα πολεμιώτατον τοῖς ἀρχηγοῖς τῶν ἔργων βουλεύμασι, τοῦ Θεοῦ τοιαύτην τινὰ τὴν κρίσιν ἄνωθεν ταλαντεύοντος. Εὐδαιμονοῦσι δ' ὁπόσοι δυστυχεῖς τινες καὶ ἀφανεῖς καὶ παραπλῆγες καὶ Ἐρινννύων πεφύκασι θρέμματα, καὶ νικῶσιν ἀνὰ κράτος τοὺς ἔμφρονας ἄφρονες, καὶ κυριεύουσι τῶν κοσμίων καὶ εὐσχημόνων ἀνδρῶν ἐμπαῖκταί τινες καὶ οἰκότριβες ἄνθρωποι.

130 Nikephoros Gregoras, *Roman History*, ed. Schopen, vol. 2, p. 641: Οὕτω ῥᾴδιον ἡ συνήθεια καὶ κοῦφον καὶ οὐ σφόδρα ἐπίπονον, ὥστε καὶ εἴ τις, ἐκ προθέσεως ἀγαθῆς ὡρμημένος, τὸν ἄριστον ἕλοιτο βίον, ἀταλαίπωρον ἂν εἶναί οἱ εὐθὺς τοῦ λοιποῦ βίον τε ἀνύειν ἀνώδυνον καὶ ἡδονὴν ἀθάνατον ἐν θνητῷ κτᾶσθαι σώματι.

131 Theodore Metochites, *Orations*, no. 10, 47, eds. Polemis/Kaltsogianni, p. 381, lines 8–10: ὥστε οὐ μόνον κατὰ τὸν Πυθαγόραν ἔξεστιν εἰπεῖν, ὡς «ἑλοῦ βίον τὸν ἄριστον· τοῦτον δὲ ἡδὺν ἡ συνήθεια ποιήσει».

318 POLEMIS

George Sphranzes, *Chronicle*, ed. R. Maisano, *Giorgio Sfranze Cronaca* (Corpus Fontium Historiae Byzantinae, 29), Rome 1990.

Matthew of Ephesos (Manuel Gabalas), *Letters*, ed. & trans. D. Reinsch, *Die Briefe des Matthaios von Ephesos im Codex Vindobonensis Theol Gr. 174*, Berlin 1974.

Maximos Planoudes, *Letters*, ed. P.L.M. Leone, *Maximi monachi Planudis epistulae* (Classical and Byzantine Monographs, 18), Amsterdam 1991.

Michael Gabras, *Letters*, ed. G. Fatouros, *Die Briefe des Michael Gabras* (*ca. 1290–nach 1350*) (Wiener Byzantinistische Studien, 10), 2 vols., Vienna 1973.

Mousokles, eds. O./E. Schönberger, *Anonymus Byzantinus, Lebenslehre in drei Dialogen, Hermodotos, Musokles, Hermippos. Griechischer Text, Einleitung und Übersetzung*, Würzburg 2010.

Nicholas Lampenos, *Imperial oration for the emperor Andronikos*, ed. I. Polemis, Ὁ λόγιος Νικόλαος Λαμπηνὸς καὶ τὸ ἐγκώμιον αὐτοῦ εἰς Ἀνδρόνικον Β´ Παλαιολόγον, Athens 1992.

Nikephoros Choumnos, *On matter and species*, ed. L.G. Benakis, «Νικηφόρου Χούμνου, Περὶ τῆς ὕλης καὶ τῶν ἰδεῶν. Εἰσαγωγή, Κριτικὴ Ἔκδοση καὶ Νεοελληνικὴ μετάφραση», Φιλοσοφία 3 (1973), 339–81.

Nikephoros Gregoras, *Florentius*, ed. P.L.M. Leone, *Niceforo Gregora, Fiorenzo o Intorno alla Sapienza. Testo critico, introduzione, traduzione e commentario*, Naples 1975.

Nikephoros Gregoras, *Letters*, ed. P.A.M. Leone, *Nicephori Gregorae Epistulae*, 2 vols., Matino 1982–83.

Nikephoros Gregoras, *Roman History*, ed. L. Schopen, *Nicephori Gregorae Byzantina Historia* (Corpus Scriptorum Historiae Byzantinae, 19), 2 vols., Bonn 1829–30.

Philo Judaeus, *Opera*, eds. L. Cohn/P. Wendland, *Philonis Alexandrini opera quae supersunt*, 6 vols., Editio minor, Berlin 1896–1915.

Philo Judaeus, *Works*, ed. & trans. F.H. Colson (The Loeb Classical Library), vol. 7, Cambridge, MA/London 1984.

Plotinus, *Enneads*, eds. P. Henry/H.-R. Schwyzer, *Plotini opera*, vol. 1, Leiden 1951.

Presocratics, *Fragments*, ed. H. Diels, *Die Fragmente der Vorsokratiker*, vol. 1, Berlin [4]1922.

Sophocles, *The Oedipus Coloneus*, in R. Jebb (ed. & transl.), *Sophocles, The Plays and Fragments*, vol. 2, Cambridge 1928.

Theodore Metochites, *Miscellanea*, ed. & transl. K. Hult, *Theodore Metochites on the Human Condition and the Decline of Rome. Semeioseis Gnomikai 27–60. Critical Edition with Introduction, Translation, Notes, and Indexes* (Studia Graeca et Latina Gothoburgensia, 70), Gothenburg 2016.

Theodore Metochites, *Miscellanea*, eds. C.G. Müller/T. Kiessling, *Theodori Metochitae Miscellanea philosophica et historica*, Leipzig 1821 (repr. Amsterdam 1966).

Theodore Metochites, *Miscellanea*, ed. S. Wahlgren, *Theodore Metochites' Sententious Notes Semeioseis Gnomikai 61–70 & 72–81. A Critical Edition with Introduction,*

Translation, Notes, and Indexes (Studia Graeca et Latina Gothoburgensia, 71), Gothenburg 2018.

Theodore Metochites, *On Morals (Ethikos)*, ed. & trans. S. Xenophontos, *On Morals or Concerning Education Theodore Metochites* (Dumbarton Oaks Medieval Library, 61), Cambridge, MA/London 2020.

Theodore Metochites, *Orations*, eds. I. Polemis/E. Kaltsogianni, *Theodorus Metochites Orationes* (Bibliotheca Scriptorum Graecorum et Romanorum Teubneriana, 2031), Berlin/Boston 2019.

Theodore Metochites, *Poems*, ed. I. Polemis, *Theodori Metochitae carmina* (Corpus Christianorum. Series Graeca, 83), Turnhout 2015.

Theodore Metochites, *Poems*, trans. I. Polemis, *Theodore Metochites, Poems. Introduction, translation and notes* (Corpus Christianorum in Translation, 26), Turnhout 2017.

Theodore Metochites, *Stoicheiosis Astronomike*, ed. B. Bydén, *Theodore Metochites' Stoicheiosis Astronomike and the Study of Natural Philosophy and Mathematics in Early Palaiologan Byzantium* (Studia Graeca et Latina Gothoburgensia, 66), Gothenburg 2003.

Secondary Literature

Arendt, H., *The Life of the Mind*, San Diego/New York/London 1978.

Beck, H.-G., *Theodoros Metochites. Die Krise des byzantinischen Weltbildes im 14. Jahrhundert*, Munich 1952.

Betz, H.D., *Plutarch's Theological Writings and Early Christian Literature*, Leiden 1975.

Bousset, W., *Die Himmelreise der Seele (Sonderausgabe, Wissenschaftliche Buchgesellschaft)*, Darmstadt 1960.

Cacouros, M., "La philosophie et les sciences du *trivium* et du *quadrivium* à Byzance de 1204 à 1453 entre tradition et innovation: les textes et l'enseignement, les cas de l'école du Prodrome (Pétra)", in id./M.-H. Congourdeau (eds.), *Philosophie et Sciences à Byzance de 1204 à 1453. Les textes, les doctrines et leur transmission*. Actes de la Table Ronde organisée au XXᵉ Congrès International d'Études Byzantines (Paris 2001) (Orientalia Lovaniensia Analecta, 146), Leuven/Paris/Dudley, MA 2006.

Chenu, M.-D., *Nature, Man, and Society in the Twelfth-Century*, Toronto/Buffalo/London 1997.

Courcelle, P., *Connais-toi toi-même de Socrate à saint Bernard*, Paris 1974.

Culianu, I.P., *Psychanodia I. A Survey of the Evidence concerning the Ascension of the Soul and its Relevance*, Leiden 1983.

Daniélou, J., *Message évangelique et culture hellénistique aux IIᵉ et IIIᵉ siècles*, Paris 1961.

de Vries-van der Velden, E., *Théodore Métochite. Une réévaluation*, Amsterdam 1987.

Dreyfus, H.L./M.A. Wrathall (eds.), *A Companion to Heidegger*, Malden/Oxford/Victoria 2005.

Dreyfus, H.L./S.D. Kelly, *All Things Shining. Reading the Western Classics to Find Meaning in a Secular Age*, New York 2011.

Fenster, E., *Laudes Constantinopolitanae* (Miscellanea Byzantina Monacensia 9), Munich 1968.

Festugière, A.-J., *La Révélation d'Hermès trismégiste. II. Le Dieu cosmique*, Paris 1949.

Fryde, E., *The Early Palaeologan Renaissance (1261–c. 1360)* (The Medieval Mediterranean, 27), Leiden/Boston 2000.

Gaul, N., *Thomas Magistros und spätbyzantinische Sophistik. Studien zum Humanismus urbaner Eliten in den frühen Palaiologenzeit* (Mainzer Veröffentlichungen zur Byzantinistik, 10), Wiesbaden 2011.

Gigante, M., *Scritti sulla civilta letteraria bizantina*, Naples 1981.

Hohlweg, A., "Astronomie und Geschichtsbetrachtung bei Nikephoros Gregoras", in W. Seibt (ed.), *Geschichte und Kultur der Palaiologenzeit. Referate des Internationalen Symposions zu Ehren von Herbert Hunger (Wien, 30. November bis 3. Dezember 1994)* (Philosophisch-Historische Klasse Denkschriften, 241), Vienna 1996, 51–63.

Hohlweg, A., "Drei anonyme Texte suchen einen Autor", *Βυζαντιακά* 15 (1995), 15–45.

Hunger, H., "Theodoros Metochites als Vorläufer des Humanismus in Byzanz", *Byzantinische Zeitschrift* 45 (1952), 4–19.

Jaeger, W., *Aristotle. Fundamentals of the History of his Development*, transl. R. Robinson, Oxford 1962.

Joly, R., *La thème philosophique des genres de vie dans l'Antiquité Classique* (Académie Royale de Belgique, Mémoires, 51, Fasc. 3), Brussels 1956.

Kermanidis, M., *Episteme und Ästhetik der Raummodelierung in Literatur und Kunst des Theodoros Metochites. Ein frühpalaiologischer Byzantiner im Bezug zur Frühen Neuzeit* (Byzantinisches Archiv, 37), Berlin/Boston 2020.

Kourousis, S.I., "Ὁ ἀκτουάριος Ἰωάννης Ζαχαρίας συγγραφεὺς ἀποδοθέντων αὐτῷ μὴ ἰατρικῶν πονημάτων", *Ἀθηνᾶ* 82 (1997/1998), 27–77.

Kourousis, S.I., *Τὸ ἐπιστολάριον Γεωργίου Λακαπηνοῦ-Ἀνδρονίκου Ζαρίδου (1299–1315ca.) καὶ ὁ ἰατρός-ἀκτουάριος Ἰωάννης Ζαχαρίας (1275 ca.–1328/;). Μελέτη φιλολογική* (Ἀθηνᾶ. Σειρὰ διατριβῶν καὶ μελετημάτων, 23), Athens 1984.

Lovejoy, A.O., *The Great Chain of Being. A Study of the History of an Idea*, Cambridge, MA 1936.

Medvedev, I.P., "Neue philosophische Ansätze im späten Byzanz", *Jahrbuch der Österreichischen Byzantinistik* 31/2(1981), 529–48.

Medvedev, I.P., *Vizantijskij Gumanizm XIV–XV vv.*, Saint Petersburg 1997.

Melzer, A.M., *Philosophy Between the Lines. The Lost History of Esoteric Writing*, Chicago/London 2014.

Meyendorff, J., "Spiritual Trends in Byzantium in the Late Thirteenth and Early Fourteenth Century" in P.A. Underwood (ed.), *The Kariye Djami*, vol. 4: *Studies in the Art of Kariye Djami and Its Intellectual Background*, London 1975, pp. 95–106.

COSMIC VISION AND ITS SIGNIFICANCE 321

Pépin, J., *Théologie cosmique et théologie chrétienne (Ambroise, Exam. I, 1, 1–4)*, Paris 1964.

Pfeiffer, J., *Contemplatio Caeli. Untersuchungen zum Motiv der Himmelsbetrachtung in lateinischen Texten der Antike und des Mittelalters*, Berlin 2001.

Polemis, I., "Theodore Metochites' Byzantios as a Testimony to the Cosmological Discussions of the Early Palaeologan Period", *Revue des Études Byzantines* 66 (2008), 241–46.

Polemis, I., *Θεόδωρος Μετοχίτης, Ἠθικὸς ἢ Περὶ Παιδείας, Εἰσαγωγὴ-Κριτικὴ ἔκδοση-Μετάφραση-Σημειώσεις*, Athens ²2002.

Richter, D.S., *Cosmopolis. Imagining Community in Late Classical Athens and the Early Roman Empire*, Oxford 2011.

Richter, G., *Theodoros Dukas Laskaris: Die natürliche Zusammenhang. Ein Zeugnis vom Stand der byzantinischen Philosophie in der Mitte des 13. Jahrhunderts*, Amsterdam 1989.

Runia, D.T., *Philo of Alexandria and the Timaeus of Plato*, Leiden 1986.

Ševčenko, I., *Études sur la polémique entre Théodore Métochite et Nicéphore Choumnos* (Corpus Bruxellense. Historiae Byzantinae Subsidia, 3), Brussels 1962.

Ševčenko, I., *Ideology, Letters and Culture in the Byzantine World* (Variorum Reprints), London 1982.

Ševčenko, I., "Théodore Métochites, Chora et les courants intellectuels de l'époque", in id., *Ideology, Letters and Culture in the Byzantine World*, no. VIII.

Ševčenko, I., "The Decline of Byzantium Seen through the Eyes of its Intellectuals", *Dumbarton Oaks Papers* 15 (1961), 169–86.

Solmsen, F., *Aristotle's System of the Physical World. A Comparison with his Predecessors*, Ithaca, New York 1960.

Spanneut, M., *Le Stoicisme des Pères de l'Église de Clément de Rome à Clément d'Alexandrie*, Paris 1957.

Strauss, L., *Persecution and the Art of Writing*, Chicago/London 1980.

Theiler, W., *Zur Geschichte der teleologischen Naturbetrachtung bis auf Aristoteles*, Berlin 1964.

Treu, M., "Der Philosoph Joseph", *Byzantinische Zeitschrift* 8 (1899), 1–64.

Völker, W., *Maximos Confessor als Meister des geistlichen Lebens*, Wiesbaden 1965.

Wolfson, H.A., *Philo. Foundations of Religious Philosophy in Judaism, Christianity and Islam*, vol. 1, Cambridge, MA 1947.

CHAPTER 9

Monasticism and Intellectual Trends in Late Byzantium

Demetra Samara and Ilias Taxidis

At the beginning of the second millennium Byzantine monasticism was in full flower.[1] Although Arab advances in the preceding centuries had deprived Byzantium of the initial cradles of Christian monasticism in Egypt, Syria and Palestine, the balance was restored by the development of great monastic centers both in Asia Minor, such as Latros near Miletos, Galesion in the vicinity of Ephesos, and Mount Auxentios in Bithynia, and progressively in the European part of the empire, among them Mount Athos and Mount Ganos.[2] Apart from these remote complexes, monasteries also began to spring up in the cities, and especially in the two great urban centres of Constantinople and Thessaloniki. In the latter case, these were mainly founded by members or connections of the imperial family or high-ranking officials of State or Church.

1 Monastic Centers in Asia Minor

The centers in Asia Minor did not, unfortunately, flourish for long. The fate that befell the monasteries of the eastern provinces as the Arabs advanced was repeated at the end of the 11th century with the Seljuk raids on the foundations in Asia Minor, and would be repeated again at the end of the 13th and the early 14th century with the Ottoman Turks, wiping out Byzantine monasticism in Asia Minor, after the sack and evacuation of all the monastic centers.[3]

Before this final end, some of these monasteries experienced a last blossoming in the days of the Empire of Nicaea, and made a major contribution to the intellectual flowering of Byzantium in the first half of the 13th century. One of the Asia Minor monasteries that played a particular role in paving the

---

1 See in this regard Talbot, "An Introduction to Byzantine Monasticism".
2 See Smyrlis, *La fortune des grands monastères* and Kotzabassi, *Βυζαντινά χειρόγραφα*, p. 5.
3 For the Seljuk and Ottoman expansion in Asia Minor, see Vryonis, *The Decline of Medieval Hellenism*, pp. 69–142 and 403–43, as well as Kotzabassi, *ibid.*, pp. 5–6. For the devastation of the region of Maiander, see George Pachymeres, *History*, ed. Failler, vol. 2, pp. 403–05, lines 28–4.

© KONINKLIJKE BRILL NV, LEIDEN, 2023 | DOI:10.1163/9789004527089_011

MONASTICISM AND INTELLECTUAL TRENDS IN LATE BYZANTIUM   323

way for the intellectual movement of the Palaiologan era was the Monastery of the Lord-Christ-Who-Is (*Ontos Theou*), founded by Nikephoros Blemmydes near Ephesos.[4]

The great monastic centers in Asia Minor still surviving, as indicated by the manuscripts issuing from their libraries and the documents in which they are mentioned, were the monasteries of Mount Latros (Monastery of Kellibara and Monastery of the Theotokos *tou Stylou*), of Galesion (Monastery of the Theotokos), of Sosandron (near Magnesia), of the Theotokos Lembiotissa (between Smyrna and Nymphaion, on Mount Lembos),[5] of the Theotokos of Bolax (possibly between Smyrna, Ephesos and Philadelphia), and some in Bithynia, such as those of Christ the Saviour *tou Kophou* in Nicaea and of the Archangel Michael on Mount Auxentios.[6] A special case in the same location is the Monastery of the Holy Five (*Hagion Pente*), for which we have the information that it was granted, almost ruined, in the early 1290s to the scholar-monk Maximos Planoudes by the Metropolitan of Chalcedon;[7] at the same time, a group of manuscripts that was found in 1874 attests to the existence of another unknown monastery located on the island of lake Egirdir, in Pisidia.[8]

In the following decades some of these monasteries were attached by imperial chrysobulls to foundations in Constantinople, in order to ensure a means of their survival, as well as a refuge for their monks and valuables, e.g. the manuscripts in their libraries;[9] this had, of course, happened before, when monks moved away from their original foundations, one example being the transfer of manuscripts from the Monastery of the Theotokos *tou Stylou* on Mount Latros to that of St. John the Theologian on Patmos. Some of the Asia Minor monasteries had, in fact, become dependencies of monasteries in

---

4   See Munitiz, *Nicephori Blemmydae Autobiographia*.

5   For Mount Lembos, see TIB 13, pp. 730–31.

6   See Kotzabassi, *Βυζαντινά χειρόγραφα*, pp. 147–69 (Latros), 120–45 (Galesion), 105–09 (Sosandron), 113–14 (Lembiotissa), 111–12 (Bolax), 51–59 (Kophou) and 33–34 (Auxentiou).

7   See Maximos Planoudes, *Letters*, no. 24, ed. Leone, p. 51, lines 8–13 and 16–18: τῷ φροντιστηρίῳ, ὃ τῶν ἁγίων ἐπικέκληται πέντε· κεῖται δ' ὑπὸ τὴν ὑπώρειαν τοῦ βουνοῦ, ὃς τοῦ ἁγίου Αὐξεντίου ὠνόμασται, ἐν ᾧ φροντιστηρίῳ κἀγὼ νυνὶ ποιοῦμαι τὴν δίαιταν· καὶ γὰρ δεσπόζειν αὐτοῦ διὰ βίου μοι παντὸς ὁ Χαλκηδόνος ἐξέδοτο· [...] καὶ γὰρ δεῖται πολλῆς ἐπιμελείας τὸ φροντιστήριον, ἅτε ἀφρόν-τιστον ἐκ μακροῦ μεῖναν καὶ μικροῦ κινδυνεῦσαν εἰς τέλος πεσεῖν (to the monastery which is called, of the Holy Five (*Hagion Pente*); and it is placed at the foot of the mount called after St. Auxentios and to which I maintain my dwelling; besides, the Metropolitan of Chalcedon granted to me the dominance of it for my whole life; [...] of course, the monastery really needs to be taken care of, because it was left for a long time without any regard and almost about to collapse in the end). See also Constantinides, *Higher Education*, p. 68 and TIB 13, pp. 904–05.

8   See Kotzabassi, *Βυζαντινά χειρόγραφα*, pp. 6–7 and 179–88.

9   See relatively Kotzabassi, *ibid.*, p. 6 (where the previous bibliography).

Constantinople in the 12th century (e.g., Nossion, Galakrenon),[10] while others continued to exist independently throughout the 14th century, as for example a) the Monastery of Hyakinthos in Nicaea, to which Manuel Holobolos was exiled in 1273 when he fell from grace for his stand on the ecclesiastical policy of Michael VIII Palaiologos and where Gregory Palamas lived for a time in 1354,[11] b) the Monastery of the Theotokos *Eleousa tou Kritzous*, which is attested in several manuscripts of the 14th century,[12] and, c) until 1320, when the Ottomans conquered Magnesia, the Monastery of Sosandron.[13]

One of the monasteries that were attached by imperial document to monasteries in Constantinople was that of Bolax (region of Smyrna), which was joined by decree of Andronikos II Palaiologos to the Monastery of Christ Pantepoptes.[14] Maximos Planoudes refers to this monastery and to its unification with the monastery of Constantinople at length in two of his letters, the first sent to one of its monks (no. 88) and the second to the brother of Constantine Akropolites, Melchisedek (no. 115); the latter is also known to have lived as a monk in Asia Minor.[15]

The Monastery of the Theotokos of Galesion, one of the three monasteries founded north of Ephesos on Mount Galesion by St. Lazaros Galesiotes early in the 10th century, flourished for a time during the Empire of Nicaea. In the second half of the 13th century it played an important role in ecclesiastical affairs, since two of its monks, Meletios and Galaktion, vigorously opposed the efforts of Michael VIII Palaiologos towards the unification of the Churches and were punished for it, while two patriarchs of that era, Joseph Galesiotes and Athanasios, also resided there for a time. It also seems to have had a fine library. One indication of the importance of this monastery is the fact that Gregory of Cyprus, who succeeded Joseph Galesiotes as Patriarch at the end of the 13th century, wrote a *vita* of its founder, St. Lazaros. The monastery was attached by Andronikos II to the Monastery of the Resurrection in Constantinople.[16]

The Monastery of the Theotokos of Kellibara, which belonged to the Mount Latros complex, seems to have passed into the hands of the Turks shortly

---

10 These monasteries are dependencies of the Monastery of Pantokrator, according to its *Typikon*, see *Typikon Pantokratoros*, ed. Gautier, pp. 69–73, lines 685–727).

11 See Janin, *Les églises et les monastères*, pp. 121–24.

12 See Kotzabassi, Βυζαντινά χειρόγραφα, p. 102.

13 See Kotzabassi, *ibid.*, p. 105.

14 See Kotzabassi, *ibid.*, p. 111.

15 See Maximos Planoudes, *Letters*, nos. 88 and 115, ed. Leone, pp. 135–36 and 190–92, respectively. See also Taxidis, Μάξιμος Πλανούδης, pp. 55–56 and 78–79.

16 See Kotzabassi, Βυζαντινά χειρόγραφα, pp. 120–21.

before 1282, but had already been attached to the Monastery of St. Demetrios in Constantinople, according to that foundation's *Typikon*, by decree of Michael VIII.[17]

The most important of the Latros monasteries, the Monastery of the Theotokos *tou Stylou*, which had been founded by St. Paul the Younger, is associated with Constantinople in a different way, since at the end of the 13th century it had its own dependency there.[18] The Monastery of the Theotokos of *Hiera* also had a dependency there – that of Xerochoraphion. Its documents were used by George Baiophoros in the Prodromos Petra Monastery at the beginning of the 15th century as palimpsests and to bind other manuscripts, a fact which led Gamillscheg to make the hypothesis that the two monasteries were unified at the end of the 13th century by chrysobull of Andronikos II.[19]

Another of the Asia Minor monasteries that were united with monastic centers in Constantinople was that of the Theotokos of *Heliou Bomon* (or *Elegmoi*) near Kios, which at the beginning of the 14th century, after a period of decline, is mentioned as a dependency of the Monastery of Peribleptos, but was destroyed soon afterwards (after Prousa was taken by the Ottomans in 1306).[20]

In some cases the Byzantine emperors ceded monasteries to high-ranking clerics for their convenience. Thus, the *Megalou Agrou* Monastery, which had been founded by Theophanes the Confessor, was granted by Michael VIII in 1261, together with that of the Archangel Michael of Sosthenion, to Patriarch Athanasios of Alexandria, from whom Patriarch Athanasios of Constantinople later reclaimed it.[21]

The Monastery of Archangel Michael on Mount Auxentios, which was founded in the 5th century by St. Auxentios and destroyed during the Latin occupation, was re-established in the 13th century by Alexios Palaiologos, grandfather of Michael VIII.[22] It was to this monastery that the latter banished Meletios Galesiotes for his opposition to Michael's pro-unionist policy, while Constantinople's future patriarch Athanasios also lived there for a time. On 29 June 1282, the feast day of the Apostles Peter and Paul was celebrated there in the presence of Patriarch John Bekkos, the Emperor Michael VIII, and his son Andronikos II; but Meletios' position remained unchanged. A resident of the Monastery of Auxentios for some time after 1283 seems to have been the

---

17   See Kotzabassi, *ibid.*, pp. 147–48.

18   See Kotzabassi, *ibid.*, pp. 160–61 and Kresten, "Das Kloster des Heiligen Paulus".

19   See Kotzabassi, *ibid.*, p. 171 and Gamillscheg, "Zur Rekonstruktion einer Konstantinopolitaner Bibliothek", pp. 291–92.

20   See Kotzabassi, *ibid.*, pp. 73–74 and TIB 13, pp. 546–49.

21   See Kotzabassi, *ibid.*, p. 94 and TIB 13, pp. 764–66.

22   See TIB 13, p. 780.

monk Theodosios Saponopoulos, correspondent and – at first – friend of the Patriarch Gregory II of Cyprus, where he seems to have been richly hosted, before turning against the patriarch and fleeing unexpectedly to Mount Athos, with the ultimate intention of spreading rumors against him and against the Emperor Andronikos II Palaiologos.[23] At the end of the 13th century the monastery was united with that of Christ Akataleptos in Constantinople, according to a note in codex Vatican City, Biblioteca Apostolica Vaticana, Vat. gr. 844.[24]

2   Monastic Centers Outside Asia Minor

2.1   *Athos*
One of the oldest monastic centers outside Asia Minor is Mount Athos, where almost every form of monasticism is represented: *eremitic* (secluded and solitary way of life), *coenobitic* (a way of monastic life that resembles a spiritual family, organized in a community and based on equality) and *lavrite* (a middle way between eremitic and coenobitic life). Given the great mobility that has always been a feature of monasticism, the historic changes in Asia Minor, and the interest of Serb princes in this historic monastic center,[25] Athos and its monasteries – including the great foundations of Lavra, Vatopedi and Esphigmenou – were magnets for many who were drawn to asceticism and contemplation. In the 14th century numerous important spiritual figures were to be found on Mount Athos, some of whom remained there while others assumed high offices in the Church. We possess considerable knowledge regarding intellectual and spiritual life on Mount Athos, derived mainly from the *Vitae* of contemporary saints who lived there for a time, among them the Patriarchs of Constantinople, Isidore Boucheiras and Philotheos Kokkinos, Gregory Palamas, and many others.[26]

---

23   See Samara, *Θεόδωρος Μουζάλων*, pp. 192–99.

24   See Kotzabassi, *Βυζαντινά χειρόγραφα*, pp. 33–34. Regarding the monasteries on Mount Auxentios, especially in previous centuries, see Belke, "Heilige Berge Bithyniens" and TIB 13, 438–441. On the Akataleptos Monastery see *infra*, p. 332.

25   A typical case is that of the Serbian *kraal* Milutin who paid frequent visits – following the example of the Nemanja family, who at the end of the 12th century had contributed to the development of the Chilandar monastery, which had been given to them by the Byzantine Emperor Alexios III – and had taken up residence there. See also Korać, "Les fondations serbes au Mont Athos".

26   See also Paschalidis, "Εκφάνσεις τῆς λογιότητας στὸ Ἅγιον Ὄρος".

The *Vitae* of important monastic figures of the time also provide invaluable information about Athonite monasticism. Monks from other monastic centers also settled on Mount Athos, like St. Nikodemos of Vatopedi, who was a close associate of Gregory Palamas in the early days and who came from the monastic center of Mount Auxentios in Bithynia, or Athanasios of Constantinople, who lived there for a time barefoot and wearing a tunic.

Mount Athos played a particularly important role in the strife over Hesychastic theology, mental prayer and teachings concerning the uncreated light. From the beginning of this controversy, which was kindled by the criticism of Barlaam of Calabria and grew into a general dispute that took on aspects of a political crisis since it drew in emperors, the Athonites stood against those who doubted that it was possible for humans to see the uncreated light, which they considered as divine energy. After years of dispute and synod upon synod, the Synodical Tome of 1368 put an end to the controversy by confirming the doctrine of the uncreated light and canonizing Gregory Palamas. The positions of Hesychasm were disseminated beyond the borders of Byzantium by monks who visited Mount Athos, contributed to the renewal of Byzantine theology and Byzantine spirituality, and helped shape its course both within Greece and among the Slavs.[27]

The splendor of the Athonite monasteries, many of which had received generous gifts from Byzantine emperors of earlier centuries, was evident in this era too, and especially in their relations with leading political and ecclesiastical figures of the 14th century, who bestowed on them not only lands but also precious manuscripts to enrich their libraries. The most important gift was that of John VI Kantakouzenos, a fervent supporter and friend of many of the Hesychasts, who after his abdication retired to Vatopedi and donated a quantity of costly manuscripts to its library, as the notes in the codices reveal.[28]

The libraries of the great Athonite monasteries were also enriched by the work of a number of monastic scribes, who copied what was needful not only for the operation of the foundations, but also for the defence of their theological opinions, since in this period a respectable number of the Athonite monks were men of considerable education, like Gregory Palamas and Philotheos

---

[27] See for more details about Hesychasm the chapter by Polemis, "The Hesychast Controversy: Events, Personalities, Texts and Trends" in the present volume, pp. 345–82.

[28] See Lamberz, "Die Schenkung des Kaisers Johannes VI. Kantakuzenos". Id., "Beobachtungen zu den patristischen Corpora". See also, Politis, "Jean-Joasaph Cantacuzène fut-il copiste?", p. 198.

Kokkinos.[29] After the Fall of Constantinople (1453) many manuscripts from the city's monastic libraries were taken to Mount Athos.[30]

2.2 Meteora

Around this time a new monastic center began to develop within the sphere of influence of the Despotate of Epiros. The first monastery founded there was established by Athanasios of Meteora. A native of Hypate (b. Neopatras, 1302), he went to Mount Athos and became a monk. There he discovered Hesychasm and frequented some of the most important figures of the age, among them Gregory Sinaites and the subsequent Patriarchs of Constantinople, Isidore and Kallistos. Forced by Turkish aggression to leave the area, Athanasios and other monks travelled via Thessaloniki and Berroia to the safety of the sheer pinnacles of Meteora, where with the assistance of Serbian leaders he founded the region's first coenobitic monastery, on the Athonite model, in honour of the Transfiguration of the Saviour and the Theotokos. Its great library, containing hundreds of manuscripts (more than 500 remain there to this day, while a great number were transferred in the 19th century to the National Library of Greece in Athens, and other European libraries), exemplified its intellectual stature.[31]

2.3 Macedonia

A center of particular importance in the 14th century was the *Skete* of Berroia. It was situated on the banks of the Aliakmon, a short distance from the city of Berroia, which at that time was enjoying a period of remarkable intellectual and cultural eminence, being not only a safe, tranquil place closely associated with Constantinople and a number of prominent families, but also on the road between Western Macedonia and Thessaly. The *Skete* of Berroia was evidently already famous for its anchorites, so that many of the monks who fled from Mount Athos ahead of the invading Turks sought refuge there. Among them were Gregory Palamas and his brothers, and also Athanasios of Meteora. Gregory Palamas settled there sometime between 1326–1331 or 1336, and the

---

29   See Lamberz, "Die Handschriftenproduktion in den Athosklöstern" and Lamberz, "Βιβλιο-γράφοι και βιβλιογραφικά εργαστήρια".

30   See in general Wilson, "The Libraries", pp. 66–68. For the monastic libraries of the Palaeologan period see the chapter by Taxidis, "Public and Private Libraries in Byzantium", in the present volume, pp. 461–67, and Lamberz, "The Library of Vatopaidi", pp. 562–74 and 672–77.

31   See *Life of St. Athanasios Meteorita*, ed. Sophianos; see also, Nicol, *Meteora, the Rock Monasteries of Thessaly*, Nikonanos, *Μετέωρα. Τα μοναστήρια και η ιστορία τους*, and Sophianos, "Τα χειρόγραφα των Μετεώρων".

MONASTICISM AND INTELLECTUAL TRENDS IN LATE BYZANTIUM 329

fact that after his father's death he brought his brothers from Constantinople to Berroia suggests that he intended to remain there; circumstances, however, intervened to alter his plans.[32]

Two additional monasteries in Macedonia, those of Timios Prodromos in Serres and of Eikosiphoinissa, on Mount Paggaion, show an important instructive and bibliographical activity during the late Byzantine centuries.[33]

2.4 Thrace

Another monastic center of the time in the wider area of Thrace was Mount Ganos, on the shores of the Sea of Marmara, southwest of Rhaidestos.[34] It was closely associated with the Patriarch of Constantinople, Athanasios I. Athanasios (born between 1230–35) resided in turn in a number of important monastic centers, including Mount Athos, Mount Latros, Mount Auxentios and Mount Galesion, and later settled with a number of disciples on Mount Ganos and devoted himself to good works, according to his *vita*, written by his disciple Theoktistos Stoudites, and the testimony of Gregory Palamas, who describes him in his *In defence of those who practise Holy Quietude* as one of the teachers of the Hesychastic prayer. His personality attracted such large numbers of men and women to the contemplative life, that he was led to found a nunnery, too.[35]

Another great figure of Byzantine monasticism associated with Mount Ganos at this time was Maximos of Kausokalybia, who was born in Lampsakos and at the age of 17 decided to join the anchorite Mark there, an ascetic whose fame remained undimmed in the days of Maximos' biographer, Makarios Makres.[36]

---

32 For the history of the *Skete*, see Papazis, "Σύντομη ιστορία της I. Μονής του Τιμίου Προδρόμου".

33 For the history of the monasteries of Timios Prodromos and Eikosiphoinissa and their bibliographical ateliers, see Paschalides/Strates, *Τὰ μοναστήρια τῆς Μακεδονίας*, pp. 355–402 and 65–103, respectively. See also Džurova, "Les manuscrits du moine Matthieu", esp. pp. 261–62, for the role of these monasteries as intermediate for the circulation and restoration of manuscripts between Constantinople and Mount Athos, as well as other peripheral centers.

34 See TIB 12, pp. 374–76 and Külzer, "Das Ganos-Gebirge in Ostthrakien". For the monastic life in Thrace in general, see Charizanis, *Ο μοναχισμός στη Θράκη* and Charizanis, "Παπίκιον – Γάνος – Παρόρια".

35 See also Afentoulidou-Leitgeb, *Die Hymnen des Theoktistos Studites*, pp. 55–67.

36 See *Life of St. Maximos Kausokalybites*, ed. Argyriou, *Μακαρίου του Μακρή Συγγράμματα*, pp. 141–65. For Makarios Makres and his writing and intellectual activity, see Argyriou, *Μακαρίου του Μακρή Συγγράμματα*, pp. 13–43.

After Mark's death, Maximos left Mount Ganos for another important monastic center in Thrace, Mount Papikion,[37] a place where – according to Makarios Makres – monks lived an eremitic life. As attested by many documents, both the monastic communities of Mount Ganos and those of Mount Papikion were ruled by a *Protos*, which links them to the form of the monastic center developed on Mount Latros.[38] Gregory Sinaites also lived for a time on Mount Papikion, and according to his *Vita* (written by Theophanes of Peritheorion) met Maximos Kausokalybites there. Gregory Palamas also stopped at Mount Papikion on his way to Mount Athos with his brothers Makarios and Theodosios, and was so impressed by the monks there that he decided to remain with them for the winter.[39]

Gregory Sinaites is also associated with another important monastic center of the 14th century, that of Mount Paroria, on the border between Byzantine Thrace and Bulgaria.[40] The advance of the Turks had forced him to abandon Mount Athos, like Gregory Palamas, Athanasios of Meteora and many others, although he went back there some years later before returning to Paroria to found a great Lavra on the "Frozen Mountain" and later another two, thus creating an important Hesychastic center.

3   The Spiritual Role of the Monasteries in the Cities

3.1   *Constantinople*

Constantinople remained perhaps the main monastic center in Byzantium throughout the Palaiologan era, for it had a centuries-long heritage of dozens of monasteries, male and female, many of them imperial foundations. And while the monasteries suffered greatly from the Latin occupation of Constantinople in the first half of the 13th century, the restoration of the empire after 1261 led to the widespread renovation of many older churches and monasteries with

---

37   For Mount Papikion as a monastic center, see Charizanis, "Ὁ πρωτοστράτορας Ἀλέξιος Ἀξούχος" and Charizanis, "Παπίκιον – Γάνος – Παρόρια". See also TIB 6, pp. 386–87.

38   See Külzer, "Das Ganos-Gebirge in Ostthrakien", p. 48.

39   See Philotheos Kokkinos, *Encomium of Gregory Palamas*, ed. Tsames, p. 441, lines 15–19: Θράκην γε μὴν διϊόντες καὶ κατὰ τὸ Παπίκιον γεγονότες (ὄρος δι' ἱερὸν τοῦτο πάλαι μεταξὺ κείμενον Θράκης τε καὶ Μακεδονίας καὶ μονασταῖς ἀνειμένον ἀνδράσι τότε θαυμαστοῖς καὶ σπουδαίοις καὶ τὰ θεῖα φιλοσοφοῦσι καλῶς), ἐγχειμάζειν παρ' αὐτοῖς ἔγνωσαν [passing through Thrace and arriving at Mount Papikion (this was long ago a holy mount, placed between Thrace and Macedonia, set free to monks who were admirable and great men, and experts on theological issues), they decided to stay there for the winter].

40   For Paroria, see in general Delikari, "Ein Beitrag zu historisch-geographischen Fragen" and TIB 6, pp. 388–89. See also Charizanis, "Παπίκιον – Γάνος – Παρόρια".

MONASTICISM AND INTELLECTUAL TRENDS IN LATE BYZANTIUM 331

financial support either from members of the Palaiologos family or from high-ranking Byzantine officials and their wives.[41]

One of the most important monastic foundations of the Comnenian era, the Monastery of Christ Pantokrator, founded by Irene, the wife of John II Komnenos, and placed under imperial patronage, was doubtless significantly damaged during the Latin occupation, given its change of use, but must have been rapidly repaired and restored to its original purpose as a monastery. As an imperial foundation it retained its prominence under the new dynasty, and many Palaiologans chose it as their final resting place. In the final years before the city fell, the monastery became a center of opposition to the union of the Churches under the leadership of George Scholarios, later Patriarch of Constantinople under the name Gennadios.[42]

A special position among the monasteries of the imperial capital was reserved for the Chora, a monastery founded in the 6th or 7th century.[43] At the end of the 13th century, in the context of the general rebuilding that went on during the reign of Andronikos II Palaiologos, its renovation was undertaken by the *logothetes tou genikou* (the logothetes of the central public treasury), Theodore Metochites, who decorated the church with exquisite mosaics and added, as happened with other monasteries in Constantinople in that period, a mortuary chapel. He also, naturally, re-organised its library, which he and his student Nikephoros Gregoras would make use of.[44] The widespread assertion that before its renovation Maximos Planoudes stayed in the monastery for some time due to teaching activities remains a speculation, on the one hand because it is not based on the testimonies of the texts, and on the other because it is considered a given by previous research that the monastery, due to its desolation during the Latin rule, could not had been inhabited until 1305 and onwards.[45]

---

41   About restoring or re-founding monastic establishments during the last centuries of the Byzantine Empire, see Demirtiken, "Changing Profiles of Monastic Founders in Constantinople, From the Komnenoi to the Palaiologoi".

42   See Kotzabassi, "The Monastery of Pantokrator" (where the older bibliography). See also Janin, *La géographie ecclésiastique*, pp. 515–23 and Kidonopoulos, *Bauten in Konstantinopel*, pp. 30–33.

43   For the monastery, see Janin, *La géographie ecclésiastique*, pp. 531–38 and Kidonopoulos, *Bauten in Konstantinopel*, pp. 19–25.

44   See Taxidio, "Public and Private Libraries in Byzantium", in the present volume, pp. 463–64. About Theodore Metochites, Nikephoros Gregoras and their relation to the Monastery of Chora, see in general Ševčenko, "Theodore Metochites" and Sklavenite, Συμβολή στη μελέτη των επιστολών του Νικηφόρου Γρηγορά, pp. 25–76 (where the older bibliography).

45   See Taxidis, Μάξιμος Πλανούδης, pp. 20–21 (and n. 20). See also Ševčenko, "Theodore Metochites", pp. 28–29, 35–37 and 41–42.

332   SAMARA AND TAXIDIS

Although we know very little about the Monastery of Christ Akataleptos, it seems to have played a special role in the intellectual life of the Byzantine capital.[46] Two great Byzantine scholars of the early Palaiologan era resided there for a period (probably not at the same time) in the final decades of the 13th century, when there may had been no monks in residence; one of these, as we know from his correspondence, was George of Cyprus, who later became Patriarch of Constantinople as Gregory II, and the other was the great scholar Maximos Planoudes. More specifically, Gregory of Cyprus, before his ascension to the patriarchal throne, appeared to be living in the Monastery of Akataleptos with his secular name, George, according to a letter addressed to the *chartophylax* of Thessaloniki, John Staurakios, with which he asks for the dispatch of the book and its copy that he had ordered to be prepared for him. He complains about the delay in delivery and gives instructions to the bearer of the order, so as to find his place of residence and to bring him the manuscripts required personally.[47]

Moreover, we get the information from Maximos Planoudes himself and the manuscript written in his hand, Venice, Biblioteca Nazionale Marciana, Marc. gr. 481, that he also dwelled in the Monastery of Akataleptos (between 1299–1301), where he showed writing and possibly teaching activity.[48] Another eminent guest was Philotheos Kokkinos, who took up residence there for some time after his first removal from the patriarchal throne (1354/55 to 1364) and who honoured the memory of Gregory Palamas with singers from the Great

---

46   For the monastery, see Janin, *La géographie ecclésiastique*, pp. 504–06; Müller-Wiener, *Bildlexikon*, pp. 209–11; Kotzabassi, "Zur Lokalisierung des Akataleptos-Klosters" and Asutay-Effenberger/Effenberger, "Eski İmaret Camii", pp. 26–27.

47   Gregory of Cyprus, *Letters*, no. 20, ed. Eustratiades pp. 15–16: Ζητείτω δὲ ἡμᾶς ὁ κομιού- μενος τὰ βιβλία μὴ ἐν τοῖς ἀρχείοις – οὐ γὰρ εὑρήσει – ἐν τῇ μονῇ δὲ μάλιστα τοῦ Σωτῆρος – Ἀκατάληπτος ἐπονομάζεται – ἔνθα ἡμεῖς καταμένομεν (May the bearer of the books ask for us not at the archives – he will not find us there – but at the monastery of the Saviour – it also bears the name Akataleptos – where we reside). See also Constantinides, *Higher Education*, pp. 43–44 and 70, Fryde, *The Early Palaeologean Renaissance*, p. 89 and Kountoura-Galake, "Ἰωάννης Σταυράκιος", pp. 382–84.

48   See Maximos Planoudes, *Letters*, ed. Treu, pp. 182 and 189: ἐγράφη ἡ μετάφρασις αὕτη τοῦ κ(α)τ(ὰ) Ἰω(άννην) ἁγίου εὐαγγελίου. χειρὶ Μαξίμου μοναχοῦ τοῦ Πλανούδη· ἐντὸ(ς) Κωνσταντινουπόλεως. κ(α)τ(ὰ) τὴν μονὴν τοῦ σ(ωτῆ)ρ(ο)ς Χ(ριστο)ῦ. τὴν τοῦ Ἀκαταλήπτου ἐπονομαζομένην· μηνὶ σεπτ(εμβ)ρ(ίῳ)· ἰν(δικτιῶνος) ιγ· ἔτους στω' δεκ(ά)τ(ου) (this translation of the Holy Gospel according to John was composed by the monk Maximos Planoudes, in Constantinople and in the monastery of Christ the Saviour, called of the Akataleptos; month September, 13th indiction, year 6810). See also Taxidis, *Μάξιμος Πλανούδης*, p. 22 (and n. 25–26).

MONASTICISM AND INTELLECTUAL TRENDS IN LATE BYZANTIUM   333

Church and a large number of clergymen before his canonization with the Synodical Tome of 1368.[49]

Two more monasteries in Constantinople took an active part in the intellectual life of Byzantium in the 14th and early 15th centuries. One of these was the Hodegon Monastery, a 5th-century foundation whose name is associated with a particularly legible script with distinctive characteristics, which became known as the Hodegon style.[50] It is represented by numerous scribes of that age, who mostly copied liturgical texts, usually writing on parchment and using a formula of the type "Θεοῦ τὸ δῶρον καὶ Χαρίτωνος πόνος" (this is a gift of God and the labour of Chariton). Although it is not certain that all the scribes who used the Hodegon style were monks of that monastery, the script was widely imitated in the post-Byzantine era.[51]

The second of these foundations was the Prodromos Petra Monastery, founded in the 11th century, which at that time boasted some of the finest scribes of the day, including George Baiophoros and Stephen of Medeia, who used the parchment from older manuscripts (palimpsests) to write on and to preserve and bind their work.[52] In any case, it is noteworthy that more than two hundred manuscripts are connected with the scribes who were active in the Prodromos Petra Monastery, including George Chrysokokkes, Leon Atrapes, John Argyropoulos and Michael Apostoles.[53]

The women of the imperial and other aristocratic families of Byzantium also played a major role in the renovation and renewed splendour of Constantinople's monasteries in this period.

After her husband's death, Theodora, the wife of Michael VIII Palaiologos, renovated the 10th-century Lips Monastery and built a new church, dedicated to St. John the Baptist, next to the old one, which was dedicated to the

---

49   See *Synodical Tome II, Patrologia Graeca*, vol. 151, col. 711D1–6: Διὰ τοῦτο καὶ ἐγὼ ἐν τῷ μονα-
       στηρίῳ τοῦ Ἀκαταλήπτου καθήμενος, καὶ ἰδιάζων, περιφανή τινα καὶ μεγάλην ἑορτὴν ἐπετέλουν
       τῷ ἁγίῳ τούτῳ καὶ τοῖς τῆς μεγάλης Ἐκκλησίας ταύτης μελῳδοῖς ἔχων μετ' ἐμοῦ καὶ πολλοὺς
       τῶν τοῦ κλήρου (For that reason, I myself, dwelling in the monastery of Akataleptos and
       withdrawn, held a brilliant and great feast in honour of that saint, having on my side the
       singers of the Great Church itself and a number of clergymen). See also Kotzabassi, "Zur
       Lokalisierung des Akataleptos-Klosters", p. 233 (and n. 3).

50   For the monastery, see Janin, *La géographie ecclésiastique*, pp. 199–207 and Kidonopoulos,
       Bauten in Konstantinopel, pp. 77–78. See also, Pérez Martín, "El 'estilo hodegos'", including
       the older bibliography about the "Hodegon" script.

51   See Volk, *Die byzantinischen Klosterbibliotheken*, pp. 43–50 and Taxidis, "Public and
       Private Libraries in Byzantium", in the present volume, pp. 464–65.

52   For the monastery, see Janin, *La géographie ecclésiastique*, pp. 435–43 and Kidonopoulos,
       Bauten in Konstantinopel, pp. 45–49.

53   See Taxidis, "Public and Private Libraries in Byzantium", in the present volume, pp. 478–79.

Theotokos.[54] As we know from the *Typikon* of Theodora, the new female monastery was intended to house fifty nuns and a hospital with 12 beds.[55] Theodora also renovated the Monastery of the Anargyroi, where she also founded a nunnery.[56] She was praised for this activity by Constantine Akropolites, and also by Theodore Metochites, who refers in his *Monodia* to her interest in donating manuscripts and sacred vessels to monasteries.[57]

Theodora had first displayed her interest in promoting letters and the sciences in 1265, when she commissioned the monk Arsenios to translate into Greek the geometry of the Persian philosopher al-Zanati, which is preserved in the codex Naples, Biblioteca Nazionale, Neap. II C 33, with an annotation recording this commission.[58] Also associated with Theodora and her monastery is a costly manuscript, the London Codex, British Library Add. 22748, containing the *Typikon* of the Lips Monastery and a brief rule for the Monastery of the Anargyroi.[59] It seems plausible the possibility that the illuminated liturgical manuscripts that Hugo Buchtal and Hans Belting studied in 1970 and ascribed (based on the monogram of the Palaiologans appearing on one of them) to the "atelier of the Palaiologina" – tentatively identifying her as Theodora Raoulaina, the niece of Michael VIII Palaiologos who was famous for her interest in studying and copying manuscripts – should actually be associated with Theodora, the wife of Michael VIII, as proposed by Talbot.[60]

Whether it was Theodora Palaiologina or Theodora Raoulaina who commissioned this particular set of manuscripts, the latter certainly played a leading role in the intellectual life of the early Palaiologan period. She was closely connected to the imperial family, and was married to two high-ranking officials (*protovestiarioi*), first as a young girl to George Mouzalon, who was assassinated in Nicaea after the death of Theodore II Laskaris, and later to John Komnenos Petraliphes Raoul, who died *circa* 1274. Along with her mother, Michael VIII's sister, Irene-Eulogia Palaiologina, she opposed his fight for the Church union. Theodora Raoulaina devoted herself to the study and exchange of manuscripts with many of the important scholars of her day; she also renovated

---

54 For the monastery, see Janin, *La géographie ecclésiastique*, pp. 307–10 and Kidonopoulos, *Bauten in Konstantinopel*, pp. 86–87.

55 For the *typikon*, see Talbot, "Empress Theodora Palaiologina", pp. 298–301.

56 For the monastery, see Janin, *La géographie ecclésiastique*, pp. 287–89 and Kidonopoulos, *Bauten in Konstantinopel*, pp. 1–4.

57 See Talbot, "Empress Theodora Palaiologina", p. 301.

58 See Talbot, *ibid.*, p. 301.

59 See Talbot, *ibid.*, p. 301. See also Buchtal/Belting, *Patronage in Thirteenth Century Constantinople*.

60 See Talbot, *ibid.*, p. 302.

MONASTICISM AND INTELLECTUAL TRENDS IN LATE BYZANTIUM 335

the Monastery of St. Andrew *en te Krisei*, which she entered as a nun,[61] and the small Monastery of Aristene, which she granted to Gregory of Cyprus after his abdication from the patriarchal throne and with whom she maintained a scholarly friendship for many years.[62] Maximos Planoudes has composed three epigrams, dedicated to the Monastery of St. Andrew *en te Krisei*, ordered by her.[63] At her instigation also the relics of the former patriarch Arsenios, which had been transferred to Constantinople after the end of the Arsenite schism, were brought to St. Andrew's Monastery.[64] Theodora Raoulaina had a large library of both older manuscripts and various works copied by herself or other scribes. Her education is also apparent from the classical references and quotations in her *Vita* of Sts. Theodore and Theophanes the Graptoi.[65]

Another woman who played an active role in the intellectual life of the period was Irene Choumnaina, the daughter of Nikephoros Choumnos, who after the death of her husband, the Despot John Palaiologos, son of the Emperor Andronikos II, retired as the nun Eulogia to the Monastery of Christ Philanthropos Soter founded by her father.[66] Initially, she was an intellectual follower of the Metropolitan Theoleptos of Philadelphia, who was considered

---

61 See George Pachymeres, *History*, ed. Failler, vol. 3, pp. 97–99, lines 32–1: Ἐν ὑστέρῳ δὲ χρόνῳ ἡ Ῥαούλαινα πρωτοβεστιάρισσα ἐν τῇ τοῦ Ἁγίου Ἀνδρέου μονῇ τοῦ τῆς Κρίσεως ἱερὸν οἶκον, εἰς κάλλος ἐξησκημένον καὶ μέγεθος, ἀνιστᾷ (Later on, Raoulaina the *protovestiarissa* built up in the monastery of St. Andrew *en te Krisei* a holy dwelling-place, full of beauty and greatness). For the monastery, see Janin, *La géographie ecclésiastique*, pp. 28–31 and Kidonopoulos, *Bauten in Konstantinopel*, pp. 9–10.

62 See George Pachymeres, *History*, ed. Failler, vol. 3, p. 151, lines 7–10: Καί γε τῷ τῆς Ἀριστηνῆς μονυδρίῳ, ἐχόμενά που κειμένῳ τῆς τοῦ Ἁγίου Ἀνδρέου τοῦ ἐν τῇ Κρίσει μονῆς – ἐκεῖ γὰρ ἡ πρωτοβεστιάρισσα Ῥαούλαινα συνῆγεν, ἐξ ἑαυτῆς περιθάλπουσα τὰ μεγάλα –, φέρων ἑαυτὸν δίδωσιν (And he retired to the small monastery of Aristene, very close to the Monastery of St. Andrew in *Krisei* – it was that place that *protovestiarissa* Raoulaina rendered him as a shelter, and looked after him). See also Kotzabassi, "Scholarly Friendship in the Thirteenth century".

63 See Maximos Planoudes, *Epigrams*, ed. Taxidis, pp. 118–132.

64 See Nikephoros Gregoras, *Roman History*, ed. Schopen, vol. 1, p. 262, lines 1–4: ἵνα δηλαδὴ τὸ τοῦ πατριαρχεύσαντος Ἀρσενίου λείψανον ἐκ τῆς τοῦ ἁγίου Ἀνδρέου μονῆς ἐντίμως ἀνειληφότες ἐν τῷ μεγίστῳ τῆς τοῦ θεοῦ Σοφίας νεῷ μεταθῶσι (so to transfer in honour the relics of Patriarch Arsenios from the Monastery of St. Andrew to the Great Church of Hagia Sophia).

65 See in this regard Kotzabassi, "Scholarly Friendship in the Thirteenth Century", pp. 113–19 and Talbot, "Bluestocking Nuns", p. 611. For her private library, see Taxidis, "Public and Private Libraries in Byzantium" in the present volume, p. 370.

66 See Hero, "Irene-Eulogia Choumnaina Palaiologina". See also Verpeaux, "Notes prosopographiques", pp. 260–61 (no. 17). For the monastery, see Janin, *La géographie ecclésiastique*, pp. 525–29; Müller-Wiener, *Bildlexikon*, p. 109 and Kidonopoulos, *Bauten in Konstantinopel*, pp. 33–36.

336 SAMARA AND TAXIDIS

the mentor of Gregory Palamas and who addressed a series of homilies to her. Later, however, she aligned herself with Gregory Akindynos, with whom she corresponded, and shifted her allegiance to the anti-Hesychasts, as is apparent from the accusations Gregory Palamas levelled against her.

Finally, a nunnery in Constantinople for which information is limited, is the Monastery of Pertze, known from a letter by Gregory of Cyprus addressed to the *megas logothetes*, Theodore Mouzalon. The name of the nunnery is mentioned in the context of financial irregularities on the part of the *apografeus* (fiscal official) of Macedonia and Thrace, John Theologites, who seems to be acting against the patriarch, but in favour of the monastery, showing plain indifference to the imperial order of Andronikos II Palaiologos.[67]

3.2   Thessaloniki

The Palaiologan era was a period of particular brilliance for the second largest city of the Byzantine empire. Thessaloniki, as an intellectual center that had presented significant spiritual achievements throughout its long history despite always being in the shadow of the capital, often just honourably as a queen city, became a special case mostly during the late Byzantine period. More specifically, the long-standing presence in the city of Irene-Yolanda of Montferrat, the wife of the Emperor Andronikos II, from 1303 to 1317, of the co-Emperor Michael IX Palaiologos, who also remained in the city until his death in 1320, and of his widow Maria-Rita of Armenia for thirteen years more (until 1333), and finally of the Empress Anna of Savoy for fifteen years until her death in 1365/66, set the ground for the protection of scholars and monasticism. Thus, due to the occasional long-lasting presence of royal authority, Thessaloniki truly became the intellectual and monastic queen city of the Empire.

The old monasteries, like those of St. Theodora and Hosios David,[68] continued to flourish, and new ones were founded with churches distinguished for their exceptionally fine brickwork and frescoes. Among these are, within the city, the church of the Holy Apostles, which is associated with Patriarch Niphon of Constantinople (1310–1314), the Monastery of *Kyr Isaac*, the *Nea Mone*,[69] and others, such as the Monastery of Philokalou and Chortaites, on the city's outskirts.[70] Thessaloniki's involvement in the Hesychast controversy and connec-

---

67   See Samara, *Θεόδωρος Μουζάλων*, pp. 185–88. For the monastery, see Janin, *La géographie ecclésiastique*, pp. 396–97 and Kidonopoulos, *Bauten in Konstantinopel*, pp. 61–62.
68   See Janin, *Les églises et les monastères*, pp. 374–75 (St. Theodora) and 364–65 (Hosios David).
69   See Janin, *ibid.*, pp. 352–54 (Holy Apostles), 386–88 (*Kyr Isaac*) and 398–99 (*Nea Mone*).
70   See Janin, *ibid.*, pp. 418–19 (Philokalou) and 414–15 (Chortaites). See also Volk, *Die byzantinischen Klostebibliotheken*, p. 132.

MONASTICISM AND INTELLECTUAL TRENDS IN LATE BYZANTIUM   337

tion with some of Hesychasm's leading figures, e.g., Gregory Palamas, is linked to the dedication of two new monasteries to the Transfiguration of Christ the Saviour. One of these was a small foundation almost directly opposite the Monastery of *Kyr Isaac*, and the other was the Blatadon Monastery adjacent to the city's north wall, which was founded by the brothers Dorotheos and Mark Blates, who were students and friends of Gregory Palamas.[71]

Moreover, the patriarchal nunnery of Gerontiou is traced in a letter sent by Gregory of Cyprus to Theodore Mouzalon, according to which the nuns of it address to the patriarch their written protest against their abbess. Another monastery, that of Akapniou, is also reported in the same letter.[72]

These monasteries maintained close relations with those of Mount Athos and Constantinople, as is confirmed by the visits paid by important figures of the time to all three centers, and they transmitted the intellectual climate of both Thessaloniki and Constantinople to the Slavic nations. Particularly in the case of Thessaloniki, after all, such a verification is reinforced by the operation of high-level educational foundations and smaller-places of learning during the 14th century, in which scholars (clergy and non-clergy), such as Nikephoros Choumnos, Demetrios Triklinios, Demetrios Kydones, Thomas Magistros, Gregory Palamas and Philotheos Kokkinos, were born and flourished.[73]

If one were to summarize the contribution of Palaiologan monasticism to the intellectual movement of the period, one might trace two principal lines: one is its role, direct or indirect, in what is described as the "Palaiologan renaissance", the systematic study of classical antiquity, copying and collecting manuscripts, and indeed the translation of Latin texts, since many of the scholars of the day lived and worked in monasteries, among others the Chora, Akataleptos

---

71   See Janin, *ibid.*, pp. 417 (Transfiguration) and 356–58 (Blatadon). See also Volk, *ibid.*, p. 132.
72   See Gregory of Cyprus, *Letters*, no. 144, ed. Eustratiades p. 135: Ἔστι μὲν ἐν Θεσσαλονίκῃ τῇ πόλει καὶ ἄλλα δή τινα μοναστήρια ὑπὸ τὴν πατριαρχικὴν ἐξουσίαν τελοῦντα, ἔστι δὲ καὶ τὸ τοῦ Γεροντίου λεγόμενον, οὐκ ἄνδρες ἐν αὐτῷ, μοναχαὶ δὲ γυναῖκες οἰκοῦσιν· ἐκ δὴ τούτου πρό τινων οὐ πάνυ πολλῶν ἡμερῶν ἧκέ μοι γράμμα ἔχον μὲν ἐπιγραφήν, αἱ ἅπασαι μοναχαὶ τῷ πατριάρχῃ, ἔχον δὲ καὶ τὴν κατηγορίαν ὅσην ἂν εἴποις κατὰ τῆς ἡγουμένης πολλήν (In the city of Thessaloniki there also exist other monasteries under patriarchal authority, like the so-called Monastery of Gerontiou, in which reside not monks, but nuns; a letter arrived from this monastery the other day, bearing the title: "From all the nuns to the Patriarch", and containing their many complaints against the abbess). See also Samara, Θεόδωρος Μουζάλων, p. 182 (n. 327). For the monasteries, see Janin, *ibid.*, pp. 358 (Gerontiou) and 347–49 (Akapniou).
73   For the intellectual movement of Thessaloniki during the Palaeologan era in general, see Bianconi, *Thessalonica*. See also Constantinides, "Οι απαρχές της πνευματικής ακμής" and Tinnefeld, "Intellectuals in Late Byzantine Thessalonike".

and Prodromos Petra. The other is its role in supporting and disseminating Hesychasm both within the Byzantine Empire and beyond its borders.

In an age when the empire was dying, monasticism experienced a new blossoming at the intellectual, ideological and artistic levels. Many of the monastic foundations that were founded or renovated at this time were decorated with some of the most superb examples of Byzantine architecture, painting and minor arts – work that reflects the splendour of the Byzantine art and spirituality and bequeaths it to the world, even after the fall of Constantinople and the end of the empire.

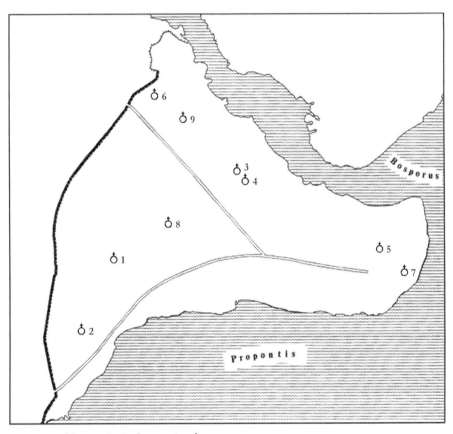

MAP 9.1   Monasteries in Constantinople
1. Monastery of the Holy Anargyroi
2. Monastery of St. Andrew *en te Krisei*
3. Monastery of Christ Akataleptos
4. Monastery of Christ Pantokrator
5. Monastery of Christ Philanthropos Soter
6. Chora Monastery
7. Hodegon Monastery
8. Lips Monastery
9. Prodromos Petra Monastery

MONASTICISM AND INTELLECTUAL TRENDS IN LATE BYZANTIUM

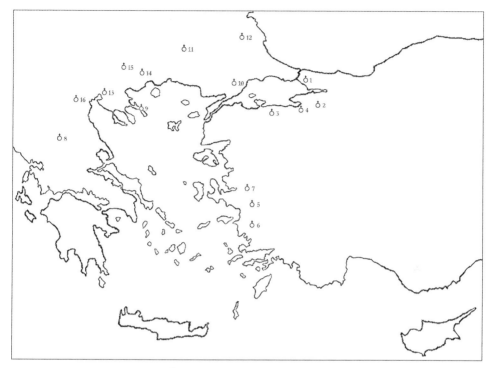

MAP 9.2   Monastic centers outside of Constantinople

1. Monasteries on Mount Auxentios [Archangel Michael, Holy Five (*Hagion Pente*)]
2. Monasteries in Nicaea (Christ the Saviour *tou Kophou*, Hyakinthos)
3. Monastery of the *Megalou Agrou*
4. Monastery of the Theotokos of *Heliou Bomon* (or *Elegmoi*)
5. Monasteries in the region of Ephesos [Theotokos of Galesion, Lord-Christ-Who-Is (*Ontos Theou*)]
6. Monasteries on Mount Latros (Kellibara, Theotokos of *Hiera*, Theotokos *tou Stylou*)
7. Monasteries in the region of Smyrna/Magnesia (Sosandron, Theotokos of Bolax, Theotokos Lembiotissa)
8. Monasteries on Meteora
9. Monasteries on Mount Athos
10. Monasteries on Mount Ganos
11. Monasteries on Mount Papikion
12. Monasteries on Mount Paroria
13. Monasteries in Thessaloniki
14. Monastery of Eikosiphoinissa (Mount Paggaion)
15. Monastery of Timios Prodromos (Serres)
16. *Skete* of Berroia

340 SAMARA AND TAXIDIS

Bibliography

Primary Sources

George Pachymeres, *History*, ed. A. Failler, *Georges Pachymérès, Relations historiques* (Corpus Fontium Historiae Byzantinae, 24), 5 vols., Paris 1984–2000.

Gregory of Cyprus, *Letters*, ed. S. Eustratiades, Γρηγορίου τοῦ Κυπρίου οἰκουμενικοῦ πατριάρχου ἐπιστολαὶ καὶ μῦθοι, Alexandria 1910.

Life of St. Athanasios Meteorita, ed. D. Sophianos, Ο Όσιος Αθανάσιος ο Μετεωρίτης: βίος – ακολουθία – συναξάρια, Athens 1990.

Life of St. Maximos Kausokalybites, ed. Argyriou, Μακαρίου τοῦ Μακρῆ Συγγράμματα, pp. 141–65.

Maximos Planoudes, *Epigrams*, ed. and trans. I. Taxidis, *Les épigrammes de Maxime Planude. Introduction, édition critique, traduction française et annotation* (Byzantinisches Archiv, 32), Berlin/Boston 2017.

Maximos Planoudes, *Letters*, ed. M. Treu, *Maximi monachi Planudis epistulae*, Breslau 1890 (repr. Amsterdam 1960).

Maximos Planoudes, *Letters*, ed. P.A. Leone, *Maximi monachi Planudis epistulae* (Classical and Byzantine Monographs, 18), Amsterdam 1991.

Nikephoros Gregoras, *Roman History*, eds. L. Schopen/I. Bekker, *Nicephori Gregorae Byzantina Historia* (Corpus Scriptorum Historiae Byzantinae, 19), 3 vols., Bonn 1829–55.

Philotheos Kokkinos, *Encomium of Gregory Palamas*, ed. D.G. Tsames, Φιλοθέου Κωνσταντινουπόλεως τοῦ Κοκκίνου ἁγιολογικὰ ἔργα. Α΄. Θεσσαλονικεῖς ἅγιοι (Θεσσαλονικεῖς Βυζαντινοὶ Συγγραφεῖς, 4), Thessaloniki 1985, pp. 427–591.

Synodical Tome II (Against Prochoros Kydones), in *Patrologia Graeca*, vol. 151, cols. 693–716.

Typikon Pantokratoros, ed. P. Gautier, "Le typikon du Christ Sauveur Pantocrator", *Revue des Études Byzantines* 32 (1974), pp. 1–145.

Secondary Literature

Afentoulidou-Leitgeb, E., *Die Hymnen des Theoktistos Studites auf Athanasios I. von Konstantinopel. Einleitung, Edition, Kommentar* (Wiener Byzantinistische Studien, 25), Vienna 2008.

Argyriou, A., Μακαρίου τοῦ Μακρῆ Συγγράμματα (Βυζαντινὰ Κείμενα καὶ Μελέται, 25), Thessaloniki 1996.

Asutay-Effenberger, N./A. Effenberger, "Eski İmaret Camii, Bonoszisterne und Konstantinsmauer", *Jahrbuch der Österreichischen Byzantinistik* 58 (2008), 13–44.

Auzépy, M.-F., "Les Monastères", in B. Geyer/J. Lefort (eds.), *La Bithynie au Moyen Âge*, Paris 2003, pp. 431–58.

MONASTICISM AND INTELLECTUAL TRENDS IN LATE BYZANTIUM 341

Belke, Kl., "Heilige Berge Bithyniens", in Soustal (ed.), *Heilige Berge und Wüsten*, pp. 15–24.

Bianconi, D., *Tessalonica nell'età dei Paleologi. Le pratiche intellettuali nel riflesso della cultura scritta* (Dossiers Byzantins, 5), Paris 2005.

Buchtal H./H. Belting, *Patronage in Thirteenth Century Constantinople. An Atelier of Late Byzantine Book Illumination and Calligraphy* (Dumbarton Oaks Studies, 16), Washington 1978.

Charizanis, G., *Ο μοναχισμός στη Θράκη κατά τους Βυζαντινούς αιώνες*, PhD thesis, Aristotle University of Thessaloniki 2003.

Charizanis, G., "*Ο πρωτοστράτορας Αλέξιος Αξούχος, ο σεβαστοκράτορας Αλέξιος Κομνηνός και το μοναστικό κέντρο του Παπικίου όρους (β΄ μισό του 12ου αι.). Προσωπογραφικά και άλλα ζητήματα*", *Byzantinische Forschungen* 30 (2011), 671–93.

Charizanis, G., "Παπίκιον – Γάνος – Παρόρια. Τα περίλαμπρα μοναστικά κέντρα της Βυζαντινής Θράκης", in M.G. Varvounes (ed.), *Πολυχρόνιον. Τιμητικό αφιέρωμα στον Μακαριώτατο Αρχιεπίσκοπο Αθηνών και πάσης Ελλάδος, κ. Ιερώνυμο Β΄*, Komotini 2017, pp. 63–72.

Constantinides, C.N., *Higher Education in Byzantium in the Thirteenth and Early Fourteenth Centuries (1204–ca 1310)* (Texts and Studies of the History of Cyprus, 11), Nicosia 1982.

Constantinides, C.N., "Οι απαρχές της πνευματικής ακμής στη Θεσσαλονίκη κατά τον 14ο αιώνα", *Δωδώνη* 1 (1992), 135–36.

Delikari, A., "Ein Beitrag zu historisch-geographischen Fragen auf dem Balkan: "Paroria". Neue Angaben zur Lokalisierung des Klostergebietes von Gregorios Sinaites", in Soustal (ed.), *Heilige Berge und Wüsten*, pp. 71–76.

Demirtiken, E., "Changing Profiles of Monastic Founders in Constantinople, From the Komnenoi to the Palaiologoi: The Case of the Theotokos Pammakaristos Monastery in Context", in M. Kinloch/A. MacFarlane (eds.), *Trends and Turning Points. Constructing the Late Antique and Byzantine World* (The Medieval Mediterranean, 117), Leiden/Boston 2019, pp. 266–86.

Džurova, A., "Les manuscrits du moine Matthieu dans la collection du Centre Dujcev (Le Cod. D.279=Olim. Kos. 54 et le Cod. 217=Olim. Kos. 49) (Les sorts de manuscrits médiévaux)", in *Η Δράμα και η περιοχή της. Ιστορία και πολιτισμός, Πρακτικά Β΄ Επιστημονικής Συνάντησης, Δράμα 18–22 Μαΐου 1994*, vol. 1, Drama 1998, pp. 257–78.

Fryde, E., *The Early Palaeologean Renaissance (1261–c.1360)* (The Medieval Mediterranean, 27), Leiden/Boston/Köln 2000.

Gamillscheg, E., "Zur Rekonstruktion einer Konstantinopolitaner Bibliothek", *Rivista di Studi Bizantini e Slavi* 1 (1981), 283–93.

Hero, A.C., "Irene-Eulogia Choumnaina Palaiologina, Abbess of the Convent of Philanthropos Soter in Constantinople", *Byzantinische Forschungen* 9 (1985), 119–48.

Janin, R., *La géographie ecclésiastique de l'empire byzantin*. I. *Le siège de Constantinople et le patriarcat œcuménique*. III. *Les églises et les monastères*, Paris 1969.

Janin, R., *Les églises et les monastères des grands centres byzantins (Bithynie, Hellespont, Latros, Galèsios, Trébizonde, Athènes, Thessalonique)*, Paris 1975.

Kidonopoulos, V., *Bauten in Konstantinopel 1204–1328. Verfall und Zerstörung, Restaurierung, Umbau und Neubau von Profan- und Sakralbauten* (Mainzer Veröffentlichungen zur Byzantinistik, 1), Wiesbaden 1994.

Korać, V., "Les fondations serbes au Mont Athos et les origines athonites de l'architecture serbe", in *Το Άγιο Όρος χθες-σήμερα-αύριο, Διεθνές Συμπόσιο, Θεσσαλονίκη 29 Οκτωβρίου–1 Νοεμβρίου 1993* (Μακεδονική Βιβλιοθήκη, 84), Thessaloniki 1996, pp. 145–56.

Kotzabassi, S., *Βυζαντινά χειρόγραφα από τα μοναστήρια της Μικράς Ασίας*, Athens 2004.

Kotzabassi, S., "Scholarly Friendship in the Thirteenth Century: Patriarch Gregorios II Kyprios and Theodora Raoulaina", *Parekbolai* 1 (2011), 117–70.

Kotzabassi, S., "The Monastery of Pantokrator between 1204 and 1453", in S. Kotzabassi (ed.), *The Pantokrator Monastery in Constantinople* (Byzantinisches Archiv, 27), Boston/Berlin 2013, pp. 57–69.

Kotzabassi, S., "Zur Lokalisierung des Akataleptos-Klosters in Konstantinopel", *Revue des Études Byzantines* 63 (2005), 233–35.

Kountoura-Galake, E., "Ἰωάννης Σταυράκιος: "Ἕνας λόγιος στὴ Θεσσαλονίκη τῆς πρώιμης Παλαιολόγειας ἐποχῆς" *Βυζαντινὰ Σύμμεικτα* 16 (2003), 379–94.

Kresten, O., "Das Kloster des Heiligen Paulus am Berge Latros oder vom Berge Latros?", *Jahrbuch der Österreichischen Byzantinistik* 50 (2000), 187–204.

Külzer, A., "Das Ganos-Gebirge in Ostthrakien (Isiklar Dagi)", in Soustal (ed.), *Heilige Berge und Wüsten*, pp. 41–52.

Lamberz, E., "Beobachtungen zu den patristischen Corpora in der Schenkung des Johannes Kantakuzenos an das Kloster Vatopedi und ihren Vorlagen", in A. Berger/S. Mariev/G. Prinzing/A. Riehle (eds.), *Koinotaton Doron. Das späte Byzanz zwischen Machtlosigkeit und kultureller Blüte (1204–1461)* (Byzantinisches Archiv, 31), Berlin/Boston 2016, pp. 87–99.

Lamberz, E., "Βιβλιογράφοι και βιβλιογραφικά εργαστήρια στο Άγιον Όρος κατά την εποχή των Παλαιολόγων", in Th. Zeses/P. Asemakopoulou-Atzaka/B. Katsaros (eds.), *Η Μακεδονία κατά την εποχή των Παλαιολόγων, Β´ Συμπόσιο, Θεσσαλονίκη 14–20 Δεκεμβρίου 1992* (Διεθνή Συμπόσια για τη Μακεδονία), Thessaloniki 2002, pp. 143–72.

Lamberz, E., "Die Handschriftenproduktion in den Athosklöstern bis 1453", in G. Cavallo/G. De Gregorio/M. Maniaci (eds.), *Scritture, libri e testi nelle aree provinciali di Bisanzio, Atti del seminario di Erice, 18–25 Settembre 1988*, Spoleto 1991, pp. 25–78.

Lamberz, E., "Die Schenkung des Kaisers Johannes VI. Kantakuzenos an das Kloster Vatopedi und die Schreiberzentren Konstantinopels im 14. Jahrhundert", in I. Ševčenko/G.G. Litavrin/W.K. Hanak (eds.), *Acts [of the] XVIIIth International*

Congress of Byzantine Studies. Selected Papers, Moscow 1991, vol. 4: *Literature, Sources, Numismatics and History of Sciences* (Byzantine Studies/ Études Byzantines, New Series, Supplementum, 4), Shepherdstown, WV 1996, pp. 155–67.

Lamberz, E., "The Library of Vatopaidi and Its Manuscripts", in *The Holy and Great Monastery of Vatopaidi. Tradition – History – Art,* vol. 2, Mount Athos 1998.

Müller-Wiener, W., *Bildlexikon zur Topographie Istanbuls: Byzantion-Konstantinupoli s-Istanbul bis zum Beginn des 17. Jahrhunderts,* Tübingen 1977.

Munitiz, J.A., *Nicephori Blemmydae Autobiographia sive curriculum vitae necnon Epistola universalior* (Corpus Christianorum. Series Graeca, 13), Turnhout 1984.

Nicol, D.M., *Meteora, the Rock Monasteries of Thessaly,* London 1963.

Nikonanos, N., *Μετέωρα. Τα μοναστήρια και η ιστορία τους,* Athens ³2009.

Papazis, D., "Σύντομη ιστορία της Ι. Μονής του Τιμίου Προδρόμου (Σκήτη) Βεροίας", *Nicolaus* 25 (1998), 363–95.

Paschalidis, S., "Ἐκφάνσεις τῆς λογιότητας στὸ Ἅγιον Ὅρος κατὰ τὴν Παλαιολόγεια περίοδο", in D. Kaklamanos (ed.), *Πρακτικὰ Η΄ Διεθνοῦς Ἐπιστημονικοῦ Συνεδρίου: Ἅγιον Ὅρος καὶ Λογιοσύνη, Θεσσαλονίκη 24–24 Νοεμβρίου 2013,* Thessaloniki 2014, pp. 43–52.

Paschalidis, S./D. Strates, *Τὰ μοναστήρια τῆς Μακεδονίας. Α΄ Ἀνατολικὴ Μακεδονία,* Thessaloniki 1996.

Pérez Martín, I., "El 'estilo hodegos' y su proyección en las escrituras constantinopolitanas", *Segno e Testo* 6 (2008), 389–458.

Politis, L., "Jean-Joasaph Cantacuzène fut-il copiste?", *Revue des Études Byzantines* 14 (1956), 195–99.

Samara, D., *Θεόδωρος Μουζάλων. Ἡ ζωὴ καὶ τὸ συγγραφικὸ ἔργο ἑνός λογίου τοῦ 13ου αἰώνα* (Βυζαντινά Κείμενα και Μελέτες, 64), Thessaloniki 2018.

Ševčenko, I., "Theodore Metochites, the Chora and the Intellectual Trends of his Time", in P.A. Underwood (ed.), *The Kariye Djami, IV. Studies in the art of the Kariye Djami and its intellectual background,* Princeton 1975, pp. 17–55.

Sklavenite, A., Συμβολή στη μελέτη των επιστολών του Νικηφόρου Γρηγορά, Athens 2019.

Smyrlis, K., *La fortune des grands monastères byzantins (fin du Xe–milieu du XIVe siècle)* (Monographies, 21), Paris 2006.

Sophianos, D.Z., "Τα χειρόγραφα των Μετεώρων. Ιστορική επισκόπηση – Γενική θεώρηση", *Τρικαλινά* 8 (1988), 35–89.

P. Soustal (ed.), *Heilige Berge und Wüsten. Byzanz und sein Umfeld, Referate auf den 21. Internationalen Kongress für Byzantinistik, London 21–26 August 2006* (Veröffentlichungen zur Byzanzforschung, 16), Vienna 2009.

Talbot, A.M., "An Introduction to Byzantine Monasticism", *Illinois Classical Studies* 12 (1987), 229–41 (repr. in ead., *Women and Religious Life in Byzantium,* Aldershot 2001, no. XI).

Talbot, A.M., "Bluestocking Nuns: Intellectual Life in the Convents of Late Byzantium", in *Okeanos: Essays presented to Ihor Ševčenko on his Sixtieth Birthday by his Colleagues and Students, Harvard Ukrainian Studies* 7 (1983), 604–18 (repr. in ead., *Women and Religious Life in Byzantium*, Aldershot 2001, no. XVIII).

Talbot, A.M., "Empress Theodora Palaiologina, Wife of Michael VIII", *Dumbarton Oaks Papers* 46 (1992), 295–303 (repr. in ead., *Women and Religious Life in Byzantium*, Aldershot 2001, no. V).

Taxidis, I., *Μάξιμος Πλανούδης: Συμβολή στη μελέτη του corpus των επιστολών του* (Βυζαντινά Κείμενα και Μελέτες, 58), Thessaloniki 2012.

Tinnefeld, F., "Intellectuals in Late Byzantine Thessalonike", *Dumbarton Oaks Papers* 57 (2003), 153–72.

Verpeaux, J., "Notes prosopographiques sur la famille Choumnos", *Byzantinoslavica* 20 (1959), 252–66.

Volk, O., *Die byzantinischen Klosterbibliotheken von Konstantinopel, Thessalonike und Kleinasien*, PhD thesis, University of Munich 1954.

Vryonis, S., *The Decline of Medieval Hellenism in Asia Minor and the Process of Islamization from the Eleventh through the Fifteenth Century*, Berkeley 1986.

Wilson, N.G., "The Libraries of the Byzantine World", *Greek Roman and Byzantine Studies* 8 (1967), 53–80.

CHAPTER 10

The Hesychast Controversy: Events, Personalities, Texts and Trends

Ioannis Polemis

1 Introduction

The term "hesychast controversy"[1] refers to a quarrel that broke out in Byzantium around the year 1335. The two main protagonists were Gregory Palamas (*PLP* 21546), later metropolitan of Thessaloniki, and Barlaam of Calabria (*PLP* 2284). The quarrel started as a disagreement on a question concerning the proper way of refuting the Latins: whether apodictic arguments were permitted or not during theological discussions. However, very soon the initial disagreement was forgotten and the discussions focused on two issues that became critical: whether through prayer man may obtain a vision of the uncreated light of God in the way the disciples of Christ had the opportunity to see it on Mount Tabor during the Transfiguration, and whether there is a real distinction between God's uncreated essence and His uncreated energies, in which man may participate. These problems are certainly dogmatic, involving the perennial question of man's union with God. The Byzantine ascetic literature of the previous centuries avoided clear-cut doctrinal formulations of the relevant problems. The term "hesychast" is not misleading, since the quarrel had to do with the contemporary practices of hesychast prayer and the goal of that prayer which, according to certain monastic circles, was the vision of the divine. As Louth points out, the hesychast tradition "is a tradition of (originally monastic) prayer based on repetition of the Jesus prayer

---

1 An extensive bibliography on hesychasm up to 2003 was compiled by Horujy, *Isihasm. Annotirovannaja bibliografia*. A bibliography on Palamas was compiled by Knežević, *Gregory Palamas*. On earlier literature on Palamism, see Stiernon, "Bulletin sur le palamisme", pp. 232–341. The relevant chapter in Beck, *Kirche*, pp. 712–73, remains indispensable. An excellent summary of the most recent trends in the vast bibliography, especially in the orthodox world, concerning Palamas is to be found in Russell, *Gregory Palamas and the making of Palamism*, pp. 210–30. Russell has recently published a very useful collection of the main texts referring to Hesychasm in translation, see Russell, *The Hesychast Controversy and the Debate with Islam*. Some important texts pertaining to the Palamite controversy have been recently translated by Russell, *The Hesychast Controversy and the Debate with Islam*.

© KONINKLIJKE BRILL NV, LEIDEN, 2023 | DOI:10.1163/9789004527089_012

("Lord Jesus Christ, Son of God, have mercy on me, a sinner"), under the direction of a spiritual father, which leads to a conscious experience of the presence of God, often in the form of a vision of light".[2] Equally justifiable is the term "Palamite controversy",[3] if we take into account the fact that Palamas' theories were at the center of all relevant discussions and quarrels. A rough outline of the main events of this controversy will be drawn over the following lines. It is impossible to summarize all the results of earlier and recent research on the controversy; the bibliography is immense. My ambition is to give the readers the opportunity to form an idea of their own on the issues involved in the controversy. I shall refrain from dealing with the social aspects of the controversy or with the impact of the discussions on Byzantine art, but the reader must be aware that these aspects are also present.[4] Unfortunately, I lack the necessary qualifications to discuss the influence exerted by hesychasm on the thought of Russian, Bulgarian and Serbian theologians of the 14th–15th c., which is an important aspect of the hesychast controversy.

2 The Beginnings of the Controversy (1334–1340)

The beginnings of the hesychast controversy are somewhat obscure. It all began with a rather trivial disagreement between Gregory Palamas, a well-educated scion of an aristocratic family of Constantinople who was a monk on Mount Athos,[5] and Barlaam of Calabria, a Greek-speaking monk from Southern Italy. The latter, who had come to Byzantium in order to study the

---

2 Louth, "Light, Vision, and Religious Experience in Byzantium", p. 89.

3 Fyrigos, *Dalla controversia palamitica*, p. 158, introduces a distinction between the terms "Palamite controversy", which refers to the discussion of Palamas with Barlaam concerning the proper terminology to be employed in anti-Latin polemics, and "hesychast controversy" which refers to the discussion about the hesychast prayer and the divine light. Beyer (ed. & trans., Kallistos I of Constantinople, *The Life of Gregory Sinaites*, p. 7), strongly protests against any identification of hesychasm with Palamism, which is just a doctrinal interpretation and defence of the hesychast phenomenon. He even refers to Palamas as a pseudo-hesychast (ibid., p. 12), arguing that in his case the genuine religious experience of such true hesychasts as Gregory Sinaites, gives way to ideology (ibid., pp. 25–26). See also, Nikephoros Gregoras, *Antirrhetic works*, ed. id., p. 92.

4 See, respectively, e.g., Sekulovski, "The Social Aspects of Fourteenth-Century Hesychasm", pp. 373–377, Charalampidis, "La rappresentazione della Lux increata", pp. 41–50, and Andreopoulos, *Metamorphosis*, pp. 209–42.

5 A full list of the works of Palamas is to be found in Sinkewicz, "Gregory Palamas", pp. 138–55 and in Vernačkii, "Grigorii Palama", pp. 17–26.

THE HESYCHAST CONTROVERSY   347

ancient authors more closely,[6] and had been involved already in a controversy with Nikephoros Gregoras (*PLP* 4443),[7] being more familiar than most
Byzantine scholars with the intricate doctrinal positions of the Roman Church,
was entrusted by the Emperor Andronikos III (*PLP* 21437) and his influential
collaborator, the *megas domestikos* John Kantakouzenos (*PLP* 10973), with the
laborious task of negotiating with the legates of Pope John XXII (*PLP* 8664),
Franciscus de Camerino (*PLP* 30163) and Richard, bishop of Cherson; the discussions took place in the early months of 1334.[8] At that time, at the instigation of his friend Gregory Akindynos (*PLP* 495), Gregory Palamas undertook
the composition of his two *Apodictic Treatises against the Latins*.[9] It is to be
surmised that Palamas had been informed about the negotiations taking place
at the time and wanted to express his own views on the most thorny issue,
that of the procession of the Holy Spirit, and possibly to present himself as
the ideal interlocutor of the Latins, undermining Barlaam's position. Certain
passages in his *Second Apodictic Treatise against the Latins* clearly anticipate
his theory on the distinction between God's essence and His uncreated energies. However, there is some doubt whether Palamas had already at this stage
formulated a clear version of his teaching. Kakridis,[10] and Nadal,[11] based on
the Slavonic translation of this treatise of Palamas, which omits certain passages of the Greek text referring to the divine energies, came to the conclusion that these passages were later additions, made by the author many years
afterwards, and that consequently we are not permitted to postulate a clear
formulation of Palamas' teaching at this stage. However, even if this is true,
it is clear that Palamas in his *Second Apodictic Treatise against the Latins*
made use of Nikephoros Blemmydes' (*PLP* 2897) distinction between the eternal procession of the Spirit from the Father and the temporal distribution of

---

6   On the motives of Barlaam's coming to Byzantium see Fyrigos, *Dalla controversia palam-*
     itica, pp. 162–63, and Quaranta, "Un profugo a Bisanzio prima di Barlaam", pp. 88–89.
7   On this controversy, see Nikephoros Gregoras, *Antirrhetic works*, ed. Beyer, pp. 36–54.
8   Nadal, *La résistance d'Akindynos*, pp. 23–28. I adhere to the chronology of events suggested
     by Nadal, and not the one adopted by Meyendorff, *Introduction à l'étude de Grégoire*
     Palamas, pp. 65–94, or that of Chrestou (ed.), Gregory Palamas, *Works*, vol. 1, pp. 180–99,
     and 315–54, which is outdated. Slightly different, but very close to that of Nadal, is the
     chronology proposed by Sinkewicz, "The doctrine of the knowledge of God", pp. 183–93.
9   Nadal, *La résistance d'Akindynos*, pp. 28–30, and 104. The text is published by Chrestou
     (ed.), Gregory Palamas, *Works*, vol. 1, pp. 23–153. See an analysis of those two texts by Beyer
     (ed.), Nikephoros Gregoras, *Antirrhetic works*, pp. 72–76.
10   Kakridis, *Codex 88 des Klosters Dečani*, pp. 56–62, 82–85. See also Kaltsogianni, «Δύο ἄγνω-
     στα ἀποσπάσματα», pp. 89–100.
11   Nadal, *La résistance d'Akindynos*, pp. 105–07.

His gifts through the Son.[12] This theory, later adopted by Gregory of Cyprus (*PLP* 4590) and other Byzantine theologians of the 13th c., was clearly the basis for Palamas' introducing the distinction between God's essence and His energies, which could be communicated to the creatures.

It is not certain whether Palamas was familiar at the time of his composing the two anti-Latin treatises with the anti-Latin works of Barlaam, and if so, with which one of them.[13] In any case, sometime after 15 May 1335,[14] Palamas wrote his *First Letter to Akindynos* accusing Barlaam of denying the value of apodictic arguments referring to the divine realities.[15] It is most probable that Palamas had misunderstood Barlaam's position. However, in his letter Palamas speaks quite clearly about a distinction existing between what belongs to God Himself and those things that are to be found around Him.[16] In the later writings of Palamas what belongs to God was identified with His essence, while His energies were called "the things that are around God". At the same time Palamas made an ominous statement that was to have serious consequences afterwards: there are two ways of knowing God. Those who are close to Him are granted a spiritual illumination, which is the most perfect sort of knowledge; those who are not yet purified, may attain a certain knowledge of God by studying the creatures.[17]

Akindynos tried to negotiate between the two opponents, and Barlaam wrote his *First Letter to Palamas*[18] explaining to him his method of dealing with the Latins and his view on the uselessness of apodictic syllogisms for those discussing theological subjects.[19] Near the end of his letter Barlaam, on the basis of a text of the Neoplatonic philosopher Syrianos, argues that even the pagan

---

12   Polemis, "Nikephoros Blemmydes and Gregorios Palamas", pp. 179–89. See also Ioannidis, Ὁ Νικηφόρος Βλεμμύδης, p. 261, and Stavrou, *Nicéphore Blemmydès, Oeuvres théologiques*, pp. 116–18.

13   See Barlaam of Calabria, *Works*, ed. Fyrigos, pp. 228–30, and Nadal, *La résistance d'Akindynos*, pp. 109–110. Sinkewicz, "The Doctrine of the Knowledge of God", p. 196, believes that Palamas, while writing his *First Letter to Akindynos*, had read the fifth anti-Latin treatise of Barlaam.

14   Beyer (ed., Nikephoros Gregoras, *Antirrhetic works*, p. 76), dates that letter to 1336.

15   Gregory Palamas, *Works*, ed. Chrestou, vol. 1, pp. 203–19. See also Fyrigos, *Dalla controversia palamitica*, pp. 76–82, and Sinkewicz, "The Doctrine of the Knowledge of God", pp. 202–15. See also the fundamental analysis of Podskalsky, *Theologie und Philosophie*, pp. 124–73.

16   See Sinkewicz, "The Doctrine of the Knowledge of God", pp. 210–15.

17   Ibid., pp. 222–23.

18   Barlaam of Calabria, *Greek Letters*, ed. & trans. Fyrigos, pp. 194–272.

19   On this subject there is an extensive bibliography. See mainly Ierodiakonou, "The Anti-Logical Movement in the Fourteenth Century", pp. 219–36, and Athanasopoulos, "Demonstration", 361–73.

THE HESYCHAST CONTROVERSY

349

sages were illuminated by God, at least to a certain degree.[20] Palamas replied with his *First Letter to Barlaam*,[21] while at the same time writing his *Second Letter to Akindynos*.[22] Palamas accuses Barlaam of believing that the Greek philosophers were illuminated by God; this was a privilege of the Christian saints and ascetics, who were united with God and taught by Him in an ineffable manner, having been illuminated by Him with an intelligible and divine light.[23]

Barlaam answered without delay: in his *Second Letter to Palamas*[24] he questioned Palamas about the exact nature of the light the hesychasts received from God: did it resemble fire, having the same colour with it, did it enter man in an inexplicable manner, as some people maintained? At this stage, "Barlaam's doctrine of the knowledge of God is characterised by a pronounced intellectualist emphasis".[25] He seems to deny the gifts of the divine grace,[26] and thus places himself outside mainstream Byzantine Orthodoxy: while he initially expressed his mistrust towards the apodictic syllogisms of secular philosophy, he ended as a supporter of the purely philosophic way of approaching God, neglecting the charismatic aspect of that approach.[27] In his *Second Letter to Barlaam*,[28] Palamas further clarified his position: the light was one of those realities which were to be found around God, like His wisdom and life, which, although distinct from God's essence, were also uncreated, and identical to His energies. The hesychast controversy is formulated more or less clearly in this letter for the first time: there is an uncreated light distinct from God's essence, but identical to His energy, which can be communicated to men. He also made some insinuations at the acquaintances of Barlaam, who informed him concerning the hesychast practices of the monks.[29]

In two of Barlaam's *Letters* to a certain hesychast named Ignatios [*PLP* 8058],[30] the Calabrian had vaguely referred to certain people who maintained that the mind of man might enter into his heart through his nostrils.[31] Who were these men? According to the testimony of Gregory Palamas and most other authors

---

20 See Sinkewicz, "The Doctrine of the Knowledge of God", p. 224.
21 Gregory Palamas, *Works*, ed. Chrestou, vol. 1, pp. 225–59.
22 Ibid., pp. 220–24. See also Fyrigos, *Dalla controversia palamitica*, pp. 91–92.
23 Fyrigos, *Dalla controversia palamitica*, pp. 94–95.
24 Ibid., pp. 298–368.
25 Sinkewicz, "The Doctrine of the Knowledge of God", p. 241.
26 Ibid., p. 237.
27 Ibid., p. 242.
28 Gregory Palamas, *Works*, ed. Chrestou, vol. 1, pp. 260–95.
29 Sinkewicz, "The Doctrine of the Knowledge of God", p. 228.
30 On his identity see Fyrigos, *Dalla controversia palamitica*, pp. 105–06.
31 Ibid., pp. 100–01.

dealing with the events, sometime around 1335 Barlaam was astonished to hear certain illiterate and ignorant monks in Thessaloniki affirming that man had the capability to see an uncreated light through his bodily eyes during his prayer, provided that he followed certain psycho-somatic practices (e.g. sitting with the head gazing upon the area of the navel and restraining breathing, so that the mind might return to its original place, which was the heart[32]) supposedly taught by certain ascetic fathers, and he rushed to accuse them of Messalianistic leanings. Rigo has identified Barlaam's informant as Ignatios the hesychast, who, in his turn, was familiar with the teaching of Gregory Sinaites (*PLP* 4601). In his view, Barlaam's informants were not ignorant monks, but certain prominent monastics of Thessaloniki, who belonged to the circle of Ignatios. At a later stage Barlaam read Palamas' *First Triad* and responded to it by writing his works, which were in turn refuted by Palamas in his *Second Triad*.[33] It is evident that Barlaam had in mind the so-called "Jesus-prayer", an ascetic practice of older times,[34] which had become prominent once more in the 13th c., when two treatises advertising it were written, the *Method of the Holy Prayer* falsely attributed to Symeon the New Theologian[35] and the *Discourse on Prayer* by Nikephoros the Athonite (*PLP* 20325).[36] These treatises, which were widely circulated and enjoyed a certain popularity among the monks of Athos,[37] were known to both Barlaam and Palamas.[38] One should not forget the writings of the aforementioned Gregory Sinaites, who was also a supporter of these practices,[39] and whose students had come into contact with Barlaam.[40] The authors of these ascetic works advocated a new way of approaching God and being united with Him by constantly repeating "O Lord Jesus Christ have mercy on me"; the union involved the drawing of

---

32   Sinkewicz, "The Doctrine of the Knowledge of God", p. 232.

33   Fyrigos, *Dalla controversia palamitica*, pp. 147–49.

34   On the "Sinaitic" background of the Jesus prayer, see Pseudo-Symeon the New Theologian, *Oration*, ed. Hausherr, pp. 142–48, Rigo, "Gregorio il Sinaita", Conticello/Conticello, *La théologie byzantine*, pp. 94–95, and Gunnarson, *Mystical Realism*, p. 67.

35   Pseudo-Symeon the New Theologian, *Oration*, ed. Hausherr, pp. 150–209. See also Rigo, *Mistici bizantini*, pp. 401–402.

36   Nikephoros the Athonite, *Philokalia*, pp. 18–28. See also Rigo, "Niceforo l'Esicasta", pp. 78–81, and Ware, "The Hesychasts", pp. 244–46.

37   A very useful list of those monks practicing hesychast prayer on Mount Athos in the first half of the 14th c. has been drawn by Rigo, "Massimo il Kausokalyba", pp. 194–96. On the views on hesychastic prayer of Maximos of Kausokalybia (*PLP* 16810), a contemporary of Palamas, see Ware, "St Maximos of Kapsokalyvia", pp. 409–30.

38   Rigo, *Monaci esicasti e monaci bogomili*, pp. 50–56.

39   Id., "Le tecniche d'orazione esicastica", pp. 92–95.

40   Id., *Mistici bizantini*, p. LXXV.

THE HESYCHAST CONTROVERSY   351

the intellect of the ascetic into his heart through the control of the ascetic's own respiration and sometimes the concentration of his gaze on the navel,[41] thus restoring the mind's position that had been destroyed as a result of the original sin.[42] However, the texts are far removed from any Bogomilistic tendencies. Based on a detailed study of the relevant texts, Rigo came to the conclusion that Barlaam accused these monks of "Messalianism" on the basis of certain superficial similarities of the teaching of the monks of Thessaloniki with the standard accusations levelled against the Messalians by earlier Byzantine heresiologists.[43] However, taking into account the fact that Bogomilism, identified by Byzantine heresiologists with Messalianism, was widespread among the monks of Athos, Rigo argues for the existence of a certain similarity in the ascetic practices of the Orthodox and the Bogomil monks; this was almost inevitable. A case of a certain overlapping of Orthodox and "Messalian" practices is that of the circle of Isidore Boucheiras (*PLP* 3140), the future Patriarch of Constantinople (1347–1350).

Barlaam composed two extensive treatises concerning the teaching of the monks, where he refuted the relevant theories in detail, attempting to prove their Messalianistic background, but these treatises are unfortunately lost. Palamas composed his *First Triad on the Defence of the Holy Hesychasts*,[44] with which he refuted the doctrinal positions of Barlaam, defending the teaching of those monks who, due to their ineptitude for doctrinal discussions, were unable to answer Barlaam's objections themselves; it is on the basis of the first two *Triads* of Palamas that we are able to reconstruct Barlaam's argumentation to a certain extent. The *First Triad* dealt with three subjects: the uselessness of secular education, the way of uniting the mind with the heart during prayer, and the exact nature of the light which illumined the hesychasts. Palamas identified this light with the one seen by the Disciples of Christ on Mount Tabor, during the Lord's Transfiguration. It seems that Palamas, while writing the *First Triad*, did not have direct access to any of Barlaam's texts, instead relying on the information given to him by certain monks who knew the Calabrian's

---

41   On the background of this specific point, see id., "Le tecniche d'orazione esicastica", pp. 114–15, and Meyendorff, "Le thème du 'retour en soi'", pp. 188–206.

42   Rigo, *Mistici bizantini*, pp. LXVI–LXXII. One should take care to distinguish the variants of this technique: some authors combine the repetition of Jesus' name with the control of human respiration, while others recommend only the repetition of Jesus' name, see id., "Le tecniche d'orazione esicastica", pp. 85, 90–92, and 98–103.

43   Id., *Monaci esicasti e monaci bogomili*, pp. 86–88, and 274.

44   On the details, see Rigo, *Monaci esicasti e monaci bogomili*, pp. 41–42. The two *Triads* have been published by Chrestou (ed.), Gregory Palamas, *Works*, vol. 1, pp. 359–613.

views.[45] Only when composing his *Second Triad* was he able to obtain copies of Barlaam's writings, to which he explicitly referred.[46] Barlaam, in contrast to Palamas' distinction between a human and a divine philosophy, maintained that there was only one philosophy: both secular knowledge and the divine revelation have a common starting point and a common end.[47] Anyone who wishes to become similar to God, must purify his soul both morally and intellectually through the acquisition of knowledge.[48] As far as the hesychast prayer was concerned, Barlaam insisted that the human body played no part in the procedure of man's unification with God,[49] decrying the hesychast practices (e.g. the control of one's respiration) recommended by the monks as violent.[50] Barlaam attacked them for pretending to see a divine light which was perceivable: if perceivable, it could not be divine. Only the intelligible light of man's own mind, or the light of the angels, may be so described;[51] the light of Tabor was just a created symbol of the divinity which might be comprehended by man's senses. He also pointed out that the mind should not return to the body during prayer, but must be as far away from it as possible.[52]

Barlaam had visited Italy in 1339 as a legate of the Emperor Andronikos III. In his absence Palamas had composed his *Second Triad*. Barlaam returned to Thessaloniki in the autumn of the same year and composed his lost treatise *Against the Messalians*, which was published near the end of 1339. Some extracts from it are preserved in Palamas' *Third Triad*,[53] written in 1340.[54] Barlaam affirmed that the light of Tabor is merely a sensible light; whatever was not identical to God's essence, was created. Barlaam accused Palamas and his followers that by admitting the existence of many uncreated divine energies, they introduced a new polytheism into the Church. Palamas returned to Athos, where in 1340 he managed to persuade several leading monks of the monasteries and the hermitages to publish a pamphlet denouncing Barlaam

---

45 Fyrigos, *Dalla controversia palamitica*, pp. 118–19.

46 Ibid., pp. 122–25, where the problem of the titles of Barlaam's writings is thoroughly discussed.

47 Ibid., pp. 125–28.

48 Ibid., p. 130.

49 Ibid., pp. 133–34.

50 Ibid., p. 133, n. 101.

51 ibid., p. 139.

52 Rigo, *Mistici bizantini*, p. LXXVI.

53 Gregory Palamas, *Works*, ed. Chrestou, vol. 1, pp. 615–94. See also the analysis of this problem by Fyrigos, *Dalla controversia palamitica*, pp. 149–59, and Gunnarson, *Mystical Realism*, pp. 147–50.

54 Fyrigos, *Dalla controversia palamitica*, p. 159.

THE HESYCHAST CONTROVERSY   353

and vindicating his own position. This is the so called *Hagioretic Tome*.[55] It is noteworthy that the teaching on the distinction between God's essence and His energies is presented as a doctrine, not previously known to everybody but revealed by God at that particular time.[56]

3   The Further Development of the Crisis and the Controversy between Palamas and Akindynos (1341–1347)

Despite the attempts of their mutual friend Gregory Akindynos to reconcile Barlaam with Palamas, the gap between the two opponents was further widened through Barlaam's denouncing Palamas to the Patriarch John XIV Kalekas (*PLP* 10288), who had no other solution than to summon Palamas to Constantinople in order to defend himself in front of the Church authorities. After writing his third Letter to Akindynos, aggressively accusing Barlaam,[57] Palamas, accompanied by Isidoros Boucheiras, arrived in Constantinople probably in January of 1341, where he was soon joined by his friend David Dishypatos (*PLP* 5532), who had played a role in the early phase of Palamas' quarrel with Barlaam. The patriarch was inclined to convoke a council to settle the matter, but at that time the Emperor Andronikos III and John Kantakouzenos were absent from Constantinople. Barlaam, afraid of the outcome of the council, asked for the intervention of the emperor, who was favorably disposed towards him. When the emperor finally returned to the capital in May 1341, the road for the convocation of the council was open. It was convoked on 10 June 1341. Emperor Andronikos III's death five days after the convocation was a great misfortune for Barlaam. The outcome of the council was thus unfavourable to Barlaam, who had failed to convince the Church authorities that the monks defended by Palamas were Messalians. However, in the meantime a rift opened between Palamas and his friend Gregory Akindynos, who refused to recognize the validity of the former's main teaching concerning the distinction between divine essence and energies. He urged Palamas to adopt a more conciliatory attitude, refraining from further doctrinal discussions and avoiding certain phrases that had scandalized his opponents (for example that the

---

55   Gregory Palamas, *Works*, ed. Chrestou, vol. 2, pp. 567–78. That edition has now been superseded by the edition of Rigo, Gregory Palamas, *The Hagioretic Tome*, pp. 108–26.

56   Nadal, *La résistance d'Akindynos*, p. 151.

57   See Nadal, "La redaction premier", pp. 235–85, who points out that Palamas later reworked his letter, in order to expurgate certain ambiguous expressions from it. For similar cases, see Candal, "Escrito de Palamas desconocido", 357–440, and Polemis, *Theologica varia inedita*, pp. LXVI–LXX.

light of Tabor was a lesser divinity). Palamas, anxious to secure the support of Akindynos before the council, had promised to correct his most extreme theories, but his intransigence only increased after the council.[58] Akindynos consequently denounced him as a liar. The council was convoked once more in July of 1341, after Barlaam had abandoned Constantinople, recognizing his own defeat at the hands of the Palamites. John Kantakouzenos, the most powerful man of the state after the death of the emperor, was favorable to Palamas. The Palamites claimed afterwards that Akindynos had been condemned by the second council of 1341, but this is far from certain.[59] The synodical *Tome* of 1341,[60] which was written by the followers of Palamas in July 1341 after the official closing of the works of the second council,[61] at the insistence of Kantakouzenos and despite the objections of Patriarch Kalekas, adopted Palamas' position on the light of Tabor and the hesychast prayer and condemned Barlaam. But there was a caveat: no more discussions on these subjects were permitted.[62] Despite the affirmations of the Palamites, the *Tome* of 1341 did not vindicate all the positions of their teacher, as Orthodox scholars maintain to this day. That is why Kantakouzenos, after he became emperor, ordered patriarch Philotheos Kokkinos (*PLP* 11917) to remove this document from the patriarchal register.[63]

A civil war broke out in the autumn of 1341. A coup d'état organized by the opponents of Kantakouzenos during his absence from Constantinople placed all power in the hands of the Empress Anna of Savoy (*PLP* 21347) and Alexios Apokaukos (*PLP* 1180). Kantakouzenos, who was in Didymoteichon at the time, proclaimed himself emperor. Patriarch John Kalekas supported the ruling clique of Anna and Apokaukos. Palamas' relations with the patriarch deteriorated, while Akindynos, presenting himself as a supporter of the empress and the patriarch, gained the latter's favor. Palamas was ultimately arrested on Kalekas' orders in the early autumn of 1342. In late 1341 and early 1342 Palamas, neglecting the prohibition of any further doctrinal disputes by the *Tome* of 1341, composed a number of treatises against Akindynos: a. The treatise, *On how many senses one can speak of the divine union and distinction*,[64] b. *An apology*

---

58 This is affirmed by Akindynos himself in his extensive letter to patriarch John Kalekas, Gregory Akindynos, *Oration against John Kalekas*, ed. Nadal, pp. 260, 87–120.

59 Nadal, *La résistance d'Akindynos*, pp. 217, and 226–230. See also id., "Denys l'Aréopagite", p. 537.

60 *Tomes of 1341 and 1347*, eds. Hunger/Kresten et al., pp. 208–56. The text has been translated by Russell, *The Hesychast Controversy and the Debate with Islam*, pp. 214–30.

61 On the chronological problems connected with the date of the *Tome*'s publication, see Kresten, "Studien", pp. 45–46, and. n. 2.

62 Nadal, *La résistance d'Akindynos*, pp. 223–24.

63 Ibid., p. 226.

64 Gregory Palamas, *Works*, ed. Chrestou, vol. 2, pp. 69–95.

THE HESYCHAST CONTROVERSY   355

addressed to those who think they can demonstrate that there are two gods,[65]
c. *On divine and divinizing participation,*[66] d. *A dialogue of an Orthodox with a
Barlaamite,*[67] e. The dialogue titled, *Theophanes,*[68] f. The treatise titled, *That
Barlaam and Akindynos are the ones who are dividing the one divinity into two
unequal divinities.*[69] As is evident from the titles of these works, Palamas was
anxious to answer Akindynos' objection that by distinguishing between God's
essence and His uncreated energies he destroyed the simplicity of God, thus
denying one of the fundamental doctrines of the Church.[70] Akindynos, encouraged by John Kalekas, decided to abandon his passivity and launched an open
attack against Palamas. In four of his treatises *Against Palamas* Akindynos
refuted the Palamite positions as those where expounded in his work, *A dialogue of an Orthodox with a Barlaamite*. He also composed a *Shorter Refutation*
of the same Palamite dialogue.[71] Palamas responded to those treatises with a
series of seven *Antirrhetic Treatises against Akindynos.*[72]

In November 1344 Akindynos' efforts to have Palamas condemned were
crowned with success: John Kalekas convoked a council which excommuni-
cated Palamas and deposed his friend Isidoros Boucheiras, who in the meantime had been elected bishop of Monemvasia.[73] Kalekas was ready to ordain
Akindynos a bishop, but was opposed by both the Empress Anna and the *megas
doux* Apokaukos, who defended Palamas. The patriarch went as far as composing an exegesis of the *Tome* of 1341, claiming that it had been falsely interpreted
by Palamas and his followers to further their own plans.[74] In his turn Palamas
refuted the text of Kalekas. Although imprisoned, he also wrote several letters to his friends and other prominent members of the clergy, attempting to
influence them in his favor and to undermine the position of Akindynos and
Kalekas. On 2 February 1347 the Empress, who took the side of Palamas, openly
convoked a council which deposed Kalekas and vindicated the Palamites. That
same night Kantakouzenos, Palamas' devoted friend, entered Constantinople,

---

65   Ibid., pp. 96–136.
66   Ibid., pp. 137–63.
67   Ibid., pp. 164–218.
68   Ibid., pp. 219–62. On this work, see also Kapriev, "Systemelemente", pp. 263–90.
69   Gregory Palamas, *Works*, ed. Chrestou, vol. 2, pp. 263–77. According to Nadal, *La résistance
      d'Akindynos*, p. 237, this treatise was written somewhat later.
70   Sinkewicz, "Gregory Palamas", pp. 134–35, and 140–41. I offer their titles abbreviated.
71   Nadal (ed.), *Gregoru Acindyni*, pp. XXX–XXXI. All these works of Akindynos have been
      published by Nadal in this volume.
72   Gregory Palamas, *Works*, ed. Chrestou, vol. 3, pp. 39–506.
73   On the activity of Isidoros on behalf of Kantakouzenos, see Weiss, *Joannes Kantakuzenos*,
      pp. 113–14.
74   Meyendorff, *Introduction à l'étude de Grégoire Palamas*, pp. 110–18.

356　　　　　　　　　　　　　　　　　　　　　　　　　　　　　　　　　POLEMIS

seizing the reins of power. In May 1347 Isidoros Boucheiras became patriarch and Palamas was ordained metropolitan of Thessaloniki. Akindynos disappeared without a trace. A new *Tome* vindicating Palamas' positions was promulgated in 1347.[75] The second phase of the hesychast controversy had come to its close.

4　The Involvement of Nikephoros Gregoras and the Council of 1351

Palamas was unable to reach Thessaloniki, which at the time was held by the opponents of Kantakouzenos. He only managed to do so three years after his ordination. Before coming to his see, Palamas composed the *One Hundred and Fifty Chapters on Topics of Natural and Theological Science, the Moral and Ascetic Life, intended as a Purge for the Barlaamite Corruption*,[76] adopting the literary genre of the ascetic *kephalaia*, in order to explain his doctrines to an audience which was in all probability monastic. Palamas had realized earlier than most of his opponents, that the support of the monks was crucial for anyone who wished to gain the upper hand in a doctrinal controversy. Even at this late stage, when his position seemed to be secure, Palamas sought to continue influencing the monks of the empire, since his problems were far from over. At this time Palamas also composed his *Three chapters on prayer*[77]

75　Hunger/Kresten et al. (eds.), *Das Register des Patriarchats*, pp. 346–82. A detailed account of those events in Rigo, *1347. Isidoro patriarca di Constantinopoli*, pp. 16–63. The text has been recently translated by Russell, *The Hesychast Controversy and the Debate with Islam*, pp. 294–322.

76　Gregory Palamas, *The One Hundred and Fifty Chapters*, ed. Sinkewicz, and Gregory Palamas, *Works*, ed. Chrestou, vol. 5, pp. 37–119. See also Sinkewicz, "Christian Theology", pp. 334–51. A detailed analysis of this work is attempted by Müller-Schauenburg, *Religiöse Erfahrung*, pp. 161–282. On the use of several extracts of Augustine's *De trinitate* by Palamas in this work, see Flogaus, "Die heimliche Blick nach Westen", pp. 275–97, and Demetrakopoulos, *Αὐγουστῖνος καὶ Γρηγόριος Παλαμᾶς*. See also Flogaus, "Inspiration-Exploitation-Distortion", pp. 63–80. Neo-Palamite theologians are greatly disturbed by this case of direct dependence of Palamas on Augustine, see, e.g., how Kapriev, *Vizantiiskata Filosofia*, p. 347, tries in vain to diminish the importance of this discovery. See also Sopko, "Scholasticism and Orthodoxy", pp. 383–98. More bibliography on this subject is to be found in Biriukov, "Sv. Grigorii Palama", pp. 456–57, n. 25. Krausmüller, "Banishing Reason", pp. 60–68, has convincingly argued that Palamas exploited Augustine's restriction of God's image to the man's highest part in order to exclude discursive reasoning from the divine image in man. On other aspects of Palamas' dependence on Augustine see Kappes, "Gregory Palamas' Reception on Augustine's Doctrine", pp. 207–57.

77　Gregory Palamas, *Works*, ed. Chrestou, vol. 5, pp. 157–59.

THE HESYCHAST CONTROVERSY   357

and his *Discourse* addressed to the nun Xene,[78] where, interestingly enough, no
mention of the psycho-somatic technique he had defended a few years previously is to be found.[79]

In July of 1347 certain anti-Palamite bishops, the most prominent of whom
was Matthew Gabalas (*PLP* 3308) of Ephesos, denounced the new patriarch
and refuted the doctrines of Palamas, publishing a formal *Tome* against the
new authorities of the Church. Their driving force was the prominent philosopher Nikephoros Gregoras. A student of Theodore Metochites (*PLP* 17982) and
a faithful partisan of the old Emperor Andronikos II Palaiologos (1282–1328,
PLP 21436), Gregoras had been involved in a controversy with Barlaam of
Calabria as soon as Barlaam arrived in Constantinople in the late thirteen-twenties; Gregoras defended Plato and rejected the Aristotelianism represented by Barlaam. He had not been involved in the early phase of the Palamite
controversy, but it seems that the Empress Anna of Savoy urged him to take an
active part in it as early as 1346, admonishing him to write down his views on
the teaching of Palamas, though she was aware that Gregoras did not share her
late enthusiasm for him. A product of her instigation was a short text against
Palamas entitled *Chapters*.[80] His more extensive *First Antirrhetic Treatises
against Palamas* were published in 1350.[81] John VI Kantakouzenos, who maintained close relations with both Palamas and Gregoras, tried to intervene in
their dispute but was unable to pacify them. Thus a new council was convoked
in Constantinople on 27 May 1351, presided over by Kantakouzenos himself.
As was to be expected, Gregoras and his followers were condemned. In July of
the same year a new *Tome*,[82] written by Neilos Kerameus (*PLP* 11648) (or Neilos
Kabasilas, *PLP* 10102)[83] and Philotheos Kokkinos, was promulgated, in which
the teaching of Palamas on the distinction between God's essence and energies was definitively recognized as the official teaching of the Church.[84]

---

78   Ibid., pp. 193–230.

79   Rigo, *Mistici bizantini*, pp. LXXIX–LXXX.

80   Nikephoros Gregoras, *Antirrhetic works*, ed. Beyer, p. 111. A detailed account of the activities of the opponents of Palamas after the victory of Kantakouzenos has been recently
     sketched by Rigo, *1347. Isidoro patriarca di Constantinopoli*, pp. 16–94.

81   Sinkewicz, "Gregory Palamas", p. 136.

82   *Patrologia Graeca* 151, col. 717–70, and *Tome of 1351*, ed. Karmiris, pp. 374–410. The text
     has been translated by Russell, *The Hesychast Controversy and the Debate with Islam*,
     pp. 327–76.

83   On the identity of the second author of the *Tome* of 1351 see Kotzabassi, "Eine Akoluthie",
     p. 302, n. 11.

84   The decisions of the council are summarized by Ware, "God Hidden and Revealed", p. 130.

It was the triumph of Palamas. Gregoras was imprisoned and was liberated only in 1353 after John Kantakouzenos had been deposed by John v Palaiologos (*PLP* 21485). It is noteworthy that almost concurrently Palamas, who was travelling from Tenedos to Constantinople, was taken prisoner by the Turks, with a representative of whom he had an interesting theological discussion.[85] In 1355/6 Gregoras completed his *Second Antirrhetic Treatises against Palamas*, which were incorporated into his *Roman History*.[86] Palamas responded to them with his four treatises against Gregoras.[87] The two implacable opponents departed from this world almost at the same time, Palamas in all probability in 1357, and Gregoras soon afterwards, sometime betwen 1358 and 1361.

5   The Aftermath

The condemnation of Gregoras by the council of 1351 brought an end to the controversy concerning the doctrines of Palamas but did not prevent certain Byzantine theologians from discussing these subjects, though not as openly as before. The official declaration by the Church that such an emblematic scholar as Nikephoros Gregoras was a heretic was certainly not an encouraging signal for many intellectuals who were unwilling to obey the commandments of their Church blindly, curtailing their curiosity and their desire to investigate new subjects which were outside the purview of the official Orthodoxy. This tendency, which was evident even at the time of Gregoras' teacher Theodore Metochites, led some Byzantine scholars to seek a closer contact with the Roman Catholic Church. Demetrios Kydones (*PLP* 13876) and his brother Prochoros (*PLP* 13883) learned Latin and translated the main works of Thomas Aquinas into Greek.[88] The translated texts offered the anti-Palamites new arguments against Palamas, inspired by a thorough study of the scholastic arguments concerning the divine simplicity. Prochoros Kydones, who was a monk in the monastery of the Great Lavra on Mount Athos, was denounced by his superior to the Patriarch

---

85   See Phillipidis-Braat, "La captivité de Palamas", pp. 109–222.

86   Nikephoros Gregoras, *Roman History*, ed. Bekker, vol. 3, pp. 266–500. A most welcome partial translation and an extensive summary of the untranslated parts of the six treatises of Gregoras against Palamas have been prepared by Tinnefeld, *Nikephoros Gregoras, Rhomäische Geschichte*, pp. 41–140.

87   Gregory Palamas, *Works*, ed. Chrestou, vol. 4, pp. 231–377.

88   I am not going to discuss the translations of Aquinas here. A useful summary and inventory of the main text was compiled by Papadopoulos, Ἑλληνικαὶ μεταφράσεις θωμιστικῶν ἔργων. A partial edition of that translation was undertaken by a group of Greek philologists and historians of philosophy (without any substantial discussion of the manuscript tradition), see Demetrios Kydones, *Translation*, eds. Leontsinis et al.

THE HESYCHAST CONTROVERSY 359

Philotheos Kokkinos for his anti-Palamite positions. The patriarch, an ardent Palamite, took the opportunity to convene a new council in Constantinople in 1368 which condemned Prochoros, who died soon afterwards, and proceeded to the official sanctification of Gregory Palamas. The convocation of this council and the promulgation of a new *Tome*[89] may be seen as an attempt by Philotheos Kokkinos to undermine the position of Prochoros' brother, Demetrios, who, besides being a leading personality in the intellectual milieu of the capital, was a close collaborator of the Emperor John v Palaiologos, well known for his pro-Western leanings. Prochoros' brother Demetrios wrote a long *Apology for Prochoros*, addressed to the Patriarch Philotheos.

Certain Palamites were alarmed by the apparent success enjoyed by the translations of Demetrios Kydones, even among some Orthodox circles, and rushed to refute the arguments of Thomas Aquinas. Neilos Kabasilas wrote an extensive commentary[90] on the views of Aquinas which were not compatible with the new Palamite teaching of the Byzantine Church,[91] itself immediately refuted by Demetrios Kydones.[92] Unfortunately only the writings of Kabasilas have been published, so we are not in a position to offer a clear judgement on the extent and the full implications of that controversy. However, it is noteworthy that Neilos Kabasilas, in order to ridicule Aquinas' application of philosophic arguments in theological matters, did not hesitate to take advantage of what Barlaam of Calabria had said concerning the value of apodictic arguments, while discussing the matter with Palamas. Neilos Kabasilas tacitly copied whole extracts from Barlaam's anti-Latin works.[93] The same was done by the ex-emperor John vi Kantakouzenos in his *First Antirrhetic Treatise* against Prochoros Kydones. Two other theologians who attacked Aquinas were Kallistos Angelikoudes (*PLP* 145)[94] and Matthew Angelos Panaretos (*PLP* 21649).[95] It seems that the translations of Aquinas into Greek contributed to a growing realization by both anti-Latin and pro-Latin intellectuals that the gap between the two Churches had been widened as a result of the adoption of the Palamite teaching as the official doctine by the Byzantine Church. On the other hand, it

---

89 Rigo (ed.), "Il Monte Athos e la controversia palamitica", pp. 99–134. The text has been translated by Russell, *The Hesychast Controversy and the Debate with Islam*, pp. 417–47.

90 Neilos Kabasilas, *On the Procession of the Holy Spirit*, ed. Candal, pp. 188–384.

91 See an analysis of this treatise from an Orthodox perspective by Jevtitch, *Études Hésychastes*, pp. 106–21.

92 Podskalsky, *Theologie und Philosophie*, p. 196, n. 819. See also Fyrigos, "Tomismo e anti-Tomismo", pp. 27–72.

93 Podskalsky, *Theologie und Philosophie*, p. 194.

94 Kallistos Angelikoudes Melenikiotes, *Against Thomas Aquinas*, ed. Papadopoulos, pp. 27–299.

95 On him see Blanchet, "Éliminer Thomas", pp. 452–65.

360 POLEMIS

must be pointed out that even Byzantine theologians of impeccable Orthodox credentials did not hesitate to tacitly take advantage of the theories of Aquinas while discussing theological problems.[96] This is an indication that despite the growing differences between the two parties, the lines between them could be easily crossed, even after the Palamite disputes were over.

However, the Palamite controversy was not forgotten so easily in Byzantium, even after the canonisation of Palamas. The purges and the persecution of his opponents continued until at least the end of the 14th c.[97] The Emperor Manuel II Palaiologos (1391–1425, PLP 21513), though a friend of Demetrios Kydones and other pro-Latin Byzantine intellectuals, did not lose the opportunity in his long *Dialogue with a Perse* to offer an apology of Palamism,[98] long after the relevant discussions had subsided. Manuel Kalekas (PLP 10289), who became a Dominican monk, composed a long treatise against Palamas somewhere near the end of the 14th c. Symeon of Thessaloniki (PLP 27057) dealt with the "heresy" of Barlaam and Akindynos, though in brief.[99] The leader of the Orthodox party at the council of Florence Mark Eugenikos (PLP 6193) also composed an extensive treatise criticising the doctrines of Barlaam and Akindynos (in reality the defence of those doctrines by Maximos Chrysoberges, PLP 31123), while his adversary Bessarion of Nicaea (PLP 2707) also discussed the subject from another perspective, although in a rather casual manner. Andrew Chrysoberges (PLP 31106) vehemently attacked Palamism in an attempt to refute Mark.[100] The fall of Constantinople brought an end to the theological discussions concerning the distinction between God's essence and His energies. Other subjects became more critical. A new revival of the interest in Palamas and his doctrines would have to wait until the late 18th c., when the circle of Nikodemos of Mount Athos rediscovered Palamism.

---

96 See Demetracopoulos, "Thomas Aquinas' Impact on Late Byzantine Theology", pp. 333–410, and Id., "Palamas Transformed", pp. 263–372. For an interpretation of this phenomenon see Kappes, "A Provisional Definition", 187–202. To say the least, his insistence on both the patristic foundations and the "openess" of late Byzantine theology is open to discussion.

97 Matschke/Tinnefeld, *Die Gesellschaft im späten Byzanz*, p. 229.

98 Manuel II Palaiologos, *Dialogue which was held with a certain Persian, the Worthy Mouterizes, in Angkyra of Galatia*, p. 109. See also Polemis, "Manuel II Palaiologos Between Gregory Palamas and Thomas Aquinas", pp. 353–60.

99 Pitsakis, "Barlaam Calabro e i giuristi bizantini", p. 62.

100 Delacroix-Besnier, *Les Dominicains*, pp. 374–75.

THE HESYCHAST CONTROVERSY

6   The Basic Ideas of the Protagonists

6.1   *Gregory Palamas and the Patristic Background of His Teaching*

At the beginning of the controversy Palamas' main concern was to defend the visions of the light by the monks and to offer a convincing doctrinal foundation for such a mystical experience. He tried to avoid the main trap laid for him by Barlaam, who argued that no uncreated reality may be seen by the eyes of the body in this life. According to Palamas, the monks were able to see the light during their prayer not through the power of their human senses, but through a special "spiritual perception" given to them by the grace of God; even the term "light" employed to describe the object of the monks' vision may be misleading: in reality the monks and every true hesychast saw something supernatural which could be neither compared nor described by any term referring to the realities of this world. In such a way Palamas thought that he would be able to defend the monks from any accusation of Messalian leanings: the Messalians declared that they were able to see the essence of God with their eyes; the holy hesychasts did not make such an extravagant claim; only in certain special cases were they able to see a light which was an uncreated energy of God. Palamas thus tried to explain the typical *photophaneiai* of the Eastern monks, employing certain philosophical terms (*ousia-energeia*), which were not well-suited to describe these phenomena.[101]

As we saw above, Palamas in the *Hagioretic Tome* readily presented his theory on the distinction between God's essence and His uncreated energies as a new doctrine, revealed by the Holy Spirit at that particular time. Thus, at this early phase of the controversy Palamas himself had expressed an explicit position on the problem whether there is a patristic basis for the doctrine of the distinction between God's essence and His energies: his doctrine was something new, unknown until then. Palamas was prudent enough not to adhere to this position for long. In his later works we may observe his anxious efforts to prove the opposite, adducing many texts of the fathers of the Church supposedly supporting his own position. The matter is rather thorny, because the old quarrel between the Catholic and the Orthodox Churches concerning the procession of the Holy Spirit is also involved. Most Orthodox theologians, influenced by the Russian theologians of the diaspora, especially Lossky,[102] argue even today that, far from being an innovator, Palamas is a late Byzantine defender of an old, established doctrine of the Church. On the other hand, some Catholic scholars deny the existence of a patristic foundation for

---

101   Spiteris, *Palamas*, p. 96.
102   Ibid., p. 17.

the theories of Gregory Palamas, presenting him as an innovative theologian, who in certain ways broke with the tradition of his own Church, introducing into it his novelties which became recognized, albeit with difficulty, as the doctrinal truth.[103]

Beck is certainly correct, when he claims that the Palamite controversy is basically "ein Problem der Väterinterpretation".[104] It is true that even the Cappadocians seem to make a distinction between God's essence and His energies, but as von Ivanka points out, Palamas did not take into account their purpose; Basil of Caesarea or Gregory of Nyssa wanted to refute Eunomios, who believed that through the knowledge of the creatures we can attain a sufficient knowledge of God's essence, stressing that men could not communicate with God's essence. But they were swift to emphasize that this distinction is not real and that, strictly speaking, no such distinctions are permitted in the case of God; they are just indications of our inability to discuss theological matters properly.[105] For example, Gregory of Nyssa, who in some of his passages quoted by Palamas seems to make a clear distinction between God's essence and His energies, is quite clear on this issue: the distinction of essence and energies is a characteristic of created beings, while in God's case His energies are identical to His essence; there is no distinction between God's will and His essence or His creating power; all are the same thing.[106] This, according to von Ivanka, applies to Maximos the Confessor as well,[107] who, quite emphatically, spoke about man's inability to speak about the energies of God in an objective, or metaphysical sense,[108] as Palamas does.

More recently, Bradshaw argued that if we were to interpret the relevant texts of the Cappadocians more carefully, we would realize that the energies of God "are not merely activities, but must in some sense be God Himself",[109]

---

103 See a concise review of their views, ibid., pp. 116–17. Russell, *Gregory Palamas and the making of Palamism*, pp. 169–88 gives a succinct but thoughtful account of the relevant discussions at the end of the previous century and the beginning of our own. Anyone wishing to find an account of the extensive bibliography on this subject is referred to this most important study.

104 Beck, "Humanismus und Palamismus", p. 76.

105 von Ivanka, *Plato Christianus*, pp. 429–30.

106 Ibid., pp. 430–31. This is also the result of the investigation of the matter by Williams, *The Ground of Union*, p. 164, who points out that "there is nothing to suggest that this energy exists in some sort of symbiotic or contrastive relationship to divine essence". However, she does not believe that Palamas invented a new doctrine.

107 Ibid., pp. 436–37.

108 Beck, "Humanismus und Palamismus", p. 76.

109 Bradshaw, *Aristotle East and West*, p. 165. See also Radde-Gallwitz, *Divine Simplicity*, pp. 6–14.

THE HESYCHAST CONTROVERSY   363

and that in some passages Gregory of Nyssa clearly indicated that the term
"energy" referred to a divine reality, distinct from God's essence. According to
Bradshaw this cannot be reconciled with the Western, scholastic notion of a
clear-cut division of God's uncreated substance and what is outside it, which
must be necessarily created. He also maintained that the term "things around
God", employed by Maximos the Confessor quite frequently, was essentially
identical to the term "energies" employed by the Cappadocians;[110] those things
are divine perfections, in which man may participate, having a glimpse of
the divine reality. According to him, the influence of Pseudo-Dionysios the
Areopagite is not to be overlooked either, since Palamas was greatly helped in
the formulation of his own theory on the divine energies by the (Neoplatonic)
theory of Pseudo-Dionysios on the divine procession and return.[111] But despite
this employment of terms and arguments, which would seem favorable to
Palamas, the Eastern tradition refrained from formulating a clear and unam-
biguous doctrinal teaching on man's participation in the divine realities before
the 14th c. Generally speaking, Bradshaw is willing to recognize that there are
precedents for Palamas' teaching on the uncreated energies of God, being
rather sympathetic to Palamas' attempt to synthesize the Eastern tradition.[112]
He even adopts the modern Neo-Palamite position that the question whether
there are any uncreated energies of God distinct from His essence and whether
this is compatible with the Christian teaching on the absolute simplicity of
God, is the matter par excellence that divides the Roman Catholic from the
Byzantine Church, with the other questions, like the doctrine of filioque and
the primacy of the pope, being rather trivial in comparison.[113]

In contrast to the modern defenders of Palamism, Rowan Williams in a pioneering article argued that "Palamism is, philosophically, a rather unhappy
marriage of Aristotelian and Neoplatonic systems, the characteristic extreme
realism of Neoplatonic metaphysics colouring (and confusing) a terminology better understood in terms (inadequate though they may be) of the
Aristotelian logic already applied to Christian trinitarianism".[114] Williams

---

110   Ibid., p. 190. Similar views were expressed by Savvidis, *Die Lehre von der Vergöttlichung des
       Menschen*, pp. 165–72, and Larchet, "Ὁ ἅγιος Γρηγόριος ὁ Παλαμᾶς καὶ ἡ πατερικὴ παράδοση",
       pp. 331–46. See also Lévy, *Le créé et l'incréé*, passim.
111   Blackstone, "Reading Denys in Late Byzantium", p. 51.
112   A similar view is expressed by Torrance, "Precedents for Palamas' Essence-Energies
       Theology", pp. 54–56, who emphasizes the distinction introduced by Basil of Caesarea
       between God's essence and His energies in his *Letter* 234, a key text in the hesychast con-
       troversy (Basil of Caesarea, *Letters*, ed. & trans. Courtonne, vol. 3, pp. 42–44).
113   Bradshaw, *Aristotle East and West*, p. 229.
114   Williams, "The Philosophical Structures of Palamism", p. 41.

correctly remarks that the Palamite statement that God has something in addition to His substance, i.e. His energies, is incomprehensible from an Aristotelian point of view. According to Aristotle, the term "substance" refers to what sort of thing we are dealing with, and not to "a mysterious core of essentiality to which qualities"[115] or energies may be added.[116] This distinction, which is totally alien to Aristotle, is a result of the Neoplatonic attempt to imbue the Aristotelian terms, like "substance" or "energy", with ontological, i.e. metaphysical content.[117] According to Williams, the Neoplatonic interpretation of the Aristotelian terms elevated the divine substance above everything, giving the possibility to Pseudo-Dionysius the Areopagite afterwards to refer to "an intermediate class of mysterious divine 'powers' which although they are 'God', are not included in the simplicity of his *ousia* (or *hyperousiotes*)".[118] Williams' position seems to imply that in a rather sinister sense Palamas was a continuator of Pseudo-Dionysios, although not of the Cappadocians.[119]

However, one should not forget the immediate forerunners of Palamas, those Byzantine theologians of the 13th c. who were anxious to defend the Byzantine position on the *Filioque* after the annulment of the decisions of the council of Lyon (1274), which had temporarily restored the unity between East and West. We have already mentioned Nikephoros Blemmydes. It is to Meyendorff's credit that he emphasized the importance for Palamas' thought of the theological teaching of Patriarch Gregory of Cyprus, who maintained that the Son is the eternal distributor of the uncreated gifts of the Holy Spirit, which may be identified with the energies of the divinity.[120] George

---

115 Ibid., p. 32.

116 This was explicitly taught even by some early Greek Fathers, like Anastasios of Antioch, see Bernardino (ed.), *Patrologia*, pp. 210–12.

117 Ibid., p. 32. See also Finch, "Neo-Palamism", pp. 241–42, and Podskalsy, "Gottesschau", pp. 36–37, who point out that Palamas mistakenly interpreted several Fathers, even Pseudo-Dionysios, under a false, Neoplatonic perspective. On Palamas' dependence on Proclus, see Flogaus, "Palamas and Barlaam", p. 9. On certain possible direct loans of several neoplatonic teachings in Palamas' early works, see Polemis, "Neoplatonic and Hesychastic Elements", pp. 205–21.

118 Ibid., p. 37.

119 Ibid., p. 43.

120 Meyendorff, *Introduction à l'étude de Grégoire Palamas*, pp. 25–28. See also Larchet, *La vie et l'oeuvre théologique de Géorges/Grégoire de Chypre*, pp. 119–24, and Savvatos, Ἡ θεολογικὴ ὁρολογία καὶ προβληματικὴ τῆς πνευματολογίας Γρηγορίου Β΄ τοῦ Κυπρίου, pp. 185–228, and Lison, *L'Esprit répandu*, pp. 94–97. Realizing that a direct dependence of Palamas on Gregory of Cyprus and the other theologians of the late 13th c. would be detrimental to the case of those arguing that Palamas is a continuator of the patristic traditional teaching on the divine energies, Kapriev, *Vizantiiskata Filosofija*, pp. 359–60, tries to diminish the importance of the fact.

THE HESYCHAST CONTROVERSY 365

Moschampar (PLP 19344), another anti-Latin theologian, speaks clearly in his recently published works about the distinction between God's essence and His energies.[121] So does Ierotheos (PLP 8135), another anti-Latin theologian of the late 13th c.[122] We may confidently say that Palamas is a continuator of the tradition of the Byzantine theologians of the late 13th c. concerning the distinction between God's essence and His energies. However, the patristic background of his teaching cannot be as firmly established.

As far as Palamas' teaching on the hesychast prayer is concerned, there is no consensus among modern scholars. Meyendorff presented a composite overview of the whole Eastern tradition on the problem of the participation of the body in the hesychast prayer: according to him Palamas is a clear representative of the Biblical trend, which emphasized that man is a psychosomatic unity and that his deification also involved his body, especially his heart. That trend was opposed to another, Platonizing trend, which stressed the higher quality of man's mind, refusing to recognize any intrinsic value to the body. A representative of the Biblical trend is the author of the so-called Pseudo-Macarian corpus, while, according to Meyendorff, Evagrios Pontikos is a representative of the Platonizing theological tradition. This scheme was rightly criticised even by other Orthodox theologians like Romanides.[123] Beyer has pointed out that the monastic teaching on prayer, as formulated by the immediate forerunners of Palamas and by Palamas himself, presents many points of contact both with the theological teaching of Euagrius on man's union with God[124] and with the Pseudo-Macarian corpus, through which a Messalianistic influence may be discerned even in the works of Gregory Sinaites.[125] Gregory Sinaites played a pivotal role in the dissemination of the so-called Jesus prayer on Mount Athos. Being familiar with the *Method of the Holy Prayer* of Pseudo-Symeon the New

---

121 Moniou, Γεώργιος Μοσχάμπαρ, pp. 215–26.

122 Ioannidis, Ὁ ἱερομόναχος Ἱερόθεος, pp. 65–69. See also Patacsi, "Palamism before Palamas", pp. 64–71. On the other hand, I am not entirely convinced that Gregory Sinaites introduced such a clear distinction as Veniukov, "Grigorii Sinait, Bogoslovie", p. 62, maintains.

123 Romanides, "Notes on the Palamite Controversy", pp. 225–70. More recently similar protests were voiced by Plested, *The Macarian Legacy*, pp. 26–27. See also Sinkewicz, "The Doctrine of the Knowledge of God", p. 236, n. 262.

124 On the Euagrian background of late Byzantine hesychasm see also Gunnarson, *Mystical Realism*, pp. 35–42.

125 Beyer, "Die Lichtlehre", pp. 491–510, and id., "Gregorios' des Sinaiten Rede", p. 261, and 277–82. On the influence of Evagrios Pontikos on both Palamites and anti-Palamites, see the recent study of Rigo, "De l'apologie à l'évocation de l'expérience mystique", pp. 85–108. On the influence of the Pseudo-Macarian corpus on Palamas, see Kallistos I of Constantinople, *The Life of Gregory Sinaites*, ed. & trans. Beyer, p. 23.

Theologian and with the similar treatise of Nikephoros the Athonite,[126] and coming from such an ancient centre of hesychast spirituality as Sinai,[127] he had various contacts with Gregory Palamas and his circle, and his influence on the teaching of Palamas regarding the hesychast prayer is not to be underestimated. Nadal has drawn our attention to certain contacts Palamas had with some "Macarian" or "orientalizing" circles on Mount Athos around the year 1330, which may have also exerted an influence.[128] Palamas offered a clear doctrinal formulation for the rather simplistic interpretations of the visions of the monks which were circulating on Mount Athos at the time, identifying the light seen by the ascetics with one of the uncreated energies of the Holy Trinity. In this way Palamas, according to Akindynos and other anti-Palamite authors, tried to avoid certain monastic exaggerations,[129] that the hesychasts had had visions of God Himself, or even worse of His substance, keeping his distance from the "Messalian" heretics who were certainly active on Mount Athos at the time.

We must not forget another important figure of Eastern spirituality, Symeon the New Theologian. His teaching on the union of man with God and the experience of the divine light[130] bears many similarities to the teaching of the ascetics of the early 14th c.[131] Symeon stressed that even the human body is deified by the grace of God. The heart is of paramount importance for Symeon, who considers it the centre of man's personality and the place where God is united with him.[132] The case of Sabbas Tziskos is of interest: If one is to trust Philotheos Kokkinos' *Life*, Tziskos, a monk of Vatopedi monastery (*PLP* 27991) and a contemporary of Palamas, had experienced a trance which lasted for forty days: the description of Sabbas' experience bears unmistakable affinities

---

126   See Beyer, "Gregorios' des Sinaiten Rede", p. 288.

127   Rigo, "Gregorio il Sinaita", pp. 100–01, has suggested a connection of the psychosomatic practice with Muslim Sufism.

128   See also Nikephoros Gregoras, *Antirrhetic works*, ed. Beyer, pp. 104–08. More recently Müller-Schauenburg, "Gregorios Palamas und die kulturelle Neugier", pp. 291–96 has tried to present Palamas as a man more or less consciously seeking contact with those monks, being almost friendly disposed towards them. This is really too much for such a typical representative of the Byzantine theological elite as Palamas!

129   Some of which are based on the Macarian Corpus, see, for example, Russell, "Partakers of the Divine Nature", p. 61.

130   An interesting outline of the prehistory of the divine light in early Christian thought is drawn by Gunnarson, *Mystical Realism*, pp. 152–59.

131   See ibid., pp. 58–65, and Alfeyev, *St Symeon the New Theologian*, pp. 277–78.

132   On the localization of man's spirit there was a lengthy controversy in antiquity, see Kallistos I of Constantinople, *The Life of Gregory Sinaites*, ed. & trans. Beyer, pp. 7–15, and Rossi, *I filosofi greci padri dell'esicasmo*, pp. 173–78.

THE HESYCHAST CONTROVERSY   367

with Symeon's supernatural experiences as described in his own writings.[133]
It is not without reason that the so-called *Method of the holy prayer* was
attributed to Symeon the New Theologian.

Palamas himself referred to certain important figures of the late 13th and
early 14th c. as teachers of the Jesus prayer and immediate forerunners of
the monks, the teaching of whom he attempted to defend. These were Neilos
(*PLP* 20051), Seliotes (*PLP* 25118),[134] Athanasios Lependrenos (*PLP* 14741), and
most important among them, Theoleptos of Philadelpheia (*PLP* 7509) and
Athanasios I, patriarch of Constantinople (*PLP* 415).[135] Interestingly enough,
he does not seem to mention Gregory Sinaites.[136] Unfortunately very few, if
any, details of the teaching of Athanasios I are known. On the monastic teaching of Theoleptos of Philadelpheia we are better informed due to the speeches
he addressed to the monastic community he had founded in Constantinople
under the guidance of Irene-Eulogia Choumnaina (*PLP* 30936). Theoleptos
repeatedly refers to the Jesus prayer, but almost nothing even remotely akin
to the doctrinal foundation of the prayer as developed by Palamas or to
the psycho-somatic technic recommended by Nikephoros the Athonite and
Pseudo-Symeon the New Theologian is to be found in his writings.[137] There
is a certain quotation in a fragment of a letter of Palamas to the monk Menas
(*PLP* 18033) of a work of Gregory Sinaites[138] and it must be noted that some
students of Gregory Sinaites, like the future patriarchs Isidore and Kallistos,

---

133   Polemis, "Gregorio Palamas e la spiritualita athonita dell'epoca", pp. 311–18.

134   On this personality see Rigo, "Nota su Teolepto", pp. 171–74.

135   Meyendorff, *Introduction à l'étude de Grégoire Palamas*, pp. 40–41.

136   See Kallistos I of Constantinople, *The Life of Gregory Sinaites*, ed. & trans. Beyer, p. 15.

137   In his *Catechesis on the Transfiguration* there is a faint hint at the later teaching that
      the light may be seen by human eyes, see Beyer, "Die Katechese des Theoleptos von
      Philadelpheia auf die Verklärung Christi", p. 179. Rigo, "Nota sulla dottrina", p. 199, rightly
      points out that in Theoleptos' works no recommendation of the psycho-somatic tech-
      nique of prayer so highly praised by Pseudo-Symeon the New Theologian is to be found,
      see also id., *Mistici bizantini*, p. LXXXIV. Rather different is the view of Przegorlinčii,
      Vizantiiskaja čerkov, pp. 164–67, who sees in Theoleptos a precursor of Palamas. See also
      Gunnarson, *Mystical Realism*, pp. 72–76. One must also take into account the presenta-
      tion of Theoleptos' views on contemplation by Sinkewicz, *Theoleptos of Philadelpheia*,
      pp. 32–47. The article of Krausmüller, "The Rise of Hesychasm", pp. 101–126, deals with the
      predecessors of Palamas like Pseudo-Symeon the New Theologian, Nikephoros the Monk,
      and Gregory of Sinai, and gives a succinct but pregnant with new ideas account of the
      early stages of the controversy.

138   Rigo, "L'epistola a Menas", pp. 57–80. See also Polemis, "Gregorio Palamas e la spiritualità
      athonita", pp. 297–303. On the importance of the light of Tabor in Gregory of Sinai, see
      Rigo, "La Transfigurazione di Cristo", pp. 277–91, and Balfour, *Saint Gregory the Sinaite*,
      pp. 139–58. On the hesychast aspects of Gregory's teaching see also Ware, "The Jesus
      Prayer in St Gregory of Sinai", pp. 3–22, Hisamatsu, *Gregorios Sinaites*, pp. 321–440, and

became ardent Palamites. In that respect Palamas' teaching on prayer owes much to the revival of the Jesus prayer that is to be observed in the monastic centers of Byzantium, especially on Mount Athos. However, the way he tried to expose that teaching, linking it with his teaching on the divine energies, rightly or wrongly, is his original contribution to the ascetic doctrines of the Christian East.

As Meyendorff has pointed out, Palamas in a sense corrects the apophatism of Pseudo-Dionysios the Areopagite, arguing that God is not only beyond knowledge, but also beyond ignorance.[139] This permits him to deny the extreme apophatism of Barlaam, giving to man the possibility of knowing God in this life through participating in His uncreated energies. On the other hand, Palamas, though paying a lip-service to it, greatly diminishes the importance of natural contemplation as a way of approaching God, which is the corner-stone of the theological method of humanism,[140] being rather distrustful of the attempts of the older generation of Palaeologan philosophers like Metochites to revive the study of the natural and mathematical sciences. Palamas stresses the importance of the direct experience of the divine realities; therefore, there is no room in his thought for an attempt to reach an understanding of God through the study of His creatures. Another sinister aspect of Palamas' teaching, clearly related to his neglect of natural contemplation, was his rejection of classical education and the study of the ancient Greek authors. Prompted by Barlaam's contention that the Greek thinkers were illuminated by God, Palamas vehemently attacked the pagan philosophers, going as far as to claim that Socrates was possessed by demons and arguing that the study of the pagan authors had no real value for any Christian,[141] who should limit himself to keeping the commandments of the Lord as contained in the Gospel and the writings of the Holy

---

Rigo, *Il monaco, la chiesa e la liturgia*, pp. LXXIX–LXXXVIII, where the composite nature of Gregory's teaching is underlined.

139   See, e.g., Meyendorff, "Notes sur l'influence dionysienne", pp. 547–52, and Kapriev, *Vizantiiskata Filosofia*, p. 343. See also the important study of Rigo, "Il corpus pseudo-dionisiano negli scritti di Gregorio Palamas", pp. 519–34, especially p. 529: "Gregorio ... vedeva nell' apofasi un momento preliminare e oltrepassabile". More critical of Meyendorff's positions is Ritter, "Gregor Palamas als Leser des Dionysius Ps.-Areopagita", pp. 565–79.

140   Podskalsky, *Von Photius zu Bessarion*, pp. 83–85.

141   Totally unconvincing is the attempt of Kapriev, *Vizantiiskata Filosofia*, pp. 344–57, to exonerate Palamas from the accusation justly brought against him by Podskalsky, *Theologie und Philosophie*, p. 155, of burning any bridges that existed between theology and philosophy. More indicative of the position of Palamas himself, at least in my view, is the relevant entry of the article of Asmus-Vernančkii, "Gregorii Palama, Učenie", pp. 28–29.

THE HESYCHAST CONTROVERSY   369

Fathers. Fortunately, this position of Palamas, who certainly had predecessors in the earlier centuries of Byzantium, did not become dominant, even after the official vindication of Palamism by the councils of 1351 and 1368.

6.2   *Barlaam of Calabria*

Vilified by Meyendorff as a bad nominalist theologian,[142] Barlaam was only recently recognized as a true Byzantine humanist.[143] Unfortunately, we are not so well-informed about the opinions of Barlaam as we are about those of his opponents, the main reason being that his writings referring to the hesychast controversy are lost. His anti-Latin treatises which have been preserved have little to offer concerning the matter under discussion. Only his letters to Palamas and his friends contain information of value. The main contention of Barlaam, who was an avid reader of Aristotle, was that the pagan philosophers were illuminated by God to a certain degree and that their teaching was valuable for the Christians, who, therefore, should not limit themselves to the study of the Holy Scripture and the Fathers. As far as the light of Tabor was concerned, Barlaam affirmed that it was a created symbol of the divinity; this explains why the disciples easily perceived it through their senses. This view, which contradicted a long series of patristic and hymnographic texts confirming that the light of the Transfiguration was ineffable and eternal, was criticised by both Palamas and Akindynos, but was adopted by Nikephoros Gregoras and his followers and became the canonical view of the anti-Palamites. Barlaam was unable to understand the peculiarities of Byzantine hesychasm, denying the value of the ascetic practices of his contemporary monks. Being rather unfamiliar with the theological background of these practices, he vehemently attacked the monks and thus gave his opponents the opportunity to discredit him even before his official condemnation. Barlaam's fate was sealed the moment he began criticising the monks: certain subjects in Byzantium were not open to discussion; the attack against the monks was considered an attack against the very institution of monasticism. In stating this, we do not wish to deny either the patristic foundation of Barlaam's criticism of the monks who were proud of seeing the divinity with their mortal eyes, or the value of his contribution to the revival of the discussion concerning the methodology of theology in Byzantium.

Barlaam certainly had some knowledge of Western Scholasticism and did not fail to quote Thomas Aquinas in his anti-Latin treatises, but he certainly cannot be regarded as a typical representative of Scholasticism, as some modern Orthodox theologians maintain. His knowledge of Scholasticism was rather

---

142   See, e.g., his article "Un mauvais théologien de l'unité au XIV siècle", pp. 47–64.
143   Podskalsky, "Il significato di Barlaam", pp. 14–15.

limited. The fact that Barlaam was born of Orthodox parents in South Italy, which at that time was still Byzantium-oriented, should warn us against seeing the controversy between Palamas and Barlaam as an episode in the long history of the opposition between the spirituality of Byzantium and Western rationalism. Despite his peculiarities, Barlaam was a Byzantine intellectual and the hesychast controversy was an internal Byzantine phenomenon. What is more important is that Barlaam was familiar with the late-antique Neoplatonic interpreters of Aristotle and their Byzantine continuators, drawing from them his basic idea of the soul's purification through philosophy, which he juxtaposed to the idea of man's purification through ascesis suggested by Palamas.[144]

6.3   Gregory Akindynos

Akindynos' importance as a prolific author and an important intellectual of his time is now reluctantly recognized even by Orthodox scholars.[145] Akindynos, who was initially a close friend of Palamas,[146] was the one who clearly demonstrated the inconsistencies inherent in his friend's theological system. According to Akindynos, there is no distinction between God's essence and His energies. God comes into contact with His world through His essence. The essence of God is present everywhere in an ineffable and inexplicable manner.[147] No one is permitted to ask how God creates and sanctifies man, positing the existence of intermediate energies between God's essence and His creatures: this is a denial of God's simplicity and a reintroduction of Greek polytheism. According to Akindynos, it is not permissible to ask how God appears and becomes united with those He loves. The only answer to this question is that this is done in the way God wishes to be perceived by those men who are able to approach Him, if only slightly.[148] The Palamite answer that it is through His energies that God comes into contact with human beings is just an audacious and exceedingly impudent attempt to explain the ineffable divine mysteries. Properly speaking, God's energies are His creatures.[149] The light that illuminated the disciples on Mount Tabor is not an uncreated energy of God; however, Akindynos also refrains from declaring it a created

---

144   M. Trizio, "Una è la verità", pp. 108–140. On the Neoplatonic background of certain ideas of Barlaam see also Kourousis, "Ὁ ἀκτουάριος Ἰωάννης Ζαχαρίας", pp. 386–406.

145   See, for example, Biriukov, "Grigorii Akindin", p. 493.

146   See the biography of Akindynos sketched by the editor of his letters, Constantinides Hero (Gregory Akindynos, *Letters*), pp. IX–XXXIII.

147   Nadal, "Denys l'Aréopagite", pp. 553–56.

148   Gregory Akindynos, *Dialogue*, ed. Nadal, I, 42, pp. 49–50.

149   See Nadal, "Denys l'Aréopagite", pp. 544–46.

THE HESYCHAST CONTROVERSY 371

symbol.[150] If pressed to answer what the light is, Akindynos says that the light was the Word Himself who became incarnate; Christ who is light according to the Gospel of John illuminated the minds of the disciples and offered to them a limited perception of His divinity.[151] Meyendorff, seeing the reluctance of Akindynos to discuss doctrinal matters, accused him of agnosticism; this is hardly true. Akindynos' unwillingness to let his opponents draw him into interminable theological discussions was just an expression of the apophatic spirit of Byzantine theologians.[152] Akindynos, while recognizing the existence of the uncreated divine energies,[153] was most adamant in refusing to recognize their real existence *outside* the essence of God. According to him God's energies as interpreted by Palamas ended up being mere accidents.[154] Akindynos believed that there is an uncreated grace which is identical to God, and a created grace; the latter is given to us through the mystery of the Holy Eucharist, i.e. through Christ's blood.[155] Akindynos was indignant at Palamas' assertion that there was another way of deification for man, i.e. through prayer that led to a vision of the light of Tabor.[156]

6.4   *Nikephoros Gregoras*

Nikephoros Gregoras was an eminent Byzantine intellectual,[157] whose fame does not depend entirely on his contribution to the hesychast controversy, as was the case with Palamas, Barlaam and Akindynos. The last great historian of Byzantium, a student of the polymath Theodore Metochites, and a philosopher of considerable distinction, who entertained close relations with the Byzantine court, he was drawn into the dispute after the fate of the anti-Palamites was sealed. One of his public conversations with Palamas was documented by George Phakrases (*PLP* 29575).[158] He attacked Palamas and the Emperor John VI Kantakouzenos and was imprisoned in the monastery of Chora after

---

150   See Biriukov, "Grigorii Akindin", p. 494, and Gagen, "Grigorii Akindin", p. 666.

151   Gregory Akindynos, *Dialogue*, ed. Nadal, 1, 41, p. 49.

152   See the relevant position of Nadal, "Gregorio Akindinos", p. 229: "Para Akindinos, la voluntad de no hacer teologia se fundaba en el hecho de que siempre habia creido que la contemplación estaba por encima de la teologia positiva".

153   Nadal, "Denys l'Aréopagite", p. 562.

154   Ibid., pp. 551–53.

155   Ibid., pp. 241–42.

156   On this point of Akindynos' theology, see Russell, "The 'Gods' of Psalm 81 (82)", pp. 248–51.

157   A new list of his works has been compiled by Paraskevopoulou, Τὸ ἁγιολογικὸ καὶ ὁμιλητικὸ ἔργο τοῦ Νικηφόρου Γρηγορᾶ, pp. 27–37.

158   George Phakrases, *Dialogue*, ed. M. Candal, pp. 328–56, and Gregory Palamas, *Works*, ed. Chrestou, vol. 4, pp. 191–230. See also a Russian translation of the text, accompanied by various essays on several aspects of it by Pospelova, *Georgii Fakrasis, Disput.*

the council of 1351. After his release, he wrote his *Second Antirrhetics*, which were also incorporated into his *History*. Gregoras ironically points out that the uncreated light of Tabor postulated by Palamas may be considered the fourth person of the Holy Trinity and wonders what this new God of Palamas who lacks a hypostasis really is.[159] He also accuses Palamas of resuscitating the Platonic ideas by arguing that something uncreated exists besides the divine essence.[160] Unlike Akindynos, but like Barlaam, Gregoras firmly believed that the light of Tabor was a created symbol of divinity, which was perceptible by the human eyes of the Apostles. According to him there is nothing uncreated besides the divine essence.

7 Lesser Figures

7.1 *The Followers of Palamas*
The most important figure among the followers of Palamas was beyond any doubt the patriarch Philotheos Kokkinos (1353–1354, and 1364–1376).[161] He was a student of the philologist Thomas Magistros (*PLP* 16045), before becoming a monk. He was involved in the redaction of the *Hagioretic Tome* and played a prominent role in the events that culminated in the triumph of Palamism in 1351. He was also a close collaborator of John VI Kantakouzenos, who appointed him patriarch in 1353, after the deposition of Kallistos I, who was an ally of Kantakouzenos' opponent, the Emperor John V Palaiologos. Philotheos Kokkinos composed *Fourteen Chapters against Barlaam and Akindynos*, as well as two treatises *Against Akindynos*.[162] His fifteen *Treatises against Gregoras*[163] may be considered his main work. Philotheos, who was responsible for the canonisation of Palamas in 1368, composed a series of hagiographic texts celebrating both saints of the past and several important figures of his own time[164] who belonged to the Palamite party, the most important of these being Palamas himself.

---

159 See Kapriev, *Vizantiiskata Filosofija*, p. 331.
160 Ibid., p. 331.
161 On the life of Philotheos, see mainly Kotzabassi, "Eine Akoluthie", pp. 305–11. See also Russell, "The Patriarch Philotheos Kokkinos", pp. 21–31, and Fonkič, "Avtografi konstantinopolskogo patriarcha Filofeja Kokkina", pp. 78–92.
162 Philotheos Kokkinos, *On the Light of Tabor*, ed. Janeva, pp. 25–142.
163 Philotheos Kokkinos, *Dogmatic works*, ed. Kaimakis, pp. 19–595. See also Beyer, "Der Streit um Wesen und Energie", pp. 255–82.
164 Philotheos Kokkinos, *Hagiological works*, ed. Tsamis, pp. 33–591.

THE HESYCHAST CONTROVERSY 373

Another important figure belonging to the circle of Kantakouzenos and Philotheos Kokkinos was Theophanes, bishop of Nicaea (*PLP* 7615). No details on his life are available. He wrote a treatise *On the Light of Tabor*, which was directed against some contemporary opponents of Palamas,[165] one of whom was certainly Prochoros Kydones. This treatise was connected with the preparations for the council of 1368.[166] Theophanes, despite being a follower of Palamas, did not hesitate to make use of the works of Thomas Aquinas, which had been recently translated into Greek; in some cases he even tried to offer a synthesis between Thomism and Palamism.[167] Closely connected with the Palamite controversy is his treatise *On the Eternity of Beings*, in which he attempted to refute Gregoras' argument that if we were to accept the theory of Palamas concerning the energies of God, the world which was a product of the creative energy of God should have no beginning.[168] His long *Speech on the Virgin Mary*[169] shows the influence of the Palamite theory on the energies of God too: The Virgin Mary is presented as the distributor of the energies of the Godhead to mankind. He also composed a *Letter to Paul* (*PLP* 22143), Latin titular Patriarch of Constantinople who was involved in a discussion with Kantakouzenos concerning the problem of the divine energies, which remains unpublished.[170] What should be stressed in the case of Theophanes, is that he tried to mitigate the official Palamism: this is evident both in his works which deal with the Palamite controversy, and in his treatise *Against the Latins*, where he clearly expressed his reservations concerning the Palamite teaching that there was no hierarchical order between the three persons of the Holy Trinity.

John VI Kantakouzenos, through whose political activities the Palamites managed to impose their theories as the official doctrine of the Byzantine Church, was also a prolific, though hardly original, author who, except for

---

165   There are two editions of this text, one by Sotiropoulos (ed.), Theophanes of Nicaea, *On the Light of Tabor*, pp. 175–302 and another one by Zacharopoulos (ed.), Theophanes of Nicaea, *Works*, pp. 124–304. On the latter edition, see Dunaev, "Bogoslovie evcharistii", p. 148.

166   Polemis, *Theophanes of Nicaea*, pp. 74–78.

167   Ibid., pp. 87–109.

168   Theophanes of Nicaea, *Treatise*, ed. Polemis, pp. 1–49.

169   Theophanes of Nicaea, *Oration*, ed. Jugie, pp. 2–210.

170   There is a renewed interest in Theophanes of Nicaea, particularly among Russian and Bulgarian scholars, see, e.g., Makarov, "Some Notes on the Notions of Sunergy", pp. 205–16, id., *Mariologija Feofana Nikeiskogo*, and id., "Feofan Nikeiskii", pp. 572–80. Of no value is the article of Markov, "Teofan Nikeiski", pp. 188–209, who is unable to interpret the texts free from the Neo-Palamite positions. On Theophanes' views on the Eucharist, see Van Rossum, "Holy Communion as 'Symbol'", pp. 205–10, and Louth, "The Eucharist and Hesychasm", pp. 199–205. See also Knežević, *Gregory Palamas*, p. 165.

his *History*, an important source for the 14th c., where he defended his own policies, wrote some treatises in defense of Palamas after he was deposed and took the monastic habit. The most extensive of them is a detailed refutation of the *Palamitikai parabaseis* of Gregoras' student John Kyparissiotes (*PLP* 13900), which remains unpublished.[171] He also composed two *Antirrhetic Treatises against Prochoros Kydones*,[172] and another one against Isaac Argyros (*PLP* 1285), which has been recently published.[173] His *Letter to John bishop of Carpasia* in Cyprus (*PLP* 8448),[174] his *Seven Letters to Paul*, Latin archbishop of Constantinople,[175] and his long *Letter* to a certain Raoul Palaiologos (*PLP* 24139), preserved only in an anonymous anti-Palamite treatise, also dealt with the theories of Palamas. In some respects, Kantakouzenos, like Theophanes of Nicaea, represents a mitigated Palamism. For example, in his treatise against Kyparissiotes, Kantakouzenos maintains that the visions of the prophets of the Old Testament had nothing to do with the vision of the light of Tabor, as Palamas maintained;[176] Kantakouzenos was not willing to explain all supranatural visions as direct experiences of the divine energies.

Two individuals belonging to the close circle of Palamas, who tried their hand at composing theological treatises, were David Dishypatos and Joseph Kalothetos (*PLP* 10615). Dishypatos wrote a short history of the hesychast controversy for the sake of the Empress Anna of Savoy,[177] another treatise against Barlaam and Akindynos, written in the summer of 1342[178] and a long dogmatic poem replying to a poem of similar content written by Akindynos.[179] Kalothetos composed nine treatises against Barlaam and Akindynos,[180] some

---

171 A small part of this work has been published by Moniou (ed.), John VI Kantakouzenos, *Works*, pp. 129–232.

172 John VI Kantakouzenos, *Antirrhetic Discourses*, eds. Voordeckers/Tinnefeld, pp. 3–172.

173 Isaac Argyros, *Theological Works*, ed. Polemis, pp. 93–228.

174 John VI Kantakouzenos, *Letter*, ed. Darrouzès, pp. 15–21.

175 John VI Kantakouzenos, *Antirrhetic Discourses*, eds. Voordeckers/Tinnefeld, pp. 175–239. The letters to Paul and the letter to John of Carpasia have been translated by Prochorov, *Ioann Kantakuzin, Beseda*, pp. 45–58, and 297–306, who wrote an interesting introduction to Kantakouzenos' work.

176 Polemis, *Theologica varia*, p. CXLII.

177 David Dishypatos, *Text*, ed. Candal, pp. 116–24.

178 David Dishypatos, *Oration*, ed. Tsamis, pp. 35–95. See an analysis of this work by Beyer, "David Disypatos", pp. 107–28.

179 David Dishypatos, *Poem on Akindynos*, ed. Browning, pp. 723–39. It is noteworthy that Dishypatos claims that God's energy may be called θειότης but not θεότης, see Vernačkii/ Dunaev, "David Disipat", pp. 586–87.

180 Joseph Kalothetos, *Works*, ed. Tsamis, pp. 81–341. His letters deal mainly with the hesychast controversy (ibid., pp. 363–419). Recently Rigo, "Autografi manoscritti", pp. 107–139, has identified Kalothetos's hand and clarified some aspects of his literary activity.

THE HESYCHAST CONTROVERSY 375

of which offer us important details concerning the beginnings of the hesychast controversy. A treatise against Akindynos addressed to the patriarch John Kalekas and written by Mark Kyrtos (*PLP* 17086), a student of Gregory Sinaites, seems to belong to the early phase of the controversy.[181] Two of his letters to the Emperor John Kantakouzenos are also preserved.[182]

Neilos Kabasilas, archbishop of Thessaloniki, is known for his anti-Latin works which became canonical afterwards. Candal has published a small, but nonetheless interesting treatise of Neilos Kabasilas, which interprets a passage of Gregory of Nyssa, according to which there is nothing uncreated except God: Neilos attempted to reconcile the views of the venerable father of the Church with the views of Palamas.[183] John Kyparissiotes devoted the whole fifth book of his *Palamikai parabaseis* to the refutation of Kabasilas' views. He also composed a florilege containing patristic texts supposedly favoring Palamas' positions.[184]

Kallistos I, patriarch of Constantinople (1350–1353, and 1354–1364), played a role in the hesychast controversy more as an active clergyman fighting for the case of Palamas than as a writer. A collection of Kallistos' *Homilies* is preserved, some of which are devoted to the refutation of Gregoras' views.[185] Kallistos was not an original theologian; his main purpose was to persuade his audience on the orthodoxy of Palamas' teaching, which was expounded in a rather confusing and haphazard manner. More important is the *Life* of his teacher Gregory Sinaites, which gives us a vivid picture of early 14th c. monasticism in Byzantium.[186] Also noteworthy are his ascetic *Chapters*.[187] Kallistos'

---

181 Mark Kyrtos, *Letters*, ed. Apostolopoulou, pp. 121–51. On a new publication of the letter to Kalekas by Panagiotou (ed.), Mark Kyrtos, *Works*, pp. 41–76, see the rather negative, but totally convincing review of Dunaev, "Book review of Panagiotou, A., Ἡσυχαστικά", pp. 571–93.

182 Mark Kyrtos, *Letters*, ed. Apostolopoulou, pp. 71–76, and 86–102.

183 Neilos Kabasilas, *Oration*, ed. Candal, pp. 240–56.

184 On his minor works referring to the hesychast controversy see Kislas, *Nil Cabasilas*, pp. 66–67, and 74–79.

185 Kallistos I of Constantinople, *Orations against Gregoras*, ed. Paidas, pp. 89–299 (full of all manner of mistakes, especially as far as the constitution of the Greek text and the interpretation of the author's thought are concerned), Kallistos I of Constantinople, *Orations against the Latins*, ed. id., pp. 70–400, and Kallistos I of Constantinople, *Dogmatic Discourse*, ed. id., pp. 123–30. The only serious study of the *Homilies* of Kallistos as a whole remains that of Gonin, Τὸ συγγραφικὸν ἔργον τοῦ οἰκουμενικοῦ πατριάρχου Καλλίστου Α΄, pp. 123–251.

186 There are currently two editions of this text, one by Delikari (ed.), Kallistos I of Constantinople, *Slavic Translation of the Life of Gregory Sinaites*, pp. 312–48, and another by Beyer (ed. & trans.), Kallistos I of Constantinople, *The Life of Gregory Sinaites*, pp. 106–226.

187 Kallistos I of Constantinople, *On the Purity of the Soul*, ed. Rigo, pp. 303–407.

predecessor Isidoros Boucheiras had composed certain liturgical canons, where he exposed the Palamite teaching on the distinction between God's essence and His energies. Some fragments of these now lost controversial texts are preserved in certain anti-Palamite florilegia.[188] The canonist Matthew Blastares (*PLP* 2808) had also composed a short treatise against Akindynos and two smaller works of similar content.[189] Of some philosophical importance are two treatises against Barlaam and Akindynos written by Neophytos Momitzilas (Prodromenos, *PLP* 19254).[190]

Philotheos of Selybria (*PLP* 29896), who became bishop of that city during the second patriarchate of Philotheos Kokkinos, wrote an interesting *Dialogue on the Dogmatic Theology*,[191] in which the main themes of the hesychast controversy are discussed. The interlocutors are all the important personalities who became involved in the controversy: Palamas, Barlaam, Akindynos, Gregoras, Dexios, Argyros, the emperor, Philotheos himself, and even some persons of whose works nothing survives, like Sophianos (*PLP* 26398) and Theodore Atouemes (*PLP* 1642). The dialogue seems to give an accurate account of the views of these individuals, but it lacks liveliness, resembling an anthology rather than a real dialogue.

A remarkable Palamite theologian was Kallistos Angelikoudes Melenikiotes (or Kataphygiotes).[192] His *Chapters on the Divine Union and the Contemplative Life*, published long ago in the *Philokalia*, go far beyond Palamas. Kallistos noted a weak point of Palamas' teaching: Palamas sometimes speaks of just one divine energy and sometimes of numerous energies. Kallistos argues that man at a later stage comes beyond the vision of the divine energies, being united with God Himself; therefore, the vision of the divine energies is not to be considered the final stage in the long procedure of man's deification.[193]

---

188 See Tinnefeld, *Demetrios Kydones, Briefe*, p. 160, and n. 34, and Philotheos Kokkinos, *Hagiological works*, ed. Tsamis, p. 382, n. 230.

189 See Pitsakis, "Barlaam Calabro", pp. 56–57. Some comments on the first treatise in Polemis, "Notes on Two Texts", pp. 207–09.

190 Neophytos Momitzilas Prodromenos, *Works*, ed. Kalogeropoulou-Metallinou, pp. 337–407.

191 Philotheos of Selybria, *Works*, ed. Vakalopoulou, pp. 183–294.

192 See Rigo, *Mistici bizantini*, pp. 655–56, and id., "Callisto Angelicude Catafygiota Meleniciota", pp. 251–68. See also Kallistos Angelikoudes Melenikiotes, *Treatises*, ed. Koutsas, pp. 30–61.

193 Polemis, "Notes on Two Texts", pp. 209–12, and id., "Nikolaos Kabasilas's De Vita in Christo", pp. 101–31. Somewhat different is the interpretation of Rodionov, "The *Chapters* of Kallistos Angelikoudes", pp. 141–59. Dordevic, *Nikolas Kabasilas*, pp. 129–63, tries to reconcile the positions of Kabasilas with those of Palamas, arguing that Kabasilas wanted to disprove some theories of certain Palamite extremists, though he neglects to identify them.

THE HESYCHAST CONTROVERSY   377

Aiming at terminological accuracy and developing Palamas' system, Kallistos must be placed at the same level as Theophanes of Nicaea, who also tried to give a new version of the Palamite teaching, mitigating its most extreme aspects. Theophanes of Nicaea, Kallistos Angelikoudes, and to a certain extent John VI Kantakouzenos represent a trend among the Palamites to somehow water down the most extreme affirmations of their teacher, having realized that their rigid application, far from solving any problems, further complicated matters. The same polyphony, to an even larger extent, is to be observed in the anti-Palamite camp.

7.1.1   A Special Case: Nicholas Kabasilas

Nicholas Kabasilas (*PLP* 30539), the writer of the long *Explication of the Divine Liturgy*, for which he became famous, is considered by most Orthodox theologians a faithful student of Palamas.[194] However, no traces of Palamism are to be found in his extensive treatise on the mysteries of the Church titled *On the Life in Christ*.[195] To the contrary, Kabasilas implicitly rejects Palamas' view that deification itself is uncreated, his views being closer to those of Gregory Akindynos. It should be noted that Kabasilas composed a short treatise on the usefulness of the *logoi*, which is a direct refutation of the Palamite arguments against secular education.[196] On the other hand, he wrote an epigram on the death of the Palamite Isidoros Boucheiras, while a short treatise against Gregoras is preserved under his name.[197] In all probability, Kabasilas refrained from openly supporting either Palamas or his opponents, maintaining good relations with leading personalities of both parties.[198] However, his basic idea that man attains his union with God through his good works and his faithful fulfillment of the commandments of the Lord can hardly be reconciled with the views of Palamas,[199] who, although recognizing the value of a virtuous life,[200] stressed the importance of the mystical, supernatural experience of man's contact with the divine.

---

194 See the protests of Podskalsky, *Von Photios zu Bessarion*, p. 82.
195 Nicholas Kabasilas, *The Life in Christ*, ed. Congourdeau, vol. 1, pp. 74–356, vol. 2, pp. 12–220. See also Rigo, *Mistici bizantini*, pp. LXXXVIII–XC.
196 Nicholas Kabasilas, *Arguments*, ed. Demetracopoulos, pp. 55–57. See also Polemis, "Notes on a short Treatise", pp. 155–60.
197 On the attribution of this treatise, see Podskalsky, *Von Photios zu Bessarion*, p. 41, and n. 143, and Neilos Kabasilas, *Orations*, ed. Kislas, p. 71.
198 Congourdeau, "Nicolas Cabasilas et le palamisme", pp. 191–210.
199 Polemis, "Nikolaos Kabasilas's De Vita in Christo", pp. 114–15.
200 Williams, *The Ground of Union*, pp. 106–08.

7.1.2 The Anti-Palamites

Those who maintained the banner of resistance against Palamas after the death of Gregoras were his students and friends Theodore Dexios (*PLP* 5194), John Kyparissiotes, and Isaac Argyros. Kyparissiotes is probably the most prolific author of all those involved in the hesychast controversy.[201] He composed a long treatise in five books, still not fully published,[202] entitled *Palamikai parabaseis*, which contained a short historical exposition of the main events of the controversy and a comprehensive refutation of the views of Palamas and his followers. He also composed a systematic account of the main doctrines of Christian theology, the anti-Palamite bias of which is hardly hidden,[203] nine prose *Hymns* to God,[204] and a shorter treatise dealing with various aspects of Palamas' teaching.[205] The influence of Kydones' Greek translations of the works of Thomas Aquinas on the works of Kyparissiotes is easily discernible. Isaac Argyros,[206] who shared his teacher Gregoras' astronomic interests, composed an extensive *Letter to Gedeon Zographos* refuting the views of Theodore Dexios,[207] an anti-Palamite like him, and a treatise concerning the distinction proposed by the Palamites between God's essence and His hypostatic characteristics.[208] A treatise by Argyros on the four ways of man's participating in God is a typical product of Argyros's way of interpreting Palamism.[209] In Argyros' hand is written a long, anonymous treatise refuting a letter of Kantakouzenos to a certain Raoul Palaiologos.[210] The unknown author of this treatise refers to a historical exposition of the main events of the Palamite controversy he had composed in the past. Mercati attributed the treatise to Argyros. However,

---

201 See the introduction to his works by Dentakis, Ἰωάννης Κυπαρισσιώτης, pp. 11–123.
202 A small extract from the first part is to be found in *Patrologia Graeca*, vol. 152, cols. 663–737. The second part has been published by Liakouras (ed.), John Kyparissiotes, *Against the Tome of Palamas*, pp. 137–480, the fifth by Marangoudakis (ed.), John Kyparissiotes, *Against Neilos Kabasilas*, pp. 45–288.
203 John Kyparissiotes, *Elementary Exposition of Theological Texts*, ed. Dentakis, pp. 17–655.
204 John Kyparissiotes, *Hymns*, ed. id., pp. 3–67.
205 John Kyparissiotes, *Treatise*, ed. id., pp. 15–60. See also his work on the Palamite teaching on the Holy Trinity, John Kyparissiotes, *Treatise*, ed. Candal, pp. 128–50.
206 See Pingree, "Argyros, Isaac", p. 166. On the scribal activity of Argyros connected with the hesychast controversy, see Bianconi, "La controversia palamitica", pp. 337–76, and more recently, Gioffredda, *Tra i libri di Isacco Argiro*, pp. 119–127, whose conclusions must be treated with some caution.
207 Isaac Argyros, *On the Light of Tabor*, ed. Candal, pp. 90–112.
208 Isaac Argyros, *Text*, ed. id., pp. 108–36. Argyros' theological treatises have been recently published by Polemis (ed.), Isaac Argyros, *Theological Works*, pp. 3–69.
209 Some extracts of it have been published by Mercati, *Notizie di Procoro e Demetrio Cidone*, pp. 271–73. See also Dunaev, "Isaak Argir", p. 686.
210 Polemis (ed.), *Theologica varia inedita*, pp. 55–323.

THE HESYCHAST CONTROVERSY   379

bearing in mind that another work of Kyparissiotes is written in Argyros' hand and that a historical exposition concerning the main events of the hesychast controversy is to be found in Kyparissiotes' *Palamikai parabaseis*, while no such treatise of Argyros is preserved, I am inclined to believe that this anonymous treatise was also written by Kyparissiotes.[211]

Theodore Dexios had played a minor role in the council of 1341. According to Kantakouzenos' *History*, he was involved in the negotiations between him and Anna of Savoy in 1341.[212] He was a friend of Gregoras, whom he tonsured a monk on his deathbed. Before Kantakouzenos' fall from power in 1354, he wrote a long *Invective* against the emperor accusing him of uncanonical involvement in the council of 1351, which safeguarded the triumph of Palamas. The *Invective* is divided into five books[213] and is preserved anonymously, but Mercati has attributed it to Dexios on safe grounds. After the death of Gregoras, Dexios was accused by his fellow anti-Palamite Isaac Argyros of falsifying the Orthodox doctrine on the light of Tabor, identifying it with Christ's human body. Argyros argued that the light of Tabor may be safely identified with the created splendor emanating from Adam's body in paradise. Dexios answered Argyros' objections with two long *Letters* addressed to his friends,[214] where he offered various arguments in defence of his theory that the light of Tabor may be identified with Christ's body.

Prochoros Kydones,[215] the brother of Demetrios and his fellow translator of the works of Thomas Aquinas into Greek,[216] was actively involved in the Palamite controversy. His most important work was his extensive treatise *On the Essence and Energies of God*, which was falsely attributed to Gregory Akindynos.[217] Prochoros deals with this subject in a Scholastic manner, imitating even the formal characteristics of the *Summa theologiae*. The sixth book of the treatise is devoted to the light of Tabor.[218] His minor treatises are his work *On the Cataphatic and Apophatic Way of Theology*,[219] a small fragment (or an

---

211   Ibid., pp. LIII–LXI.
212   Nikephoros Gregoras, *Roman History*, ed. Schopen, vol. 2, p. 103, lines 1–7.
213   Theodore Dexios, *Works*, ed. Polemis, pp. 3–185.
214   Ibid., pp. 189–329.
215   See the biography of Prochoros compiled by Tinnefeld, *Demetrios Kydones, Briefe*, pp. 237–44, and the important article of Dunaev, "Kidonis Prochor", pp. 657–63.
216   On the writings of Prochoros, see Mercati, *Notizie di Procoro e Demetrio Cidone*, pp. 1–61. On the reception of Aquinas in the 14th c., see Polemis, "Thomas Aquinas Reception", pp. 38–52.
217   *Patrologia Graeca*, vol. 151, cols. 1192–241.
218   Prochoros Kydones, *On the Light of Tabor*, ed. Candal, pp. 258–96.
219   Polemis (ed.), *Theologica varia inedita*, pp. 327–79.

incomplete writing) on the value of syllogisms,[220] and his *Apology* addressed to patriarch Philotheos, which was in all probability composed on his behalf by his brother Demetrios.[221] Prochoros was probably the first theologian who attempted to refute the teachings of Palamas, taking advantage of his remarkable knowledge of Western Scholastic theology.[222] His brother Demetrios composed a short treatise on the hypostatic characteristics of the Holy Trinity, a theme that had become critical due to Neilos Kabasilas' attempt to argue that the distinction between God's essence and His energies is somehow similar to the distinction between the hypostatic characteristics of the godhead.[223]

An early anti-Palamite was George Lapithes of Cyprus (*PLP* 14479), a friend of Akindynos and Gregoras, of whose treatises very few remnants survive.[224] A certain Nephon *hypopsephios* (*PLP* 20651) composed an important anti-Palamite florilegium,[225] which attempted to clarify the beginnings of the hesychast controversy, referring in deprecatory terms to Symeon the New Theologian. The text was published under the name of Demetrios Kydones.

A figure who remains somewhat of an enigma is George of Pelagonia (*PLP* 4117), who left us an extensive anti-Palamite work, the first part of which offers an important historical account of the events that led to the council of 1341.[226] This author, on whom almost nothing is known except that he wrote a *Life* of the Emperor John III Vatatzes, used certain original documents such as the works of Gregory Akindynos in order to compose his treatise, offering some details not preserved in any other contemporary source. The possibility that he made use of the lost treatises of Barlaam referring to his controversy with Palamas is not to be excluded.[227]

---

220 Prochoros Kydones, *Text in Vat. gr. 609*, ed. Tinnefeld, pp. 520–23.

221 Mercati, *Notizie di Procoro e Demetrio Cidone*, pp. 296–313.

222 On the importance of the figure of Prochoros, see Russell, "Prochoros Cydones", pp. 75–91. See also Triantafyllopoulos, "The Thomist Basis of Prochoros Kydones' anti-Palamite Treatise", pp. 411–30.

223 Demetrios Kydones, *Letter to Constantine Asan*, ed. Candal, pp. 76–110. See Williams, "The Philosophical Structures of Palamism", p. 34, who acutely points out that Palamism may lead to a notion that the essence of God exists prior to the three persons of the Trinity; in fact, this was taught by Neilos Kabasilas!

224 On the activities of Lapithes, see Sinkewicz, "The *Solutions* addressed to George Lapithes", pp. 153–54.

225 *Adversus Palamam, Patrologia Graeca*, vol. 154, cols. 837–64. See also Rigo, "L'epistola a Menas", pp. 60–61, n. 10.

226 Polemis (ed.), *Theologica varia inedita*, pp. 3–51. See also Talbot, "George the Philosopher", pp. 838–39.

227 Ibid., pp. XVIII–XXXI.

THE HESYCHAST CONTROVERSY   381

A figure of lesser importance in the anti-Palamite camp was Arsenios, bishop of Tyre (*PLP* 1407). A follower of the anti-Palamite patriarch of Antioch Ignatios (*PLP* 8073) who had denounced Palamas in 1344, Arsenios was involved in various schemes against the Palamites. An invective against Palamas supposedly written by him but in all probability composed by Isaac Argyros, providing us various details about the initial phases of the controversy, is preserved.[228] The text was probably destined to be promulgated as the official *Tome* of the patriarchate of Antioch against Palamas, but this probably never took place.

A list of various anti-Palamites is preserved in MS. Vatican City, Biblioteca Apostolica Vaticana, Vaticanus graecus 1096.[229] Some lesser names like Theodore Atouemes[230] and Sophianos are also known. Of the various Palamite or anti-Palamite florilegia I will not express an opinion, because much work remains to be done on them.[231]

8   Conclusion

The problem of the real existence of God's energies, which, though divine, are distinct from God's essence, as posed by Gregory Palamas, reminds us of the great problem of the divine attributes that arose in Islam in the first part of the 8th century, and was hotly debated by both Arabs and Jews during the Middle Ages. According to the Muslim Atrributists, certain terms which are attributed to God in the Koran stand for real incorporeal beings which exist in God from eternity, like "life", "wisdom" and "power". The Muslims and Jews, who denied the validity of such a distinction, employed arguments similar to those of the anti-Palamites: God alone is eternal, therefore no other thing besides Him may be considered eternal. Some Muslim theologians even distinguished between an eternal creating power existing in God, and His act-of-creation, which was created![232] Some others affirmed that those attributes were superimposed onto the essence of God.[233] Even the difference between God's essence and His glory seen by Moses was brought up for discussion.[234] I am not in a position

---

228   Arsenios of Tyre, *Tome*, ed. Polemis, pp. 254–76. See also Kresten, *Die Beziehungen zwischen den Patriarchaten von Konstantinopel und Antiocheia*, pp. 75–82.
229   Mercati, *Notizie di Procoro e Demetrio Cidone*, pp. 222–23. See also Weiss, *Joannes Kantakuzenos*, pp. 126–27.
230   See Blanchet, "Atoumès, un nouveau traducteur byzantin", pp. 17–37.
231   See Markesinis, "Un florilège composé pour la dèfense du concile de 1351", p. 470.
232   Wolfson, *The Philosophy of the Kalam*, pp. 112–46.
233   Id., *Repercussions of the Kalam*, p. 7.
234   Id., "Crescas on the Problem of Divine Attributes", p. 292.

to further explore this terrain, which is alien to me,[235] but I am tempted to believe that the case of the Palamite controversy is just another indication of the internal unity of medieval philosophical thought in both East and West.

The Palamite controversy is just an expression of a tendency inherent in Christian, monotheist thought to bring up for discussion the problem of the divine attributes: the question is how to harmonize the belief in God's unity and transcendence with the belief in His immanence. Palamas' thought was not devoid of weaknesses. His insistence on defending the monks who saw an uncreated light with their bodily eyes trapped him. He tried to escape the trap by identifying this light with an uncreated energy of God. Palamas was certainly not the inventor of the distinction between God's essence and His energies, which was discussed by the anti-Latin Byzantine theologians of the 13th c., but it is he who molded such teaching into a coherent theological system. It is true that despite Palamas' protests to the contrary, his theories endangered the doctrine of the simplicity of God. It is also true that the vision of the uncreated light as interpreted by Palamas had a materialistic colouring, though Palamas, when speaking of the vision of a light, clearly understood that such language is a "pointer and not a strict description".[236] But his audacity to pose the problem of God's relations with His creatures in Byzantium in the 14th c. and to apply that distinction to the problem of man's union with God in a consistent manner, using a precise, philosophical vocabulary,[237] is certainly commendable. Palamas was one of the few original thinkers of late Byzantium.

Bibliography

Primary Sources

Arsenios of Tyre, *Tome*, ed. I. Polemis, "Arsenius of Tyre and his Tome against the Palamites", *Jahrbuch der Österreichischen Byzantinistik* 43 (1993), 241–81.

Barlaam of Calabria, *Greek Letters*, ed. & trans. A. Fyrigos, *Dalla controversia palamitica alla polemica esicastica (con un'edizione critica delle "Epistole greche" di Barlaam Calabro)* (Medioevo, 11), Rome 2005, pp. 194–400.

---

235 Papademetriou, in *Maimonides and Palamas on God*, made an interesting attempt to compare Palamas with Maimonides, but I think that Papademetriou, though admitting that the immanent God of Palamas is different from the more remote God of Maimonides (ibid., p. 85), fails to the main difference between the two theologians: Maimonides denied the existence of any attributes in God.

236 Ware, "The Debate about Palamism", p. 53.

237 Tollefsen, *Activity and Participation*, p. 195.

THE HESYCHAST CONTROVERSY 383

Barlaam of Calabria, *Works*, ed. A. Fyrigos, *Barlaam Calabro, Opere contro i Latini*, vol. 1: *Introduzione, storia dei testi, edizione critica, traduzione e indici* (Studi e Testi, 347), Vatican City 1998.

Basil of Caesarea, *Letters*, ed. & trans. Y. Courtonne, *Saint Basile. Lettres*, 3 vols., Paris 1957–66.

David Dishypatos, *Oration*, ed. D.G. Tsamis, Δαβὶδ Δισυπάτου, Λόγος κατὰ Βαρλαὰμ καὶ Ἀκινδύνου πρὸς Νικόλαον Καβάσιλαν (Βυζαντινὰ Κείμενα καὶ Μελέται, 10), Thessaloniki 1973.

David Dishypatos, *Poem on Akindynos*, ed. R. Browning, "David Disypatos' Poem on Akindynos", *Byzantion* 25/27 (1955/1957), 713–45.

David Dishypatos, *Text*, ed. M. Candal, "Origen ideologico del palamismo en un documento de David Disipato", *Orientalia Christiana Periodica* 15 (1949), 85–125.

Demetrios Kydones, *Letter to Constantine Asan*, ed. M. Candal, "Demetrio Cidonio y el problema trinitario palamitico", *Orientalia Christiana Periodica* 28 (1962), 75–120.

Demetrios Kydones, *Translation*, in Θωμᾶ Ἀκυινάτου Σούμμα Θεολογικὴ ἐξελληνισθεῖσα, eds. G. Leontsinis/A. Glykofridi-Leontsini, (Corpus Philosophorum Graecorum Recentiorum, 15), Athens 1976; P. Demetrakopoulos (Corpus Philosophorum Graecorum Recentiorum, 16), Athens 1979; Id. (Corpus Philosophorum Graecorum Recentiorum, 17A), Athens 1980; S. Sideri/P. Photopoulou (Corpus Philosophorum Graecorum Recentiorum, 17B), Athens 1982; E. Kalokairinou (Corpus Philosophorum Graecorum Recentiorum, 18), Athens 2002; A. Glykofridi-Leontsini/I.D. Spyralatou (Corpus Philosophorum Graecorum Recentiorum, 19), Athens 2011.

George Phakrases, *Dialogue*, ed. M. Candal, "Fuentes Palamiticas. Dialogo de Jorge Facrasi sobre el contradictorio de Palamas con Niceforo Gregoras", *Orientalia Christiana Periodica* 16 (1950), 303–57.

Gregory Akindynos, *Dialogue*, ed. J. Nadal Cañellas, *Gregorii Acindyni Refutationes duae operis Gregorii Palamae cui titulus Dialogus inter Orthodoxum et Barlaamitam* (Corpus Christianorum. Series Graeca, 31), Turnhout/Leuven 1995.

Gregory Akindynos, *Letters*, ed. & trans. A. Constantinides Hero, *Letters of Gregory Akindynos* (Dumbarton Oaks Texts, 7 / Corpus Fontium Historiae Byzantinae, 21), Washington, D.C. 1983.

Gregory Akindynos, *Oration against John Kalekas*, ed. J. Nadal Cañellas, "Gregorio Akindinos, Discurso ante Juan Kalekas", in Conticello/Conticello (eds.), *La théologie byzantine*, pp. 257–314.

Gregory Palamas, *Letter to Akindynos*, ed. J.S. Nadal, "La rédaction première de la *Troisième lettre de Palamas à Akindynos*", *Orientalia Christiana Periodica* 40 (1974), 233–85.

Gregory Palamas, *Text*, ed. M. Candal, "Escrito de Palamas desconocido (Su "Confession de Fe", refutada por Acindino)", *Orientalia Christiana Periodica* 29 (1963), 357–440.

Gregory Palamas, *The One Hundred and Fifty Chapters*, ed. R.E. Sinkewicz, *Saint Gregory Palamas, The One Hundred and Fifty Chapters. A Critical Edition, Translation and Study*, Toronto, Ontario 1988.

Gregory Palamas, *Works*, ed. P. Chrestou et al., *Γρηγορίου τοῦ Παλαμᾶ Συγγράμματα*, 5 vols., Thessaloniki 1962–1992.

Gregory Palamas, *The Hagioretic Tome*, ed. A. Rigo, *Gregorio Palamas Tomo aghioritico. La storia, il testo e la dottrina* (Orientalia Lovaniensia Analecta, 298), Leuven 2021.

Gregory Sinaites, *Discourse on the Transfiguration*, ed. D. Balfour, *Saint Gregory the Sinaite: Discourse on the Transfiguration. First Critical Edition, with English Translation and Commentary. Reprinted from "Theologia"*, Athens 1982.

Gregory Sinaites, *Oration on the Transfiguration*, ed. H.-V. Beyer, "'Gregorios' des Sinaiten 'Rede auf die heilige Verklärung unseres Herrn Jesu Christi' als ein Dokument spätbyzantinischer Mystik. Eingeleitet, herausgegeben, übersetzt und mit Anmerkungen versehen", *Byzantinoslavica* 66 (2008), 259–327.

Isaac Argyros, *On the Light of Tabor*, ed. M. Candal, "Argiro contra Dexio (Sobre la luz taborica)", *Orientalia Christiana Periodica* 23 (1957), 80–113.

Isaac Argyros, *Text*, ed. M. Candal, "Un escrito trinitario de Isaac Argiro en la contienda palamitica del siglo XIV", *Orientalia Christiana Periodica* 22 (1956), 92–137.

Isaac Argyros, *Theological Works*, ed. I. Polemis, *Isaac Argyri Opera omnia theologica necnon Iohannis ex-imperatoris Cantacuzeni Oratio adversus Argyrum* (Corpus Christianorum. Series Graeca, 93), Turnhout 2021.

John VI Kantakouzenos, *Antirrhetic Discourses*, eds. E. Voordeckers/F. Tinnefeld, *Iohannis Cantacuzeni, Refutationes duae Prochori Cydonii et Disputatio cum Paulo patriarcha Latino epistulis septem tradita* (Corpus Christianorum. Series Graeca, 16), Turnhout/Leuven 1987.

John VI Kantakouzenos, *History*, ed. L. Schopen, *Ioannis Cantacuzeni ex Imperatoris Historiarum libri IV graece et latine*, 3 vols., (Corpus Scriptorum Historiae Byzantinae, 41), Bonn 1828–1832.

John VI Kantakouzenos, *Letter*, ed. J. Darrouzès, "Lettre inédite de Jean Cantacuzène relative à la controverse palamite", *Revue des Études Byzantines* 17 (1959), 7–27.

John VI Kantakouzenos, *Works*, ed. D.I. Moniou, *Ἰωάννης Στ΄ Καντακουζηνός-Ἰωάννης Κυπαρισσιώτης. Μία σημαντικὴ πτυχὴ τῶν ἡσυχαστικῶν ἐρίδων*, Athens 2012.

John VI Kantakouzenos, *Against Argyros*, ed. I. Polemis, *Isaac Argyri Opera omnia theologica necnon Iohannis ex-imperatoris Cantacuzeni Oratio adversus Argyrum* (Corpus Christianorum. Series Graeca, 93), Turnhout 2021.

John Kyparissiotes, *Against Neilos Kabasilas*, ed. S.T. Marangoudakis, *Ἰωάννου τοῦ Κυπαρισσιώτου, Κατὰ Νείλου Καβάσιλα Λόγοι πέντε ἀντιρρητικοί, νῦν τὸ πρῶτον ἐκδιδόμενοι. Editio princeps*, Athens 1995.

THE HESYCHAST CONTROVERSY 385

John Kyparissiotes, *Against the Tome of Palamas*, ed. K.I. Liakouras, Ἰωάννου τοῦ Κυπαρισσιώτου Κατὰ τῶν τοῦ Παλαμικοῦ Τόμου διακρίσεων καὶ ἑνώσεων ἐν τῷ Θεῷ. Τὸ κείμενον νῦν πρῶτον ἐκδιδόμενον. *Editio princeps*, Athens 1991.

John Kyparissiotes, *Elementary Exposition of Theological Texts*, ed. V.L. Dentakis, Ἰωάννου τοῦ Κυπαρισσιώτου, Τῶν θεολογικῶν ῥήσεων Στοιχειώδης Ἔκθεσις. Νῦν τὸ πρῶτον ἐκδιδόμενον. *Editio princeps*, Athens 1982.

John Kyparissiotes, *Hymns*, ed. V.L. Dentakis, Οἱ εἰς τὸν Ἰωάννην Κυπαρισσιώτην ἀποδιδόμενοι Ἐννέα Ὕμνοι εἰς τὸν τοῦ Θεοῦ Λόγον, νῦν τὸ πρῶτον ἐκδιδόμενοι. *Editio princeps*, Athens 1964.

John Kyparissiotes, *Treatise*, ed. M. Candal, "Juan Ciparisiota y el problema trinitario palamitico", *Orientalia Christiana Periodica* 25 (1959), 127–64.

John Kyparissiotes, *Treatise*, ed. V.L. Dentakis, Ἰωάννου τοῦ Κυπαρισσιώτου, Περὶ τῆς θείας οὐσίας καὶ θείας ἐνεργείας διαφορᾶς [ὅτι οὐκ ἔστι ταύτην παρὰ τῷ Θεῷ ἀνευρεῖν]. Νῦν τὸ πρῶτον ἐκδιδόμενον. *Editio princeps*, Athens 1976.

Joseph Kalothetos, *Works*, ed. D.G. Tsamis, Ἰωσὴφ Καλοθέτου Συγγράμματα (Θεσσαλονικεῖς Βυζαντινοὶ Συγγραφεῖς, 1), Thessaloniki 1980.

Kallistos Angelikoudes Melenikiotes, *Against Thomas Aquinas*, ed. S.G. Papadopoulos, Καλλίστου Ἀγγελικούδη, Κατὰ Θωμᾶ Ἀκινάτου. Εἰσαγωγή, κριτικὸν ὑπόμνημα καὶ πίνακες, Athens 1970.

Kallistos Angelikoudes Melenikiotes, *Treatises*, ed. S. Koutsas, *Callistos Angelicoudès, Quatre traités hésychastes inédits. Introduction, texte critique, traduction et notes*, Athens 1998.

Kallistos I of Constantinople, *Dogmatic Discourse*, ed. K. Paidas, "Editio princeps of an Unedited Dogmatic Discourse against the Barlaamites by the Patriarch of Constantinople Kallistos I", *Byzantinische Zeitschrift* 105 (2012), 117–30.

Kallistos I of Constantinople, *Slavic Translation of the Life of Gregory Sinaites*, ed. A. Delikari, Ἅγιος Γρηγόριος ὁ Σιναΐτης. Ἡ δράση του καὶ ἡ συμβολή του στὴ διάδοση τοῦ ἡσυχασμοῦ στὰ Βαλκάνια. Ἡ σλαβικὴ μετάφραση τοῦ Βίου του κατὰ τὸ ἀρχαιότερο χειρόγραφο, Thessaloniki 2004.

Kallistos I of Constantinople, *The Life of Gregory Sinaites*, ed. & trans. H.-V. Beyer, *Kallist I, patriarch Konstantinopolija, Zitije i dejatelnost ize vo svjatach otča nashego Grigorija Sinaita. Vedenije, kritičeskoe izdanije grečeskogo teksta i ruskii perevod* [Kallistos I, patriarch of Constantinople. The Life and Activity of our Holy Father Gregory of Sinai. Introduction, Critical Edition and Russian Translation], Ekaterinenburg 2006.

Kallistos I of Constantinople, *On the Purity of the Soul*, ed. A. Rigo, "Callisto I patriarca, I 100 (109) Capitoli sulla purezza dell'anima. Introduzione, edizione e traduzione", *Byzantion* 80 (2010), 333–407.

Kallistos I of Constantinople, *Orations against Gregoras*, ed. K. Paidas, Οἱ Κατὰ Γρηγορᾶ ὁμιλίες τοῦ πατριάρχη Κωνσταντινουπόλεως Καλλίστου Α΄. Κριτικὴ ἔκδοση, Athens 2013.

386 POLEMIS

Kallistos I of Constantinople, *Orations against the Latins*, ed. K. Paidas, *Κάλλιστος Α΄ Πατριάρχης Κωνσταντινουπόλεως. Ψευδοπροφῆτες, μάγοι καὶ αἱρετικοὶ στὸ Βυζάντιο κατὰ τὸν 14ο αἰῶνα. Ἑπτὰ ἀνέκδοτες Ὁμιλίες τοῦ πατριάρχου Κωνσταντινουπόλεως Καλλίστου Α΄*, Athens 2011.

Manuel II Palaiologos, *Dialogue which was held with a certain Persian, the Worthy Mouterizes, in Angkyra of Galatia*, ed. E. Trapp, *Manuel II Palaiologos, Dialoge mit einem "Perser"* (Wiener byzantinische Studien, 2), Vienna/Graz/Cologne 1966; W. Baum (ed.)/R. Senoner (trans.), *Kaiser Manuel II. Palaiologos. Dialog über den Islam und Erziehungsratschlage*, Vienna 2003.

Mark Kyrtos, *Letters*, ed. S. Apostolopoulou, *Markos Kyrtos. Leben und Briefe*, PhD thesis, University of Vienna 1987.

Mark Kyrtos, *Works*, ed. A.D. Panagiotou, *Ἡσυχαστικὰ Α΄*, Athens 2006.

Neilos Kabasilas, *On the Procession of the Holy Spirit*, ed. E. Candal, *Nilus Cabasilas et theologia S. Thomae de processione Spiritus Sancti. Novum e Vaticanis codicibus subsidium ad historiam theologiae Byzantinae saeculi XIV plenius elucidandam* (Studi e Testi, 116), Vatican City 1945.

Neilos Kabasilas, *Oration*, ed. M. Candal, "Le "Regla teologica" de Nilo Cabasilas", *Orientalia Christiana Periodica* 23 (1957), 237–66.

Neilos Kabasilas, *Orations*, ed. T. Kislas, *Nil Cabasilas, Sur le Saint-Esprit. Introduction, texte critique, traduction et notes*, Paris 2001.

Neophytos Momitzilas Prodromenos, *Works*, ed. V. Kalogeropoulou-Metallinou, *Ὁ μοναχὸς Νεόφυτος Προδρομηνὸς καὶ τὸ θεολογικό του ἔργο*, Athens 1996.

Nicholas Kabasilas, *Arguments*, ed. J. Demetracopoulos, "Nicholas Cabasilas' *Quaestio de rationis valore:* an anti-Palamite Defence of Secular Wisdom", *Βυζαντινά* 19 (1998), 53–93.

Nicholas Kabasilas, *The Life in Christ*, ed. M.-H. Congourdeau, *Nicolas Cabasilas, La Vie en Christ. Livres I–VII* (Sources Chrétiennes, 355 & 361), 2 vols., Paris 1989–90.

Nikephoros the Athonite, *Philokalia*, in Nikodemos of Mount Athos, *Φιλοκαλία τῶν ἱερῶν νηπτικῶν συνερανισθεῖσα παρὰ τῶν ἁγίων καὶ θεοφόρων πατέρων ἡμῶν.* vol. 4, Athens 1991, pp. 18–28.

Nikephoros Gregoras, *Antirrhetic works*, ed. H.-V. Beyer, *Nikephoros Gregoras Antirrhetika I. Einleitung, Textausgabe, Übersetzung und Anmerkungen* (Wiener Byzantinistische Studien, 12), Vienna 1976.

Nikephoros Gregoras, *Roman History*, eds. L. Schopen/I. Bekker, *Nicephori Gregorae Byzantina Historia* (Corpus Scriptorum Historiae Byzantinae, 19), 3 vols., Bonn 1829–55.

Philotheos Kokkinos, *Dogmatic works*, ed. D.B. Kaimakis, *Φιλοθέου Κοκκίνου δογματικὰ ἔργα* (Θεσσαλονικεῖς Βυζαντινοὶ Συγγραφεῖς, 3), Thessaloniki 1983.

THE HESYCHAST CONTROVERSY 387

Philotheos Kokkinos, *Hagiological works*, ed. D.G. Tsamis, *Φιλοθέου Κωνσταντινουπόλεως τοῦ Κοκκίνου Ἁγιολογικὰ Ἔργα. Α΄ Θεσσαλονικεῖς ἅγιοι* (Θεσσαλονικεῖς Βυζαντινοὶ Συγγραφεῖς, 4), Thessaloniki 1985.

Philotheos Kokkinos, *On the Light of Tabor*, ed. P. Janeva, *Filotei Kokin, Za Taborskata svetlina. Izdanije na teksta i prevod ot srednovekoven grečki* (*Bibliotheca Christiana. Series nova*, 18) [Philotheos Kokkinos, On the Light of Tabor. Edition of the Text and Translation from the Ancient Greek], Sofia 2011.

Philotheos of Selybria, *Works*, ed. M. Vakalopoulou, *Φιλόθεος Σηλυβρίας. Βίος καὶ συγγραφικὸ ἔργο*, Athens 1992.

Prochoros Kydones, *On the Light of Tabor*, ed. M. Candal, "El libro VI de Procoro Cidonio (Sobre la luz taborica)", *Orientalia Christiana Periodica* 20 (1954), 247–97.

Prochoros Kydones, *Text in Vat. gr. 609*, ed. F. Tinnefeld, "Ein Text des Prochoros Kydones in *Vat. gr. 609* über die Bedeutung der Syllogismen für die theologische Erkenntnis", in A. Schoors/P. Van Deun (eds.), *Philohistor. Miscellanea in honorem C. Laga septuagenarii* (Orientalia Lovaniensia Analecta, 60), Leuven 1994, pp. 515–27.

Pseudo-Symeon the New Theologian, *Oration*, ed. I. Hausherr, "La Méthode d'Oraison Hésychaste", *Orientalia Christiana* 9/2 (1927), 101–209.

Theodore Dexios, *Works*, ed. I. Polemis, *Theodori Dexii, Opera ommia* (Corpus Christianorum. Series Graeca, 55), Turnhout/Leuven 2003.

Theoleptos of Philadelpheia, *Katechesis*, ed. H.-V. Beyer, "Die Katechese des Theoleptos von Philadelpheia auf die Verklärung Christi", *Jahrbuch der Österreichischen Byzantinistik* 34 (1984), 171–95.

Theoleptos of Philadelpheia, *Monastic Discourses*, ed. R.E. Sinkewicz, *Theoleptos of Philadelpheia, The Monastic Discourses. A Critical Edition, Translation and Study*, Toronto, Ontario 1992.

Theophanes of Nicaea, *On the Light of Tabor*, ed. C. Sotiropoulos, *Θεοφάνους Γ΄ ἐπισκόπου Νικαίας Περὶ θαβωρίου φωτὸς Λόγοι πέντε*, Athens 1990.

Theophanes of Nicaea, *Oration*, ed. M. Jugie, *Theophanes Nicaenus, Sermo in sanctissimam Deiparam* (Lateranum N.S. An. 1), Rome 1936.

Theophanes of Nicaea, *Treatise*, ed. I. Polemis, *Θεοφάνους Νικαίας, Ἀπόδειξις ὅτι ἐδύνατο ἐξ ἀιδίου γεγενῆσθαι τὰ ὄντα καὶ ἀνατροπὴ ταύτης*. Editio princeps, εἰσαγωγή, κείμενο, μετάφραση, εὑρετήρια (Corpus Philosophorum Medii Aevi. Philosophi Byzantini, 10), Athens 2000.

Theophanes of Nicaea, *Works*, ed. G. Zacharopoulos, *Θεοφάνης Νικαίας (;-+1381). Ὁ βίος καὶ τὸ συγγραφικὸ του ἔργο* (Βυζαντινὰ Κείμενα καὶ Μελέται, 23), Thessaloniki 2003.

Tomes of 1341 and 1347, eds. H. Hunger/O. Kresten et al., *Das Register des Patriarchats von Konstantinopel*, vol. 2: *Edition und Übersetzungen der Urkunden aus den Jahren 1337–1350* (Corpus Fontium Historiae Byzantinae, 19/2), Vienna 1995.

388   POLEMIS

Tome of 1351, ed. I. Karmiris, Τὰ Δογματικὰ καὶ Συμβολικὰ Μνημεῖα τῆς Ὀρθοδόξου Καθολικῆς Ἐκκλησίας, I, Athens 1960.

Secondary Literature

Alfeyev, I., *St Symeon the New Theologian and Orthodox Tradition*, Oxford 2000.

Alfeyev, I. et al. (eds.), *Il Christo transfigurato nella tradizione spirituale ortodossa. Atti del XV Convegno ecumenico internazionale di spiritualità ortodossa, Bose, 16–19 settembre 2007*, Comunità di Bose 2008.

de Andia, Y. (ed.), *Denys l'Aréopagite et sa postérité en Orient et en Occident. Actes du Colloque International, Paris 21–24 septembre 1994*, Paris 1997.

Andreopoulos, A., *Metamorphosis. The Transfiguration in Byzantine Theology and Iconography*, Crestwood, NY 2005.

Asmus, A./M.M. Vernančkii, "Gregorii Palama, Učenie", *Pravoslavnaja Enčiklopedija* 13 (2006), 28–37.

Athanasopoulos, C., "Demonstration (ἀπόδειξις) and Its Problems for Gregory Palamas: Some Neglected Aristotelian Aspects of St. Gregory Palamas' Philosophy and Theology", in Kneževič, M. (ed.), *The Ways of Byzantine Philosophy*, Alhambra, CA 2015, pp. 361–73.

Beck, H.-G., "Humanismus und Palamismus", in *XIIe Congrès International des Études Byzantines 1961. Rapports* III, Belgrade/Ohrid 1961, pp. 63–82.

Beck, H.-G., *Kirche und theologische Literatur im byzantinischen Reich*, Munich 1959.

Bernardino, A. (ed.), *Patrologia*, vol. 5: *Dal Concilio di Calcedonia (451) a Giovanni Damasceno (+750). I padri orientali*, Genoa/Milan 2000.

Beyer, H.-V., "David Disypatos als Theologe und Vorkämpfer für den Hesychasmus (ca. 1337–ca. 1350)", *Jahrbuch der Österrreichischen Byzantinistik* 24 (1975), 107–28.

Beyer, H.-V., "Der Streit um Wesen und Energie und ein spätbyzantinischer Liedermacher. Bemerkungen zum 1 Antirrhetikos des Philotheos Kokkinos und dem ihm entsprechenden 1 Buch der Antirrhetikoi des Nikephoros Gregoras", *Jahrbuch der Österreichischen Byzantinistik* 36 (1986), 255–82.

Beyer, H.-V., "Die Lichtlehre der Mönche des vierzehnten und des vierten Jahrhunderts, erörtert am Beispiel des Gregorios Sinaïtes, des Euagrios Pontikos und des Ps.-Makarios/Symeon", in *XVI. Internationaler Byzantinistenkongress, Wien, 4–9 Oktober 1981 Akten*, vol. 1: *Hauptreferatei/2. Halbband. Themengruppen 7–11*, Vienna 1981 (=*Jahrbuch der Österreichischen Byzantinistik* 31/2), pp. 473–512.

Bianconi, D., "La controversia palamitica: figure, libri, testi e mani", *Segno e Testo* 6 (2008), 337–76.

Biriukov, D.S., "Grigorii Akindin", in *Antologija vostočno hristianskoi bogoslovskoi misli. Ortodoksia i geterodoksia* [Anthology of Eastern Christian Theological Views. Orthodoxy and Heterodoxy], vol. 2, Moscow/Saint Petersburg 2009, pp. 485–98.

Biriukov, D.S., "Sv. Grigorii Palama", in *Antologija vostočno hristianskoi bogoslovskoi misli. Ortodoksia i geterodoksia*, vol. 2, Moscow/Saint Petersburg 2009, pp. 448–66.

Blackstone, J., "Reading Denys in Late Byzantium: Gregory Palamas's Approach to the Theological Categories of "Apophasis" and "Union and Distinction", in Russell (ed.), *Spirituality*, pp. 45–53.

Blanchet, M.-H., "Atoumès, un nouveau traducteur byzantin de Thonas d'Aquin", in A. Berger/S. Mariev/G. Prinzig/A. Riehle (eds.), *Koinotaton Doron. Das späte Byzanz zwischen Machtslosigkeit und kultureller Blüte (1204–1461)* (Byzantinisches Archiv, 31), pp. 17–37.

Blanchet, M.-H., "Éliminer Thomas: le programme antithomiste de Matthieu Ange Panarétos (seconde moitié du XIVème siècle)", in Speer/Steinkrüger (eds.), *Knotenpunkt Byzanz*, pp. 452–65.

Bradshaw, D., *Aristotle East and West. Metaphysics and the Division of Christendom*, Cambridge 2004.

Charalampidis, C.P., "La rappresentazione della Lux increata nell'iconografia cristologica bizantina", in Fyrigos (ed.), *Barlaam Calabro*, pp. 41–50.

Chrysostomides, J. (ed.), *Καθηγήτρια. Essays presented to J. Hussey for her 80th Birthday*, Camberley, Surrey 1988.

Congourdeau, M.-H., "Nicolas Cabasilas et le palamisme", in Rigo (ed.) *Gregorio Palamas e oltre*, pp. 191–210.

Conticello, C.G./V. Conticello, *La théologie byzantine et sa tradition*, vol. 2: (*XIIIe–XIXe s.*), Turnhout 2002.

Delacroix-Besnier, C., *Les Dominicains et la chrétienté grecque aux XIV et XV siècles*, Rome 1997.

Demetrakopoulos, J.A., *Αὐγουστῖνος καὶ Γρηγόριος Παλαμᾶς. Τὰ προβλήματα τῶν ἀριστοτελικῶν Κατηγοριῶν καὶ τῆς τριαδικῆς ψυχοθεολογίας*, Athens 1997.

Demetrakopoulos, J.A., "Palamas Transformed. Palamite Interpretations of the Distinction between God's Essence and Energies in Late Byzantium", in M. Hinterberger/C. Schabel (eds.), *Greeks, Latins, and Intellectual History 1204–1500* (Bibliotheca, 11), Leuven/Paris/Walpole, MA 2011, pp. 263–372.

Demetrakopoulos, J.A., "Thomas Aquinas' Impact on Late Byzantine Theology and Philosophy: The Issues of Method or *Modus Sciendi* and *Dignitas Hominis*", in Speer/Steinkrüger (eds.), *Knotenpunkt Byzanz*, pp. 333–410.

Dentakis, V.L., *Ἰωάννης Κυπαρισσιώτης ὁ σοφὸς καὶ φιλόσοφος*, Athens 1965.

Dordevic, M., *Nikolas Kabasilas. Ein Weg zu einer Synthese der Traditionen*, Leuven/Paris/Bristol 2015.

Dunaev, A.G., "Bogoslovic evcharistii v kontekste palamitskich sporov" [Eucharistic Theology in the context of the Palamite controversy], *Bogoslovskie trudi* 42 (2009), 146–68.

390 POLEMIS

Dunaev, A.G., "Book review of Panagiotou, A., *Ἡσυχαστικά*, Ἀθήνα 2006", in *Bogoslovskie trudi. 50 Let. Jubileinii vapusk* 43–44 (2012), 571–93.

Dunaev, A.G., "Isaak Argir", *Pravoslavnaja Enciklopedija* 26 (2011), 686–93.

Dunaev, A.G., "Kidonis Prochor", *Pravoslavnaja Enciklopedija* 32 (2013), 657–63.

Flinch, J.D., "Neo-Palamism, Divinizing Grace, and the Breach between East and West", in M.J. Christensen/J.A. Wittung, *Partakers of the Divine Nature. The History and Development of Deification in the Christian Tradition*, Grand Rapids, MI 2007, pp. 233–49.

Flogaus, R., "Die heimliche Blick nach Westen. Zur Rezeption von Augustins *De trinitate* durch Gregorios Palamas", *Jahrbuch der österreichischen Byzantinistik* 46 (1996), 275–97.

Flogaus, R., "Inspiration-Exploitation-Distortion: The Use of St Augustine in the Hesychast Controversy", in G.E. Demacopoulos/A. Papanikolaou (eds.), *Orthodox Readings of Augustine*, Crestwood, NY 2008, pp. 63–80.

Flogaus, R., "Palamas and Barlaam Revisited. A Reassessment of East and West in the Hesychast Controversy of 14th Century Byzantium", *St Vladimir's Theological Quarterly* 42/1 (1998), 1–31.

Fonkič, B., "Avtografi konstantinopolskogo patriarcha Filofeja Kokkina", in Id., *Grečeskie rukopisi evropeiskich sobranii. Paleografičeskie i kodikologičeskie isledovanija 1988–1998 gg.* ["Autographs of Patriarch Philotheos of Constantinople", in Id., *Greek Manuscripts of European Collections. Paleographic and Codicological Research in the years 1988–1998*], Moscow 1999, pp. 78–92.

Fyrigos, A. (ed.), *Barlaam Calabro, l'uomo, l'opera, il pensiero. Atti del convegno internazionale. Reggio Calabria-Seminara-Gerace 10–11–12 dicembre 1999*, Rome 2000.

Fyrigos, A., *Dalla controversia palamitica alla polemica esicastica (con un'edizione critica delle "Epistole greche" di Barlaam Calabro)* (Medioevo, 11), Rome 2005.

Fyrigos, A., "Tomismo e anti-Tomismo a Bisanzio (con una nota sulla "Defensio S. Thomae Aquinatis adversus Nilum Cabasilam" di Demetrio Cidone)", in A. Molle (ed.), *Tommaso d'Aquino e il mondo bizantino*, Vanfro 2004, pp. 27–72.

Gagen, S., "Grigorii Akindin", *Pravoslavnaja Enčiklopedija* 12 (2006), 662–67.

Gioffreda, A. *Tra i libri di Isacco Argiro* (Transmissions, 4), Berlin/Boston 2021.

Gonis, D.V., *Τὸ συγγραφικὸν ἔργον τοῦ οἰκουμενικοῦ πατριάρχου Καλλίστου Α΄*, Athens 1980.

Gunnarson, H., *Mystical Realism in the Early Theology of Gregory Palamas. Context and Analysis*, Gothenburg 2002.

Hisamatsu, E., *Gregorios Sinaites als Lehrer des Gebetes*, Altenberge 1994.

Horujy, S., *Isihasm. Annotirovannaja bibliografia* [Hesychasm. Annotated Bibliography], Moscow 2004.

Ierodiakonou, K., "The Anti-Logical Movement in the Fourteenth Century", in ead. (ed.), *Byzantine Philosophy and its Ancient Sources*, Oxford 2002, pp. 219–36.

Ioannidis, N., *Ὁ ἱερομόναχος Ἱερόθεος (ΙΓ΄ αἰ) καὶ τὸ ἀνέκδοτο συγγραφικὸ ἔργο του. Κριτικὴ ἔκδοση*, Athens 2003.

Ioannidis, N., *Ὁ Νικηφόρος Βλεμμύδης καὶ ἡ περὶ ἐκπορεύσεως τοῦ Ἁγίου Πνεύματος διδασκαλία του*, Athens 2010.

Jevtitch, A., *Études Hésychastes*, traduit du Serbe par J.-L. Palierne, Lausanne 1995.

Kakridis, I., *Codex 88 des Klosters Dečani und seine griechischen Vorlagen. Ein Kapitel der serbisch-byzantinischen Literaturbeziehungen im 14. Jahrhundert*, Munich 1988.

Kaltsogianni, E., "Δύο ἄγνωστα ἀποσπάσματα τοῦ δευτέρου Ἀποδεικτικοῦ Λόγου τοῦ Γρηγορίου Παλαμᾶ Περὶ τῆς ἐκπορεύσεως τοῦ Ἁγίου Πνεύματος", *Ἑλληνικά* 59 (2009), 299–310.

Kappes, C.W., "A Provisional Definition of Byzantine Theology in Light of Palamite Theologians and their Sources", *Nicolaus* 40 (2013), 187–202.

Kappes, C.W., "Gregorios Palamas' Reception of Augustine's Doctrine of the Original Sin and Nicholas Kabasilas' Rejection of Aquinas Maculism as the Background to Scholarios' Immaculism", in D. Searby (ed.), *Never the Twain Shall Meet: Latins and Greeks Learning from Each Other in Byzantium*, Berlin/Boston 2017, 207–57.

Kapriev, G., "Systemelemente des philosophisch-theologischen Denkens in Byzanz. Zum Dialog "Theophanes" des Gregorios Palamas", *Recherches de Théologie et Philosophie Médiévales* 64/2 (1997), 263–90.

Kapriev, G., *Vizantiiskata Filosofia. Vtoro dopalneno izdanie* [Byzantine Philosophy. Second Edition with Supplements], Sofia 2011.

Knežević, M., *Gregory Palamas (1296–1357): Bibliography* (Bibliografija Srpske Teologije, 7), Belgrade 2012.

Krausmüller, D., "The Rise of Hesychasm", in M. Angold (ed.), *The Cambridge History of Christianity. V. Eastern Christianity*, Cambridge 2006, 101–26.

Krausmüller, D., "Banishing Reason from the Divine Image: Gregory Palamas' 150 Chapters", *Journal of Late Antique Religion and Culture* 13 (2019), 60–68.

Kotzabassi, S., "Eine Akoluthie zu Ehren des Philotheos Kokkinos", *Jahrbuch der Österreichischen Byzantinistik* 46 (1996), 299–310.

Kourousis, S.I., "Ὁ ἀκτουάριος Ἰωάννης Ζαχαρίας πρόδρομος κακοδοξιῶν Βαρλαάμ τοῦ Καλαβροῦ", *Ἀθηνᾶ* 60 (1990), 386–406.

Kresten, O., *Die Beziehungen zwischen den Patriarchaten von Konstantinopel und Antiocheia unter Kallistos I. und Philotheos Kokkinos im Spiegel des Patriarchatsregisters von Konstantinopel* (Abhandlungen der Geistes-und Sozialwissenschaftlichen Klasse, Jahrgang 2000, 6), Mainz/Stuttgart 2000.

Kresten, O., "Studien zum Tomos des Jahres 1341", in H. Hunger/O. Kresten (eds.), *Studien zum Patriarchatsregister von Konstantinopel*, vol. 2, Vienna 1997, pp. 45–191.

Larchet, J.-C., *La vie et l'oeuvre théologique de Géorges/Grégoire de Chypre (1241–1290) patriarche de Constantinople*, Paris 2012.

Larchet, J.-C., "Ὁ ἅγιος Γρηγόριος ὁ Παλαμᾶς καὶ ἡ πατερικὴ παράδοση", in G. Mantzarides (ed.), Ὁ ἅγιος Γρηγόριος ὁ Παλαμᾶς στὴν ἱστορία καὶ τὸ παρόν (Πρακτικὰ διεθνῶν ἐπιστημονικῶν συναντήσεων Ἀθηνῶν καὶ Λεμεσοῦ), Holy Monastery of Vatopedi, Mount Athos 2000, pp. 331–46.

Lévy, A., Le créé et l'incréé. Les origins de la querelle palamienne chez Maxime le Confesseur et Thomas d'Aquin, Paris 2006.

Lison, J., L'Esprit répandu. La pneumatologie de Grégoire Palamas, Paris 1994.

Louth, A., "Light, Vision, and Religious experience in Byzantium", in M.T. Kapstein. (ed.), The Presence of Light. Divine Radiance and Religious Experience, Chicago/ London 2004, pp. 85–103.

Louth, A., "The Eucharist and Hesychasm, with Special Reference to Theophanes III, Metropolitan of Nicaea", in I. Perczel/R. Forrai/G. Gereby (eds.), The Eucharist in Theology and Philosophy. Issues of Doctrinal History in East and West from the Patristic Age to the Reformation, Leuven 2005, pp. 199–205.

Makarov, D., "Feofan Nikeiskii mezdu palamizmom i antipalamizmom; vlijane Fom Akvinskogo" [Theophanes of Nicaea between Palamism and Anti-Palamism: The Influence of Thomas Aquinas], Antologija vostočno hristianskoi bogoslovskoi misli. Ortodoksia i geterodoksia, vol. 2, Moscow/Saint Petersburg 2009, pp. 572–80.

Makarov, D., Mariologija Feofana Nikeiskogo v kontekste Bizantiiskoi bogoslovskoi tradičii VII–XIV vv. [The Mariology of Theophanes of Nicaea in the Context of Byzantine Theological Tradition], Saarbrücken 2012.

Makarov, D., "Some Notes on the Notions of Synergy and Interpenetration in Theophanes of Nicaea", Studia Patristica 51 (2011), 205–16.

Markesinis, B., "Un florilège composé pour la défence du concile de 1351", in A. Schoors/ P. Van Deun (eds.), Philohistor. Miscellanea in honorem C. Laga septuagenarii (Orientalia Lovaniensia Analecta, 60), Leuven 1994, pp. 469–93.

Markov, S., "Teofan Nikeiski i prinost na palamitite v diskusiata za vecnosta na sveta" [Theophanes of Nicaea and his Contribution to the Discussion on the Eternity of the World], Archiv für mittelalterliche Philosophie und Kultur 19 (2013), 188–209.

Matschke, K.-P./F. Tinnefeld, Die Gesellschaft im späten Byzanz. Gruppen, Strukturen und Lebensformen, Cologne/Weimar/Vienna 2001.

Mercati, G., Notizie di Procoro e Demetrio Cidone, Mauele Caleca e Teodoro Meliteniota ed altri appunti per la storia della teologia e della letteratura bizantina del secolo XIV (Studi e Testi, 56), Rome 1931.

Meyendorff, J., Introduction à l'étude de Grégoire Palamas (Patristica Sorbonensia, 3), Paris 1959.

Meyendorff, J., "Le thème du "retour en soi" dans la doctrine palamite du XIV siècle", Revue de l'Histoire des Religions 145 (1954), 188–206.

Meyendorff, J., "Notes sur l'influence dionysienne en Orient", Studia Patristica 2 (1957), 547–52.

Meyendorff, J., "Un mauvais théologien de l'unité au XIV siècle: Barlaam le Calabrais", in *1054–1954: L'Eglise et les Eglises*, vol. 2, Chévetogne 1954, pp. 47–64 (repr. in id., *Byzantine Hesychasm: Historical, Theological and Social Problems*, London 1974, no. V).

Moniou, D.I., *Γεώργιος Μοσχάμπαρ, ἕνας ἀνθενωτικὸς θεολόγος τῆς πρώιμης Παλαιολόγειας περιόδου. Βίος καὶ ἔργο*, Athens 2011.

Müller-Schauenburg, B., "Gregorios Palamas und die kulturelle Neugier-Relecture einer theologischen Leitfigur", in Speer/Steinkrüger (eds.), *Knotenpunkt Byzanz*, pp. 287–307.

Müller-Schauenburg, B., *Religiöse Erfahrung, Spiritualität und theologische Argumentation. Gotteslehre und Gottebenbildlichkeit bei Gregorios Palamas*, Stuttgart 2011.

Nadal Cañellas, J., "Denys l'Aréopagite dans les traités de Grégoire Akindynos", in De Andia, *Denys*, pp. 535–64.

Nadal Cañellas, J., "Gregorio Akindinos", in Conticello/Conticello, *La théologie byzantine*, pp. 189–314.

Nadal Cañellas, J., *La résistance d'Akindynos à Grégoire Palamas. Enquête historique avec traduction et commentaire de quatre traités édités recemment*, vol. 2: *Commentaire historique*, Leuven 2006.

Papademetriou, G., *Maimonides and Palamas on God*, Brookline, MA 1994.

Papadopoulos, S.G., *Ἑλληνικαὶ μεταφράσεις θωμιστικῶν ἔργων: Φιλοθωμισταὶ καὶ ἀντιθωμισταὶ ἐν Βυζαντίῳ. Συμβολὴ εἰς τὴν ἱστορίαν τῆς Βυζαντινῆς θεολογίας*, Athens 1967.

Paraskevopoulou, I., *Τὸ ἁγιολογικὸ καὶ ὁμιλητικὸ ἔργο τοῦ Νικηφόρου Γρηγορᾶ* (Βυζαντινὰ Κείμενα καὶ Μελέται, 59), Thessaloniki 2013.

Patacsi, G., "Palamism before Palamas", *Eastern Churches Review* 9 (1977), 64–71.

Philippidis-Braat, A., "La captivité de Palamas chez les Turcs: Dossier et Commentaire", *Travaux et Memoires* 7 (1979), 109–222.

Pingree, D., "Argyros, Isaac", in A.P. Kazhdan et al. (eds.), *The Oxford Dictionary of Byzantium*, vol. 1, New York/Oxford 1991, p. 166.

Pitsakis, C., "Barlaam Calabro e i giuristi bizantini deil secoli XIV–XV", in Fyrigos (ed.), *Barlaam Calabro*, pp. 51–66.

Plested, M., *The Macarian Legacy. The Place of Macarius-Symeon in the Eastern Christian Tradition*, Oxford 2004.

Podskalsky, G., "Gottesschau und Inkarnation, zur Bedeutung der Heilgeschichte bei Gregorios Palamas", *Orientalia Christiana Periodica* 35 (1969), 5–44.

Podskalsky, G., "Il significato di Barlaam nell'ortodossia bizantino-slava (da un punto di vista cattolico)", in Fyrigos (ed.), *Barlaam Calabro*, pp. 13–23.

Podskalsky, G., *Theologie und Philosophie in Byzanz. Der Streit um die theologische Methodik in der spätbyzantinischen Geistesgeschichte (14/15.Jh.), seine systematischen Grundlagen und seine historische Entwicklung* (Byzantinisches Archiv, 15), Munich 1977.

394 POLEMIS

Podskalsky, G., *Von Photius zu Bessarion. Der Vorrang humanistisch geprägter Theologie in Byzanz und deren bleibende Bedeutung* (Schriften zur Geistesgeschichte des östlichen Europa, 25), Wiesbaden 2003.

Polemis, I., "Gregorio Palamas e la spiritualita athonita dell'epoca: esperienze soprannaturali e loro contesto", in Alfeyev et al. (eds.) *Il Cristo transfigurato*, pp. 293–333.

Polemis, I., "Manuel II Palaiologos Between Gregory Palamas and Thomas Aquinas", in M. Kneževič (ed.), *The Ways of Byzantine Philosophy*, Alhambra, CA 2015, pp. 353–60.

Polemis, I., "Neoplatonic and Hesychastic Elements in the Early Teaching of Gregorios Palamas on the Union of Man with God: The *Life of St. Peter the Athonite*", in S. Efthymiadis/C. Messis/P. Odorico/I. Polemis (eds.), *Pour une poétique de Byzance: Hommage à V. Katsaros* (Dossiers byzantins, 16), Paris 2015, pp. 205–21.

Polemis, I., "Nikephoros Blemmydes and Gregorios Palamas", in Rigo (ed.), *Gregorio Palamas e oltre*, pp. 179–89.

Polemis, I., "Nikolaos Kabasilas's De Vita in Christo and its context", *Byzantinische Zeitschrift* 106 (2013), 101–31.

Polemis, I., "Notes on a Short Treatise of Nicolas Cabasilas" *Revue des Études Byzantines* 51 (1993), 155–60.

Polemis, I., "Notes on Two Texts Dealing with the Palamite Controversy", in S. Kotzabassi/G. Mavromatis (eds.), *Realia Byzantina* (Byzantinisches Archiv, 22), Berlin 2009, 207–12.

Polemis, I. (ed.), *Theologica varia inedita saeculi XIV. Georgius Pelagonius, Adversus Palamam, Anonymus, Adversus Cantacuzenum, Prochorus Cydones, De lumine thaborico* (Corpus Christianorum. Series Graeca, 76), Turnhout 2012.

Polemis, I., *Theophanes of Nicaea: His Life and Works* (Wiener Byzantinistische Studien, 20), Vienna 1996.

Polemis, I., "Thomas Aquinas' Reception in Fourteenth-Century Byzantium", in M. Levering/M. Plested (eds.), *The Oxford Handbook of Thomas Aquinas*, Oxford 2021, 38–52.

Pospelova D.A., *Georgii Fakrasis, Disput svt. Gregorija Palami c Grigoroi filosofom. Filosofskie i bogoslovskie aspekti palamiskih sporov* [George Phakrases, The Dispute of St Gregory Palamas with Gregoras the Philosopher. Philosophical and Theological Aspects of the Palamite Controversy], Mount Athos 2009.

Prochorov, G.M., *Ioann Kantakuzin, Beseda s papskim legatom. Dialog s Iudeem i drugie sočinenija* [John Kantakouzenos, The Dialogue with the Papal Legate, The Dialogue with a Jew and Other Works], Saint Petersburg 1997.

Przegorlinčii, A., *Vizantiiskaja čerkov na rubeke XIII–XIV vv. Dejatelnost i naslednie sv. Feolipta mitropolita Filadelfiiskogo* [The Byzantine Church in the Turning between the XIII and XIV Centuries. The Activity and the Heritage of St Theoleptos of Philadelpheia], Saint Petersburg 2011.

Quaranta, F., "Un profugo a Bisanzio prima di Barlaam. L'Anonimo calabrese del Vat. gr. 316", in Fyrigos (ed.), *Barlaam Calabro*, pp. 79–90.

Radde-Gallwitz, A., *Basil of Caesarea, Gregory of Nyssa, and the Transformation of Divine Simplicity*, Oxford 2009.

Rigo, A. (ed.), *Byzantine Theology and its Philosophical Background* (Byzantioς. Studies in Byzantine History and Civilization, 4), Turnhout 2012.

Rigo, A., "Callisto Angelicude Catafygiota Meleniciota e l'esicasmo bizantino del XIV secolo. Una nota prosopografica", in N. Kauchtschischwili/G.M. Prochorov/ F. von Lilienfeld (eds.), *Nil Sorskij e l'esicasmo. Atti del II Convegno ecumenico internationale di spiritualita russa, Bose, 21–24 settembre 1994*, Magnano 1995, pp. 251–68.

Rigo, A., "De l'apologie à l'évocation de l'expérience mystique. Évagre le Pontique, Isaac le Syrien et Diadoque de Photicé dans les oeuvres de Grégoire Palamas (et dans la controverse palamite)", in Speer/Steinkrüger (eds.), *Knotenpunkt Byzanz*, pp. 85–108.

Rigo, A., "Gregorio il Sinaita", in C.G. Conticello/V. Conticello, *La théologie byzantine*, pp. 35–122.

Rigo, A. (ed.), *Gregorio Palamas e oltre. Studi e documenti sulle controversie teologiche del XIV secolo Bizantino* (Orientalia Venetiana, 16), Florence 2004.

Rigo, A., "Il corpus pseudo-dionisiano negli scritti di Gregorio Palamas (e di Barlaam) del 1336–1341", in De Andia (ed.) *Denys*, pp. 519–34.

Rigo, A., "Il Monte Athos e la controversia palamitica dal concilio del 1351 al *Tomo synodale* del 1368. Giacomo Tricanas, Procoro Cidone e Filoteo Kokkinos", in Id. (ed.), *Gregorio Palamas e oltre*, pp. 99–134.

Rigo, A., *1347. Isidoro patriarca di Constantinopoli e il breve sogno dell' inizio di una nuova epoca* (Wiener Byzantinistische Studien, 30), Vienna 2020.

Rigo, A., "La Transfigurazione di Cristo sul monte Tabor nelle opere di Gregorio il Sinaita", in Alfeyev et al. (eds.), *Il Cristo transfigurato*, pp. 277–91.

Rigo, A., "L'epistola a Menas di Gregorio Palamas e gli effetti dell'orazione", *Cristianesimo nella storia* 9 (1988), 59–79.

Rigo, A., "Le tecniche d'orazione esicastica e le potenze dell'anima in alcuni testi ascetici bizantini", *Rivista di Studi Bizantini e Slavi* 4 (1984), 75–115.

Rigo, A., "Massimo il Kausokalyba e la rinascità eremitica sul monte Athos nel XIV secolo", in A. Louf/J. Noret et al. (eds.), *Atanasio e il monachesimo al monte Athos. Atti del XII Convegno ecumenico internazionale di spiritualità ortodossa, Bose 12–14 settembre 2004*, Comunità de Bose 2005, pp. 181–216.

Rigo, A., "Autografi, manoscritti e nuove opera di Giuseppe Kalothetos (metà del XIV secolo)", *Revue d'histoire des textes* 12 (2017), 107–39.

Rigo, A. (ed.), *Mistici bizantini*, Turin 2008.

Rigo, A., *Monaci esicasti e monaci bogomili. Le accuse di messalianismo e bogomilismo rivolte agli esicasti ed il problema dei rapporti tra esicasmo e bogomilismo* (Orientalia Venetiana, 2), Florence 1989.

Rigo, A., "Niceforo l'esicasta (XIII sec.): alcune considerazioni sulla vita e sull'opera", in T. Spidlik (ed.), *Amore del bello, studi sulla Filocalia. Atti del "Simposio Internazionale sulla Filocalia", Pontificio Collegio Greco, Roma, Novembre 1989* (Spiritualità orientale), Magnano 1991, pp. 79–119.

Rigo, A., "Nota sulla dottrina ascetico-spirituale di Teolepto metropolita di Filadelfia (1250/51–1322)", *Rivista di Studi Bizantini e Neoellenici NS.* 24 (1987), 165–200.

Rigo, A., *Il monaco, la chiesa e la liturgia. I capitoli sulle gerarchie di Gregorio il Sinaita*, Florence 2005.

Ritter, A.M., "Gregor Palamas als Leser des Dionysius Ps.-Areopagita", in De Andia, *Denys*, pp. 565–79.

Rodionov, O., "The *Chapters* of Kallistos Angelikoudes", in Rigo (ed.), *Byzantine Theology*, pp. 141–59.

Romanides, J.S., "Notes on the Palamite Controversy and Related Topics", *The Greek Orthodox Theological Review* 9 (1963–1964), 225–70.

Rossi, L., *I filosofi greci padri dell'esicasmo. La sintesi di Nikodemo Aghiorita*, Turin 2000.

Russell, E. (ed.), *Spirituality in Late Byzantium: Essays Presenting New Research by International Scholars*, New Castle upon Tyne 2009.

Russell, N., *Gregory Palamas and the Making of Palamism in the Modern Age* (*Changing Paradigms in Historical and Systematic Theology*), Oxford 2019.

Russell, N., *Gregory Palamas. The Hesychast Controversy and the Debate with Islam. Documents relating to Gregory Palamas. Translated with an Introduction and Notes* (Translated Texts for Byzantinists, 8), Liverpool 2020.

Russell, N., "Partakers of the Divine Nature (2 Peter 1:4) in the Byzantine tradition", in Chrysostomides (ed.), *Καθηγήτρια*, pp. 51–67.

Russell, N., "Prochoros Cydones and the Fourteenth-Century Understanding of Orthodoxy", in A. Louth/A. Casiday (eds.), *Byzantine Orthodoxies. Papers from the Thirty-sixth Spring Symposium of Byzantine Studies, University of Durham, 22–25 March 2002*, Aldershot, Hants 2006, pp. 75–91.

Russell, N., "The "Gods" of Psalm 81 (82) in the Hesychast Debates", in A. Andreopoulos/ A. Casiday/C. Harrison (eds.), *Meditations of the Heart: The Psalms in Early Christian Thought and Practice. Essays in Honour of A. Louth*, Turnhout 2011, pp. 243–56.

Russell, N., "The Patriarch Philotheos Kokkinos and his Defense of Hesychasm", in Russell (ed.), *Spirituality*, pp. 21–31.

Savvatos, Chr., *Ἡ θεολογικὴ ὁρολογία καὶ προβληματικὴ τῆς πνευματολογίας Γρηγορίου Β΄ τοῦ Κυπρίου*, Katerini 1997.

Savvidis, K., *Die Lehre von der Vergöttlichung des Menschen bei Maximos dem Bekenner und ihre Rezeption durch Gregor Palamas* (Veröffentlichingen des Instituts für orthodoxe Theologie, 5), Abbey of St. Ottilien 1997.

Sekulovski, G., "The Social Aspects of Fourteenth-Century Hesychasm", *Studia Patristica* 48 (2010), 373–77.

Sinkewicz, R.E., "Christian Theology and the Renewal of Philosophical and Scientific Studies in the Early Fourteenth Century: The *Capita 150* of Gregory Palamas", *Mediaeval Studies* 48 (1986), 334–51.

Sinkewicz, R.E., "Gregory Palamas", in C.G. Conticello/V. Conticello, *La théologie byzantine*, pp. 131–88.

Sinkewicz, R.E., "The Doctrine of the Knowledge of God in the Early Writings of Barlaam the Calabrian", *Mediaeval Studies* 44 (1982), 181–242.

Sinkewicz, R.E., "The *Solutions* addressed to George Lapithes by Barlaam the Calabrian and their Philosophical Context", *Mediaeval Studies* 43 (1981), 151–54.

Sopko, A.J., "Scholasticism and Orthodoxy. Some Current Observations", in D. Papademetriou-A.J. Sopko (eds.), *The Church and the Library. Studies in Honor of Rev. Dr. G.C. Papademetriou*, Boston, MA 2005, pp. 383–98.

Speer, A./P. Steinkrüger (eds.), *Knotenpunkt Byzanz. Wissenformen und kulturelle Wechselbeziehungen*, Berlin/Boston 2012.

Spiteris, Y., *Palamas: la grazia e l'esperienza. Gregorio Palamas nella discussione teologica*. Introducione di M. Cacciari, Rome 1996.

Stiernon, D., "Bulletin sur le palamisme", *Revue des Études Byzantines* 30 (1972), 232–341.

Talbot, A.-M., "George the Philosopher", in A.P. Kazhdan et al. (ed.), *The Oxford Dictionary of Byzantium*, vol. 2, New York/Oxford 1991, pp. 838–39.

Tinnefeld, F., *Demetrios Kydones, Briefe*, vol. 1/1: *Einleitung und 47 Briefe* (Bibliothek der griechischen Literatur, 12), Stuttgart 1981.

Tinnefeld, F., *Nikephoros Gregoras, Rhomaische Geschichte. Historia Rhomaike, 6. Kapitel XXX–XXXVII*, (Bibliothek der griechischen Literatur, 66), Stuttgart 2007.

Tollefsen, T.T., *Activity and Participation in Late Antique and Early Christian Thought* (Oxford Early Christian Studies), Oxford 2012.

Torrance, A., "Precedents for Palamas' Essence-Energies Theology in the Cappadocian Fathers", *Vigiliae Christianae* 63 (2009), 47–70.

Triantafyllopoulos, C., "The Thomist Basis of Prochoros Kydones' anti-Palamite Treatise 'De essentia et operatione Dei' and the Reaction of the Byzantine Church", in Speer/Steinkrüger (eds.), *Knotenpunkt Byzanz*, pp. 411–30.

Trizio, M., "Una è la verità che pervade ogni cosa. La sapienza profana nelle opere perdute di Barlaam Calabro", in Rigo (ed.), *Byzantine Theology*, pp. 108–40.

van Rossum, J., "Holy Communion as "Symbol" in Pseudo-Dionysius and Theophanes of Nicaea", *Studia Patristica* 48 (2010), 205–10.

Veniukov, D., "Grigorii Sinait, Bogoslovie" [Gregory the Sinaite. His Theology], *Pravoslavnaja Enciklopedia* 13 (2006), 60–66.

Vernačkii, M.M., "Grigorii Palama, Sočinenija" [Gregory Palamas. His Writings], *Pravoslavnaja Enčiklopedija* 13 (2006), 16–26.

Vernačkii, M.M./A.G. Dunaev, "David Disipat", *Pravoslavnaja Enčiklopedija* 13 (2006), 582–90.

Ware, K., "God Hidden and Revealed: The Apophatic Way and the Essence-Energies Distinction", *Eastern Churches Review* 7/2 (1975), 125–36.

Ware, K., "St Maximos of Kapsokalyvia and Fourteenth-Century Athonite Hesychasm", in Chrysostomides (ed.), Καθηγήτρια, pp. 409–30.

Ware, K., "The Debate about Palamism", *Eastern Churches Review* 9 (1977), 45–63.

Ware, K., "The Hesychasts: Gregory of Sinai, Gregory Palamas, Nicolas Cabasilas", in C. Jones/G. Wainright/E. Yarnold (eds.), *The Study of Spirituality*, New York/Oxford 1986, pp. 242–55.

Ware, K., "The Jesus Prayer in St Gregory of Sinai", *Eastern Churches Review* 4 (1972), 3–22.

Weiss, G., *Joannes Kantakuzenos-Aristokrat, Staatsmann, Kaiser und Mönch-in der Gesellschaftsentwicklung von Byzanz im 14. Jahrhundert* (Studien zur Geistesgeschichte des östlichen Europa, 4), Wiesbaden 1969.

Williams, A.N., *The Ground of Union. Deification in Aquinas and Palamas*, New York/Oxford 1999.

Williams, R.W., "The Philosophical Structures of Palamism", *Eastern Churches Review* 9 (1977), 27–44.

Wolfson, H.A., "Crescas on the Problem of Divine Attributes", in Id., *Studies in the History of Philosophy and Religion*, vol. 2, Cambridge, MA/ London 1977, pp. 247–337.

Wolfson, H.A., *Repercussions of the Kalam in Jewish Philosophy*, Cambridge, MA/ London 1979.

Wolfson, H.A., *The Philosophy of the Kalam*, Cambridge, MA/London 1976.

CHAPTER 11

Working in the Imperial and Patriarchal Chanceries

Giuseppe De Gregorio

1 Introductory Background

As is well known, among the many unique features of Byzantine society was an elevated idea of central authority, based on a principle directly derived from Roman imperial tradition. It is not surprising, therefore, that public documentation assumed a prominent role. The forms and characters with which it was produced almost always carried strong symbolic significance and represented concrete and tangible instruments through which that same central authority, both political-institutional and religious, exercised and manifested its power. Although the papyri of late antique Egypt have furnished us with very few original documents relevant to the acts issued by public bureaux of Constantinople other than the imperial office,[1] it is likely that the primary chancery of the Byzantine state, structurally organized with more or less stable personnel, was that of the emperor, at least by some point and certainly during the Palaeologan era. Similarly, in the ecclesiastical world, it is possible to reconstruct as a permanent entity the inner office of the Great Church,[2] which was in charge of preparing documents and equipped with well-established structures, based on entrenched and enduring tradition and customs – that is to say, the chancery of the primate of Orthodoxy.[3]

Certainly, we possess numerous acts issued by officials of various ranks in the state administration and the ecclesiastical hierarchy, which concern documents of officials or of bishops, archbishops, or metropolitans,[4] as well as a similarly conspicuous mass of private documents (still much less studied for Byzantium compared to Western medieval studies), that should be traced back to notarial boards organized in various ways. Regarding the documents

---

1 Cf. e.g. Salomon, "A Papyrus from Constantinople (Hamburg Inv. No. 410)".
2 In Greek, ἡ Μεγάλη τοῦ Θεοῦ Ἐκκλησία, which refers first to the church of *Hagia Sophia* in Constantinople and, more universally, to the Ecumenical Patriarchate housed there.
3 Certainly, documentary production is also confirmed for the other eastern patriarchates (Jerusalem, Alexandria, and Antioch), though mostly indirectly; but a systematic organization of the office is conceivable only for the prior period, up until a few centuries after the Arab conquest.
4 Cf. Dölger/Karayannopulos, *Byzantinische Urkundenlehre*, pp. 23–24.

© KONINKLIJKE BRILL NV, LEIDEN, 2023 | DOI:10.1163/9789004527089_013

of officials, we know, for example, that a good part of the letters and acts that make up the work of Demetrios Chomatenos (between the late 12th century and ca. 1236, first as *apokrisiarios* from the archbishopric of Ohrid to the patriarch of Constantinople, then *chartophylax* in Ohrid and finally archbishop of the same autocephalous see at Ohrid), were not only released but also written by that same prelate, based on forms and legal customs learned in the patriarchal chancery of Constantinople. Meanwhile, the remaining pieces must have been composed and transcribed by clerics in his service in a chancery office of the archbishop in Ohrid, under the guidance of a *chartophylax*.[5] Similarly, regarding private documents, it is necessary to mention briefly the traditional role of the citizen notaryship, which, beyond the well-known example of Ravenna in the early Byzantine period, can be well illustrated, in terms of that office's corporate organization, by the regulations attested in the "Book of the Eparch" (early 10th century).[6] Moreover, regarding just the late Byzantine era, we cannot ignore the testimony of the numerous private documents conserved in cartularies, where tabellions with ecclesiastical rank – sometimes elevated – were active in a characteristic mix of functions. For example, in the cartulary of Makrinitissa and Nea Petra (13th century),[7] the bishop of Demetrias (Thessaly) operated as a "notary" in private acts (in the place of lay professionals, who must have not been available in that area), which moreover indicate an uncommon knowledge in the field of law as the result of formal study.

Nevertheless, a simple survey of, for example, the acts published in the series of the "Archives de l'Athos" reveals the presence of a somewhat extemporaneous production for the so-called minor authorities and for the notarial tradition in the realm of private documentation, where on the one hand the physical compilers seem to have been recruited just from the scribes operating in a specific region or place, mainly on the basis of their comparatively superior writing skills, and, on the other, the documentary forms appear to be modelled more or less coherently on the practices of the two central chanceries. A rapid skimming of the section "Erwähnte Urkunden und Gesetze" in the three volumes currently published in the edition of the Register of the Patriarchate of Constantinople, however, sheds some light on a not irrelevant series of private documents from the 14th century behind which likely hides an intense activity that has not yet been sufficiently investigated in terms of its organization and structure.

---

5 Prinzing, "Konvergenz und Divergenz zwischen dem Patriarchatsregister und den *Ponemata Diaphora*".

6 Leo VI the Wise, *Book of the Eparch*, ed. Koder, pp. 74–84 (Chapt. 1: Περὶ ταβουλλαρίων).

7 Cf. infra, n. 40 and context.

WORKING IN THE IMPERIAL AND PATRIARCHAL CHANCERIES   401

In general, it is useful to observe, for example, that in the 13th century the imperial chancery, though it had long dropped the tradition of the "Reservatschrift" (the script that was learned and spread exclusively within that office, especially for the privileges),[8] did not relinquish its role of controlling and selecting the types of handwriting internally employed there, depending on the various categories of documents produced (categories that can be valued correctly only with adequate knowledge of diplomatics). The same is also true, for example, of the production of imperial documents in the age of Andronikos II Palaiologos (between the 13th and 14th century) and beyond, at least until the middle of the 14th century, where, even in the presence of scripts used both for books and for documents (and thus not employed exclusively by the imperial chancery) more formalized outcomes were preferred for chrysobulls.[9] Moreover, the testimony of the Register of the Patriarchate of Constantinople will, throughout most of the 14th century, offer a similar point of departure in the present overview.

2 Chanceries in the Service of Rhetoric and Ideology

Without doubt, the primary feature of the ideological programme of Michael VIII Palaiologos (1259–1282) – at least in this respect followed faithfully by his son Andronikos II Palaiologos (1282–1328) – was restoration. Reaffirming imperial dignity, thus legitimizing the dynastic power of the Palaiologoi, promoting the restoration and reconstruction of buildings in the capital, thus returning them to ancient splendour, and, last but not least, reconstructing the monastic communities dispersed during the Latin occupation (1204–1261), were some of the objectives of the policies of the dynasty's first two emperors, as is highlighted, with justifiable pride, in certain prefaces to documents issued by the same Michael VIII in favour of ecclesiastic institutions that were re-established and renewed – one example is the chrysobull for the restoration of the church of *Hagia Sophia* in Constantinople (1267–1271).[10] But it is the

---

8   Cf. Dölger, "Die Kaiserurkunde der Byzantiner als Ausdruck ihrer politischen Anschauungen", pp. 236–39 (repr., pp. 17–20); Dölger/Karayannopulos, *Byzantinische Urkundenlehre*, pp. 31–34; Hunger, "Schriftästhetik in den drei originalen kaiserlichen Auslandsschreiben der Komnenenzeit".

9   "Großprivilegienurkunden": cf. Dölger/Karayannopulos, *Byzantinische Urkundenlehre*, pp. 119–27; Burgmann, "Chrysobull gleich Privileg?".

10   Dölger/Wirth, *Regesten*, vol. 3, no. 1941a (transmitted in copy). An interesting contribution is now offered by Smyrlis, "Priesterhood and Empire". Cf. more generally Talbot, "The Restoration of Constantinople under Michael VIII".

402 DE GREGORIO

rhetorical construction of the acts – that is, the high tenor, the forms and the conventions of the chancery's *dictamen* – that reinforces these instruments for apology and propaganda. For example, it is telling that in some of these documentary sources (unfortunately only seldom transmitted in the original for this first period after Latin rule), the western yoke is described with intentionally vague and generic expressions, since, as is well-known, the Byzantines did not like to talk of contingent situations, especially unfavourable ones. Thus (confining ourselves to the customs of the patriarchal chancery), the disruption and the dispersion of monastic communities in the first half of the 13th century, which the Palaeologan dynasty now attempted to remedy, are revealed in an unedited documentary fragment, Vatican City, Biblioteca Apostolica Vaticana, MS Vat. gr. 100 B, with an ambiguous and reticent circumlocution in genitive absolute: "the die of fate of the events having rolled over differently" (or "the course of events having changed").[11] Moreover, regarding the institutional crises – economic and social – that from the end of the 13th century and throughout the entire 14th century shook the empire (as a consequence, additionally, of a progressive loss of territory, especially in Asia Minor), the documentation alludes simply to the "confusion and the irregularity of the state of things",[12] although the progressive decline of the administrative and civil structures left the Church to assume an ever increasing role, as much moral as political, in late Byzantine society.

2.1 Prefaces to Documents as Expressions of Intellectual Production

Beyond relaying historical information of fundamental importance, chancery documents can often be evaluated in the same way as literary works, at times attaining a high level of form and style. The highest expression – rhetorically and content-based – of imperial ideology, as well as of patriarchal intervention in theological matters or in the realm of monastic and ecclesiastical discipline, is normally found in prefaces (or arengas), that is, the introductory sections of the documentary text – which have already been analysed in terms of structure and tradition in a few esteemed contributions in the corpus of Byzantine studies[13] – where the ideological motivations (universally valid from the ethi-

---

11 Vat. gr. 100 B, line 4: ... τοῦ πε⟨σ⟩σοῦ τῶν πραγμάτων ἄλλως μεταπεσόντος (I attribute this fragment to the first term of Patriarch Ioseph I Galesiotes, late 1266–early 1275).

12 *Patriarchal Register*, vol. 1, no. 51 (1315, July), lines 14–15: ... ἡ τῶν πραγμάτων σύγχυσις καὶ ἀνωμαλία ... .

13 Hunger, *Prooimion* (with the addition of Browning, *Notes on Byzantine Prooimia*); Mazal, *Die Prooimien der byzantinischen Patriarchenurkunden*. Observations on the compositional style of the documents transmitted in the Register of the Patriarchate of

WORKING IN THE IMPERIAL AND PATRIARCHAL CHANCERIES   403

cal point of view) behind the legal action are made explicit. To write these
arengas, in part due to the necessity of adhering in the *dictamen* to established
habits and conventional formularies that would reinforce and confirm the
validity of the act, the chancery servants, and those called on from time to
time to collaborate with the office, were able to use pre-existing models. One
interesting collection of 20 *clichés* for prefaces to chrysobulls is conserved in
MS Heidelberg, Universitätsbibliothek, Palat. gr. 356, copied towards the end
of the 13th century, most likely in Constantinople.[14] Furthermore, one example of a document composed following the highest rhetorical rules, though it
was never actually delivered to its recipient (perhaps because it was rendered
obsolete by the hectic succession of events), is the letter (1265, ca. June) from
the Emperor Michael VIII Palaiologos to the newly elected Pope Clement IV
aimed at re-proposing agreement with Rome on the dogmatic level.[15] The
text is passed down to us for its literary value in a *dossier* (contained in MS
Vienna, Österreichische Nationalbibliothek, Vindob. Phil. gr. 321, from the second half of the 13th century) of works by Manuel Holobolos, the well-known
court rhetor and teacher in the patriarchal school who also had noteworthy
experience in documentary *dictamen*, with particular reference to the dictation of prefaces.[16] Here we find numerous constructions, common in this kind
of document, which derive from a pre-existing chancery formulary that was
from time to time combed through for letters to be sent to the Roman pope.

It is not surprising that even intellectuals of a high level engaged in the composition of prefaces for documents, as this is a custom that was well established in Byzantium. For older periods, as prime examples one can quote
Michael Psellos (11th century) and the brothers George and Demetrios Tornikes
(12th century, second half/end).[17] For the age of the Palaeologan dynasty we

---

Constantinople can be found in Hunger, "Zum Stil und zur Sprache des Patriarchatsregisters von Konstantinopel"; id., "Zur scheinbaren Nonchalance der Kanzleisprache des
Patriarchatsregisters"; Gastgeber, "Rhetorik in der Patriarchatskanzlei von Konstantinopel"; on the formulary of the patriarchal chancery see now id., "Das Formular der Patriarchatskanzlei". On the prefaces and chancery formulas of the "letters of union" (the
foreign letters and documents connected to the negotiations with the Church of Rome
before and after the Council of Lyon of 1274) cf. Pieralli, *La corrispondenza diplomatica
dell'imperatore bizantino*, pp. 61–69.

14   Cf. Hunger, *Prooimion*, pp. 217–45 (with 1 pl.); Heid, Palat gr 356, fols 65ᵛ 69ᵛ, tit.
      "Various chrysobull's proems excerpted from older chrysobulls" (Προοίμια χρυσοβούλλων
      διάφορα παρεκβληθέντα ἀπὸ παλαιοτέρων χρυσοβούλλων).
15   Pieralli, *La corrispondenza diplomatica dell'imperatore bizantino*, pp. 167–83 (no. 8).
16   On Manuel Holobolos cf. PLP 21047; De Gregorio, "Una lista di commemorazioni di
      defunti", 142–44, 180–81; Fisher, "Manuel Holobolos and the Role of Bilinguals".
17   Cf. Michael Psellos, *Orations*, ed. Dennis, pp. 143–81; George/Demetrios Tornikes, *Letters
      and Orations*, ed. Darrouzès, pp. 189–201, 324–53 (nos. 30, 32–34) (also in the case of

also possess numerous testimonies of this type of text composed by the most eminent scholars of the time, who were in service as *mesazontes* (trusted advisors of the emperor and intermediaries of his will with the people). These scholars could inspire and sometimes formulate the text of the acts produced in the imperial chancery and submitted to the highest authority for signature. Thus, we are able to identify at least four highly elegant prefaces composed by Nikephoros Choumnos (1250/55–1327), which were inserted into four chrysobulls also drafted by the scholar and transmitted in several manuscripts with his works. Among these, MS Milan, Biblioteca Ambrosiana, Ambros. C 71 sup. (gr. 185) stands out, a collection of writings by Choumnos datable between 1320 and 1327 and copied in his own entourage by, among others, the primary scribe of the imperial chancery in this period, George Boullotes.[18] The latter was also the scribe of the only surviving original of these four chrysobulls, which are also preserved in the manuscript tradition,[19] as well as the scribe of another original, whose formal composition and style connect it, too, with certainty, to Choumnos, indisputably the head of the imperial chancery at the time. This last testimony also carries on its *verso* a typical entry of this office in Choumnos' own hand.[20]

For Choumnos' great rival, too, the scholar and politician Theodore Metochites (1270–1332) who managed and interpreted the policies of Andronikos II during the second half of his long reign, we have the testimony of at least one arenga, also intended for an imperial chrysobull and attested as a rhetorical exercise and compositional model in the well-known witness of the *mesazon's* Discourses (*Logoi*), MS Vienna, Österreichische Nationalbibliothek, Vindob. Phil. gr. 95 (fol. 329r–v), copied by his scribe, the imperial notary Michael Klostomalles. From certain stereotypical expressions characteristic of rhetorical composition in documentary practice, we can recognize the style adopted

---

George Tornikes MS Vindob. Phil. gr. 321 counts as *codex unicus*; see also Pieralli, *La corrispondenza diplomatica dell'imperatore bizantino*, pp. 9–10, 63).

18 Cf. Papatriantaphyllou-Theodoridi, *Choumnos*, pp. 28–31 (nos. 23, 24, 25, 29 [= Dölger, *Regesten*, vol. 4, nos. 2158, 2348, 2323, 2085]), 128–46 (for the codex Ambrosianus). I shall return to Boullotes below.

19 Papatriantaphyllou-Theodoridi, *Choumnos*, p. 29, no. 24 (1313, October: *Documents Chilandar*, eds. Živojinović/Kravari/Giros, no. 29; Dölger, *Regesten*, vol. 4, no. 2348); Lamberz, "Georgios Bullotes", p. 37 with n. 15, pl. 8.

20 *Documents Lavra*, eds. Lemerle/Guillou/Svoronos/Papachryssanthou, vol. 2, no. 89 A (1298, June; Dölger, *Regesten*, vol. 4, no. 2208); it is the oldest known document in Boullotes' hand: Lamberz, "Georgios Bullotes", p. 36, pl. 3. The document of Chilandar cited here (cf. previous footnote) also carries on its *verso* the chancery note inserted by Choumnos; to these originals, I shall return below.

WORKING IN THE IMPERIAL AND PATRIARCHAL CHANCERIES 405

in other chrysobulls from the first decades of the 14th century for which Metochites was in all likelihood responsible.[21]

Finally, remaining with the office in charge of preparing and copying acts for the emperor, we may mention three formularies of prefaces composed by Demetrios Kydones (ca. 1324–1397/98). Kydones was the most noted anti-Palamite theologian and scholar of the second half of the 14th century, as well as an advocate for union with the Roman Church. He was in service as *mesazon* both from 1347–1354 under John VI Kantakouzenos and during the reign of John V Palaiologos from around 1356 to 1386 – precisely the period from which the three prefaces date (one being attributable to the end of 1371, and the other two probably simple drafts still without date).[22] Demetrios Kydones also played a decisive role in composing and transcribing the Greek text of the profession of Roman Faith (as well as partially in drawing up the related Latin version), that John V Palaiologos presented on 18 October 1369 in the Roman church of Santo Spirito in Sassia.[23]

Nikephoros Gregoras (1293–1361) is an equally significant case.[24] We know that the author of the *Historia Rhomaike* must have attempted, especially in his youth, the composition of some arengas, extremely refined rhetorically, that are now collected along with other literary works of his in MS Vatican City, Biblioteca Apostolica Vaticana, Vat. gr. 1086.[25] Examples of his activity in the realm of *dictamen* come from the documentation relating to the years of Patriarch John XIII Glykys (1315–1319).[26] Gregoras must have established a close relationship with the chancery of this primate of the Orthodox Church thanks, above all, to the good offices of his uncle John, metropolitan

---

21   Cf. Hunger, *Prooimion*, pp. 39 (with n. 99), 196 (no. 303) (= Dölger, *Regesten*, vol. 4, no. 2600 [without date]). Theodore Metochites, *Orations*, eds. Polemis/Kaltsogianni, pp. 609–10 (no. 15).

22   Hunger, *Prooimion*, pp. 39 (with n. 98); 113 and 129 (no. 162); 55, 141 and 157 n. 2 (no. 52) (he assigns these three rhetorical exercises to the beginning of the reign of Manuel II Palaiologos [1391–1425]); cf. Dölger, *Regesten*, vol. 5, nos. 3130 (AD 1371), 3217 e 3222 (both without date); cf. also above, chapter 10.

23   See now Pieralli, "Un imperatore di Bisanzio a Roma".

24   PLP 4443; Beyer, "Eine Chronologie der Lebensgeschichte des Nikephoros Gregoras"; De Gregorio, "Un'aggiunta su copisti greci del secolo XIV", 261–68.

25   Cf. Kresten, in *Patriarchal Register*, vol. 1, pp. 43–45 (*Einleitung*, 11: *Überlieferungsgeschichte*). In Vat. gr. 1086 the hand of Gregoras is attested on several folios; cf. especially Ševčenko, "Some Autographs of Nicephorus Gregoras", pp. 444–46 (with figs. 4–5); further bibliography is provided in Bianconi, "La biblioteca di Cora tra Massimo Planude e Niceforo Gregora", 417 (no. 39) (more recently Bianconi, "I libri di Niceforo Gregora", p. 35 [no. 27] limits himself to mentioning Ševčenko); see also Pérez Martín, *El patriarca Gregorio de Chipre*, pp. 49–50, 326 with n. 7, pl. 11; ead., "El «estilo Hodegos»", pp. 113–14, 118–21, pl. 7.

26   PLP 4271.

of Herakleia Pontike (1295–1328).[27] John took care of his nephew's education, introducing him to the circle of John Glykys. Thus, his young and promising relative composed, with great stylistic effect, the preface for an act issued by this patriarch in favour of the city of Herakleia Pontike (AD 1317–1318), which is transmitted in a dual tradition, both in the collection of Gregoras' works in Vat. gr. 1086 (fol. 213r) and in the series of documents included in the Register of the Patriarchate of Constantinople (MS Vienna, Österreichische Nationalbibliothek, Vindob. Hist. gr. 47, fols. 33v–34v).[28] Some images foreshadow the complex rhetorical architecture of the writer's major works: for example, the construction of the preface's conclusion, modelled chiastically and alluding to the ties of spiritual brotherhood (such as those between the patriarch and his metropolitan) that are stronger than ties of blood:

> there, in fact, one is perhaps accused only for the harshness of the heart and one distances oneself after adequate pain has been established; here, instead, in addition one is blamed before the person from whom one has received the entrustment of the office of administration, in cases in which, though being able to offer a helping hand, one permits, through indolence, one's brother [in Christ] to be oppressed with violence.[29]

Moreover, we know of texts of this literary genre composed by Gregoras and conserved exclusively in the partial autograph of his works.[30] It is worth noting first another arenga, also for a patriarchal *sigillion*, likewise attributable to the period of John Glykys and addressed to an (unspecified) monastic community, which is otherwise unknown in the documentary tradition.[31] There are also two more prefaces for imperial chrysobulls,[32] demonstrating that barriers

---

27   *PLP* 8609. Gregoras was also a native of Herakleia Pontike.

28   *Patriarchal Register*, vol. 1, no. 51 (from the Vat. gr. 1086, Nikephoros Gregoras, *Opuscules*, ed. Leone, pp. 769–70 [no. VII]); Darrouzès, *Les regestes*, vol. 5, no. 2081.

29   *Patriarchal Register*, vol. 1, no. 51, lines 11–16: ... παρ' ὅσον καὶ κρείττων ἡ τοῦ πνεύματος τῆς ἐξ αἵματος συναφείας. ἐκεῖ μὲν γὰρ ἴσως σκληρότητα γνώμης καταγνωσθεὶς τὶς εἶτα ἀπῆλθεν ἐς τοσοῦτον αὐτῷ τῆς καταδίκης ὁρισθείσης, ἐνταῦθα δὲ πρὸς τούτοις καὶ δίκας ὀφλήσει παρὰ τῷ τὰ τῆς οἰκονομίας πιστεύσαντι, εἰ δυνάμενος χεῖρα βοηθείας παρέχεσθαι, ἔπειτα ῥᾳστώνῃ δεδωκὼς τὸ πρᾶγμα τῇ βίᾳ συνωθεῖσθαι τὸν ἀδελφὸν συγκεχώρηκεν.

30   For an overview and exhaustive bibliographic references cf. Kresten, in *Patriarchal Register*, vol. 1, p. 44 n. 29.

31   Vat. gr. 1086, fols. 211v–212r; Nikephoros Gregoras, *Opuscules*, ed. Leone, pp. 766–67 (no. IV); cf. also Darrouzès, *Les regestes*, vol. 5, no. 2081 ("Critique").

32   Vat. gr. 1086, fols. 216v–217v, 235r–v; Nikephoros Gregoras, *Opuscules*, ed. Leone, pp. 778–81 (nos. XIII–XIV); also see the introduction to Nikephoros Gregoras, *History*, trans. van Dieten, vol. 1, p. 47 (nos. 19–20).

between the two central Byzantine institutions were practically non-existent in terms of the activity of the intellectual class and often also for those who, thanks to their acknowledged skills, performed there the function of scribe and physical compiler of acts. Finally, the arengas the scholar composed for the wills of several ecclesiastics appear in the same Vatican manuscript relating to Gregoras,[33] among which the literarily and historically most important is without doubt the *diatheke* of the same John Glykys (1319), a composition that would later be included in his major work.[34]

It is plausible that other prefaces to patriarchal documents might be attributed to Gregoras and that his contribution to the drawing up of texts issued by his mentor John Glykys is not limited to the examples contained in Vat. gr. 1086.[35] In this respect, one can understand why in 1321, right after he had personally met Gregoras and thus shortly after the death of the patriarch who marked the rise of this emerging figure in intellectual circles, Emperor Andronikos II Palaiologos intended to offer him the title of *chartophylax* of the Great Church (corresponding, in practice, to the head of the chancery), a position of great significance, from which, however, the scholar shielded himself.[36]

All this, however, does more than reflect the intersection, characteristic of Byzantium, between the caste of officials and the most elevated intellectual circles. It also demonstrates that the latter most definitely did not disdain the idea of concerning themselves with the production of documents, which, beyond the stereotypical formulary, served as a training ground for rhetorical education (a true pillar in the literary conception of the Byzantines). Moreover, it is clear that these exercises – certainly not secondary in value but always more limited in length – often merged (directly or indirectly) into the major works. The testimonies connected to documentary practices also often help bring to the fore figures otherwise less known, or entirely unknown, whose work and influence were primarily confined to the chancery. In this regard, we have some other invaluable attestations of preface authors in the documents

---

33   It is probable that some of these pieces collected in Vat. gr. 1086 represent rhetorical exercises or variations on a theme and compositional sketches.

34   Vat. gr. 1086, fols. 210r–211v; ed. in Kourousis, "Ὁ λόγιος οἰκουμενικὸς πατριάρχης Ἰωάννης ΙΓ´ ὁ Γλυκύς", 403–05; Nikephoros Gregoras, *History* 8, 2, ed. Schopen, vol. 1, pp. 289, line 23–292, line 11; cf. Nikephoros Gregoras, *History*, trans. van Dieten, vol. 1, p. 48 (no. 22); Beyer, "Eine Chronologie der Lebensgeschichte des Nikephoros Gregoras", 131 (no. 6).

35   Cf. Darrouzès, *Les regestes*, vol. 5, no. 2081 ("Critique"); Kresten, in *Patriarchal Register*, vol. 1, p. 44 n. 29.

36   Nikephoros Gregoras, *History* 8, 8–9, ed. Schopen, vol. 1, pp. 339, line 22–340, line 10; cf. Beyer, "Eine Chronologie der Lebensgeschichte des Nikephoros Gregoras", 131 (no. 10); Kresten, in *Patriarchal Register*, vol. 1, pp. 44–45.

of the Register of the Patriarchate of Constantinople from the 14th century.[37] Among these, of particular importance are the arengas composed (and physically transcribed in the Register) by the scribe and patriarchal notary John Holobolos, who rose up through the ecclesiastical hierarchy to the level of (*megas*) *chartophylax* and later metropolitan (of whom, more later). In these last documents, it is evident that the notary/*dictator* drafted a text not only for the recipient directly involved ("addressed audience") but also for an "unaddressed audience". To study the rhetorical education of the patriarchal notaries, one need only glance at the private collections of John Chortasmenos (ca. 1370–ca. 1436/37).[38]

3 Officials and Intellectuals in the Imperial and Patriarchal Chanceries

As we have just seen, the osmosis between the offices of the two central chanceries and the scholarly circles was continuous: not only were those who held positions in these centres of documentary production themselves protagonists in the intellectual life of the time, but also well-known writers occasionally could lend their services to the preparation of acts. Similarly, alongside the most notable scholar-officials, from time to time "minor" figures linked to documentary production also emerge from oblivion, shedding light on an equally important cultural substratum. In this respect, useful information is furnished by, for example, *typika* (i.e. documents of foundation that contain the rules of community discipline) and cartularies (i.e. collections of documentary copies) relating to "imperial" monasteries. In fact, these are texts that illustrate how the activity of the chancery of the Byzantine ruler could extend beyond the tight organization of that office to include the more or less occasional work of officials not formally employed for practices directly linked to documentary production, although they were members of the court's entourage, such as those who held generic secretarial offices.[39] A significant example is provided by the cartulary of the Thessalian monasteries of Makrinitissa and Nea Petra (AD 1280–82, validated by the emperor in 1285/1286), aristocratic foundations under the patronage of the Malias(s)enos family and under the aegis of the first members of the Palaeologan dynasty. The collection's compiler, holder of the imperial office of "*logothetes* of the herds", skilfully interspersed the

---

37   Cf. Gastgeber, "Rhetorik in der Patriarchatskanzlei von Konstantinopel", pp. 191–97.

38   Cf. Hunger, *Chortasmenos*, pp. 29–31; see chapter 12 in this volume.

39   Cf. e.g. Dölger/Karayannopulos, *Byzantinische Urkundenlehre*, p. 64; Oikonomidès, "La chancellerie impériale", 170.

transcription of documents with a series of paratexts, in prose and in verse, composed for the occasion as introduction to and commentary on the acts, thus creating rhetorical and literary linking devices that also enhance enjoyment of the documentary codex.[40] The same technique of combining brief metric prologues with the transcription of acts appears in other volumes of a documentary character, also compiled in the imperial chancery: for example, in the *typikon* of the well-known male monastery dedicated to the archangel Michael and re-founded by Emperor Michael VIII Palaiologos on Mount Auxentios in the vicinity of Chalcedon, each chapter opens with a dodecasyllabic couplet referring to the content of the precept expounded below.[41]

Nevertheless, both the imperial and the patriarchal chanceries required qualified staff to fix in documentary form the wishes and deliberations of the emperor or of the Orthodox primate and the permanent Synod (σύνοδος ἐνδημοῦσα). We must therefore now examine more closely the structure of these two offices.

3.1   *The Imperial Chancery*

The Byzantine imperial chancery changed over the centuries in terms of its organization and, consequently, of the denomination and tasks of the officials working there. A coherent reconstruction of the diverse roles is at times complicated by the fact that the sources do not always provide us with an entirely homogenous picture. For the Palaeologan age, we can distinguish between functionaries connected to the chancery who assumed a high-level political role there and personnel who primarily looked after the concrete mechanisms of setting up the acts. Naturally, there was continuous interaction between the two levels, so that the leading figures of the first category could (and often did) also hold the highest offices of the second.

Among those closest to the emperor, with whom he shared foreign policy and who assumed the responsibility of preparing acts addressed to foreign powers and institutions, we find the grand *logothetes*,[42] a title that at the end of the 12th century is used to indicate the functions of the *logothetes* of the

---

40   Cf. De Gregorio, "Epigrammi e documenti" pp. 58–06. Ibid., pp. 90–96, it has been proposed to identify the compiler of the *codex diplomaticus* of Makrinitissa and Nea Petra with the *logothetes* of the herds Pepagomenos (PLP 22350) mentioned in Gregory of Cyprus, *Letters*, no. 52, ed. Eustratiades, pp. 36–37.

41   Cf. De Gregorio, "Epigrammi e documenti", pp. 79–84; engl. trans. of the *typikon* by G. Dennis, in Thomas/Constantinides-Hero/Constable (eds.), *Byzantine Monastic Foundation Documents*, vol. 3, pp. 1215–34 (no. 37).

42   Μέγας λογοθέτης.

sekreta[43] and in the 13th century replaces the *logothetes* of the Course.[44] It is not possible to speak *stricto sensu* of the head of the imperial chancery, but rather of an even higher rung – an official who looked after the entire foreign correspondence, a sort of head of the Byzantine "Foreign Office".[45] However, the role of the grand *logothetes* seems to have diminished over the course of the 14th century as that of the *mesazon* rose in importance.

The latter represented the veritable éminence grise in the Byzantine court, with direct influence over the production of acts.[46] In fact, the *mesazon* (which literally means "intermediary")[47] was the trusted man closest to the emperor, who received the petitions of those, individuals or institutions, who intended to appeal to the highest authority in order to obtain privileges or confirmations of previous concessions, to resolve lawsuits or to receive justice or satisfaction in various disputes and so forth – and this through the last sanction that was submitted to a written draft in documentary form. It was not, therefore, a position in the true sense,[48] but rather a title to which an extraordinary power was linked. Precisely because of his proximity to the throne, the *mesazon* collected petitions and interceded with the *basileus*, personally submitting to him the request (or even the document already compiled) with a recommendation in favour of its acceptance by the emperor or interposing his good offices for a positive result. The involvement of this high court dignitary could also translate into the conceptual formulation of the act itself, or at least into control over its writing: his intervention (as well as that of any other official, for example the grand *logothetes* himself, who might have brought about the legal action which was then translated into a document) could be registered in a specific autograph note on the *recto* of the document (the so-called *notitia interventionis* or *intercessionis*).[49] Over the course of the 14th century, the importance of the

---

43   Λογοθέτης τῶν σεκρέτων, coordinator of various departments.

44   Λογοθέτης τοῦ δρόμου. Cf. Guilland, "Les logothètes".

45   Cf. Pseudo-Kodinos, *On the offices*, ed. Verpeaux, p. 174, lines 1–9.

46   The most suggestive portrait of this figure is provided by Beck, "Der byzantinische Ministerpräsident".

47   Μεσάζων τοῖς πράγμασι is the definition, referred to Nikephoros Choumnos, that we find in Nikephoros Gregoras, *History*, 7, 5, ed. Schopen, vol. 1, p. 241, lines 1–2; on the other hand, George Pachymeres, *History*, 6, 26, ed. Failler, vol. 2, p. 627, line 6, speaks of μεσιτεία τῶν κοινῶν, discussing one of the posts held by Theodore Mouzalon, the first, at least to judge from the testimonies dating back to the Palaeologan period, to combine simultaneously, from a certain moment on, the fuctions of grand *logothetes* and those of *mesazon*.

48   Actually, e.g. in Pseudo-Kodinos, *On the offices*, the *mesazon* is only present in connection with the grand *logothetes* (cf. above, n. 45).

49   "Intervenientenvermerk" in German diplomatics: cf. Karayannopulos, "Zu den «διά-Vermerken»". It might be translated in English as "note of intevention" or "intercession".

mesazon increased at the expense of the grand *logothetes*, so that from around the middle of the century there were two *mesazontes*, one of whom might concern himself with foreign affairs (as is the case, for example, with Demetrios Kydones). Thus, they increasingly assumed the functions of official counsellors to the emperor, appearing less associated with the daily work of the chancery.

Regarding this last aspect, it is necessary to draw a distinction. While for the reporting of single issues necessitating imperial intervention – and later the dictation of the relevant document – we have seen the grand *logothetes* and the *mesazon* at work, for all the formal aspects relating both to the physical copying of the acts and to their validation, since the 9th century there had been another figure in Byzantium with whom the direction of the proper chancery work lay: that is, the *epi tou kanikleiou* – literally, the official in charge of the custody and the use of the imperial inkstand (*kanikleion*) containing the red ink reserved to the *basileus*. The role of the *epi tou kanikleiou* is effectively described in a document predating the period discussed here, which attests to his extreme proximity to the emperor, a status which was also retained in subsequent periods.[50] This official was entrusted with the task of *recognitio*, i.e. the insertion, within the text, of the words in red ink (that is, the *kanikloma*), such as the substantives *logos, sigillion, graphe*, which, accompanying the first part of the act's denomination (*chrysoboullos*), officially connoted the documentary typology and fulfilled a corroborative function, that is, confirming the act's validity. In a previous period, the *epi tou kanikleiou* was also in charge of applying the annotation *Legi* or *Legimus* (a statement of careful inspection and imperial approval), which remains in force, still in Latin, in documents of the highest tenor throughout the 12th century. Meanwhile, for cases requiring the actual signature of the sovereign (certainly during the Palaeologan era), the emperor himself would append the autograph formula of validation at the end of the text in the guise of a signature. It cannot be totally excluded that at times the *epi tou kanikleiou* (as well as other authorities or officials temporarily assigned to this task) may have taken the place of the *basileus* not so much in the insertion of the name signature (usually reserved for the highest authority), but rather in cases that required final sanction in the form of a notation of

---

50   Cf. *Documents Lavra*, eds. Lemerle/Guillou/Svoronos/Papachryssanthou, vol. 1, no. 32 (AD 1057), lines 12–17. The best fine-tuning about this official (resumed then in Dölger/ Karayannopulos, *Byzantinische Urkundenlehre*, pp. 29–30, 34–40, 56, 62–67, 118–20) remains that of Dölger, "Der Kodikellos des Christodulos in Palermo", pp. 44–57 (= repr., pp. 50–65); but the list of people who held the office of *epi tou kanikleiou* in the Palaeologan period, which is found ibid., p. 50 (= repr., p. 57), is incomplete and sometimes inaccurate. Moreover, not even the devaluation of this role, theorized in Oikonomidès, "La chancellerie impériale", 181, in the wake of a previous tradition of studies, seems justified.

the month and the indiction, the so-called *menologema* – a type of subscription used for imperial documents such as the *prostagmata* and the *horismoi*.[51] Certainly, the *epi tou kanikleiou* was appointed both to correct the text and to supervise the physical work of the chancery's team of scribes, and in the case of Choumnos at least was also responsible for safeguarding the document from forgery and surreptitious insertions via the addition, on the *verso*, of chancery notes at the junctures (*kolleseis*) between the single folios (*kollemata*), on parchment or paper, making up the documentary scroll.[52] It was perhaps not by chance (precisely in virtue of this key role that the *epi tou kanikleiou* played in the daily activities of the imperial chancery) that the trusted scribe of Nikephoros Choumnos – that same George Boullotes who collected the works of the celebrated official in the manuscript edition shortly before his death (Ambros. C 71 sup.) – carried out, even independently of his mentor's fortunes, the task of primary compiler of imperial documents. Indeed, Boullotes played a much more significant role in their physical writing than the scribe at the service of Theodore Metochites, that is Michael Klostomalles, even though the latter was given the title of imperial *notarios* – and this despite the rivalry with Metochites, who in his irresistible rise, as *mesazon* and grand *logothetes*, progressively marginalized Choumnos within the higher sphere of court officials under Andronikos II.

Precisely with regard to figures working in this eminent bureaucratic realm, who exemplify the activity and the role of chancery officials within the court and, more generally, in Byzantine society (from the intellectual perspective as well), I shall now present an overview of two notable pairs of rivals. The first is George Akropolites[53] and Theodore Mouzalon,[54] between whom the baton of grand *logothetes* metaphorically passed at the end of the reign of Michael VIII. The second is Nikephoros Choumnos[55] and Theodore Metochites,[56] who both served at the highest levels in the imperial chancery (Choumnos as *epi tou kanikleiou* and *mesazon*, a post subsequently ceded to Metochites, the grand *logothetes* responsible for the exaltation of this last office), as well as being the

---

51 Cf. Kresten, "Μηνολόγημα. Anmerkungen zu einem byzantinischen Unterfertigungstyp", pp. 32–42; De Gregorio, "Epigrammi e documenti", p. 93 with n. 409.

52 These annotations are the "Klebevermerke", so-called in German diplomatics: Dölger/ Karayannopulos, *Byzantinische Urkundenlehre*, pp. 35–37; Karayannopulos, "Zu den «διά-Vermerken»", pp. 203–04, 213–17, 230–32.

53 *PLP* 518.

54 *PLP* 19439; on Mouzalon see more recently Samara, Θεόδωρος Μουζάλων.

55 *PLP* 30961.

56 *PLP* 17981.

WORKING IN THE IMPERIAL AND PATRIARCHAL CHANCERIES 413

protagonists of a well-known polemic during the second half of the reign of Andronikos II.

George Akropolites is the author of the *Chronike Syngraphe*, a primary source for the period of the Fourth Crusade and the Empire of Nicaea.[57] During this epoch, he began his education (under Nikephoros Blemmydes, among others) and started to exercise his influence at court under the Laskaridai. Other than as an important historian of the Nicaean era, Akropolites is also known as a teacher of philosophy and mathematics in Constantinople immediately after the city's re-conquest in 1261.[58] Indeed, Gregory of Cyprus – the future patriarch whose name is linked with the anti-unionist reaction – studied under his tutelage. Akropolites, by contrast, was a staunch defender of the deliberations of the *Lugdunense* II (the council in which he participated as ambassador of Michael VIII),[59] as his activity as panegyrist also shows. We find him also among the legates charged with delivering to Rome the Latin letters the Byzantine emperor addressed to Pope Gregory X in the same year, 1274.[60] His total acceptance of the unionist policies of Michael VIII Palaiologos, to whom Akropolites remained a faithful servant throughout his reign, is striking. Akropolites held the post of grand *logothetes* from the time of Theodore II Laskaris (in 1255) until his own death, at an advanced age, in the same year as Michael VIII (1282), and more specifically just after the conclusion of a diplomatic mission to John II Komnenos of Trebizond to arrange a marriage between the latter and the emperor's daughter, Eudokia Palaiologina Komnene.[61] Akropolites' two most prominent characteristics – his great knowledge and his lack of scruples – are noted by the great sketcher of characters and personalities, the historian George Pachymeres, reporting the repression of the Arsenites in 1267:

---

57   Cf. George Akropolites, *History*, trans. Macrides.

58   George Pachymeres, *History*, 4, 14, ed. Failler, vol. 2, p. 369, lines 14–18.

59   Cf. Pieralli, *La corrispondenza diplomatica dell'imperatore bizantino*, p. 259 (no. 17 [Lyon, 1274, July 6]: abjuration of the schism and profession of Roman Faith; a text repeated within the renewed profession of faith of Michael VIII in 1277: ibid., p. 312 [no. 20]). A deep analysis of the Byzantine emperors' correspondence with the West is now provided by Gastgeber, "Changes in Documents of the Byzantine Chancery in contact with the West".

60   For all the texts sent to Rome on this occasion, cf. Pieralli, *La corrispondenza diplomatica dell'imperatore bizantino*, pp. 219–57 (nos. 12–16). On this diplomatic mission, shortly before the beginning of the Council of Lyon, cf. George Pachymeres, *History*, 4, 17 and 21, ed. Failler, vol. 2, pp. 490–95, 506–09.

61   George Pachymeres, *History*, 6, 34, ed. Failler, vol. 2, pp. 653–59 (ibid., p. 655, lines 18–19, the historian refers to Akropolites as "still living" [ἔτι ζῶν]); on the function of Akropolites see also Guilland, "Les logothètes", pp. 104–06 (no. 2, within the wider discussion about the figure of the grand *logothetes*, ibid., pp. 100–15).

414   DE GREGORIO

the questions regarding these [scil. the Arsenites] are entrusted to George
Akropolites, grand *logothetes* and eminent wise man, though unconcerned about matters of the conscience.[62]

We have at least one concrete trace of this unionist intellectual's activity in the
imperial chancery: a document (*chrysoboullon sigillion*) issued by Michael VIII
in 1277 with which the *basileus* sanctioned, among other things, the independence of the Chilandar monastery on Mount Athos from the authority of the
protos.[63] An autograph note (*notitia interventionis*, with the formula introduced by διά) written by the grand *logothetes* George Akropolites is conserved
on the *recto* of this original:[64] in this way Akropolites – that is to say, the person
to whose intercession we owe the issue of the document itself – immortalized
this pious action with his own hand, under the imperial signature (here obviously in the form of a *menologema*).

Similarly significant, even if reversed on the theological and doctrinal level,
is the example furnished by the figure of Theodore Mouzalon. In the letter
(no. 52, ed. Eustratiades) addressed by Gregory of Cyprus to the *logothetes* of
the herds Pepagomenos (the probable compiler of the cartulary of Makrinitissa
and Nea Petra),[65] the future patriarch reminds the addressee to send him the
"wonderful discourse of the very wise *logothetes*".[66] The editor of this epistolary
collection, Sophronios Eustratiades, has interpreted here the author's indication as a clear reference to a work by the grand *logothetes* Theodore Mouzalon,
who played a major role in the correspondence of Gregory of Cyprus.[67] This
hypothesis is confirmed, in the letters that immediately follow (nos. 53–56
Eustratiades), by the flattering stylistic judgements on Mouzalon's oratory
expressed by Gregory himself, who repaid the gift of the *logos* with one of his
own rhetorical compositions.[68] Letter 52 can be linked to a particular turn-

---

62   George Pachymeres, *History*, 4, 28, ed. Failler, vol. 2, p. 409, lines 23–25: Ἀνατίθεται τοί-
      νυν τὰ περὶ τούτων τῷ Ἀκροπολίτῃ Γεωργίῳ καὶ εἰς λογοθέτας μεγάλῳ καὶ σοφῷ τὰ μάλιστα,
      πλὴν κατημελημένως τῶν εἰς συνείδησιν ἔχοντι. The Arsenites were supporters of the former
      Patriarch Arsenios Autoreianos (*PLP* 1694), who opposed Michael VIII Palaiologos' usur-
      pation of the imperial throne at the expense of John IV Laskaris in 1261.
63   *Documents Chilandar*, eds. Živojinović/Kravari/Giros, no. 10 (Dölger/Wirth, *Regesten*,
      vol. 3, no. 2031).
64   Cf. Karayannopulos, "Zu den «διά-Vermerken»", p. 229 (no. 35).
65   Cf. supra, n. 40.
66   Gregory of Cyprus, *Letters*, no. 52, ed. Eustratiades, p. 37, lines 5–6: ὡς εὐφράναι με καλλίστῳ
      λόγῳ τοῦ πάντα σοφοῦ λογοθέτου ὑπέστης.
67   Ibid., pp. ιγ´–ιδ´.
68   See the rich analysis of Laiou, "The Correspondence of Gregorios Kyprios", pp. 92–95,
      98–100, 102–06.

WORKING IN THE IMPERIAL AND PATRIARCHAL CHANCERIES 415

ing point in the history of Byzantium, on the watershed between the reigns of Michael VIII and Andronikos II, that is to say shortly before the nomination of the Cypriot to patriarch of Constantinople (early spring, 1283) and in a moment in which Theodore Mouzalon had already been promoted to grand *logothetes*. And the latter obtained this recognition – after not a few hardships caused by his opposition to the decree of Lyon on the union with Rome – in 1282 in person from Michael VIII, the emperor who, at the death of George Akropolites and a few months before his own unexpected demise, wanted to reward Mouzalon for his submission.

This emblematic affair involving Mouzalon – who, thanks to his rhetorical education, was certainly becoming an expert, even in the *dictamen* of documents – illustrates well the conditions under which the activity of the great officials in charge of supervising the imperial chancery took place. Again Pachymeres' description faithfully reflects the times.[69] A protégé of Michael VIII Palaiologos, who, after having guided his studies and his military career, raised him (in 1277) to the rank of *logothetes* of the public treasury[70] and even found him a wife from the Kantakouzenos family, Mouzalon simultaneously became the intermediary for public affairs.[71] As *logothetes* of the public treasury, we see him at work in 1277 (the same year in which Akropolites records his intervention for the release of a document in favour of Chilandar)[72] on a treaty with Venice, in the related chancery note on the *verso*, at the level of the junctures, intended to safeguard the document's integrity.[73] In the text, the grand *logothetes* George Akropolites and the *logothetes* of the public treasury Theodore Mouzalon are mentioned, among others, as witnesses to the pact. Between the summer of 1280 and the first months of 1281 (due to George Akropolites' hostility) Mouzalon was temporarily distanced from the court: the emperor, persuaded to test Mouzalon's fidelity to the unionist policy, provocatively attempted to include him in a diplomatic mission to Rome and received a refusal without explicit motivation (the emperor then responded in anger and ordered Mouzalon's own brother Leo to beat him until he bled). Theodore thus fell into disgrace and was removed from his offices, especially that of *mesites* (= *mesazon*) which had placed him among the closest to the emperor. Prostrated by the harsh punishment inflicted upon him, he finally

---

69 George Pachymeres, *History*, 6, 26, ed. Failler, vol. 2, pp. 625, line 15–627, line 11.
70 Λογοθέτης τοῦ γενικοῦ; cf. Guilland, "Les logothètes", 11–24 (ibid., p. 22, no. 16).
71 It is the μεσιτεία τῶν κοινῶν, on which cf. supra, n. 47.
72 Cf. supra, nn. 63–64 and context.
73 Dölger/Wirth, *Regesten*, vol. 3, no. 2026; cf. Karayannopulos, "Zu den «διά-Vermerken»", p. 230 (no. 2); new ed. by Pieralli, *La corrispondenza diplomatica dell'imperatore bizantino*, pp. 267–301 (no. 19).

accepted the peace with the Church of Rome and was reinstated to all his functions. Newly appointed to the post of grand *logothetes*, Mouzalon was then the most influential of the counsellors used by Andronikos II Palaiologos, immediately after he was proclaimed emperor in December 1282, for the fulfilment of the most urgent affairs and likely for the first steps towards revoking the union with Rome.[74] On the strength of his friendship with Gregory of Cyprus – in a changed political-religious climate (which is also evident in some of his anti-unionist dogmatic writings), and freed from the hostility of the court – and although he was ill, Mouzalon became the *longa manus* of Andronikos II in the imperial chancery during the first years of his reign, combining for the first time, at least in the Palaeologan era, the functions of *mesazon* and grand *logothetes* and serving until his death in 1294. This is reflected in documentary practice, too, for five further dorsal notes survive, inserted at the *kolleseis* by Mouzalon on five original chrysobulls dating from 1283 to 1292,[75] which bear witness to the characteristic effort of the first Palaiologan emperors to favour the monasteries through the issue of privileges. Thus, here too we find traces of intervention – albeit of a merely technical nature – by the highest chancery official of the day.

But, as I have already noted, the rivalry that was most significant and weighty in terms of its impact on the organization of the imperial chancery itself was that between Nikephoros Choumnos and Theodore Metochites – two figures, both leaders in the intellectual and political life of Byzantium from the end of the 13th century through the first three decades of the 14th century, whose relationship is highlighted in a masterful study published by Ihor Ševčenko by now sixty years ago.[76] This is not the place to discuss the role of these two officials from a literary point of view, even though the breadth of

---

74 George Pachymeres, *History* 7, 1, ed. Failler, vol. 3, p. 19, lines 16–19; from this passage it is possible to deduce that Mouzalon was awarded the high office of grand *logothetes* – at the death of his archrival George Akropolites in 1282 – by the same Michael VIII. Cf. also Guilland, "Les logothètes", pp. 106–08 (no. 3).

75 *Documents Iviron*, eds. Lefort/Oikonomidès/Papachryssanthou/Kravari, vol. 3, no. 62 (AD 1283; Dölger, *Regesten*, vol. 4, no. 2095); *Documents Philotheou*, eds. Regel/Kurtz/Korablev, no. 3 (AD 1287; Dölger, *Regesten*, vol. 4, no. 2121); Dölger, *Regesten*, vol. 4, no. 2131 (AD 1289, Lykousada monastery); *Documents Zographou*, eds. Regel/Kurtz/Korablev, no. 11 (AD 1289; Dölger, *Regesten*, vol. 4, no. 2136); *Documents Patmos*, ed. Vranussi, no. 15 (AD 1292; Dölger, *Regesten*, vol. 4, no. 2149). Cf. Karayannopulos, "Zu den «διά-Vermerken»", pp. 230 (nos. 3–5), 232 (nos. 17–18). In these acts, the title Mouzalon used in the corresponding dorsal note (in most of the cases introduced by διά) is mainly that of μέγας λογοθέτης. For a last note (AD 1293), this time on the *recto* and attested in a *prostagma* which is transmitted in copy, cf. Karayannopulos, "Zu den «διά-Vermerken»", p. 230 (no. 37).

76 Ševčenko, *La vie intellectuelle et politique à Byzance*.

WORKING IN THE IMPERIAL AND PATRIARCHAL CHANCERIES   417

their interests and their production are well known.[77] Here I shall focus on one specific aspect, which also reflects a bending of the court's hierarchical order that impacted the very office entrusted with the charge of writing acts issued by the emperor. Their two careers developed following inverse paths of ascent and descent.[78] Choumnos reached the apex of his influence right at the end of the 13th century: in 1294, he was appointed *mesazon* by Andronikos II (replacing Mouzalon), and in the following year he added the function of head of the chancery (*epi tou kanikleiou*), a post that he held probably until his death (1327), although, as we will soon see, it had by then lost the prestige that Choumnos himself had helped to confer upon it. Metochites began the first stages of his dizzying ascent in the years during which his friend/rival was consolidating his position. Younger than Choumnos by 15 to 20 years, Metochites charged through the various levels of *logothetes* until finally he reached the rank of grand *logothetes* (μέγας λογοθέτης), starting in 1321. It was in this last year that he finally surpassed Choumnos, whose star had begun to wane a few years before, when in 1315/1316 Metochites was appointed *mesazon* in his place. In 1321, then, Metochites combined the two most important roles in political leadership directly connected to the documentary production, as had been the case a few years earlier with Mouzalon. Their fates thus played out within the chancery: Choumnos technically remained the head of the office, but lost his political and diplomatic prestige as principal counsellor to the *basileus*.

One source of primary importance – the treatise *De officiis* by Pseudo-Kodinos – describes with embarrassment the impossibility of placing the office of *epi tou kanikleiou* within the ranks of the court's hierarchy, as reflected by the position the officials occupied during public visits at the Palace, specifically because of the awkward case of Choumnos:

> *Epi tou kanikleiou* was the emperor's co-father-in-law, Choumnos, and he never attended the ceremony of the reception nor was he present at that of the kiss; therefore, his position was unknown.[79]

---

77   On Choumnos' oeuvre and the range of its transmission, see Papatriantaphyllou-Theodoridi, *Ἡ χειρόγραφη παράδοση τῶν ἔργων τοῦ Νικηφόρου Χούμνου*; on Metochites, see Ševčenko's still fundamental study "Theodore Metochites, the Chora, and the Intellectual Trends of His Time".

78   Essential bibliography on the stages of their two careers: for Choumnos, Verpeaux, *Nicéphore Choumnos, homme d'état et humaniste*; for Metochites, id., "Le *cursus honorum* de Théodore Métochite", as well as Guilland, "Les logothètes", 18, 22, 74, 100, 110–13.

79   Pseudo-Kodinos, *On the offices*, ed. Verpeaux, p. 140, lines 1–7: Ἐπὶ τοῦ κανικλείου ἦν ὁ συμπένθερος τοῦ βασιλέως ὁ Χοῦμνος καὶ οὔτε εἰς παράστασιν ἐστάθη ποτέ, οὔτε εἰς ἀσπασμὸν παρεγένετο· διὸ καὶ ἦν ὁ τόπος αὐτοῦ ἀνεπίγνωστος. It should be recalled that Choumnos' daughter, Irene, married the despot John Palaiologos, son of Andronikos II (however,

418 DE GREGORIO

After having replaced Mouzalon, during the first part of the reign of Andronikos II, and serving as a state official at the highest rank, Choumnos no longer took part in court ceremonies after 1321 (the year in which Metochites was appointed grand *logothetes*), remaining out of sight as a bureaucrat in the chancery. In that year, we observe a reversal of hierarchical order, with the grand *logothetes* moving from twelfth to ninth position[80] while the *epi tou kanikleiou* dropped to thirteenth.[81] Certainly, Choumnos did not want to be subjected to the humiliation of publicly confronting his rival,[82] even though the situation reflected in the *De officiis* should be applied to this clamorous but circumscribed case: the lack of ranking for the *epi tou kanikleiou* does not imply a vacancy in this office until 1354 (with Manuel Angelos), for we can now point to John Gabras Meliteniotes as Choumnos' probable immediate successor.[83]

The traumatic turnover between Choumnos and Metochites is described – in a cryptic manner (as is often the case in Byzantine sources) and with apparent nonchalance – in some verses of the anepigraphic list of *officia* published by Jean Verpeaux in an appendix:

> We have met the illustrious Choumnos *epi tou kanikleiou*, who occupied a more important position than previously [i.e. with respect to others who held the same office], and after him [i.e. in a temporal sense] the dear Metochites, grand *logothetes*, to whom fate granted wisdom, wearing a

---

Metochites also married into the reigning dynasty, as his daughter, also named Irene, wed John *panhypersebastos*, the emperor's nephew). The first of the two ceremonies mentioned was when the emperor received all of the dignitaries and the *archontes* in a general audience (ibid., pp. 190–94). The second regards the circumstance by which courtiers kissed the emperor's right foot, left hand and right cheek (ibid., pp. 234–35). A re-edition of Pseudo-Kodinos, *On the offices*, with English translation and commentary has been more recently provided by Macrides/Munitiz/Angelov.

80 Pseudo-Kodinos, *On the offices*, ed. Verpeaux, pp. 136, 137, line 8.

81 Ibid., pp. 300, lines 9–10; 320, lines 29–30.

82 Cf. Ševčenko, *La vie intellectuelle et politique à Byzance*, pp. 157–61; Pseudo-Kodinos, *On the offices*, ed. Verpeaux, pp. 28–29.

83 The current interpretation derives from the analysis exhibited in Pseudo-Kodinos, *On the offices*, ed. Verpeaux, pp. 27–30 (introduction): cf. e.g. Oikonomidès, "La chancellerie impériale", 181 n. 71. On Manuel Angelos (*epi tou kanikleiou* from 1354 to 1370, to be identified with Agathangelos, an anti-Palamite companion of Nikephoros Gregoras) cf. PLP 91040; for John Gabras Meliteniotes (who is also documented in the first half of the 14th century and is mentioned as *mesazon* in 1341) cf. PLP 17853–17854 (to be identified probably also with PLP 17847).

WORKING IN THE IMPERIAL AND PATRIARCHAL CHANCERIES

gilded red headdress, which the emperor, the illustrious Andronikos, conferred as a gift upon him, for his support in governing.[84]

Here dwells the essence of this replacement: the anonymous source recalls with pride having experienced the times in which Choumnos was *epi tou kanikleiou*, a function which he raised to the highest level, and having lived through Metochites' ascent. The latter was rewarded for his action at the side of the *basileus* with the insignia (here most especially the hat) that we see reproduced, for example, in the celebrated mosaic of the Chora monastery, which the grand *logothetes* himself had re-founded. But it is especially in the production of acts that these two figures – on the one hand Choumnos, above all in his older role as head of the chancery office, on the other hand Metochites, as the closest and most faithful servant and supporter of the *basileus*, in terms of both internal and external policy – influenced the concrete work of the imperial bureaucracy.

With regard to the material preparation of documents, within the chancery's personnel we can distinguish the copyists in charge of transcribing texts from the notaries public in the emperor's service.[85]

The first, the simple scribes of the imperial chancery, were recruited – at least in the late Byzantine period – based on their professional skills and often following contingent criteria (more or less illustrious acquaintances and relatives, collaboration with officials of a higher level at the forefront within the Palace at a specific moment, and so forth), without any real selection through formal training. Although the notion of a script learned and used exclusively within the imperial chancery as a "reserved" element of validation was long lost, we can argue that in the age of Michael VIII Palaiologos and the first years of the reign of his son, Andronikos II, the privileges surviving in original form display a script based on the *Fettaugen* ("fat-blob") style, of a high formal level and a more balanced and solemn structure compared to common examples, as well as a disciplined and airy layout.[86]

Right at the height of Choumnos' success at court, the scribe George Boullotes emerged in the imperial chancery. It is to Boullotes that we owe the first decisive step towards a "graphic reform", which unfolded simultaneously

---

84   Pseudo-Kodinos, *On the offices*, ed. Verpeaux, p. 338, lines 127–135: Ἔγνωμεν λαμπρὸν τὸν Χοῦμνον κανικλείου / στάσιν ἔχοντα μείζονα τῆς προτέρας, / καὶ δὴ μετ' αὐτὸν τὸν καλὸν Μετοχίτην / λογοθετῶν μέγιστον, σοφίας λῆξιν, / φοροῦντα χρυσῆν ἐρυθρὰν τὴν καλύπτραν, / ἣν δῶρον αὐτῷ συνανέχοντι κράτος / ἄναξ ὁ λαμπρὸς παρέσχεν Ἀνδρόνικος.

85   On the chancery's personnel, cf. Oikonomidès, "La chancellerie impériale", 170–73.

86   Cf. Pieralli, "Le scritture dei documenti imperiali del XIII secolo"; De Gregorio, "La scrittura greca di età paleologa", pp. 83–86.

420 DE GREGORIO

(though case by case in different ways) in the scribal habits of the Byzantine world.[87] We can characterize his handwriting as one of the most distinctive and successful examples of that tendency to control and modulate – in a masterfully balanced and calligraphic manner – the baroque elements of the *Fettaugenmode*, still recognizable as an allusion to a vogue that was not yet entirely passé. Boullotes must have had a brilliant career as scribe of documents in the imperial chancery, becoming its "spearhead" and remaining in service for more than thirty years, from 1298 to 1329, to judge from the surviving documentation. Erich Lamberz has reconstructed a picture of Boullotes' activity in that office thanks to a series of new attributions: overall, Boullotes copied 33 "grand privileges", to which we can also add some imperial documents of a lower tenor – that is, at least six *prostagmata* from the period between 1299 and 1321. Much less consistent, on the contrary, is his activity in copying books: up to now, only three manuscripts in his hand have been identified.[88]

Among the chrysobulls copied by Boullotes, two contain the characteristic chancery note at the junctures on the *verso*, introduced by the preposition διά and appended by Choumnos (διὰ τοῦ ἐπὶ τοῦ κανικλείου Νικηφόρου τοῦ Χούμνου). Chronologically the first surviving documents in Boullotes' hand, they are a chrysobull issued by Andronikos II in 1298 for the Great Lavra of Mount Athos and an analogous act addressed to the Serbian monastery of Chilandar, also on the Holy Mountain, by the same emperor in 1313. Both contain prefaces composed by the same *epi tou kanikleiou*, a tangible sign of an also otherwise fruitful closeness.[89] There are also four documents by Boullotes, still in the form of privileges, that carry the *notitia interventionis* on the *recto* inserted by Metochites (διὰ τοῦ μεγάλου λογοθέτου Θεοδώρου τοῦ Μετοχίτου).[90]

---

87 Cf. Lamberz, "Georgios Bullotes", as well as more recently De Gregorio, "Filone Alessandrino tra Massimo Planude e Giorgio Bullotes", pp. 206–11.

88 Wolfenbüttel, Herzog August Bibliothek, MS Guelf. 42 Gud. graec. (AD 1314/1315), Milan, Biblioteca Ambrosiana, MS Ambros. C 71 sup. (gr. 185, from the years 1320–1327), to which I have added more recently Florence, Biblioteca Medicea Laurenziana, MS Laur. Plut. 10.23 (not dated). Cf. bibliography in the previous footnote (for the *Ambrosianus supra*, n. 18).

89 Cf. supra, nn. 19–20 and context; Karayannopulos, "Zu den «διά-Vermerken»", p. 230 (nos. 6–7); Lamberz, "Georgios Bullotes", pp. 36–37, pls. 3, 8.

90 *Documents Vatopedi*, eds. Lefort/Kravari/Giros/Smyrlis, vol. 2, no. 62 (1324, June; Dölger, *Regesten*, vol. 4, no. 2512); *Documents Chilandar*, eds. Petit/Korablev, no. 100 (1324, December; Dölger, *Regesten*, vol. 4, no. 2519); ibid., no. 101 (1324, December; Dölger, *Regesten*, vol. 4, no. 2520); *Documents Zographou*, eds. Regel/Kurtz/Korablev, no. 23 (1325, September; Dölger, *Regesten*, vol. 4, no. 2538). Cf. Karayannopulos, "Zu den «διά-Vermerken»", pp. 226–27 (nos. 1–2, 4); Lamberz, "Georgios Bullotes", pp. 37–38; De Gregorio, "Epigrammi e documenti", pp. 110–11 with n. 500.

Contrary to the conventions of the Latin medieval world, no Byzantine chancery scribe normally mentioned his own name explicitly in his documentary transcriptions (but see the cases of Klostomalles and Babiskomites mentioned immediately afterwards). The anonymity is obviously a reflection of the Byzantine mentality, which erased any manifestation of individuality before the supreme authority and the act that pertains to it as a unique prerogative. In his only surviving subscription, inserted, moreover, in a manuscript with literary content, Boullotes simply declares his ecclesiastical title of deacon,[91] without any reference to his activity in the office of the emperor. It is therefore evident that although Boullotes was one of the most expert "technical operators" within the imperial chancery, his position must not have had an entirely organic status among the office's personnel. More generally, the scribe, i.e. the person in charge of the material effort of putting the act in written form, did not seem to fulfil an official role in the hierarchy, although he possessed a specific graphic education that was appreciated as an essential element in the preparation and validation of the document. His task was rather that of a mere physical executor, called upon (and obviously compensated) for his acknowledged technical skills – in short, a manual labourer who remained anchored to the more general status of scribe in Byzantium. In a fairly literate society, as the Byzantine world was, the acquisition of a technical skill, such as that of an amanuensis, and the capacity to manage at a certain level copying literary texts and/or documents, allowed such persons to practice a recognized profession, even if it was considered to be of a purely technical nature.

Different is the case of Michael Klostomalles, identified for several years now with the "scribe of Theodore Metochites", to whom we owe, for example, the *mundum* – the fair copy – with the Discourses of the great statesman in a codex that also conserves the stratification in the various phases of its own creation and writing.[92] We know his name thanks to an explicit reference in a foreign letter missive, a deed of covenant in Greek and in Latin from the year 1324, addressed by Emperor Andronikos II Palaiologos to the Republic of Venice:

---

91   MS Guelf. 42 Gud. graec.: cf. Harlfinger/Sicherl et al., *Griechische Handschriften und Aldinen*, pp. 40–42 (no. 11); Papatriantaphyllou-Theodoridi, *Ἡ χειρόγραφη παράδοση τῶν ἔργων τοῦ Νικηφόρου Χούμνου*, pp. 137–38; Lamberz, "Georgios Bullotes", pp. 35–44, pl. 7.

92   MS Vindob. Phil. gr. 95 (Theodore Metochites, *Orations*, eds. Polemis/Kaltsogianni). For the identification with Klostomalles cf. Lamberz, "Das Geschenk des Kaisers Manuel II. an das Kloster Saint-Denis". For an overview on this scribe of books and documents, who represents an important chapter in the history of studies, cf. especially Prato, "I manoscritti greci dei secoli XIII e XIV: note paleografiche", pp. 140–48; Lamberz, "Georgios Bullotes", pp. 44–48, pl. 15; id., "Johannes Kantakuzenos und die Produktion von Luxushandschriften", pp. 140–45, 149, 151–53, 155–56; Hutter, "Schreiber und Maler der Palaiologenzeit in Konstantinopel", pp. 172–76; Bianconi, "Il Laur. Plut. 28.26 ovvero la storia di Bisanzio nella storia di un codice", pp. 39–40, 46–52.

"... written in Romaic [i.e. Greek] letters by the hand of the notary of my majesty, Michael Klostomalles".[93] Such an indication occurs here exceptionally, for the scribe of the Greek section intended to comply with the Latin text, where customarily the name of the notary appears. It has been rightly highlighted that Klostomalles was primarily active as a scribe of manuscripts rather than documents.[94] Certainly, the eight documents in his hand that have been identified up to now, which cover the period from 1311 to 1342, demonstrate that he was employed as simple scribe in the imperial chancery only sporadically, and extending into the reign of John v Palaiologos (therefore rather beyond the apogee of the Andronikos II/Metochites duo). Klostomalles' activity in the realm of book production, however, was much more consistent: the hitherto known codices in his hand (around 20) display the art of an "all-round calligrapher and decorator"[95] and leading figures of the aristocratic elite availed themselves of his work, among them – apart from his mentor Metochites – the future Emperor John VI Kantakouzenos (when he still held the post of *megas domestikos*), as well as, in all probability, members of the Palaiologos family.

Nevertheless, it is possible to add a few considerations that are helpful in terms of understanding certain mechanisms in the production of acts. Undoubtedly at the beginning, between the first and second decades of the 14th century, Klostomalles, who was younger than and perhaps a pupil of Boullotes, participated in the intellectual climate that gave rise to the new graphic trend (attested as much in the realm of books as in documentary production) that associates him with Boullotes as well as with further chancery scribes and also with other figures – mostly unknown up till now and often circulating within the court milieu – who were active only in manuscripts.[96] Moreover, Klostomalles, trained in this ambience, developed the new writing style to the highest perfection, freeing himself definitively from the imbalance

---

93   Venice, Archivio di Stato, Miscell. Atti Diplomat. e Priv., busta 12, doc. no. 432 ('Ορκωμοτικὸν χρυσόβουλλον, 1324, October; Dölger, *Regesten*, vol. 4, no. 2515 [on this documentary type cf. Dölger/Karayannopulos, *Byzantinische Urkundenlehre*, pp. 99–100]): ... γραφὲν Ῥωμαϊκοῖς γράμμασι διὰ χειρὸς τοῦ νοταρίου τῆς βασιλείας μου Μιχαὴλ τοῦ Κλωστομάλλου ... [the first-person pronoun is obviously a reference to the author of the act, that is to say the *basileus*]. See the analogue case (with identical wording) of Nicholas Babiskomites, also in a treaty with Venice of November 1332 (Dölger, *Regesten*, vol. 4, no. 2787): cf. Kresten, "Zur Datierung, zum Schreiber und zum politischen Hintergrund dreier Urkunden des Kaisers Andronikos III. Palaiologos", 87.

94   Lamberz, "Georgios Bullotes", p. 46; id., "Beobachtungen zu den patristischen Corpora".

95   Hutter, "Schreiber und Maler der Palaiologenzeit in Konstantinopel", p. 176.

96   Lamberz, "Georgios Bullotes", p. 47. On the imperial chancery, also see the problem of scribal attribution (helpful in defining the boundaries of a veritable style) which is examined in Müller, "Weder Klostomalles noch Babiskomites".

WORKING IN THE IMPERIAL AND PATRIARCHAL CHANCERIES   423

of the *Fettaugen* fashion and creating a truly admirable formal equilibrium in the tissue of his flowing script and in page construction. But, despite his success in the preparation of books of the highest craftsmanship, it is in the imperial chancery that he must have built up his fame as a calligrapher, so that he carved himself a privileged space among Byzantium's elite patrons of the arts. In fact, it is not contradictory for an imperial notary to have left many fewer acts in his hand compared to a colleague who did not boast such a title (for example Boullotes). It is plausible that, just after starting as a simple scribe of the imperial chancery – the first three surviving documents are encompassed within a time span of a little less than three years (September 1311–February 1314)[97] – Klostomalles moved on, probably as a result of Metochites' rise through the ranks of the bureaucracy all the way to the top (grand *logothetes*, 1321), to occupy the post of imperial notary. This figure (under the control of a *protonotarios*) assumed the role of notary public during the Palaeologan era, and was no longer a simple scribe. Besides holding the imperial *potestas* ("notary by imperial authority")[98] that rendered the signed acts valid for the whole empire, in the realm of foreign policy (and, therefore, in close connection with the grand *logothetes* himself) the *basilikos notarios* was employed in sending letters missive from the *basileus* and on missions outside the borders of the empire, as well as drafting treaties with foreign powers. Naturally, there were other *notarii* who were concerned with preparing the Latin text in these foreign letters missive, as the career of the Genoese Ogerio Boccanegra, *protonotarius imperatoris Graecorum* in the service of Michael VIII Palaiologos,

---

97   *Documents Panteleemon*, eds. Lemerle/Dagron/Ćircović, no. 10 (1311, September; Dölger, *Regesten*, vol. 4, no. 2333); *Documents Protaton*, ed. D. Papachryssanthou, no. 12 (1312, November; Dölger, *Regesten*, vol. 4, no. 2342); *Documents Lavra*, eds. Lemerle/Guillou/Svoronos/Papachryssanthou, vol. 2, no. 103 (1314, February; Dölger, *Regesten*, vol. 4, no. 2353); from this same period, we have only one document copied by Boullotes (1313, October: cf. supra, n. 19), who, however, whether before or whether mostly thereafter must have nevertheless earned the role of the office's principle scribe. There are also three originals attributed to Klostomalles for the years 1317–1321: *Documents Chilandar*, eds. Živojinović/Kravari/Giros, nos. 34 (1317, July; Dölger, *Regesten*, vol. 4, no. 2390) and 35 (1317, July; Dölger, *Regesten*, vol. 4, no. 2649); *Documents Koutloumousiou*, ed. Lemerle, no. 10 (1321, September; Dölger, *Regesten*, vol. 4, no. 2469); for this same epoch, in contrast, we have at least 14 acts transcribed by Boullotes. That Klostomalles' activity in copying imperial chrysobulls drastically thinned out later is demonstrated by the fact that the last two surviving documents in his hand were transcribed at a considerable interval from each other, i.e. the Ὀρκωμοτικὸν χρυσόβουλλον of 1324 (supra, n. 93) and the chrysobull for the Lavra on Mount Athos of 1342 (*Documents Lavra*, eds. Lemerle/Guillou/Svoronos/Papachryssanthou, vol. 3, no. 123; Dölger, *Regesten*, vol. 4, no. 2885). Meanwhile, between 1323 and 1329, Boullotes copied 10 documents still extant today.

98   Βασιλικὴ ἐξουσία: cf. Oikonomidès, "La chancellerie impériale", 172–73 (with n. 30).

424 DE GREGORIO

illustrates.[99] It is therefore not by chance that Klostomalles was responsible for the material preparation – for example, among the extant documents – of precisely the aforementioned deed of covenant with the Republic of Venice in 1324: his participation in scribal activity must no longer have been part of his duties except in relatively infrequent circumstances connected to the higher function he was entrusted with.

3.2   The Patriarchal Chancery

The organization of the patriarchal chancery's personnel is described in detail in Jean Darrouzès' foundational work on the *officia* of the Byzantine Church.[100] The leading role for this department (*sekreton*) was assigned to the *chartophylax*, usually a deacon.[101] Through his insignia, the *chartophylax* conferred authenticity upon the acts of the patriarch, participated in the work of the Synod as secretary of the primate, oversaw the material aspects of transcribing, signing, and sealing patriarchal documents, and held judiciary power in the investigation of disciplinary and canonical procedures. In the *notitiae* listing the *officia* of the Great Church, the *chartophylax* normally occupies the fourth position, after the *megas oikonomos*, the *sakellarios*, and the *skeuophylax* and before the *sakelliou* – thus in the first pentad, namely the band of excellence of the *exokatakoiloi*, to whom a sixth was added at the end of the 12th century (the *protekdikos*). One of these *notitiae* specifies that the tasks of the *chartophylax* were focused on playing the role of intermediary (*mesazon*) and writing reports,[102] while elsewhere it is pointed out that "the (*megas*) *chartophylax* is not, as some say, a custodian and janitor of the *sekreton* ... but rather the curator of the episcopal rights, namely as legal representative of the patriarch in affairs pertaining to the latter".[103]

---

99   Cf. Pieralli, *La corrispondenza diplomatica dell'imperatore bizantino*, pp. 88–95; see now Gastgeber, "Changes in Documents of the Byzantine Chancery in contact with the West", pp. 195–200, 213, 231–32, 234, 238, 248–49, 253–55; ibid., pp. 205–06, 232, 234–35, 260–62 we have also some considerations on George Kaballaropoulos (ἑρμηνεύς) and Stephen Syropoulos (*interpres*), one as scribe of the Latin text and the other as imperial envoy preparing the deed of covenant with the Republic of Venice (1324) mentioned above (see n. 93 and context).

100   Darrouzès, *Recherches sur les ὀφφίκια*, pp. 333–87. On the patriarchal documents themselves I newly had the opportunity to see very quickly the most recent contribution by Gastgeber, "Diplomatics of the Patriarchate of Constantinople".

101   Darrouzès, *Recherches sur les ὀφφίκια*, pp. 334–53: 338–44.

102   Ibid., pp. 345, 546 (*notitia* F): 4. Ὁ χαρτοφύλαξ, εἰς τὸ μεσάζειν καὶ εἰς τὰς σημειώσεις.

103   Ibid., p. 565: Ὁ δὲ μέγας χαρτοφύλαξ οὐκ ἔστιν, ὥς τινές φασι, φύλαξ τοῦ σεκρέτου καὶ θυρωρός [...], ἀλλ' ἔστιν ἐπισκοπικῶν δικαίων φροντιστὴς καὶ οἱονεὶ δικαίῳ τῶν ἀνηκότων τῷ πατριάρχῃ.

WORKING IN THE IMPERIAL AND PATRIARCHAL CHANCERIES   425

Then there are officials who were subordinate to the *chartophylax*, or who supported him, such as the *protonotarios* (the coordinator of the notaries) – the seventh official in the hierarchy to whom the patriarch was able to directly entrust the writing of acts and other tasks, while the *primicerius* was in practice only a specialized notary.[104] And from there trickle down all the other *archontes*: *logothetes, hypomnematographos* (for the drafting of solemn acts and for the composition of the final records of synodal sessions), *hieromnemon, epi ton deeseon* and so on.[105] Here, among the simple employees, I will focus briefly on the *notarioi*, the primary labour force in any chancery, and on their prerogatives, which are generally distinct from the classic traits of the tabellion.[106] Normally numbering twelve, the notaries waited in the vicinity of the patriarchal throne during synodal assemblies and concisely registered their content. It was then their task to write the corresponding act for issue as well as to supply additional paperwork. Here too the difference between simple chancery scribe and patriarchal notary is not always clear. As professional writers, the first could be called upon (at times in occasional forms) even autonomously from the second (as we shall soon see in the case of George Galesiotes, who was for a long period the head scribe in the patriarchal chancery but was never officially designated in the sources as *notarios*), although it is likely that the *dictator* of the text and the one who materially wrote it were very often one and the same. As simple executors, notaries almost always remained anonymous, as we have already seen with the corresponding imperial office. Exceptional skills in the *dictamen* and "rhetorization" of the documents issued by the patriarchal chancery very often served to foster appreciation and favour among the "audience" and the addressees of the acts,[107] in so far as the activity of copying within the office helped scribes to procure profitable, high-rank book commissions from outside.

From this chancery office we can also identify numerous figures who stand out in the fervid intellectual climate of this era through their participation, in various ways, in the theological disputes that cut through the almost two hundred years of the Palaeologan dynasty's reign from beginning to end. Here we will examine in particular the struggles connected to union with the Church of Rome, sanctioned by Michael VIII in Lyon in 1274 and revoked by his son

---

Cf. also Schminck, "Wörtliche Zitate des weltlichen und kirchlichen Rechts", p. 240. On the introduction of the adjective *megas* to the title of *chartophylax* (also added in the Palaeologan era to nearly all the posts in the first pentad) cf. infra, n. 140 and context.

104 Darrouzès, *Recherches sur les ὀφφίκια*, pp. 353–59.

105 Ibid., pp. 359–79.

106 Ibid., pp. 379–87.

107 Cf. Gastgeber, "Rhetorik in der Patriarchatskanzlei von Konstantinopel", pp. 189–97; an accurate analysis is now provided by id., "Das Formular der Patriarchatskanzlei".

426 DE GREGORIO

Andronikos II in 1282, as well as the Palamite controversy that swept through the Byzantine world for a large part of the 14th century.

Regarding the relationship with the Latins, let us compare and contrast two exceptional documents, which carry the signatures of many officials of the Great Church, including the representatives of the patriarchal chancery. The first is the "guarantee document" of 1277, with which the patriarchal *archontes* (numbering 40) officially recognized the deliberations of Lyon, under the pressure of Michael VIII and the guidance of Patriarch John XI Bekkos.[108] Among the first signatories we find Constantine Meliteniotes,[109] the archdeacon of the Palace clergy[110] who precisely during this crucial period – from the deposition of the anti-unionist Patriarch Joseph I Galesiotes through the rise and fall of Bekkos (1275–1282) – also filled the top post in the patriarchal chancery (that of *chartophylax*), succeding Bekkos himself: Meliteniotes thus provided the concrete impetus to the writing of this act, to which the leading exponents of the Constantinopolitan clergy were committed, in support of imperial policy.[111] Moreover, within his chancery Bekkos had also appointed one of his relatives – George Bekkos, correspondent first of Maximos Planoudes and later of Nikephoros Gregoras – to the strategic post of *primicerius* of the notaries. The young George appears in the tenth position of the patriarchal *archontes* on the list of 1277 (in the absence of the *protonotarios*).[112]

The guarantee document of 1277 bears the signature of other figures who were also protagonists in this phase. For example, appearing immediately after Meliteniotes is the well-known historian Theodore Skoutariotes (with the dual role of *dikaiophylax*, a judicial officer nominated by the emperor for ecclesiastical matters,[113] and *sakelliou*, with jurisdiction over places of wor-

---

108 Ἔγγραφος ἀσφάλεια τῶν κληρικῶν τῆς Μεγάλης Ἐκκλησίας ἐπὶ τῇ εἰρήνῃ δῆθεν τῶν ἐκκλησιῶν. Cf. *Dossier Lyon*, eds. Laurent/Darrouzès, pp. 468–73 (no. 17); Darrouzès, *Recherches sur les ὀφφίκια*, pp. 112, 532.

109 *PLP* 17856.

110 Ἀρχιδιάκονος τοῦ βασιλικοῦ κλήρου.

111 It should be pointed out that Meliteniotes, still as archdeacon of the Palace clergy, and Bekkos himself, who at that time was the *chartophylax* of the Great Church, were present, during a diplomatic mission, at the death of Louis IX, King of France, in Tunis (1270): George Pachymeres, *History* 5, 9, ed. Failler, vol. 2, pp. 463–67. Meliteniotes was therefore the immediate successor of Bekkos as head of the patriarchal chancery, when the latter became primate of Orthodoxy.

112 *PLP* 2547, probably identical with 2546 (George Bekkos must have risen through the patriarchal hierarchy to the rank of *megas oikonomos*); on this matter, cf. Darrouzès, *Recherches sur les ὀφφίκια*, pp. 115–16, 356, 532.

113 Darrouzès, *Recherches sur les ὀφφίκια*, pp. 109–10.

ship and their ministers),[114] who in this same year was also appointed metropolitan of Kyzikos.[115] Skoutariotes must have been followed as signatory by George Metochites, father of Theodore Metochites as well as polemicist and writer of a history of the dogmatic controversies ignited after 1274, who was also an archdeacon of the Palace clergy and official "assigned to supplications" in the patriarchal chancery.[116] Indeed, a George is listed as *epi ton deeseon* in the 16th place of the presences, an entry which, considering his biographical dates, can refer only to the well-known author of the *Historia dogmatica*. Again in 1277, a highly eventful year in the negotiations with the Latins, all three officials (Skoutariotes, already in the post of metropolitan of Kyzikos, Meliteniotes and George Metochites, one as *chartophylax* and the other as *epi ton deeseon*) participated in the diplomatic mission Michael VIII sent to Pope John XXI to strengthen the agreement with Rome.[117] In addition to the imperial foreign letters missive, on this occasion the embassy also presented a document weighty in its consequences – the letter addressed by the Patriarch John XI Bekkos to Pope John XXI himself, which, in adherence with the sanctions of 1274 in Lyon, issued a profession of Roman Faith (including the *Filioque*) and affirmed the primacy of the Church of Rome and the complete doctrinal identity between the two Churches, with a renunciation of the schism.[118] This exceptional document, whose Greek text is conserved in original at the Vatican Apostolic

---

114   Ibid., pp. 318–22.

115   *PLP* 26204; Theodore Skoutariotes, *Chronicle*, ed. Tocci; on manuscripts which belonged to him and most likely were also written in the patriarchal milieu, cf. e.g. D'Aiuto, "Note ai manoscritti del Menologio Imperiale", pp. 215–22 ("Appendice I. Per la biblioteca di Teodoro Scutariota"); Zorzi, "Lettori bizantini della «Bibliotheca» di Fozio", pp. 836–44; Bianconi, "Sui copisti del Platone Laur. Plut. 59.1 e su altri scribi d'età paleologa", pp. 265–71.

116   *PLP* 17979; see now Samorì, "A Self-Portrait of an Unyielding Unionist"; ead., "I codici autografi del diacono Giorgio Metochites". On the figure of the ἐπὶ τῶν δεήσεων – the intermediary who, like the corresponding offical in the Palace for the emperor, presented the patriarch with the supplications and oversaw their writing in the chancery office – cf. Darrouzès, *Recherches sur les ὀφφίκια*, pp. 378–79; Skoutariotes also held this post before George Metochites.

117   Cf. Pieralli, *La corrispondenza diplomatica dell'imperatore bizantino*, pp. 349–57 (no. 22: the emperor entrusted his legates, mentioned by name, with the documents requested by Rome [in Latin only]); the dossier displayed on that occasion by the Byzantine embassy also provided for the renewed professions of faith by Michael VIII (in Latin) and by his son Andronikos II (in Greek and Latin) as imperial documents to be delivered to Rome: ibid., pp. 303–48 (nos. 20–21).

118   Cf. ibid., pp. 415–31 (App. No. 3), pl. 16 (1277, April; Laurent, *Les regestes*, vol. 4, no. 1433); a brief palaeographic discussion of the text's script can be found in De Gregorio, "La scrittura greca di età paleologa", pp. 86–87, pl. 6.

428 DE GREGORIO

Archives, also bears the dorsal chancery note inserted by Meliteniotes at the juncture between the two segments of parchment.[119]

Skoutariotes, Meliteniotes and George Metochites were among Bekkos' closest collaborators, with whom they shared the tenet of the reunion with the Roman Church both during the years of Michael VIII and after his successor Andronikos II had repudiated the Lyon decree.[120] Although he lost the metropolitan see, Skoutariotes was somehow spared from the anti-unionist reaction following Bekkos' sudden deposition, whereas a different fate befell the two chancery officials. Immediately after the condemnation enacted at the second Council of Blachernae in 1285, both George Metochites (along with his son Theodore, who was still quite young) and the (former) *chartophylax* Meliteniotes were imprisoned in the fortress of St. Gregory in the Gulf of Nicomedia, along with Bekkos himself, due to the annoyance caused by the steadfastness and obstinacy they demonstrated during the theological dispute. They were transferred back to Constantinople in 1290 and interned in the Great Palace.[121]

Aside from bearing witness to the involvement of Byzantine intellectuals with chancery work, these documents – and in particular the guarantee document of 1277 – also reflect their inner turmoil in the face of the regime's directives. The acceptance of such diktats, obviously a good rule for survival in the Byzantine world, reveals a not irrelevant intimidation and conditioning during the age of such a strong figure as Michael VIII Palaiologos, who demanded an explicit declaration of adherence to his unionist policies, even though opposition remained tenacious within the Church.[122] A case that exemplifies this dichotomy is that of the historian George Pachymeres. As a teacher in the patriarchal school[123] he signed the guarantee document of 1277, while as

---

119   Vatican City, Archivio Apostolico Vaticano, A. A. Arm. I–XVIII, doc. no. 1740; on the *verso* διὰ τοῦ χαρτοφύλακος Κωνσταντίνου [scil. τοῦ Μελιτηνιώτου]. The name signature of the patriarch was inserted by Bekkos in the form of a monocondyle (i.e. executed in a single motion, without lifting the writing instrument from the support surface), an absolutely uncommon method in patriarchal documents. I shall return to this point shortly.

120   In the works of the two major scholars – i.e. Skoutariotes and George Metochites – there are numerous pro-unionist references. Moreover, before 1282 Meliteniotes wrote two discourses on the Procession of the Holy Spirit and, after Andronikos II's anti-unionist turn, a polemical treatise against the Patriarch Gregory of Cyprus.

121   Cf. George Pachymeres, *History*, 7, 35; 9, 29; ed. Failler, vol. 3, pp. 117, line 20–119, line 2; 299, lines 1–5. On the location of the fortress of St. Gregory (in which Bekkos remained until his death in 1297) cf. Failler, "Chronologie et composition dans l'Histoire de Georges Pachymère [III]", pp. 21–22.

122   Cf. Constantinides, "Byzantine Scholars and the Union of Lyons (1274)".

123   Διδάσκαλος τοῦ Ἀποστόλου: Darrouzès, *Recherches sur les ὀφφίκια*, p. 532.

WORKING IN THE IMPERIAL AND PATRIARCHAL CHANCERIES 429

hieromnenon of the Great Church (a high official in the patriarchal chancery in charge of the procedures of sacerdotal ordination)[124] he appears in the list of signatories to the final deliberation (*Tomos*) of the Council of Blachernae in 1285, which sanctioned the condemnation of Bekkos and the officials loyal to him.[125]

The *Tomos* of Blachernae from 1285 – antithetical in respect to that of 1277 – is the second document on which I shall focus here. Two patriarchal notaries also followed the same path as Pachymeres: Theodore Hypatios and Andrew Holobolos, who appear in the lists of witnesses in both documents.[126] Naturally, the evaluation of presences and absences in the two contrasting documents (of 1277 and 1285) also gives us an idea of the ecclesiastical officials who were purged for not bending to authority, or for being too involved in the losing side's policy. On the other hand, Pachymeres' silence on the facts of 1277 in his historical work[127] reveals the discretion (or better, embarrassment) of the offi-

---

124   Ibid., pp. 368–73.

125   On this synodal assembly see more generally Papadakis, *Crisis in Byzantium*. The relevant τόμος συνοδικός has been most recently discussed and edited by Stavrou, "Une réévaluation du *Tomos* du Deuxième Concile des Blachernes"; the same author has also printed the text of 1285 (without the list of signatories) for the editorial enterprise of the Fondazione per le scienze religiose (Bologna): Stavrou, M. (ed.), "Concilium Constantinopolitanum – 1285. Synod of Constantinople – 1285. Second Council of Blachernae", in *Ecumenical Councils*, eds. Alberigo/Melloni et al., vol. 4/1, pp. 103–30; the sole subscriptions had already been published in Laurent, "Les signataires du second concile des Blakhernes". For the signatures of the ἐκκλησιαστικοί see Stavrou, "Une réévaluation du *Tomos* du Deuxième Concile des Blachernes", pp. 90–93 (= Laurent, "Les signataires du second concile des Blakhernes", pp. 148–49: Εἴχε καὶ ὑπογραφὰς τῶν ἐκκλησιαστικῶν ταύτας κτλ.); in the fourth place we read: Ὁ ἱερομνήμων τῆς ἁγιωτάτης τοῦ Θεοῦ Μεγάλης Ἐκκλησίας Γεώργιος διάκονος ὁ Παχυμέρης, ὑπέγραψα (Stavrou, "Une réévaluation du *Tomos* du Deuxième Concile des Blachernes", pp. 90 [lines 62–63], 91 [with nn. 134–35]; Laurent, "Les signataires du second concile des Blakhernes", p. 148 [no. 4]); cf. Darrouzès, *Recherches sur les ὀφφίκια*, pp. 117, 533. The synodal document against Bekkos was initially subscribed by Emperor Andronikos II Palaiologos (Dölger, *Regesten*, vol. 4, no. 2108), by Patriarch Gregory of Cyprus (Laurent, *Les regestes*, vol. 4, no. 1490) and then by the bishops and metropolitans; the other ecclesiastical dignitaries (i.e. for the most part the *archontes* of the Great Church, including Pachymeres himself) signed only after having received assurance from higher-up in the synodal hierarchy: George Pachymeres, *History*, 8, 1–2, ed. Failler, vol. 3, pp. 127, line 28–131, line 9; 131, lines 27–30. Shortly after 1285, Pachymeres reached the rank of *protekdikos* of the Great Church, which fell into the *exokatakoiloi*.

126   *PLP* 29492; *PLP* 21043. Darrouzès, *Recherches sur les ὀφφίκια*, pp. 532–33. For the *Tomos* of 1285 see Stavrou, "Une réévaluation du *Tomos* du Deuxième Concile des Blachernes", pp. 92 (lines 79, 82), 93 (with nn. 157, 161) (Laurent, "Les signataires du second concile des Blakhernes", p. 149 [nos. 17, 20]).

127   Cf. *Dossier Lyon*, eds. Laurent/Darrouzès, pp. 464, 468.

430 DE GREGORIO

cial and man of letters, though he must have borne the unionist impositions with considerable difficulty.

The guarantee document of 1277 is preserved, *inter alia*, in MS Vatican City, Biblioteca Apostolica Vaticana, Chigi R.VI.a² (gr. 54, fols. 139r–140v). This codex, which can be dated to the first quarter of the 14th century and is certainly of Constantinopolitan origin, also contains works of the theologian and anti-Latin pamphleteer George Moschampar.[128] The latter, "Teacher of the Gospels" at the patriarchal school,[129] appears as the first signatory – among the ecclesiastical *archontes* – of the *Tomos* against Bekkos and the other unionists issued at the conclusion of the second Council of Blachernae in 1285. Here, we see him at work as *chartophylax*, in the place of Meliteniotes.[130] Moschampar – one of the instigators and certainly the person in charge of the preparation of this document containing the definitive condemnation of the union as well as the reconciliation among the parties that were opposed to Michael VIII – indissolubly fused his lead role in directing the patriarchal chancery with his activity as a polemicist. This latter is expressed in ferocious anti-Latin pamphleteering (published anonymously before 1282, to avoid suppression) and afterwards in a diatribe against Patriarch Gregory II of Cyprus himself, who, after he removed Moschampar from the post of *chartophylax*, endured not only his invectives but also an attempt (orchestrated by, among others, his old chancery official) to depose him from the highest seat in the Orthodox Church.

We have seen how the highest scholar-officials of the patriarchal chancery customarily inserted their name signatures in documents that marked the religious policy of the time. These subscriptions were often affixed with a single motion, without lifting the writing instrument from the support surface (the technical term used by modern scholars for this practice is "monocondyle", from ancient and medieval Greek μονοκόνδυλος); and the occurrences are

---

128 The Chigi manuscript, which has been severely damaged by humidity and is nearly indecipherable in many places, may have originated in the milieu of the Patriarchate of Constantinople; the chronology is confirmed by the presence of a type of Italian paper with a watermark datable to around 1320 (*Cercle*, cf. Mošin/Traljić, no. 2015). On George Moschampar cf. *Dossier Lyon*, eds. Laurent/Darrouzès, pp. 19–24; PLP 19344; Silvano, "L'origine dello scisma in un dialogo di Giorgio Moschampar"; id., "Per l'edizione della «Disputa tra un ortodosso e un latinofrone seguace di Becco sulla processione dello Spirito Santo» di Giorgio Moschampar"; Moniou, Γεώργιος Μοσχάμπαρ, ἕνας ἀνθενωτικὸς θεολόγος.

129 Διδάσκαλος τοῦ Εὐαγγελίου; on his tasks cf. *Dossier Lyon*, eds. Laurent/Darrouzès, p. 21.

130 Stavrou, "Une réévaluation du *Tomos* du Deuxième Concile des Blachernes", pp. 90 (lines 57–58), 91 (with nn. 128–29) (= Laurent, "Les signataires du second concile des Blakhernes", p. 148 [no. 1]: Ὁ χαρτοφύλαξ τῆς ἁγιωτάτης τοῦ Θεοῦ Μεγάλης Ἐκκλησίας Γεώργιος ὁ Μοσχάμπαρ συναινῶν ὑπέγραψα).

WORKING IN THE IMPERIAL AND PATRIARCHAL CHANCERIES 431

naturally numerous.[131] However, there are also patriarchal documents show-ing, exceptionally, only the signature and the seal of the official who served as head of the patriarchal chancery – that is, the *chartophylax* – instead of the analogous instruments of validation that were usually the prerogative of the primate. It is those acts that bear the formula indicating their extraction, or better redaction, from the draft minutes of the proceedings for which the *char-tophylax* was responsible.[132] But the rule required that it should be the patri-arch in person who appended his signature at the bottom of the acts copied by his chancery. These subscriptions could be presented in name form or with the sole mention of the month and the indiction (*menologema*), depending on the type of document and its legal value, which is not always identifiable through internal evidence (i.e. distinguishing between acts of the patriarch alone, of the patriarch as archbishop of Constantinople and of the patriarch as head of the synodal assembly).[133] They were usually of indifferent quality, reflect-ing an often sloppy scribal education: the monocondyle signature of Patriarch John xi Bekkos[134] stands as an exception, precisely because he came from the ranks of the bureaucracy – his last post being just that of *chartophylax* of the Great Church – rather than from the long-established ecclesiastical apparatus or the monastic class, from which patriarchs were generally elected. From the late Byzantine era on, and more frequently after the fall of Byzantium, one may observe an increasing interaction between the customs of the ecclesiastical

---

131 Especially concerning the Register of the Patriarchate of Constantinople, suffice it to refer both to the officials' signatures, which are to be found appended at the bottom of some documents recorded there, and to the lists of the *exarchoi* (which I shall address shortly). For μονοκόνδυλος, attested in classical Greek as an adjective and in Byzantine sources also as a substantive (up to the modern Greek terms μονοκονδύλιον and μονοκονδυλιά/μονοκο-ντιλιά), cf. Trapp (ed.), *Lexikon zur byzantinischen Gräzität*, fasc. 5: λ-παλιάνθρωπος, p. 1040 (s.v. μονοκόνδυλος, ὁ).

132 It is the so-called formula ταῦτα παρεκβληθέντα: cf. Darrouzès, *Le registre synodal*, pp. 281, 304, 324; id., *Recherches sur les ὀφφίκια*, pp. 517–21; Pieralli, "I «protocolli» delle riunioni sinodali". The originals which are still conserved for this typology (occurring already in the Comnenian era) are, for our time period, Laurent, *Les regestes*, vol. 4, nos. 1549 (1290–1293, under the Patriarch Athanasios i) and 1567 (1295, 5 October, Patriarch John xii). A fragment in a third analogous document, datable to 1354, 28 March (under the Patriarch Philotheos Kokkinos, first term), was discovered by Otto Kresten; moreover, it should be noted that the (*megas*) *chartophylax* who signed the document is John Ampar, while the scribe of the text has been identified as George Galesiotes: two protagonists in the patri-archal chancery during the 14th century who will be discussed in more detail below.

133 Cf. Darrouzès, *Le registre synodal*, pp. 140–43; id., *Recherches sur les ὀφφίκια*, pp. 395–426.

134 Cf. supra, pp. 427–28 with nn. 118–19.

432 DE GREGORIO

hierarchy and the scribal habits that were once the exclusive prerogative of patriarchal officials, as the diffusion of the monocondyle in the signatures of metropolitans testifies.

As outlined above, one of the functions of the *chartophylax* was that of coordinating all the operations of the office that was appointed to the production of acts, "for the writing of the reports",[135] a procedure that was solemnly emphasized in the ceremonial of the Great Church. A concrete trace of this can be found in the Register of the Patriarchate of Constantinople. It should be pointed out here that, unlike any other public institution (including the imperial chancery), the patriarchal chancery provided, as a key step, for the transcription of the issued documents in a common register, which the Byzantines called the "Register of the sacred *chartophylakeion*" or, more simply, the "Holy Register" or "Register of the Church".[136] An exceptional record of this activity has been preserved thanks to the erudite interest in the relics of Byzantine culture that animated the Flemish bibliophile Ogier Ghislain de Busbecq, well-known Habsburg ambassador to the Sublime Porte in Ottoman Constantinople (1555–1562). In fact, two original volumes of the Register (for the years 1315–1376 and 1379–1404) are preserved in Vienna in, respectively, the MSS Österreichische Nationalbibliothek, Vindob. Hist. gr. 47 and 48.[137] MS Vindob. Hist. gr. 47, for example, transmits at fol. 48r the annotation at the start of the records referring to the *chartophylax* Gregory Koutales,[138] who began to serve under Patriarch Hesaias at the end of the reign of Andronikos II Palaiologos:

> Register of the proceedings of the synodal sessions kept in the days of our mostly holy Lord and Ecumenical Patriarch, *kyr* Hesaias, starting from the moment in which the most honourable *chartophylax* of the most holy

---

135 Εἰς τὰς σημειώσεις (cf. above, n. 102 and context).

136 Κωδίκιον τοῦ ἱεροῦ χαρτοφυλακείου (where χαρτοφυλακεῖον obviously means the office of the *chartophylax*, namely the patriarchal chancery itself) or ἱερὸν κωδίκιον or also ἐκκλησιαστικὸν κωδίκιον.

137 See, above all, the introductions to the three volumes of *Patriarchal Register* that have so far appeared, as well as the monograph by Darrouzès, *Le registre synodal* (which, though outdated in some palaeographical and codicological aspects, is still relevant). Cf. also the overview in Hunger, "Das Patriarchatsregister von Konstantinopel", and more recently the contributions which appeared in the proceedings edited by Gastgeber/Mitsiou/Preiser-Kapeller, *The Register*.

138 *PLP* 13617.

WORKING IN THE IMPERIAL AND PATRIARCHAL CHANCERIES   433

Great Church of God, the *panhyperentimotatos kyr* Gregory Koutales, was awarded the office of *chartophylax*.[139]

With this reference to the act of entering upon his duties by the *chartophylax*, we are thrown directly into the work of the office of the patriarchal chancery. Koutales belonged to an influential Byzantine family which was very active in the milieu of the intellectual elite during the Palaeologan age. He was, for example, a correspondent of Matthew of Ephesos and a contributor to the political climate during the years of high tension between Andronikos II and Andronikos III, which escalated into the civil war between the grandfather and his grandson. Imprisoned when Patriarch Hesaias sent him to Andronikos II right after being appointed *chartophylax*, Gregory was liberated by Andronikos III when the latter succeeded his grandfather in 1328. In recompense, the young emperor promptly elevated the designation of Koutales' title, which from then on was *megas chartophylax*.[140] Koutales' ecclesiastical *cursus honorum* then culminated with his rise to the metropolitan throne of Thessaloniki (1334), a further demonstration that in many cases working in the chancery served as a springboard that could launch officials towards the highest rungs of the Orthodox Church hierarchy.

Thanks to a codicological examination of MS Vindob. Hist. gr. 47 conducted by Otto Kresten, we have been able to uncover manipulations in the structure of the patriarchal Register.[141] Of particular interest are the actions connected with the Palamite controversy and the dynastic struggles following the death of Andronikos III Palaiologos, as well as those relating to the alternating succession on the patriarchal throne, where the chancery of the Orthodox primate played a primary role in intrigues that resulted in censure and in the skilful disguise of the sequence of the acts.

The *Tomos* of 1341 – the document with which Patriarch John XIV Kalekas and the Synod condemned the writings of the monk Barlaam of Calabria against Gregory Palamas – is a noteworthy case. The various phases of the assembly's

---

139   *Patriarchal Register*, vol. 1, no. 65 (1327, March–September; Darrouzès, *Les regestes*, vol. 5, no. 2134): † Κωδίκιον τῶν συνοδικῶν παρασημειώσεων γεγονὸς ἐπὶ τῶν ἡμερῶν τοῦ παναγιωτάτου ἡμῶν δεσπότου καὶ οἰκουμενικοῦ πατριάρχου, κῦρ Ἡσαΐου, ἐξότου ὁ τιμιώτατος χαρτοφύλαξ τῆς ἁγιωτάτης Μεγάλης τοῦ Θεοῦ Ἐκκλησίας, πανυπερεντιμότατος κῦρ Γρηγόριος ὁ Κουτάλης, τῷ τοῦ χαρτοφύλακος ὀφφικίῳ ἐτιμήθη. The scribe of this record is George Galesiotes, whom I shall discuss at length below.

140   Cf. John VI Kantakouzenos, *History*, ed. Schopen, vol. 1, p. 313, lines 9–16. See also Gastgeber, "Das Patriarchatsregister als Spiegel der Religionspolitik", pp. 100–01.

141   Kresten, in *Patriarchal Register*, vol. 2, pp. 17–74 (*Einleitung*, II: *Zur Kodikologie des Patriarchatsregisters von Konstantinopel unter Ioannes XIV. Kalekas und Isidoros I.*). See also Gastgeber, "Das Patriarchatsregister als Spiegel der Religionspolitik", pp. 122–30.

progress (which was convened before the death of Emperor Andronikos III Palaiologos [15 June 1341] and led to the first affirmation of the Palamitic doctrine) can be reconstructed fairly easily thanks to the intersection of diverse sources.[142] The focal point for these events falls in the eighteenth and nineteenth quires of the patriarchal Register (now fols. 103–107 and 108–109 of the *Vindobonensis* manuscript).[143] These seven folia constitute the remains of an extensive intervention, which included the removal of at least seven other folia from the original quires. The resulting lacuna appears after fol. 107, right at the conclusion of the *Tomos* of 1341, in the version released in July of that year, which lacks the participants' signatures (the death of Andronikos III Palaiologos and the dynastic difficulties in the succession must have caused initial disorientation).[144]

Otto Kresten's reconstruction of this puzzle reads like a true crime novel within the walls of the patriarchal chancery. First and foremost, we can say for certain that the missing portion of the Register did not contain the August version of the same *Tomos*, which, today transmitted in copy, was nearly identical to the preceding version, with the signatures added. What was originally on these folia is difficult to say. Probably, the documents removed had something to do with the Palamite controversy (and they may have bothered the winning hesychastic side) or with the regency of the empire in support of the underage John V Palaiologos (for example, Patriarch John XIV Kalekas' excommunication of John Kantakouzenos at the end of 1341).[145] Who may have been responsible for this action and why, however, is easily understood, for it is a diversion intended to conceal an extreme tampering with the Register through the defamation of the *chartophylax* John Ampar,[146] who was active in the patriarchal chancery a few years after the *Tomos* of 1341 was issued – at the time of the first affirmation of Palamism, Ampar was in the service of the empress Anna Palaiologina (Giovanna of Savoy), the regent for her son John V and protagonist in the struggle with John Kantakouzenos.

---

142 Cf. Darrouzès, *Les regestes*, vol. 5, nos. 2210–14.

143 Kresten, in *Patriarchal Register*, vol. 2, pp. 32–45; on the issue that is dealt with here, see the two contributions, also by Kresten, "Der sogenannte „Absetzungsvermerk" des Patriarchen Ioannes XIV. Kalekas" and id., "Fünf nachgezeichnete Metropolitenunterschriften".

144 The text of the *Tomos* of July (*Patriarchal Register*, vol. 2, no. 132; Darrouzès, *Les regestes*, vol. 5, no. 2213) begins already on fol. 102v, the final page of the seventeenth quire of MS Vindob. Hist. gr. 47. Andronikos III Palaiologos must have participated in the discussion during this first phase (cf. e.g. the emperor's intervention recorded in *Patriarchal Register*, vol. 2, no. 132, lines 424–463), but was already deceased by the time of the final act.

145 Darrouzès, *Les regestes*, vol. 5, no. 2218.

146 *PLP* 800.

WORKING IN THE IMPERIAL AND PATRIARCHAL CHANCERIES 435

To fully understand the events, for which the patriarchal chancery was just the fulcrum, we must leap forward a few years, from 1341 to 1355 – a chronological span full of upheaval for Byzantium: from the discussions connected to the *Tomos* of 1341, with the attempts to reinterpret and distort its outcomes carried out by John XIV Kalekas and Gregory Akindynos,[147] to the resulting deposition of the patriarch (the *Tomos* of February 1347);[148] from the enthronement of the new Orthodox primate (Isidore I Boucheiras)[149] to the conclusion of the civil war with Kantakouzenos' appointment as co-emperor (both of which occurred in May 1347); from the *Tomos* of the Council held at the Blachernae in 1351 under the patriarch Kallistos I (elected in 1350[150]), with the definitive condemnation of Barlaam and Akyndinos, to the renewal of the dynastic conflict, with John VI Kantakouzenos' claim to nominate his son Matthew as co-emperor, the subsequent removal of Kallistos I from the patriarchal see and the election, in his place, of Philotheos Kokkinos (August 1353), who was willing to accept a line of imperial succession that, in practice, ousted John V Palaiologos, relegating him to a subordinate position; and finally, from the conclusion of the second dynastic conflict, with the abdication of John VI Kantakouzenos and the subsequent abandonment of Philotheos Kokkinos (at the end of 1354), to the return of Kallistos I on the throne of the Apostle Andrew (at the beginning of 1355).

Indeed, the note announcing the resumption of the entries in the *kodikion* with the second term of Patriarch Kallistos in the first half of 1355 helps us to understand this event, which exemplifies the "working methods" in the

---

147   Cf. e.g. *Patriarchal Register*, vol. 2, no. 145 (1344, November; Darrouzès, *Les regestes*, vol. 5, no. 2251), with the annotation *Patriarchal Register*, vol. 2, no. 146, inserted in the Register by an adversary of Kalekas after his deposition and erased by a supporter of the ex-patriarch (Kresten, "Der sogenannte „Absetzungsvermerk" des Patriarchen Ioannes XIV. Kalekas"; id., in *Patriarchal Register*, vol. 2, pp. 51–52).

148   *Patriarchal Register*, vol. 2, no. 147 (1347, February; Darrouzès, *Les regestes*, vol. 5, no. 2270); it should be noted that the text of the *Tomos* of 1347, as it appears in the *Patriarchal Register*, is particularly damaged by scrapping and mutilations: Kresten, in *Patriarchal Register*, vol. 2, pp. 52–69. See also most recently Lauritzen, F. (ed.), "Concilium Constantinopolitanum – 1347. Synod of Constantinople – 1 February 1347", in *Ecumenical Councils*, eds. Alberigo/Melloni et al., vol. 4/1, pp. 153–70.

149   Cf. the annotation at the start of the entries under Isidoros I in the *hieron kodikion*, *Patriarchal Register*, vol. 2, no. 153 (1347, May 17; Darrouzès, *Les regestes*, vol. 5, no. 2273); George Galesiotes' hand appears here again. For these events see now Rigo, *1347: Isidoro patriarca di Costantinopoli*.

150   *Patriarchal Register*, vol. 3, no. 176 (1350, June 10: beginning of the entries; cf. Darrouzès, *Les regestes*, vol. 5, no. 2311), where we see George Galesiotes again at work.

chancery of the Orthodox primate in one of Byzantium's most dramatic moments.[151] This detailed declaration – which also recalls the reasons for which Kallistos was compelled to leave the patriarchal throne in the first place, given his refusal to contravene the rules of dynastic succession – without doubt conceals a chancery official, who, in concert with Kallistos himself, distorted the composition of the patriarchal Register, eliminating not only the folia following the *Tomos* of July 1341 but also, and above all, the "undesired" documents transcribed during the brief period of the first patriarchal term of Philotheos Kokkinos. And in the executor of this wild manipulation we can easily recognize the primary scribe of the patriarchal chancery, who remained afloat in that office, despite the dramatic upheavals, from the 1320s to the 1370s: that is to say, George Galesiotes, who in this circumstance must have represented the *longa manus* of the reinstated patriarch (Kallistos I). In fact, the plan required throwing dust in the eyes, thus distracting attention from the real manoeuvres of censorship and identifying a plausible scapegoat. In the Register's annotation, transcribed and perhaps also composed by Galesiotes himself, the blame for these grave alterations in the *Vindobonensis* manuscript is shifted onto the *megas chartophylax* John Ampar (who was no longer able to defend himself, as he had been recently removed from his position on account of a turbid affair of simony).[152] Ampar, therefore, served as a sacrificial victim, ready to be delivered to the outside world as the designated culprit. We need only look at the words used here, which must be conceived as a true denigration of a person already discredited by the investigations launched against him (the end of the following passage stands as a magnificent example of "smoke and mirrors"!):

---

151   *Patriarchal Register*, vol. 3, no. 211 (1355, February/August; cf. Darrouzès, *Les regestes*, vol. 5, no. 2376); see the reconstruction by Kresten, in *Patriarchal Register*, vol. 2, pp. 41–44, as well as id., "Der sogenannte „Absetzungsvermerk" des Patriarchen Ioannes XIV. Kalekas", pp. 214–17, and id., "Fünf nachgezeichnete Metropolitenunterschriften", 170–71. Gastgeber, "Das Patriarchatsregister als Spiegel der Religionspolitik", pp. 102–03.

152   On the fate of Ampar, who was accused of malfeasance in office and, indeed, of φιλαργυρία (the cases of corruption concerned conduct and practices that were against the ecclesiastical canons regarding both sacerdotal consecrations and celebrations of marriage), cf. Hunger, "Amtsmißbrauch im Patriarchat von Konstantinopel". Ampar's trial and dismissal must likely have taken place during Philotheos Kokkinos' first term as patriarch. The text of the pertinent synodal deliberation was replaced (probably in Galesiotes' hand) by a generic list of accusations, now *Patriarchal Register*, vol. 3, no. 202 (between February and the end of 1354) (cf. also Darrouzès, *Les regestes*, vol. 5, no. 2375), which appears at a point where the manipulations conducted at the beginning of Kallistos' second patriarchate are particularly extensive; cf. also Kresten, "Fünf nachgezeichnete Metropolitenunterschriften", 168–72.

WORKING IN THE IMPERIAL AND PATRIARCHAL CHANCERIES 437

In the meantime,[153] however, one or a few evil men, fellows of the former *megas chartophylax* Ampar and then belonging to the ranks of the [Great] Church, arrived at such temerity and insolence that they not only severed and removed the synodal *tomos* issued in devout respect of the sacred dogmas, for which the much celebrated and most pious emperor, father of our powerful and holy lord and emperor, had supremely striven, exerting no small effort, as everyone knows, for the reward bestowed by God [...],[154] that is to say that holy synodal *tomos* transcribed in the Register of the Church, but they also destroyed the synodal acts once occurring in the same Register, as one by now can see.[155]

Alongside his office activities, Ampar had played an important role in the intellectual life of the Byzantine capital in the middle of the 14th century, among other things filling the imperial post of "consul of the philosophers" (*hypatos ton philosophon*). The passage quoted above portrays the *megas chartophylax* as the leader of a circle of ecclesiastical scholars – the "evil men" who in the stratagem are said to have assisted him in the destruction of the *Tomos* from 1341 and of the other documents – who in all likelihood actively participated in the theological disputes of the time. The episode narrated in this extract is particularly instructive since it occurs entirely within the patriarchal chancery, with fidelity and a sense of belonging giving way to intrigue and slander, above all when the senior official had already fallen into disgrace. Ampar and Galesiotes operated side by side during the period in which the former served as *chartophylax*. We see them active together, for example, in the *Tomos* of the Council held at Blachernae in 1351 (with the solemn recognition of the hesychastic doctrine and the definitive condemnation of the anti-Palamites,

---

153   The first part of the document retraces the events of the civil war, with the dynastic rights of John v Palaiologos infringed by Kantakouzenos and the banishment of Kallistos I, who would not bend to the usurper's will.

154   The passage omitted here, for the sake of brevity, recalls that the Synod of 1341 had been convened at the church of *Hagia Sophia* in an extreme longing by Andronikos III Palaiologos, who was then dying.

155   *Patriarchal Register*, vol. 3, no. 211, lines 19–32: Ἐντῷμεταξὺ δὲ τίς καί τινες χαιρέκακοι μετὰ τοῦ ποτὲ μεγάλου χαρτοφύλακος, τοῦ Ἄμπαρι, κατειλεγμένοι τηνικαῦτα τῇ ἐκκλησίᾳ, εἰς τοῦτο τόλμης καὶ αὐθαδείας ἦλθον, ὥστε οὐ μόνον τὸν ἐπ' εὐσεβείᾳ τῶν ἱερῶν δογμάτων ἐκτεθειμένον συνοδικὸν τόμον, ὑπὲρ οὗ ὁ ἀοίδιμος καὶ εὐσεβέστατος βασιλεύς, ὁ πατὴρ τοῦ κραταιοῦ καὶ ἁγίου ἡμῶν αὐθέντου καὶ βασιλέως [...], πλεῖστα ἐμόγησε καί, ὡς ἅπαντες ἴσασιν, οὐ μικρὸν πόνον ὑπέστη διὰ τὰς ἀπὸ τοῦ Θεοῦ μισθαποδοσίας [...], τοῦτον τὸν ἱερὸν συνοδικὸν τόμον ἐν τῷ ἐκκλησιαστικῷ κωδικίῳ καταγεγραμμένον διέρρηξαν καὶ κατέλυσαν, ἀλλὰ καὶ τὰς ἐν τῷ αὐτῷ κωδικίῳ κειμένας συνοδικὰς πράξεις ἠφάνισαν, καθάπερ ἤδη ὁρᾶται. See also more recently Gastgeber, "Das Patriarchatsregister als Spiegel der Religionspolitik", p. 103.

438   DE GREGORIO

from the already-deceased Barlaam and Gregory Akindynos to the polemicists active at that moment, such as Nikephoros Gregoras): Ampar as the first signatory among the *exokatakoiloi*,[156] Galesiotes as one of the official readers of the text and, above all, as the scribe of the original.[157] This did not prevent the skilled and devious calligrapher from demolishing his old boss, contriving for the Patriarch Kallistos I – who meanwhile had been restored to the throne – the stratagem that drew a veil over the unscrupulous action of censure (induced by the primate), by cancelling from the Register the most troublesome traces left by Philotheos Kokkinos.

The transcription of the acts in the Register being a "work in progress", the patriarchal chancery also constituted a sort of training ground for the scribal education of those who worked therein. And in this sense, it stood as a true

---

156   *Patrologia Graeca*, vol. 151, col. 763B, lines 5–7 (text of the *Tomos* of 1351 [Darrouzès, *Les regestes*, vol. 5, nos. 2324, 2326], signatures): Ὁ μέγας χαρτοφύλαξ τῆς ἁγιωτάτης τοῦ Θεοῦ Μεγάλης Ἐκκλησίας καὶ ὕπατος τῶν φιλοσόφων, ὁ Ἔμπαρις [= Ἄμπαρις] ("The *megas chartophylax* of the most holy Great Church of God and consul of the philosophers Ampar"); cf. Darrouzès, *Recherches sur les ὀφφίκια*, pp. 133, 319 n. 1. In the edition of the *Tomos* of 1351 printed by Karmires (*Dogmatic Monuments of the Orthodox Church*, vol. 1, pp. 374–407: 406), we find only the first six signatories (the two emperors, John VI Kantakouzenos and John V Palaiologos, Patriarch Kallistos I, the metropolitan of Herakleia in Thrace [Philotheos Kokkinos: see the next footnote], the metropolitan of Thessaloniki [Gregory Palamas] and the metropolitan Arsenios of Kyzikos), while in Lauritzen, F. (ed.), "Concilium Constantinopolitanum – 1351. Synod of Constantinople – 1351", in *Ecumenical Councils*, eds. Alberigo/Melloni et al., vol. 4/1, pp. 171–218, who based his text on that established by Karmires, there are no signatures published, as is normally the case in the Bologna series.

157   Philotheos Kokkinos, *First Antirrhetic against Nikephoros Gregoras*, ed. Kaimakes, p. 33, lines 304–306: Τρεῖς δ᾽ ἦμεν οἱ κατὰ διαδοχὴν ἀνεγνωκότες ἐκεῖνον [scil. τὸν Τόμον], Γαλησιώτης, φημί, καὶ Μάξιμος ὁ σοφὸς καὶ τρίτος ἐπ᾽ ἐκείνοις καὶ τελευταῖος ὁ Ἡρακλείας ("We were three, those who in turn read the *tomos*, I mean to say Galesiotes, the wise Maximos [probably Maximos Laskaris Kalopheros, PLP 10733] and third among them and last the metropolitan of Herakleia [in Thrace, namely Philotheos Kokkinos himself, who in 1351, shortly before his election to the patriarchal throne, held precisely that post: PLP 11917]"). Two original fragments, perfectly overlapping, of this *Tomos* – without doubt redacted by Philotheos Kokkinos among others (cf. e.g. ed. Kaimakes, p. 33, line 274) – survive today: they contain the final part of the text and a portion of the signatures (MS Basel, Öffentliche Bibliothek der Universität, N I 6 no. 16: Darrouzès, *Les regestes*, vol. 5, no. 2326; Hieronymus, *Griechischer Geist aus Basler Pressen*, pp. 727–36 [no. 446]): from the available facsimiles it is easy to identify George Galesiotes as the text's scribe (cf. Dölger, "Ein byzantinisches Staatsdokument in der Universitätsbibliothek Basel"; Dold, *Das Geheimnis einer byzantinischen Staatsurkunde aus dem Jahre 1351* [with 6 pls.]); see more recently Harlfinger, "Autographa aus der Palaiologenzeit", pp. 49–50 (with pl. 22). It should also be noted that Ampar and Galesiotes are attested together, the first as signatory, the second as scribe, in the documentary fragment of 1354 (Patriarch Philotheos Kokkinos, first term) mentioned above (supra, n. 132).

WORKING IN THE IMPERIAL AND PATRIARCHAL CHANCERIES   439

crossroads for the trends and innovations introduced in Greek script during
that period, which are inevitably reflected in the realm of book production,
since, as I have already emphasized, professional copyists of manuscripts and
scribes-notaries were very often the same persons. Indeed, as a "gathering
place" for writing practices, the patriarchal chancery can be seen as a laboratory
in which many great transformations were heralded and produced. Moreover,
the Register bears witness to different levels of literacy in the late Byzantine
period, for instance, among those who signed the lists of the *exarchoi* (ecclesiastic officials assigned to internal discipline and control), a concrete example
of the action of moral renewal and recovery of the Constantinopolitan clergy
undertaken by Patriarch Kallistos I in 1357.[158]

I shall now briefly examine the organization of the physical work of copying within this office, based just on the two volumes of the Register of the
Patriarchate of Constantinople (MSS Vindob. Hist. gr. 47 and 48). Supported
by a study, still in progress, of the scribes in the patriarchal chancery starting
from the mid-14th century,[159] I have been able to reconstruct a precise "line of
descent" consisting of three figures who passed on to one another the baton
as the primary physical compilers of the Register entries. Two of these three
also served as patriarchal notaries and pursued brilliant careers in the ecclesiastical hierarchy. Moreover, all three are known as scribes of manuscripts and
participated to various degrees in the intellectual climate during the second
Palaeologan age, over a chronological span of more than one hundred years,
from the third decade of the 14th century through the 1430s.

The first of this triad is George Galesiotes, who was particularly appreciated for his scribal skills, being able to move from an extremely calligraphic
style to a much more rapid, informal and at times "dishevelled" ductus.[160] Well
known in the patriarchal milieu – where he was customarily referred to simply as "Galesiotes" and never designated by an official title or role – and the
relative of a homonymous literary author who was also a high ecclesiastical
dignitary,[161] he entered the patriarchal chancery at a very young age in 1323

---

158   Cf. Hunger, "Die Exarchenlisten des Patriarchen Kallistos I."; De Gregorio, "La scrittura
       greca di età paleologa", pp. 98–99.
159   Cf. De Gregorio, "La scrittura greca di età paleologa", pp. 97–101, 115, and now id.,
       "Un'aggiunta su copisti greci del secolo XIV".
160   Cf. De Gregorio, "Καλλιγραφεῖν/ταχυγραφεῖν", pp. 441–45.
161   We can distinguish George Galesiotes the Elder, probably the scribe's uncle, thanks to
       a cross-reference between biographical data (cf. the single lemma *PLP* 3528) and the
       activity of our chancery servant. Born around 1278/80, Galesiotes the Elder initially filled
       the post of πρωτέκδικος (approximately from 1310 to 1334, as the successor of George
       Pachymeres) and then that of σακελλίου (*post* 1334–*ante* 1344) of the Great Church (i.e. an
       ἐξωκατάκοιλος). He was also the author of, among other works, a well known *Metaphrasis*

440 DE GREGORIO

under the Patriarch Hesaias (1323–1332). There he became, from the start, the principal scribe both for the Register entries (32 out of the 35 acts inserted there in this first period are in his hand)[162] and for the few surviving original documents. The situation is somewhat different for the documents recorded in MS Vindob. Hist. gr. 47 during the age of the Patriarchs John XIV Kalekas (1334–1347) and Isidore I (1347–1350), when Galesiotes – perhaps choosing to keep his head down in the turbid general situation prevailing during this phase of the Palamite controversy – transcribed about half of the acts attested in the *kodikion* (33 out of 69, approximately 22 folia out of the 55 corresponding to that period in the *Vindobonensis* manuscript). Nevertheless, even while essentially serving as the coordinator of a team of around ten scribes, he did not dominate the scene: among the documents he was not entrusted with transcribing into the Register were, for example, the two *Tomoi* of 1341 and 1347 and the will of Isidore I.[163] Nonetheless, Galesiotes continued to gravitate towards the more restricted patriarchal orbit under John XIV Kalekas as well, as may be inferred from his part in the copying of the "house book" of Matthew, metropolitan of Ephesos, and from his high-level book production in MS Sinait. gr. 152 (commissioned by the powerful Isaac Palaiologos Asanes but probably

of Nikephoros Blemmydes' Βασιλικὸς Ἀνδριάς (cf. Hunger/Ševčenko, *Des Nikephoros Blemmydes Βασιλικός Ἀνδριάς*). A confirmation of the hypothesis (already put forth ibid., pp. 33–34, upon suggestion of O. Kresten) that an ἐξωκατάκοιλος could not serve as a simple chancery scribe – furthermore at the venerable age of seventy-plus years old – can be found in the *Tomos* of 1351. In fact, thanks to the testimonies mentioned above (supra, n. 157 and context), we know that this document was written and, in part, read aloud publicly by George Galesiotes (therefore, as a servant operating in the patriarchal chancery, without any title or epithet corresponding to the rank), whereas the offices of σακελλίου, and, higher up in the first πεντάς, of the μέγας χαρτοφύλαξ and of the μέγας σκευοφύλαξ of the Μεγάλη Ἐκκλησία, were held at that time by other well-known figures, respectively Michael Kabasilas (*PLP* 10101, σακελλίου at least from 1344!), John Ampar (μέγας χαρτοφύλαξ: cf. supra, pp. 434–38) and Euthymios Apokaukos (*PLP* 1185, μέγας σκευοφύλαξ precisely in 1351), who all signed the *Tomos*. In 1351, therefore, Galesiotes the Elder, i.e. the Church official of high rank and learned rhetor known in Constantinople, was, in all likelihood, already dead. The scribe Galesiotes, on the other hand, appears in the patriarchal Register at least until 1371. His date of birth can therefore be placed around 1300. A different reconstruction (following the older interpretation) is offered by Gastgeber, "Das Patriarchatsregister als Spiegel der Religionspolitik", pp. 115–17.

162 Cf. Hunger, in *Patriarchal Register*, vol. 1, pp. 65–71; Gastgeber, "Das Patriarchatsregister als Spiegel der Religionspolitik", p. 118 (pl. 2).

163 See the distinction of hands proposed by Hunger, in *Patriarchal Register*, vol. 2, pp. 75–80; for the two *Tomoi* cf. supra, pp. 433–37, while the διαθήκη of Isidoros I is *Patriarchal Register*, vol. 2, no. 156 (1350, February; Darrouzès, *Les regestes*, vol. 5, no. 2309); see also Gastgeber, "Das Patriarchatsregister als Spiegel der Religionspolitik", pp. 118–19 (pls. 3–4), 130–31.

WORKING IN THE IMPERIAL AND PATRIARCHAL CHANCERIES 441

initiated by the patriarch himself).[164] Galesiotes then returns as undisputed protagonist in the patriarchal chancery in the two terms of Kallistos I (1350– 1353 [August], 1355–1363) and in the brief interval of the first patriarchate of Philotheos Kokkinos (August 1353 through the end of 1354): according to the data collected in my ongoing study, I can argue that during these years Galesiotes remained practically the only scribe attested in the *kodikion*, as well as in the few surviving originals. For the *Vindobonensis* manuscript, we are dealing with, in total, around sixty folia between fol. 137r and fol. 230r, excluding the folia with the lists of the *exarchoi* that originally circulated loose among the signatories.[165]

By contrast, the physiognomy of the patriarchal chancery must have changed radically at the beginning at least of the second term of Philotheos Kokkinos (1364–1376). In fact, from October 1364 to December 1365[166] there is no trace of George Galesiotes' hand in the Register, since he had temporarily fallen into disgrace and had been removed by Philotheos on account of his compromising ties with the policies of the previous patriarch (Kallistos I). In the Register entries from this era we see five fairly occasional and inexpert copyists alternating in the transcription, who highlight the trend towards an increasing personalization of the writing outcomes in Byzantine chanceries and, more generally, towards an impoverishment of the professional figure of the scribe in Byzantium, which foreshadows the following period's extreme variety. It is therefore not surprising that already in March 1366[167] the irreplaceable (though elderly) Galesiotes was reinstated in his role of coordinator of the patriarchal scribes. Starting from that date, and extending at least until May 1371,[168] his handwriting appears with a certain continuity in the *kodikion*, although it is found alongside another hand, more accurate and rounded compared to the later work of the elderly scribe. Thanks to an insight in Jean Darrouzès'

---

164 On the two manuscripts, cf. infra, nn. 179, 183 and context.

165 Cf. supra, n. 158. For these lists, I have identified Galesiotes' handwriting in the decree that describes the patriarchal action, as well as the script of two primary hands (Michael Balsamon, *PLP* 2121, and Michael Skoutariotes, *PLP* 26211, both known by the professional title of ταβουλλάριος), which appear in the introductory texts.

166 *Acta et diplomata*, eds. Miklosich/Müller, pp. 448–79 (nos. 194–222 [incomplete numbering] = *Patriarchal Register*, vol. 4 [forthcoming], nos. 272–302).

167 *Acta et diplomata*, eds. Miklosich/Müller, pp. 479–83 (no. 223 = *Patriarchal Register*, vol. 4 [forthcoming], no. 303; Darrouzès, *Les regestes*, vol. 5, no. 2510).

168 *Acta et diplomata*, eds. Miklosich/Müller, pp. 578–80 (no. 319 = *Patriarchal Register*, vol. 4 [forthcoming], no. 402; Darrouzès, *Les regestes*, vol. 5, no. 2622).

442 DE GREGORIO

pioneering work[169] we are able to attach a name to Galesiotes' collaborator, who seems to have been trained exactly as his successor: John Holobolos.

A reference to this latter scribe has been handed down to us thanks both to a note of redaction that appears as marginal insert in a few prefaces of documents comprised in the Register and to the subscription in MS Mount Athos, Lavra K 112 (AD 1369), which contains Constantine Harmenopoulos' *Hexabiblos* (with Philotheos Kokkinos' refutation of some synodal *tomoi* quoted by the same canonist) and other texts, such as one *Notitia episcopatuum* and some lists of ecclesiastical as well as imperial offices. Holobolos is indeed one of the chancery scribes for whom we can assume a specific activity as *dictator* (i.e. drafter of documents, as shown by the *prooimia* explicitly attributed to himself in the patriarchal Register) in the role of patriarchal notary (as indicated, for example, in the Athonite Codex).[170] I have been able to assign 34 entries in the *kodikion*, between 1366 and 1372, to Holobolos with certainty, to which we can add at least four original documents also dating from the second term of Philotheos Kokkinos.[171] His *cursus honorum* was brilliant: from *notarios patriarchikos* and scribe of the chancery (as well as, later, *kanstrisios*, the servant in charge of ceremony belonging to the middle class of patriarchal officials), John Holobolos was even placed at the head of the patriarchal chancery as *megas chartophylax* from 1389 to 1399, the year in which he was promoted to the metropolitan throne of Gotthia in Crimea. In 1402–1403, he was a protagonist in the deposition of his mentor, the Patriarch Matthew I, who, however,

---

169 Darrouzès, *Le registre synodal*, pp. 54, 56, 75, 77, 89, 114–15, 200, 261, 283, 330, pl. 37; id., *Recherches sur les ὀφφίκια*, pp. 246 n. 3, 364–65, 384.

170 After Darrouzès, it is now possible to consult Gastgeber, "Rhetorik in der Patriarchatskanzlei von Konstantinopel", pp. 192–94, and Schminck, "Wörtliche Zitate des weltlichen und kirchlichen Rechts", pp. 239–40, 243; cf. also the record in PLP 21044. For this paper, I could not consider the very recent articles by Estangüi Gómez, "Pour une étude prosopographique des fonctionnaires", and by Pieralli, "Gli originali copiati da due notai"; besides the comprehensive investigation I am conducting on the scribes of the patriarchal chancery (1350–1376), I shall return to the figure of Holobolos in a contribution, to be published soon, entitled "Un manoscritto agiografico dal Patriarcato di Costantinopoli nel XIV secolo: il Vat. gr. 809, Filoteo Kokkinos e gli scribi della sua cancelleria". – For MS Athon. Lavra K 112 see e.g. Burgmann/Fögen/Schminck/Simon, *Repertorium der Handschriften des byzantinischen Rechts*, pp. 42–43 (no. 33); its subscription is worded as follows: τὸ παρὸν πρόχειρον τῶν νόμων ἐγράφη χειρὶ τοῦ ἀπὸ τῶν πατριαρχικῶν νοταρίων Ἰωάννου τοῦ Ὁλοβώλου ἐν τῷ πατριαρχείῳ καὶ ἐτελειώθη κατὰ μῆνα μάρτιον τῆς ζ΄ ἰνδικτιῶνος τοῦ ϛωοζ΄ ἔτους (fol. 311r: "the present Handbook of the Laws was written by the hand of the patriarchal notary John Holobolos at the Patriarchate and it was completed in the month of March of the seventh indiction of the year 6877 [= AD 1369]").

171 A further twenty acts, inserted in the patriarchal Register and also belonging to the same period, are most likely attributable to this scribe-notary.

WORKING IN THE IMPERIAL AND PATRIARCHAL CHANCERIES 443

was immediately reinstated by Emperor Manuel II Palaiologos. Holobolos' path, which through the redaction of prefaces and the material preparation of documents and entries in the Register brought him to the intrigues of "high" politics, concludes with his retirement to a monastery and his death in 1406.

John Chortasmenos follows directly on the heels of Holobolos in the notarial tradition.[172] Starting from the monograph by Herbert Hunger,[173] we know quite a bit about this intellectual, well-read and educated although from low social rank, who with his salary as a patriarchal notary (from 1391 to around 1415) managed to buy a few manuscripts on which to study texts, epitomize and fill them with annotations. Traces of his activity in the patriarchal chancery remain primarily in the second volume of the Register (MS Vindob. Hist. gr. 48), still for the patriarchate of Matthew I (more specifically covering the years 1399–1401),[174] and on fols. 200r–215v of MS Vatican City, Biblioteca Apostolica Vaticana, Urb. gr. 80, a personal copy, probably from his youth, with older documents from the Register today partially missing in MS Vindob. Hist. gr. 47.[175] Simultaneously with his work as notary, and also after he assumed the monastic habit (as *hieromonachos* Ignatios, 1415–1430), Chortasmenos secured other sources of income both as a teacher (his students included protagonists of the following era, such as the tenacious anti-unionist Mark Eugenikos, the future cardinal of the Roman Church Bessarion and the future patriarch of Constantinople George Gennadios II Scholarios) and as a restorer of the older manuscripts discovered in the Byzantine capital (it is worth mentioning at least the Dioskourides manuscript of Vienna, Österreichische Nationalbibliothek, Vindob. Med. gr. 1, from the beginning of the 6th century).[176]

---

172   Cf. the reference already occurring in Darrouzès, *Le registre synodal*, p. 77.

173   Hunger, *Johannes Chortasmenos* (particularly interesting is his picture of late Byzantine society, ibid., pp. 44–48). For the manuscripts that contain notes of possession or acquisition by Chortasmenos indicating his profession as *notarios* cf. ibid., pp. 14, 52–53 (for the years from 1391 to 1402). On Chortasmenos see more recently Acerbi/Bianconi, "L'*Organon* a fisarmonica di Giovanni Cortasmeno".

174   Hunger, *Johannes Chortasmenos*, p. 51; Darrouzès, *Le registre synodal*, pp. 76–77, pls. 58–60, 64; cf. also Canart/Prato, "Les recueils organisés par Jean Chortasménos", pp. 165–66, pls. 4–5.

175   On the miscellany transmitted by the Codex Urbinas, which contains numerous sections in the hand of Chortasmenos, in addition to Hunger, *Johannes Chortasmenos*, pp. 24, 51, see, above all, the considerations in Canart/Prato, "Les recueils organisés par Jean Chortasménos", passim, especially pp. 173–75 and pls. 15–17 for the folia in question ("U 5"), as well as Kresten, "Zu Darrouzès, Regest *N. 2041".

176   For the legends and other annotations inserted by Chortasmenos (AD 1405/6) in the Dioskourides manuscript of Vienna cf. e.g. Hunger, *Johannes Chortasmenos*, pp. 15, 26, 51; Canart/Prato, "Les recueils organisés par Jean Chortasménos", p. 163, pl. 3; the significance of the whole restoration work on this cimelium by our notary has been more recently

444   DE GREGORIO

He also continued to cultivate his interests as a scholar, focusing on mathematics and astronomy, rhetoric, and Aristotelian philosophy. Moreover, he managed to build relationships with his numerous and influential correspondents, a network that allowed him to ascend to the metropolitan throne of Selymbria in 1431. His fame, laboriously gained starting from his apprenticeship in the patriarchal chancery, earned him a leading place in the intellectual life of this era. Here is a brief portrait of him by his pupil Bessarion:

> I was also acquainted with the metropolitan of Sely(m)bria, Chortasmenos, who was one of the scholars and of the great teachers, to wit, as I well know, to a particularly high degree.[177]

Galesiotes, Holobolos, Chortasmenos: with these figures we have entered the last Byzantine age, between tradition and the transformation, or, to some degree, the dissolution, of formal and socio-cultural models. From a strictly palaeographical point of view, we can propose the following considerations. The first half of the 14th century had already seen the flourishing of the "scribe of Metochites", Michael Klostomalles, who inaugurated a trend with the evident intention of rendering the script normally used for chancery practices (and now suitable even for modern high-level manuscripts) more calligraphic and ordered. Starting from around the middle of the same century, this multifunctional feature was heightened, breaking down more decisively the already thin barriers between the documentary and manuscript realms. On the one hand, a copyist like Galesiotes, who certainly entered the profession in connection with Klostomalles, made his own script increasingly more personal and informal. Cases in which the use of the calligraphic variant, directly connected with the chancery styles employed during the immediately preceding period (e.g. the *Metochitesstil*), was required – for the particular function of the act or for the high patronage in manuscripts – stand as exceptions. Thus, the script of Galesiotes' pupil Holobolos is equally characterized by a high aesthetic level, in the wake of a chancery tradition that had evolved and modernized. And the early attempts of Chortasmenos are also indebted to this tendency derived from the *Metochitesstil*. On the other hand, a graphic variant similar to the so-called *ton Hodegon* style, usually reserved for liturgical codices and scrolls

---

pointed out by Gamillscheg, "Johannes Chortasmenos als Restaurator des Wiener Dioskurides".

177   Cf. Hunger, *Johannes Chortasmenos*, pp. 14 n. 7, 19: εἶδον δὲ καὶ τὸν Σηλυβρίας τὸν Χορτασμένον, ὃς ἦν τῶν λογίων καὶ τῶν μεγάλων διδασκάλων εἷς, καὶ οἶδα καλῶς ὅτι λίαν.

of "pomp and circumstance" – the same style referenced in Chortasmenos' "liturgical script" – is employed, for example, in the lists of the *exarchoi* within the Register of the Patriarchate of Constantinople.[178] And it is precisely Chortasmenos, with his chameleon-like "multigraphism", who represents the point of arrival, between the 14th and 15th centuries, of these phenomena, as well as reflecting the changes that occurred in the hotbed of experimentation that was the patriarchal chancery during the long period examined here.

These three patriarchal scribes also copied manuscripts, and the number of exemplars attributable to them grows with the refinement of palaeographical techniques. Here, I shall limit myself to noting, first of all, their activity in the preparation of so-called "house books" – for Galesiotes the volumes of well-known leading exponents (e.g. Matthew of Ephesos in MS Vienna, Österreichische Nationalbibliothek, Vindob. Theol. gr. 174)[179] as well as in private copies (e.g. MS Vatican City, Biblioteca Apostolica Vaticana, Vat. gr. 112),[180] for Chortasmenos above all in this latter category (the case of MS Vienna, Österreichische Nationalbibliothek, Vindob. Suppl. gr. 75 is particularly instructive);[181] and then their manuscript production under patronage – Galesiotes was asked to create precious and refined exemplars for personalities of the highest rank such as John Kantakouzenos (in the Gregory of Nazianzos MS Mount Athos, Vatopedi Monastery, Vatop. 105, from 1326, in the Basil of Caesarea MS Vatop. 65 and in the Four Gospels MS Vatop. Skeuoph. 17)[182] and the *panhypersebastos* Isaac Palaiologos Asanes, great-uncle of the Emperor John v Palaiologos and perhaps also his *mesazon* (in the Four Gospels MS Mount Sinai, Saint Catherine's Monastery, Sinait. gr. 152, from 1346, commissioned by

---

178   Canart/Prato, "Les recueils organisés par Jean Chortasménos", pp. 166–67, pl. 7. On this stylization, which started from the scribes active in the Constantinopolitan monastery *ton Hodegon*, cf. for the cases of the *exarchoi* De Gregorio, "La scrittura greca di età paleologa", pp. 99–100, 116; the contribution of Pérez Martín, "El «estilo Hodegos»" is, by contrast, controversed and problematic.

179   Cf. e.g. De Gregorio, "Καλλιγραφεῖν/ταχυγραφεῖν", pp. 442–44, pl. 9a.

180   Ibid., pp. 444–45, pl. 9b.

181   Cf. Hunger, *Johannes Chortasmenos*, pp. 54–63 et alibi (with 8 pls.); Canart/Prato, "Les recueils organisés par Jean Chortasménos", pp. 120–25 et alibi, pl. 1.

182   Cf. Lamberz, "Johannes Kantakuzenos und die Produktion von Luxushandschriften", pp. 135–38, 140, 142, 146, 148–49, 153, 155–56, figs. 15–17 (and now id., "Beobachtungen zu den patristischen Corpora", where, moreover, the hand of Galesiotes is identified in the Gregory of Nyssa MS Mytilene, Mone Ioannou tou Theologou tou Hypselou 6, which displays the same characteristics of the de luxe manuscripts produced on the initiative of Kantakouzenos; cf. especially ibid., p. 95 with nn. 25–26); Hutter, "Schreiber und Maler der Palaiologenzeit in Konstantinopel", pp. 160 nn. 6 and 9–10, 162 nn. 15–16, 172 n. 55, 179, 182 n. 96, 188 n. 117, figs. 44–45.

the influential politician most likely through the good offices of the Patriarch John XIV Kalekas).[183] Holobolos, by contrast, was employed primarily in volumes prepared in the Patriarchate of Constantinople itself (probably commissioned by Philotheos Kokkinos) and in connection with the Palamite controversy. From my still ongoing census, I shall confine myself to mentioning here only the following two exemplars: MS Vatican City, Biblioteca Apostolica Vaticana, Vat. gr. 809, the first part of which was copied by Galesiotes (in the 1350s–1360s) and the second and third parts (1370s), containing hagiographic texts composed by Philotheos Kokkinos and two orations by Palamas himself, by Holobolos;[184] and MS Mount Athos, Vatopedi Monastery, Vatop. 262, which dates from 1369–70 and transmits, among other texts and documents, the complete series of synodal *tomoi* on Palamism (from 1341, 1347 and 1351) and lastly that from 1368 with the condemnation of Prochoros Kydones, also signed by John Holobolos as patriarchal notary.[185]

But in the intellectual life of the Palaeologan age, the fortunes and the influence of these three brilliant bureaucrats – who were in contact with the highest political and religious spheres – are inextricably linked to their professional training in the chancery of the Great Church, the Ecumenical Patriarchate of Constantinople, which even today in the few relics of the South Gallery of Ayasofya Müzesi (such as the "Marble Door") reveals traces of its charm and vestiges of its ancient splendour.[186]

---

183   Cf. now De Gregorio, "Un'aggiunta su copisti greci del secolo XIV", esp. pp. 169–84, 192–201, pls. 1, 3.

184   Cf. the contribution announced supra, n. 170.

185   Rigo, "Il Monte Athos e la controversia palamitica", pp. 55–60, 69, 76–77, 134, pls. I, IV. [*Addendum*: Estangüi Gómez, "Pour une étude prosopographique des fonctionnaires", p. 149 seems not to agree with the identification of the scribe with Holobolos. As already stated before (supra, n. 170), I shall return to Holobolos in a study currently under preparation. I just would like to point out here that the two plates provided by Rigo, *pace* Estangüi Gómez, do really show the same hand: the only difference, which a palaeographer would easily recognize, lies in the circumstance that the script displayed in pl. IV (Vatop. 262, fol. 151v) is simply airier and more spacious because this page contains (beginning from line 3, after the chronology) the copy of the subscriptions under the *Tomos* of 1347; *de hoc satis*, at least in the present contribution.]

186   The role of the Great Church on the eve of the Fall of Constantinople has been more recently outlined by Harris, "The Patriarch of Constantinople and the last Days of Byzantium".

WORKING IN THE IMPERIAL AND PATRIARCHAL CHANCERIES

447

Bibliography

Primary Sources

Acta et diplomata, eds. F. Miklosich/I. Müller, *Acta et diplomata graeca medii aevi sacra et profana*, vol. 1, Vienna 1860.

Documents Chilandar, eds. L. Petit/B. Korablev, *Actes de Chilandar. Actes grecs* (Actes de l'Athos, 5/1), Saint Petersburg 1911.

Documents Chilandar, eds. M. Živojinović/V. Kravari/Ch. Giros, *Actes de Chilandar*, vol. 1: *Des origines à 1319* (Archives de l'Athos, 20), Paris 1998.

Documents Iviron, eds. J. Lefort/N. Oikonomidès/D. Papachryssanthou/V. Kravari (avec la collaboration d'H. Métrévéli), *Actes d'Iviron*, vol. 3: *De 1204 à 1328* (Archives de l'Athos, 18), Paris 1994.

Documents Koutloumousiou, ed. P. Lemerle, *Actes de Kutlumus* (Archives de l'Athos, 2), Paris ²1988.

Documents Lavra, eds. P. Lemerle/A. Guillou/N. Svoronos/D. Papachryssanthou, *Actes de Lavra*, vol. 1: *Des origines à 1204* (Archives de l'Athos, 5), Paris 1970; vol. 2: *De 1204 à 1328* (Archives de l'Athos, 8), Paris 1977; vol. 3: *De 1329 à 1500* (Archives de l'Athos, 10), Paris 1979.

Documents Panteleemon, eds. P. Lemerle/G. Dagron/S. Ćirković, *Actes de Saint-Pantéléèmôn* (Archives de l'Athos, 12), Paris 1982.

Documents Patmos, ed. E. Vranussi, Βυζαντινὰ ἔγγραφα τῆς Μονῆς Πάτμου, vol. 1: Αὐτοκρατορικά, Athens 1980.

Documents Philotheou, eds. W. Regel/E. Kurtz/B. Korablev, *Actes de Philothée* (Actes de l'Athos, 6), Saint Petersburg 1913.

Documents Protaton, ed. D. Papachryssanthou, *Actes du Prôtaton* (Archives de l'Athos, 7), Paris 1975.

Documents Vatopedi, eds. J. Lefort/V. Kravari/Ch. Giros/K. Smyrlis, *Actes de Vatopédi*, vol. 2: *Des 1330 à 1376* (Archives de l'Athos, 22). Paris 2006.

Documents Zographou, eds. W. Regel/E. Kurtz/B. Korablev, *Actes de Zographou* (Actes de l'Athos, 4), Saint Petersburg 1907.

Dogmatic Monuments of the Orthodox Church, ed. I. Karmires, Τὰ δογματικὰ καὶ συμβολικὰ μνημεῖα τῆς Ὀρθοδόξου Καθολικῆς Ἐκκλησίας, 2 vols, Athens ²1960 [repr. Graz 1968].

Dossier Lyon, eds. V. Laurent/J. Darrouzès, *Dossier grec de l'union de Lyon (1273–1277)* (Archives de l'Orient chrétien, 16), Paris 1976.

Ecumenical Councils, eds. G. Alberigo/A. Melloni et al., *Conciliorum oecumenicorum generaliumque decreta. Editio critica*, vol. 4/1: *The Great Councils of the Orthodox*

448 DE GREGORIO

Churches. Decisions and Synodika. From Constantinople 861 to Constantinople 1872 (Corpus Christianorum), Turnhout 2016.

George Akropolites, *History*, trans. R. Macrides, *George Akropolites, the History. Introduction, Translation and Commentary*, Oxford 2007.

George Pachymeres, *History*, ed. A. Failler, *Georges Pachymérès, Relations historiques* (Corpus Fontium Historiae Byzantinae, 24), 5 vols., Paris 1984–2000.

George/Demetrios Tornikes, *Letters and Orations*, ed. J. Darrouzès, *Georges et Dèmètrios Tornikès. Lettres et discours*, Paris 1970.

Gregory of Cyprus, *Letters*, ed. S. Eustratiades, *Γρηγορίου Κυπρίου οἰκουμενικοῦ Πατριάρχου ἐπιστολαὶ καὶ μῦθοι*, Alexandria 1910.

John VI Kantakouzenos, *History*, ed. L. Schopen, *Ioannis Cantacuzeni Eximperatoris Historiarum libri IV, Graece et Latine*, (Corpus Scriptorum Historiae Byzantinae, 41), 3 vols., Bonn 1828–32.

Leo VI the Wise, *Book of the Eparch*, ed. J. Koder, *Das Eparchenbuch Leons des Weisen* (Corpus Fontium Historiae Byzantinae, 33), Vienna 1991.

Michael Psellos, *Orations*, ed. G.T. Dennis, *Michaelis Pselli Orationes forenses et acta* (Bibliotheca Scriptorum Graecorum et Romanorum Teubneriana), Stuttgart/ Leipzig 1994.

Nikephoros Gregoras, *History*, eds. L. Schopen/I. Bekker, *Nicephori Gregorae Byzantina Historia, Graece et Latine* (Corpus Scriptorum Historiae Byzantinae, 19), 3 vols., Bonn 1829–55.

Nikephoros Gregoras, *History*, German trans. J.L. van Dieten, *Rhomäische Geschichte. Historia Rhomaike*, (Bibliothek der griechischen Literatur, 4), 6 vols., Stuttgart 1973–2003.

Nikephoros Gregoras, *Opuscules*, ed. P.L.M. Leone, "Nicephori Gregorae Opuscula nunc primum edita", *Annali della Facoltà di Lettere e Filosofia dell'Università di Macerata* 3–4 (1970/71), 729–82.

Patriarchal Register, eds. H. Hunger/O. Kresten [vol. 2: H. Hunger/O. Kresten/ E. Kislinger/C. Cupane; vol. 3: J. Koder/M. Hinterberger/O. Kresten; Indices: C. Cupane/E. Schiffer], *Das Register des Patriarchats von Konstantinopel*, vol. 1: *Edition und Übersetzung der Urkunden aus den Jahren 1315–1331*; vol. 2: *Edition und Übersetzung der Urkunden aus den Jahren 1337–1350* [+ *Indices zu den Urkunden aus den Jahren 1315–1350*]; vol. 3: *Edition und Übersetzung der Urkunden aus den Jahren 1350–1363* (Corpus Fontium Historiae Byzantinae, 19/1–3), Vienna 1981, 1995, 2001; vols., 4 (*Edition und Übersetzung der Urkunden aus den Jahren 1364–1376*) and 5 (*Edition und Übersetzung der Urkunden aus den Jahren 1379–1390*) are announced as forthcoming.

WORKING IN THE IMPERIAL AND PATRIARCHAL CHANCERIES 449

Philotheos Kokkinos, *First Antirrhetic against Nikephoros Gregoras*, ed. D.B. Kaimakes, Φιλοθέου Κοκκίνου δογματικὰ ἔργα, vol. 1 (Θεσσαλονικεῖς Βυζαντινοὶ Συγγραφεῖς, 3), Thessaloniki 1983, pp. 25–43.

Pseudo-Kodinos, *On the offices*, ed. & French trans. J. Verpeaux, *Pseudo-Kodinos, Traité des offices* (Le monde byzantin, 1), Paris 1966; ed. & English trans. R. Macrides/ J.A. Munitiz/D. Angelov, *Pseudo-Kodinos and the Constantinopolitan Court: Offices and Ceremonies* (Birmingham Byzantine and Ottoman Studies, 15), Farnham 2013.

Theodore Metochites, *Orations*, eds. I. Polemis/E. Kaltsogianni, *Theodorus Metochites, Orationes* (Bibliotheca Scriptorum Graecorum et Romanorum Teubneriana, 2031), Berlin/Boston 2019.

Theodore Skoutariotes, *Chronicle*, ed. R. Tocci, *Theodori Scutariotae Chronica* (Corpus Fontium Historiae Byzantinae, 46), Berlin/Boston 2015.

Secondary Literature

Acerbi, F./D. Bianconi, "L'*Organon* a fisarmonica di Giovanni Cortasmeno", *Segno e testo* 18 (2020), 223–82.

Atsalos, B./N. Tsironi (eds.), *Πρακτικά του ΣΤ΄ Διεθνούς Συμποσίου Ελληνικής Παλαιογραφίας (Δράμα, 21–27 Σεπτεμβρίου 2003)* (Βιβλιοαμφιάστης – Παράρτημα, 1), Athens 2008 [2009].

Beck, H.-G., "Der byzantinische Ministerpräsident", *Byzantinische Zeitschrift* 48 (1955), 309–38.

Berger, A./S. Mariev/G. Prinzing/A. Riehle (eds.), *Koinotaton Doron. Das späte Byzanz zwischen Machtlosigkeit und kultureller Blüte (1204–1461)* (Byzantinisches Archiv, 31), Berlin/Boston 2016.

Beyer, H.-V., "Eine Chronologie der Lebensgeschichte des Nikephoros Gregoras", *Jahrbuch der Österreichischen Byzantinistik* 27 (1978), 127–55.

Bianconi, D., "I libri di Niceforo Gregora. Un aggiornamento", in D'Agostino/Pieralli (eds.), *Φιλόδωρος εὐμενείας*, pp. 29–61.

Bianconi, D., "Il Laur. Plut. 28.26 ovvero la storia di Bisanzio nella storia di un codice," in M. D'Agostino/P. Degni (eds.), *Alethes philia. Studi in onore di Giancarlo Prato*, (Collectanea, 23), 2 vols., Spoleto 2010, vol. 1, pp. 39–63.

Bianconi, D., "La biblioteca di Cora tra Massimo Planude e Niceforo Gregora. Una questione di mani", *Segno e testo* 3 (2005), 391–438.

Bianconi, D., "Sui copisti del Platone Laur. Plut. 59.1 e su altri scribi d'età paleologa. Tra paleografia e prosopografia", in Id./L. Del Corso (eds.), *Oltre la scrittura. Variazioni sul tema per Guglielmo Cavallo* (Dossiers byzantins, 8), Paris 2008, pp. 253–88.

Blanchet, M.-H./M.-H. Congourdeau/D.I. Mureşan (eds.), *Le patriarcat œcuménique de Constantinople et Byzance hors frontières (1204–1586). Actes de la table ronde*

450   DE GREGORIO

organisée dans le cadre du 22e Congrès International des Études Byzantines, Sofia, 22–27 août 2011 (Dossiers byzantins, 15), Paris 2014.

Browning, R., *Notes on Byzantine Prooimia* (Wiener Byzantinistische Studien, 1/Suppl.), Vienna 1966.

Burgmann, L., "Chrysobull gleich Privileg? Beobachtungen zur Funktion einer byzantinischen Urkundenform", in B. Dölemeyer/H. Mohnhaupt (eds.), *Das Privileg im europäischen Vergleich*, vol. 1 (Ius commune. Veröffentlichungen des Max-Planck-Instituts für Europäische Rechtsgeschichte. Sonderhefte. Studien zur Europäischen Rechtsgeschichte, 93), Frankfurt am Main 1997, pp. 69–92.

Burgmann, L./M.T. Fögen/A. Schminck/D. Simon, *Repertorium der Handschriften des byzantinischen Rechts, part 1: Die Handschriften des weltlichen Rechts (Nr. 1–327)* (Forschungen zur byzantinischen Rechtsgeschichte, 20), Frankfurt am Main 1995.

Canart, P./G. Prato, "Les recueils organisés par Jean Chortasménos et le problème de ses autographes", in Hunger (ed.), *Studien zum Patriarchatsregister von Konstantinopel*, vol. 1, pp. 115–78.

Constantinides, C.N., "Byzantine Scholars and the Union of Lyons (1274)", in R. Beaton/C. Roueché (eds.), *The Making of Byzantine History. Studies dedicated to Donald M. Nicol* (Centre for Hellenic Studies, King's College London, Publications, 1), Aldershot 1993, pp. 86–93.

D'Agostino, M./L. Pieralli (eds.), *Φιλόδωρος εὐμενείας. Miscellanea di studi in ricordo di Mons. Paul Canart* (Littera Antiqua 21), Città del Vaticano 2021.

D'Aiuto, F., "Note ai manoscritti del Menologio Imperiale. I. Un monogramma nel Menologio di Mosca", *Rivista di Studi Bizantini e Neoellenici* N. S. 39 (2002), 189–228.

Darrouzès, J., *Le registre synodal du patriarcat byzantin au XIVe siècle. Étude paléographique et diplomatique* (Archives de l'Orient chrétien, 12), Paris 1971.

Darrouzès, J., *Les regestes des actes du patriarcat de Constantinople I. Les actes des patriarches*, vol. 5: *Les regestes de 1310 à 1376*, Paris 1977.

Darrouzès, J., *Recherches sur les ὀφφίκια de l'Église byzantine* (Archives de l'Orient chretien, 11), Paris 1970.

De Gregorio, G., "Epigrammi e documenti. Poesia come fonte per la storia di chiese e monasteri bizantini", in C. Gastgeber/O. Kresten (eds.), *Sylloge Diplomatico-Palaeographica. Studien zur byzantinischen Diplomatik und Paläographie I* (Österreichische Akademie der Wissenschaften, philosophisch-historische Klasse, Denkschriften, 392, Veröffentlichungen zur Byzanzforschung, 19), Vienna 2010, pp. 9–134.

De Gregorio, G., "Filone Alessandrino tra Massimo Planude e Giorgio Bullotes. A proposito dei codici Vindob. Suppl. gr. 50, Vat. Urb. gr. 125 e Laur. Plut. 10, 23", in C. Brockmann/D. Deckers/L. Koch/S. Valente (eds.), *Handschriften- und Textforschung heute. Festschrift zu Ehren von Dieter Harlfinger* (Serta Graeca, 30), Wiesbaden 2014, pp. 177–230.

De Gregorio, G., "Καλλιγραφεῖν/ταχυγραφεῖν. Qualche riflessione sull'educazione grafica di scribi bizantini", in E. Condello/Id. (eds.), *Scribi e colofoni. Le sottoscrizioni di copisti dalle origini all'avvento della stampa. Atti del seminario di Erice – X Colloquio del Comité international de paléographie latine (23–28 ottobre 1993)* (Biblioteca del "Centro per il collegamento degli studi medievali e umanistici in Umbria", 14), Spoleto 1995, pp. 423–48.

De Gregorio, G., "La scrittura greca di età paleologa (secoli XIII–XIV). Un panorama", in F. Magistrale (ed.), *Scrittura memoria degli uomini. In ricordo di Giuliana Cannataro (Lezioni tenute presso la Facoltà di Lettere e Filosofia dell'Università degli Studi, Bari, 3 maggio 2004)*, Bari 2006, pp. 81–138.

De Gregorio, G., "Un'aggiunta su copisti greci del secolo XIV: a proposito di Giovanni Duca Malace, collaboratore di Giorgio Galesiota nell'*Athen. EBE 2*", *Nea Rhome* 16 (2019), 161–276.

De Gregorio, G., "Una lista di commemorazioni di defunti dalla Costantinopoli della prima età paleologa. Note storiche e prosopografiche sul *Vat. Ross. 169*", *Rivista di Studi Bizantini e Neoellenici* N. S. 38 (2001), 103–94.

Dold, A., *Das Geheimnis einer byzantinischen Staatsurkunde aus dem Jahre 1351*, Beuron in Hohenzollern 1958.

Dölger, F., *Byzantinische Diplomatik. 20 Aufsätze zum Urkundenwesen der Byzantiner*, Ettal 1956.

Dölger, F., "Der Kodikellos des Christodulos in Palermo. Ein bisher unerkannter Typus der byzantinischen Kaiserurkunden", in *Archiv für Urkundenforschung* 11 (1929), 1–65 (repr. in id., *Byzantinische Diplomatik*, pp. 1–74).

Dölger, F., "Die Kaiserurkunde der Byzantiner als Ausdruck ihrer politischen Anschauungen", *Historische Zeitschrift* 159 (1938/1939), 229–50 (repr. in id., *Byzanz und die europäische Staatenwelt. Ausgewählte Vorträge und Aufsätze*, Ettal 1953 [Darmstadt ²1964], pp. 9–33).

Dölger, F., "Ein byzantinisches Staatsdokument in der Universitätsbibliothek Basel: Ein Fragment des Tomos des Jahres 1351", *Historisches Jahrbuch* 72 (1953), 205–21 (repr. in id., *Byzantinische Diplomatik*, pp. 245–61, pls. XXIV–XXV).

Dölger, F., *Regesten der Kaiserurkunden des oströmischen Reiches von 565–1453*, vol. 4: *Regesten von 1282–1341*, Munich/Berlin 1960.

Dölger, F./J. Karayannopulos, *Byzantinische Urkundenlehre 1. Die Kaiserurkunden.* (Handbuch der Altertumswissenschaft, XII.3.1.1.), Munich 1968.

Dölger, F./P. Wirth, *Regesten der Kaiserurkunden des oströmischen Reiches von 565–1453*, vol. 3: *Regesten von 1204–1282*, Munich ²1977.

Dölger, F./P. Wirth, *Regesten der Kaiserurkunden des oströmischen Reiches von 565–1453*, vol. 5: *Regesten von 1341–1453*, Munich/Berlin 1965.

Estangüi Gómez, R., "Pour une étude prosopographique des fonctionnaires de la chancellerie patriarcale: la carrière du secrétaire Iôannes Chrysoképhalos Holobôlos", in O. Delouis/K. Smyrlis (eds.), *Lire les Archives de l'Athos. Actes du colloque réuni à Athènes du 18 au 20 novembre 2015 à l'occasion des 70 ans de la collection refondée par Paul Lemerle* (Travaux et mémoires, 23/2), Paris 2019, pp. 111–84.

Failler, A., "Chronologie et composition dans l'Histoire de Georges Pachymère [III] (livres VII–XIII)", *Revue des Études Byzantines* 48 (1990), 5–87.

Fisher, E.A., "Manuel Holobolos and the Role of Bilinguals in Relations between the West and Byzantium", in A. Speer/P. Steinkrüger (eds.), *Knotenpunkt Byzanz. Wissensformen und kulturelle Wechselbeziehungen* (Miscellanea Mediaevalia, 36), Berlin/Boston 2012, pp. 210–22.

Gamillscheg, E., "Johannes Chortasmenos als Restaurator des Wiener Dioskurides", *Biblos* 55/2 (2006), 35–40.

Gastgeber, C., "Changes in Documents of the Byzantine Chancery in contact with the West (Michael VIII and Andronikos II Palaiologos). Language, Material, and Address", in N. Drocourt/É. Malamut (eds.), *La diplomatie byzantine, de l'Empire romain aux confins de l'Europe (Vᵉ–XVᵉ s.). Actes de la Table-Ronde « Les relations diplomatiques byzantines (Vᵉ–XVᵉ siècle): Permanences et/ou changements », XXIIIᵉ Congrès International des Études byzantines – Belgrade, Août 2016* (The Medieval Mediterranean, 123), Leiden/Boston 2020, pp. 175–272.

Gastgeber, C., "Das Formular der Patriarchatskanzlei", in Gastgeber/Mitsiou/Preiser-Kapeller/Zervan (eds.), *The Patriarchate*, pp. 197–302.

Gastgeber, C., "Das Patriarchatsregister als Spiegel der Religionspolitik: Registerführung unter dem Palamiten Isidoros I. (1347–1350)", in Blanchet/Congourdeau/Mureşan (eds.), *Le patriarcat œcuménique de Constantinople et Byzance hors frontières (1204–1586)*, pp. 99–131.

Gastgeber, C., "Diplomatics of the Patriarchate of Constantinople: The State of Research on Byzantine Documents of the Patriarchs of Constantinople", in Id./E. Mitsiou/J. Preiser-Kapeller/V. Zervan (eds.), *A Companion to the Patriarchate of Constantinople* (Brill's Companions to the Byzantine World, 9), Leiden/Boston 2021, pp. 246–85.

Gastgeber, C., "Rhetorik in der Patriarchatskanzlei von Konstantinopel", in Gastgeber/Mitsiou/Preiser-Kapeller (eds.), *The Register*, pp. 175–97.

Gastgeber, C./E. Mitsiou/J. Preiser-Kapeller (eds.), *The Register of the Patriarchate of Constantinople. An Essential Source for the History and Church of Late Byzantium. Proceedings of the International Symposium, Vienna, 5th–9th May 2009* (Österreichische Akademie der Wissenschaften, philosophisch-historische Klasse, Denkschriften, 457. Veröffentlichungen zur Byzanzforschung, 32), Vienna 2013.

Gastgeber, C./E. Mitsiou/J. Preiser-Kapeller/V. Zervan (eds.), *The Patriarchate of Constantinople in Context and Comparison. Proceedings of the International Conference Vienna, September 12th–15th 2012. In memoriam Konstantinos Pitsakis (1944–2012) and Andreas Schminck (1947–2015)* (Österreichische Akademie der Wissenschaften, philosophisch-historische Klasse, Denkschriften, 502. Veröffentlichungen zur Byzanzforschung, 41), Vienna 2017.

Guilland, R., "Les logothètes. Études sur l'histoire administrative de l'Empire byzantin", *Revue des Études Byzantines* 29 (1971), 5–115.

Harlfinger, D., "Autographa aus der Palaiologenzeit", in Seibt (ed.), *Geschichte und Kultur der Palaiologenzeit*, pp. 43–50.

Harlfinger, D./M. Sicherl et al., *Griechische Handschriften und Aldinen. Eine Ausstellung anläßlich der XV. Tagung der Mommsen-Gesellschaft in der Herzog August Bibliothek Wolfenbüttel* (Ausstellungskataloge der Herzog August Bibliothek, 24), Wolfenbüttel-Braunschweig 1978.

Harris, J., "The Patriarch of Constantinople and the last Days of Byzantium", in Gastgeber/Mitsiou/Preiser-Kapeller/Zervan (eds.), *The Patriarchate*, pp. 9–16.

Hieronymus, F., *Griechischer Geist aus Basler Pressen* (Publikationen der Universitätsbibliothek Basel, 15), Basel 1992.

Hunger, H., "Amtsmißbrauch im Patriarchat von Konstantinopel um die Mitte des 14. Jahrhunderts: Der Megas Chartophylax Ioannes Amparis", *Illinois Classical Studies* 18 (1993), 335–44.

Hunger, H., "Das Patriarchatsregister von Konstantinopel als Spiegel byzantinischer Verhältnisse im 14. Jahrhundert", *Anzeiger der philosophisch-historischen Klasse der Österreichischen Akademie der Wissenschaften* 115 (1978), 117–36.

Hunger, H., "Die Exarchenlisten des Patriarchen Kallistos I. im Patriarchatsregister von Konstantinopel", in J. Chrysostomides (ed.), Καθηγήτρια. *Essays presented to Joan Hussey for her 80th Birthday*, Camberley/Surrey 1988, pp. 431–80.

Hunger, H., *Johannes Chortasmenos (ca. 1370–ca. 1436/37). Briefe, Gedichte und kleine Schriften. Einleitung, Regesten, Prosopographie, Text* (Wiener Byzantinistische Studien, 7), Vienna 1969.

Hunger, H., *Prooimion. Elemente der byzantinischen Kaiseridee in den Arengen der Urkunden* (Wiener Byzantinistische Studien, 1), Vienna 1964.

Hunger, H., "Schriftästhetik in den drei originalen kaiserlichen Auslandsschreiben der Komnenenzeit", *Römische Historische Mitteilungen* 40 (1998), 187–96.

Hunger, H. (ed.), *Studien zum Patriarchatsregister von Konstantinopel*, 2 vols., Vienna 1981–97.

Hunger, H., "Zum Stil und zur Sprache des Patriarchatsregisters von Konstantinopel. Rhetorik im Dienste der orthodoxen Hierarchie", in id. (ed.), *Studien zum Patriarchatsregister von Konstantinopel*, vol. 1, pp. 11–60.

Hunger, H., "Zur scheinbaren Nonchalance der Kanzleisprache des Patriarchatsregisters. Verschleierung, Absicherung und Ironie in Urkunden des Patriarchats von Konstantinopel", in id. (ed.), *Studien zum Patriarchatsregisters von Konstantinopel*, vol. 2, pp. 11–43.

Hunger, H./I. Ševčenko, *Des Nikephoros Blemmydes Βασιλικὸς Ἀνδριάς und dessen Metaphrase von Georgios Galesiotes und Georgios Oinaiotes. Ein weiterer Beitrag zum Verständnis der byzantinischen Schrift-Koine* (Wiener Byzantinistische Studien, 18), Vienna 1986.

Hutter, I., "Schreiber und Maler der Palaiologenzeit in Konstantinopel", in Atsalos/Tsironi (eds.), *Πρακτικά*, pp. 159–90.

Karayannopulos, J., "Zu den «διά-Vermerken» der byzantinischen Kaiserurkunden", in G. De Gregorio/O. Kresten (eds.), *Documenti medievali greci e latini. Studi comparativi, Atti del seminario di Erice (23–29 ottobre 1995)* (Incontri di studio, 1), Spoleto 1998, pp. 203–32.

Kourousis, S.I., "Ὁ λόγιος οἰκουμενικὸς πατριάρχης Ἰωάννης ΙΓ΄ ὁ Γλυκύς (Συναγωγὴ εἰδήσεων καὶ ἀνέκδοτα αὐτοῦ ἔργα)", *Ἐπετηρὶς Ἑταιρείας Βυζαντινῶν Σπουδῶν* 41 (1974), 297–405.

Kresten, O., "Der sogenannte „Absetzungsvermerk" des Patriarchen Ioannes XIV. Kalekas im Patriarchatsregister von Konstantinopel (Cod. Vind. hist. gr. 47, f. 116v)", in W. Hörandner/J. Koder/Id./E. Trapp (eds.), *Βυζάντιος. Festschrift für Herbert Hunger zum 70. Geburtstag*, Vienna 1984, pp. 213–19.

Kresten, O., "Fünf nachgezeichnete Metropolitenunterschriften aus der ersten Amtsperiode des Patriarchen Philotheos Kokkinos im Patriarchatsregister von Konstantinopel", *Österreichische Osthefte* 33 (1991), 167–200.

Kresten, O., "Μηνολόγημα. Anmerkungen zu einem byzantinischen Unterfertigungstyp", *Mitteilungen des Instituts für Österreichische Geschichtsforschung* 102 (1994), 1–52.

Kresten, O., "Zu Darrouzès, Regest *N. 2041. Beobachtungen zum Beginn des ersten Bandes des Patriarchatsregisters von Konstantinopel (Cod. Vind. hist. gr. 47) und zu dessen Abschrift im Cod. Vat. Urb. gr. 80", in Hunger (ed.), *Studien zum Patriarchatsregister von Konstantinopel*, vol. 1, pp. 85–113.

Kresten, O., "Zur Datierung, zum Schreiber und zum politischen Hintergrund dreier Urkunden des Kaisers Andronikos III. Palaiologos für das Serbenkloster Chilandariu", *Anzeiger der philosophisch-historischen Klasse der Österreichischen Akademie der Wissenschaften* 130 (1993), 67–99.

Laiou, A.E., "The Correspondence of Gregorios Kyprios as a Source for the History of Social and Political Behaviour in Byzantium or, on Government by Rhetoric", in Seibt (ed.), *Geschichte und Kultur der Palaiologenzeit*, pp. 91–108.

Lamberz, E., "Beobachtungen zu den patristischen Corpora in der Schenkung des Johannes Kantakuzenos an das Kloster Vatopedi und ihren Vorlagen", in Berger/Mariev/Prinzing/Riehle (eds.), *Koinotaton Doron*, pp. 87–99.

Lamberz, E., "Das Geschenk des Kaisers Manuel II. an das Kloster Saint-Denis und der 'Metochitesschreiber' Michael Klostomalles", in B. Borkopp/T. Steppan (eds.), *Λιθόστρωτον. Studien zur byzantinischen Kunst und Geschichte. Festschrift für Marcell Restle*, Stuttgart 2000, pp. 155–65.

Lamberz, E., "Georgios Bullotes, Michael Klostomalles und die byzantinische Kaiserkanzlei unter Andronikos II. und Andronikos III. in den Jahren 1298–1329", in B. Mondrain (ed.), *Lire et écrire à Byzance. XXᵉ Congrès International des Études Byzantines, 19–25 août 2001. [Actes de la] Table ronde*, (Collège de France – CNRS. Centre de recherche d'histoire et civilisation de Byzance. Monographies, 19), Paris 2006, pp. 33–64.

Lamberz, E., "Johannes Kantakuzenos und die Produktion von Luxushandschriften in Konstantinopel in der frühen Palaiologenzeit", in Atsalos/Tsironi (eds.), *Πρακτικά*, pp. 133–57.

Laurent, V., *Les regestes des actes du patriarcat de Constantinople, I. Les actes des patriarches*, vol. 4: *Les regestes de 1208 à 1309*, Paris 1971.

Laurent, V., "Les signataires du second concile des Blakhernes (Été 1285)", *Échos d'Orient* 26 (1927), 129–49.

Mazal, O., *Die Prooimien der byzantinischen Patriarchenurkunden* (Byzantina Vindobonensia, 7), Vienna 1974.

Moniou, D.I., *Γεώργιος Μοσχάμπαρ, ἕνας ἀνθενωτικὸς θεολόγος τῆς πρώιμης Παλαιολόγειας περιόδου. Βίος καὶ ἔργο*, Athens 2011.

Mošin, V.A./S.M. Traljić, *Vodeni znakovi XIII. i XIV. vijeka* [= *Filigranes des XIIIᵉ et XIVᵉ ss.*], I–II, Zagreb 1957.

Müller, A., "Weder Klostomalles noch Babiskomites: Beobachtungen zur Schreiberhand von DR 2684 und DR 2775", in Berger/Mariev/Prinzing/Riehle (eds.), *Koinotaton Doron*, pp. 115–23.

Oikonomidès, N., "La chancellerie impériale de Byzance du 13ᵉ au 15ᵉ siècle", *Revue des Études Byzantines* 43 (1985), 167–95.

Papadakis, A., *Crisis in Byzantium. The* Filioque *Controversy in the Patriarchate of Gregory II of Cyprus (1283–1289)*, Crestwood/NY ²1997.

Papatriantaphyllou-Theodoridi, N., *Ἡ χειρόγραφη παράδοση τῶν ἔργων τοῦ Νικηφόρου Χούμνου (1250/55–1327)* (Ἀριστοτέλειο Πανεπιστήμιο Θεσσαλονίκης. Ἐπιστημονικὴ Ἐπετηρίδα τῆς Φιλοσοφικῆς Σχολῆς, Παρ. 32), Thessaloniki 1984.

Pérez Martín, I., "El «estilo Hodegos» y su proyección en las escrituras constantinopolitanas", in Atsalos/Tsironi (eds.), *Πρακτικά*, pp. 71–130.

Pérez Martín, I., *El patriarca Gregorio de Chipre (ca. 1240–1290) y la transmisión de los textos clásicos en Bizancio* (Nueva Roma, 1), Madrid 1996.

Pieralli, L., "Gli originali copiati da due notai attivi presso la cancelleria patriarcale costantinopolitana del XIV sec.: Giovanni Holobolos ed il copista C del patriarca Matteo", in D'Agostino/Id. (eds.), *Φιλόδωρος εὐμενείας*, pp. 591–614.

Pieralli, L., "I «protocolli» delle riunioni sinodali (*Regestes*, no 1549, 1567, 3424 [= 2352a])", in Blanchet/Congourdeau/Mureşan (eds.), *Le patriarcat œcuménique de Constantinople et Byzance hors frontières (1204–1586)*, pp. 133–57.

Pieralli, L., *La corrispondenza diplomatica dell'imperatore bizantino con le potenze estere nel XIII secolo (1204–1282). Studio storico-diplomatistico ed edizione critica* (Collectanea Archivi Vaticani, 54), Vatican City 2006.

Pieralli, L., "Le scritture dei documenti imperiali del XIII secolo", in G. Prato (ed.), *I manoscritti greci tra riflessione e dibattito. Atti del V Colloquio internazionale di Paleografia greca (Cremona, 4–10 ottobre 1998)* (Papyrologica Florentina, 31), Florence 2000, vol. 1, pp. 273–93.

Pieralli, L., "Un imperatore di Bisanzio a Roma: la professione di fede di Giovanni V Paleologo", in M.-H. Blanchet/F. Gabriel (eds.), *L'Union à l'épreuve du formulaire. Professions de foi entre Églises d'Orient et d'Occident (XIIIᵉ–XVIIIᵉ s.)* (Collège de France – CNRS. Centre de recherche d'histoire et civilisation de Byzance. Monographies, 51), Leuven/Paris/Bristol 2016, pp. 97–144.

Prato, G., "I manoscritti greci dei secoli XIII e XIV: note paleografiche", in D. Harlfinger/Id. (eds.), *Paleografia e codicologia greca. Atti del II Colloquio internazionale (Berlino – Wolfenbüttel, 17–21 ottobre 1983)* (Biblioteca di Scrittura e Civiltà, 3), Alessandria 1991, pp. 131–49.

Prinzing, G., "Konvergenz und Divergenz zwischen dem Patriarchatsregister und den *Ponemata Diaphora* des Demetrios Chomatenos von Achrida/Ohrid", in Gastgeber/Mitsiou/Preiser-Kapeller (eds.), *The Register*, pp. 9–32.

Rigo, A., "Il Monte Athos e la controversia palamitica dal Concilio del 1351 al *Tomo* sinodale del 1368. Giacomo Trikanas, Procoro Cidone e Filoteo Kokkinos", in id. (ed.), *Gregorio Palamas e oltre. Studi e documenti sulle controversie teologiche del XIV secolo bizantino* (Orientalia Venetiana, 16), Florence 2004, pp. 1–177.

Rigo, A., *1347: Isidoro patriarca di Costantinopoli e il breve sogno dell'inizio di una nuova epoca* (Wiener Byzantinistische Studien, 31), Vienna 2020.

Salomon, R.G., "A Papyrus from Constantinople (Hamburg Inv. No. 410)", *The Journal of Egyptian Archaeology* 34 (1948), 98–108 (with pl. XVIII).

Samara, D., *Θεόδωρος Μουζάλων. Ἡ ζωὴ καὶ τὸ συγγραφικὸ ἔργο ἑνὸς λογίου τοῦ 13ου αἰώνα* (Βυζαντινὰ Κείμενα καὶ Μελέτες, 64), Thessaloniki 2018.

Samorì, F., "A Self-Portrait of an Unyielding Unionist: The *Historia dogmatica* of George Metochites and the Fight for Church Unity", *Parekbolai* 12 (2022), 67–103.

Samorì, F., "I codici autografi del diacono Giorgio Metochites e la tradizione manoscritta delle sue opere", *Revue des Études Byzantines* 80 (2022), 5–68.

Schminck, A., "Wörtliche Zitate des weltlichen und kirchlichen Rechts im Register des Patriarchats von Konstantinopel", in Gastgeber/Mitsiou/Preiser-Kapeller (eds.), *The Register*, pp. 235–43.

Seibt, W. (ed.), *Geschichte und Kultur der Palaiologenzeit. Referate des Internationalen Symposions zu Ehren von Herbert Hunger (Wien, 30. November bis 3. Dezember 1994)* (Österreichische Akademie der Wissenschaften, philosophisch-historische Klasse,

Denkschriften, 241. Veröffentlichungen der Kommission für Byzantinistik, 8), Vienna 1996.

Ševčenko, I., *La vie intellectuelle et politique à Byzance sous les premiers Paléologues: Études sur la polémique entre Théodore Métochite et Nicéphore Choumnos* (Corpus Bruxellense Historiae Byzantinae. Subsidia, 3), Brussels 1962.

Ševčenko, I. "Some Autographs of Nicephorus Gregoras", *Zbornik Radova Vizantološkog Instituta* 8/2 (1964), 435–50 (repr. in id., *Society and Intellectual Life in Late Byzantium* [Variorum Collected Studies Series, 137], London 1981, no. XII).

Ševčenko, I. "Theodore Metochites, the Chora and the Intellectual Trends of His Time", in P.A. Underwood (ed.), *The Kariye Djami*, vol. 4: *Studies in the Art of the Kariye Djami and Its Intellectual Background* (Bollingen Series, 70), Princeton 1975, pp. 17–91.

Silvano, L., "L'origine dello scisma in un dialogo di Giorgio Moschampar", *Porphyra* 6, 13/2 (2009), 13–23.

Silvano, L., "Per l'edizione della «Disputa tra un ortodosso e un latinofrone seguace di Becco sulla processione dello Spirito Santo» di Giorgio Moschampar. Con un inedito di Bonaventura Vulcanius", *Medioevo greco* 14 (2014), 229–65.

Smyrlis, K., "Priesthood and Empire: Ecclesiastical Wealth and Privilege under the early Palaiologoi", in Gastgeber/Mitsiou/Preiser-Kapeller/Zervan (eds.), *The Patriarchate*, pp. 95–103.

Stavrou, M., "Une réévaluation du *Tomos* du Deuxième Concile des Blachernes (1285): commentaire, tradition textuelle, édition critique et traduction", in Gastgeber/Mitsiou/Preiser-Kapeller/Zervan (eds.), *The Patriarchate*, pp. 47–93.

Talbot, A.-M., "The Restoration of Constantinople under Michael VIII", *Dumbarton Oaks Papers* 47 (1993), 243–61.

Thomas, J./A. Constantinides-Hero/G. Constable (eds.), *Byzantine Monastic Foundation Documents. A Complete Translation of the Surviving Founders' Typika and Testaments*, (Dumbarton Oaks Studies, 35/1–5), 5 vols., Washington DC 2000.

Trapp, E. (ed.), *Lexikon zur byzantinischen Gräzität besonders des 9.–12. Jahrhunderts* (Veröffentlichungen der Kommission für Byzantinistik, VI/1–8), 8 vols., Vienna 1994–2017.

Verpeaux, J., "Le *cursus honorum* de Théodore Métochite", *Revue des Études Byzantines* 18 (1960), 195–98.

Verpeaux, J., *Nicéphore Choumnos, homme d'état et humaniste (ca 1250/1255–1327)*, Paris 1959.

Zorzi, N., "Lettori bizantini della «Bibliotheca» di Fozio: *marginalia* del Marc. gr. 450", *Syculorum Gymnasium* N. S. 57 (2004) (= *Atti del VI Congresso Nazionale dell'Associazione Italiana di Studi Bizantini*), 829–44.

CHAPTER 12

Public and Private Libraries in Byzantium

Ilias Taxidis

The sack of Constantinople following the Crusader conquest of the city in 1204 was so ruthless that what Michael VIII Palaiologos recaptured in 1261 was a virtual wasteland,[1] its religious and secular foundations, among them libraries, dissolved and stripped of their treasures, which had either been destroyed or shipped to the West.

1   Imperial Library

One of the first concerns of the Byzantines once Constantinople had been retaken was to rebuild the ruined institutions and monasteries and restore higher education, which meant re-establishing and re-stocking the libraries with old manuscripts and new copies of classical texts.[2] These efforts were

---

1   See Nikephoros Gregoras, *Roman History*, eds. Schopen/Bekker, vol. 1, p. 87, line 23–p. 88, line 9. See also Kidonopoulos, *Bauten in Konstantinopel*, pp. XI and 227–30 and Fryde, *Palaeologean Renaissance*, pp. 3–5.

2   For the public and private libraries in Byzantium from the recapture of Constantinople (1261) to the Fall of the city (1453), see Staikos, *Ιστορία της βιβλιοθήκης*, pp. 421–65. For the efforts to obtain mansuscripts, see Maximos Planoudes, *Letters*, no. 67, ed. Leone, p. 101, lines 1–2: πρὸς τὴν βασιλίδα πόλιν ὁθενδήποτε μετηνέχθησαν αἱ βίβλοι (books were brought to Constantinople from anyplace). See also Browning, "Recentiores non deteriores", p. 12; Constantinides, "The Scholars and their Books", p. 13 and Constantinides, *Higher Education*, p. 134. When manuscripts were in poor condition every effort was made to restore and correct them, see e.g. Maximos Planoudes, *Letters*, no. 67, ed. Leone, p. 99, lines 26–29: ἐπανήκει νῦν ἐκ τῶν πάλαι ῥυτίδων ἡβῶσα. τὰ μὲν ἔξωθεν ὄφιν ἂν εἴποι τις τὴν παλαιὰν ἀποξυσάμενον λεβηρίδα, τὰ δ' ἐντός, οἵαν ἂν ἴδοιμεν οἰκίας ἐκ μακροῦ πεπονηκυίας ἐπισκευὴν καὶ ἀνάκτησιν [(the book) was reborn from its old wrinkles. One might say that it was externally transformed as the snake changes its old skin, and internally repaired and renovated just like a timeworn residence], and if they could not be copied, to bind them with others; see in this regard Browning, "Recentiores non deteriores", p. 14. See also Manaphes, *Αἱ ἐν Κωνσταντινουπόλει βιβλιοθῆκαι*, pp. 53–54; Kotzabassi, "Kopieren und Exzerpieren", pp. 473–74, who observes that one factor in the great production of manuscripts in the Palaeologan period was the widespread use of paper, which was much less costly than parchment, and Mondrain, "Der Transfer griechischer Handschriften", pp. 109–22, who concludes that the period following the interlude of Frankish rule was generally much more favourable to the production of new codices than the time after the Fall of 1453.

© KONINKLIJKE BRILL NV, LEIDEN, 2023 | DOI:10.1163/9789004527089_014

PRIVATE AND PUBLIC LIBRARIES IN BYZANTIUM 459

advanced by the return of many men of letters from Nicaea and the creation of a new circle of scholars, initially around George Akropolites, and the interest of the Emperor Andronikos II Palaiologos in art and literature.

These efforts proved fruitful, judging by the testimony of the historian Doukas that in 1453, when Constantinople fell to the Turks, there were books beyond number in the city.[3] The imperial library, which after 1261 was housed in the Blachernae Palace, had apparently been restored to a least a degree of its old splendour, judging from the account of the Spanish traveller Pero Tafur, who was in Constantinople in 1437–38 and reported it to be a great hall with marble furniture and many extremely valuable manuscripts,[4] and the evidence of Constantine Laskaris, who stated that shortly after the Fall he found the entire works of Diodorus Siculus there.[5] Although we do not know how many volumes the imperial library contained or what they were, it must have been sufficiently well-furnished to meet the needs of those who used it.[6]

---

3   See Doukas, *History*, ed. Grecu, p. 393, lines 6–10: τὰς δὲ βίβλους ἁπάσας ὑπὲρ ἀριθμὸν ὑπερβαι-νούσας, ταῖς ἁμάξαις φορτηγώσαντες ἁπανταχοῦ ἐν τῇ ἀνατολῇ καὶ τῇ δύσει διέσπειραν. Δι᾽ ἑνὸς νομίσματος δέκα βίβλοι ἐπιπράσκοντο, Ἀριστοτελικοί, Πλατωνικοί, Θεολογικοὶ καὶ ἄλλο πᾶν εἶδος βίβλου. Εὐαγγέλια μετὰ κόσμου παντοίου ὑπὲρ μέτρον, ἀνασπῶντες τὸν χρυσὸν καὶ τὸν ἄργυρον, ἀλλ᾽ ἐπώλουν, ἀλλ᾽ ἔρριπτον [Innumerable books were loaded onto the wagons and hauled in all directions; they were dispersed throughout East and West. For a single gold coin ten books were sold – the works of Aristotle and Plato, books of theological content and on every subject. Gold and silver were pulled from the Evangelistaries which were adorned with many different jewels; some were sold and the rest were thrown away, see Magoulias, *Doukas*, p. 240 (XLII, 1)]. Kritoboulos gives a similar account, see Michael Kritoboulos, *History*, ed. Reinsch p. 73, lines 6–10. See also Manaphes, *Αἱ ἐν Κωνσταντινουπόλει βιβλιοθῆκαι*, p. 145 and Staikos, *Ἱστορία τῆς βιβλιοθήκης*, p. 451.

4   See Pero Tafur, *Adventures and travels*, ed. Jiménez de la Espada, p. 180, lines 20–28: *á la entrada del palaçio debaxo de unas cámaras está una lonja sobre mármoles, abierta, de arcos con poyos en torno bien enlosados é junto con ellos como mesas puestas de cabo á cabo sobre pilares baxos, ansí mesmo cubiertos de losas, en que están muchos libros é escrituras antiguas é estorias.* See also Wilson, "The Libraries", p. 54 (and n. 1) and Manaphes, *Αἱ ἐν Κωνσταντινουπόλει βιβλιοθῆκαι*, p. 60.

5   See Constantine Laskaris, *On Greek Writers from Sicily*, ed. in *Patrologia Graeca*, vol. 161, col. 918, lines 6–8: *Ego autem omnes ejus (Diodori) libros vidi in biblioteca imperatoris CPolitani*. See also Manaphes, *Αἱ ἐν Κωνσταντινουπόλει βιβλιοθῆκαι*, p. 60.

6   One of the manuscripts that we know for certain, from the annotation "ἐναπετέθη ἐν τῇ βασιλικῇ βιβλιοθήκῃ", belonged to the imperial library is the 1276 codex of theological texts now in Paris, Bibliothèque nationale de France, Par. gr. 1115, see Omont, *Inventaire*, vol. 1, p. 223. For J.A. Munitiz' detailed description of this codex, see Astruc/Astruc-Morize/Géhin/ Guérard/Hoffmann/ Mondrain/Munitiz, *Manuscrits grecs*, pp. 46–48. See also Alexakis, *Parisinus graecus 1115*, p. 46 and *infra* p. 479. For the imperial library, see Wendel, "Die erste kaiserliche Bibliothek", pp. 193–209; Wilson, "The Libraries", pp. 54–57 and Manaphes, *Αἱ ἐν Κωνσταντινουπόλει βιβλιοθῆκαι*, pp. 41–61 (esp. pp. 55–61, for the state of the library in the Palaeologan period).

460   TAXIDIS

2   The Patriarchal Library and the Library of Hagia Sophia

Very little solid information exists about the patriarchal library in Constantinople.[7] After 1261 the Patriarchate returned to its old seat in the Thomaite triclinium, next to Hagia Sophia,[8] and efforts were evidently made to reconstitute its library.

The chief source of information on the collection of books in the patriarchal library is, in Manaphes' view, the *Ecclesiastical History* composed by Nikephoros Kallistos Xanthopoulos and the historian's account in the preface of the books he used in writing it.[9] His statement, however, that he found everything he needed to write his *History* in Hagia Sophia,[10] casts doubt on the identification of his resource as the patriarchal library and consequently undermines Manaphes' surmise that it was indeed the patriarchal library and not that of Hagia Sophia.[11] Given, moreover, that the question of the sources used by Nikephoros has not yet been explored in depth, any attempt to reconstitute the content of the patriarchal library on the basis of the works he used in composing his *History* is unsafe.[12]

The so-called "Katholikon Museion" (or "Museion of the Xenon") must also have had a library, but information about it is scanty. We know that from the end of the 14th century and until the middle of the 15th the "Katholikon Museion" was associated with the Prodromos Petra Monastery and the Xenon of the Kral and operated as a school where Western scholars, particularly from

---

7   For the patriarchal library, see Wilson, "The Libraries", pp. 58–59 and Manaphes, *Αἱ ἐν Κωνσταντινουπόλει βιβλιοθῆκαι*, pp. 62–148 (esp. pp. 130–48, for the library in the Palaeologan period). See also Staikos, *Ιστορία της βιβλιοθήκης*, pp. 432–33.

8   See in this regard Stichel, "Sechs kolossale Säulen", pp. 23–24.

9   See Manaphes, *Αἱ ἐν Κωνσταντινουπόλει βιβλιοθῆκαι*, pp. 133–34.

10   See Nikephoros Kallistos Xanthopoulos, *Ecclesiastical History*, ed. in *Patrologia Graeca*, vol. 145, col. 609, lines 30–35.

11   The same occurs elsewhere as well, such as in the case of the testament of Joseph Bryennios, in which he expressly declares that his books are left to the Church of Hagia Sophia, see *infra* p. 478 (and n. 137), or that of a manuscript in the Hagia Sophia library that is mentioned in an annotation to the Vatican City codex, Biblioteca Apostolica Vaticana, Vat. gr. 830 of 1447 on fol. 474v, see Devreesse, *Codices vaticani graeci*, p. 378: μετεγράφη τὸ παρὸν βιβλίον τῶν πρακτικῶν τῆς οἰκουμενικῆς τρίτης συνόδου ἀπὸ βιβλίου παλαιοτάτου βαμβικίνου τῆς βιβλιοθήκης τῆς ἁγίας Σοφίας (the present book containing the proceedings of the third Ecumenical Synod had been transcribed from a very old bombycin codex originated from the library of Hagia Sophia) and Manaphes, *Αἱ ἐν Κωνσταντινουπόλει βιβλιοθῆκαι*, pp. 156–58.

12   See Manaphes, *Αἱ ἐν Κωνσταντινουπόλει βιβλιοθῆκαι*, pp. 140–41. See also Karpozilos, *Βυζαντινοί ιστορικοί*, pp. 99–120 and Berger, "Nikephoros Kallistou Xanthopoulos", pp. 9–16.

PRIVATE AND PUBLIC LIBRARIES IN BYZANTIUM 461

Italy, could learn Greek and study Aristotelian philosophy.[13] Its library must, then, presumably have contained manuscripts useful for such teaching.[14]

3 Monastery Libraries

The monastic library in Constantinople about which we know most is that of the Prodromos Petra Monastery, which was remarkable for the number and variety of books it contained and for the systematic efforts that were made to enrich it in the late Byzantine period.[15]

The characteristic patronal inscription, written in Byzantine dodecasyllabic metre, credits the library with twenty-eight manuscripts.[16] Apart from the famous Vienna manuscript of Dioscourides,[17] these were almost exclusively collections of theological and liturgical texts (Gospels, homilies of Church Fathers, *Lives* of saints, Old Testaments and *Menaia*), suggesting that the contents of the library reflected only, as indeed was customary, the spiritual and liturgical needs of the brethren and the monastery.[18]

Assessing the remarkable activity of the scholars who wrote and the scribes who copied books in the monastery, Cataldi Palau has shown in recent studies that roughly two hundred and fifty manuscripts of varied content can be

---

13 The Xenon of the Kral, which was built early in the 14th century by Stefan Uroš II Milutin of Serbia, functioned as a hospital and hostel serving primarily Serbian and Russian visitors to the city, see Kidonopoulos, *Bauten in Konstantinopel*, pp. 218–21 and Staikos, *Ιστορία της βιβλιοθήκης*, p. 428 (and n. 48–51). For the Xenon and its connection with the Prodromos Petra Monastery and the "Katholikon Mouseion", see also Živojinović, "Bolnica Milutina", pp. 105–17; Miller, *Hospital*, pp. 195–97 and *infra* p. 462.

14 As e.g. in cases of manuscripts relating to George Baiophoros, Stephen of Medeia, George Chrysokokkes and John Argyropoulos, see *infra* p. 462 (and n. 19).

15 For the monastery and its library, see Cataldi Palau, "The Manuscript Production", pp. 197–207 and Cataldi Palau, "The Library of the Monastery of Prodromos Petra", pp. 209–18. See also Volk, *Die byzantinischen Klosterbibliotheken*, pp. 64–79 and Kakoulidi, "Η βιβλιοθήκη της μονής Προδρόμου-Πέτρας", pp. 3–39.

16 Ἡ βίβλος αὕτη τῆς μονῆς τοῦ Προδρόμου/τῆς κειμένης ἔγγιστα τῆς Ἀετίου·/ἀρχαϊκὴ δὲ τῇ μονῇ κλῆσις Πέτρα [This book belongs to the Monastery of St. John the Baptist that stood near the (cistern of) Aetios and was formerly called Petra]. For a list of the manuscripts, see Kakoulidi, "Η βιβλιοθήκη της μονής Προδρόμου-Πέτρας", pp. 7–15. See also Cataldi Palau, "The Manuscript Production", pp. 198–201 and Cataldi Palau, "The Library of the Monastery of Prodromos Petra", pp. 210–11.

17 For this manuscript, which was refreshed and bound by John Chortasmenos, see *infra* p. 477, n. 129.

18 See Kakoulidi, "Η βιβλιοθήκη της μονής Προδρόμου-Πέτρας", p. 38.

associated with the foundation and its library.[19] The size of this collection is partially due to the close relations the monastery had developed with the Xenon of the Kral and the "Katholikon Museion", which meant that from the 14th century onwards the library was open not only to senior state officials but also to Western visitors and students at the "Katholikon Museion".[20] It was precisely the same reason that in the final century before the Fall of Constantinople led to a significant change in the content of the monastery's library, by then no longer exclusively theological but containing mainly scientific, medical and philosophical texts.[21]

Founded in the mid 11th century by the Emperor Constantine IX Monomachos, the Monastery of St. George Mangana was from the outset one of the most important religious houses in Constantinople.[22] During the period of Frankish occupation it adopted the Latin Rule and was spared pillaging. Its library must have thus remained fairly rich even after the reconquest of the city in 1261, although the number of the extant manuscripts is not particularly large.[23] Of its nine known codices, eight contain works and homilies of Basil of Caesarea, John Chrysostom, Gregory of Nazianzos, Philotheos Kokkinos and Gregory Palamas, and liturgical texts; only one contains a secular work, namely

---

19   As in the case of Neophytos Prodromenos, George Baiophoros, Stephen of Medeia, George Chrysokokkes, Leo Atrapes and John Argyropoulos, see Gamillscheg/Harlfinger, *Repertorium*, vol. 1, nos. 55, 158, 366 and vol. 2, nos. 74, 95, 212, 328, 411, 503 and Gamillscheg/Harlfinger/Eleuteri, *Repertorium*, nos. 90, 127, 263, 383, 481, 584. See also Cataldi Palau, "*Mazaris*", pp. 367–97; Cataldi Palau, "The Manuscript Production", pp. 203–07; Cataldi Palau, "The Library of the Monastery of Prodromos Petra", pp. 211–18; Cataldi Palau, "I colleghi di Giorgio Baiophoros", pp. 305–16 (for Stephen of Medeia), 317–32 (for George Chrysokokkes) and 332–43 (for Leo Atrapes); Cataldi Palau, "Un nuovo manoscritto", pp. 281–302 and *infra* pp. 478–79. Gamillscheg came to much the same conclusion in his study of the subject, saying that the library that George Baiophoros used, based on the manuscripts that he wrote, corrected or restored, must have been that of the Prodromos Petra Monastery; see Gamillscheg, "Zur Rekonstruktion", pp. 283–93. The number should be augmented by the codices that are bound in the same way as the manuscripts that are known to have come from the Monastery, see Cataldi Palau, "Legature constantinopolitane", pp. 235–80.

20   Examples include Giovanni Aurispa, Cristoforo Garatone and Francesco Filelfo, see Cataldi Palau, "I colleghi di Giorgio Baiophoros", pp. 321–32. For the Xenon of the Kral and the "Katholikon Mouseion", see also *supra* pp. 460–61 (and n. 13).

21   See Cataldi Palau, "The Manuscript Production", p. 204.

22   See Janin, *La géographie ecclésiastique*, pp. 70–76 and Kidonopoulos, *Bauten in Konstantinopel*, pp. 39–41.

23   See Mercati, "Un testament inédit", pp. 41–43; Volk, *Die byzantinischen Klosterbibliotheken*, pp. 22–35 and Janin, *La géographie ecclésiastique*, p. 75.

PRIVATE AND PUBLIC LIBRARIES IN BYZANTIUM 463

the *Antiquitates Judaicae* of Flavius Josephus.[24] To these manuscripts must be added the eleven books bequeathed to the monastery by the monk and steward Gabriel, who also left books to the abbot of the Mangana Monastery and the Church of the Theotokos of Blachernae.[25]

The history of the Chora Monastery and its library in the Palaeologan period is interwoven with those of Theodore Metochites, who renovated it (1316–1321), and his student Nikephoros Gregoras, who spent his final years there.[26] The monastery had been so badly damaged during the period of Frankish occupation that it was uninhabitable until Metochites had completed his restoration, and thus its library contains very few manuscripts earlier than the 13th century and even fewer that are likely to have belonged to the monastery before it was sacked; these few are an 11th century Gospel lectionary, a copy of the *Ladder* of St. John Klimax, and codices containing Platonic dialogues and works by Diodorus Siculus and Ptolemy.[27]

The monastery's library also had a codex with the Acts of the First Ecumenical Council,[28] while the palaeographic and particular features of some other manuscripts of secular texts point to their having been among its acquisitions.[29] The most important part of the Chora Monastery's library, however, was the collection of books donated by Theodore Metochites – and

---

24   To the eight codices that have been established by earlier research as belonging to the monastery must be added, as S.G. Mercati correctly concludes, the codex Vatican City, Biblioteca Apostolica Vaticana, Vat. Pal. gr. 138 dated to 1299 (the erroneous reference to number 128 at the beginning of Mercati's study is surely a slip), which contains a copy of the testament by which the monk Gabriel left his personal library to the Monastery of St. George Mangana, see Mercati, "Un testament inédit", p. 43.
25   For a detailed account of the content of Gabriel's personal library, see *infra* pp. 473–74.
26   For this monastery, see Janin, *La géographie ecclésiastique*, pp. 531–38 and Kidonopoulos, *Bauten in Konstantinopel*, pp. 19–25, while for its library see Volk, *Die byzantinischen Klosterbibliotheken*, pp. 168–69 and Bianconi, "La biblioteca di Cora", pp. 391–438. See also Ševčenko, "Chora", pp. 28–29, 35–37 and 41–42 and Taxidis, *Μάξιμος Πλανούδης*, pp. 20–21 (and n. 20) and 22–23 (and n. 27), who also examines the question of the doubtful conclusion of earlier research that Planoudes lived in the monastery and that the royal library he mentions in his letter to Theodore Mouzalon (Letter 67) was that of the Chora.
27   See Pérez Martín, "El scriptorium de Cora", pp. 209–12.
28   According to an annotation in codex Vat. gr. 830 dated to 1447 on fol. 105r, see Devreesse, *Codices vaticani graeci*, p. 378: μετεγράφη τὸ παρὸν βιβλίον τῶν πρακτικῶν τῆς οἰκουμενικῆς πρώτης συνόδου ἀπὸ βιβλίου παλαιοῦ μεμβράνου τοῦ μοναστηρίου τῆς Χώρας (the present book containing the proceedings of the first Ecumenical Council had been transcribed from an old parchment codex originating from the Chora monastery). See also *supra* p. 460, n. 11.
29   See Pérez Martín, "El scriptorium de Cora", pp. 212–13.

464 TAXIDIS

possibly later by Nikephoros Gregoras.[30] According to the personal testimony of the *grand logothetes* expressed in two texts written in exile to the abbot of the Chora Monastery and Gregoras, his extensive and varied collection was initially placed in the monastery for safekeeping;[31] later, it was absorbed into the monastery's own collection, which Metochites had in any case helped to enrich.

The Stoudios Monastery also had a fine library prior to the Frankish conquest of Constantinople, and the copies produced in its scriptorium were as a rule works of theology.[32] Twenty-four manuscripts from this library still survive, twenty-two of them from before 1204, and just two, one of homilies written by Abbot Makarios – in the early 15th century – and one of the Acts of the Council of Chalcedon, from the Palaeologan age.[33] After 1261, however, and despite the despoliation of the library, there must have been other manuscripts in the monastery apart from those mentioned, which have either not survived or simply remain unknown.

Manuscripts of the theological and ecclesiastical texts necessary to their operation existed, of course, in all the monasteries in Constantinople and its environs, while the most important of these, e.g. the Theotokos Hodegetria,[34] the Pammakaristos,[35] the Peribleptos[36] and the Charsianeites[37] as well as

---

30   For the personal libraries of Theodore Metochites and Nikephoros Gregoras, see *infra* pp. 476–77. See also Pérez Martín, "El scriptorium de Cora", pp. 214–23 and Bianconi, "La ‚biblioteca' di Niceforo Gregora", pp. 227–28.

31   See e.g. Theodore Metochites, *Letter to the Monks of the Chora*, ed. Ševčenko, p. 80 (§23), lines 2–3: ὅπως φυλάσσοιτέ μοι τὰ ταμιεῖα τοῦ καλλίστου πλούτου, τῶν πολυτιμήτων βίβλων, ἐν ἀσφαλεῖ καὶ ἄσυλα, πάσης ἐπηρείας ἀνώτερά τε καὶ κρείττω (so as to keep in safety for my account the treasures of the most beautiful wealth, that is, my invaluable books, beyond any recklessness), and Theodore Metochites, *Poems*, no. 4 (on Gregoras), ed. Polemis, p. 97, line 341: Χώρα τέ μοι, γένε ἄσυλος ἀμφὶ τέκεσσ' ἀμεδαποῖς [Chora, be a shelter for me and my "children" (= books)]. See also *infra* p. 476 (and n. 124).

32   For the monastery's library and scriptorium, see Volk, *Die byzantinischen Klosterbibliotheken*, pp. 80–91; Eleopoulos, *Ἡ βιβλιοθήκη*, pp. 16–36; Janin, *La géographie ecclésiastique*, pp. 430–40 and Kidonopoulos, *Bauten in Konstantinopel*, pp. 49–51.

33   These are the codices Athens, National Library of Greece, Metochiou Panagiou Taphou 455 dated to the early 15th century and Vatican City, Biblioteca Apostolica Vaticana, Vat. gr. 831 dated to 1446, see Eleopoulos, *Ἡ βιβλιοθήκη*, pp. 35–45 (esp. p. 44).

34   See Volk, *Die byzantinischen Klosterbibliotheken*, pp. 43–50. See also Janin, *La géographie ecclésiastique*, pp. 199–207 and Kidonopoulos, *Bauten in Konstantinopel*, pp. 77–78.

35   See Volk, *ibid.*, pp. 51–52. See also Janin, *ibid.*, pp. 208–13 and Kidonopoulos, *ibid.*, pp. 80–86.

36   See Volk, *ibid.*, pp. 55–58. See also Janin, *ibid.*, pp. 218–22 and Kidonopoulos, *ibid.*, pp. 91–93.

37   See Volk, *ibid.*, pp. 95–98 and Janin, *ibid.*, pp. 501–02. See also *infra* p. 478.

PRIVATE AND PUBLIC LIBRARIES IN BYZANTIUM 465

the monasteries of Christ Akataleptos,[38] Christ Panoiktirmon[39] and Christ Pantepoptes[40] would have had larger libraries. Based on the patronal annotations on manuscripts and the inventories of extant books,[41] it seems that these monastic foundations had well-stocked libraries with sizeable numbers of theological and liturgical texts,[42] which were most likely enriched during the Palaeologan period by the collections of the monasteries in Asia Minor with which they were amalgamated.[43]

The growth of the monasteries in and around Constantinople in the Palaeologan period was paralleled in reverse by the decline of the once flourishing monastic centres in Asia Minor. By as early as the end of the 11th century they were gradually shrinking under the effects of Seljuk and Ottoman raids, while by the beginning of the 14th century they had been sacked and abandoned.[44] Many of the manuscripts in their libraries were removed to the capital or other regional monasteries, taken to the West, or simply destroyed.[45]

The result was that there were few remarkable monastic libraries in Asia Minor which still existed in the early Palaeologan period and from which more

38 See Volk, *ibid.*, pp. 99–101 and Janin, *ibid.*, pp. 504–06. Except for the manuscripts mentioned by Volk, there is also an important attestation by Constantine Akropolites, according to which there also existed in the library of the monastery the work of Pseudo-Dionysius the Areopagite, *The Mystical Theology* (Περὶ μυστικῆς θεολογίας), see Constantine Akropolites, *Letters*, no. 173, ed. Romano, p. 243, lines 12–14. For the teaching and writing that occupied Planoudes in the monastery in 1299–1301, see Taxidis, *Μάξιμος Πλανούδης*, p. 22.

39 See Volk, *ibid.*, pp. 102–06. See also Janin, *ibid.*, pp. 512–13.

40 See Constantine Akropolites, *Letters*, no. 173, ed. Romano, pp. 242–43, lines 10–13, which mentions that in the library of the monastery there existed a manuscript containing the hermeneutical work on the *Psalms* by John Chrysostom.

41 As in the case of the inventory of books in the Monastery of Christ Panoiktirmon, see *Inventory of the monastery of Christ Panoiktirmon*, eds. Miklosich/Müller, vol. 5. See also Volk, *Die byzantinischen Klosterbibliotheken*, pp. 102–04.

42 Particularly the Hodegon Monastery, from which came at least sixteen manuscripts (see Volk, *Die byzantinischen Klosterbibliotheken*, pp. 43–50), and the Monastery of Christ Panoiktirmon, which seems to have had a fairly extensive library, given that its *brebion* (see also preceding note) lists some fifty books.

43 One such example is the Auxentios Monastery which amalgamated with the Akataleptos Monastery during the reign of Andronikos II Palaiologos, see in this regard Kotzabassi, *Βυζαντινὰ χειρόγραφα*, p. 6.

44 See, e.g., for the devastation of the Maiander region, George Pachymeres, *History*, ed. Failler, vol. 1, p. 403, line 20–p. 405, line 4. See also Vryonis, *The Decline of Medieval Hellenism*, pp. 69–142 and 403–43 and Kotzabassi, *Βυζαντινὰ χειρόγραφα*, p. 6.

45 See e.g. the case of the books from the library of the Stylos Monastery which went to the Monastery of St. John the Theologian in Patmos, in Kotzabassi, *ibid.*, p. 2, n. 6. The transfer of libraries to the West may have occurred indirectly, via other cities or monasteries within the empire.

than two or three manuscripts were preserved. Thirteen codices of theological texts came from the library of the Theotokos Monastery on Mount Galesion in Ephesos,[46] which survived until the reign of Andronikos II Palaiologos, and we know of seven theological books that came from the library of the Milesian Monastery of Kellibara,[47] which was dissolved after 1282. Our knowledge of the library of the Monastery of Kotine, near Philadelphia, which contained mainly liturgical manuscripts, comes from the testament of its abbot and founder, Maximos, drawn up in 1247,[48] while the case of the twenty-five manuscripts from Egirdir (Pisidia) is unique, in that they were part of the library of an unknown monastery that survived in its initial location until the 19th century.[49]

On the other hand, the five known theological codices of the Stylos Monastery near Miletos should perhaps be considered in the Palaeologan period as part of the library of the Monastery of St. John the Theologian on Patmos, to which they were removed probably in the early part of the 14th century.[50] Additional information about the content of that library, which is known to have been adorned with significant manuscripts, as for example the codex Oxford, Bodleian Library, Clark. 39 (895/96) containing Plato's works, is supplied by the ledger of books taken out, which has survived, and which suggests that most of the manuscripts contained liturgical texts.[51]

Apart from the important monastic libraries of Asia Minor, mention should also be made of two of the wealthiest monasteries in the vicinity of Thessaloniki, namely the Akapniou Monastery and the Monastery of St. Anastasia Pharmacolytria.[52] The manuscripts known, chiefly on the basis of their patronal inscriptions, to have come from these monasteries – six from the former and thirty-eight from the latter – are primarily liturgical in nature and contain

---

46   See for details Kotzabassi, *ibid.*, pp. 120–46. See also Volk, *Die byzantinischen Klosterbibliotheken*, pp. 150–58.

47   See for details Kotzabassi, *ibid.*, pp. 147–159. See also Volk, *ibid.*, pp. 163–66 and Janin, *Les églises et les monastères*, p. 226.

48   See Kotzabassi, *ibid.*, p. 4, n. 15, with the older bibliography. See also Volk, *ibid.*, pp. 173–78 and for the text of the testament of Maximos the Monk, *Testament*, ed. Gedeon, pp. 271–90 (esp. 280–83 and 288–89).

49   See for more detail Kotzabassi, *ibid.*, pp. 6–7 and 179–88.

50   See for more detail Kotzabassi, *ibid.*, pp. 2 and 160–69. See also Volk, *Die byzantinischen Klosterbibliotheken*, pp. 167–69 and Janin, *Les églises et les monastères*, p. 227.

51   See Waring, "Literacies of Lists", pp. 181–83.

52   See also Wilson, "The Libraries", pp. 65–72. In the absence of specific information about the existence of libraries and the more general transfer of books to Mistra in the Palaeologan period one can only hypothesize, see in this regard Staikos, *Ιστορία της βιβλιοθήκης*, pp. 438–45.

PRIVATE AND PUBLIC LIBRARIES IN BYZANTIUM 467

homilies of Church Fathers,[53] although several of the manuscripts from the Monastery of St. Anastasia also preserve secular texts, including works of poetry and texts on grammar, rhetoric and law, and are now part of the collection of the National Library of France.[54]

Other important libraries include those of the Pontic monasteries,[55] and of course the libraries of the Athonite monasteries, particularly Vatopedi and Megiste Lavra which had exceptionally large collections,[56] part of which was transferred to the Synodical Library of Moscow and the National Library of France.

4   Private Libraries

Although we know more about the private libraries than the public ones, our information is still insufficient to form a clear picture of their extent or importance. Nonetheless, there can be no doubt that many learned church and state officials owned impressive collections of books. The most telling witness to the size and variety of their libraries is the correspondence between them on the subject. These scholars, we learn, sent each other books to be copied, or bestowed as gifts, or corrected.[57] Additional information about these private libraries comes from the testaments some bibliophiles left, and from manuscript notes concerning, usually, the loan of a book.[58]

---

53   See Volk, *Die byzantinischen Klosterbibliotheken*, pp. 112–29 and Janin, *Les églises et les monastères*, pp. 347–51. For the equally well-furnished private library of an anonymous individual in Thessaloniki in the early 14th century, see *infra* p. 474, and for the production of books in that city in the context of the Hesychast controversy, see Staikos, *Ιστορία της βιβλιοθήκης*, pp. 436–37.

54   See Darrouzès, "Sainte-Anastasie", pp. 45–57.

55   Ioanna Kolia's unpublished doctoral dissertation (*Les bibliothèques de la region de Trébizonde*) is a seminal study of the manuscripts of monastic libraries in the region of Trebizond. See also Kolias, "Bibliothèques", pp. 282–89.

56   Although a fair number of their surviving manuscripts were written after the Fall of Constantinople, see Wilson, "The Libraries", pp. 66–68.

57   In his in-depth study of 14th-century collections of letters, Karpozilos ("Books and Bookmen", p. 271) finds that a) many of the books in the personal libraries of scholars of that period were works written by friends and acquaintances, sent to them with a request for their critical opinion, and b) since lending was not common, these scholars either had fine libraries of their own or had access to the books upon which their opinion was requested. See also on this issue the contribution of A. Riehle in the present volume.

58   As for example in the case of the testaments of John Bekkos and Joseph Bryennios, see *infra* pp. 468–69 and 478 respectively.

468 TAXIDIS

Information about the library of a relative by marriage of the Xiphilinos family, possibly Michael Eskammatismenos,[59] is furnished by the annotation on the 13th century codex Vatican City, Biblioteca Apostolica Vaticana, Vat. gr. 207 (fol. VII), which gives a detailed list of the books he lent to friends, relatives and acquaintances over the period 1268–82.[60] From it we learn that he owned at least thirteen codices, containing works of Homer, Aristotle (*Organon*), Basil of Caesarea (chiefly ascetic texts), Theodoret of Cyrrhus, John of Damascus and John Doxopatres (commentary on Hermogenes), as well as texts on rhetoric, mathematics, music and canon law.[61]

Similar annotations on the codex Vatican City, Biblioteca Apostolica Vaticana, Vat. gr. 765 (fol. II) yield information about the smaller library of the roughly contemporary Michael of Cappadocia, which contained mainly theological works,[62] while similar information is provided by the annotation, written in a 14th-century hand, to the 13th-century manuscript Vatican City, Biblioteca Apostolica Vaticana, Vat. gr. 269 (fol. III), on the eight secular and religious books belonging to a man called Andronikos Phakrases.[63]

The sole source for the content of the library of the exiled patriarch John XI Bekkos is his testament, which is preserved in its entirety in the manuscript Florence, Biblioteca Medicea Laurenziana, Laur. Plut. 7.31 dated to the late 13th or the early 14th century.[64] From it we learn that Bekkos owned twenty-nine books, both theological and secular in nature, which he left to his "spiritual son" Constantine Sinaites.[65] Among these were a set of Gospels, two hagiographical collections, the letters of John Chrysostom, Aristotle's *Rhetoric* and *Organon*, the commentaries of Simplikios on Aristotle's *Categories*, the *Histories* of Thucydides and Herodotus, some *Meletai* of Libanios, works by

---

59 The *megas chartophylax* of the Great Church. See in this regard Constantinides, "The Scholars and their Books", pp. 16–17 and Constantinides, *Higher Education*, p. 139.

60 See Mercati/Franchi de' Cavalieri, *Codices vaticani graeci*, pp. 249–50. See also Trapp, "Probleme der Prosopographie", pp. 198–99 and Canart, "Vaticanus graecus 207", pp. 271, 274 and 279–83.

61 See Mercati/Franchi de' Cavalieri, *Codices vaticani graeci*, pp. 249–50 and Staikos, Ἱστορία τῆς βιβλιοθήκης, p. 431.

62 Containing hermeunetical works of Cyril of Alexandria, dogmatical works of Athanasios of Alexandria and the homilies *On the Statues* (Εἰς τοὺς ἀνδριάντας) by John Chrysostom. The codex was written in the 12th century, but the annotation is in a 13th-century hand, see in this regard Devreesse, *Codices vaticani graeci*, p. 281.

63 In the annotation are mentioned, between others, manuscripts bearing works of Aristotle and Anastasios Sinaites, Gregory's of Cyprus letters, the hermeneutical work to the letters of St. Paul by Theophylact of Bulgaria and the letters of John Chrysostom *To Olympiad* (Πρὸς Ὀλυμπιάδα), see Mercati/Franchi de' Cavalieri, *Codices vaticani graeci*, p. 355.

64 See Kotzabassi, "The Testament", pp. 25–26.

65 See John Bekkos, *Testament*, ed. Kotzabassi, p. 34, lines 52–53.

PRIVATE AND PUBLIC LIBRARIES IN BYZANTIUM 469

Lucian and Homer, commentaries on Hermogenes' *On Issues* (Περὶ στάσεων) and *On Types of Style* (Περὶ ἰδεῶν), commentaries on *Progymnasmata*, a collection of medical texts, a Psalter, an Octoechos, a Typikon and two volumes of poetry.[66]

Patriarch Gregory II of Cyprus also had an extensive and varied library and a great love of books, as evidenced not least by the fact of his constant search for paper and parchment on which to copy the works he wanted to study.[67] Although relatively few of the manuscripts he wrote himself and those containing only his own notes have survived,[68] the information to be gleaned from his letters concerning the kind of books he owned, lent or borrowed is revealing, for it tells us that his library included dialogues of Plato, speeches of Demosthenes and Aelius Aristides,[69] letters of Gregory of Nazianzos, the *Ethics* of Basil of Caesarea and a volume with the books of the prophets.[70]

From the manuscript tradition we also learn that he was interested in Aristotle,[71] while it is clear from Letter 58 that he was looking for a book with the commentaries of Syrianos on Plato's *Parmenides*. The person to whom this letter was addressed, whose name was Skoutariotes, was apparently someone from whom he frequently borrowed books,[72] perhaps Theodore Skoutariotes, Metropolitan of Kyzikos during the final years of the reign of Michael VIII,[73] whose private library was, judging by the manuscripts we know that he owned, justly famous for its size and diversity.[74]

---

66 See John Bekkos, *Testament*, ed. Kotzabassi, p. 34, lines 53–58 and 69–71.

67 See e.g. Gregory of Cyprus, *Letters*, no. 39, ed. Eustratiades, p. 28, lines 22–24 and no. 38, p. 27, lines 21–23. See also Constantinides, "The Scholars and their Books", p. 14 and Constantinides, *Higher Education*, p. 136–37 (and n. 18).

68 See Pérez Martín, *El patriarca Gregorio de Chipre*, pp. 17–50. See also Gamillscheg/Harlfinger, *Repertorium*, vol. 2/A, nos. 99 and 115.

69 See e.g. Gregory of Cyprus, *Letters*, no. 28, ed. Eustratiades, p. 20, lines 16–19; no. 100, p. 77, line 6 and no. 38, p. 27, lines 18–19. See also Constantinides, *Higher Education*, p. 138 (and n. 27–29).

70 See e.g. Gregory of Cyprus, *Letters*, no. 98, ed. Eustratiades, p. 75, lines 7–8 and no. 30, p. 22, lines 5–6. See also Gregory of Cyprus, *Letters to Theodora Raoulaina*, no. 17, ed. Kotzabassi, p. 158, lines 22–24 and Constantinides, *Higher Education*, p. 138 (and n. 30–32).

71 See Pérez Martín, *El patriarca Gregorio de Chipre*, pp. 19–24. See also Kotzabassi, "Aristotle's *Organon*", p. 53 (and n. 9) and Kotzabassi, "Kopieren und Exzerpieren", p. 475, n. 10.

72 See Gregory of Cyprus, *Letters*, no. 58, ed. Eustratiades, p. 40, lines 23–28.

73 The hasty identification of the Patriarch's correspondent as Theodore is unsupported, see Constantinides, *Higher Education*, p. 138 and Pérez Martín, *El patriarca Gregorio de Chipre*, p. 28.

74 These include codices containing, among other things, Aristotle's *Rhetoric* and *Poetics*, Photios' *Library*, Euthymios Zigabenos' paraphrases of the Letters of St. Paul, and works by John Chrysostom and Michael and Nicetas Choniates, see in this regard Constantinides, *Higher Education*, p. 139 (and n. 34).

470   TAXIDIS

Our information about the library of Theodora Raoulaina is derived indirectly. Of the manuscripts that she copied herself only two survive: one of speeches of Aelius Aristides and one with Simplikios' commentary on Aristotle's *Physics*.[75] Although her own letters are lost, it is clear from those written to her that she had an important collection of manuscripts,[76] including one of Demosthenes,[77] the *Ethics* of Basil of Caesarea,[78] a book on harmonics[79] and a codex on mathematics,[80] while she received from Choumnos a manuscript of Aristotle's *Meteorology* with the commentary by Alexander of Aphrodisias.[81] She also apparently owned a considerable number of old manuscripts of Ancient Greek literature, including the codices Munich, Bayerische Staatsbibliothek, Monac. gr. 485 with the speeches of Demosthenes dated to the 11th century and Monac. gr. 430 dated to the 10th–11th centuries, a copy of Thucydides' *History*.[82]

Another fine late 13th/early 14th century library, and one which testifies to the material wealth of its owner, was that of Nikephoros Moschopoulos, appointed Metropolitan of Crete in 1285.[83] Detailed information about the

---

75   Codices Vatican City, Biblioteca Apostolica Vaticana, Vat. gr. 1899 and Moscow, Istoriceskij Muzej, Mosqu. Muz. 3649 dated to the second half of the 13th century, see Gamillscheg/ Harlfinger/Eleuteri, *Repertorium*, no. 206 and Harlfinger, "Einige Aspekte", p. 267. See also Kotzabassi, "Scholarly Friendship", pp. 116–17 (and n. 12–13).

76   She received twenty-nine letters from Gregory of Cyprus, two from Choumnos, one from Planoudes and one from Akropolites, see also Kotzabassi, "Scholarly Friendship", p. 115. In one of his letters, Gregory of Cyprus confesses that the books he has borrowed from Raoulaina have displaced his own books from his shelves, see Gregory of Cyprus, *Letters to Theodora Raoulaina*, no. 17, ed. Kotzabassi, p. 157, lines 1–2: Παρώσαντο μὲν βίβλους τὰς ἡμετέρας αἱ σαί, κἀκ τῆς ἀνειμένης αὐταῖς κεῖσθαι χώρας, εἴς τι στενὸν τῆς οἰκίας συνήλασαν (Your books displaced my own from their place in a narrow part of the house).

77   See Gregory of Cyprus, *Letters to Theodora Raoulaina*, no. 17, ed. Kotzabassi, p. 158, lines 18–19.

78   See *supra* p. 469, n. 70.

79   See Maximus Planoudes, *Letter 68*, ed. Leone, p. 103, lines 11–14: ἐχρῆν τὴν ἁρμονικὴν ἡμᾶς διορθοῦν ... ἥ γε μὴν ἡμετέρα βίβλος ἀπῆν, πρὸς ἣν ἔδει βλέποντα τὴν ὑμετέραν εὐχερῶς διορθοῦν (I should have emended your book on harmonics ... but I did not have my own book anymore, based on which I should easily emend yours). See also *infra* p. 472 (and n. 90).

80   See Constantine Akropolites, *Letters*, no. 60, ed. Leone, p. 155, lines 1–5. See also Kotzabassi, "Scholarly Friendship", p. 115, n. 6.

81   See Nikephoros Choumnos, *Letters*, no. 76, ed. Boissonade, p. 92, lines 16–20. See also Karpozilos, "Books and Bookmen", p. 262 and *infra* p. 475 (and n. 111).

82   See in this regard Kugeas, "Augustanus F", pp. 590–91 and Pérez Martín, "Planudes", pp. 303–07. For the richness of her library, see Gregory of Cyprus, *Letters*, no. 17, ed. Kotzabassi, p. 157, lines 1–3. See also Kotzabassi, "Scholarly Friendship", p. 116 and Taxidis, *Μάξιμος Πλανούδης*, pp. 75–76.

83   See Papadopoulos-Kerameus, "Νικηφόρος Μοσχόπουλος", pp. 215–23 and Papaeliopoulou-Photopoulou, *Νικηφόρος Μοσχόπουλος*, pp. 115–18. See also Taxidis, *Μάξιμος Πλανούδης*, pp. 79–80.

PRIVATE AND PUBLIC LIBRARIES IN BYZANTIUM 471

purchase, treatment, copying or dedication of the manuscripts preserved
from that library may be derived from the epigrams and prose dedications
accompanying them[84] and the letters written to him by his nephew Manuel
Moschopoulos[85] and Manuel Gabalas (later Matthew, Metropolitan of
Ephesos).[86]

Moschopoulos, it seems, collected books by purchasing them, by commissioning copies and by copying them himself, while in his latter years,
which he spent in Constantinople, he decided to donate some of his books
to various monasteries outside the capital.[87] The complete list of manuscripts
Nikephoros Moschopoulos is known to have possessed with certainty – or
in a few instances with reservations – shows that his library contained both
ecclesiastical and secular works, among them Gospels, *Menaia*, *Lives* of saints,
homilies of John Chrysostom, a hermeneutical series on the minor prophets
and commentaries on Job, as well as the epics of Homer and the commentaries
of Pseudo-Nonnos on the homilies of Gregory of Nazianzos.[88]

In the case of the scholarly monk and teacher Maximos Planoudes, among
his letters, his autograph manuscripts and the codices he edited that have been
firmly associated with his students,[89] we have a fairly complete picture of the

---

84 See Manousakas, "Νικηφόρου Μοσχόπουλου επιγράμματα", pp. 232–46.

85 His nephew makes specific mention of the size of his uncle's library, saying that when
he undertook to move it to Lesbos four horses were required for its transportation, see
Manuel Moschopoulos, *Letters*, no. 3, ed. Levi, p. 61, lines 27–33.

86 Manuel Gabalas alludes indirectly to the wealth of Moschopoulos' library in the context of the return of a book he had lent him, see Matthew of Ephesos, *Letters*, no. 61,
ed. & trans. Reinsch, p. 188, lines 2–3 and 27–29. See also Kourousis, *Μανουήλ Γαβαλᾶς*,
pp. 269–70.

87 Beneficiary monasteries included St. Athanasios in Phokaia, St. John the Baptist on the
Jordan, and the Brontochion Monastery in Mistra, see Papaeliopoulou-Photopoulou,
Νικηφόρος Μοσχόπουλος, pp. 118 (1), 120 (7), 123–24 (11).

88 Having thoroughly studied Gamillscheg's catalogue of the seventeen (sixteen certain and one with reservations) manuscripts ("Eine Platonhandschrift des Nikephoros
Moschopulos", pp. 99–100), Papaeliopoulou-Photopoulou drew up a list of twenty-two
(three with reservations) codices that belonged to the library of Nikephoros Moschopoulos,
see Papaeliopoulou-Photopoulou, *Νικηφόρος Μοσχόπουλος*, pp. 118–30, and Gamillscheg/
Harlfinger, *Repertorium*, vol. 1, no. 303 and vol. 2, no. 417. See also the annotation in the
codex Vatican City, Biblioteca Apostolica Vaticana, Vat. gr. 1822 (fol. 100v) dated to the
19th 11th centuries (Canart, *Codices vaticani graeci*, p. 223), where it is reported from an
unknown scribe, that he was given an order from a certain Moschopoulos (Nikephoros?)
[and from a Mouzalon (Theodore?) also] for copying *Menaia*.

89 See in this regard Gamillscheg/Harlfinger, *Repertorium*, vol. 1, no. 259bis and vol. 2,
no. 357. See also Browning, "Recentiores non deteriores", p. 17; Gamillscheg, "Autoren und
Kopisten", pp. 390–94; Constantinides, "The Scholars and their Books", p. 15; Pérez
Martín, "Nuevos códices planudeos", pp. 385–403; Pérez Martín, "Maxime Planude et le

breadth and diversity of his writings and consequently of the personal library he must surely have had.

In four letters to different correspondents Planoudes enquires about a collection of texts on *Harmonics* that he had edited and had lent to the monk Arsenios Autoreianos.[90] From two others it appears that he had a codex of the mathematician Diophantus,[91] while Letter 46 shows that he had borrowed a book on Indian arithmetic from George Bekkos, presumably in relation to his study of the subject, which resulted in the writing of the *Psephophoria kat' Indous* [Arithmetic according to the Indians].[92] From his letters we also learn that he lent a physician from Ephesos a manuscript with his own translation of Boethius' *De consolatione philosophiae*,[93] that his library also contained Theodosius' *Spherics* and a collection of the works of Diophantus, Nicomachus, Zosimos and Euclid,[94] and that he was about to copy the works of Plutarch,[95] while from his epigrams we are informed that he had discovered a manuscript of Ptolemy's *Geography*.[96]

Knowing the variety of his own writings, some of which were associated with his work as a teacher, we may assume that Planoudes had direct access to manuscripts of ancient Greek and Latin texts, although we cannot be sure whether they all belonged to his own personal library or to the royal library of the monastery he was living in, although the latter, according to what he wrote in a letter to the *protovestiarios* Theodore Mouzalon (no. 67), was in very poor condition.[97]

    'Diophantus Matritensis'", pp. 433–62 and Mondrain, "Les écritures", pp. 160–61. For his life and work, see Taxidis, *Μάξιμος Πλανούδης*, pp. 17–29.

90 See Maximos Planoudes, *Letters*, no. 64, ed. Leone, p. 94, line 5; no. 65, p. 96, line 6; no. 68, p. 103, lines 13–16 and no. 106, p. 169, lines 12–13. See also Taxidis, *ibid.*, pp. 59–60, 123, 75–76 and 109 respectively, and also *supra* p. 470 (and n. 79).

91 See Maximos Planoudes, *Letters*, no. 33, ed. Leone, p. 66, lines 14–15 and no. 67, p. 99, lines 24–27. See also Taxidis, *ibid.*, pp. 66 (and n. 129) and 81 respectively.

92 See Maximos Planoudes, *Letters*, no. 46, ed. Leone, p. 80, lines 8–12. See also Taxidis, *ibid.*, p. 65 (and n. 122).

93 See Maximos Planoudes, *Letters*, no. 5, ed. Leone, p. 15, lines 18–20. See also Taxidis, *ibid.*, p. 63.

94 See Maximos Planoudes, *Letters*, no. 67, ed. Leone, p. 102, lines 3–12. See also Taxidis, *ibid.*, p. 81.

95 See Maximos Planoudes, *Letters*, no. 106, ed. Leone, p. 169, line 18. See also Pérez Martín, "Nuevos códices planudeos", pp. 385–403 and Taxidis, *ibid.*, pp. 108–09 (and n. 365).

96 See Maximos Planoudes, *Epigrams*, no. 5, ed. Taxidis, p. 88, lines 28–29.

97 See Maximos Planoudes, *Letters* no. 67, ed. Leone, p. 100, lines 17–20. See also Taxidis, *ibid.*, p. 82, while for the unsupported hypothesis that it was the library of the Chora Monastery, see Taxidis, *ibid.*, p. 23 (and n. 27–28) and *supra* p. 463, n. 26. Maximos Planoudes edited works of Aesop, Aratus, Theocritus, Pindar and Ptolemy, wrote commentaries on works by

PRIVATE AND PUBLIC LIBRARIES IN BYZANTIUM

Most of what we know about the library of Constantine Akropolites, too, comes from its owner's correspondence. A single brief letter, in fact, is enough to suggest its wealth, for in it he relates that he inherited many of his father's books, and mentions a private room in the upper part of his house where he kept them and where he liked to go and read.[98] From other letters we learn that his library contained Andronikos Kamateros' *Sacred Arsenal* and George Pisides' *Hexaemeron*,[99] codices with works of Plato and Plotinus,[100] while, according to the evidence of a letter from Gregory of Cyprus, he also had a manuscript of Aelius Aristides.[101]

Another interesting case is that of the library owned in the late 13th century by a monk called Gabriel, whose testament, which is preserved anonymously in the codex Vatican City, Biblioteca Apostolica Vaticana, Vat. Pal. gr. 138 (fol. III), records that he had at least eighteen books, which he bequeathed to the church of the Monastery of St. George Mangana.[102] His collection included the letters of St. Paul with the commentary by Euthymios Zigabenos, treatises on Old Testament books (*Isaiah*, *The Song of Songs*, *Proverbs*, *The Wisdom of Solomon* and *Ecclesiastes*), a book of canon law with commentary by John Zonaras, liturgical books, the works of John Mauropous, and Philip Monotropos' *Dioptra*.[103] Gabriel also left a codex with the letters of Isidore of

---

Aristophanes, Euclid, Euripides, Hesiod, Thucydides and Sophocles, and translated works by St. Augustine, Boethius, Cicero, Macrobius, Ovid, Pseudo-Augustine and Pseudo-Cato, see Taxidis, *ibid.*, pp. 28–29 (and n. 59).

98 See Constantine Akropolites, *Letters*, no. 80, ed. Romano, p. 169, lines 1–3 and 11–13 and no. 59, p. 155, lines 39–40. See also Constantinides, *Higher Education*, pp. 138 (and n. 25) and 141 (and n. 42–43); *supra* p. 470, n. 76 for the narrow part of Gregory of Cyprus' house, where he transferred some of his books and *infra* p. 475 (and n. 115) about the case of a country house, where Michael Gabras kept a good number of books and where he used to go. No information concerning the content of George Akropolites' library has survived.

99 See Constantine Akropolites, *Letters*, no. 61, ed. Romano, p. 156, line 1 and no. 78, ed. Romano, p. 167, lines 1–3.

100 See Constantine Akropolites, *Letters*, no. 59, ed. Romano, p. 154, lines 12–13 and no. 95, p. 189, line 20.

101 See Gregory of Cyprus, *Letters*, no. 38, ed. Eustratiades, p. 28, lines 7–8 and no. 169, p. 167, lines 9–11.

102 For the identification of the author of this testament as the monk Gabriel (based on dedicatory notes on three manuscripts which S.G. Mercati identified as three of the books mentioned in the text of the testament), see Mercati, "Un testament inédit", pp. 39–41. For the codex, see also *supra* p. 463, n. 24.

103 See Gabriel monk, *Testament*, ed. Mercati, p. 46, line 20–p. 47, line 4. As regards the books belonging to the library of the Monastery of St. George Mangana, see also *supra* pp. 462–63.

474 TAXIDIS

Pelusion to the abbot of the Mangana Monastery[104] and six liturgical books to the Church of the Theotokos at Blachernae.[105]

A number of other manuscripts also contain completions, on blank sheets, in Gabriel's hand, indicating that he must have had them in his possession; these manuscripts seem, however, to have been part of the library of John Kritopoulos, at least for a period of time, for they bear his cipher. While both men lived in the early part of the 14th century, it is not yet clear what the relation between them may have been.[106] These codices are the miscellany Vatican City, Biblioteca Apostolica Vaticana, Chis. R.IV.12 dated to the 14th century with works by Gregory of Cyprus, Gregory of Nazianzos and others, the 14th century codex Paris, Bibliothèque nationale de France, Par. gr. 1220 with theological and philosophical texts, the 13th century codex Venice, Biblioteca Nazionale Marciana, Marc. gr. 613 of Homer, the 14th century codex Florence, Biblioteca Medicea Laurenziana, Laur. Plut. 57.45 with orations of Lysias, and the codex Munich, Bayerische Staatsbibliothek, Monac. gr. 564 (13th/14th centuries) with works of Julius Pollux.[107]

One remarkably rich and far-ranging collection of books of roughly the same period was that owned by an unidentified Thessalonian. According to the annotation on the codex Vatican City, Biblioteca Apostolica Vaticana, Vat. gr. 64 (fol. 289), this library contained liturgical and theological works, the letters of Basil of Caesarea, Gregory of Nazianzos and John Chrysostom, classical works of Ancient Greek literature (e.g. Sophocles, Euripides, Aeschines, Isocrates and Arrian), and medical manuscripts with texts of Homer, Hippocrates, Galen and Paul of Aegina.[108] Having sifted the codex for any indications pointing to the identity of its owner, Bianconi posited that this library must have belonged to someone in the milieu of John Pediasimos Pothos, whose books he acquired (perhaps by inheritance) after his death.[109]

In the late 13th and the first half of the 14th century a network of epistolographers, including Nikephoros Choumnos, Theodore Hyrtakenos and Michael Gabras, seem to have exchanged books from their personal libraries among

---

104   See Gabriel monk, *Testament*, ed. Mercati, p. 47, lines 29–30.
105   See Gabriel monk, *Testament*, ed. Mercati, p. 47, lines 15–27.
106   See in this regard Kotzabassi, "Kopieren und Exzerpieren", p. 480 and Kotzabassi, *Die handschriftliche Überlieferung*, pp. 208–09 (and n. 217).
107   See Kotzabassi, *Die handschriftliche Überlieferung*, pp. 207–09 and Kotzabassi, "Kopieren und Exzerpieren", p. 480 (and n. 45).
108   The codex dates to 1269/70, but the annotation to the early 14th century, see Bianconi, *Tessalonica nell'età dei Paleologi*, pp. 69–70. See also Kotzabassi, "Kopieren und Exzerpieren", p. 481.
109   See Bianconi, *Tessalonica nell'età dei Paleologi*, pp. 70–72, with the older related bibliography.

PRIVATE AND PUBLIC LIBRARIES IN BYZANTIUM 475

themselves and with other contemporary scholars.[110] Choumnos, as we have seen, owned a copy of Aristotle's *Meteorology* with the commentaries of Alexander of Aphrodisias, as well books with works by Theodore Metochites and Leo Bardales,[111] while many of his books seem also to have been in the libraries of – apart from Hyrtakenos and Gabras – his son John Choumnos, the Emperor Andronikos II Palaiologos, Theodore Xanthopoulos, Theodore Metochites, the *hypatos of the philosophers* Niketas Kyprianos, and the less well known Manuelites and Phakrases.[112]

From the letters of Choumnos we also learn that Theodore Hyrtakenos often gave books to others, asking for their opinion, and also frequently borrowed books.[113] His own personal library must have contained works of classical literature in addition to books by his scholar friends, despite the fact that in one letter he declares categorically that, even though he has books by Gregory of Nazianzos, Basil of Caesarea and John Chrysostom, he has none of the works of the three great tragic poets of antiquity.[114]

Michael Gabras kept a good number of his books at his country house, suggesting that his library must have been particularly extensive.[115] He certainly owned several works of ancient Greek literature, for manuscripts of Homer, Herodotus, Plato and Demosthenes are mentioned in his correspondence.[116] He also had codices with the letters of St. Paul, works of Plutarch and Aelius Aristides, and books by his own contemporaries.[117] Moreover, his eagerness to find and acquire manuscripts in any possible way is expressed in a letter to

---

110　See in this regard Karpozilos, "Books and Bookmen", pp. 272–76, with a detailed table of the books loaned and borrowed by each.

111　See *supra* p. 470 (and n. 81). See also Nikephoros Choumnos, *Letters*, no. 38, ed. Boissonade, p. 47, lines 4–7 and no. 75, p. 90, lines 8–10. See also Karpozilos, *ibid.*, p. 262.

112　See e.g. Nikephoros Choumnos, *Letters*, no. 4, ed. Boissonade, p. 5, lines 5–6; no. 37, p. 45, lines 2–4 and no. 145, p. 168, lines 26–28. See Karpozilos, *ibid.*, pp. 259–62.

113　See e.g. Theodore Hyrtakenos, *Letters*, no. 51, eds. Karpozilos/Fatouros, p. 198, lines 2–4 and no. 6, p. 84, lines 2–5. See also Karpozilos, *ibid.*, pp. 257–59.

114　See Theodore Hyrtakenos, *Letters*, no. 30, eds. Karpozilos/Fatouros, p. 150, lines 2–8. See also Karpozilos, *ibid.*, p. 259 and Karpozilos, "The Correspondence of Theodoros Hyrtakenos", p. 291.

115　See Michael Gabras, *Letters*, no. 359, ed. Fatouros, vol. 2, pp. 562–63, lines 2–37 (esp. 27–37). See also Karpozilos, "Books and Bookmen", p. 268.

116　See e.g. Michael Gabras, *Letters*, no. 100, ed. Fatouros, vol. 2, p. 162, lines 2–3 and no. 3, p. 12, lines 2–3. See also Karpozilos, *ibid.*, pp. 267 and 270.

117　See e.g. Michael Gabras, *Letters*, no. 337, ed. Fatouros, vol. 2, p. 533, lines 2–4; no. 252, p. 409, lines 2–4; no. 260, p. 416, lines 2–3 and no. 431, p. 664, lines 3–5. See also Karpozilos, *ibid.*, pp. 267–68.

476 TAXIDIS

Nikephoros Kallistos Xanthopoulos, asking the latter to lend him certain books from the library he apparently had.[118]

Another particularly fine library of this first half of the 14th century was that owned by the Thessalonian scholar Demetrios Triklinios. His primary philological interest was copying and writing commentaries on classical Greek literature and, as indicated by the twenty-three manuscripts known to be in his hand, he owned codices of Hesiod, Aeschylus, Sophocles, Euripides and Aristophanes.[119] He also possessed works of Ptolemy, Libanios and Theodoret of Cyrrhus, as well as two of Maximos Planoudes' translations of Ovid (*Heroides, Metamorphoses*).[120] The more than fifty-five manuscripts copied – presumably under his guidance – by his students, among them John Katrares, must also be associated with his personal library.[121]

Our information about the extent and content of the library of Theodore Metochites comes from his own works. In a letter to the monks of the Chora Monastery, written while he was in exile at Didymoteichon (1328–1330), he draws attention to the particular value of his books and asks for special care to be taken of them.[122] One of his poems speaks of a great library of mostly secular books,[123] while in his poem *Εἰς τὸν σοφὸν Νικηφόρον τὸν Γρηγορᾶν ὑποθῆκαι καὶ περὶ τῶν οἰκείων συνταγμάτων* he specifies that his collection is mostly of works of philosophy, science, rhetoric and poetry.[124] His student Nikephoros Gregoras, judging by the manuscripts written identifiably in his hand, had a similar library, containing mainly works of science and philosophy,[125] including some

---

118 See Michael Gabras, *Letters*, no. 2, ed. Fatouros, vol. 2, p. 11–12, lines 7–9. No further information about the private library of Nikephoros Kallistos Xanthopoulos survives. For his relation with the patriarchal library, see *supra* p. 460.

119 Six of these manuscripts were written wholly or in part by Triklinios; the other eleven bear marginalia and annotations in his hand, see Bianconi, *Tessalonica nell'età dei Paleologi*, pp. 102–07 and 248–49. See also Gamillscheg/Harlfinger, *Repertorium*, vol. 1, no. 104 and vol. 2, no. 136 and Gamillscheg/Harlfinger/Eleuteri, *Repertorium*, no. 170.

120 See Bianconi, *ibid.*, pp. 102–07.

121 Katrares copied thirty of these manuscripts, see Bianconi, *ibid.*, pp. 250–51 and Gamillscheg/Harlfinger/Eleuteri, *Repertorium*, no. 279. For the other twenty-five manuscripts, copied in unknown hands, see Bianconi, *ibid.*, pp. 252–54.

122 See Theodore Metochites, *Letter to the Monks of the Chora*, ed. Ševčenko, pp. 80–82 (§23), lines 2–8. See also *supra* p. 464, n. 31.

123 See Theodore Metochites, *Poems*, no. 1, ed. Polemis, p. 45, lines 1147–53.

124 See Theodore Metochites, *Poems*, no. 4 (on Gregoras), ed. Polemis, pp. 93–94, lines 250–55 and pp. 96–97, lines 353–61.

125 Including works of Aristotle, Plutarch, John Lydus and Nicomachus of Gerasa, see Bianconi, "La ,biblioteca' di Niceforo Gregora", pp. 228–30. See also Gamillscheg/Harlfinger, *Repertorium*, vol. 2, no. 416 and Gamillscheg/Harlfinger/Eleuteri, *Repertorium*, no 491; Pérez Martín, "El scriptorium de Cora", pp. 214–23 and Mondrain, "Les écritures", pp. 162–65.

PRIVATE AND PUBLIC LIBRARIES IN BYZANTIUM 477

of Metochites' own books (the *Introduction to Astronomy* and commentaries on Ptolemy's *Mathematical Treatise*).

An otherwise unknown figure who must also have had his own library was the physician John Konstantes, who lived in the last half of the 14th and the early part of the 15th century and who, as attested by the inscriptions on them, owned at least six codices containing mainly theological works by Basil of Caesarea, Cyril of Alexandria, Prokopios of Gaza, Gregory of Nyssa, Maximos the Confessor and Andronikos Kamateros' *Sacred Arsenal*, as well as synodic texts and works of canon law.[126] These six manuscripts were later acquired by Cardinal Bessarion and ended up in the Biblioteca Marciana.[127]

On the evidence of the manuscripts associated with him, early 15th century scholar and bibliophile John Chortasmenos must also have had a large and wide-ranging library.[128] According to Hunger seven of these manuscripts, mainly palimpsest *Menaia* and collections of works on geography and astronomy, are written entirely or almost entirely in his hand.[129] Shorter texts, marginalia and autograph inscriptions, mostly patronal, in Chortasmenos' hand are recognised in most of the other twenty codices that presumably belonged to his – primarily secular – library and which contain works of history, rhetoric, philosophy and science.[130]

Later research, however, has added to Hunger's list at least five more codices that, on the evidence of the commentaries and notes in his hand, must certainly have belonged to his library. These are the codices Munich, Bayerische Staatsbibliothek, Monac. gr. 358 dated to the late 9th century (or in the early 10th century), which contains Prokopios of Gaza's *Ekloge epitomon*,[131]

---

126 Codices Venice, Biblioteca Nazionale Marciana, Marc. gr. 22 (13th c.), 57 (12th c.), 136 (13th c.), 158 (14th c.), 164 (mid. 14th c.) and 170 (12th c.), see in this regard Mioni, *Thesaurus antiquus*, vol. 1, pp. 36–37, 82, 189–91, 230–31, 241–43 and 253–56.

127 For greater detail on Bessarion's library, see *infra* pp. 479–80.

128 For the catalogue of manuscripts copied by Chortasmenos or containing shorter texts or notes of his own, and those simply containing his own works, see Hunger, *Johannes Chortasmenos*, pp. 51–53. See also Gamillscheg/Harlfinger, *Repertorium*, vol. 1, no. 191 and vol. 2, no. 252 and Gamillscheg/Harlfinger/ Eleuteri, *Repertorium*, no. 315.

129 Hunger includes in his catalogue the famous Vienna *Dioscourides*, which belonged, according to its inscription, to the Prodromos Petra Monastery, see *supra* p. 161. The work in question, however, is a 6th-century manuscript which Chortasmenos simply refreshed and rebound but which never belonged to him, see Hunger, *Johannes Chortasmenos*, p. 51 and Mondrain, "Un nouveau manuscrit", p. 356, n. 22.

130 These manuscripts contain works of, e.g., Aristotle, Euclid, Euripides, Theon, Libanios, Lucian, Theodore Metochites, Plutarch, Ptolemy and Michael Psellos, see Hunger, *Johannes Chortasmenos*, pp. 51–53.

131 See Mondrain, "Un nouveau manuscrit", pp. 351–58.

478   TAXIDIS

Princeton, Princeton University Library, Princ. MS. 173 and 173A dated to the
late 13th century and the first quarter of the 15th century respectively, which
contain Aristotle's *Organon*,[132] and two 14th-century manuscripts of philosophical texts, Paris, Bibliothèque nationale de France, Par. gr. 1846, and
Vatican City, Biblioteca Apostolica Vaticana, Vat. gr. 1018.[133] Additionally, based
on an autograph annotation of 1430 to codex Oxford, Library of Christ Church
College, Oxon. Aed. Chr. 56 (fol. 402ᵛ), Chortasmenos owned another ten liturgical manuscripts, which he had copied himself and which, as Metropolitan
Ignatios of Selybria, he donated to his cathedral.[134]

The sole source for the personal library of the distinguished monk, writer
and scholar Joseph Bryennios is the testament he drew up in 1421,[135] by which
he bequeathed eleven books, all of secular literature, to the library of Hagia
Sophia.[136] This number seems small in relation to his career, and he may well
have owned more books than these few volumes of grammar, rhetoric, philosophy, mathematics and music, including works by Planoudes, Moschopoulos,
Thomas Magistros, Aristotle, Nicomachus, Blemmydes, Ptolemy and Manuel
Bryennios, which he presumably used in teaching.[137] The explanation for this
apparent paucity, however, may be that Bryennios chiefly used the library of
the Charsianeites Monastery, in which he was living at the time.[138]

Most of the known teachers and copyists associated with the Prodromos
Petra Monastery and the "Katholikon Museion" in the 15th century[139] must also
have had their own larger or smaller libraries, although it is not always clear
which of the codices connected with them were their personal property or
had been commissioned to adorn some other library. These scribes included

132   See Kotzabassi/Patterson Ševčenko/Skemer, *Greek Manuscripts at Princeton*, pp. 147–50
      and Kotzabassi, "Aristotle's *Organon*", pp. 57–60 (and n. 22).
133   See Cataldi Palau, "The Library of the Monastery of Prodromos Petra", p. 213 (with the
      older bibliography) and Cacouros, "Marginalia", pp. 271–78. See also Cacouros, "Jean
      Chortasménos", pp. 185–225.
134   See in this regard Gamillscheg, "Die Handschriftenliste", pp. 52–56.
135   For a detailed account of his life and work, see Tomadakes, Ὁ Ἰωσήφ Βρυέννιος, pp. 11–36.
136   See Joseph Bryennios, *Testament*, ed. Papadopoulos-Kerameus, p. 295, lines 26–28. For
      the dubious hypothesis formulated by Manaphes that this collection, which in his view
      comprised only liturgical books, was left not to Hagia Sophia but to the patriarchal
      library which was housed in the neighbouring Thomaite triclinium, see Manaphes,
      Αἱ ἐν Κωνσταντινουπόλει βιβλιοθῆκαι, pp. 156–57. See also Tomadakes, Ὁ Ἰωσήφ Βρυέννιος,
      p. 33 and *supra* p. 460.
137   See Joseph Bryennios, *Testament*, ed. Papadopoulos-Kerameus, p. 295, line 28–p. 296,
      line 11.
138   See Tomadakes, Ὁ Ἰωσήφ Βρυέννιος, p. 33 and *supra* p. 464 (and n. 37).
139   For the monastery and the "Katholikon Mouseion", see *supra* pp. 460–61.

PRIVATE AND PUBLIC LIBRARIES IN BYZANTIUM 479

George Baiophoros, Stephen of Media, George Chrysokokkes, Leo Atrapes, John Argyropoulos and Michael Apostoles, whose names are associated with more than two hundred manuscripts.[140]

The interest in manuscripts Doukas betrays in his *History* is also attested by the modest collection of books owned by the historian, who lived in Nea Phokaia and Lesbos.[141] It has been shown that the only exemplar of his *History*, the manuscript Paris, Bibliothèque nationale de France, Par. gr. 1310 dated to the last half of the 15th century, is most probably an autograph copy,[142] while the content of the other five codices written in the same hand allow us to form some idea of the books he had in his possession.[143] The number and variety of the texts he copied into codex Par. gr. 1310, and the texts that complete into codex Paris, Bibliothèque nationale de France, Par. gr. 1115 of 1276 and the 14th-century codex Oxford, Bodleian Library, Bodl. Canon. 41 show that he must have had access to an extensive and well-furnished library.[144] He also owned an 11th-century codex of the Old Testament, the codex Florence, Biblioteca Medicea Laurenziana, Laur. Plut. 10.8, a miscellany of mainly dogmatic works, the codex Paris, Bibliothèque nationale de France, Par. gr. 1303 dated to the first half of the 14th century and probably a) the 14th-century manuscript Vatican City, Biblioteca Apostolica Vaticana, Vat. gr. 12, which in addition to the *Lexicon vindobonense* contains also a number of other texts (grammatical and lexico-graphical, proverbs, passages from ecclesiastical and comic writers),[145] and b) the 15th-century codex London, British Library, Lond. Burn. 92, devoted exclusively to texts on astronomy.

Two of the finest private libraries of the Palaeologan period, although created partially after the Fall of Constantinople and thus after the end of the Byzantine era, were those of Cardinal Bessarion and Constantine Laskaris. By his own account Bessarion set about building up a substantial library from a very early age, collecting as many manuscripts as he could and copying what

---

140 See Gamillscheg/Harlfinger, *Repertorium*, vol. 1, nos. 55, 158, 278, 366 and vol. 2, nos. 74, 95, 212, 328, 379, 503 and Gamillscheg/Harlfinger/Eleuteri, *Repertorium*, nos. 90, 127, 263, 383, 454, 584. See also *supra* pp. 460–61.

141 See also *supra* p. 459, n. 3.

142 See Kotzabassi, "Ist der Kopist?", pp. 679–83. See also Reinsch, "Warum der Text", pp. 185–92.

143 See Kotzabassi, "Der Kopist", pp. 309 and 311–14. See also Kotzabassi, "Ist der Kopist?", p. 679.

144 For the codex Par. gr. 1115, see also *supra* p. 459, n. 6.

145 See Kotzabassi, "Doukas", p. 399. For a recent description of the codex, see Guida, *Lexicon vindobonense*, pp. xxx–xxxi (with the older bibliography).

he could not afford to buy.[146] After 1439, in particular, as an expatriate living in Italy, he managed to acquire many manuscripts of ancient Greek works – chiefly, given his particular interest in philosophy, Aristotle and Plato – and commissioned copies and translations into Latin. A few years before his death he bequeathed hundreds of volumes of Greek and Latin manuscripts to the city of Venice, where they became the nucleus of the Biblioteca Marciana.[147]

Scholar and grammarian Constantine Laskaris, another Byzantine expatriate living in Italy, also built up an extensive library starting from the books he acquired in different parts of Greece (Rhodes, Pherae, Crete) in the first years after the Fall and before he settled in Milan.[148] He bequeathed his collection, which numbered at least 149 autograph manuscripts, mainly of classical literature, to the Senate of Messina in Sicily, where he had been living and where many of them had been written. Two centuries later they were taken to Spain, and are now part of the Royal Library in Madrid.[149]

There can be no doubt that at least the known scholars of the age, and probably many others as well, had their own personal libraries, large or small, whether or not any evidence of them now remains. At the same time, the wide-ranging nature of those Palaeologan libraries (apart from the monastic ones, which were overwhelmingly theological) demonstrates the lively interest of their scholarly owners in collecting and preserving primarily secular books, with the ancient classics and particularly the works of Aristotle occupying a pre-eminent position in the intellectual activity of the last two centuries of the Byzantine empire.

---

146   See Bessarion, *Letter to the Doge and Senate of Venice*, ed. Labowsky, p. 147, lines 1–3: *Equidem semper a tenera fere puerilique aetate omnem meum laborem, omnem operam, curam studiumque adhibui ut quotcumque possem libros in omni disciplinarum genere comparem.*

147   See Labowsky, *Bessarion's Library*, pp. 1–144 (esp. pp. 5–23); Mioni, "La formazione", pp. 229–40 and Mondrain, "Le cardinal Bessarion", pp. 187–202. See also Leporace/Mioni, *Cento codici Bessarionei*, pp. 3–95; Gamillscheg/Harlfinger, *Repertorium*, vol. 1, no. 41 and vol. 2, no. 61 and Gamillscheg/Harlfinger/Eleuteri, *Repertorium*, no. 77.

148   See Martínez Manzano, *Constantino Láscaris*, pp. 6–9. Generally for the transfer of Greek manuscripts to the West after the Fall of Constantinople in 1453, see Mondrain, "Der Transfer griechischer Handschriften", pp. 109–22.

149   See Martínez Manzano, *Constantino Láscaris*, pp. 31–81 (esp. pp. 32–45 and 55–68). See also Gamillscheg/Harlfinger, *Repertorium*, vol. 1, no. 223 and vol. 2, no. 313 and Gamillscheg/ Harlfinger/Eleuteri, *Repertorium*, no. 362.

PRIVATE AND PUBLIC LIBRARIES IN BYZANTIUM

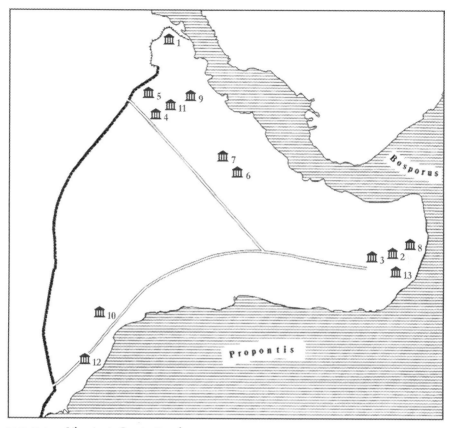

MAP 12.1   Libraries in Constantinople

1. Imperial Library (Blachernae Palace)
2. Patriarchal Library
3. Library of Hagia Sophia
4. Library of the "Katholikon Museion" (or "Museion of the Xenon")
5. Library of the Chora Monastery
6. Library of the Christ Akataleptos Monastery
7. Library of the Christ Pantepoptes Monastery
8. Library of the Monastery of St. George Mangana
9. Library of the Pammakaristos Monastery
10. Library of the Peribleptos Monastery
11. Library of the Prodromos Petra Monastery
12. Library of the Stoudios Monastery
13. Library of the Theotokos Hodegetria Monastery

MAP 12.2   Monastic Libraries in Asia Minor

1. Egirdir (Pisidia)
2. Monastery of Kellibara (Miletos)
3. Monastery of Kotine (Philadelphia)
4. Monastery of the Theotokos of Galesion (Ephesos)
5. Monastery of the Theotokos tou Stylou (Miletos)

PRIVATE AND PUBLIC LIBRARIES IN BYZANTIUM 483

Bibliography

Primary Sources

Bessarion, *Letter to the Doge and Senate of Venice*, ed. Labowsky, *Bessarion's Library*, pp. 147–151.

Constantine Akropolites, *Letters*, ed. R. Romano, *Constantino Acropolita. Epistole*, Naples 1991.

Constantine Laskaris, *On Greek Writers from Sicily*, in *Patrologia Graeca*, vol. 161, cols. 915–924.

Doukas, *History*, ed. V. Grecu, *Ducas, Historia Turco – Byzantina (1341–1462)* (Scriptores Bizantini, 1), Bucharest 1958.

Gabriel monk, *Testament*, ed. S.G. Mercati, "Un testament inédit en faveur de Saint-Georges des Manganes", *Revue des Études Byzantines* 6 (1948), 46–47.

George Pachymeres, *History*, ed. A. Failler, *Georges Pachymérès, Relations historiques* (Corpus Fontium Historiae Byzantinae, 24), 5 vols., Paris 1984/2000.

Gregory of Cyprus, *Letters*, ed. S. Eustratiades, Γρηγορίου τοῦ Κυπρίου οἰκουμενικοῦ πατριάρχου ἐπιστολαὶ καὶ μῦθοι, Alexandria 1910.

Gregory of Cyprus, *Letters to Theodora Raoulaina*, ed. S. Kotzabassi, "Scholarly Friendship in the Thirteenth Century: Patriarch Gregorios II Kyprios and Theodora Raoulaina", *Parekbolai* 1 (2011), 145–67.

Inventory of the monastery of Christ Panoiktirmon, eds. F. Miklosich/J. Müller, *Acta et diplomata graeca medii aevi sacra et profana*, vol. 5, Vienna 1887, pp. 322–27.

John Bekkos, *Testament*, ed. S. Kotzabassi, "The Testament of Patriarch John Bekkos", Βυζαντινά 32 (2012), 32–35.

Joseph Bryennios, *Testament*, ed. A. Papadopoulos-Kerameus, *Varia graeca sacra. Sbornik grečeskich neizdannych bogoslovskich tekstov IV–XV vekov* [Collection of Unedited Greek Theological Texts of the 4th–15th c.], Saint Petersburg 1909 (repr. *Subsidia Byzantina lucis ope iterate*, 6, Leipzig 1975), pp. 295–96.

Manuel Moschopoulos, *Letters*, ed. L. Levi, "Cinque lettere inedite di Emanuele Moscopulo (Cod. Marc. CI. XI, 15)", *Studi Italiani di Filologia Classica* 10 (1902), 60–63.

Matthew of Ephesos (Manuel Gabalas), *Letters*, ed. & trans. D. Reinsch, *Die Briefe des Matthaios von Ephesos im Codex Vindobonensis Theol. Gr. 174*, Berlin 1974.

Maximos the Monk, *Testament*, ed. M. Gedeon, "Διαθήκη Μαξίμου μοναχοῦ, κτήτορος τῆς ἐν Λυδίᾳ μονῆς Κοτινῆς (1247)", *Μικρασιατικά Χρονικά* 2 (1939), 263–91.

Maximos Planoudes, *Epigrams*, ed. & trans. I. Taxidis, *Les épigrammes de Maxime Planude: introduction, édition critique, traduction française et annotation* (Byzantinisches Archiv, 32), Berlin 2017.

484   TAXIDIS

Maximos Planoudes, *Letters*, ed. P.A. Leone, *Maximi monachi Planudis epistulae* (Classical and Byzantine Monographs, 18), Amsterdam 1991.

Michael Gabras, *Letters*, ed. G. Fatouros, *Die Briefe des Michael Gabras* (*ca. 1290–nach 1350*) (Wiener Byzantinistische Studien, 10), 2 vols., Vienna 1973.

Michael Kritoboulos, *History*, ed. D.R. Reinsch, *Critobuli Imbriotae Historiae* (Corpus Fontium Historiae Byzantinae, 22), Berlin 1983.

Nikephoros Choumnos, *Letters*, ed. J.F. Boissonade, *Anecdota nova*, Paris 1844 (repr. Hildesheim 1962), pp. 1–190.

Nikephoros Gregoras, *Roman History*, eds. L. Schopen/I. Bekker, *Nicephori Gregorae Byzantina Historia* (Corpus Scriptorum Historiae Byzantinae, 19), 3 vols., Bonn 1829–55.

Nikephoros Kallistos Xanthopoulos, *Ecclesiastical History*, in *Patrologia Graeca*, vols., 145–147.

Pero Tafur, *Adventures and travels*, ed. M. Jiménez de la Espada, *Andanças é viajes de Pero Tafur por diversas partes del mundo avidos (1435–1439)* (Colección de libros españoles raros ó curiosos, 8), Madrid 1874.

Theodore Hyrtakenos, *Letters*, ed. & trans. A. Karpozilos/G. Fatouros, *The Letters of Theodoros Hyrtakenos, Greek Text, Translation, and Commentary*, Athens 2017.

Theodore Metochites, *Letter to the Monks of the Chora*, ed. I. Ševčenko, "Πρὸς τοὺς μοναχοὺς τῆς Χώρας ἐπὶ τῇ τελευτῇ τοῦ πρώτου καθηγουμένου αὐτῶν Λουκᾶ· μονῳδία τε ἐπ᾽ αὐτῷ καὶ προτροπὴ αὐτοῖς εἰς τὴν ἐπιμέλειαν τοῦ καλοῦ", in P.A. Underwood (ed.), *The Kariye Djami, vol. 4: Studies in the Art of the Kariye Djami and Its Intellectual Background* (Bollingen Series, 70), Princeton 1975, pp. 57–84.

Theodore Metochites, *Poems*, ed. I. Polemis, *Theodori Metochitae carmina* (Corpus Christianorum, Series Graeca, 83), Turnhout 2015.

Theodore Metochites, *Poems*, trans. I. Polemis, *Theodore Metochites, Poems. Introduction, translation and notes* (Corpus Christianorum in Translation, 26), Turnhout 2017.

Secondary Literature

Alexakis, A., *Parisinus graecus 1115 and its Archetype* (Dumbarton Oaks Studies, 34), Washington, DC 1996.

Astruc, Ch./G. Astruc-Morize/P. Géhin/M.-G. Guérard/Ph. Hoffmann/B. Mondrain/ J.A. Munitiz, *Les manuscrits grecs datés des XIIIᵉ et XIVᵉ siècles conservés dans les bibliothèques publiques de France. I. XIIIᵉ siècle*, Paris 1989.

Berger, A., "Nikephoros Kallistou Xanthopoulos und seine Quellen in den Büchern I bis VI", in Chr. Gastgeber/S. Panteghini (eds.), *Ecclesiastical History and Nikephoros Kallistou Xanthopoulos. Proceedings of the International Symposium, Vienna, 15th–16th December 2011* (Österreichische Akademie der Wissenschaften. Denkschriften der

PRIVATE AND PUBLIC LIBRARIES IN BYZANTIUM 485

philosophisch.-historischen Klasse, 477. Veröffentlichungen zur Byzanzforschung, 37), Vienna 2015, pp. 9–16.

Bianconi, D., "La biblioteca di Cora tra Massimo Planude e Niceforo Gregora. Una questione di mani", *Segno e Testo* 3 (2005), 391–438.

Bianconi, D., "La 'biblioteca' di Niceforo Gregora", in B. Atsalos/N. Tsironi (eds.), *Πρακτικά του ΣΤ´ Διεθνούς Συμποσίου Ελληνικής Παλαιογραφίας (Δράμα, 21–27 Σεπτεμβρίου 2003)* [= *Βιβλιοαμφιάστης – Παράρτημα*, 1], Athens 2008, vol. 1, pp. 225–33.

Bianconi, D., *Tessalonica nell'età dei Paleologi. Le pratiche intellettuali nel riflesso della cultura scritta* (Dossiers Byzantins, 5), Paris 2005.

Browning, R., "Recentiores non detentiores", *Bulletin of the Institute of Classical Studies* 7 (1960), 11–21 (repr. in id. Studies on Byzantine history, literature and education, London 1977, no. 12).

Cacouros, M., "Jean Chortasménos katholikos didaskalos, annotateur du Corpus logicum dû à Néophytos Prodromènos", *Bollettino della Badia greca di Grottaferrata* 52 (1998), 185–225.

Cacouros, M., "Marginalia de Chortasménos dans un opuscule logique dû à Prodromènos (Vatic. gr. 1018)", *Revue des Études Byzantines* 53 (1995), 271–78.

Canart, P., *Codices vaticani graeci. Codices 1745–1962*, Vatican City 1970.

Canart, P., "A propos du Vaticanus graecus 207. Le recueil scientifique d'un érudit constantinopolitain du XIIIᵉ siècle et l'emploi du papier "à zig-zag" dans la capitale byzantine", *Illinois Classical Studies* 7/2 (1982), 271–98.

Cataldi Palau, A., "I colleghi di Giorgio Baiophoros: Stefano di Medea, Giorgio Crisococca, Leon Atrapes", in B. Atsalos/N. Tsironi (eds.), *Πρακτικά του ΣΤ´ Διεθνούς Συμποσίου Ελληνικής Παλαιογραφίας (Δράμα, 21–27 Σεπτεμβρίου 2003)*, [= *Βιβλιοαμφιάστης – Παράρτημα*, 1], Athens 2008, vol. 1, pp. 191–224 (repr. in ead., *Studies in Greek Manuscripts*, vol. 1, pp. 303–44).

Cataldi Palau, A., "Legature constantinopolitane del monastero di Prodromo Petra tra I manoscritti di Giovanni di Ragusa († 1453)", Codices manuscripti 37/38 (2001), 11–50 (repr. in ead., *Studies in Greek Manuscripts*, vol. 1, pp. 235–80).

Cataldi Palau, A., "*Mazaris*, Giorgio Baiophoros e il monastero di Prodromo Petra", *Nea Rhome* 7 (2010), 367–97.

Cataldi Palau, A., *Studies in Greek Manuscripts* (Testi, Studi, Strumenti, 24), 2 vols., Spoleto 2008.

Cataldi Palau, A., "The Library of the Monastery of Prodromos Petra in the Fifteenth Century (to 1453)", in ead., *Studies in Greek Manuscripts*, vol. 1, pp. 209–18.

Cataldi Palau, A., "The Manuscript Production in the Monastery of Prodromos Petra (Twelfth–Fifteenth Centuries)", in ead., *Studies in Greek Manuscripts*, vol. 1, pp. 197–207.

486

Cataldi Palau, A., "Un nuovo manoscritto palinsesto di Giorgio Baiophoros", in S. Lucà (ed.), *Libri palinsesti greci: conservazione, restauro digitale, studio. Monte Porzio Catone (Villa Mondragone) – Università degli Studi di Roma "Tor Vergata" – Biblioteca del Monumento Nazionale di Grottaferrata. Atti del Convegno internazionale 21–24 aprile 2004*, Roma 2008, pp. 263–78 (repr. in ead., *Studies in Greek Manuscripts*, vol. 1, pp. 281–302).

Constantinides, C., "The Scholars and their Books in the Late Thirteenth Century", *Jahrbuch der Österreichischen Byzantinistik* 32/4 (1982), 13–21.

Constantinides, C., *Higher Education in Byzantium in the Thirteenth and Early Fourteenth Centuries (1204–ca 1310)* (Texts and Studies of the History of Cyprus, 11), Nicosia 1982.

Darrouzès, J., "Les manuscrits du monastère Sainte-Anastasie Pharmacolytria de Chalcidique", *Revue des Études Byzantines* 12 (1954), 45–57.

Devreesse, R., *Codices vaticani graeci, Tomus III: Codices 604–866*, Vatican City 1950.

Eleopoulos, N.X., Ἡ βιβλιοθήκη καὶ τὸ βιβλιογραφικὸν ἐργαστήριον τῆς μονῆς τῶν Στουδίου, Athens 1967.

Fryde, E., *The Early Palaeologan Renaissance (1261–c. 1360)* (The Medieval Mediterranean, 27), Leiden/Boston 2000.

Gamillscheg, E., "Autoren und Kopisten", *Jahrbuch der Österreichischen Byzantinistik* 31/2 (1981), 379–94.

Gamillscheg, E.,"Die Handschriftenliste des Johannes Chortasmenos im Oxon. Aed. Chr. 56", *Codices Manuscripti* 7 (1981), 52–56.

Gamillscheg, E.,"Eine Platonhandschrift des Nikephoros Moschopulos (Vind. Phil. Gr. 21)", in W. Hörandner/J. Koder/O. Kresten/E. Trapp (eds.), *BYZANTIOΣ. Festschrift für H. Hunger zum 70. Geburtstag*, Vienna 1984, pp. 95–100.

Gamillscheg, E.,"Zur Rekonstruktion einer Konstantinopolitaner Bibliothek", *Rivista di Studi Bizantini e Slavi* 1 (1981), 283–93.

Gamillscheg, E./D. Harlfinger, *Repertorium der griechischen Kopisten 800–1600. 1. Teil. Handschriften aus Bibliotheken Grossbritanniens; 2. Teil. Handschriften aus Bibliotheken Frankreichs und Nachträge zu den Bibliotheken Grossbritanniens*, 2 vols., Vienna 1981–89.

Gamillscheg, E./D. Harlfinger/P. Eleuteri, *Repertorium der griechischen Kopisten 800–1600. 3. Teil. Handschriften aus Bibliotheken Roms mit dem Vatikan*, Vienna 1997.

Guida, A., *Lexicon vindobonense* (Biblioteca dell'"Archivum Romanicum", 2: Linguistica, 62), Florence 2018.

Guilland, R., "Les poésies inédites de Théodore Métochite", *Byzantion* 3 (1926), 265–302.

Harlfinger, D., "Einige Aspekte der handschriftlichen Überlieferung des Physikkommentars des Simplikios", in I. Hadot (ed.), *Simplicius, sa vie, son œuvre, sa survie. Actes du Colloque international de Paris (28 Sept.–1 Oct. 1985)*, Berlin 1987, pp. 267–86.

PRIVATE AND PUBLIC LIBRARIES IN BYZANTIUM

Hunger, H., *Johannes Chortasmenos* (*ca. 1370–ca. 1436/37*). *Briefe, Gedichte und kleine Schriften. Einleitung, Regesten, Prosopographie, Text* (Wiener Byzantinistische Studien, 7), Vienna 1969.

Janin, R., *La géographie ecclésiastique de l'empire byzantin. I. Le siège de Constantinople et le patriarcat œcuménique. III. Les églises et les monastères*, Paris 1969.

Janin, R., *Les églises et les monastères des grands centres byzantins* (*Bithynie, Hellespont, Latros, Galèsios, Trébizonde, Athènes, Thessalonique*), Paris 1975.

Kakoulidi, E.D., "Ἡ βιβλιοθήκη τῆς μονῆς Προδρόμου-Πέτρας στὴν Κωνσταντινούπολη", *Ἑλληνικά* 21 (1968), 3–39.

Karpozilos, A., "Books and Bookmen in the 14th c. The Epistolographical Evidence", *Jahrbuch der Österreichischen Byzantinistik* 41 (1991), 255–76.

Karpozilos, A., *Βυζαντινοὶ Ἱστορικοὶ καὶ Χρονογράφοι, Δ΄ (1305–1505 αἰ.)*, Athens 2015.

Karpozilos, A., "The Correspondence of Theodoros Hyrtakenos", *Jahrbuch der Österreichischen Byzantinistik* 40 (1990), 275–94.

Kidonopoulos, V., *Bauten in Konstantinopel 1204–1328. Verfall und Zerstörung, Restaurierung, Umbau und Neubau von Profan- und Sakralbauten* (Mainzer Veröffentlichungen zur Byzantinistik, 1), Wiesbaden 1994.

Kolias, I., "Bibliothèques et manuscrits de Trébizonde", *Ἀρχεῖον Πόντου* 35 (1978), 282–89.

Kolias, I., *Les bibliothèques de la region de Trébizonde et leurs manuscrits grecs*, PhD thesis, Université Paris Nanterre 1971.

Kotzabassi, S., "Aristotle's *Organon* and Its Byzantine Commentators", *Princeton University Library Chronicle* 65 (2002), 51–62.

Kotzabassi, S., *Βυζαντινά χειρόγραφα από τα μοναστήρια της Μικράς Ασίας*, Athens 2004.

Kotzabassi, S., "Der Kopist des Geschichtswerkes von Dukas", in F. Berger/C. Brockmann/ G. De Gregorio/M.I. Ghisu/ead./B. Noack/ (eds.), *Symbolae Berolinenses für Dieter Harlfinger*, Amsterdam 1992, pp. 307–23.

Kotzabassi, S., *Die handschriftliche Überlieferung der rhetorischen und hagiographischen Werke des Gregor von Zypern* (Serta graeca, 6), Wiesbaden 1998.

Kotzabassi, S., "Doukas and codex Vat. gr. 12", in A. Binggeli/V. Déroche/M. Stavrou (eds.), *Mélanges Bernard Flusin* (Travaux et Mémoires, 23/1), Paris 2019, pp. 399–406.

Kotzabassi, S., "Ist der Kopist von Dukas Dukas selbst?", *Byzantinische Zeitschrift* 96 (2003), 679–83.

Kotzabassi, S., "Kopieren und Exzerpieren in der Palaiologenzeit", in A. Bravo García/ I. Pérez Martín (eds.), *The Legacy of Bernard de Montfaucon: Three Hundred Years of Studies on Greek Handwriting. Proceedings of the Seventh International Colloquium of Greek Palaeography* (*Madrid – Salamanca, 15–20 September 2008*) (Bibliologia, 31A), Turnhout 2010, pp. 473–82.

Kotzabassi, S., "Scholarly Friendship in the Thirteenth Century: Patriarch Gregorios II Kyprios and Theodora Raoulaina", *Parekbolai* 1 (2011), 115–70.

Kotzabassi, S., "The Testament of Patriarch John Bekkos", *Βυζαντινά* 32 (2012), 25–35.

488 TAXIDIS

Kotzabassi, S., /N. Patterson Ševčenko/D.C. Skemer, *Greek Manuscripts at Princeton, Sixth to Nineteenth Century. A Descriptive Catalogue*, Princeton 2010.

Kourousis, S.I., *Μανουὴλ Γαβαλᾶς, εἶτα Ματθαῖος μητροπολίτης Ἐφέσου (1271/2–1355/ 60). Α΄: Τὰ βιογραφικά* (Ἀθηνᾶ. Σειρὰ διατριβῶν καὶ μελετημάτων, 12), Athens 1972.

Kugeas, S., "Zur Geschichte der Münchener Thukydideshandschrift Augustanus F", *Byzantinische Zeitschrift* 16 (1907), 588–609.

Labowsky, C., *Bessarion's Library and the Biblioteca Marciana. Six Early Inventories* (Sussidi Eruditi, 31), Rome 1979.

Leporace, T.G./E. Mioni, *Cento codici Bessarionei. Catalogo di mostra*, Venice 1968.

Magoulias, H.J., *Decline and Fall of Byzantium to the Ottoman Turks by Doukas. An Annotated Translation of «Historia Turco-Byzantina»*, Detroit 1975.

Manaphes, K.A., *Αἱ ἐν Κωνσταντινουπόλει βιβλιοθῆκαι, αὐτοκρατορικαὶ καὶ πατριαρχική, καὶ περὶ τῶν ἐν αὐταῖς χειρογράφων μέχρι τῆς ἁλώσεως (1453)* («Ἀθηνᾶ», Σειρὰ διατριβῶν καὶ μελετημάτων, 14), Athens 1972.

Manousakas, M., "Νικηφόρου Μοσχοπούλου ἐπιγράμματα σὲ χειρόγραφα τῆς βιβλιοθήκης του (Πίν 3–4)", *Ἑλληνικά* 15 (1957), 232–46.

Martínez Manzano, T., *Constantino Láscaris. Semblanza de un humanista bizantino* (Nueva Roma, 7), Madrid 1998.

Mercati, S.G., "Un testament inédit en faveur de Saint-Georges des Manganes", *Revue des Études Byzantines* 6 (1948), 36–47.

Mercati, I./Franchi de' Cavalieri, P., *Codices vaticani graeci. I: Codices 1–329*, Rome 1923.

Miller, T.S., *The Birth of the Hospital in the Byzantine Empire*, Baltimore ²1997.

Mioni, E., *Bibliothecae divi Marci Venetiarum. Codices graeci manuscripti. Thesaurus antiquus*, 2 vols., Rome 1985.

Mioni, E., "La formazione della biblioteca greca di Bessarione", in G. Fiaccadori (ed.), *Bessarione e l'Umanesimo* (Istituto Italiano per gli Studi Filosofici. Saggi e Ricerche, 1), Naples 1994, pp. 229–40.

Mondrain, B., "Der Transfer griechischer Handschriften nach der Eroberung Konstantinopels", in K. Arnold/F. Fuchs/S. Füssel (eds.), *Osmanische Expansion und europäischer Humanismus. Akten des Symposions, Wiener-Neustadt 29.–31. Mai 2003* (Prickheimer-Jahrbuch für Renaissance- und Humanismusforschung, 20), Wiesbaden 2005, pp. 109–22.

Mondrain, B., "Le cardinal Bessarion et la constitution de sa collection de manuscrits grecs – ou comment contribuer à l'intégration du patrimoine littéraire grec et byzantin en Occident", in Cl. Märtl/Chr. Kaiser/Th. Ricklin (eds.), *„Inter graecos latinissimus, inter latinos graecissimus". Bessarion zwischen den Kulturen* (Pluralisierung & Autorität, 39), Berlin/Boston 2013, 187–202.

Mondrain, B., "Les écritures dans les manuscrits byzantins du XIVᵉ siècle", *Rivista di Studi Bizantini e Neoellenici* 44 (2007), 157–96.

PRIVATE AND PUBLIC LIBRARIES IN BYZANTIUM 489

Mondrain, B., "Un nouveau manuscrit de Jean Chortasménos", *Jahrbuch der Öster-reichischen Byzantinistik* 40 (1990), 351–58.

Omont, H., *Inventaire sommaire des manuscrits grecs de la Bibliothèque nationale de Paris et des Départements*, 4 vols., Paris 1886–98.

Papadopoulos-Kerameus, A., "Νικηφόρος Μοσχόπουλος", *Byzantinische Zeitschrift* 12 (1903), 215–23.

Papaeliopoulou-Photopoulou, E., *Ο Νικηφόρος Μοσχόπουλος και το ανέκδοτο ποιητικό έργο του*, PhD thesis, National and Kapodistrian University of Athens 1991.

Pérez Martín, I., *El patriarca Gregorio de Chipre (ca. 1240–1290) y la transmisión de los textos clásicos en Bizancio* (Nueva Roma, 1), Madrid 1996.

Pérez Martín, I., "El scriptorium de Cora: un modelo de acercamiento a los centros de copia bizantinos", in P. Bádenas/A. Bravo/ead. (eds.), *Ἐπίγειος Οὐρανός. El cielo en la tierra. Estudios sobre el monasterio bizantino* (Nueva Roma, 3), Madrid 1997, pp. 205–23.

Pérez Martín, I., "Maxime Planude et le 'Diophantus Matritensis' (Madrid, Biblioteca Nacional, MS 4678): un paradigme de la récupération des textes anciens dans la 'Renaissance Paléologue'", *Byzantion* 76 (2006), 433–62.

Pérez Martín, I., "Nuevos códices planudeos de Plutarco", in C. Schrader/V. Ramón/J. Vela (eds.), *Plutarco y la historia. Actas del V simposio español sobre Plutarco. Zaragoza, 20–22 de junio de 1996* (Monografias de la filología griega, 8), Zaragoza 1997, pp. 385–403.

Pérez Martín, I., "Planudes y el monasterio de Acatalepto. A propósito del Monacensis Gr. 430 de Tucidides (ff. 4–5 y 83–85)", *Erytheia* 10 (1989), 303–07.

Reinsch, D.R., "Warum der Text im cod. Parisinus gr. 1310 nicht das Autographon des Autors Dukas sein kann", *Medioevo greco* 19 (2019), 185–92.

Ševčenko, I., "Theodore Metochites, the Chora and the Intellectual Trends of His Time", in P.A. Underwood (ed.), *The Kariye Djami, vol. 4: Studies in the Art of the Kariye Djami and Its Intellectual Background* (Bollingen Series, 70), Princeton 1975, pp. 17–55.

Staikos, K.S., *Η ιστορία της βιβλιοθήκης στον δυτικό πολιτισμό, III: από τον Μέγα Κωνσταντίνο έως τον καρδινάλιο Βησσαρίωνα. Αυτοκρατορικές, μοναστηριακές, σχολικές και ιδιωτικές βιβλιοθήκες στον βυζαντινό κόσμο*, Athens 2006.

Stichel, R., "Sechs kolossale Säulen nahe der Hagia Sophia und di Curia Justinians am Augusteion in Konstantinopel", *Architectura* 30 (2000), 1–25.

Taxidis, I., *Μάξιμος Πλανούδης: συμβολή στη μελέτη του corpus των επιστολών του* (Βυζαντινά Κείμενα και Μελέτες, 58), Thessaloniki 2012.

Tomadakes, N.B., *Ὁ Ἰωσὴφ Βρυέννιος καὶ ἡ Κρήτη κατὰ τὸ 1400. Μελέτη φιλολογικὴ καὶ ἱστο-ρική*, Athens 1947.

Trapp, E., "Probleme der Prosopographie der Palaiologenzeit", *Jahrbuch der Österreichi-schen Byzantinistik* 27 (1978), 181–201.

Volk, O., *Die byzantinischen Klosterbibliotheken von Konstantinopel, Thessalonike und Kleinasien*, PhD thesis, University of Munich 1954.

Vryonis, S., *The Decline of Medieval Hellenism in Asia Minor and the Process of Islamization from the Eleventh through the Fifteenth Century*, Berkeley 1986.

Waring, J., "Literacies of Lists: Reading Byzantine Monastic Inventories", in C. Holmes/ead. (eds.), *Literacy, Education and Manuscript Transmission in Byzantium and beyond* (The Medieval Mediterranean, 42), Leiden 2002, pp. 165–85.

Wendel, C., "Die erste kaiserliche Bibliothek in Konstantinopel", *Zentralblatt für Bibliothekswesen* 59 (1942), 193–209.

Wilson, N.G., "The Libraries of the Byzantine World", *Greek Roman and Byzantine Studies* 8 (1967), 53–80.

Živojinović, M., "Bolnica Kralja Milutina u Carigradu" [The Hospital of King Milutin in Istanbul], *Zbornik Radova Vizantološkog Instituta* 16 (1975), 105–17.

General Bibliography

Primary Sources

Athanasios I, *Letters to the Emperor*, ed. & trans. A.-M. Maffry Talbot, *The Correspondence of Athanasius I, Patriarch of Constantinople. Letters to the Emperor Andronicus II, Members of the Imperial Family, and Officials* (Corpus Fontium Historiae Byzantinae, 7), Washington, DC 1975.

Barlaam of Calabria, *Greek Letters*, ed. & trans. A. Fyrigos, *Dalla controversia palamitica alla polemica esicastica (con un'edizione critica delle "Epistole greche" di Barlaam Calabro)* (Medioevo, 11), Rome 2005, pp. 194–400.

Barlaam of Calabria, *Works*, ed. A. Fyrigos, *Barlaam Calabro, Opere contro i Latini*, vol. 1: *Introduzione, storia dei testi, edizione critica, traduzione e indici* (Studi e Testi, 347), Vatican City 1998.

Bessarion, *Letters*, ed. L. Mohler, *Kardinal Bessarion als Theologe, Humanist und Staatsmann*, vol. 3 (Quellen und Forschungen aus dem Gebiete der Geschichte, 24), Paderborn 1942, pp. 415–571.

Byzantine Alexander Poem, ed. W.J. Aerts, *The Byzantine Alexander Poem* (Byzantinisches Archiv, 26), 2 vols., Boston/ Berlin 2014, vol. 1, pp. 33–232.

Chronicle, ed. P. Schreiner, *Die byzantinischen Kleinchroniken* (Corpus Fontium Historiae Byzantinae. Series Vindobonensis, 12/1), Vienna 1975.

Chronicle of Morea, ed. J.M. Egea, *La crónica de Morea* (Nueva Roma, 2), Madrid 1996.

Chronicle of the Tocco, ed. G. Schirò, *Cronaca dei Tocco di Cefalonia di anonimo. Prolegomeni, testo critico e traduzione* (Corpus Fontium Historiae Byzantinae, 10), Rome 1975.

Constantine Akropolites, *Letters*, ed. R. Romano, *Constantino Acropolita. Epistole*, Naples 1991.

Constantine Laskaris, *Letters*, ed. T. Martínez Manzano, *Konstantinos Laskaris: Humanist – Philologe – Lehrer – Kopist* (Meletemata, 4), Hamburg 1994, pp. 156–74.

Demetrios Chrysoloras, *One Hundred Letters*, ed. F. Conti Bizzarro, *Demetrio Crisolora. Cento epistole a Manuele II Paleologo*, Naples 1984.

Demetrios Kydones, *Letters*, ed. R.-J. Loenertz, *Démétrius Cydonès. Correspondance* (Studi e Testi, 186 & 208), 2 vols., Vatican City 1956–60.

Demetrios Kydones, *Letters*, trans. F. Tinnefeld, *Demetrios Kydones. Briefe* (Bibliothek der griechischen Literatur, 12, 16, 33, 50 & 60), 5 vols., Stuttgart 1981–2003.

Demetrios Kydones, *Monody on Those who Fell in Thessaloniki*, in *Patrologia Graeca*, vol. 109, cols. 639–52.

Demetrios Kydones, *Translation*, in Θωμᾶ Ἀκυινάτου Σούμμα Θεολογικὴ ἐξελληνισθεῖσα, eds. G. Leontsinis/A. Glykofridi-Leontsini, (Corpus Philosophorum Graecorum

Recentiorum, 15), Athens 1976; P. Demetrakopoulos (Corpus Philosophorum Graecorum Recentiorum, 16), Athens 1979; Id. (Corpus Philosophorum Graecorum Recentiorum, 17A), Athens 1980; S. Sideri/P. Photopoulou (Corpus Philosophorum Graecorum Recentiorum, 17B), Athens 1982; E. Kalokairinou (Corpus Philosophorum Graecorum Recentiorum, 18), Athens 2002; A. Glykofridi-Leontsini/I.D. Spyralatou (Corpus Philosophorum Graecorum Recentiorum, 19), Athens 2011.

Doukas, *History*, ed. V. Grecu, *Ducas, Historia Turco – Byzantina (1341–1462)* (Scriptores Bizantini, 1), Bucharest 1958.

Gennadios II Scholarios, *Opera*, eds. L. Petit/X.A. Sidéridès/M. Jugie, *Oeuvres complètes de Gennade Scholarios*, 8 vols., Paris 1928–1936.

George Akropolites, *History*, trans. R. Macrides, *George Akropolites, the History. Introduction, Translation and Commentary*, Oxford 2007.

George Akropolites, *History/Works*, ed. A. Heisenberg, *Georgii Acropolitae opera*, 2 vols., Leipzig 1903.

George Pachymeres, *Commentary on Plato's Parmenides*, eds. L.G. Westerink et al., *George Pachymeres. Commentary on Plato's Parmenides [Anonymous Sequel to Proclus' Commentary]* (Philosophi Byzantini, 4), Athens 1989.

George Pachymeres, *History*, ed. A. Failler, *Georges Pachymérès, Relations historiques* (Corpus Fontium Historiae Byzantinae, 24), 5 vols., Paris 1984–2000.

George Sphrantzes, *Chronicle*, ed. R. Maisano, *Giorgio Sfranze, Cronaca* (Corpus Fontium Historiae Byzantinae, 29), Rome 1990.

Gregory Akindynos, *Dialogue*, ed. J. Nadal Cañellas, *Gregorii Acindyni Refutationes duae operis Gregorii Palamae cui titulus Dialogus inter Orthodoxum et Barlaamitam* (Corpus Christianorum. Series Graeca, 31), Turnhout/Leuven 1995.

Gregory of Cyprus, *Autobiography*, ed. W. Lameere, *La tradition manuscrite de la correspondance de Grégoire de Chypre Patriarche de Constantinople*, Brussels 1937, pp. 173–91.

Gregory of Cyprus, *Autobiography*, trans. A. Pelendrides, *The Autobiography of George of Cyprus (Ecumenical Patriarch Gregory II)*, London 1993.

Gregory of Cyprus, *Letters*, ed. S. Eustratiades, *Γρηγορίου τοῦ Κυπρίου οἰκουμενικοῦ πατριάρχου ἐπιστολαὶ καὶ μῦθοι*, Alexandria 1910.

Gregory of Cyprus, *Letters to Theodora Raoulaina*, ed. S. Kotzabassi, "Scholarly Friendship in the Thirteenth Century: Patriarch Gregorios II Kyprios and Theodora Raoulaina", *Parekbolai* 1 (2011), 115–70.

Gregory Palamas, *Defense of the Holy Hesychasts*, ed. J. Meyendorff, *Grégoire Palamas. Défense des saints hésychastes* (Spicilegium Sacrum Lovaniense. Études et documents, 30), Louvain 1973.

Gregory Palamas, *The One Hundred and Fifty Chapters*, ed. R.E. Sinkewicz, *Saint Gregory Palamas, The One Hundred and Fifty Chapters. A Critical Edition, Translation and Study*, Toronto, Ontario 1988.

GENERAL BIBLIOGRAPHY 493

Gregory Palamas, *Works*, ed. P. Chrestou et al., *Γρηγορίου τοῦ Παλαμᾶ Συγγράμματα*, 5 vols., Thessaloniki 1962–1992.

Irene Choumnaina, *Correspondence with an Anonymous Monk*, ed. & trans. A.C. Hero, *A Woman's Quest for Spiritual Guidance: The Correspondence of Princess Irene Eulogia Choumnaina Palaiologina* (The Archbishop Iakovos Library of Ecclesiastical and Historical Sources, 11), Brookline, Mass. 1986.

John VI Kantakouzenos, *Antirrhetic Discourses*, eds. E. Voordeckers/F. Tinnefeld, *Iohannis Cantacuzeni, Refutationes duae Prochori Cydonii et Disputatio cum Paulo patriarcha Latino epistulis septem tradita* (Corpus Christianorum. Series Graeca, 16), Turnhout/Leuven 1987.

Joseph Kalothetos, *Works*, ed. D.G. Tsamis, *Ἰωσὴφ Καλοθέτου Συγγράμματα* (Θεσσαλονικεῖς Βυζαντινοὶ Συγγραφεῖς, 1), Thessaloniki 1980.

Laonikos Chalkokondyles, *History*, ed. E. Darkó, *Laonici Chalcocondylae Historiarum Demonstrationes*, 2 vols., Budapest 1922/23.

Manuel Kalekas, *Letters*, ed. R.-J. Loenertz, *Correspondance de Manuel Calecas* (Studi e Testi, 152), Vatican City 1950.

Manuel II Palaiologos, *Dialogue which was held with a certain Persian, the Worthy Mouterizes, in Angkyra of Galatia*, ed. E. Trapp, *Manuel II Palaiologos, Dialoge mit einem "Perser"* (Wiener Byzantinische Studien, 2), Vienna/Graz/Cologne 1966; W. Baum (ed.)/R. Senoner (trans.), *Kaiser Manuel II. Palaiologos. Dialog über den Islam und Erziehungsratschlage*, Vienna 2003.

Manuel II Palaiologos, *Letters*, ed. & trans. G.T. Dennis, *The Letters of Manuel II Palaeologus* (Corpus Fontium Historiae Byzantinae, 8), Washington, DC 1977.

Manuel II Palaiologos, *Verses to an Atheist*, ed. I. Vassis, "Ἀνέκδοτοι στίχοι προς ἄθεον ἄνδρα του Μανουὴλ Β´ Παλαιολόγου", *Βυζαντινά* 32 (2012), 37–100.

Manuel Philes, *Poems*, ed. E. Braounou-Pietsch, *Beseelte Bilder. Epigramme des Manuel Philes auf bildliche Darstellungen* (Veröffentlichungen zur Byzanzforschung, 26), Vienna 2010.

Maximos Planoudes, *Epigrams*, ed. & trans. I. Taxidis, *Les épigrammes de Maxime Planude: introduction, édition critique, traduction française et annotation* (Byzantinisches Archiv, 32), Berlin 2017.

Maximos Planoudes, *Letters*, ed. P.A. Leone, *Maximi monachi Planudis epistulae* (Classical and Byzantine Monographs, 18), Amsterdam 1991.

Michael Kritoboulos, *History*, ed. D.R. Reinsch, *Critobuli Imbriotae Historiae* (Corpus Fontium Historiae Byzantinae, 22), Berlin 1983.

Nicholas Kabasilas, *The Life in Christ*, ed. M.-H. Congourdeau, *Nicolas Cabasilas, La Vie en Christ. Livres I–VII* (Sources Chrétiennes, 355 & 361), 2 vols., Paris 1989–1990.

Nikephoros Blemmydes, *Autobiography*, ed. J.A. Munitiz, *Nicephori Blemmydae Autobiographia sive Curriculum vitae necnon Epistula universalior* (Corpus Christianorum. Series Graeca, 13), Turnhout/Louvain 1984.

494 GENERAL BIBLIOGRAPHY

Nikephoros Gregoras, *Florentius*, ed. P.L.M. Leone, *Niceforo Gregora, Fiorenzo o Intorno alla Sapienza. Testo critico, introduzione, traduzione e commentario*, Naples 1975.

Nikephoros Gregoras, *Letters*, ed. P.A.M. Leone, *Nicephori Gregorae Epistulae*, 2 vols., Matino 1982–83.

Nikephoros Gregoras, *Roman History*, trans. J.L. van Dieten, *Rhomäische Geschichte. Historia Rhomaike*, 6 vols., (Bibliothek der griechischen Literatur), Stuttgart 1973–2003.

Philotheos Kokkinos, *Dogmatic works*, ed. D.B. Kaimakis, *Φιλοθέου Κοκκίνου δογματικὰ ἔργα* (Θεσσαλονικεῖς Βυζαντινοὶ Συγγραφεῖς, 3), Thessaloniki 1983.

Philotheos Kokkinos, *Hagiological works*, ed. D.G. Tsamis, *Φιλοθέου Κωνσταντινουπόλεως τοῦ Κοκκίνου Ἁγιολογικὰ Ἔργα. Α´ Θεσσαλονικεῖς ἅγιοι* (Θεσσαλονικεῖς Βυζαντινοὶ Συγγραφεῖς, 4), Thessaloniki 1985.

Prochoros Kydones, *Works*, ed. I. Polemis, *Theologica varia inedita saeculi XIV. Georgius Pelagonius, Adversus Palamam, Anonymus, Adversus Cantacuzenum, Prochorus Cydones, De lumine thaborico* (Corpus Christianorum. Series Graeca, 76), Turnhout 2012.

Stephanos Sachlikes, *Poems*, eds. G.K. Mavromatis/N.M. Panagiotakis, *Στέφανος Σαχλίκης, Τὰ ποιήματα. Χρηστικὴ ἔκδοση μὲ βάση καὶ τὰ τρία χειρόγραφα*, Athens 2015.

Sylvester Syropoulos, *Memoirs*, ed. V. Laurent, *Les "mémoires" de Sylvestre Syropoulos sur le concile de Florence (1438–1439)*, Rome 1971.

Theodore Dexios, *Works*, ed. I. Polemis, *Theodori Dexii, Opera ommia* (Corpus Christianorum. Series Graeca, 55), Turnhout/Leuven 2003.

Theodore Hyrtakenos, *Letters*, ed. & trans. A. Karpozilos/G. Fatouros, *The Letters of Theodoros Hyrtakenos, Greek Text, Translation, and Commentary*, Athens 2017.

Theodore Metochites, *Orations*, eds. I. Polemis/E. Kaltsogianni, *Theodorus Metochites, Orationes* (Bibliotheca Teubneriana, 2031), Berlin/Boston 2019.

Theodore Metochites, *Poems*, ed. I. Polemis, *Theodori Metochitae carmina* (Corpus Christianorum. Series Graeca, 83), Turnhout 2015.

Theodore Metochites, *Poems*, trans. I. Polemis, *Theodore Metochites, Poems. Introduction, translation and notes* (Corpus Christianorum in Translation, 26), Turnhout 2017.

Theodore Metochites, *Stoicheiosis Astronomike*, ed. B. Bydén, *Theodore Metochites' Stoicheiosis Astronomike and the Study of Natural Philosophy and Mathematics in Early Palaiologan Byzantium* (Studia Graeca et Latina Gothoburgensia, 66), Gothenburg 2003.

Theophanes of Nicaea, *Treatise*, ed. I. Polemis, *Θεοφάνους Νικαίας, Ἀπόδειξις ὅτι ἐδύνατο ἐξ ἀιδίου γεγενῆσθαι τὰ ὄντα καὶ ἀνατροπὴ ταύτης*. Editio princeps, εἰσαγωγή, κείμενο, μετάφραση, εὑρετήρια (Corpus Philosophorum Medii Aevi. Philosophi Byzantini, 10), Athens 2000.

Theseid, Book I, ed. E. Follieri, *Il Teseida Neogreco. Libro I. Saggio di edizione*, Athens/Rome 1959.

GENERAL BIBLIOGRAPHY

Theseid, Book VI, ed. B. Olsen, "The Greek Translation of Boccaccio's *Theseid*, Book 6", *Classica et Mediaevalia* 41 (1990), 275–301.

Secondary Literature

Acerbi, F., "Logistic, Arithmetic, Harmonic Theory, Geometry, Metrology, Optics and Mechanics", in Lazaris (ed.), *A Companion to Byzantine Science*, pp. 105–59.

Atsalos, B./N. Tsironi (eds.), *Πρακτικά του ΣΤ΄ Διεθνούς Συμποσίου Ελληνικής Παλαιογραφίας (Δράμα, 21–27 Σεπτεμβρίου 2003)* [= *Βιβλιοαμφιάστης – Παράρτημα*, 1], Athens 2008 [2009].

Balfour, D., *Politico-Historical Works of Symeon Archbishop of Thessalonica* [*1416/17 to 1429*]. *Critical Greek Text with Introduction and Commentary* (Wiener Byzantinistische Studien, 13), Vienna 1979.

Beaton, R., "Byzantine Verse Romances", in Hörandner/Rhoby/Zagklas (eds.), *A Companion to Byzantine Poetry*, pp. 539–55.

Beck, H.-G., *Theodoros Metochites. Die Krise des byzantinischen Weltbildes im 14. Jahrhundert*, Munich 1952.

Belting, H./D. Mouriki/C. Mango, *Mosaics and Frescoes of St. Mary Pammakaristos (Fethiye Camii) at Istanbul*, Washington, DC 1978.

Benakis, L., *Michael Psellos: Kommentar zur Physik des Aristoteles* (Commentaria in Aristotelem Byzantina, 5), Athens 2008.

Berger, A., "Nikephoros Kallistu Xanthopulos und die jüdische Geschichte", in Berger/Mariev/Prinzing/Riehle (eds.), *Koinotaton Doron*, pp. 1–15.

Berger, A./S. Mariev/G. Prinzing/A. Riehle (eds.), *Koinotaton Doron. Das späte Byzanz zwischen Machtlosigkeit und kultureller Blüte (1204–1461)* (Byzantinisches Archiv, 31), Berlin/Boston 2016.

Bianconi, D., "La biblioteca di Cora tra Massimo Planude e Niceforo Gregora. Una questione di mani", *Segno e Testo* 3 (2005), 391–438.

Bianconi, D., "La controversia palamitica: figure, libri, testi e mani", *Segno e Testo* 6 (2008), 337–76.

Bianconi, D., *Tessalonica nell'età dei Paleologi. Le pratiche intellettuali nel riflesso della cultura scritta* (Dossiers Byzantins, 5), Paris 2005.

Blanchet, M.-H., "Atoumès, un nouveau traducteur byzantin de Thomas d'Aquin", in Berger/Mariev/Prinzing/Riehle (eds.), *Koinotaton Doron*, pp. 17–37.

Blanchet, M.-H., "Éliminer Thomas: le programme antithomiste de Matthieu Ange Panarétos (seconde moitié du XIVème siècle)", in Speer/Steinkrüger (eds.), *Knotenpunkt Byzanz*, pp. 452–465.

Blanchet, M.-H., *Georges-Gennadios Scholarios (vers 1400–vers 1472). Un intellectuel orthodoxe face à la disparition de l'Empire byzantin* (Archives de l'Orient Chrétien, 20), Paris 2008.

Bouras-Vallianatos, P., *Innovation in Byzantine Medicine. The Writings of John Zacharias Aktouarios (c.1275–c.1330)* (Oxford Studies in Byzantium), Oxford 2020.

Bravo García, A./I. Pérez Martín (eds.), *The Legacy of Bernard de Montfaucon: Three Hundred Years of Studies on Greek Handwriting* (Bibliologia, 31), Turnhout 2010.

Buchtal, H./H. Belting, *Patronage in Thirteenth Century Constantinople. An Atelier of Late Byzantine Book Illumination and Calligraphy* (Dumbarton Oaks Studies, 16), Washington, DC 1978.

Bydén, B., "'Strangle Them with These Meshes of Syllogisms': Latin Philosophy in Greek Translations of the Thirteenth Century", in J.O. Rosenqvist (ed.), *Interaction and Isolation in Late Byzantine Culture* (Swedish Research Institute in Istanbul Transactions, 13), Stockholm 2004, pp. 133–57.

Candal, M., *Nilus Cabasilas et theologia S. Thomae de processione Spiritus Sancti* (Studi e Testi, 116), Vatican City 1945.

Caudano, A.-L., "Astronomy and Astrology", in Lazaris (ed.), *A Companion to Byzantine Science*, pp. 202–30.

Cavallo, G. (ed.), *Lo spazio letterario del Medioevo, 3. Le culture circostanti, vol. I: La cultura bizantina*, Rome 2004.

Çelik, S. *Manuel II Palaiologos (1350–1425). A Byzantine Emperor in a Time of Tumult*, Cambridge 2021.

Chrysostomides, J. (ed.), *Καθηγήτρια. Essays presented to J. Hussey for her 80th Birthday*, Camberley, Surrey 1988.

Congourdeau, M.-H. (ed.), *Les Zélotes. Une révolte urbaine à Thessalonique au 14e siècle. Le dossier des sources*, Paris 2013.

Constantinides, C.N., *Higher Education in Byzantium in the Thirteenth and Early Fourteenth Centuries (1204–ca 1310)* (Texts and Studies of the History of Cyprus, 11), Nicosia 1982.

Conticello, C.G./V. Conticello, *La théologie byzantine et sa tradition*, vol. 2: (*XIIIe–XIXe s.*), Turnhout 2002.

Cupane, C., *Romanzi cavallereschi bizantini* (Classici Greci. Autori della tarda antiquità e dell'età bizantina), Torino 1995.

Cupane, C./B. Krönung (eds.), *Fictional Storytelling in the Medieval Eastern Mediterranean and Beyond* (Brill's Companions to the Byzantine World, 1), Leiden/Boston 2016.

de Vries-van der Velden, E., *Théodore Métochite: une réévaluation*, Amsterdam 1987.

Estangüi Gómez, R., "Pour une étude prosopographique des fonctionnaires de la chancellerie patriarcale: la carrière du secrétaire Iôannes Chrysoképhalos Holobôlos", in *Lire les Archives de l'Athos* (Travaux et mémoires, 23/2), Paris 2019, pp. 111–84.

GENERAL BIBLIOGRAPHY

Fischer, E., "Manuel Holobolos and the role of bilinguals in relations between the West and Byzantium", in Speer/Steinkrüger (eds.), *Knotenpunkt Byzanz*, pp. 210–22.

Fryde, E., *The Early Palaeologan Renaissance (1261–c. 1360)* (The Medieval Mediterranean, 27), Leiden/Boston 2000.

Gaul, N., *Thomas Magistros und die spätbyzantische Sophistik: Studien zum Humanismus urbaner Eliten der frühen Palaiologenzeit* (Mainzer Veröffentlichungen zur Byzantinistik, 10), Wiesbaden 2011.

Goldwyn, A.J./I. Nilsson (eds.), *Reading the Late Byzantine Romance. A Handbook*, Cambridge 2019.

Golitsis, P., "Georges Pachymère comme didascale. Essai pour une reconstitution de sa carrière et de son enseignement philosophique", *Jahrbuch der Österreichischen Byzantinistik* 58 (2008), 53–68.

Harlfinger, D., "Autographa aus der Palaiologenzeit", in Seibt (ed.), *Geschichte und Kultur der Palaiologenzeit*, pp. 43–50.

Harlfinger, D., "Einige Aspekte der handschriftlichen Überlieferung des Physikkommentars des Simplikios", in I. Hadot (ed.), *Simplicius, sa vie, son œuvre, sa survie. Actes du Colloque international de Paris (28 Sept.–1 Oct. 1985)*, Berlin 1987, pp. 267–86.

Hero, A.C., "Irene-Eulogia Choumnaina Palaiologina, Abbess of the Convent of Philanthropos Soter in Constantinople", *Byzantinische Forschungen* 9 (1985), 119–48.

Hinterberger, M., Autobiographische Traditionen in Byzanz (Wiener Byzantinistische Studien, 22), Vienna 1999.

Hörandner, W./A. Rhoby/N. Zagklas (eds.), *A Companion to Byzantine Poetry* (Brill's Companions to the Byzantine World, 4), Leiden/Boston 2019.

Hunger, H., *Johannes Chortasmenos (ca. 1370–ca. 1436/37). Briefe, Gedichte und kleine Schriften. Einleitung, Regesten, Prosopographie, Text* (Wiener Byzantinistische Studien, 7), Vienna 1969.

Hunger, H./I. Ševčenko, *Des Nikephoros Blemmydes Βασιλικὸς Ἀνδριάς und dessen Metaphrase von Georgios Galesiotes und Georgios Oinaiotes. Ein weiterer Beitrag zum Verständnis der byzantinischen Schrift-Koine* (Wiener Byzantinistische Studien, 18), Vienna 1986.

Kalopissi-Verti, S., "Patronage and Artistic Production in Byzantium during the Palaiologan Period", in S.T. Brooks (ed.), *Byzantium: Faith and Power (1261–1557). Perspectives on Late Byzantine Art and Culture*, New Haven/London 2006, pp. 76–97.

Kaltsogianni, E./S. Kotzabassi/I. Paraskevopoulou, *Η Θεσσαλονίκη στη βυζαντινή λογοτεχνία. Ρητορικά και αγιολογικά κείμενα* (Βυζαντινά κείμενα και μελέτες, 32), Thessaloniki 2002.

Karpozilos, A., "Books and Bookmen in the 14th c. The Epistolographical Evidence", *Jahrbuch der Österreichischen Byzantinistik* 41 (1991), 255–76.

498 GENERAL BIBLIOGRAPHY

Kermanidis, M., *Episteme und Ästhetik der Raummodelierung in Literatur und Kunst des Theodoros Metochites. Ein frühpalaiologischer Byzantiner im Bezug zur Frühen Neuzeit* (Byzantinisches Archiv, 37), Berlin/Boston 2020.

Kianka, F., *Demetrius Cydones (c.1324–c.1397): Intellectual and Diplomatic Relations between Byzantium and the West in the Fourteenth Century*, PhD thesis, Fordham University 1981.

Kidonopoulos, V., *Bauten in Konstantinopel 1204–1328. Verfall und Zerstörung, Restaurierung, Umbau und Neubau von Profan- und Sakralbauten* (Mainzer Veröffentlichungen zur Byzantinistik, 1), Wiesbaden 1994.

Kiousopoulou, T., *Βασιλεύς ή Οικονόμος. Πολιτική εξουσία και ιδεολογία πριν την Άλωση*, Athens 2007 (trans. P. Magdalino, *Emperor or Manager: Power and Political Ideology in Byzantium before 1453*, Genoa 2011).

Kotzabassi, S., "Eine Akoluthie zu Ehren des Philotheos Kokkinos", *Jahrbuch der Österreichischen Byzantinistik* 46 (1996), 299–310.

Kotzabassi, S., "Gregorios Kyprios as Reader and Critic", in ead./G. Mavromatis (eds.), *Realia Byzantina* (Byzantinisches Archiv, 22), Berlin 2009, pp. 76–88.

Kotzabassi, S., "Scholarly Friendship in the Thirteenth Century: Patriarch Gregorios II Kyprios and Theodora Raoulaina", *Parekbolai* 1 (2011), 115–70.

Kubina, K., *Die enkomiastische Dichtung des Manuel Philes. Form und Funktion des literarischen Lobes in der frühen Palaiologenzeit* (Byzantinisches Archiv, 38), Berlin/Boston 2020.

Kyritses, D.S., *The Byzantine Aristocracy in the Thirteenth and Early Fourteenth Centuries*, PhD thesis, Harvard University 1997.

Lamberz, E., "Das Geschenk des Kaisers Manuel II. an das Kloster Saint-Denis und der ‚Metochitesschreiber' Michael Klostomalles", in B. Borkopp/T. Steppan (eds.), *Λιθόστρωτον. Studien zur byzantinischen Kunst und Geschichte. Festschrift für Marcell Restle*, Stuttgart 2000, pp. 155–65.

Lamberz, E., "Die Handschriftenproduktion in den Athosklöstern bis 1453", in *Scritture, libri e testi nelle aree provinciali di Bisanzio, Atti del seminario di Erice, 18–25 Settembre 1988*, Spoleto 1991, pp. 25–78.

Lamberz, E., "Johannes Kantakuzenos und die Produktion von Luxushandschriften in Konstantinopel in der frühen Palaiologenzeit", in Atsalos/Tsironi (eds.), *Πρακτικά*, pp. 133–57.

Lampros, S.P., *Παλαιολόγεια καὶ Πελοποννησιακά*, 4 vols., Athens 1912–30.

Lazaris, S. (ed.), *A Companion to Byzantine Science* (Brill's Companions to the Byzantine World, 6), Leiden/Boston 2020.

Leonte, F., *Imperial Visions of Late Byzantium. Manuel II Palaiologos and Rhetoric in Purple* (Edinburg Byzantine Studies), Edinburgh 2020.

GENERAL BIBLIOGRAPHY 499

Lindberg, D.C./M.H. Shank (eds.), *The Cambridge History of Science. Vol. 2: Medieval Science*, Cambridge 2013.

Magoulias, H.J., *Decline and Fall of Byzantium to the Ottoman Turks by Doukas. An Annotated Translation of « Historia Turco-Byzantina »*, Detroit 1975.

Martínez Manzano, T., *Constantino Láscaris. Semblanza de un humanista bizantino* (Nueva Roma, 7), Madrid 1998.

Martínez Manzano, T., "Malaquías Mónaco, alias *Anonymus Aristotelicus*: filosofía, ciencias y exégesis bíblica en la Constantinopla de la controversia palamita", *Aevum* 93 (2019), 495–558.

Matschke, K.-P./Tinnefeld, F., *Die Gesellschaft im späten Byzanz. Gruppen, Strukturen und Lebensformen*, Cologne/Weimar/Vienna 2001.

Mergiali, S., *L'enseignement et les lettrés pendant l'époque des Paléologues (1261–1453)* (Ἑταιρεία τῶν Φίλων τοῦ Λαοῦ: Κέντρον Ἐρεύνης Βυζαντίου, 5), Athens 1996.

Mondrain, B., "Der Transfer griechischer Handschriften nach der Eroberung Konstantinopels", in K. Arnold/F. Fuchs/S. Füssel (eds.), *Osmanische Expansion und europäischer Humanismus. Akten des Symposions, Wiener-Neustadt 29.–31. Mai 2003* (Prickheimer-Jahrbuch für Renaissance- und Humanismusforschung, 20), Wiesbaden 2005, pp. 109–22.

Mondrain, B. (ed.), *Lire et écrire à Byzance. Actes de la table ronde tenue à Paris à l'occasion du XXᵉ Congrès International des études byzantines, 19–25 août 2001* (Association des amis du Centre de Byzance), Paris 2006.

Necipoğlu, N., *Byzantium between the Ottomans and the Latins. Politics and Society in the Late Empire*, Cambridge 2009.

Papatriantaphyllou-Theodoridi, N., Ἡ χειρόγραφη παράδοση τῶν ἔργων τοῦ Νικηφόρου Χούμνου (1250/55–1327) (Ἀριστοτέλειο Πανεπιστήμιο Θεσσαλονίκης. Ἐπιστημονικὴ Ἐπετηρίδα τῆς Φιλοσοφικῆς Σχολῆς, Παρ. 32), Thessaloniki 1984.

Paraskevopoulou, I., Τὸ ἁγιολογικὸ καὶ ὁμιλητικὸ ἔργο τοῦ Νικηφόρου Γρηγορᾶ (Βυζαντινὰ Κείμενα καὶ Μελέτες, 59), Thessaloniki 2013.

Paschalides, S. "Ἐκφάνσεις τῆς λογιότητας στὸ Ἅγιον Ὄρος κατὰ τὴν Παλαιολόγεια περίοδο", in D. Kaklamanos (ed.), Πρακτικὰ Η΄ Διεθνοῦς Ἐπιστημονικοῦ Συνεδρίου: Ἅγιον Ὄρος καὶ Λογιοσύνη, Θεσσαλονίκη 24–24 Νοεμβρίου 2013, Thessaloniki 2014, pp. 43–52.

Paschos, P.B., Ὁ Ματθαῖος Βλάσταρης καὶ τὸ ὑμνογραφικὸν ἔργον του, Thessaloniki 1978.

Pérez Martín, I., *El patriarca Gregorio de Chipre (ca. 1240–1290) y la transmisión de los textos clásicos en Bizancio* (Nueva Roma, 1), Madrid 1996.

Pingree, D., *The Astronomical Works of Gregory Chioniades, I, The Zīj al-ʿAlāʾī, part 1, Text, translation, commentary; part 2, Tables, Corpus des astronomes byzantine II*, 2 vols., Amsterdam 1985–86.

Podskalsky, G., *Theologie und Philosophie in Byzanz. Die Streit um die theologische Methodik in der spätbyzantinischen Geistesgeschichte (14/15.Jh.), seine systematischen*

Grundlagen und seine historische Entwicklung (Byzantinisches Archiv, 15), Munich 1977.

Polemis, I., "Nikolaos Kabasilas's De Vita in Christo and its context", *Byzantinische Zeitschrift* 106 (2013), 101–31.

Polemis, I., "Notes on a Short Treatise of Nicolas Cabasilas", *Revue des Études Byzantines* 51 (1993), 155–60.

Polemis, I., *Theophanes of Nicaea: His Life and Works* (Wiener Byzantinistische Studien, 20), Vienna 1996.

Polemis, I., "Two Praises of the Emperor Manuel II Palaiologos: Problems of Authorship", *Byzantinische Zeitschrift* 103 (2010), 699–714.

Prato, G., "I manoscritti greci dei secoli XIII e XIV: note paleografiche", in D. Harlfinger/Id. (eds.), *Paleografia e codicologia greca. Atti del II Colloquio internazionale (Berlino – Wolfenbüttel, 17–21 ottobre 1983)* (Biblioteca di Scrittura e Civiltà, 3), Alessandria 1991, pp. 131–49.

Prosopographisches Lexikon der Palaiologenzeit (= *PLP*), 12 vols., ed. E. Trapp et al., Vienna 1976–96.

Rhoby, A., "Poetry on Commission in Late Byzantium (13th–15th Century)", in Hörandner/ Id./Zagklas (eds.), *A Companion to Byzantine Poetry*, pp. 264–304.

Rhoby, A./E. Schiffer (eds.), *Imitatio – Aemulatio – Variatio* (Veröffentlichungen zur Byzanzforschung, 21), Vienna 2010.

Rhoby, A./N. Zagklas (eds.), *Middle and Late Byzantine Poetry: Texts and Contexts* (Byzantioς. Studies in Byzantine History and Civilization, 14), Turnhout 2019.

Riehle, A. (ed.), *A Companion to Byzantine Epistolography* (Brill's Companions to the Byzantine World, 7), Leiden/Boston 2020.

Riehle, A., *Funktionen der byzantinischen Epistolographie. Studien zu den Briefen und Briefsammlungen des Nikephoros Chumnos (ca. 1260–1327)*, PhD thesis, University of Munich 2011.

Riehle, A., "*Καί σε προστάτιν ἐν αὐτοῖς τῆς αὐτῶν ἐπιγράψομεν σωτηρίας*. Theodora Raulaina als Stifterin und Patronin", in L. Theis/M. Mullett/M. Grünbart (eds.), *Female Founders in Byzantium and Beyond*, Vienna 2014 = *Wiener Jahrbuch für Kunstgeschichte* 60/61 (2011/12), pp. 299–315.

Riehle, A., "Theodoros Xanthopulos, Theodoros Metochites und die spätbyzantinische Gelehrtenkultur. Zu einem unbeachteten Brief im Codex Laur. Plut. 59.35 und den Xanthopulos-Briefen im Codex Vat. gr. 112", in Berger/Mariev/Prinzing/Riehle (eds.), *Koinotaton Doron*, pp. 161–83.

Rigo, A. (ed.), *Byzantine Theology and its Philosophical Background* (Byzantioς. Studies in Byzantine History and Civilization, 4), Turnhout 2012.

Rigo, A. (ed.), *Gregorio Palamas e oltre: studi e documenti sulle controversie teologiche del XIV secolo bizantino* (Orientalia Venetiana, 16), Florence 2004.

Rigo, A. (ed.), *Mistici bizantini*, Turin 2008.

GENERAL BIBLIOGRAPHY 501

Rigo, A., *Monaci esicasti e monaci bogomili. Le accuse di messalianismo e bogomilismo rivolte agli esicasti ed il problema dei rapporti tra esicasmo e bogomilismo* (Orientalia Venetiana, 2), Florence 1989.

Runciman, S., *The Last Byzantine Renaissance*, Cambridge 1970 (repr. 2008).

Russell, N., *Gregory Palamas. The Hesychast Controversy and the Debate with Islam. Documents relating to Gregory Palamas. Translated with an Introduction and Notes* (Translated Texts for Byzantinists, 8), Liverpool 2020.

Russell, N. (ed.), *Spirituality in Late Byzantium: Essays Presenting New Research by International Scholars*, New Castle upon Tyne 2009.

Ryder, J.R., *The Career and Writings of Demetrius Kydones. A Study of Fourteenth Century Byzantine Politics, Religion and Society* (The Medieval Mediterranean, 85), Leiden/ Boston 2010.

Samara, D., *Θεόδωρος Μουζάλων. Ἡ ζωὴ καὶ τὸ συγγραφικὸ ἔργο ἑνὸς λογίου τοῦ 13ου αἰώνα* (Βυζαντινὰ Κείμενα καὶ Μελέτες, 64), Thessaloniki 2018.

Savvatos, Chr., *Ἡ θεολογικὴ ὁρολογία καὶ προβληματικὴ τῆς πνευματολογίας Γρηγορίου Β΄ τοῦ Κυπρίου*, Katerini 1997.

Schönauer, S., *Untersuchungen zum Steinkatalog des Sophrosyne-Gedichtes des Meliteniotes mit kritischer Edition der Verse 1107–1247* (Meletemata, 6), Wiesbaden 1996.

Seibt, W. (ed.), *Geschichte und Kultur der Palaiologenzeit. Referate des Internationalen Symposions zu Ehren von Herbert Hunger (Wien, 30. November bis 3. Dezember 1994)* (Philosophisch-Historische Klasse Denkschriften, 241), Vienna 1996.

Ševčenko, I., *Ideology, Letters and Culture in the Byzantine World* (Variorum Reprints), London 1982.

Ševčenko, I., *La vie intellectuelle et politique à Byzance sous les premiers Paléologues: Études sur la polémique entre Théodore Métochite et Nicéphore Choumnos* (Corpus Bruxellense Historiae Byzantinae. Subsidia, 3), Brussels 1962.

Shawcross, T., *The Chronicle of Morea: Historiography in Crusader Greece* (Oxford Studies in Byzantium), Oxford 2009.

Sklavenite, A., Συμβολή στη μελέτη των επιστολών του Νικηφόρου Γρηγορά, Athens 2019.

Smyrlis, K., *La fortune des grands monastères byzantins (fin du Xe–milieu du XIVe siècle)* (Monographies, 21), Paris 2006.

Speer, A./P. Steinkrüger (eds.), *Knotenpunkt Byzanz. Wissensformen und kulturelle Wechselbeziehungen*, Berlin 2012.

Talbot, A.-M., *Women and Religious Life in Byzantium*, Aldershot 2001.

Taxidis, I., *Les épigrammes de Maxime Planude: introduction, édition critique, traduction française et annotation* (Byzantinisches Archiv, 32), Berlin/Boston 2017.

Thorn-Wickert, L., *Manuel Chrysoloras, ca. 1350–1415: Eine Biographie des byzantinischen Intellektuellen von dem Hintergrund der hellenistischen Studien in der italienischen Renaissance* (Bonner romanistische Arbeiten, 92), Frankfurt am Main/Berlin/Bern 2006.

Tihon, A., *Études d'astronomie byzantine* (Variorum Reprints), Hampshire 1994.

Tihon, A., "Science in the Byzantine Empire", in Lindberg/Shank, *The Cambridge History of Science. Vol. 2: Medieval Science*, pp. 190–206.

Timplalexi, P., *Medizinisches in der byzantinischen Epistolographie (1110–1453)* (Europäische Hochschulschriften. Reihe VII. Abt. B Geschichte der Medizin, 9) Frankfurt am Main 2002.

Tinnefeld, F., *Die Briefe des Demetrios Kydones. Themen und literarische Formen* (Mainzer Veröffentlichungen zur Byzantinistik, 11), Wiesbaden 2010.

Toth, I., *Imperial Orations in Late Byzantium (1261–1453)*, PhD Thesis, University of Oxford 2003.

Trapp, E., "Probleme der Prosopographie der Palaiologenzeit", *Jahrbuch der Österreichischen Byzantinistik* 27 (1978), 181–201.

Underwood, P.A. (ed.), *The Kariye Djami, vol. 1: Historical Introduction and Description of the Mosaics and Frescoes, vol. 2: The Mosaics, vol. 3: The Frescoes*, New York 1966, *vol. 4: Studies in the Art of the Kariye Djami and Its Intellectual Background* (Bollingen Series, 70), Princeton 1975.

Verpeaux, J., *Nicéphore Choumnos. Homme d'état et humaniste byzantin (ca. 1250/1255–1327)*, Paris 1959.

Vryonis, S., *The Decline of Medieval Hellenism in Asia Minor and the Process of Islamization from the Eleventh through the Fifteenth Century*, Berkeley 1986.

Ware, K., "St Maximos of Kapsokalyvia and Fourteenth-Century Athonite Hesychasm", in Chrysostomides (ed.), Καθηγήτρια, pp. 409–430.

Ware, K., "The Debate about Palamism", *Eastern Churches Review* 9 (1977), 45–63.

Ware, K., "The Jesus Prayer in St Gregory of Sinai", *Eastern Churches Review* 4 (1972), 3–22.

Weiss, G., *Joannes Kantakuzenos – Aristocrat, Staatsmann, Kaiser und Mönch – in der Gesellschaftsentwicklung von Byzanz im 14. Jahrhundert* (Studien zur Geistesgeschichte des östlichen Europa, 4), Wiesbaden 1969.

Wilson, N.G., *From Byzantium to Italy: Greek Studies in the Italian Renaissance*, Baltimore 1992.

Wilson, N.G., "The Libraries of the Byzantine World", *Greek Roman and Byzantine Studies* 8 (1967), 53–80.

Yiavis, K., "The Adaptations of Western Sources by Byzantine Vernacular Romances", in Cupane/Krönung (eds.), *Fictional Storytelling*, pp. 127–56.

Yiavis, K., "The Categories of 'Originals' and 'Adaptations' in Late Byzantine Romance. A Reassessment", in Goldwyn/Nilsson (eds.), *Reading the Late Byzantine Romance*, pp. 19–39.

Index of Manuscripts and Documents

Athens, National Library of Greece
Metochiou Panagiou Taphou 106   257
Metochiou Panagiou Taphou 455
464n33

Athos
Monastery of Megiste Lavra
K 112   442&n170
Monastery of Vatopedi
65   445
105   445
262   446
Skeuoph. 17   445

Basel, Öffentliche Bibliothek der Universität
N I 6 no 16   438n157

El Escorial, Real Biblioteca
R.I.20   23
Y.II.10   24

Florence
Biblioteca Medicea Laurenziana
plut. 7.31   468
plut. 10.8   479
plut. 10.23   420n88
plut. 57.45   474
plut. 80.19   23
plut. 85.1   257
plut. 85.6   258
plut. 87.5   258
Biblioteca Riccardiana
gr. 58   22

Heidelberg, Universitätsbibliothek
Palat. gr. 356   403&n14

Leiden, Bibliotheek der Rijksuniversiteit
B.P.G. 49   114

London, British Library
Add. 22748   334
Burn. 92   479
Harley 5697   22

Milan, Biblioteca Ambrosiana
C 71 sup. (gr. 185)   404, 412, 420n88
G 14 sup. (gr. 383)   35n140
L 64 sup. (gr. 485)   24

Modena, Biblioteca Estense
α.R.6.19   114

Moscow, Istoriceskij Muzej
Muz. 3649   470n75
Synod. 489   23

Munich, Bayerische Staatsbibliothek
gr. 358   477
gr. 430   3, 225, 470
gr. 485   470
gr. 505   22
gr. 564   474

Mytilene, Monastery of St. John the Theologian of Hypselou
6   445n182

Naples, Biblioteca Nazionale
II C 33   334
II.E.17   23
III. E. 17   258

Oxford
Bodleian Library
Barocci 131   24
Canon. 41   479
Clark. 39   466
Christ Church College
Aed. Chr. 56   478
New College Library
New College 258   21

Paris, Bibliothèque nationale de France
gr. 1115   459n6, 479&n144
gr. 1220   474
gr. 1303   479
gr. 1310   479
gr. 1810   258

INDEX OF MANUSCRIPTS AND DOCUMENTS

Paris (*cont.*)
  gr. 1846   478
  gr. 2830   21
  gr. 2998   23
  Coisl. gr. 128   3
  Mazarine 4453   23

Princeton, University Library
  MS. 173   478
  MS. 173   478

Rome, Biblioteca Angelica
  gr. 42 (C. 3. 13)   258

Sinai, Saint Catherine's Monastery
  gr. 152   440, 446

Turin, Biblioteca Nazionale Universitaria
  C VI 26   307

Vatican City, Biblioteca Apostolica Vaticana
  Chis. R.IV.12 (gr. 12)   474
  Chis. R.VI.a^2 (gr. 54)   430
  Chis. R.VI.43 (gr. 35)   24
  Pal. gr. 138   463n24, 473
  Urb. gr. 80   443
  Urb. gr. 133   214
  gr. 12   479
  gr. 64   474
  gr. 83   23
  gr. 100 B   402&n11
  gr. 101   214
  gr. 112   445
  gr. 175   307n94
  gr. 207   468
  gr. 224   23
  gr. 241   257
  gr. 261   258
  gr. 269   468
  gr. 765   468
  gr. 809   442n170, 446
  gr. 830   460n11, 463n28
  gr. 831   464n33
  gr. 844   326
  gr. 939   24
  gr. 1018   478
  gr. 1086   405, 406, 407
  gr. 1096   381

  gr. 1299   23
  gr. 1822   471n88
  gr. 1899   470n75
  gr. 2207   130n41

Venice, Biblioteca Nazionale Marciana
  gr. 22   477n126
  gr. 203   257
  gr. 481   332
  gr. 613   474

Vienna, Österreichische Nationalbibliothek
  hist. gr. 3   130n41
  hist. gr. 47   406, 432, 433, 434n144,
     439, 440, 443
  hist. gr. 48   432, 439, 443
  med. gr. 1   443
  phil. gr. 95   404, 421n92
  phil. gr. 321   24, 403, 404n17
  suppl. gr. 64   134
  suppl. gr. 75   22, 445
  theol. gr. 174   445

Wolfenbüttel, Herzog August Bibliothek
  Guelf. 42 Gud. graec.   420n88, 421n91

Documents

Athos

Chilandar, eds. Petit/Korablev
  100   420n90
  101   420n90

Chilandar, eds. Živojinović/Kravari/Giros, vol. 1
  10   414n63
  29   404n19
  34   423n97
  35   423n97

Koutloumousiou, ed. Lemerle
  10   423n97

Lavra, eds. Lemerle/Guillou/Svoronos/
Papachryssanthou
  vol. 1
    32   411n50

INDEX OF MANUSCRIPTS AND DOCUMENTS

vol. 2
 89 A   404n20
 103   423n97
vol. 3
 123   423n97

Panteleemon, eds. Lemerle/Dagron/Ćircović
 10   423n97

Philotheou, eds. Regel/Kurtz/Korablev
 3   416n75

Protaton, ed. Papachryssanthou
 12   423n97

Vatopedi, eds. Lefort/Kravari/Giros/Smyrlis
 vol. 2
 62   420n90

Zographou, eds. Regel/Kurtz/Korablev
 11   416n75
 23   420n90

Patmos
 ed. Vranussi
 15   416n75

Venice
 Archivio di Stato, Miscell. Atti Diplomat.
  e Priv.
 busta 12, no 432 [DR, vol. 4, no
  2515]   422n93

Acta et diplomata, eds. Miklosich/Müller
 194–222   441n166
 223   441n167
 319   441n168

Dossier Lyon, eds. Laurent/Darrouzès
 17   413n59, 426n108

Patriarchal Register, eds. Hunger/Kresten et
 alii

vol. 1
 51   406n28 & n31, 407n35
 65   433n139

vol. 2
 132   434n144
 145   435n147
 146   435n147
 147   435n148
 153   435n149
 156   440n163

vol. 3
 176   435n150
 202   436n152
 211   436n151

vol. 4 [forthcoming]
 272–302 [Miklosich/Müller, nos 194–222]
  441n167
 303   441n167
 402   441n168

**Pieralli, *La corrispondenza diplomatica
dell'imperatore bizantino***
 8   403n15
 12–16   413n60
 17   413n59
 20   413n59
 22   427n117
 App. 3   428n119

Index of Regest Numbers

Darrouzès, *Les regestes*, vol. 5
 2081   406n28 & n31, 407n35
 2134   433n139
 2210–2214   434n142
 2213   434n144
 2218   434n145
 2251   435n147
 2270   435n148
 2273   435n149
 2309   440n163
 2311   435n150
 2324   438n156
 2326   438n156
 2375   436n152
 2376   436n151
 2510   441n167
 2622   441n168

INDEX OF MANUSCRIPTS AND DOCUMENTS

Dölger, *Regesten*, vol. 4

2085	404n18
2108	429n125
2121	416n75
2131	416n75
2136	416n75
2149	416n75
2158	404n18
2208	404n20
2323	404n18
2333	423n97
2342	423n97
2348	404n18 & n19
2353	423n97
2390	423n97
2469	423n97
2512	420n90
2515	422n93
2519	420n90
2520	420n90
2538	420n90

2600	405n21
2649	423n97
2787	422n93
2885	423n97

Dölger/Wirth, *Regesten*, vol. 3

1941a	401n10
2026	415n73
2031	414n63

Dölger/Wirth, *Regesten*, vol. 5

3130	405n22
3217	405n22
3222	405n22

Laurent, *Les Regestes*, vol. 4

1433	427n118
1490	429n125
1549	431n132
1567	431n132

Index of Places

Antioch 50, 399n3

Asia Minor 3, 11, 32, 35, 99, 126, 136, 137, 138, 144, 146, 150, 152, 163, 177, 187, 226, 290, 322–26, 402, 465, 466

Athos, Mount 11, 139, 253, 268, 322, 326–28, 329, 330, 337, 339, 346, 350, 351, 352, 358, 360, 365, 366, 368, 400, 414, 420, 423n97, 442, 445, 446

Auxentios, Mount 11, 322, 323, 325, 326n24, 327, 329, 339, 409

Beirut 242

Berroia/skete of 236,328, 339

Bithynia 11, 138, 322, 323, 327

Blachernae Palace 459, 481

Bosporos 150, 153

Bukhārā 90

Bulgaria 330

Cappadocia, -ans 362, 363, 364

Caria 137

Catania 242

Cephallonia 193

Chalcedon 323, 409, 464

Chios 242

Churches (Constantinople)
Hagia Sophia 129, 335n64, 460–461, 478, 481
Holy Apostles 262, 336
Maria-Martha, chapel in Pammakaristos Monastery 178
St. John the Baptist, in Lips Monastery 333
Sts. Peter and Paul, in Constantinople 130
Theotokos, in Lips Monastery 334
Theotokos of Blachernae 463, 474

Constantinople 2, 4, 7, 10, 11, 17, 22, 24, 31, 32, 33, 35, 36, 37, 38, 39, 41, 47, 48, 49, 50, 51, 52, 54, 55, 56, 77, 84, 88, 89, 91, 92, 94n90, 96, 97, 116, 120, 121, 122, 124, 125, 126, 128, 129, 133, 134, 135, 136, 139, 140, 141, 144, 145, 146, 148, 149, 150, 151, 155, 156, 157, 158, 159, 160, 174, 175, 178, 181, 183, 187, 188n80, 192, 193, 197, 198,

217, 222, 224, 226, 228, 229, 230, 235, 236, 239, 240, 241, 242, 243, 257, 263, 265, 267, 291, 292, 293, 294, 295, 296

Corfu 156

Corinth 37, 53

Crete 45, 182, 184, 187, 188, 192, 233, 240, 242, 470, 480

Crimea 442

Cyprus 116, 122, 125, 135, 187, 188, 233, 240, 242, 374, 380

Demetrias (Thessaly) 400

Didymoteichon 81, 143, 354, 476

Egirdir 323, 466, 482

Egypt 211, 286, 322, 399

England 239

Ephesos 6, 11, 44, 116, 228, 238n105, 264, 322, 323, 324, 339, 466, 472, 482

Epiros, despotate of 134, 135, 191, 193, 315, 328

Euboea 126

Ferrara 240

France 96, 239

Galata 141

Galesion, Mount 11, 322, 323, 324, 339, 466, 482

Ganos, Mount 11, 322, 329, 330, 339

Georgia 177

Gotthia 442

Herakleia (Thrace) 438n156 et 157

Herakleia Pontike 406

Hexamilion 37, 145, 162

Hypate (Neopatras) 328

Imbros 53, 153

Ioannina 135

Ionian islands 193

Italy 8, 22, 47, 95, 96, 129, 150, 226, 239, 240, 241, 242, 243, 270, 346, 352, 370, 461, 480

Jerusalem 47, 124, 155, 186, 399

Kallipolis 139
Katholikon Museion; *see* Museion of the
  Xenon 460, 462, 478, 481
Kios 325

Lakonia 53, 232
Lampsakos 329
Latros, Mount 11, 125, 322, 323, 324, 325, 329,
  330, 339
Lembos, Mount 323
Leontarion 160, 161n43
Lesbos 471n85, 479

Macedonia 138, 328–329, 330n39, 336
Mesopotamia 226
Messina 242, 480
Meteora 11, 328, 339
Milan 240, 242, 480
Miletos 11, 322, 466, 482
Mistra(s) 38n165, 39, 43, 44, 45, 48, 59, 230,
  232, 233, 236, 242, 466n52, 471n87
Monasteries
  Akapniou (Thessaloniki) 337, 466
  Anargyroi (Constantinople) 334, 339
  Anastasia St., Pharmacolytria (near
    Thessaloniki) 466
  Archangel Michael of Auxentios
    (Bithynia) 323, 325, 339, 409
  Archangel Michael of Sosthenion 325
  Andrew St., *en te Krisei*,
    (Constantinople) 224, 335, 338
  Athanasios, St. (Phokaia) 471n87
  Aristene (Constantinople) 335
  Blatadon (Thessaloniki) 337
  Brontochion (Mistra) 471n87
  Charsianeites (Constantinople) 129,
    464, 478
  Chilandar (Athos) 326n25, 404n20, 414,
    415, 420
  Chora (Constantinople) 1, 124, 138, 140,
    181, 258, 285n11, 331, 337, 338, 371, 419,
    463, 464, 472n97, 476, 481
  Chortaites (near Thessaloniki) 336
  Christ Akataleptos (Constantinople)
    326, 332–333, 337–338, 465, 481
  Christ Krataios (Constantinople) 4
  Christ Panoiktirmon (Constantinople)
    465
  Christ Pantepoptes (Constantinople)
    324, 465, 481

Christ Pantokrator (Constantinople)
  324n10, 331, 338
Christ Philanthropos Soter
  (Constantinople) 4, 225, 338
Christ the Saviour *tou Kophou*
  (Nicaea) 323, 339
David, Hosios (Thessaloniki) 336
Demetrios, St. (Constantinople)
  125–126, 325
Esphigmenou (Athos) 326
Galakrenon 324
George, St., Mangana (Constantinople)
  462, 463n24, 473–474, 481
Gerontiou (Thessaloniki) 337
Hodegon (Constantinople) 333, 338,
  445n178, 464, 465n42, 481
Holy Five (*Hagion Pente*) 323, 339
Hyakinthos (Nicaea) 324, 339
John the Baptist, (on the Jordan) 471n87
John the Theologian (Patmos) 125, 323,
  465n45, 466
Kellibara (Mount Latros) 125–126,
  323–324, 339, 466, 482
Kotine, (near Philadelphia) 466, 482
Kyr Isaac (Thessaloniki) 336, 337
Lips (Constantinople) 333, 334, 338
Lord-Christ-Who-Is (*Ontos Theou*), (near
  Ephesos) 323, 339
Makrinitissa (Thessaly) 400, 408,
  409n40, 414
Megalou Agrou (Bithynia) 325, 339
Megiste/Great Lavra (Athos) 3, 253, 326,
  358, 420, 467
Nea Petra (Thessaly) 400, 408, 409n40,
  414
Nea Mone (Thessaloniki) 336
Nossion (Bithynia) 324
Pertze (Constantinople) 336
Philokalou (Thessaloniki) 336
Prodromos Petra (Constantinople) 325,
  333, 338, 460, 461, 462n19, 477n129,
  478, 481
Prodromos (near Serres) 329, 339
Resurrection, of the (Constantinople)
  324
Sosandron (Magnesia) 323, 324, 339
Stoudios (Constantinople) 129, 464, 481
Theodora, St. (Thessaloniki) 4, 336
Theotokos (Meteora) 328

INDEX OF PLACES

Theotokos *Bebaias Elpidos*
(Constantinople) 4
Theotokos Eikosiphoinissa (Mount
Paggaion) 329, 339
Theotokos Eleousa *tou Kritzous* 324
Theotokos *Heliou Bomon* (or
Elegmoi) 325, 339
Theotokos Hodegetria; *see* Hodegon
Theotokos Lembiotissa 323, 339
Theotokos Pammakaristos
(Constantinople) 8, 178, 464, 481
Theotokos Peribleptos
(Constantinople) 325, 464, 481
Theotokos of Bolax (near Smyrna)
323–24, 339
Theotokos of Galesion 323–24, 339, 466,
482
Theotokos of *Hiera* (Mount Latros) 325,
339
Theotokos tou Stylou (Mount Latros)
323, 325, 339, 482
Transfiguration of Christ
(Thessaloniki) 337
Transfiguration of Christ (Meteora) 328
Vatopedi (Athos) 326, 327, 366, 467
Xerochoraphion 325
Monemvasia 355
Morea 59, 145, 233
Moscow 148
Mytilene 240

Naples 242
Nicaea, Empire of 17, 48, 49, 113, 116, 126,
128n39, 133, 134, 192, 263, 264, 282n7,
322, 323, 324, 334, 339, 413, 459
Nicomedia 428
Nicopolis 144
Nymphaion 323

Ohrid 222, 400

Paggaion, Mount 329, 339
Palatitzia 129
Palestine 116, 152, 322
Papikion, Mount 330, 339
Paris 100
Paroria, Mount 330, 339
Patmos 125, 323, 465n45, 466
Pelagonia 126

Peloponnese 37, 39, 43, 59, 126, 135, 138,
161n43, 193, 226, 232, 233, 240
Pera 94, 240
Pherae 480
Philadelphia 4, 160, 228, 323, 466, 482
Phokaia 471n87
Phokaia, Nea 479
Pisidia 323, 466, 482
Prousa 325

Ravenna 45, 400
Rhaidestos 329
Rhodes 242, 480
Rome 50, 51, 96, 133, 147, 149, 153, 156, 157,
239, 240, 403, 413, 415, 416, 427
Rumeli Hisar, fortress 150
Russia 177

Sangarius 137
Sebasteia 160
Serres 223, 329, 339
Sicily 126, 480
Skyros 188
Smyrna 323, 324, 339
Spain 239, 480
Syria 322

Tabor, Mount 262, 345, 351, 352, 354,
367n138, 369, 370, 371, 372, 374, 379
Tabriz 88, 89, 90, 91
Tenedos 149, 358
Thessaloniki 4, 5–6, 11, 21, 23, 37, 41, 46,
47, 48, 50, 54, 55, 56, 92, 99, 112n4, 117,
122, 141, 145, 146, 150, 153, 161, 176, 194,
217n19, 226, 230, 231, 232, 235, 242, 288,
322, 328, 332, 336–338, 339, 345, 350,
351, 352, 356, 433, 466, 467n53
Thessaly 328, 400
Thomaite triclinium 460, 478n136
Thrace 11, 126, 138, 140, 161, 329–330, 336,
438
Trebizond, Empire of 45, 51, 52, 53, 88, 89,
90, 91, 175, 183, 233, 467n55
Troy 47, 153, 197
Tunis 426
Tzympe, fortress of 139

Venice 149, 161, 415, 421, 422n93, 424, 480

Xenon of the Kral 460, 462

General Index

Achilles 39n166, 197
Achilles Tatius 195
Adam 187, 379
Aelian 186
Aelius Aristides 220, 469–70, 473, 475
Aeschines 23, 474
Aesop 194, 473n97
Agathangelos *see* Manuel Angelos
Alexander of Aphrodisias 219, 257–58, 470, 475
Alexander the Great 29, 153, 197
Alexios III Angelos, emperor 326n25
Alexios II Komnenos, emperor of Trebizond 89, 90, 175, 326n25
Alexios IV Komnenos, emperor of Trebizond 51n257
Alexios Apokaukos 227, 354, 355
Alexios Iagoup 98n103
Alexios Lampenos 41, 185
Alexios Makrembolites 46
Alexios Palaiologos, grandfather of Michael VIII Palaiologos 325
Alexios Philanthropenos 315
Alexios Strategopoulos, caesar 315, 316n126
al-Zanati 334
Ammonios 257
Anastasios of Antioch 364n116
Anastasios Sinaites 468n63
Anaxagoras 281
Andrew Asan 176
Andrew Chrysoberges 360
Andrew Holobolos 429
Andrew Libadenos 183
Andronikos II Palaiologos, emperor 2, 4, 19, 30n106, 31, 33–36, 38, 40–42, 49, 54, 57–58, 60, 78, 80–81, 84–85, 91, 115n16, 118–21, 126, 136–38, 142, 154, 160, 290, 303, 312, 315, 324, 325, 326, 331, 335, 336, 347, 357, 401, 404, 407, 412, 413, 415, 416, 417, 418, 419, 420, 421, 422, 426, 427n117, 428, 429n125, 432, 433, 459, 465n43, 466, 475
Andronikos III Palaiologos, emperor 36, 42, 54, 57, 84n39, 138–39, 142, 160, 174, 181, 227, 228, 229, 347, 352, 353, 433, 434, 437n154

Andronikos Kallistos 47, 241, 242
Andronikos Kamateros 473, 477
Andronikos Komnenos Doukas Palaiologos 189
Andronikos Phakrases 468
Angeli Jacopo 240
Angelos Kalothetos 233
Angelos Vergikios 186n69
Anna Komnene 112n4, 143
Anna Komnene Raoulaina Strategopoulina 4
Anna Palaiologina (wife of John II Orsini) 191
Anna Palaiologina (Giovanna of Savoy) 434
Anselm of Canterbury 94
anthology 178, 189, 376
anti-Hesychasts 5, 336
anti-Palamites 184–85, 233–34, 261n32n34, 262, 357–59, 365–66, 369, 371, 374, 376–81, 405, 418n83, 437
Antony IV, patriarch of Constantinople 148
Apollonius of Perga 119, 120
Apollonius of Tyre 197
Arabs 322, 381
Aratus 473n97
arenga 16, 402–08
Aristophanes 473n97, 476
Aristotle 3, 7, 10, 23, 30, 32, 119, 123, 219–20, 254–55, 256–59, 260–64, 267–74, 286, 291n32, 292, 296, 300, 364, 369–70, 459n3, 468–70, 475, 476n125, 477n130, 478, 480
Arrian 474
Arsenios Autoreianos, patriarch of Constantinople 126, 335, 414n62, 472
Arsenios, bishop of Tyre 381
Arsenios, metropolitan of Kyzikos 438n156
Arsenios, monk 334
asceticism, ascetics 86, 127, 179, 188–89, 252–53, 269, 326, 329, 345, 349–51, 356, 366, 368–69, 375, 468
Aspasios 257
astrolabe 91
astrology 378–79, 384, 386–91
astronomy 7, 9, 78–81, 84–91, 120–23, 187, 281, 306, 313–14, 378, 444, 477, 479

GENERAL INDEX 511

Athanasios of Alexandria 325, 468n62
Athanasios I, patriarch of Constantinople
 125, 183, 218n21, 268, 329, 367, 431n132
Athanasios Lependrenos 367
Athanasios of Meteora 328, 330
Attic (discourse, rhetors) 16, 32, 53, 97, 115,
 237
Atticising/Atticism 190, 218
Augustine 4, 7, 8, 94, 356n76, 473n97
Aurispa Giovanni 241, 462n20
autobiography 112–19, 121–29, 180
autograph 23–24, 406, 410–11, 414, 471,
 477–80
Auxentios, Saint 325
Averroes 255
Avicenna 255

Barbaro Ermolao 241
Barlaam of Calabria 139, 233, 234, 260,
 261n31et32, 262, 264n47, 311, 345, 346–
 53, 354–57, 359–60, 361, 368, 369–370,
 371–72, 374, 376, 380, 433, 435, 438
Basil I, grand prince of Moscow 148
Basil of Caesarea 362, 363n112, 445, 462,
 468, 469, 470, 474, 475, 477
Bayezid I 99, 100
Beccadelli Antonio 242
Benoît de St. Maure 197n122
Bessarion of Nicaea 44–45, 51–52, 148, 235,
 241, 242, 254, 256, 271, 274, 305, 360,
 443–44, 477, 479
Blachernae, Council of 1285 118, 428,
 429–30
 Council of 1351 435–37
Boccaccio Giovanni 197n125
Boccanegra Ogerio 423
Boethius 2, 472, 473n97
Branas, family 127
brebion 465n42
Bruni Leonardo 239, 240
Bryennios (Gregory or John?) 231
Bulgarians 126, 226
Busbecq Ogier Ghislain de Caligula 432

calendar (metrical) 183–84
captatio benevolentiae 54
Carlo I Tocco 193
cartulary 400, 408, 414

Catalans 137
Cato 4; see also Pseudo-Cato
Charles of Anjou 126
Charles VI of France 100
chreia 25
Christodoulos, Saint 125
Christophoros Mytilenaios 183
chrysobull 323, 325, 401, 403
Cicero 286, 473n97
classicism 22, 147n19, 151, 163
Clement IV, pope 403
Cleomedes 5
commentary,-ies 3, 20, 35, 219, 256, 257,
 258, 266, 267, 268, 271, 359, 409, 468,
 470, 473
Constantine I the Great, emperor 26, 50,
 148, 159
Constantine VII Porphyrogennetos,
 emperor 2
Constantine IX Monomachos, emperor 462
Constantine XI Palaiologos, emperor
 38–39, 58, 154, 156, 237, 255, 462
Constantine Akropolites 2, 3, 6, 19, 26, 30,
 50, 125, 129, 218, 222, 324, 334, 465n38
 et 40, 470n80, 473
Constantine Harmenopoulos 6, 442
Constantine Hermoniakos 191
Constantine Kephalas 178
Constantine Koumas 243
Constantine Laskaris 241–42, 459, 479, 480
Constantine Manasses 192
Constantine Meliteniotes 426
Constantine Palaiologos, despot 57
Constantine Sinaites 23, 468
Copernicus 91
Cyril of Alexandria 468n62, 471

David Dishypatos 185, 353, 374
David, king of Israel 143, 148, 191
David, philosopher 257
Decembrio Umberto 240
Demetrios Chalkokondyles 241
Demetrios Chomatenos 400
Demetrios Chrysoloras 28, 37, 97n100, 98,
 235
Demetrios Kastrenos 241
Demetrios Kydones 2, 4, 6, 7, 9, 19, 36, 46,
 55, 78, 92–96, 97n100, 98–99, 103, 114,

512 GENERAL INDEX

Demetrios Kydones (*cont.*)
115, 117–18, 122, 123, 145, 147, 149, 213–14, 232, 235, 239, 240, 262n36, 269, 270n66, 304, 337, 358–60, 378–80, 405, 411
Demetrios Palaiologos   39n171
Demetrios Tornikes   403
Demetrios Triklinios   5, 21, 23, 194, 337, 476
Demetrios, Saint   6, 50, 289, 303
Demosthenes   22–23, 25, 27, 29, 30, 93, 98, 469, 470, 475
Dio of Prousa   294
Dion Chrysostomus   304
Diodorus Siculus   313, 459, 463
Diogenes of Apollonia   286
Diogenes Laertius   292
Dionysios of Halikarnassos   27
Dionysius Periegetes   185
Diophantus   472
Dioscourides   461
dodecasyllable, -ic   176, 180, 183, 184, 186, 187, 190, 191, 192, 196, 409, 461
Dominicans   263
Dorotheos Blates   337
Doukas   144, 145, 148, 152, 154–56, 158, 160, 161, 163, 459, 479
Doukas Neophytos   243

ekphrasis (description)   46, 51, 52, 100
elegy   172
Elijah, Prophet   178n29
encomium   25, 28, 31, 32, 34, 36n147, 37n151, 38n159n165, 39, 41, 42, 43, 47, 48, 49, 50, 52, 54, 130, 172, 289
energeia, energy   138, 139, 185, 263, 273, 327, 349, 361, 362n106, 363, 364, 370, 373, 374n179, 376, 382
Ephraim Ainios   134, 135, 192
Epicurus   212
epistolography   10, 60, 78, 211, 214, 216, 217n16, 223, 226, 232–35, 241n116, 243
Ertogrul   160
ethopoiia (characterization)   24, 26, 27, 28, 30, 187
Euclid   7, 119, 120, 472, 473n97, 476n130
Eudokia Palaiologina Komnene   413
Eugenius IV, pope   240
Eunomios   362
Euplos, Saint   130
Euripides   304, 473n97, 474, 476, 477n130

Eustathios of Berroia   236
Eustratios, metropolitan of Nicaea   257, 267n56
Euthymios Apokaukos   440n161
Euthymios Zigabenos   469n74, 473
Evagrios Pontikos   365
exegesis, exegete   255, 256, 266, 273, 355

Ficino Marsilio   241
Filelfo Francesco   240, 241n116, 242, 462n20
Flavius Josephus   186, 463
Florence, Council of   8, 45, 123, 240, 242, 360
Franciscus de Camerino   347

Gabriel of Mangana, monk   463, 473–74
Gabriel of Thessaloniki   101
Galaktion Galesiotes   324
Galen   89n69, 474
Garatone Cristoforo   462n20
Gattilusio, family   163
Gazes   43
Gazes Theodore   28, 241, 242, 243
Genghis Khan   89
Gennadios II Scholarios *see* George/ Gennadios II
genos symbouleutikon   19, 53
George Akropolites   2, 7, 17, 22, 26, 29, 33, 116, 122, 133, 134–36, 159n39, 162, 193, 219, 222, 265, 266, 267, 274, 412, 413–14, 415, 416n74, 459, 473n98
George Amiroutzes   153, 175
George Baiophoros   325, 333, 461n14, 462n19, 479
George Bekkos   426, 472
George Boullotes   404, 412, 419–21, 422, 423
George Chionades *see* Gregory Chioniades
George Choumnos   192
George Chrysokokkes   7, 88, 89n67 & 69, 333, 461n14, 462n19, 479
George Galesiotes   12, 46, 220, 425, 431n132, 433b139, 434n149 et 150, 436–41
George Gemistos Plethon   44, 45, 59, 77n5, 147, 148, 158, 159n38, 233, 235, 236, 237, 240, 242, 254–53, 256, 272
George/Gennadios II Scholarios, patriarch of Constantinople   7, 8, 123, 148, 235, 236, 237, 240, 254–55, 256–57, 271, 272–73, 274, 331, 443
George Kaballaropoulos   424n99

GENERAL INDEX   513

George Lapithes 15, 187–88, 380
George Metochites 118, 122, 427, 428
George Moschampar 364, 430
George Mouzalon 135, 219, 334
George Oinaiotes 81n19
George of Pelagonia 380
George Pachymeres 7, 25, 29, 113n6, 124, 134,
    136–38, 162, 181, 193, 256, 258, 263, 267,
    268–69, 271, 274, 306, 413, 415, 428, 429
    et 429n125, 439n161
George Phakrases 371
George the Philosopher 269–70
George Phobenos 6
George Pisides 180n39, 473
George Sphrantzes 148, 156–58, 305
George Tornikes 403, 404
George Trapezountios 241, 254
Ghāzān Khān 90, 91
Giannoulis Eugenios 243
Giovanni Gatto, bishop of Catania 242
gnome 25
gnomologion 58, 188
grammar 18, 19, 22, 76, 116, 119, 123, 185, 235,
    242, 467, 478
Gregory X, pope 413
Gregory Akindynos 4, 5, 139, 185, 188n80,
    225, 233–34, 261n32, 336, 347–48,
    353–56, 360, 366, 369, 370–371, 372,
    374, 375, 376, 377, 379, 380, 435, 438
Gregory Chioniades 9, 78–79, 88–92
Gregory of Cyprus, patriarch of
    Constantinople 3, 7, 17, 22–23, 24–25, 29,
    33, 34, 77n5, 114, 115–117, 122–23, 125,
    180, 218–23, 225, 257, 264, 274, 324,
    326, 332, 335–36, 337, 348, 364, 413–16,
    428n120, 429n125, 430, 468n63, 469,
    470n76, 473, 474
Gregory Koutales 432–33
Gregory of Nazianzos 1, 12, 179, 181, 220, 224,
    265, 266, 445, 462
Gregory of Nyssa 362–63, 375, 445n182, 477
Gregory Palamas, metropolitan of
    Thessaloniki 6, 12, 42, 139, 140, 141, 184–
    85, 233–34, 260, 261n31, 262, 264–
    265n47, 324, 326, 327, 328–30, 332, 336,
    337, 345, 346–82, 433, 438n156, 446, 462
Gregory Sinaites 328, 330, 346n3, 350, 365,
    367, 375

Guarino, Veronese 43, 239, 240, 241
Guy de Lusignan 233n87

Helen Kantakouzene 4, 100
Helen (Eleni) Palaiologina 39n171
Heliodorus 195
Hellas (Hellenes, Hellenism) 18, 76, 77, 97,
    133, 151, 158, 159, 254, 270, 271, 272
Hermogenes of Tarsos 15, 20, 21, 22, 23, 24,
    27, 29, 35, 37, 60, 468, 469
Herodotus 52, 159, 304, 468, 475
Hesaias, patriarch of Constantinople 432,
    433, 440
Hesiod 185, 473n97, 476
Hesychasm 13, 138–39, 185, 255, 269n65, 327,
    328, 337, 338, 345–82
hexameter 124, 172, 175, 176, 180–85
Hippocrates 89n69, 474
Homer 32, 181, 192, 308, 468, 469, 471, 474,
    475
Hugues IV de Lusignan 188n80
Hūlāgū, Il-Khan 89, 91n79
hymnography 6, 182
hyperousiotes 364
hypostasis 372

Iamblichos 265, 288, 300
iambic trimeter 112, 124, 180n39
Ierotheos, anti-Latin theologian 365
Ignatios hesychast 349, 350
Ignatios, patriarch of Antioch 381
Ignatios of Sely(m)bria see John
    Chortasmenos
Ignatios, metropolitan of Thessaloniki 231
Ignatios Vatopedinos 183
Innocent VII, pope 240
Irene-Eulogia Choumnaina 4, 5, 176, 225,
    335, 367, 417n79
Irene-Eulogia Palaiologina 3, 5, 334
Irene Komnene, empress 331
Irene Metochitissa 176, 418n79
Irene-Yolanda of Montferrat 175, 176, 336
Isaac Argyros 7, 374, 376, 378–79, 381
Isaac Palaiologos Asanes 440, 445
Isidore I Boucheiras, patriarch of
    Constantinople 140, 326, 328, 351, 353,
    355–56, 376, 377, 435, 440
Isidore Glabas 60n308, 232

514 GENERAL INDEX

Isidore of Kiev 36, 37–38, 43
Isidore of Pelusion 474
Isocrates 16, 212, 474

Jews 154, 186, 253n3, 381
Joel, Chronicle of 134–35
John II Komnenos, emperor 331
John II Komnenos, emperor of
 Trebizond 175, 413
John III Vatatzes, emperor 126, 135, 380
John IV Laskaris, emperor 414n62
John V Palaiologos, emperor 4, 36, 43, 46,
 55, 93, 100, 117, 129, 140, 149, 161, 174, 185,
 239, 358, 359, 372, 405, 422, 434, 435,
 437n153, 438n156, 445
John VI Kantakouzenos, emperor 2, 4, 36,
 46, 93, 94, 95, 113n6, 114, 117, 118, 129,
 138, 139, 140, 141, 142–44, 154, 162–63,
 175, 185, 227, 229, 230, 232, 239, 259,
 327, 347, 353–59, 371, 372–74, 375, 377,
 378–79, 405, 422, 434, 435, 438n156,
 445
John VIII Palaiologos, emperor 18, 36, 37,
 38n158, 58, 100, 129, 145, 149, 150, 157,
 159, 161, 237
John XI Bekkos, patriarch of Constantinople
 23, 118, 122, 125, 137, 325, 426, 427,
 428–29, 430, 431, 467n58, 468
John XII, patriarch of Constantinople
 431n132
John XIII Glykys, patriarch of
 Constantinople 218, 219, 220, 224,
 405–07
John XIV Kalekas, patriarch of
 Constantinople 185, 353, 354–355, 375,
 433, 434, 435, 436n151, 440, 446
John XXII, pope 347
John II Orsini, despot of Epiros 191
John Aktouarios see also, John Zacharias
John Ampar 128, 431n132, 434, 436–38,
 440n161
John Anagnostes 46, 146
John Argyropoulos 18, 22, 58–59, 241, 305,
 333, 461n14, 462n19, 479
John, bishop of Carpasia (Cyprus) 374
John Charsianeites (Job) 128–29
John/Ignatios Chortasmenos, metropolitan
 of Sely(m)bria 22, 24, 28, 37, 145, 176,

 184, 235– 36, 242, 256, 408, 443–45,
 461n17, 477–78
John Choumnos 475
John Chrysokephalos Holobolos 408, 442,
 443, 444, 446
John Chrysoloras 240
John Chrysostom 51, 185, 462, 465n40, 468,
 469n74, 471, 474, 475
John of Damascus 76n2, 86, 87n54, 183,
 252n1, 264, 266, 468
John Doxapatres 20, 22
John Eugenikos 47, 52, 237–38
John Gabras 220
John Gabras Meliteniotes 418
John, metropolitan of Herakleia Pontike
 405–06
John Kalothetos 269n65
John Kaminiates 112n4, 146
John Kananos 145, 146
John Katakalon 174
John Katrares 23, 85n46, 194, 476
John Katrones 307
John Klimax 189, 463
John Komnenos Petraliphes Raoul 3, 334
John Konstantes 477
John Kritopoulos 474
John Kyparissiotes 140, 374, 375, 378–79
John Lydus 476n125
John Mauropous 112n4, 473
John Palaiologos, caesar 175–76
John Palaiologos, despot 4, 41, 176, 335,
 417n79
John panhypersebastos 418n79
John Pediasimos Pothos 5, 219, 222–23, 256,
 474
John Philoponos 257–58
John Staurakios 119n23, 332
John Theologites 336
John Tzetzes 177n25, 186, 192
John Xenos 125
John Zacharias 9, 78, 81n19, 84–88, 103, 307
John Zonaras 186, 473
Joseph I Galesiotes, patriarch of
 Constantinople 426
Joseph II, patriarch of Constantinople 150
Joseph Bryennios 56, 460n11, 478 & 478n136
Joseph Kalothetos 374

GENERAL INDEX   515

Joseph Rhakendytes   6, 20, 21, 40, 115, 121–22,
  218, 228, 180, 304, 306–07
Josephus Flavius   152, 186, 463
Julius Pollux   474

Kallistos I, patriarch of Constantinople   129,
  328, 346n3, 365n125, 366n132, 367, 372,
  375–77, 435–36, 437n153, 438–39, 441
Kallistos Angelikoudes   359, 376–77
Kallistos, deacon   220
kanikleion/kanikloma   411
kodikion (hieron)   435, 440, 441, 442
kollema, kollesis   412, 416
Korydaleus Theophilos   243

Laonikos Chalkokondyles   144, 145, 158–62
Laskarids, family   133, 134–37, 413
Latins   55, 95, 156, 240, 242, 261, 263, 271,
  345, 347, 348, 373, 426, 427
Lazaros Galesiotes, Saint   324
Leo Atrapes   333, 462n19, 479
Leo Bardales   218, 220, 221, 475
Leo Magentenos   257
Leo Mouzalon   415
Leonardos Dellaportas   182
Libanios   22, 23, 24, 29, 46, 51, 52, 112, 213,
  468, 476, 477n130
logos epibaterios (speech of arrival)   39n169;
  epitaphios (funeral oration/
  epitaph)   40, 46; *prosphonetikos*
  (laudatory address)   35
Louis IX, king of France   426n111
Loukas Notaras   156, 236–37
Lucian   23, 27, 182n50, 307, 469, 477n130
Lusignan   233
Lyon(s), Council of 1274   8, 34, 122, 135, 137,
  147, 188, 262, 364, 403n13, 413n58 & 60,
  415, 425–28

Macrobius   473n57
Maimonides   382n235
Makarios Makres   37, 44, 329–30
Makarios Palamas   330
Makarios, abbot   464
Malachias, priest (*Anonymous aristotelicus*/
  Matthew Kantakouzenos)   259
Malias(s)enos, family   408

Manuel I Komnenos, emperor   33, 173b4
Manuel II Palaiologos, emperor   2, 18,
  28, 30, 36, 37, 43–44, 50, 55–56, 58,
  59, 96–103, 117, 129, 144–45, 148–49,
  153, 154, 157, 159n38, 187, 214n10, 235,
  239n108, 240, 360, 405n22, 443
Manuel Angelos (Agathangelos)   418
Manuel Asan   176
Manuel Bryennios   3, 80, 120, 122, 478
Manuel Chrysoloras   43, 50–51, 235, 239–40
Manuel/Matthew Gabalas, metropolitan of
  Ephesos   184, 218, 228, 306, 309n103, 357,
  433, 440, 445, 471
Manuel/Maximos Holobolos   3, 7, 17–18,
  25n65, 31–33, 174, 183, 222, 239, 263n41,
  324, 403
Manuel Kalekas   214, 235, 240, 360
Manuel Kantakouzenos   232–33
Manuel Moschopoulos   5, 471, 478
Manuel Neokaisareites   222
Manuel Philes   8, 174, 175, 176, 177–180, 183,
  186, 191, 194
Manuel Raoul   232–33
Manuelites   475
Maria-Martha Tarchaneiotissa   4, 178
Maria-Rita of Armenia   336
Mark Blates   337
Mark Eugenikos   6, 47, 124n32, 235, 238n105,
  360, 443
Mark Kyrtos   375
Mark, anchorite   329–30
Mark, monk   128, 129
mathematics   7, 21, 81, 119, 120, 123, 219, 300,
  413, 444, 468, 470, 478
Matthew I, patriarch of Constantinople   125,
  127–30, 443
Matthew Angelos Panaretos   359
Matthew Blastares   6, 21, 183, 233n87, 376
Matthew Kantakouzenos   36, 259n25, 435;
  see Manuel Angelos
Maurokordatos Alexandros   243
Maurokordatos Nicholas   243
Maximos Chrysoberges   360
Maximos the Confessor   265, 266, 285,
  362–63, 477
Maximos of Kausokalybia   329, 350n37
Maximos, founder of Kotine monastery   466

516   GENERAL INDEX

Maximos Laskaris Kalopheros 438n157
Maximos Neamonites 218
Maximos/Manuel Planoudes 3, 5, 7, 8,
 20–22, 26, 35, 53, 57, 84, 178, 183,
 219–20, 223, 224–25, 239, 304, 306, 323,
 324, 331–32, 335, 426, 458n2, 463n26,
 465n38, 470n76 & 79, 471–73, 476, 478
medicine 7, 84, 85, 89, 91, 185
Mehmed II the Conqueror 150, 152, 154, 156,
 161, 162
Melchisedek Akropolites 324
Meletios Galesiotes, the Confessor 188, 325
Meliteniotes *see* John Gabras 418
Menander of Laodikeia, *see*
 Pseudo–Menander
Menas, monk 367
Metrodoros 311; *see also*, Theodore
 Methochites
menologema 412, 414, 431
messalianism 351
metrical epitaphs 43
Michael II Angelos, despot of Epiros 126
Michael VIII Palaiologos, emperor 3, 4, 7,
 17–18, 31–33, 38, 40, 60, 91n79, 115n16,
 116, 118, 125–26, 127, 135–36, 138, 147,
 154, 155, 159n39, 174, 180, 188, 192, 193,
 217, 218, 263, 265, 324–25, 333–34, 401,
 403, 409, 412, 413, 414, 415, 416n74, 419,
 423, 425–28, 430, 458, 469
Michael IX Palaiologos, emperor 35, 41, 57,
 175, 186, 336
Michael Apostoles 45, 184, 241, 333, 479
Michael Balsamon 441n165
Michael of Cappadocia (Kappadox) 468
Michael Choniates 469n74
Michael of Ephesos 258, 267n56
Michael Eskammatismenos 468
Michael Glabas Tarchaneiotes 178
Michael Glycas 177n25
Michael Kabasilas 440n161
Michael Klostomalles 12, 404, 412, 421–24,
 444
Michael Kritoboulos 147, 152–54, 158,
 160–63, 459n3
Michael Psellos 27, 28, 112n4, 142, 143, 185,
 252n1, 255, 256n10, 257, 266–67, 403,
 477n130
Michael Skoutariotes 441n165

Milutin Stefan Uroš II 326n25, 461n13
Mistra(s) *see* Morea
monasticism 11, 12, 269, 322, 326, 327, 329,
 336, 337, 338, 369, 375; coenobitic 128,
 326, 328; eremitic 326, 330; lavrite 326
Mongols 91, 100, 126
monocondyle 428n119, 430, 431, 432
monody 40, 41, 42, 46, 175n15, 176
monologue 187, 196
Morea, Despotate of 59, 100, 135, 145, 193,
 232–33, 236
Murad II 145, 153, 155, 161
mythology 29, 30
mythos 24, 195

Neilos Kabasilas 261, 357, 359, 375, 377n197,
 378n202, 380
Neilos Kerameus, patriarch of
 Constantinople 128–29, 357
Neilos, monk 367
Nemanja, family 326n25
Neo-Palamite 356n76, 363, 373n170
Neophytos Momitzilas (Prodromenos) 4,
 376, 462n19
Neophytos the Recluse, Saint 125
Neophytos, monk 194
Nephon, *hypopsephios* 380
Neoplatonic,-ism 256, 258, 266, 267, 348,
 363, 364, 370
Nicholas Babiskomites 423n93
Nicholas Kabasilas Chamaetos 1, 4, 6, 7,
 232, 260n28, 377
Nicholas Lampenos 294n42
Nicholas Myrepsos 7
Nicholas Rhabdas 7
Nicholas, Saint 183, 190–91
Nicomachus of Gerasa 119, 472, 476n125,
 478
Nikephoros Blemmydes 112–13, 114, 115, 116,
 119n22, 133, 134n1, 264–66, 323, 347,
 348n12, 364, 413, 440n161, 478
Nikephoros Bryennios 143
Nikephoros Choumnos 1, 2, 4, 6, 12, 19,
 34, 41–42, 54, 175–76, 214n10, 218, 219,
 220–21, 224, 225, 227, 228, 260n28,
 291n33, 292, 335, 337, 404, 410n47,
 412–420, 470, 474–75

GENERAL INDEX   517

Nikephoros Gregoras   4, 6, 7, 12, 35, 36, 42,
    50, 123, 138–42, 143, 159, 162–63, 188n80,
    218, 226, 227, 228–30, 231, 232, 233,
    253–54, 258, 259n25, 261n31 & 32, 262,
    271n67, 274, 281, 307, 311–12, 313–17, 331,
    335n64, 346n3, 347, 356–58, 366n128,
    369, 371–72, 373, 374, 375, 376, 377, 378,
    379, 380, 405–07, 410n47, 418n83, 426,
    438, 463–64, 476
Nikephoros Kallistou/Kallistos
    Xanthopoulos   25–26, 178, 179n34, 183,
    184, 186–87, 190, 460, 476
Nikephoros Moschopoulos, metropolitan of
    Crete   184, 470, 471
Nikephoros the Athonite   350, 366, 367
Nikephoros the Hesychast   269n65
Niketas Choniates   142, 143, 193, 489n74
Niketas Kyprianos   475
Niketas Soteriotes, *protonotarios*   231
Nikodemos of Mount Athos (Hagioreites)
    360
Nikodemos of the Vatopedi, Saint   327
Nikostratos   311; *see also* Nikephoros
    Gregoras
Niphon, patriarch of Constantinople   336

Odysseus   25, 121
Olǧäitü   91n79
Olympiodoros   258
Oppian   185
Orhan, sultan   139
Ottomans   226, 232, 241, 324, 325
ousia   361, 364
Ovid   7

Palaiologos/-oi, family   60, 157, 217, 401
Palamism   262, 271, 345n1, 346n3, 360, 363,
    369, 372, 373, 374, 377, 380n223, 434, 446
Palamite(s)   184, 185, 253, 260, 269n65,
    271n67, 354, 355, 359, 365n125, 368, 373,
    376, 377, 378, 381
Pardo Juan   242
Paris (of Troy)   197
Paul of Aegina   474
Paul Tagaris   124
Paul the Younger, Saint   325
Paul, Latin titular patriarch of
    Constantinople   373–74

Pepagomenos   409n40, 414
Petrarch   83
Phakrases   475
Phalieros Marinos   188
Philip Monotropos   191, 473
Philo Judaeus   34, 283, 286, 288, 297n54
Philotheos Kokkinos, patriarch of
    Constantinople   6, 50, 253–54, 259, 262,
    326, 328, 330n39, 332, 337, 354, 357,
    359, 366, 372, 373, 376, 431n132, 435–36,
    438, 441–42, 446, 462
Philotheos of Selybria   376
Photios, patriarch of Constantinople   27,
    469n74
photophaneiai   361
physics   21, 264, 266n52
physis   281
Pindar   32, 134, 181, 473n97
Plato   7, 10, 32, 35, 36, 45, 59, 93, 98, 101, 212,
    254, 256, 258, 259, 260, 263–74, 282,
    286, 306n89, 357, 365, 459n3, 463, 466,
    469, 473, 475, 480
Plotinus   260n28, 294, 473
Plutarch   5, 27, 32, 52, 287, 472, 475, 476n125,
    477n130
poetry   10, 18, 76, 78, 116, 119, 121, 124, 172, 173,
    174, 180, 182–85, 198, 467, 469, 476
political panegyric   35
Porphyry   257
praise   9, 27n80, 33, 35, 37, 40, 41, 43, 47–50,
    221, 224, 271, 291
preamble   16, 45, 114, 115, 116, 127
Prochoros Kydones   261–62, 269, 358–59,
    373–74, 379–80, 446
Prodicus   304
Prodromos Manganeios   177
Prokopios   163
Prokopios of Gaza   477
prooimion, -a   268n60, 442
pro-Palamites   259, 262
prosody   182, 189
prosphonemation (short address)   39
Pseudo-Alexander of Aphrodisias   257, 290
Pseudo-Augustine   473n97
Pseudo-Cato   473n97
Pseudo-Demetrios   213
Pseudo-Dionysios the Areopagite   363, 364,
    368

Pseudo-Kodinos   410n45 et 48, 417, 418n79
& 80, 82, 83, 419n84
Pseudo-Libanios   213
Pseudo-Maximos   188
Pseudo–Menander   15, 20, 21, 24, 31, 33, 34,
40, 42, 48, 49, 54, 60
Pseudo-Nonnos   471
Pseudo-Proklos   213
Pseudo-Symeon the New Theologian   365,
367
Ptochoprodromos   177n25
Ptolemy Claudius   5, 7, 79, 80, 88, 89n69,
120, 123n29, 463, 472, 473n97, 476,
477n130, 478
Pythagoras   292

Quadrivium   8, 122

Raoul Palaiologos   374, 378
Rhetoric   8, 9, 15–22, 24, 28, 31, 38, 40, 50, 56,
60, 61, 76, 78, 116, 119, 120, 122, 123, 172,
185, 401, 444, 467, 468, 476, 478
rhetorical education   16, 21, 407, 408, 415;
exercise(s) 19, 20, 24, 25, 26, 28, 52,
195, 404, 405n22, 407n33; genre 19,
31, 44, 45, 47, 53n269; handbooks
26;   manuals 21, 31n110, 60;
manuscript(s) 20; performance 18, 33;
theatron 49n245, 52n258; theory 33,
40, 50, 51, 52training 20, 24, 223
Richard, bishop of Cherson   347
romance   188, 190, 195, 196, 197
Romans   32, 40, 157, 158, 159, 187, 238

Sabbas Tziskos   366
Seliotes   367
Seljuks   11, 126
sekreton   410, 424
Serbs   226
Serenus   119, 120
Shams al-Dīn al-Bukhārī   90–91
Sigismond of Hungary   144
Simon, Dominican monk   233n87
Simonis   42
Simplikios   3, 257, 258, 468, 470
Socrates   25, 45, 264n44, 270, 304, 368
Sophianos   376, 381
Sophocles   253, 304, 473n97, 474, 476

Sophonias , monk   30, 256, 263
speech   9, 20, 28, 29, 30, 31n111, 35, 37,
39n169, 40, 46, 49, 51–59, 83n32, 135,
163, 172, 192, 220, 228, 236, 282, 298, 367,
469, 470
spirituality   12, 86, 172, 284, 286, 327, 338,
366, 370
stasis   29
Stoic, -ism   286, 292, 294
Stephen of Medeia   333, 461n14, 462n19, 479
Stephen Sachlikes   182, 188
Stephen Sgouropoulos   175
Stephen Syropoulos   424
Strozzi Palla   239
substance   87, 179, 185, 363, 364, 366
symbouleutic oratory   45n212
Symeon Metaphrastes   190
Symeon of Thessaloniki   6, 60n308, 360
Symeon the New Theologian   350, 366–67,
380
synaxarion   184, 187, 195
Synesios of Cyrene   23, 29, 34, 57, 213
synkrisis (comparison)   25, 27, 37
Syrgiannes   228
Syrianos   348, 469

Tafur Pero   459
tale   24, 25, 189, 194, 195, 196
theatron (a)   49n245, 52n258, 57, 102n122,
215
Themistios   23
Theocritus   473n97
Theodora Palaiologina, wife of Michael VIII
40, 333, 334
Theodora Palaiologina Synadene   4, 125,
126–27
Theodora Raoulaina   3–4, 5, 8, 218, 219, 221,
224, 225n53, 334–35, 470
Theodora, daughter of John VI
Kantakouzenos   139
Theodore I Laskaris, emperor   135
Theodore II Doukas Laskaris, emperor   126,
133, 134, 135, 136, 264n44, 306, 334, 413
Theodore I Palaiologos, despot of Morea   43
Theodore II Palaiologos, despot of Morea
44, 59, 236
Theodore Agallianos   124
Theodore Atouemes   376, 381

GENERAL INDEX

519

Theodore Dexios 376, 378–79
Theodore Graptos, Saint (vita) 335
Theodore Hypatios 429
Theodore Hyrtakenos 218, 220, 224, 227, 474–75
Theodore Metochites 1, 2, 6, 7, 9, 11, 12, 18, 19, 27, 34, 35, 40, 42, 48, 49, 50, 51, 77, 78–83, 84, 87, 103, 115, 118–121, 122, 123, 124–125, 139, 175–176, 180–182, 218, 220, 221n39, 224, 227, 228, 229, 256, 258, 269, 274, 281–321, 331, 334, 357, 358, 368, 371, 404–05, 412, 416–19, 420, 421, 422, 423, 427, 444, 463–64, 475, 476, 477n130
Theodore Modenos 223
Theodore Mouzalon 2, 218–19, 222, 224, 336, 337, 410n47, 412, 414–16, 417–18, 463n26, 471n88, 472
Theodore Phialites 191
Theodore Potamios 226, 232
Theodore Prodromos 174, 175, 176, 177n225, 183, 257
Theodore Sarantenos 125
Theodore Skoutariotes 134, 135, 426–28, 469
Theodore Xanthopoulos 83n32, 228, 475
Theodoret of Cyrrhus 468, 476
Theodosios Palamas 330
Theodosios Saponopoulos 326
Theodosius of Bithynia 119, 120
Theognis 304
Theoktistos Stoudites 183, 329
Theoleptos of Philadelpheia 4, 218, 228, 335, 367
Theon 80, 120, 477n130
Theophanes the Confessor 325
Theophanes Graptos, Saint (vita) 335
Theophanes, bishop of Nicaea 373, 374, 377
Theophanes, bishop of Peritheorion 330

Theophylact of Bulgaria/Ohrid 3, 468n63
theoria 285, 286, 306
theoria ton onton 313
Thomaïs 4
Thomas Aquinas 8, 94, 95, 118, 239, 255, 261n34, 262n36, 263, 269n63, 270, 271, 272–74, 358, 359, 369, 373, 378, 379
Thomas Magistros 5, 30, 54–55, 57, 58, 217n19, 231, 232n82, 295n48, 337, 372, 478
Thomism, Thomists 269, 271, 273
Thucydides 3, 153, 163, 225, 468, 470, 473n97
Timur 144, 160
Titus, emperor 186
Tome/-os of Blachernae 1285 429–30; of 1341: 354, 355, 433–37, 438n156 & 157; of 1347: 354n60, 356, 446n185; of 1351: 357, 359, 440n161; of 1368 262n35, 327, 333; *Hagioretic Tome* 353, 361, 372
Trajan, emperor 49
Traversari Ambrogio 239, 240, 241
Typikon 4, 125, 126, 127, 325, 334, 409, 469

Umur, emir of Aydin 139

Valla, Giorgio 242
Virgil 32

Xene, nun 357
Xenophanes 311; *see also* Barlaam of Calabria
Xiphilinus, family 468

Zealots 141
Zosimos 472
Zygomalas John 243
Zygomalas Theodosios 243

Printed in the United States
by Baker & Taylor Publisher Services